The Forgotten Centuries

The Forgotten Centuries

Indians and Europeans in
the American South,

1521–1704

EDITED BY

Charles Hudson

AND

Carmen Chaves Tesser

The University of Georgia Press

ATHENS & LONDON

© 1994 by the University of Georgia Press
Athens, Georgia 30602
All rights reserved
Designed by Kathi L. Dailey
Set in Sabon by Tseng Information Systems, Inc.
Printed and bound by Thomson-Shore, Inc.
The paper in this book meets the guidelines for
permanence and durability of the Committee on
Production Guidelines for Book Longevity of the
Council on Library Resources.

Printed in the United States of America

98 97 96 95 94 C 5 4 3 2 1
98 97 96 95 94 P 5 4 3 2 1

Library of Congress Cataloging in Publication Data

The Forgotten centuries : Indians and Europeans in the American
   South, 1521–1704 / edited by Charles Hudson and Carmen Chaves
   Tesser.
      p.   cm.
      Includes bibliographical references and index.
      ISBN 0-8203-1473-0 (alk. paper). — ISBN 0-8203-1654-7 (pbk.:
alk. paper)
      1. Southern States—History—Colonial period, ca. 1600–1775.
2. Indians of North America—Southern States—History—Colonial
period, ca. 1600–1775.   3. Indians of North America—Southern
States—First contact with Europeans.   4. Southern States—Discovery and exploration—Spanish.   I. Hudson, Charles M.   II. Tesser,
Carmen Chaves.
   F212.F67   1994
   975'.02—dc20   92-8616

British Library Cataloging in Publication Data available

CONTENTS

PREFACE

The quincentenary of Columbus's voyages to the New World has sparked interest in the early history of the southeastern United States. The observance of this momentous historical encounter has highlighted the lack of information on the early Southeast that is available for dissemination in college and high school classrooms. In 1989, the University of Georgia received a major grant from the National Endowment for the Humanities to conduct a five-week institute for college teachers, "Spanish Explorers and Indian Chiefdoms: The Southeastern United States in the Sixteenth and Seventeenth Centuries." This institute, like the research upon which it was based, was interdisciplinary, combining history, social anthropology, archaeology, and geography. We brought together many of the scholars who are currently working in this area to make presentations at this institute, and their essays for the present volume are based on their presentations.

In addition to these scholars, the "Spanish Explorers and Indian Chiefdoms" institute brought together twenty-five college teachers from throughout the country. Their criticism and discussion of the scholars' presentations made during the institute have contributed greatly to this volume, and we wish to thank them. The participants in the institute included George H. Ashley, Mary J. Berman, Robert Bryant, Marie E. Danforth, David Eliades, Gregory Gagnon, Perry Gnivecki, David Head, Nicholas Honerkamp, Richard Kania, John Kelly, Joseph L. Kirk, George Lankford, Joel Martin, David Moore, Lamar Pearson, Richard Persico, Marion Rice, Helen Rountree, George Sabo, Richard Shenkel, Russell Skowronek, Rebecca Storey, Thomas Watson, and Randolph Widmer. The coordination of the institute daily activities was handled admirably by Teresa Smotherman, administrative assistant to the institute director.

In 1990, the University of Georgia received an additional grant from the Georgia Humanities Council and the National Endowment for the Humanities to fund an institute for twenty-five Georgia secondary school teachers. The institute was entitled "Before Oglethorpe: Hispanic and Indian Cultures in Early Georgia." We compiled a manuscript from the 1989 institute lectures along with four additional papers, and we used this as the primary text for the "Before Oglethorpe" institute. We are indebted to the following teachers, who were our first reviewers and who provided us with valuable suggestions for the manuscript: W. Anderson Baker, Riley Brown, Connie Cooper, Erik Engel, Margaret Foil, Lisa Futch, Beverly Gascoigne, Dona Hayes Gordon, Robert Graper, Marcia L. Grimes, Delories Epps Horton, Marian S. Horton, James L. Jones, Cheryl Maceda, Daren Osvald, Anna M. Pace, Ron Nelson, Patricia W. Rhoden, Jackie Sales, Jan Saunders, Janet Schwartz, Claire Stracke, Marvin Taylor, Joyce Humphries Vest, and Ed Whitson.

CHARLES HUDSON AND
CARMEN CHAVES TESSER

Introduction

For all but specialist scholars, the history of the American South begins in the eighteenth century after no more than a sixteenth-century foreword and a seventeenth-century introduction. Only a few episodes from the total history of this earliest period of American history have found their way into textbooks. For the sixteenth century, the history of the first successful Spanish colony—St. Augustine—and the first unsuccessful English colony—Roanoke—have been well researched, and both have won secure places in historical surveys of early American history. The same can be said of the history of seventeenth-century Virginia and to a lesser extent of the seventeenth-century activities of Spanish missionaries among the Indians of the lower Atlantic coast and northern Florida. It is a story of social beginnings, of Europeans founding a precarious enterprise in the New World, and it is replete with accounts of their relationships with the native peoples who were unfortunate enough to live near the coast.

But this leaves a very large piece of early American history missing—that of the native peoples of the interior. The history of these peoples may be said to begin after 1521, when Spanish slavers landed on the South Carolina coast and captured an Indian from the "province of Chicora." This Indian, whom the Spaniards subsequently named "Francisco of Chicora," was taken to Spain where he had conversations with the humanist historian Peter Martyr (Pietro Martiere d'Anghiera). Martyr subsequently used this information in his important book *De Orbe Novo*. Even more, the native peoples of the interior enter the historical record through the documents of the Hernando de Soto expedition of 1539–43 and the follow-up expeditions of Tristán de Luna in 1559–61 and Juan Pardo in 1566–68. These expeditions penetrated every major geographic province in the South, clear to the fringe of the West, making contact with most of the important native societies.

After these initial explorations in the sixteenth century, Europeans did not venture into the interior in any significant way until the end of the seventeenth century. When they did, they found that the native peoples had been transformed by vast demographic and social changes. The story of the native peoples of the American South in these early years is so thoroughly missing from general surveys of American history, it can with little exaggeration be said that they are forgotten centuries. The reasons these centuries have evaded us until now are not hard to discern. First of all, the native people of the South have not told this story themselves because their sixteenth- and seventeenth-century ancestors were preliterate. Their ancestors' knowledge of the past was not written down, but resided in memory. By the eighteenth century, the Indians of the Southeast had lost almost all memory of the Spanish explorers and quite probably of their own ancient ancestors. A second reason, as we shall see, is that the records kept by the sixteenth-century Spanish explorers are scanty and are replete with biases and inconsistencies. Finally, as is well known, history is written by the victors, not by the vanquished. Until quite recently, English-speaking American historians have had relatively little interest in the Spanish-speaking explorers and colonists of the early South.

In recent years, certain texts from this era of Spanish explorers and conquistadores were received primarily as literary pieces with little, if any, historical validity. Indeed, literary critics have used texts from the early explorations as a means of developing theories of discovery and as a way of describing the New World seen from European eyes. For the literary critic, the text is more important than the facts upon which it is based. To these scholars, it matters not where the early explorers actually went or what they observed. What matters are the metaphors used in descriptive passages, whether they be factual or imaginary.[1]

But this should not obscure the fact that these historical documents contain priceless information about social and cultural worlds that existed in the past. The problems of doing research on this early era of southern history are so special that it almost deserves a special designation— the protohistoric. Historians are ill at ease with this protohistoric era because the documents are so skimpy, so incomplete, so difficult to interpret, and so lacking in corroboration. Historians also have difficulty in perceiving how the minutiae contained in archaeological reports add to the total picture. And, for their part, archaeologists are ill at ease with the individuals, events, and particularities that appear in the written documents of the protohistoric era. Archaeologists are intent on discovering patterns and generalities, and questions of who did what, and when, and where, are not compelling to them. Hence, in the protohistoric era neither the historian nor the archaeologist feels at ease, and this is unfortunate, because progress can only come when the two collaborate.

In addition to these intrinsic difficulties of the protohistoric era, there are additional reasons why the history of these two earliest southern centuries has not yet been written. The first is the problem of interpreting historical evidence. Cartography and navigation were in their infancy in the sixteenth and seventeenth centuries, and the earliest Spanish explorers were soldiers and adventurers who wished to make their fortunes, not scientists or historians who wished to bequeath to posterity an accurate and full record of all that they experienced. For this reason it has been extremely difficult to reconstruct the routes of the Spanish explorers of the South, and lacking this, one cannot even be certain where the major Indian societies were located.

Reconstructions of the routes followed by the Spanish explorers are fundamental to any understanding of the two earliest centuries of the history of the southern United States. In the past ten years, some notable advances have been made in achieving better reconstructions. The most crucial of these is the route of Hernando de Soto's expedition of 1539–43 and the follow-up expeditions of Tristán de Luna in 1559–61 and Juan Pardo in 1566–68.[2] The Pardo expedition produced the richest accounts, and this documentation together with Roland Chardon's research on the Spanish land league have made possible a detailed reconstruction of Pardo's route, providing landmarks in the interior that have been important in reconstructing de Soto's route.[3] Within a twenty-eight year period, these three expeditions made contact with, and in some cases revisited, the largest and most powerful native societies in the Southeast.

A new reconstruction of the de Soto route is included in this volume. The claim of this reconstruction is not that it is the last word on where de Soto went, but that it is more consistent with the total body of evidence—both documentary and archaeological—than is any other reconstruction to date. This new reconstruction of de Soto's route departs in a major way from the last major reconstruction, that of John Swanton and the United States de Soto Expedition Commission in 1939.[4] Swanton and his collaborators were severely handicapped in that they did not have benefit of reliable archaeological information. Swanton had no way of knowing which areas of the Southeast were inhabited in the sixteenth century, and even more important, which were uninhabited. Because this older route is entrenched in the thinking of many local historians as well as some scholars, controversy over which of the two routes is closer to the trail de Soto actually followed is likely to continue for some time.[5]

Reconstructions of the routes of the Tristán de Luna and Juan Pardo expeditions have recently been published in scholarly and popular books and articles, and except in passing, they are not recounted in this volume. These reconstructions are likewise controversial.[6]

Historians interested in the earlier expeditions of Lucas Vásquez de Ayllón in 1526 and Pánfilo de Narváez in 1528 must cope with very serious problems of documentation. In the first of his two papers in this volume,

Paul Hoffman recounts the events leading up to Ayllón's colony, and he gives a summary of the reasoning behind his proposed new location for Ayllón's first landing in 1526 at the mouth of the South Santee River and for Ayllón's second landing in the territory of the Guale Indians, in the Sapelo Sound area of Georgia. The historical importance of these locations can scarcely be overstated because Ayllón built the first European colonial town in the territory of the United States—San Miguel de Gualdape. As Hoffman acknowledges, verification of his placement of San Miguel de Gualdape awaits archaeological discovery of the site.

In 1528, Pánfilo de Narváez made a landfall in the neighborhood of Tampa Bay, near the place where de Soto would land eleven years later. In his second paper in this volume, Paul Hoffman proposes an interpretation of the confusion evident among members of the Narváez expedition after they missed the entrance to Tampa Bay, their intended landing place. Moreover, because Narváez marched north from this landing place in search of a bay that did not exist, his route lay closer to the coast than did de Soto's. Hoffman argues that unlike de Soto, Narváez and his army failed to reach the central town of Apalachee, arriving instead at an outlying village where they met with unremitting hostility from the Apalachees.

After the large military expeditions of de Soto, Luna, and Pardo in the middle of the sixteenth century, all of which were intent on discovering riches and exercising military control, the Spaniards did not attempt to repeat these efforts. As John Worth shows in his paper, the Spaniards did send several expeditions into the interior in the late sixteenth and early seventeenth centuries, but all of them were small, and they were increasingly dominated by clergy. Moreover, particularly after the founding of the Jamestown colony in 1607, the actions of the Spanish in Florida became increasingly defensive. The age of the bold conquistadores had ended.

Even if, eventually, the routes of the sixteenth-century explorers can be reconstructed exactly, these routes still must be linked to specific sixteenth-century archaeological sites. These linkages will allow historians and archaeologists to define the boundaries of the domains of the major native societies and will facilitate an accurate reconstruction of the total social and cultural landscape.

It is impossible to enter the world of the southeastern Indians without special explanation, and this is another of the reasons the sixteenth and seventeenth centuries are not well represented in southern history. It is just that the Indians were culturally and socially very different from sixteenth-century Spaniards and even more so from ourselves. The southeastern Indians were preliterate, and because of the way the social sciences have carved up humankind into separate scholarly domains, preliterate peoples (including Indians) became subjects of anthropological study. And because anthropologists have, by and large, thought of themselves as scientists writing for other scientists, they have not taken pains to explicate Native American culture to historians and others outside the field.

Getting inside the minds of these sixteenth-century Indians is not an easy matter. The Spanish explorers not only were little interested in the cultural details of southeastern Indian life, they did not grasp the basic structural principles that governed their societies. In fact, only in the last fifty years have scholars developed an understanding of the type of society that dominated the sixteenth-century Southeast: the chiefdom. Anthropologists understand now that in the sixteenth century (as in the eighteenth century, when historical and ethnographic documentation becomes much fuller), the lives of southeastern Indians were dominated by kinship. Most of an individual's relationships were with kinsmen or with in-laws, and so pervasive was kinship in their lives that they used kin relationships as a model for thinking about relationships quite outside kinship. This is why the documents of the eighteenth century and later are so replete with Indians referring to Europeans as "brothers," "fathers," and so on. They even used kinship analogically as a means of conceptualizing relationships in the natural world.[7]

But their kinship system could not satisfy all of their social needs. After about A.D. 1000, populations grew to the extent that internal conflicts must have become too great to be accommodated within families, extended families, and even within larger kinship groupings such as lineages or clans. As Randolph J. Widmer shows in his paper, the southeastern Indians did what people in many other parts of the world did when they found themselves in similar circumstances. They took a principle that was embedded in their kinship system—the principle of ranking by birth order—and they used this as the basis of building a more complicated social order, the chiefdom. Essentially, chiefdoms were based upon the same principle that lay behind primogeniture in English law. Namely, the first son or daughter, by the mere fact of being born first, had status and entitlements over all subsequent sons or daughters. In the chiefdom this principle of rank was extended to an entire society, and it was further extended to build an even more heterogeneous kind of society, the paramount chiefdom.

In some ways the chiefdoms of the Southeast must have seemed familiar to the Spaniards. They perceived social inequality in these societies, and they tended to regard the chiefs as *señores,* or lords, in something of the way they regarded *señores* in their own society. But in so doing, they misconstrued the true nature of these chiefdoms. As Widmer shows, these chiefdoms were not composed of ranked social classes based upon wealth and privilege, but upon an intricate system of ranking by birth order and kinship. We have no cause to be smug about the ways in which the Spanish explorers misinterpreted the Indians. The problems entailed in grasping the full sense and significance of what people in preindustrial cultures do and say are formidable, and the advances we have made in this understanding are no more than partial. It most certainly cannot be done merely by substituting a simple relativism in the place of the ethnocentrism that often dominates the thinking of naive people. The southeastern Indians were alien to sixteenth-century Spaniards, but not wholly alien. As members of the species *Homo sapiens,* the southeastern Indians exhibited some of the same broad cognitive patterns that all members of the species possess. Indeed, some of the same social and economic transformations experienced by the southeastern Indians had been experienced centuries earlier by the Spaniards' Iberian and Celtic ancestors, who likely would have understood Indian chiefdoms quite well.

A further impediment in achieving a full understanding of the southeastern Indians is that the sixteenth-century Spaniards are also exotic to us. Their technology, though perhaps state of the art for the sixteenth century, was far from what we might consider "modern." Their social institutions and habits of mind were very different from ours. The sixteenth-century Spaniards who travelled throughout the Southeast were driven by an adventuring spirit kindled by legends handed down through generations primarily, but not exclusively, through an oral tradition. Belief in these legends was strengthened after some, like de Soto, had participated in earlier expeditions through South America, during which marvelous societies and fabulous riches had been discovered. Spanish story-telling and the lure of the earlier texts of exploration added to the magic of the times and to the mythic element in the minds of the early Spanish explorers in the Southeast. Thus the legend of Chicora—a land of milk and honey (like Andalucia) supposedly located in present South Carolina—lured Spaniards to the Southeast, as did the later legend of Los Diamantes, a mountain of diamond believed to be located somewhere in the South Carolina back country. Hence, with some justification it can be said that for modern people the sixteenth-century Southeast is exotic twice over: neither of the two sets of players is intelligible to us without special explanation.[8]

As demonstrated in John F. Scarry's paper, the Spanish explorers of the Southeast did not—as some people might believe—march through a trackless wilderness, but through a landscape that had been modified for more than ten thousand years by the activities of earlier immigrants. Archaeologists have evidence showing that the human population of the Southeast rose very slowly throughout this long period of time, during which people developed new solutions to the problems of survival and growth. The earliest people in the Southeast, whom we call the Paleoindians, lived exclusively by hunting and gathering wild foods, and they probably had little more impact on the landscape than did other large carnivores. The sole exception was their possible use of fire to drive game and to increase the amount of browse for their prey animals.

After several millennia, the Indians began collecting certain wild seeds and vegetables more intensively, and by 2500 B.C. some of these seeds and vegetables began showing signs of domestication, most particularly, sunflower, sumpweed, goosefoot, and possibly a native squash. By A.D. 600–1000, some southeastern Indians, particularly in the Mississippi Valley, may have been obtaining a significant portion of their food from cultivation. Corn, a cultigen that was domesticated in Mexico as early as 5000 B.C., first showed up in the southeastern United States at about A.D. 200, but for hundreds of years it was only a minor part of the diet.[9]

About five hundred years before the Europeans arrived, momentous changes began to occur among the Indians of the Southeast. This was the beginning of the Mississippian period, when people began deriving a substantial part of their food from cultivating corn in cleared fields, a more intensive cultivation of the land that made more food available to an expanding population. These Mississippian people organized themselves into chiefdoms, which must have solved some of the social problems attendant with growth. At the same time, chiefdoms spawned new problems that led to internal conflicts and to conflicts between chiefdoms.

This is not to say that native societies of the Southeast were everywhere the same. As John Scarry shows in his paper, the Southeast contains a number of markedly different environmental areas, and these areas posed different problems and opportunities for the people who lived in them. The Indians of south Florida were different from the Timucuans of north Florida, and the Timucuans were different from the people who lived along the Fall Line and in the Tennessee Valley. These people in turn were different from those who lived in the central Mississippi Valley.

For the past fifty years, archaeologists have been piecing together information on the Mississippian period, and since first defining the Mississippian culture type, they have gradually become aware that Mississippian culture was not everywhere the same. But even though they have come to appreciate some of the varieties of Mississippian material culture, and of differing adaptations to different environments, they have not been notably successful in delineating native polities on a map. Polities are composed of people who think of themselves as somehow distinct from other people, and who will cooperate in defending themselves against outsiders. A people's sense of political identity need not be directly reflected in the material culture unearthed by archaeologists. As a consequence, when one has none but archaeological evidence, one is able to define Mississippian polities only in a hypothetical way.

New and more accurate reconstructions of the routes of explorations of de Soto, Luna, and Pardo are making it possible to locate and map the territories of a number of sixteenth-century native polities.[10] As research proceeds, archaeologists should be able to fill in many details about various aspects of the culture of these polities. This is not to say that this task of social and cultural reconstruction can be done conclusively and without argument. The papers in this volume by John Scarry, Mark Williams, Chester DePratter, and David Hally will make it abundantly clear that differences of interpretation already exist and that the synthesizing and criticism of this information is just beginning.

The Apalachee chiefdom was the first Mississippian chiefdom the Spaniards encountered. Pánfilo de Narváez had already encountered the Apalachees in 1528, and they put up a very determined and sustained military resistance to the invaders. The Apalachees played a role in the failure of Narváez's expedition. Their domain, as John Scarry shows in his paper in this volume, lay between the Aucilla and Ochlockonee rivers. One of the peculiarities of the Apalachees was that the territory of their chiefdom was not strung out along a river valley as were many of the southeastern chiefdoms in the interior. Instead, the Apalachee towns were arrayed on the land in a compact pattern, which Scarry calls two-dimensional. This may, as he points out, have conferred an organizational advantage on the Apalachees. That is, because of their compact settlement patterns, they lived in closer proximity to their chief than was the case in a linear chiefdom, some of whose towns were several days distant from the center. Perhaps the Apalachee chief was better able than most chiefs to exercise power and influence over his people. De Soto and his men were certainly impressed by the solidarity and the valor shown by the Apalachee warriors.

The de Soto expedition encountered the chiefdom of Ocute when they reached the upper Oconee River in Georgia. Mark Williams, who has taken a leading role in the archaeological investigation and interpretation of this polity, disagrees with Hudson and others on several points. For example, he believes that it was Patofa, not Ocute, that was the dominant chiefdom. For this reason, Williams prefers the neutrality of a geographical term in referring to Ocute as the "Oconee Province," the analytical designation given to it when it was first identified by Marvin Smith and Stephen Kowalewski.[11]

Because of the determined and systematic research of Williams and his co-workers, the chronology of the Ocute chiefdom, as well as the total picture of its development, is the best developed for any sixteenth-century southeastern polity. Using this information, Williams is able to plan an agenda for research in the "Oconee Province" that is capable of guiding survey and excavation for decades to come. One important question about the Ocute chiefdom is whether the power of the paramount chief extended to other areas, such as to the small nameless polity that lay on the western headwaters of the Savannah River, the Ichisi chiefdom on the Ocmulgee River, and the Guale chiefdom on the coast. That Ocute could have been a paramount chiefdom with these dimensions has been proposed by Hudson as a theoretical possibility.[12]

Of all the societies encountered by de Soto, the chiefdom of Cofitachequi has achieved the most historical notoriety. In part this was because de Soto's route north from Apalachee was based on his expectation that he would find gold, silver, and pearls at Cofitachequi. Cofitachequi has also been romanticized because of its female chief and because of the ceremonious way in which her niece greeted de Soto and his men.

It is clear that Cofitachequi was at one time a paramount chiefdom that must have been comparable to Coosa and other large paramount chiefdoms. But as can be seen in Chester DePratter's paper in this volume, interpretations differ as to how large the Cofitachequi chiefdom was and on whether it had declined significantly at the time of the de Soto and Pardo expeditions. DePratter argues that Cofitachequi was a geographically small polity, stretching from about the junction of the Congaree and Wateree rivers to about the present North Carolina state line, while Hudson has argued that the power and influence of the paramount chiefdom of Cofitachequi extended from the Atlantic Coast to the mountains.[13] But, in fact, this disagreement is more terminological than substantive. Hudson would agree that the principal or core territory of Cofitachequi was probably as DePratter indicates, and throughout this area the chief exercised real power. But Hudson would additionally argue that the Ayllón and de Soto documents indicate that the chief of Cofitachequi had, at the very least, influence over people in the much larger area.

Even the epidemic disease that the de Soto chroniclers report having afflicted Cofitachequi two years before the expedition arrived is open to interpretation. DePratter argues that this disease may never have occurred. It is a misinterpretation, he says, by the Spaniards who saw towns that had long been deserted for unknown reasons and corpse-filled houses that were simply ossuaries. Randolph Widmer offers yet another interpretation. Namely, the loss of life in the chiefdom of Cofitachequi was actual, but the cause was a famine that had perhaps been caused by a severe drought. It is simply the nature of the de Soto narratives that these kinds of differing interpretations are possible, and that differing interpretations such as these may never be decisively resolved.

Coosa, which was visited by all three of the major sixteenth-century explorers, is the paramount chiefdom that has so far been most fully reconstructed. De Soto and his men marched through the entire length of Coosa, from Chiaha in the north to Talisi in the south. A detachment of Luna's soldiers traveled through the southern towns of Coosa before reaching the capital town, where they remained for several months. In so doing, they were able to describe several aspects of the Coosa town layout and military organization. Finally, Juan Pardo penetrated the northern towns of Coosa, visiting towns that de Soto had visited as well as two or three other towns. From the Pardo documents it can be seen that the paramount chief was still functioning as late as 1567.

Along with this historical documentation, the archaeological record for Coosa is unusually well developed. Archaeological work of excellent quality has been conducted in Dallas phase sites in the upper Tennessee Valley since the 1940s, and excellent archaeological research in north Georgia has been done under the direction of David Hally for the past twenty years. The analytical work that Hally and his associates have done on the archaeological specifics of the paramount chiefdom of Coosa is ground-breaking. And in addition to this, Hally's reconstruction at the micro level of behavior that occurred within households is likewise of very high quality. Of Coosa it can be said that we currently have a fuller and more rounded picture of everyday life at every social level than we have for any other sixteenth-century southeastern polity.[14]

Spain maintained a continuous colonial presence in the Southeast after 1564, but the activities of Spanish colonists were mainly confined to the missions in Florida and the coast of Georgia and South Carolina. After Juan Pardo's expeditions in 1566–68, very few Spaniards penetrated the interior. Similarly, the English maintained a continuous presence in Virginia after the founding of Jamestown in 1607. But again, these English colonists were mainly confined to the tidewater area of Virginia, though their later economic penetration southward into the Carolina piedmont was a harbinger of things to come.

It was not until the English founded Charles Towne in 1670 and the French explored the Mississippi valley in 1673 that Europeans again penetrated the interior of the Southeast in a significant way. When they did, they encountered a social landscape that had been profoundly altered, though they themselves had no way of knowing that it had been altered. The paramount chiefdoms were nowhere to be seen. And with the partial exception of the Natchez, even simple chiefdoms were absent. The native population of the Southeast was much smaller in the late seventeenth century than it had been in the sixteenth century, and areas that had been densely populated in the period 1540–68 were depopulated a hundred years later.

What were the forces that produced such far reaching changes? The activities of the explorers themselves must have had some effect on the native people. This must have been especially the case along the Alabama River in Alabama, where thousands of Indians were killed by de Soto and his men at the battle at Mabila. And something of the same must have been true of the native societies along the Mississippi River near its junction with the Arkansas River, where members of the expedition spent two winters and where de Soto and his soldiers waged warfare against the native people to terrorize and hold them in awe.

But a far more powerful cause of mortality among the Indians was the germs and viruses brought by Europeans and Africans from the Old World to the New. The overall demographic decline caused by these diseases has been known for many years, but Marvin Smith in this volume documents the effects of these epidemics in a delimited area of the Southeast. Along with the Indians' inability to achieve a level of social organization higher than the paramount chiefdom, the greatest factor in shaping the outcome of their long-term encounter with Europeans was their biological vulnerability. In the face of the diseases, they had no real options. Whether they moved, dispersed, or remained in place, their population declined inexorably. Most particularly, as the European and African population began soaring in the late eighteenth century, the Indians became incapable of fielding armies of equivalent strength.[15]

A second force that transformed the Indians was the mission system founded by the Spaniards. First the Jesuits and then the Franciscans founded missions whose purpose was to transform the Indians into Spanish subjects using specific techniques and regimens. The Spanish missionaries wished to win the hearts and minds of the native people, and as Jerald Milanich shows in his paper, they generally succeeded in doing so. Indians became Catholics, learned European occupations, learned to speak Spanish, and some even learned to read and write Spanish. However, the ability of the missionaries to transform the Indians by design was limited to the small sphere of influence in the immediate vicinity of each mission. Indeed, it is possible that the Spanish missions had more total impact on the southeastern Indians by serving as conduits of infectious disease than by all of their proselytizing.

Compared with the impact of the Spanish missionaries on the Indians, the forces unleashed after 1670 by the English entrepreneurs in Carolina were infinitely greater. The English, by and large, cared little about winning the hearts and minds of the Indians. As Joel Martin shows in his paper, the English approach to dominion in the Southeast was to extract a profit from the Indians, and they did so by causing them to be dependent on trade goods manufactured in England. The English felt that if they could make the Indians dependent on woolen cloth, knives, axes, and most particularly guns, then the hearts and minds of the Indians would follow. When a particular southeastern Indian society found that their enemies were armed with guns, and particularly if these enemies were slave catchers, they had to acquire guns of their own if they were to defend their wives and children from enslavement. To purchase these guns, the Indians in turn became slave catchers, professional hunters, horse thieves, and mercenaries in order to acquire necessary capital. In this way, the English were able to transform native social and economic structures at little expense—in fact, at a profit—and with few bureaucratic costs. This English approach to colonial domination was not without its dangers. Armed with guns, the Indians were tempted to turn them against their English overlords, as they did in the Yamasee War of 1715. But as the war proceeded, the Yamasee ran out of powder and shot and thus were forced to the bargaining table. The reality of their dependent position in the modern world became all too plain.

The English approach to dominating the Indians of the Southeast first took shape in Virginia, but it was perfected in Carolina and Georgia. Compared with the Spanish approach, the English approach to domination was far more capable of transforming native societies in the interior. Even Virginia may have played a greater role in their transformation than we have realized. There is no better case with which to compare the English and Spanish approaches to domination than the raids waged by James Moore and his Indian mercenaries in 1702-4. Within two years Moore devastated what it had taken the Spanish missionaries over a century to build.

When the historical record for the southeastern Indians opens up again at the close of the seventeenth century, the so-called Indians of the Old South—the Catawbas, Creeks, Choctaws, Chickasaws, and Cherokees— are more or less in place. And when these Indian societies are compared with the native chiefdoms of the sixteenth-century Southeast, one can appreciate the massive nature of the transformation that had occurred. A full examination of the way in which the Indians of the South reorganized themselves to meet the challenges of the modern world remains to be researched and written. But its general character can be seen in this volume in the papers by John Hann, Helen Rountree and E. Randolph Turner III, Vernon J. Knight, Jr., and Patricia Galloway.

The various forces unleashed by the Europeans affected the Indians differently in different places. The effects of the deerskin and slave trade can be seen most clearly in Knight's paper on the formation of the Creeks and in Galloway's paper on the formation of the Choctaws. In both cases, people from remnants of the great chiefdoms in the interior coalesced to increase their numbers and to fashion a *modus vivendi* on the edge of the modern world. The coalescent societies that formed during the seventeenth century nucleated around old southeastern social forms. Knight refers to them as "provincial chiefdoms." But it was very much a case of new wine in old wineskins: as the seventeenth century drew to an end, even though a late seventeenth-century chief may have held a traditional title, his effectiveness depended upon his ability to cope with a new world economic order that placed no value on local traditions, and which in fact saw them as impediments in the ceaseless quest for profit. Research similar to that of Knight on the Creeks and Galloway on the Choctaws needs to be done on such people as the Catawbas, the Cherokees, the Chickasaws, the Quapaw, and the Caddo.

The Powhatans are unusual because they were a people who only organized themselves into a chiefdom in the late sixteenth century, possibly in response to the appearance of Europeans, and they had the misfortune of being located too close to the English colonists. Because the tobacco plantations exhausted land quickly, colonists and Indians competed for land very early in Virginia. The life span of the Powhatan chiefdom was a short one, and subsequently their role as players in frontier politics was decidedly less than that of the Creeks or the Cherokees.

The Apalachee are distinctive in that they lived wholly within the sphere of the Spanish missions. Hence, their historical experience in the seventeenth century was very different from that of the groups already mentioned. The Apalachees continued to live in the same territory they occupied at the time of the Narváez and de Soto expeditions. Superficially, the Apalachees exhibited more continuity than did the Creeks, but in fact, as John Hann shows, far-reaching changes had occurred among the Apalachees by the late seventeenth century. When the Apalachee missions were destroyed in 1704 by the Carolinian James Moore and his Indian mercenaries, the Apalachees were well on their way to becoming Christianized peasants. They were possibly more similar to peasants elsewhere in the world than they were to the Creeks and other Indians who were in contact with Carolina and Virginia traders.

Today, for the first time, we can see the broad outlines of the history of the first two centuries of European contact with the Indians of what is now the southeastern United States. The early texts, a ready source of controversial dialogue among literary critics, are now providing a glimpse into the societies encountered by the first Europeans to penetrate the Southeast. Historians, archaeologists, and anthropologists are beginning to see the need for a more interdisciplinary approach in research on these forgotten centuries. Debate will continue for some time. But once the dust has settled, and once enough progress has been made in working out the details of the vast changes that occurred during this time, a new synthesis of the social history of the early Southeast will be written. Until that time, this present book can serve as a survey of the new terrain.

NOTES

1. Todorov, *Conquest of America;* Pastor, *Discursos narrativos de la conquista.*
2. For de Soto, see Hudson, Smith, and DePratter, "The Hernando de Soto Expedition: From Apalachee to Chiaha"; DePratter, Hudson, and Smith, "The Hernando de Soto Expedition: From Chiaha to Mabila"; Hudson, Smith, and DePratter, "The Hernando de Soto Expedition: From Mabila to the Mississippi"; Hudson, "De Soto in Arkansas"; Schambach, "The End of the Trail"; Jerald Milanich and Charles Hudson, *Hernando de Soto and the Indians of Florida.*

For Luna, see Hudson, Smith, DePratter, and Kelley, "The Tristan de Luna Expedition"; Hudson, "A Spanish-Coosa Alliance."

For Pardo, see DePratter, Hudson, and Smith, "Route of Juan Pardo's Explorations"; Hudson, "Juan Pardo's Excursion."
3. The Pardo documents have been transcribed and newly translated by Paul E. Hoffman in Hudson, *The Juan Pardo Expeditions.* See Chardon, "Linear League" and "Elusive Spanish League."
4. Swanton, *Final Report,* first published in 1939 as United States House of Representatives Document no. 71, 76th Congress, 1st Session.
5. For an example of this controversy, see Boyd and Schroedl, "In Search of Coosa" and Hudson, Smith, Hally, Polhemus, and DePratter, "Reply to Boyd and Schroedl."

For an exchange on de Soto's route from Apalachee to Chiaha, see Eubanks,

"Studying de Soto's Route"; Anderson, "The Mississippian Occupation"; Hudson and Smith, "Reply to Eubanks"; Chardon, "Response to Eubanks."

6. For an interpretation of the Luna expedition different from Hudson et al., see Curren, Little, and Holstein, "Aboriginal Societies."

For an exchange on the Pardo expedition, see Larson, "The Pardo Expedition"; DePratter, Hudson, and Smith, "The Juan Pardo Expeditions."

7. Hudson, *Southeastern Indians,* 60, 184–85.

8. For the legend of Chicora, see Hoffman, *A New Andalucia.* For the legend of Los Diamantes, see Hudson, *Juan Pardo Expeditions,* 189–95.

9. Chapman, Delcourt, and Delcourt, "Strawberry Fields, Almost Forever," 55.

10. See, for example, Hudson, Smith, Hally, Polhemus, and DePratter, "Coosa."

11. Smith and Kowalewski, "Identification of a Prehistoric 'Province'."

12. Charles Hudson, "The Social Context of the Chiefdom of Ichisi."

13. Hudson, *Juan Pardo Expeditions,* 68–91.

14. Hally, Smith, and Langford, "de Soto's Coosa."

15. Wood, "The Changing Population of the Colonial South."

Exploration of the Southeast

JOHN F. SCARRY

The Late Prehistoric Southeast

The early Spanish explorers and settlers found La Florida to be a vast mosaic, a patchwork quilt of environments and peoples. The diversity of the land and its peoples profoundly affected European efforts to explore and settle the newly discovered lands of the Southeast. The Spaniards themselves recognized the difficulties posed by some environments and peoples and tried to avoid them, concentrating their efforts on those areas and peoples most amenable to conquest, exploitation, and settlement.

The native peoples of the Southeast were well adapted to their environments. They efficiently exploited locally available wild plant and animal resources, and where these were most abundant and reliable, the people used them almost exclusively. Where domesticated crops provided significant amounts of food, people and settlements concentrated in those areas containing the most fertile soils. But even where agriculture was important, predictable and concentrated wild resources such as nuts, fish, and migratory waterfowl continued to be important.

Adaptations to specific environments helped shape the cultural diversity of the Southeast. But environmental diversity was not the only factor leading to the cultural diversity of the southeastern peoples; there were historical and social factors as well. The sixteenth-century native societies of the Southeast were the products of long-term historical developments, and historical contexts shaped cultural developments as profoundly as environmental contexts.

Long before Juan Ponce de León "discovered" La Florida, the southeastern United States was discovered and settled by Native Americans. In fact, there is a ten thousand-year sequence of human occupation in the Southeast that precedes the earliest European accounts of the area.[1] (See figure 1.)

Archaeologists have divided the prehistory of the eastern United States into a series of periods that roughly correlate with major technological,

Date	Period		
A.D. 1000		Mississippi	
A.D. 600	Late		
A.D. 1	Middle	Woodland	
700 B.C.	Early		
4000 B.C	Late		
6000 B.C.	Middle	Archaic	
8000 B.C.	Early		
		Paleoindian	

FIGURE I

Archaeological periods in the Southeast

economic, and political changes. From earliest to latest these periods are the Paleoindian, the Archaic, the Woodland, and the Mississippi.[2]

Our earliest evidence of human settlement in the Southeast dates to the Paleoindian period (ca. 12,000–10,000 years ago). Radiocarbon dates associated with human activities in southern Florida stretch back over ten thousand years, and Paleoindian peoples may have first entered the Southeast several thousand years before that. These earliest inhabitants of the Southeast were foragers, hunters and gatherers of wild plants and animals, including Pleistocene megafauna such as mammoths and mastodons. Their groups were small—a typical Paleoindian band probably consisted of no more than fifty people—and widely scattered, so population densities across the region were low. Their societies likely were egalitarian systems where personal status and authority depended upon gender, age, experience, and ability, and where most decisions were made by consensus. Leaders probably were temporary and situational, depending on the activity. Our archaeological evidence of Paleoindian peoples is limited, particularly when compared to more recent inhabitants of the Southeast. What we know best are the stone tools they made and left behind.[3]

The Archaic period (8000–700 B.C.) encompassed profound environmental changes in the Southeast, beginning with the end of the glacial climate, continuing through a warm, dry period from ca. 8000 B.C. to 5000 B.C., and culminating in the establishment of an essentially modern climate and vegetation by about 3000 B.C. The environmental changes were accompanied by important economic and social changes. There was an increase in regional variation in stone tool styles suggesting that this was a time of increasing cultural differentiation and regional interaction.[4]

During the Early and Middle Archaic periods (8000–4000 B.C.), people continued as mobile foragers, although the plants and animals on which they relied were the same as those encountered by the earliest European explorers of the Southeast. Groups remained small, although population densities increased across the region. The lack of evidence for substantial structures and food storage facilities and the apparent absence of formal cemeteries suggest that settlements were small and temporary. In turn, the small size of the social groups and the absence of any evidence of status differentiation argues for social organizations similar to those of the Paleoindian period.

The Late Archaic period (4000–700 B.C.) was marked by several extremely important demographic and economic changes: plants were first cultivated in the Southeast and there were increases in the size, density, and stability of social groups. We see evidence of these changes in the appearance of large, dense midden sites; evidence of substantial structures; pits apparently used to store large amounts of food; heavy, less portable containers of stone and pottery; and formal cemeteries containing many individuals. The larger, more sedentary social groups of the Late Archaic presumably were associated with more complex social and political organizations than were in existence during earlier periods.[5]

Cultivated squash and gourd appear in the Southeast during the Late Archaic, by at least 2500 B.C. Traditionally, it has been thought that they were first domesticated in Mesoamerica, but recent studies suggest that squash may have been domesticated independently in the Southeast.[6] In addition to the "tropical" cultigens, Late Archaic peoples relied more and more on the seeds of a number of annual plants including sunflower, sumpweed, little barley, goosefoot, maygrass, and knotweed. We now have evidence that at least three of these plants were domesticated during the Late Archaic: sunflower (by 2000 B.C.), sumpweed (by 1000–500 B.C.), and goosefoot (by 1500–1000 B.C.).[7]

The Woodland period (700 B.C.–A.D. 1000) witnessed further increases in settlement size and permanence and in the importance of cultivated plants in the diet. It also saw marked increases in the complexity of mortuary rituals, including the construction of earthen mounds to cover or house the dead, and the use of elaborate, exotic, and highly symbolic artifacts as grave accompaniments. In many cases, mortuary practices and grave offerings seem to reflect status differentiation beyond that seen in the Archaic and, perhaps, greater authority and prestige of community leaders. The Woodland period also saw greater regional variation in material culture (particularly in ceramic decoration) that may reflect the emergence of more closely bounded social groups.[8]

During the Early and Middle Woodland (ca. 700 B.C.–A.D. 600), maize was introduced to the Southeast, but isotopic studies indicate that it did not form a significant portion of diet until much later. The indigenous domesticated and cultivated crops continued to be grown, but in many areas (for example, the Coastal Plain in Alabama, Georgia, and Florida) they played only minor roles in the subsistence economy. In the Middle Woodland we see evidence of widespread movement of specialized goods (exotic stones, copper, marine shell) over hundreds or even thousands of kilometers.[9] Many of these goods appear in mortuary contexts, and Middle Woodland mortuary rituals were even more elaborate than those of the Early Woodland. In some cases individuals were clearly singled out for special treatment (as at the Kolomoki site), although we lack clear evidence of the ascribed status differentiation and formal political hierarchies seen in the later Mississippian societies.[10] Presumably these special individuals were leaders who acquired their status and positions through competition with other aspiring leaders based on personal abilities. By the end of the Middle Woodland, permanent, year-round settlements appeared in many parts of the Southeast.

The Late Woodland period (A.D. 600–1000) is often depicted as a time of cultural decline between the "climaxes" of the earlier Middle Woodland societies and the later Mississippian chiefdoms. Large ceremonial centers with their impressive mounds disappeared for the most part, and there is little evidence that exotic artifacts were exchanged or used. Mortuary rituals show less evidence of status differentiation.

What we do see evidence of during the Late Woodland is a continuation of earlier economic and political adaptations. Wild resources continue to be major food sources, although indigenous crops and maize were grown and some groups in the Mississippi Valley might be characterized as farmers who derived much of their subsistence from domesticated crops.[11] Societies were structured politically along egalitarian lines. Leadership positions appear weakly developed (perhaps even more so than in Middle Woodland societies) and widely accessible. Social integration was maintained not through political hierarchies but through kinship, ritual, and tribal ties of association. We also see evidence of widespread growth and dispersal of populations. In some riverine habitats, local increases in population densities may have led to population/resource imbalances as the ability of subsistence procurement strategies to provide needed foods was exceeded.[12]

A major exception to this picture of Late Woodland societies can be seen in the Mississippi Valley. The Coles Creek groups of Arkansas, Mississippi, and Louisiana appear to have been larger and politically more complex than their contemporaries in the Southeast. Beginning about A.D. 700, the Coles Creek peoples built civic-ceremonial centers with earthen mounds arranged around open plazas. The mounds often supported buildings that may have served as temples, charnel houses, or the residences of elite individuals. These large sites suggest that the Coles Creek societies may have had a greater degree of status differentiation than other Late Woodland societies. In particular, the presence of residential structures on mounds suggests the existence of a stable elite segment of the population that was able to use community labor. There is also evidence that Coles Creek groups relied on agricultural crops (but not maize) for much of their diet.[13]

The Mississippi period (A.D. 1000–Contact) encompasses the emergence and evolution of the societies encountered by the European explorers of the interior Southeast. The critical feature of Mississippi period subsistence economies was that they yielded surpluses. Food producers and collectors were able to provide food to individuals who were not directly involved in subsistence activities. In turn, the economic surpluses were used to support permanent political hierarchies. During this period, societies developed that were larger and considerably more complex than those of earlier times. Many societies of the Mississippi period were chiefdoms, societies with hierarchical political organizations, formal political offices, institutionalized ascriptive status differentiation, and individuals with the ability to command the labor, and the products of the labor, of others. Several distinct groups of chiefdoms—the Mississippian polities of the inland Southeast, the Timucuan polities of north Florida, the Calusa of south Florida, and the polities of the Middle Atlantic coastal plain—developed during this time. These regional groupings can be differentiated on the basis of material cultures, subsistence economies, and iconographic complexes.

In many inland societies, cleared-field agriculture with maize as the dominant crop became the most important subsistence activity. This stands in marked contrast to the economies of most earlier groups. As maize production was intensified, other resources, both wild and cultivated, appear to have declined in importance (although there are European accounts describing the cultivation of chenopodium in the lower Mississippi Valley). Maize became a central element in the lives of Mississippian peoples. It contributed the bulk of the diet, particularly among commoners. Its importance was reflected in important rituals such as the historic Green Corn Ceremony or Busk. Later during the Mississippi period, beans first appeared in the Southeast, and provided a valuable complement to maize. Along the Atlantic and Gulf coastal zones, however, maize agriculture did not dominate the diet to the extent it did in inland groups. In south Florida, wild plants and animals continued to provide nearly all of the food of the peoples there.[14]

The economic and political changes of the Late Woodland-Mississippian transition were accompanied by changes in settlement patterning. In inland groups, settlements concentrated in riverine areas containing extensive tracts of fertile soils. In all areas, settlements were located in areas capable of yielding abundant and predictable subsistence resources. Increases in political complexity were mirrored in increases in the complexity of settlements. Distinct political capitals appeared for the first time. Settlements containing major public construction projects (mounds, plazas, fortifications) appear to mark the political centers of independent polities.[15] In the larger, more complex societies several levels of capital sites can be found, apparently marking district as well as polity centers. Changes in subsistence economies of inland peoples were paralleled by changes in storage facilities and technological changes in ceramic vessels. Underground storage facilities (pits), so common on Woodland period sites, were frequently abandoned, to be replaced by aboveground cribs, which were more suitable for storing maize. Technological changes in ceramics allowed the construction of larger cooking vessels better able to withstand thermal shock.[16]

While many have viewed the Late Woodland as the "gray period," it was also the period when the stage was set for the development of the chiefdoms of the Mississippi period.[17] Even the disappearance of the elaborate ceramics of the Middle Woodland period and the simplification of mortuary programs can be related to the strengthening of social integration in the face of stress.[18] In many areas of eastern North America, including portions of the Southeast, the Late Woodland period was a time of social and demographic stress.

Population increases in some areas caused changes in the costs of food procurement, altering the relationships of various strategies for obtaining food. As some sources of food became more difficult or costly to obtain, societies employed a variety of strategies to maintain their subsistence bases. In some areas they expanded into previously underutilized habitats and continued their traditional procurement strategies. In some areas they altered the mix of resources they exploited, increasing efforts devoted to less expensive resources and directing labor away from more expensive resources. In many areas, they did both. Eventually, efforts were increasingly directed toward resources whose yields could be increased with lesser increases in labor input. Maize was the most important of these resources.[19]

Even in areas where demographic stress does not appear to have been an important factor, subsistence change took place. In many instances, the changes may be attributable to the demand for food surpluses resulting from competition between individuals and groups. Competition for prestige and status involving feasting and gift giving, perhaps similar to the Mokas of the New Guinea Highlands, might well have contributed to the intensification of agriculture in the Southeast. Once demand for agricultural products was established, regardless of the reason, labor was directed away from wild resources and toward cultivated crops, large areas were cleared, and the shift in the subsistence economies might well have been irreversible.[20]

Regardless of its ultimate cause, intensive maize agriculture and the economic surpluses it provided served as the basis for most of the complex societies of the Mississippi period. While a picture of the causes and processes of the evolution of intensive maize agriculture in the Southeast is beginning to appear, our view of the emergence of the complex political structures that characterize most of the societies of the Mississippi period is much less clear. In part, the absence of a general model of political evolution in the late prehistoric Southeast can be seen as a product of the diversity of the specific historical trajectories that led to the individual chiefdoms of the Mississippi period. Thus, in one area, demographic pressure might have been ameliorated by the managerial strengths of chiefly political organization; in another area, warfare might have led to the consolidation of independent and relatively egalitarian communities under the control of a single strong leader from one community; in still another, social competition among community level leaders might have resulted in increasing demands for surplus production and the eventual institutionalization of wealth-based status differences.

Unfortunately, in most areas of the Southeast we are unable to answer many of the questions we have about the emergence of the Mississippi period chiefdoms. In only a few areas is our archaeological database adequate for examining the detailed sequences of events and processes that led from egalitarian Late Woodland societies to the hierarchical Mississippian chiefdoms.[21]

The Southeast is an environmentally diverse area. Stretching from the Florida Keys to the Ohio River valley and from the Atlantic Coast to the edges of the Great Plains, its environmental variety presented challenges and opportunities to the European explorers and colonists of the sixteenth century and to the native peoples who preceded them.

For the purpose of this discussion, we can divide the Southeast into five major environmental zones: South Florida; the Coastal Plain; the Piedmont (including the Ozarks); the Mississippi Alluvial Valley; and the Appalachian Highlands. (See figure 2.) Each of these areas offered different challenges and opportunities to the people who occupied them. Each was characterized in late prehistoric times by distinctive economic patterns, population densities, material culture patterns, and interaction networks. Each contained local habitats that varied considerably from each other.

South Florida, roughly the area from Ocala southward, includes true subtropical habitats found nowhere else in the Southeast. There is considerable ecological variation within this region. In the interior, the wet prairies of the Everglades provided seasonally abundant and easily obtainable faunal resources. Also in the interior, great cypress swamps covered much of the southwestern part of the peninsula. In both of these areas, settlement was restricted to higher, drier areas, particularly the small scattered tree islands. Scattered pinelands covered old dune ridges and were most extensive along the east coast. Along the coasts, especially the southwest coast, there were extensive mangrove forests. These provided preferred firewood, mangrove fruit, and aquatic food resources. The hardwood islands with their lush subtropical vegetation were the richest terrestrial environments and provided plant and animal foods year round. Near the coasts, these dif-

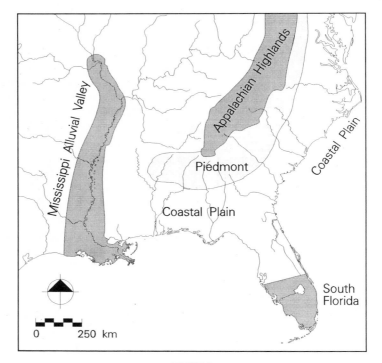

FIGURE 2
Environmental zones in the Southeast

ferent environments occur in close proximity to one another and could be
easily exploited. In part because of this, late prehistoric population densities were significantly greater along the coasts. Another reason population
densities were greater along the coast is the richness of the marine and
estuarine habitats. It is this richness that allowed the complex societies
of South Florida to develop without the agricultural subsistence base that
supported the chiefdoms over most of the Southeast.[22]

The Coastal Plain extends from the Fall Line to the Atlantic and Gulf
coasts. This region is geographically the largest of the major environmental
zones of the Southeast. It also subsumes a number of different ecological zones, although it is dominated by southern pine forests. The coastal
zones, with ready access to marine and estuarine habitats supported relatively high population densities despite the fact that they were at best only
marginally suitable for agriculture. The alluvial valleys of the larger rivers
entering the Coastal Plain from the Piedmont also supported high population densities and were the homes of many of the agricultural chiefdoms
of the late prehistoric period. The interriverine areas were less densely
occupied, especially during the late prehistoric period. From a human sub-

sistence viewpoint, these pine covered areas were less productive than the agricultural lands of the alluvial river valleys or the marine and estuarine habitats along the coast. Thus during the late prehistoric period, they typically served as buffer areas between polities. An exception to this general picture occurred in northern Florida where most of the rivers did not carry heavy silt loads and therefore did not create levees, and where fertile inter-riverine areas were the preferred settlement locations for peoples like the Apalachee, Potano, Utina, and Yustega.[23]

The Piedmont occupies the area above the Fall Line and below the Appalachian Highlands. The dominant forest cover in the Piedmont consists of mixed hardwood forests that produce abundant plant and animal food resources. Many of the larger late prehistoric polities of the Southeast occupied the larger river valleys of the Piedmont area. In these valleys, the people had access to rich agricultural soils in the alluvial valleys and the wild resources of the rolling hills of the interriverine uplands.

The Appalachian Highlands contain rugged terrain, much of which is poorly suited for agricultural lifestyles. Nevertheless, the region did support significant populations during the late prehistoric period. Most settlements were located in the narrow river valleys. Presumably the ancestors of the historic Cherokee occupied portions of the Appalachian Highlands during the late prehistoric period.[24]

The Mississippi Alluvial Valley differs from the other environmental zones of the Southeast in several ways. It contains much larger tracts of fertile agricultural lands than the other zones. Throughout its history it appears to have supported much higher population densities than the other areas, although we cannot be sure this is true before the Late Archaic since the constantly changing Mississippi River has erased much of the archaeological record for earlier times. These population densities are revealed not only in the numbers of sites recorded but in the size and complexity of the polities seen in the Mississippi Valley. It is true that large chiefdoms existed elsewhere in the Southeast during the late prehistoric period (for example, Moundville, Etowah, Coosa, the Apalachee, and the Calusa), but even the largest sites outside the Mississippi Valley are dwarfed by Cahokia, and sites such as Emerald, Anna, Winterville, and Lake George rival any sites outside the Valley. Finally, nowhere in the Southeast is there a concentration of mound sites (presumably the political centers of chiefdoms) that compares to the lower Mississippi Valley.[25]

The cultural diversity of the sixteenth-century native societies of the Southeast matched the environmental diversity. (See figure 3.) Individual polities were generally quite small, so there were a great many of them. Languages varied, although there were groups of related languages. Material cultures varied, although many were so similar that we have come to group them into broader regional units. Subsistence economies varied; while most sixteenth-century groups practiced cleared-field agriculture, the

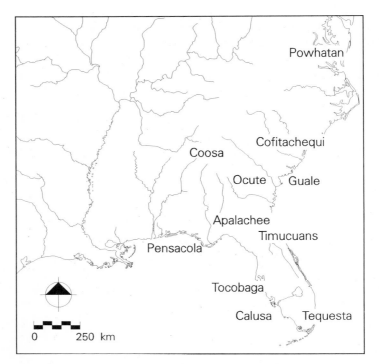

FIGURE 3
Cultural groupings in the protohistoric Southeast

specific mix of crops they planted and the degree to which they relied on them varied, and some groups appear never to have relied on domesticated plants as their primary source of food. Political organizations varied in scale and complexity, although we would classify most as chiefdoms.

The groups of southern Florida were among the first of the southeastern polities to encounter Europeans. Juan Ponce de León landed in southern Florida in 1513, and there is considerable evidence to suggest that he was not the first European to do so.

The peoples of southern Florida are poorly known. Despite, or perhaps because of, the early contact with Europeans, our ethnohistoric data on them is surpassed by many groups who were visited much later. We know the names of several groups—the Tocobaga around Tampa Bay, the Tequesta near Miami, the Ais and Jeaga on the southeast coast, and the Calusa on the southwest coast—but we cannot say for certain how their languages were related to those of groups farther north.[26]

The Calusa and their neighbors in southern Florida had subsistence economies that differed markedly from those of the chiefdoms of the interior Southeast. While corn may have been used in the interior of South

Florida a thousand years before European contact, we have no evidence that it played any significant role in Calusa subsistence in the sixteenth century. The same is true for the Ais, Jeaga, and Tequesta. The Tocobaga grew maize, but apparently not to the extent of the Timucuan or Mississippian chiefdoms. Instead, the native peoples of South Florida were fisher-foragers who relied on the abundant wild resources of the area. The Calusa in particular were blessed with a rich environment.[27]

The abundant estuarine resources seem to have allowed some of the groups of South Florida to establish permanent settlements with large populations and high population densities. While some seasonal movement is indicated for the Tequesta (and was probably the case for the Ais and Jeaga), the Calusa and Tocobaga lived in large communities with impressive public constructions. The Calusa and Tocobaga also had settlement hierarchies consisting of a variety of site types and sizes.

The richness of the coastal environments of South Florida also allowed the peoples of the area to obtain the surpluses needed to support elites. Ethnohistoric accounts for all of the groups mention "chiefs" who controlled several communities and who appear to have had considerable power. The Calusa and Tocobaga, the largest and most powerful of the South Florida groups, had hereditary rulers who exercised great power within their societies, and who had considerable influence over neighboring groups. The Calusa were particularly powerful.

The Calusa also were politically complex. The paramount chief, who inherited his office, filled religious as well as secular roles. To insure that high offices and social status were retained within the ruling kin groups, there was some marriage within that group, including sibling marriage within the royal family. While the paramount chief held considerable power and authority, he was not the only political or religious officeholder. There were subordinate chiefs of other communities. Within the chief's own community there were also a chief priest, a captain general, and a group of principal nobles who advised the chief.[28]

In the sixteenth century, the Calusa appear to have been larger and militarily more powerful than the other groups of South Florida. They seem to have been able to dominate their neighbors and extract tribute from such groups as the Tequesta. The Calusa's position of dominance over their neighbors appears to have been a tenuous one. In the sixteenth century there were internal political problems involving succession to high office, tributary polities rebelled (or at least refused to pay tribute), and there were military difficulties with their rivals the Tocobaga.

At the time of earliest European contact in the Southeast, north peninsular Florida and adjacent areas of south Georgia were occupied by peoples speaking closely related languages of the Timucuan family. Based on stylistic continuities in ceramics, it appears that they had been residents of this area at least since the beginning of the Woodland period. The division between the Timucuan peoples and the peoples of the interior Southeast must have been a long-standing one, for their languages are quite distinct from the Muskogean languages of their neighbors to the north and west.[29]

The Timucuan groups can be divided into eastern and western groups. These groups broadly correspond to the St. Johns and Alachua archaeological cultures. The eastern Timucuans included the Saturiwa, the Agua Dulce, and the Acuera. The western Timucuans included the Ocale, the Potano, the Utina, and the Yustega.

The Timucuan groups of the sixteenth century practiced maize agriculture, although it is not known to what extent they relied on agricultural crops for subsistence. The chroniclers of the de Soto expedition describe extensive fields for the western Timucuans, but some of the eastern groups along the St. Johns River and the Atlantic coast may have obtained a significant portion of their diet from aquatic resources. Western Timucuan groups appear to have adopted maize agriculture early in the Mississippi period to judge from the cob-marked pottery found on late prehistoric Alachua tradition sites in the areas occupied by the Potano and Ocale in the sixteenth century.

Many of the Timucuan groups were organized as chiefdoms in the sixteenth century. That much is clear from the accounts of the de Soto expedition. What is not clear is when chiefly organizations first appear among the Timucuans. The question simply has not been studied as intensively as it has for the Calusa or many of the Mississippian chiefdoms. There is little evidence of chiefly organization in the archaeological record from the Potano and Ocale areas. Elaborate mortuary offerings from the St. Johns area may indicate the status differentiation expected of chiefdoms, but unfortunately the excavations that yielded those artifacts were done before the development of modern theoretical frameworks and the analytical tools needed to examine social organization from such remains.[30]

The Timucuan chiefdoms were among the first southeastern natives to encounter Europeans, and they were the first to feel the full weight of European colonization and missionary efforts. Narváez and de Soto both passed through Timucuan territory and encountered several groups, including the Ocale, the Potano, the Utina, and the Yustega. Pedro Menéndez de Avilés established St. Augustine in the territory of the Saturiwa in 1565. Timucuan peoples were the first southeastern natives to be converted to Christianity. Franciscan missionaries established missions among the eastern Timucuans beginning in 1584, and by 1633 the mission chain reached across Timucuan territory to the Apalachee. And, they were the first to feel the full impact of European diseases; Timucuan populations were reduced long before those of the Apalachee.[31]

Along the Atlantic and Gulf coasts there were numerous groups that had material cultures and perhaps political organizations that resembled those of the Mississippian chiefdoms of the interior but that had subsistence economies that placed much greater reliance on wild resources than they did on domesticated crops. Prominent among these groups were the Guale and Cusabo of the Atlantic Coast and the Pensacola, Ochuse, and other, unnamed peoples of the Gulf Coast, for example, those visited by Narváez after he left Apalachee. It is clear that these peoples interacted with the Mississippian chiefdoms. They may have shared elements of belief systems and social organization as well. The best known of these groups are those that occupied the Georgia coast. The Georgia groups include the Guale, among whom the Spaniards established the mission of Santa Catalina de Guale.[32]

While Spaniards encountered other peoples in the sixteenth century, and some of those groups played important roles in the European settlement of the Southeast, the most numerous and visible of the sixteenth-century native societies were the Mississippian chiefdoms of the interior. Since several of these societies are described in detail in later chapters, I will limit this discussion to a few general features of the Mississippian polities.[33]

The definition of Mississippian societies has changed over the years. Originally, the term was used to refer to prehistoric groups that possessed a limited set of material traits including shell-tempered pottery, rectangular wall-trench houses, and flattop pyramidal mounds. More recent definitions have focused on economy, political organization, and religious cult institutions. For our purposes here, we can restrict the term to those societies that practiced cleared-field agriculture with maize as the dominant crop, that had hierarchical political organizations with evidence of ascriptive status differentiation, and that shared a set of cult institutions marked by a consistent iconographic complex and pyramidal earthen mounds.[34]

Societies that are generally classed as Mississippian existed from northern Florida to southern Illinois and from the Atlantic Coastal Plain to eastern Oklahoma. They constructed some of the largest and most impressive archaeological sites in eastern North America, such as the Cahokia site in Illinois with perhaps one hundred mounds, including the great Monks Mound that measures 1000 feet by 300 feet at the base and rises 100 feet into the air. Other large sites include Spiro in Oklahoma, Moundville in Alabama, Etowah in Georgia, and Lake George in Mississippi. Sixteenth-century Mississippian polities included Apalachee, Ocute, Cofitachequi, Coosa, and Pacaha. In many instances we can now tie sixteenth-century groups mentioned in European accounts with the archaeological remains of pre- and protohistoric Mississippian chiefdoms. (See, for example, the chapters by John F. Scarry, Mark Williams, Chester B. DePratter, and David J. Hally in this volume.)

The Mississippian peoples were farmers. They raised a diverse set of crops that provided adequate diets for the bulk of their populations. The exact mix of crops varied from group to group and area to area, but always included corn as the dominant source of calories.[35] The agricultural systems of the Mississippian societies were capable of producing substantial surpluses beyond the amount needed to support the individuals involved in crop production. The chroniclers of the earliest Spanish expeditions clearly indicate this. The capabilities of a single chiefdom to produce agricultural surpluses can be seen in the case of the seventeenth-century Apalachee province. Apalachee not only exported food to Havana and St. Augustine, there are indications that Spaniards residing in the province had better diets and greater access to expensive European goods than many of their contemporaries in the capital at St. Augustine.[36] There is some evidence that in areas where soils were less productive or agriculture less reliable the diet of Mississippian peoples may have produced nutritional stress. But in the heart of the area, in the alluvial valleys of the Southeast, Mississippian peoples appear to have been as healthy as, or healthier than their ancestors or their descendants.[37]

The Mississippian chiefdoms were capable of producing surpluses needed to support chiefs and their entourages. The most important form of material surplus was undoubtedly food, but other goods were also produced in amounts greater than that needed by the producers themselves. The economic systems of Mississippian chiefdoms were closely linked to their political systems. Surpluses not only served to support the elite, they also helped support part-time craft specialists who made items such as elaborate copper plates, engraved shell pendants and cups, and nonutilitarian artifacts of stone. In turn, elites used these items to establish links to other polities, legitimate their own authority and status, and control their potential rivals among the elite of their own society.[38]

The Mississippian societies appear to have shared a set of cult institutions visible in the archaeological record over much of the Southeast. Vernon Knight has identified three such institutions that were particularly widespread (and which he uses to identify "Mississippian" societies). There was a warfare/cosmogony cult closely tied to elites and positions of power and marked by artifacts used for display including representations of weapons or bearing representational images of imaginary animals or humans with animal characteristics. There was a communal cult focused on the earth and its periodic purification and closely linked to agricultural fertility. This cult incorporated the pyramidal Mississippian mounds. Finally, there was a priestly cult associated with mortuary ritual and ancestor worship. This cult was associated with human (temple) statuary, and Knight suggests that it mediated between the warfare/cosmogony cult that sanctified chiefly authority and the communal fertility/world purification cult. These institutions reflect the importance of the agricultural economy and served to legitimate the hierarchical structure of the Mississippian chiefdoms.[39]

In the Middle Atlantic region, particularly in the tidewater area of Virginia and Maryland, a number of chiefdoms developed that were distinct from those to the south. These societies include several—for example, the Powhatan, the Monacan, and the Patawomeke—that were described by early European explorers and colonists. Perhaps the best known of these is the Powhatan chiefdom.[40]

The Powhatan polity was clearly organized as a complex chiefdom at the time of European contact. There were hierarchies of settlements and of people. There was the paramount center, and beneath it there were district capitals, villages, and hamlets. There were the paramount chief and the district chiefs. Below the chiefly elite, the social hierarchy continued with priests and shamans, counsellors and distinguished warriors, and finally, at the bottom, the commoners.[41]

The Powhatan chiefdom incorporated over thirty distinct subgroupings in 1607 when English settlers established the Jamestown settlement. Some of these were inherited by Powhatan, the paramount chief, but over twenty were incorporated into the chiefdom through conquest or the threat of conquest. Powhatan installed relatives in high office in incorporated units and allied himself and his family to others through marriage.[42]

The elite of the Powhatan chiefdom (and presumably the other Algonquian chiefdoms of the Middle Atlantic region) inherited their status and offices matrilineally. A werowance's (chief's) heirs were, in approximate order, his brothers, his sisters, and his eldest sister's children. From Powhatan himself, the paramount office passed to his brother Opitchapan, then to another brother Opechancanough, then to Necotowance, then to Totopotomoy, and then to Cockacoeske (wife of Totopotomoy and a descendent of Opechancanough and Powhatan).[43]

The Powhatan, and presumably the other Middle Atlantic chiefdoms as well, were agricultural societies although they incorporated other foods into their diet to an apparently greater extent than their Mississippian contemporaries to the south. Nevertheless, it seems that the Powhatan grew enough corn to support themselves and a political and social elite.[44]

Like the Mississippian elites, the chiefs of the Middle Atlantic chiefdoms relied on material culture markers of status and authority. Like the Mississippian elites, the chiefs of the Middle Atlantic chiefdoms used exotic raw materials such as copper. And like the Mississippian elites, the chiefs of the Middle Atlantic chiefdoms attempted to control supplies and distribution of copper to subordinates within their polity and rivals in other polities. In fact, a major destabilizing factor in the entrance of English colonists into the Middle Atlantic was the new source of copper that they provided, a source that soon escaped the control of the native werowances.[45]

The native chiefdoms of the Southeast were extremely successful societies. Some survived for hundreds of years without major disruption or collapse. Nevertheless, none of them managed to survive the appearance of European explorers, colonists, and missionaries in the sixteenth and seventeenth centuries. Some groups, such as the Cherokee and Creek, survived, but their social and political organizations were radically transformed. Others, such as the Apalachee, Calusa, and Powhatan, disappeared completely.

NOTES

1. Two recent overviews of the prehistory of the Southeast are B. D. Smith, "The Archaeology of the Southeastern United States," and Steponaitis, "Prehistoric Archaeology."

2. This quadripartite division of the prehistory of the Southeast seems to hold for much of the region and parts of the Midwest as well. It does not seem to fit the archaeological record for southern Florida, however. There, the native peoples never seem to have adopted agriculture, although in the late prehistoric period at least one group, the Calusa, achieved a level of sociopolitical complexity comparable to those of the societies of the inland Southeast. For an overview of the chronology for South Florida, see Griffin, *Everglades National Park*.

3. Anderson, "Paleoindian Colonization"; Meltzer, "Late Pleistocene Human Adaptations"; Meltzer and Smith, "Paleo-Indian"; Clausen et al., "Little Salt Spring"; and Cockrell and Murphy, "Pleistocene Man in Florida."

4. Neusius, *Foraging, Collecting, and Harvesting*. Phillips and Brown, *Archaic Hunters and Gatherers,* is an excellent collection of papers on the Archaic period, although its focus is on the midwestern United States. Nevertheless, it provides a good basis for understanding Archaic period developments in the Southeast. See also B. D. Smith, "Archaeology of the Southeastern United States," 5.

5. Bullen and Stoltman, *Fiber-tempered Pottery*. Perhaps the best known of the Archaic period cemetery sites is Indian Knoll in Kentucky. A general descriptive report on the site may be found in Webb, *Indian Knoll,* and a more specialized examination of the mortuary complex can be found in Rothschild, "Mortuary Behavior," 658.
For a discussion of the emergence of complex social organizations during the Archaic period, see J. A. Brown, "Long-term Trends"; and Marquardt, "Fisher-gatherers-hunters."

6. Decker, "Origin(s), Evolution, and Systematics."

7. Fritz, "Multiple Pathways," 392–93; Fritz and Smith, "Old Collections and New Technology"; and Yarnell, "Domestication of Sunflower," 296.

8. There are several excellent overviews of the Woodland period currently available. Farnsworth and Emerson, *Early Woodland Archaeology,* focuses on the Early Woodland period in the eastern United States. Brose and Greber, *Hopewell Archaeology,* contains papers that concentrate on the Middle Woodland. Keegan, *Emergent Horticultural Economies,* addresses the emergence of food production in the eastern United States, particularly during the Woodland period.
While our evidence of status differentiation during the Middle Woodland period suggests greater differentiation than existed earlier, the Middle Woodland societies were neither as complex nor as hierarchically differentiated as the later chiefdoms of the Mississippi period. See Braun, "Illinois Hopewell Burial Practices."

9. Ford, "Gathering and Gardening"; Fritz, "Crops before Corn"; C. M. Scarry, "Plant Remains from the Walling Truncated Mound"; and Goad, "Middle Woodland Exchange."

10. The Kolomoki site is one of the most extreme examples of mortuary elaboration seen in the Middle Woodland period of the Southeast, although it pales next to the richest of the Ohio Hopewell burials in the American midwest. For descriptions of the Kolomoki mortuary complex (unfortunately marred by misinterpretations of its chronological position), see Sears, *Excavations at Kolomoki, Season II;* and Sears, *Excavations at Kolomoki, Season III and IV.* For a more recently excavated, less elaborate Woodland mortuary site roughly contemporaneous with Kolomoki, see Milanich et al., *McKeithen Weeden Island.*

11. Johannessen, "Farmers of the Late Woodland."

12. For a discussion of the social and political processes operating during the Late Woodland, see Braun and Plog, " 'Tribal' Social Networks." For riverine habitats, see, for example, J. F. Scarry, "Fort Walton Development."

13. Rolingson, *Plum Bayou Culture,* 7; Gayle J. Fritz, "Adding the Plant Remains to Assessments of Late Woodland/Early Mississippi Period Plant Husbandry" (Paper presented at the Fifty-third Annual Meeting of the Society for American Archaeology, Phoenix, Ariz., 1988); and Rose and Marks, "Bioarcheology of the Alexander Site," 98.

14. Witthoff, *Green Corn Ceremonialism,* and C. M. Scarry, "Mississippian Crop Production Strategies."

15. B. D. Smith, *Mississippian Settlement Patterns,* 488–90.

16. Steponaitis, *Ceramics,* 37–45.

17. For discussions of the emergence of specific Mississippian chiefdoms, see individual chapters in Marshall, *The Emergent Mississippian,* and B. D. Smith, *Mississippian Emergence.* B. D. Smith, "Mississippian Expansion," traces the theoretical development of models of the emergence of the Mississippian chiefdoms. The evolution of the Calusa chiefdom is discussed in Widmer, *Evolution of the Calusa.* The Middle Atlantic chiefdoms are discussed in Turner, "Evolution of Rank Societies."

18. Braun and Plog, " 'Tribal' Social Networks," 516–18.

19. For a case study of an area where demographic stress seems to have been involved in the emergence of Mississippian polities, see J. F. Scarry, "Mississippian Emergence."

20. Ford, "Evolutionary Ecology," 179–82.

21. Possibly the best picture we have of the emergence of a Mississippian society comes from the American Bottom area near St. Louis, Missouri; see J. E. Kelly, "Range Site Community Patterns" and "The Emergence of Mississippian." Other areas where we have reasonably detailed pictures are described in Rolingson, "Toltec Mounds Site," and Morse and Morse, "The Zebree Site."

22. C. M. Scarry, "Paleoethnobotany of the Granada Site," 187; Widmer, *Evolution of the Calusa,* 277–81.

23. The most comprehensive discussion of late prehistoric human adaptations to the Coastal Plain is L. Larson, *Aboriginal Subsistence Technology.*

24. Dickens, *Cherokee Prehistory,* and Keel, *Cherokee Archaeology,* 245.

25. Brain, "Late Prehistoric Settlement Patterning"; Fowler, "Cahokia"; Mil-

ner, "Late Prehistoric Cahokia"; Williams and Brain, *Lake George Site;* P. Phillips, *Lower Yazoo Basin;* and Phillips, Ford, and Griffin, *Lower Mississippi Alluvial Valley.*

26. The archaeological data concerning the Calusa are synthesized in a series of publications by Widmer and Marquardt. Particularly important among these are Marquardt, "Calusa Social Formation," and Widmer, *Evolution of the Calusa.* The Tequesta are discussed in Griffin et al., *Granada Site.* Finally, an overall synthesis of South Florida archaeology can be found in J. W. Griffin, *Everglades National Park.*

27. For the evidence for corn use in prehistoric South Florida, see Sears and Sears, "Prehistoric Corn Pollen." For a discussion of the absence of corn in South Florida, see Milanich, "Corn and Calusa." For more general discussions of plant food subsistence in South Florida, C. M. Scarry, "Paleoethnobotany of the Granada Site," and C. Margaret Scarry, Lee Newsom, and Marilyn Masson, "Calusa and Tequesta Plant Use: Evidence Gleaned from Archaeobotanical Data" (Paper presented at the Forty-sixth Annual Southeastern Archaeological Conference, Tampa, Fla., 1989).

28. Goggin and Sturtevant, "The Calusa," and Marquardt, "Calusa Social Formation," 98.

29. The archaeology of the Timucuan peoples is less well understood than that of many other groups in the Southeast, largely because of the limited amount of recent research. The classic reference on the archaeology of the eastern Timucua area is Goggin, *Space and Time.* The archaeology of the prehistoric Alachua tradition tied to western Timucuans is described in Milanich, *The Alachua Tradition.* Important recent sources on the late prehistoric and early historic Timucuan groups are Deagan, "Cultures in Transition," and Milanich, "The Western Timucua." Much of our knowledge of Timucuan culture comes from ethnohistoric sources. Among the best known and important of these is Milanich and Sturtevant, *Francisco Pareja's 1613 Confessionario.*

30. See, for example, the Mount Royal site in Moore, "Certain Sand Mounds," 16–35.

31. Hann, "Demographic Patterns" and "DeSoto, Dobyns, and Demography."

32. Crook, *Mississippi Period Archaeology;* Davis, *Gulf Coast Prehistory;* R. L. Smith, "Coastal Mississippian Period Sites"; and Thomas et al., *Anthropology of Mission Santa Catalina.*

33. Important general references on the archaeology of the Mississippian chiefdoms include Dye and Cox, *Towns and Temples;* B. D. Smith, *Mississippian Settlement Patterns* and *Mississippian Emergence;* and Williams and Shapiro, *Lamar Archaeology.*

34. J. B. Griffin, "Prehistoric Mississippian Cultures," provides a review of archaeological thought regarding the Mississippian societies. Griffin also proposes a definition similar in scope to the one used here. Recent alternative definitions, which I have combined into the one used here, have been proposed by Peebles and Kus, "Some Archaeological Correlates," 435; B. D. Smith, "Mississippian Patterns," 64–67; Knight, "Mississippian Religion"; and Knight, "Hierarchy in Southeastern Chiefdoms."

35. Chmurny, "Middle Mississippian Occupation," and C. M. Scarry, "Change in Plant Procurement."

36. For discussions of the economic contribution of Apalachee province to

seventeenth-century La Florida, see Matter, "Seventeenth-century Florida Missions"; and Hann, *Apalachee*. The contribution of native crops and wild foods to the diet of Spanish colonists in the Southeast is detailed in Reitz and Scarry, *Reconstructing Historic Subsistence,* 79–99, and C. M. Scarry and Reitz, "Herbs, Fish, Scum, and Vermin." Our picture of the personal wealth of Spaniards in Apalachee province is emerging from ongoing excavations by Bonnie McEwan in the Spanish village at San Luis, the provincial capital.

37. On nutritional stress, see Cassidy, "Nutrition and Health," Lallo, "Skeletal Biology," and C. S. Larsen, *Anthropology of St. Catherine's Island,* 159–207. On the alluvial valleys of the Southeast, see Milner, "Prehistoric Levels of Health," and Powell, *Status and Health.*

38. Muller, "Mississippian Specialization and Salt"; Pauketat, "Mississippian Domestic Economy"; Prentice, "Economic Differentiation"; Welch, *Moundville's Economy;* and Yerkes, "Mississippian Craft Specialization." For a more general discussion of the political economies of chiefdoms, see Wright, "Prestate Political Formations."

39. See Knight, "Mississippian Religion," for a thorough discussion of Mississippian cult institutions. Many of the artifacts and much of the iconography of Knight's Mississippian warfare/cosmogony sacra were subsumed within the Southeastern Ceremonial Complex first defined by Waring and Holder, "Prehistoric Ceremonial Complex." The iconography and material culture of the Mississippian warfare/cosmogony cult are thoroughly discussed in Galloway, *Southeastern Ceremonial Complex,* and Phillips and Brown, *Pre-Columbian Shell Engravings.* For an analysis of the "cult" that emphasizes its political and economic aspects rather than its religious aspects, see J. A. Brown, "The Southern Cult Reconsidered."

40. The Powhatan are described in great detail in documents dating to the early seventeenth century. (See Rountree and Turner, this volume.) Other sources on the Powhatan include Alex Barker, "Powhatan's Purse Strings"; McCartney, "Cockacoeske"; Turner, "Evolution of Rank Societies"; and Turner, "Socio-political Organization." Other chiefdoms in the Middle Atlantic region and its interior are discussed in Binford, "Aboriginal Cultures of Coastal Virginia"; Hantman, "Between Powhatan and Quirank"; Potter, "Chicacoan Settlement Patterns"; and "Early English Effects"; and Turner, "Archaeological Identification of Chiefdoms."

41. Turner, "Powhatan Socio-political Organization," 204, 207–8.

42. Ibid., 193, 197–99.

43. Ibid., 197; McCartney, "Cockacoeske," 173–75; and Turner, "Powhatan Socio-political Organization."

44. See Barker, "Powhatan's Purse Strings," 62–65, for a discussion of the importance of corn in Powhatan diet and society.

45. Hantman, "Between Powhatan and Quirank," 685.

PAUL E. HOFFMAN

Lucas Vázquez de Ayllón's Discovery and Colony

On June 24, 1521, Francisco Gordillo and Pedro de Quejo discovered land at the entrance to the South Santee River. Slightly over five years later, Lucas Vázquez de Ayllón, judge of the royal Audiencia of Santo Domingo and Gordillo's employer in 1521, also saw that shore. His plans called for founding a colony that would trade with and eventually convert and make Spanish subjects of the native Americans of the area. Later that summer he was to found just such a colony, but further south, on the shore of or near Sapelo Sound. That colony was the first attempt by Europeans to settle on the southeastern coast of North America. Its location in coastal Georgia meant that the "youngest" colony of the thirteen English colonies also has the distinction of being the site of the earliest European settlement.

Gordillo and Quejo had expected to find land. An unknown number of years before, Captain Pedro de Salazar had sailed north northwest from the Bahama Islands and landed on a coastal island from which he kidnapped a number of tall native Americans whom he took to Hispaniola where they were sold as slaves.[1] So far as is now known, this "land of giants" was not exploited by the slave raiders who followed Salazar to the Bahamas, probably because they did not know its location. As well, the Spanish government had outlawed raids in the Bahamas and, by extension, all lands north of the greater Antilles. The political turmoil of the 1514–20 period made slaving politically dangerous, because abuse of native Americans was a serious charge in the days when the "struggle for justice" was first influencing royal policy.[2] But knowledge of Salazar's discovery remained alive with Lucas Vázquez de Ayllón, one of Salazar's employers. In 1521, he imparted the secret to Gordillo along with instructions that if slaves were not found in the Bahamas, he should follow Salazar's route to the northwest. Gordillo met Quejo in the Bahamas, where Quejo too was seeking slaves for his employer, the Licenciado Juan Ortiz de Matienzo. Quejo had enough ship biscuit so that when it was added to Gordillo's slender supply, they would have enough for the voyage to the northwest in pursuit of the truth of Gordillo's information about Salazar's voyage. They agreed to divide evenly any slaves they might capture.[3]

After entering and anchoring in the South Santee River, the Spaniards not only came into contact with a village of native Americans, they also explored the immediate vicinity. Finding the entrance to a bay just to the west of the "cape" that they had skirted when coming to land from the northeast, they moved the ships to that better anchorage. There on June 28 or 29, 1521, Gordillo took possession of the new land for his employer, Ayllón. Quejo did the same for his employer, Matienzo, on June 30. Quejo recorded the latitude as 33°30′ north, an estimate to the nearest half of a degree. He seems to have taken a solar declination at noon, which means that the accuracy of his reading was limited only by the quality of his instrument(s) and skill with the calculation.

When the new moon of July 3–4 and the possibility of bad weather had come and gone, the Spaniards decided that it was time to return to the Antilles. They induced some sixty of the native Americans from the area to board the ships, and then raised anchor and hoisted sail, enslaving their guests. On the way home, Gordillo quarreled with the master of his ship and moved himself and his prisoners to Quejo's ship.[4] Thus it was that on August 11, 1521, Quejo's ship put into the river at Santo Domingo with a cargo of sixty North American natives. When the principals of each expedition were summoned, they divided the new slaves as the two pilots had agreed. Ayllón's slaves were sent to work on an estate he had near the city, or, perhaps, sold to Spaniards resident in the interior of the island. The fates of Matienzo's slaves are unknown except that one was later reported to be a diver at the pearl beds off Venezuela.[5] What is certain is that all but that man and one known as Francisco "El Chicorano" had died by 1526.

The two judges, and a third partner, the Audiencia's secretary, Diego Cavallero, subsequently agreed to form a company to exploit the new discovery. As a first step, they obtained an exclusive license to do so from the *Real Acuerdo,* a committee composed of Governor Diego Colón (Christopher Columbus's son), the other judges of the Audiencia, and the royal treasury officials.[6] This license was useful for keeping other persons in the Indies from jumping the claim, but was worthless without approval from the king. Accordingly, when Ayllón was sent to Spain on official business, he agreed to seek a royal license.

In due course, the Emperor Charles V granted the license, but he named Ayllón as his sole agent. Dated June 12, 1523, the contract allowed one year for exploration along the coast (the voyagers of 1521 had not gone far from the Santee-Winyah Bay area) before Ayllón had to establish a town from which trade and missions would reach to the native Americans. As Ayllón now told the tale, the discovery had been at the latitudes of Andalucia, in

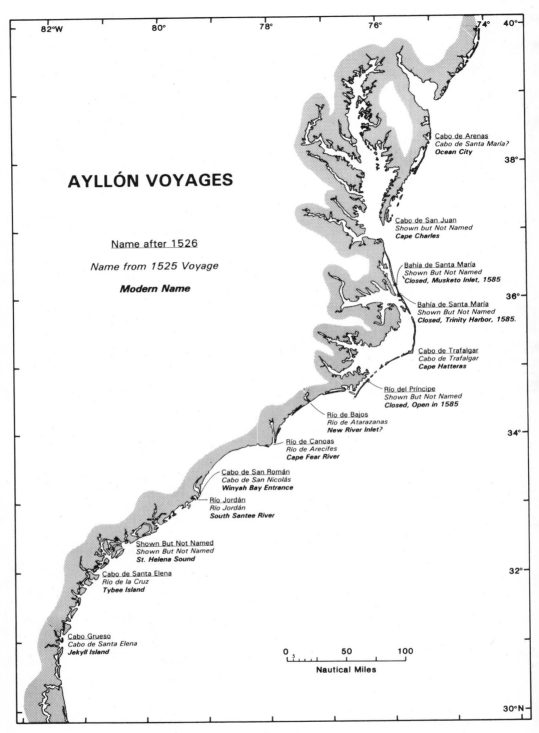

AYLLÓN VOYAGES

Name after 1526

Name from 1525 Voyage

Modern Name

Cabo de Arenas
Cabo de Santa María?
Ocean City

Cabo de San Juan
Shown but Not Named
Cape Charles

Bahía de Santa María
Shown But Not Named
Closed, Musketo Inlet, 1585

Bahía de Santa María
Shown But Not Named
Closed, Trinity Harbor, 1585.

Cabo de Trafalgar
Cabo de Trafalgar
Cape Hatteras

Río del Príncipe
Shown But Not Named
Closed, Open in 1585

Río de Bajos
Río de Atarazanas
New River Inlet?

Río de Canoas
Río de Arecifes
Cape Fear River

Cabo de San Román
Cabo de San Nicolás
Winyah Bay Entrance

Río Jordán
Río Jordán
South Santee River

Shown But Not Named
Shown But Not Named
St. Helena Sound

Cabo de Santa Elena
Río de la Cruz
Tybee Island

Cabo Grueso
Cabo de Santa Elena
Jekyll Island

0 5 50 100
Nautical Miles

FIGURE I
The South Atlantic Coast in the age of Ayllón

southern Spain, and was near the territories of a lord named Du-a-e, whose people were said to live *en policía,* that is "politically" or like civilized persons. Various Indian groups were named as residing within the area of the grant (35°–37° north latitude). Those that can be identified are, from south to north: Orista and Coçayo, whose towns lay just north of St. Helena Sound, perhaps on the Edisto River or on the Cosapoy River; Sona, near modern Stono Inlet; Cayagua, a form of Kiawa, the name of the Indians who lived around Charleston Harbor; Chicora, the name now assigned to the native captured in 1521; and Xoxi and Pasque, upriver from Chicora. Inland were Du-a-e and the Anicatixe, who were probably the Aní Kutání of Cherokee legend.[7]

Ayllón apparently hoped to enlist royal and, possibly, investor interest with this mixture of the ethnogeography of the South Carolina coast north of Saint Helena Sound, of a report of a hegemonic chief in the interior (to the northwest of Winyah Bay), and of his own notion that the discovery was a "new Andalucia." Because of the then-current debate over how native Americans should be brought into the empire and whether any native Americans were capable of living like civilized Europeans (that is, like Castilians), he stressed that a civilized native state existed in his discovery and that peaceful approaches could be used.[8] To underline the agricultural possibilities of the area—Quejo reported grape vines and "olive trees" among other things—Ayllón deliberately moved the area of the discovery from 33°30' north to 35°–37° north latitude, placing it due west of Andalucia. Additional references to "terrestrial gems" and pearls completed his picture of wealth for the taking.

Ayllón's falsification of where the discovery had taken place and what the agricultural resources of the area were—he had little direct information, remember—might not have mattered in the long run had it not been for conversations he had with Peter Martyr, the chronicler of many of the early Spanish discoveries. Martyr wrote an account of the voyage of 1521 and of what Ayllón told him about the location and resources of the new area. He also noted fantastic stories of the customs of the natives—from mortuary practices to how they stretched the bones of their prospective rulers so that they became unusually tall. All of this wound up in his *Decades* when they were published in 1530 in a complete, posthumous edition. As such, they became what I have called the "Chicora Legend," which described the American Southeast as a new Andalucia.[9] The French under Jean Ribault and the English under Sir Walter Raleigh and the two Richard Hakluyts were influenced by this legend when they planned locations for attempted colonies along the southeastern coast.[10]

When Ayllón returned to the Antilles he did not at once prepare the exploring party mandated by his contract. Rather he spent most of 1524 in Puerto Rico conducting investigations of its government, auditing treasury accounts, and in general attempting to get the island's government back onto a sound footing after a period of disorders. In anticipation of this service, the Emperor had granted him a year's extension on the time during which he had to send his exploring party.[11]

Finally, in the spring of 1525 Ayllón sent Pedro de Quejo north with one ship carrying various trade goods, seeds for European plants, and some of the Indians from Chicora to serve as interpreters. According to Ayllón's later testimony, Quejo surveyed the coast during a voyage of over 200 leagues, taking soundings over various sand bars, entering bays and rivers, and contacting four linguistic groups.[12] His report was forwarded to Spain where it became the basis for the North American portions of the Juan Vespucci map of early 1526 and seems as well to have been incorporated into Alonso de Chaves's somewhat later manuscript rutter. Both of these sources, but especially Chaves, indicate a voyage from near the Delaware Bay on the north to St. Andrews Sound on the south. Among the points explored were Chesapeake Bay—called Bahía de Santa María or St. Mary's Bay—and the river-bay-cape complex visited in 1521. The latter were recorded by Vespucci as the Jordan River and Cape San Nicolás.[13]

A voyage from near the Delaware Bay to St. Andrews Sound would indeed have brought Quejo into contact with four linguistic groups. From north to south they were: 1) the Algonquian speakers of the Chesapeake Bay and North Carolina coasts; 2) the Catawban (or Siouan) speakers of the area around Chicora; 3) the Muskogean speakers who lived from roughly St. Helena Sound southward to central Georgia; and 4) the Timucuan speakers of Cumberland Island and St. Andrews Sound. From each except the Catawban speakers, persons were seized to learn Spanish so that later colonists would have translators. Ayllón already had at least one Catawban speaker, the man Francisco "El Chicorano."[14]

By the time of Quejo's return to Santo Domingo in July 1525, Ayllón had already begun to gather the supplies and men who would be needed for his colony. Some details of this are known, although the full cost of his preparations is not. The low estimate, which is probably close to the actual figure, was twenty thousand ducats, the high estimate was one hundred thousand ducats. In either case, this was a fortune that even the wealthy Ayllón had to raise by mortgaging his properties and making loans with business associates in Spain and Santo Domingo. He also used his sugar plantation at Puerto Plata as a source of foods and animals.[15]

At some point in these preparations, Ayllón decided not to sail to the Bahía de Santa María, which was at the latitudes specified in his contract, but instead opted to return to the Jordan River and Chicora. He did not record why he made this decision, but we can infer that Quejo's report indicated that the entire coast was sandy and that one part of it offered no apparent physical or biological advantages over any other part. Accordingly, it made sense to return to the area for which interpreters were available and which was thought to give access to Du-a-e's inland kingdom and its pearls and "terrestrial gems."

One other matter required Ayllón's attention that spring. Matienzo had complained to the emperor that he also had a right to the new discovery. He demanded and obtained a royal order for the Audiencia to gather information about his claim. Accordingly, on March 28, 1526, the Audiencia began to hear a formal suit.[16] The record of this case is one of the more important sources of information about the voyage of 1521 and the reason that Ayllón held the contract, and about Quejo's voyage of 1525. In the end, Ayllón left Santo Domingo without fully replying to Matienzo's interrogatories or obtaining depositions from all of the witnesses his own attorney called. Matienzo subsequently took the record of the suit to Spain where he used it, and his prior service to the king, to obtain appointment as a judge of the audiencia of New Spain (Mexico).[17]

The fleet cleared Puerto Plata in mid-July 1526. It consisted of six ships and about six hundred persons, including a few women and some black slaves. Horses and supplies for a few months were aboard. Ayllón intended to use his estate at Puerto Plata and other sources in the Antilles to feed his colonists until their first crop came in. He left behind a wife and five young children, all under the age of twelve.[18]

When the fleet arrived at the entrance to the new land—the narratives do not say whether this was the South Santee River or Winyah Bay entrance—the *capitana* or flagship ran aground. Her passengers and crew were saved but a major part of the expedition's supplies were lost.[19] Soon after, Francisco El Chicorano and any other surviving natives of the area fled, leaving the Spaniards without interpreters or guides. Scouting expeditions into the interior showed it to be devoid of human habitation and agriculturally sterile, although abundantly supplied with pine trees.

In reaction to these events, Ayllón sent exploring parties southward along the coast. Two members of the expedition later recalled that these ships had sailed 200 leagues going and coming, which would give them a voyage to roughly St. Andrews Sound, the southern limit of Quejo's exploration of 1525.[20] A third ship, perhaps piloted by Quejo as part of a plan developed in Santo Domingo, seems to have worked its way north from St. Augustine Beach to the Jordan River during these explorations, or perhaps on the voyage from Hispaniola. Among the places it stopped was one that became known as Sapelo Sound.[21] Sapelo Sound was the home of the Guale people, who lived along its shores, on the shores of various rivers that fed into the sound, and on St. Catherines Island just to the north of the entrance to the sound. Here was the "good land" that the Spaniards needed for their colony. The large number of Indians suggested adequate agricultural land and offered the opportunities for trade and missionary work that were at the heart of Ayllón's contract. Others in the party probably recognized the possibility of forcing the Guale to provide food and labor, much as other Indians were doing in other places where the Spanish conquest was occurring.

While these exploring parties were seeking a better site for the colony,

Ayllón had his men build a boat to replace the lost *capitana*. They finished it late in August.[22]

With the new ship and a new destination, Ayllón divided his party into the sick, women, and less able—who were sent on the ships—and a land party of mounted men and those foot soldiers able to withstand the march overland. While the former made the relatively quick trip by sea, the latter set off inland, perhaps following Indian paths, perhaps simply working their way south by compass heading in the pine barrens that are thought to have existed within a few dozen miles of the coast. The major rivers that flow to the sea along this line of march would have been crossed fairly far inland and in a time when the sea was as much as a meter lower than it is today, meaning that the swampy margins of the modern rivers might not have been as wide nor have extended inland from the coast as far as they do today.[23]

Reassembled at Sapelo Sound or on the shore of one of the waterways that feeds into the sound, the Spaniards set about building their town and suffering the effects of their lack of supplies and experience in creating a European community in a strange, not to say hostile, physical and human environment. They named their town San Miguel de Gualdape, for St. Michael the Archangel. If the name is derived from the founding of the town or from the dedication of its church on the feast day of that saint, then San Miguel was founded on September 29, 1526. The meaning of Gualdape is unknown.

The Spaniards probably used timbers and wattle-and-daub construction for the walls of their buildings, with some form of thatch for the roofs. Shallow, barrel-lined wells probably provided drinking water—and dysentery due to poor sanitary practices. The tidal streams of the estuary provided abundant fish for those with the will and energy to catch them. Various mammals and birds were seen and perhaps killed for food.[24] But what the Spaniards lacked was carbohydrates. The maize they had brought from Hispaniola may not have survived the wreck of the *capitana,* but even if it did it was soon exhausted. Local Indian stores of maize, tapped by trade and threats, could not have supplied the colony for long. The Indians are known to have supplemented their maize harvests with acorns and a number of different kinds of roots, an indication that the maize harvest usually was small.[25] But acorns and roots were not acceptable food to Spaniards. In a short time, the colonists were hungry and disease-ridden. They began to die. Among the casualties was Lucas Vázquez de Ayllón, who died on St. Luke's day, October 18, 1526.[26]

Following Ayllón's death, a period of disorder descended on the colony as ambitious men temporarily displaced the leaders he had left in command, and they, once restored to power, debated whether to abandon the colony or to wait for the orders of Ayllón's designated successor, Juan Ramirez, who was in Puerto Rico. In the end, the colonists decided to abandon the inhospitable shore, whose native residents had been provoked into attacking the town from long range.[27]

The first ship to return to Hispaniola carried the Dominican friars who had formed the missionary complement of the expedition. Other ships made port in other parts of the Antilles, whence the 150 or so survivors of the original 600 persons made their ways to other destinations. In later years a number continued to reside in Hispaniola, but others settled in New Spain (Mexico) and Peru.[28]

The majority of the survivors had little good to say about the southeastern coast of North America. Their opinion became the "official" view during the 1540s and early 1550s: that the entire coast from Cape Florida to the River of Deer (the Hudson?) was useless and a desert, that is, not inhabitable.[29] On the other hand, Gonzalo Fernández de Oviedo, the chronicler who recorded most of what is known about the colony of 1526, says that some of the survivors thought that the new land would be a good place for Spanish settlement if proper preparations were made to sustain a colony until its residents obtained an understanding of the land. The climate was more like Spain's than was the case elsewhere in the Caribbean.[30] Oviedo did not add that the possibilities of Du-a-e's pearls and terrestrial gems had yet to be explored. Hernando de Soto's men were to go in search of the district where those riches were supposed to be. Among his party may have been at least one man who was with Ayllón.[31]

Locating San Miguel de Gualdape depends on first establishing the location of Ayllón's Jordan River. With that done, Oviedo's statement that San Miguel was 40–45 leagues westward from the Jordan establishes a direction (west, actually southwest) and a distance, depending on what length of league one chooses to use.[32] The locational thesis presented herein, like the others to be discussed below, depends on the location of the Jordan River, but uses previously unused evidence to show where that river was and to corroborate Oviedo's statement of distance.

Perhaps the oldest thesis on the location of San Miguel was first expressed by Oviedo with his observation that San Miguel de Gualdape was not on any map.[33] That is, its location could not be known from available evidence. (However, he goes on to provide the distance and direction noted.) The modern statement of this position is based on the supposed nonidentity of the river discovered in 1521 and the Jordan River, to which Ayllón returned in 1526. John G. Shay stated that view in 1884 because he misread the act of possession of 1521, which specifies that the name of the "land" is San Juan Bautista, to say that the river was so named. In fact, the act of possession does not name the river. Woodbury Lowery repeated this thesis in 1901.[34]

The second thesis, presented by Lowery and Paul Quattlebaum, holds that while Gordillo and Quejo were on the shore of Winyah Bay when Gordillo took possession of the land and recorded his latitude as 32°30′

north, Ayllón nonetheless did not return to that location in 1526, but instead landed on the Cape Fear River, whence he marched south along the strand to Waccamaw Neck, where he built San Miguel de Gualdape.[35] This thesis rests on the first, so far as the name of the river of 1521 is concerned and, perhaps, on Villafañe's erroneous (or even fraudulent) identification of the Jordan with a river that likely was the Cape Fear River.

The second thesis has several flaws. First, it does not take account of Ayllón's statement in the lawsuit of 1526 that in 1525 Quejo had returned to the river discovered in 1521. If he were as good a pilot as he seems to have been, he could easily have found that river again barely a year later! And this seems especially true because of the unique combination of river, bay, and "cape" that defines the discovery of 1521. A second flaw is that the league proposed is vastly shorter than any of the leagues known to have been in use in the new world in this period.[36] Finally, there is no need to assume that Ayllón would have had to have or have wanted to maintain contact with his ships, or that the ships could not have passed the land party from one shore of Winyah Bay—or any other body of water met along the way—to the other.

A variant of this "Cape Fear equals Jordan" thesis was proposed by Shea, who suggested that Ayllón went *north* from an unnamed river at 33°40′ north latitude and founded his colony at the site of Jamestown, said in one later Spanish document to be called "Guandape," the name that Alonso de Espinosa Cervantes used in his testimony of 1561 when naming the town that Ayllón founded.[37] Shea's thesis is itself a variant on the work of the great Spanish historian Martín Fernández de Navarette, who located the 1526 landing at Port Royal Sound with a march north to Cape Lookout, and of the nineteenth-century historian Johann Kohl, who located the 1526 landing at Saint Helena Sound with a march north to the Cape Fear River.[38] These variants can be dismissed as incompatible with all the other known facts.

The third thesis, to which the one presented here is similar, recognizes that the name bestowed in 1521 was on the land, not a river. The Land of St. John Bautista might well contain a river called the Jordan. Thus the Jordan was discovered, but not named, in 1521, revisited in 1525 and named on the Vespucci map of early 1526, and finally revisited in 1526. Close study of the geography and of Peter Martyr's account indicates that the river had to be the South Santee River, with Winyah Bay and the "cape" of the entrance to Winyah Bay being the Cape of San Nicolás on Vespucci's map and the Cape of San Román on the Ribero maps that became the standard Spanish map. With this location of the Jordan River firmly established, San Miguel de Gualdape can be found 40–45 leagues to the southwest, as Oviedo says.

This third thesis was first proposed by John Swanton and has since been repeated by Carl Sauer. They argued that San Miguel was on the Savannah River. In support of this, Swanton noted that de Soto's men reported a river at Cofitachequi that they assumed was the Santa Elena, on which they thought Ayllón had died. Cofitachequi was two or three days upriver from the sea, and thus from the presumed site of Ayllón's colony. Since Swanton believed that Cofitachequi was near Silver Bluff on the Savannah, the parts of the puzzle fitted together. Swanton's league was 2.5 miles long. The most recent archaeological research indicates that Cofitachequi was probably near modern Camden or Columbia, South Carolina, on a tributary of the Santee River.[39]

The thesis presented herein agrees with the Swanton identification of the Jordan River as the South Santee but argues that the site of San Miguel was further south, at Sapelo Sound. This thesis rests on the evidence of distances and points visited found in Alonso de Chaves's rutter, a source not used heretofore.[40] Chaves records Quejo's 1525 voyage and the three voyages of 1526. His materials show that the correct league was the nautical league of 17.5 to the degree, or 3.1998 modern nautical miles.[41] With that value, Oviedo's 40–45 leagues bracket Sapelo Sound, which Chaves shows was visited by one of the explorers whose materials he incorporated into his rutter. Because the Ayllón voyages are the only voyages known to have visited those latitudes during the years before 1533, when Chaves finished his manuscript, it follows that Chaves's information is a record of Ayllón's activities and hence critical new evidence about the locations of the Jordan River and San Miguel de Gualdape.

Other evidence that supports this thesis is drawn from recent archaeological studies of the Georgia coast. Fred Cook has shown that burial mounds of the correct period cluster around Sapelo Sound, whereas north of St. Catherines Sound all the way to Chesapeake Bay, and south of Sapelo Sound to Cumberland Island, the coastal zone was virtually empty, with only a few Indian settlements well up the rivers (for example, Orista) or well "hidden" inside the sounds (as at Roanoke Island).[42] While not proving that San Miguel had to be at Sapelo Sound, this evidence of population distribution points strongly to the likely spot Ayllón would select once in possession of enough evidence. His colony was intended to trade with and convert Indians, and it required a large population to carry out that purpose.

A second line of archaeological evidence is provided by Lewis Larson's study of aboriginal subsistence strategies. Larson shows that the coastal strand was rich in proteins but offered limited carbohydrate supplies. The Indians knew how to exploit the latter to the maximum, but their populations were strictly limited by the available carbohydrates. Spaniards, who fed acorns to pigs and preferred wheat flour to all other carbohydrates, would not have done well anywhere on the coastal strip, but might have thought that they would have enough food around Sapelo Sound, where small pockets of soils suitable for maize are plentiful. Not knowing about these soils, the Spaniards would have judged the food potential of the area by its native American population. Winyah Bay, where the soils are acid and not suitable for most crops, had few Indians, and even those few had fled.[43]

Three objections have been raised to the Hoffman thesis. Some students of the problem are still not convinced that the available evidence indicates that the Jordan River was the South Santee. Their doubts appear to arise because the name "Jordan River" was applied in 1525 or even 1526, not in 1521. Examination of the Act of Possession and Chaves's rutter clarifies the history of the name and the location of the river of 1521. Another objection is to the length of league, although no one else has shown that another value better fits with Chaves's data. Finally, objection is made to the idea of the Spaniards moving overland across the numerous rivers, swamps, and other obstructions that would impede movement. This objection usually assumes that the land party of 1526 would have wanted to be close to the coast, which is an unwarranted assumption. Further, Larson has shown that an extensive pine belt lay just behind the coast, an area sterile of humans and animals and, in areas where the trees were of climax growth, nearly devoid of undergrowth. In this pine belt movement would have been easy, except at river crossings, and even they may have been easier when a lower sea level meant that the swampy margins of rivers did not reach as far inland from the coast as they do today.[44]

In the end, the final proof of any of these theses will be the archaeological discovery of the site of San Miguel de Gualdape. Its signature will likely be the cemetery, some wells, and perhaps the burned remains of its houses.

Three bodies of ethnographic information are associated with the Ayllón accounts. Martyr's account provides what he claimed are notes on the customs of the Chicorans and a partial list of peoples (or towns) in the vicinity of Chicora. Ayllón's contract expanded the list of names, making it the second body of information. The third body of information is provided by Oviedo's few notes on Indians in the vicinity of San Miguel de Gualdape.

Martyr's report of the customs of the Chicorans and their neighbors focuses on mortuary practices; the purported means by which they caused the rulers of Du-a-e to be so tall; why the Indians were beardless; and certain imagined agricultural practices such as herding deer for their milk. The curious reader is referred to Martyr's seventh decade, book three, for the fantastic details.

Note was made above of the names of Indian groups between St. Helena Sound and Winyah Bay and inland from the latter that are found in Ayllón's contract. The full list is as follows: Du-a-e, Chicora, Xapira, Yta tancal, Anicatixe, Coçayo, Guacaya, Xoxi, Sona, Pasqui, Aranbe, Xamunanbe, Huaque, Tançaca, Yenhohol, Pahor, Yamiscaron, Orixa inisyguanin, and Anoxa. As has been noted, Orista inisyguanin, Coçayo, Sona, Guacaya (that is, Cayagua), and Chicora can be located along the coast from St. Helena Sound northwards. Xoxi, Pasque, Du-a-e, Anicatixe, and Xapira were located inland at various distances from the Santee–Winyah Bay area.

Du-a-e and Anicatixe were described as a hegemonic chiefdom, the former as the ruling town, the latter as the town(?) of shamans whose existence is reflected in later Cherokee legend. Mooney identifies Du-a-e as Duksai or Dukwsai, the later Toxaway.[45] This town was probably not inhabited by Cherokee in the 1520s. Hudson's analysis of the chiefdoms Juan Pardo met in 1566–68 raises questions about the Ayllón-Martyr suggestion that a town named Du-a-e had a hegemonic relationship over a coastal group, the Chicorans, unless Du-a-e and Cofitachequi were the same, as Hudson suggests. In the 1560s, Cofitachequi's power reached the coast.[46]

Finally, Oviedo provided bits of information about the customs of the Indians around San Miguel de Gualdape, that is, about the Guale peoples. He noted that their houses were dispersed, like rural farms in southern Spain, rather than gathered into nucleated villages. He indicated that they were hospitable until provoked, when they would defend home and kin. They used bows and arrows, but did not poison the tips of their arrows like the forest Indians of South America.[47]

In sum, except for the lengthy and largely unbelievable discussions in Martyr, which rest on uncertain authority, the Ayllón materials provide only a bit of ethnographic information about peoples on two stretches of the southeastern coast and in the interior of what is now South and North Carolina. This information seems consistent with later Spanish descriptions and with available archaeological evidence, suggesting that if used with caution, it may be presented as the first record of these peoples.

NOTES

This essay is based on Hoffman, *A New Andalucia*, chaps. 1–3.

1. Hoffman, "A New Voyage," 415–26.

2. Hanke, *Spanish Struggle*, is a useful introduction to the debate about the nature of the Indians and their treatment by the Spaniards.

3. Archivo General de Indias (hereafter cited as AGI), Justicia 3, No. 3, fol. 40–41.

4. AGI, Justicia 3, No. 3, fols. 41v, 49–50, 62v, 68, 70v. See also Anghiera, *Decadas del Nuevo Mundo* 2: 594–95.

5. AGI, Justicia 3, No. 3, fols. 8, 35–36v, 38, 47, 62v–63, 66, 69.

6. AGI, Justicia 3, No. 3, fol. 88.

7. The contract was printed in an imperfect transcription in the *Colección de documentos inéditos* 14: 504–15. For identification of the places named, see Swanton, *Creek Indians*, 37–38, which should be used with caution since not all of his identifications are correct. For the Anicatixe, see Fogelson, "Who were the Aní Kuatáni?", 255–63.

8. The choices were between war and peaceful preaching, conversion, and voluntary acceptance of the Emperor's sovereignty.

9. Anghiera, *De Orbe Nouo*. An English translation is d'Anghiera, *Eight De-*

cades. Unhappily, this translation is rather rare. I have cited a Spanish translation: Anghiera, *Decadas.* See also, Hoffman, "The Chicora Legend."

10. This thesis is more fully developed in my book, *A New Andalucia.* . . .

11. Note of entry in the records of the House of Trade at Seville, AGI, Justicia 3, No. 3, fol. 19.

12. Ayllón in AGI, Justicia 3, No. 3, fol. 7. Emperor to Ayllón, Toledo, December 1, 1525, AGI, Indiferente General 420, book 10, fols. 190–190v.

13. The Vespucci map is owned by the Hispanic Society of America in New York. It is reproduced in Cumming, *Southeast in Early Maps,* plate 2. Also Chaves, *Alonso de Chaves,* 124–25.

14. For a linguistic map of the southeastern United States, see Voegelin, *North American Indian Languages.* The languages are also discussed in Crawford, "Southeastern Indian Languages." See also, Karen Booker, Charles Hudson, and Robert Rankin, "Place Name Identification and Multilingualism in the Sixteenth-Century Southeast," *Ethnohistory,* 1992.

15. Hoffman, *New Andalucia,* chapt. 3.

16. This is preserved as AGI, Justicia 3, No. 3.

17. Matienzo's career is partially outlined in cedulas of March 23, 1535, AGI, Contratación 5009, appointing him to the Audiencia of Santo Domingo after his stint in Mexico.

18. Oviedo, *Historia general* 4: 537. AGI, Justicia 13, No. 1, R. 4, fols. 5v–7v, 31v–35.

19. In one version this is at night, during a storm. See testimony of Alonso de Espinosa Cervantes, Seville, 1561, AGI, Santo Domingo 11, No. 43 bis, fol. 29. Oviedo does not mention the time of day in *Historia general* 3: 628.

20. Antón de Cervantes and Alonso de Espinosa Cervantes, Seville, 1561, AGI, Santo Domingo 11, No. 43 bis, fols. 27, 29 verso.

21. Chaves, *Alonso de Chaves,* 124–25.

22. AGI, Santo Domingo 11, No. 43 bis, fol. 28 verso.

23. Ovideo, *Historia general* 3: 628. For Indian trails behind the coast, see Meyer, "Indian Trails of the Southeast," plate 15, especially trails 117, 83, and 84.

24. Oviedo, *Historia general* 3: 631–33.

25. Larson, *Aboriginal Subsistence,* 20, discusses Indian foodways in the coastal zone in general, with more details about particular foods later in his book.

26. Oviedo, *Historia general* 3: 629. Also noted in AGI, Santo Domingo 11, No. 43 bis, fols. 26, 28 verso.

27. Oviedo, *Historia general* 3: 629–32.

28. Hoffman, *New Andalucia,* chapt. 3, provides particulars.

29. Council of Indies, 1540, AGI, Patronato 267, No. 13. Santa Cruz, *Islario General* 1: 441–42, describes the coast as a "desert."

30. Oviedo, *Historia general* 3: 630.

31. Hernández de Biedma, "Relación de la isla de la Florida," 1: 52. This passage could also be read to the effect that Biedma and others had talked to an Ayllón expedition survivor who was not necessarily with them at Cofitachequi.

32. Oviedo, *Historia general* 3: 628.

33. Ibid., 630.

34. Shea, "Ancient Florida," 239–41, 285–86. Lowery, *Spanish Settlements* 1: 155, 165, 448–51.

35. Lowery, *Spanish Settlements*, 1: 155, 448–51. Quattlebaum, *The Land Called Chicora*, 10–11, 21–23, 126–29. Quattlebaum lived at Georgetown, South Carolina, on the shore of Winyah Bay.

36. Chardon, "The Linear League," 140–42, 151.

37. Shea, "Ancient Florida," 285–86. For Espinosa Cervantes's testimony, see AGI, Santo Domingo 11, No. 43 bis, fol. 29 verso.

38. Navarrete, *Viages y descubrimientos*, 3: 166–73. Kohl, *Discovery of the East Coast*, 1: 247, 396–401.

39. Swanton, *Early History of the Creek Indians*, 35, 41. Sauer, *Sixteenth Century North America*, 72–73.

40. Chaves, *Alonso de Chaves*, 124–25.

41. See Chardon, "Linear League," 140–42, 151.

42. Fred C. Cook, "Archaeological Evidence for the Distribution of Sixteenth-Century Irene and Guale People on the Georgia Coast and Relationships to Socio-Political Organization," typescript, collection of the author.

43. Larson, *Aboriginal Subsistence*, 20.

44. Ibid., 43–47.

45. Mooney, *Siouan Tribes*, 412. It is unclear from Martyr and Cherokee legends if the Anicatixe (Aní-kutânî) lived in a separate community.

46. Hudson, *Juan Pardo Expeditions*, 68–78, esp. 75.

47. Oviedo, *Historia general*, 3: 629. For more details, see Garcilaso de la Vega, *Florida of the Inca*, 11.

PAUL E. HOFFMAN

Narváez and Cabeza de Vaca in Florida

One day in March 1536, four Spanish horsemen riding near the Sinaloa River in western Mexico were overtaken by a deeply tanned, Spanish-speaking pedestrian dressed in Indian garments and accompanied by a negro, similarly attired, and eleven Indians from the region. The riders were so startled that for a time they could not speak. The apparition then asked them, in Spanish, to take him to their captain. Thus did Alvar Núñez Cabeza de Vaca and his three companions return to the Spanish world after an epic journey that had begun in Spain in 1527 when they joined Pánfilo de Narváez's expedition for the conquest of Amichel. Along the way, they had been forced to spend some time in Florida in the spring of 1528.

Historians generally have misinterpreted Pánfilo de Narváez's activities in Florida during 1528 because they have failed to pay attention to the details of his contract and the larger historical context in which he moved. In addition, they have misunderstood Alvar Núñez Cabeza de Vaca's account of the expedition, especially as it relates to Narváez's landing place. They also have failed to make as much as they might of both the limited ethnographic information in Cabeza de Vaca's account and of what that account may have taught Hernando de Soto about how to proceed in Florida. This essay addresses all of these matters.

Pánfilo de Narváez reached the New World from his native Valladolid province in 1499 or 1500. A tall, muscular man, he had a fair (blond) complexion and a red beard. His voice was deep and resonant, his conversation agreeable. His lineage was noble. Contemporaries agreed that he had a commanding presence.[1] By the beginning of the conquest of Cuba, in 1511, he had become a leader on Hispaniola. He and his followers soon went to Cuba where he and Bartolomé de las Casas, among others, spent nearly two years aiding Governor Diego de Velázquez in the "pacification" of the island. For his services he was awarded extensive estates.[2] He seems also to have had *encomienda* Indians to supply labor for his household and fields and mines.

The tranquil life that Narváez might have enjoyed as a wealthy man was soon interrupted. In 1519, Hernán Cortés, selected to carry out the conquest of Mexico for Velázquez, seized independent command before the expedition left Cuban waters. To reimpose his personal authority on the new conquest, Velázquez began preparing a fleet to be commanded by Pánfilo de Narváez. However, the Licenciado Lucas Vázquez de Ayllón appeared at Santiago de Cuba before Narváez could get to sea. On behalf of the Audiencia of Santo Domingo and the King, Ayllón demanded that Velázquez desist from his project and, when he would not, persuaded Velázquez to remain in Cuba, according to Ayllón's own account, while sending Narváez to Mexico.[3]

Narváez was able to land his force at Vera Cruz because Cortés had stationed only a skeleton garrison at the port. Ayllón, who had accompanied the fleet, continued to demand that Narváez leave a resolution of the question of who "owned" the new conquest to the courts. For his trouble, Narváez arrested Ayllón and sent him by ship to Cuba. Not long afterwards, Cortés arrested Narváez and some of his associates, after having persuaded a majority of his men that they should join Cortés's army if they wanted a share of the loot being collected from throughout the Mexica-Azteca empire. Narváez resisted, losing an eye in the fight that preceded his being chained up.[4]

Released by Cortés in 1525 as the conqueror was preparing for his expedition to Central America, Narváez hastened to court in Spain. After arriving at Toledo, he complained of his treatment at the hands of Cortés, and he asked for compensation for his losses, imprisonment, and a quarter of a century of service in the New World.

When no reward in Mexico was forthcoming, he altered his petition to request permission to settle in the territory that stretched from the Río de las Palmas (today called the Soto de la Marina River) eastward along the Gulf coast to the Point of La Florida (Cape Sable). He proposed to trade with the natives and to support missionaries who would work among them. He promised to equip his expedition with persons from Spain, rather than from the New World colonies. There already had been complaints that the various expeditions of conquest mounted in the Antilles had drained that area of its Spanish population.

The details of what Narváez asked for indicate that he was familiar with the contract that had been granted to his old antagonist, Lucas Vázquez de Ayllón, in 1523.[5] On December 11, 1526, the emperor signed the contract naming Narváez captain-general and governor of the new conquest. On February 15, 1527, Alvar Núñez Cabeza de Vaca was named royal treasurer of the expedition. Other officials were appointed at the same time.[6]

Because the subsequent history of the Narváez expedition can convey a wrong impression, it is important to note that his petition and contract give the Río de las Palmas primacy over the coast running eastward to the cape of La Florida. That is, Narváez's principal interest was in the ill-defined province (roughly the modern Mexican state of Tamaulipas) that lay just to the north of the province of Pánuco (now split between the Mexican states of Tamaulipas and Veracruz). This was, with Pánuco, the area that Francisco de Garay had claimed as the province of Amichel under his contract of 1521.[7]

Narváez's interest in the Río de las Palmas/Amichel area is understandable not only in terms of the hopes for rich native populations that Garay had held but also in terms of its access to northern Mexico. It may be that Narváez was planning, like Garay, to "jump" Cortés's claim to central Mexico and Pánuco by establishing a foothold just to the north of Cortés's conquest. Certainly the political moment was right. Cortés was in Central America chasing down Cristobal de Olid, who had proclaimed his independence from his former captain. In Mexico, the new royal treasury officials were at work questioning grants of land and *encomienda* Indians that Cortés had given to his followers. An *audiencia* was about to be established, the prelude to yet more action to diminish Cortés's power and possessions. Moreover, as a loyal supporter of the Velázquez faction in the Antillean politics of the 1520s, Narváez may have seemed an ideal candidate to challenge Cortés's claims in the name of the crown, as Velázquez earlier had challenged Christopher Columbus's son and heir Diego Colón's claims to Cuba. The Velázquez faction was a proxy for patrons at court whose interests were, on the surface at least, those of the crown. Whatever the politics behind his contract, the point is that Narváez, like Garay, intended to settle in northern Mexico. Only the accidents of his voyage along the coast of Cuba in the spring of 1528 caused him to make a landing on the west coast of Florida.[8]

A commanding presence, wealth, and physical courage did not necessarily mean that a man would be a successful leader in the difficult task of creating a European settlement in an unfamiliar natural and human environment. As was his custom, Gonzalo Fernández de Oviedo, who had met Narváez in Toledo in 1525, used the benefits of hindsight to advise his readers: "So, though I have in my prologue praised Pánfilo as a skilled soldier and afterwards as a captain, it is but just that I should give account of him, as I view him in this case. . . . there are more captains who can fight and give orders to a few than who can govern an army. There are more captains to be commanded than who know how to command. Pánfilo, when he served under the command of Diego Velázquez, in the island of Cuba, knew how to serve, and how to do as he was commanded. But when he left there. . . [he showed himself unfit for command]."[9] Narváez's old companion in arms in the conquest of Cuba, Bartolomé de las Casas, was equally unfavorable in his judgments that Narváez was "indiscreet" and "very careless." Bernal Diaz added that he was "penurious," another indication of qualities of mind that might make a person less fit for command.[10]

At present little is known about the preparations of the Narváez fleet in Spain. He sailed from San Lucar de Barrameda at the mouth of the Guadalquivir River on June 17, 1527. He had some six hundred colonists and soldiers, including secular priests, Franciscan friars, black slaves, and a few women. Cabeza de Vaca recorded some of the officer's names, and others are known from the copies of their titles of office that have been preserved in the Archive of the Indies at Seville. There were five ships.

Narváez and his company made port at Santo Domingo, where he spent forty-five days (forty according to one report) acquiring horses for his expedition, but losing 140 men to desertion. From Santo Domingo, he next sailed to Santiago de Cuba. From there the ships sailed for Trinidad, a town located in the middle of the southern coast of Cuba, to obtain provisions offered by Vasco Porcallo (or Porcalle), a resident of that town who later briefly took part in Hernando de Soto's expedition. Narváez chose to anchor four of the ships at the Cabo de Santa Cruz (Camagüey) and to send two others, including one under Cabeza de Vaca's command, to Trinidad for the supplies Porcallo had promised. These ships were sunk in a tropical storm that passed over the port in October. Sixty crewmen and twenty horses were lost.[11]

When Narváez and the four remaining ships arrived at Trinidad, the crews persuaded him to winter in Cuba. Accordingly, the ships were anchored in the nearby, sheltered harbor of Jagua. It was from there, on February 20, 1528, that Narváez set out with five ships for Havana, where he planned to resupply his fleet before departing for the Gulf Coast. In addition to a brigantine he had bought at Trinidad, Narváez had hired Diego de Miruelo to be his chief pilot. Miruelo "said that he knew and had been to the Río de las Palmas and was also a good pilot for all the northern coast [of the Gulf of Mexico]."[12] This man is sometimes confused with Garay's pilot, Diego de Morillo, and is said erroneously to be a nephew of one of Ayllón's pilots of the same name (Ayllón had no such pilot), but was probably a man who had sailed with Alonso Alvarez de Pineda in 1519 when Pineda explored the Gulf Coast for Garay. It is also possible that he had been to the Río de las Palmas on some other occasion or was simply a pilot whose claims fitted with Narváez's needs.[13]

Working westward through the Golfo de Batabano, which lies between Cuba and the Island of Pines, the ships repeatedly ran aground.[14] When finally free to round the western capes of Cuba, the fleet was traveling with nearly empty supply casks. Then, just within sight of Havana and the possibility of a renewal of provisions, the fleet was struck by a storm whose strong southerly winds drove it northward, away from the coast of Cuba into the open Gulf of Mexico.[15] Although Cabeza de Vaca does not say so, it seems obvious that Narváez was compelled by his shortage of supplies to seek a port on the west coast of Florida rather than continue on to the Río de las Palmas or attempt to return to Havana. Miruelo apparently said he knew just the place.

Cabeza de Vaca says that the fleet sighted land "on Tuesday, the 12th day of the month of April. We coasted the way of Florida, and on Holy Thursday cast anchor at the mouth of a bay, at the head of which we saw certain houses and habitations of Indians."[16]

Within days of landing, the Spaniards set out overland to the north or, more likely, northeast. In less than a day's march they came to the shore of a great bay. On a second trip they explored the western side of that bay and possibly a distance inland in an unspecified (but likely northerly) direction. Although Cabeza de Vaca does not give precise distances, the second exploration seems to have covered not less than 14 leagues, north to south, and possibly as many as 20, depending on the league he was using.

In between these land explorations, Narváez decided to send a brigantine, and Miruelo, to coast "the way of Florida" in search of the port that Miruelo had said he knew about but that he now admitted he could not find because he did not know where he was. After searching the coast, the ship was to sail to Havana to seek another ship that was to join the fleet with supplies, men, and horses. Both were then to return to the landing place.[17]

Finally, on May 1, 1528, Narváez called a council of his officers, the religious leader of the expedition (Father Juan Suarez), a seaman named Bartolomé Fernández, and the notary, Jerónimo de Alañiz. Over Cabeza de Vaca's protests, the meeting decided to take up the march toward the north in hope that they might find the port they were seeking and that Miruelo had said would be adequate as a base for their explorations.

Where were they and why did they undertake these actions? Modern scholarship offers a number of opinions as to the landing place (see Appendix I) but generally agrees that it was in the vicinity of Tampa Bay. For reasons to be noted, the most likely place was at Johns Pass at the northern end of Boca Ciega Bay.

The literature is curiously silent as to why the Narváez party sailed south along the coast and then marched north on land. Careful examination of Cabeza de Vaca's text in light of Alonso de Chaves's nearly contemporary rutter for the west coast of Florida helps to clear up both where Narváez had landed and why these explorations were undertaken.

The first question to be answered is what bay were they seeking? Cabeza de Vaca quotes the Commissary Suarez as saying that the pilots said that the bay that they were seeking entered a dozen leagues into the land, which clearly indicates Bahía Honda (Tampa Bay), described by Chaves as "large, ten leagues long and five leagues wide at the mouth."[18] Thus although Miruelo was the pilot, he was not seeking the bay that subsequently bore his name and that Chaves locates at 30°30' north latitude, roughly the loca-

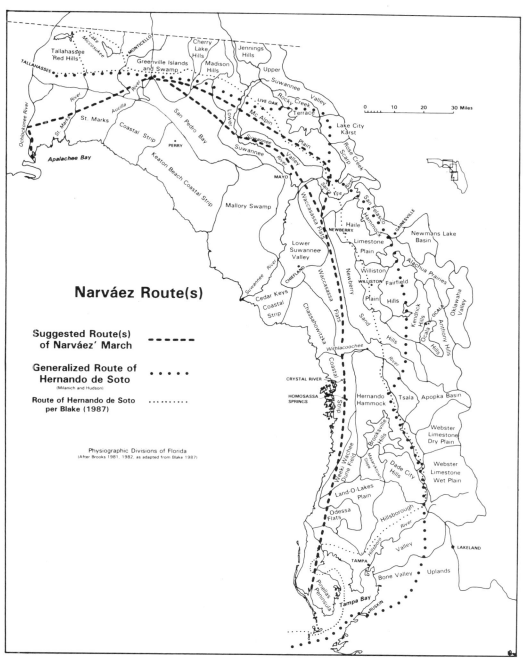

Narváez Route(s)

Suggested Route(s)   - - - - -
of Narváez' March

Generalized Route of   · · · · ·
Hernando de Soto
(Milanich and Hudson)

Route of Hernando de Soto   · · · · · · · ·
per Blake (1987)

Physiographic Divisions of Florida
(After Brooks 1981, 1982, as adapted from Blake 1987)

FIGURE I
The Route(s) of Pánfilo de Narváez

tion of Apalachee Bay.[19] Rather, he was looking for Bahía Honda. Tampa Bay is at latitude 27°35′ north.

If then, Miruelo was seeking Bahía Honda, why the confession that "he had erred and did not know where we were nor where the port was," and why could Cabeza de Vaca say that the other members of the council should "look [at the fact that] the pilots were uncertain, nor did they affirm the same thing, nor did they know where they were."[20] Surely fixing a latitude was within their abilities, and with a latitude they could decide which direction to go.

The clue to this riddle is in Chaves. According to his table, Bahía Honda was at 29° north latitude. Evidently this latitude was the one favored by those pilots who asserted, according to Father Suarez, that the port was only 10 to 15 leagues away in the direction of Pánuco; that is, to the north northwest. If the council took place on the shore of Johns Pass, as some authors have concluded, the local latitude would have been not quite 10 minutes short of 28° north. A degree was reckoned to contain 17.5 leagues, slightly more than the longer of the two distances in the pilot's estimates. Miruelo, on the other hand, may have believed that the port was at a lower latitude. He may have expected to find it at about 28° north, which would explain his confusion but also the two days sail *southward* from the point at which the fleet first made landfall. His expectation of a southern location may also explain why he was sent with the brigantine on a southerly voyage, a voyage that also removed his "expert" objections to the views of the other pilots, thereby simplifying the politics of making a decision about what to do next.[21]

In fact, Miruelo's ideas, if properly reconstructed here, were correct. After returning to Mexico, Cabeza de Vaca learned that when the fleet had sailed northward (while the land party went overland in the same direction) it failed to find the port, but upon returning southward to the point of landing and then further south, it found the entrance 5 leagues, or about 16 nautical miles, south of the harbor where the landing had been made. Johns Pass is sixteen nautical miles north of Egmont Key, on either side of which is a passage into Tampa Bay.[22]

We may thus reconstruct events as follows: The fleet was driven north from the coast of Cuba by a storm to a latitude that the pilots made out to be above 28° north. This determination was made aboard ships under what may have been less than ideal weather and sea conditions. But the approximate latitude was good enough so that Miruelo, or someone, could say with confidence that they were *north* of the bay that could serve as a port where the expedition could resupply itself or begin exploration, if that were decided upon. Accordingly, the fleet coasted south ("the way of [the cape of] Florida") for two days until a port was found.[23] Why that particular entrance was selected is not stated; perhaps the fleet needed water so badly that a stop had to be made, or perhaps the sight of the Indian village, or of the smoke from its fires, determined that stopping place.

Once anchored, and ashore, the pilots could obtain a solar declination reading and then calculate their latitude or a direct stellar altitude. In place of the estimate made aboard ship, the pilots could arrive at figures that should have been beyond dispute. Yet they were not. Some of the pilots affirmed that the port they were seeking was further north, on the way to the Río de las Palmas, but very near. Miruelo may have argued for a more southerly location, while admitting his puzzlement at not having found the entrance to the bay at the latitude he expected.

Once Miruelo was out of the way, and in view of his failure to return with a report confirming that the bay discovered by the march overland, or some other further south, was the bay they sought, Narváez was persuaded to seek it to the north. Probably because of the lack of supplies, he wanted to leave the ships and take the men and horses overland in search of this port. Cabeza de Vaca says that he objected to entering the land with inadequate supplies, no translators or intelligence data on its peoples and resources, and without a firmly established base camp on the shore of a bay where the ships would be safe from storms. Rather, he proposed a reembarkation and search for a suitable port aboard ship. Aside from considerations of prudence, which he clearly implies were his motives, why might he have taken this position? (He may also have noted his objections as part of the literary structure of the story and his development of his own role as hero.)

What Cabeza de Vaca probably noticed was that this distance of 10 to 15 leagues was contradicted by the direction and duration of the coasting they had just made and by the distance that the party had marched northward along the western shore of the bay that lay just east of their landing place, across a peninsula. Both trips (coasting and on land) must have covered the better part of the 15-league distance. The port, if it were further north, would have to be more than 15 leagues away. Cabeza de Vaca may also have suspected that they had already found the port they were seeking in the form of the bay that was across the peninsula.

But whether the port being sought, or another, the bay whose western shore they had partially explored was not suitable for a base because that port and the land "that we have seen were in themselves as depopulated and poor as any that had ever been found in those parts."[24] No one else in the junta disagreed with that assessment, although they did disagree with Cabeza's conclusion about what should be done next largely because they believed that they had not as yet found the bay that Miruelo and the pilots had promised would meet their needs for a base of operations. Rather than face the uncertainties of a new voyage at sea, these men, whose experience with the tropical storm the previous fall had motivated them to winter in Cuba, elected to try their luck on land, where their own courage and knowledge as soldiers would allow them to make their own fates, so they must have thought.

One final note about the identification of the landing place as Johns Pass.

This identification must remain approximate. The channels between the sand islands along the Florida west coast are sometimes subject to dramatic shifts because of hurricanes. Geological study of the Johns Pass area may reveal that it has changed a lot in even four hundred years. A second caution is that our knowledge of the dating of the Indian mounds that A. D. Phinney introduced as "proof" that the Johns Pass area fits the narrative is limited, although Safety Harbor assemblages have been found in them.[25] As with the various de Soto routes, the mere existence of a "mound" at an appropriate spot on a proposed route does not mean that anyone lived there at any given time during the sixteenth century. Occupation of such sites at any point in history has to be verified by appropriate archaeological evidence. Since the three villages that the Narváez party visited were quite small in the eyes of the Spaniards, and widely separated, the area of search for three villages of the right cultural horizon (Safety Harbor) and general relationship is correspondingly large.

Having decided to move the men and horses overland, while the ships went north to seek the bay that was thought to be so near, the Narváez party set out into the unknown. For fifteen days, beginning on May 2, the 260 infantry, 5 priests, 35 or so officers, and 40 horses walked and foraged through a deserted countryside where they found only palmettos ("like those of Andalucia") to eat as supplementary rations to the two pounds of ship's biscuit and half a pound of salted pork (*tocino*) that had been issued to each man. At the end of this time they came to a river that required rafts for crossing. This river was almost certainly the Withlacoochee. On its northern bank, the party was attacked by a force of two hundred Indians from a town half a league, or about 1.7 miles at most, from the crossing point. At the town, the Spaniards found a large amount of maize ready for harvest. This town was half a day's journey (perhaps no more than 7 miles) up the river from the seacoast, where the mouth opened onto a wide, shallow bay. The date would have been May 17 or 18. Garcilaso de la Vega claimed that de Soto and Narváez crossed this river at the same place, but that seems unlikely because of Cabeza de Vaca's statement that the town was half a day's journey from the sea, whereas de Soto is thought by Jerald Milanich to have crossed in the vicinity of the cove of the Withlacoochee, about 40 miles upstream. Allan Blake puts de Soto's crossing at Stokes Ferry, a good 25 miles from the Gulf of Mexico.[26]

The absence of any Indian settlement until this river was reached contrasts with de Soto's experiences further to the east. Although Blake, Milanich, and other students of de Soto's route disagree on specific locales, all of their routes place de Soto's track east of the Dade Hills, Brooksville Hills, and Hernando Hammock "ridge." There de Soto found a number of Indian towns with adequate supplies of corn, as would be expected for an area of river terraces and fairly good soils.[27]

Using Blake's maps, I suggest that Narváez went north across the Odessa

Flats and Land-O-Lakes Plain, across the Weeki Wachee Dune Field, and then up the Chassahowitzka Coastal Strip. This route carried him west of the "line" of the Dade and Brooksville Hills and the Hernando ridge. Its proximity to the coast was dictated by the expectation of meeting the 12-league (25–36 miles) deep bay. The sterility of the route is accounted for by the sands and mixed pine and palmetto vegetation that is still to be found along U.S. Route 19, which follows the general track of the Narváez force. Except for the Crystal River area, there are few archaeological sites in this stretch of coast.

Roughly a week was spent at the town located near this crossing. On the fourth day, Cabeza de Vaca led a party of men down the northern side of the river toward the sea. Probably marching in the more open country away from the hardwoods and dense vegetation along the river's course, the party came to some *placeles* "of the sea, that appeared to enter far into the land." [28] This curious geological feature, usually identified as "sand banks" or even "sand keys," was associated with water up to the knee and oyster beds. The party waded and walked for 1.5 leagues or 3–6 miles through this terrain until they arrived at the channel of the river. The following day, another party was sent to cross the river and follow its southern bank to the sea. Returning two days later, this party reported that the river emptied into a shallow bay (up to the knee deep) on which Indians in canoes had been seen. Clearly this river did not lead to a port of any value.

Departing this place on about May 23, the party moved north and a bit inland for two weeks. They used Indians as guides. Others were seen, but none "would dare to wait for us." [29] At some point on this march, the Spaniards crossed the Santa Fe River.

On June 17, the Spaniards were met by a chief carried by another Indian and dressed in a painted deerskin. He was preceded by Indians playing cane flutes and followed by a large number of other persons. Informed that the Spaniards were on their way to Apalachee, this chief let them know that he, Dulchanchellin, was the enemy of the Apalachee and would help the Spaniards attack them. Following him, the party came that night to a "broad and deep river, the current of which was very strong." The next day, June 18, the Spaniards built a canoe (fearing to use a raft) and ferried the men across. One horseman, Juan Velázquez from Cuellar, who tried to ride his horse as it swam across, was swept off of it and, becoming tangled in the reins, drowned along with his animal. [30] A day later, the Spaniards and Indians reached the chief's village. After the evening meal, the Spaniards were warned of a change in the Indians' attitude by an attack on men who went for water. On the next day, June 20, the village was deserted except for the Spaniards and their animals.

This "broad, deep river" was the Suwannee. From their crossing of the Withlacoochee, the Spaniards had continued north across the Waccasassa Flats. As before, the first leg of the route was west of the "ridge" (the Newberry Sand Hills) along whose eastern side most authors place de Soto's route. Once north of the sand hills, the route is less certain. At some point on this portion of the march they may have left the Waccasassa Flats–Lower Suwannee Valley route and crossed onto the McAlpin Plain to follow a route northwards along the same or a similar track that de Soto later used. Less likely, the march may have been up the Lower Suwannee Valley along the eastern side of that river. The point of crossing the Suwannee is unknown but may not have been near de Soto's later crossing.[31] In either case, the chief and village were almost surely Timucuan-speaking people.

Departing this village a day's march beyond the Suwannee on June 20, the army seems to have followed a line of march up the west bank of the Suwannee towards the Madison Hills area, if the crossing were as far south as the vicinity of Mayo, or more directly west toward the Hills if near where de Soto crossed. Shadowed at first by Indians who may have been from the village just visited, the Spaniards laid an ambush that captured as many as four, who were then used as guides. These persons then led the Spaniards into a "country difficult to traverse and strange [marvelous] to look at, for it had very great forests, the trees being wonderfully tall and so many of them fallen that they obstructed our way so that we had to make long detours and with great trouble."[32] They were probably following the same general route that de Soto followed across the Madison Hills into the Greenville Islands and Swamp area, although it is possible that they initially were farther south, in the northern part of the San Pedro Bay area, noted even today for its difficult terrain. The fallen trees may also be evidence that a tropical storm had passed over the forest. Whatever the route, on June 25, they arrived at "Apalachee." Scholarly opinion has long been unanimous that this town was the Apalachee of de Soto, located near or in modern Tallahassee. This identification is doubtful. Three pieces of evidence point to a different location.[33]

First, the chronicles indicate that the Apalachee de Soto visited was a head town of as many as 250 houses whose inhabitants had not had previous contact with Spaniards. Cabeza de Vaca, on the other hand, states that "Apalachee" consisted of 40 huts. In size, Narváez's Apalachee was more like one of the satellite towns described by the de Soto accounts.[34]

Second, Cabeza de Vaca's numbers of days of march from the Suwanee to "Apalachee" and from there to the sea suggest a location for Narváez's Apalachee town that was east or southeast of Tallahassee. Cabeza says that the army took six days to march from the Suwannee to the Apalachee village where it camped (including the day from the Suwannee to the town where they spent the night of June 19–20). After leaving the Apalachee village the army marched eight or nine days across initially difficult country before reaching the sea. In other words, the Apalachee village where Narváez camped was five-and-a-half to six days from the Suwannee River and eight to nine days from the sea.

On the journey from the landing site to the Withlacoochee River, the Spaniards averaged roughly 7 miles per day on a slow, foraging walk through country nearly devoid of Indian settlement. The army's speed between the Withlacoochee River and the Suwannee River cannot be calculated because the crossing point on the Suwannee is not known. Still, if the army maintained the same average daily rate of 7 miles per day it could have easily reached a point on the Suwannee near most of the proposed de Soto crossing points. A faster rate of advance, while not out of the question, is unlikely in light of Cabeza's statements that most of the men were tired and hungry, even though they found maize fields at intervals of 7 to 8 leagues.[35] If the army had moved faster—say at the rate of 17½ miles per day that Hudson has calculated for Juan Pardo's troops—it would have ended most days of marching at a source of food.

Granting then that 7 miles per day may have been the average rate of progress, this would indicate a five-and-a-half day or six day trip of no more than 42 miles from the Suwannee to the Apalachee village. De Soto's "Apalachee"—Tallahassee—is 80–130 miles, depending on route, from the Suwannee River. The army would have had to have made as many as 20 miles per day to cover the longer of those two distances in the time that Cabeza allows, and almost 14 miles per day to cover the shorter distance. After leaving Apalachee, the army marched eight or nine days across initially difficult country before reaching the sea. If the troops were able to maintain an average progress of 7 miles per day, this leg of the trip would have taken them a distance of 56 to 64 miles. Tallahassee, however, is only 40 miles from the Gulf of Mexico. In short, Cabeza de Vaca's timetable suggests that an average rate of progress of 7 miles per day may be close to the mark and, if that was so, then Narváez's Apalachee village was well to the east or southeast of Tallahassee.[36]

The third piece of evidence is that archaeological and ethnohistorical data indicate that the eastern boundary of the chiefdom of the Apalachee was at or just east of the Aucilla River, which is approximately 30–35 miles from the Suwannee, about the right distance for a five and a fraction day's march at an average rate of 7 miles a day.[37] Placing Narváez's Apalachee village near the Aucilla River also gives a distance of about 50 miles to any of the likely places where the Spaniards built their boats, again a distance that agrees with Cabeza de Vaca's timetable and the assumed rate of march of the army.

In short, Cabeza de Vaca's account documents the eastern extent of the area of the Apalachee chiefdom. His town of "Apalachee" was one of the first towns of that chiefdom to be met when coming from the Suwannee River valley. It was a poor village, not the populous, wealthy head town in or near which de Soto spent the winter of 1539–40.[38]

The Spaniards stayed at this Apalachee village for twenty-five days, eating what food they found and making at least three side journeys to learn more about the countryside. (These must have been short and led away from the other Apalachee towns.) They seem also to have picked up at least the rudiments of the local language because Cabeza de Vaca tells us that the Spaniards learned from the Indians that the land further west was as barren as what they had found when out scouting. The Spaniards failed to expose this lie. To the south (southwest), the town of Aute was spoken of as possessing abundant supplies of food.

The Spaniards departed "Apalachee" on about July 20, according to Cabeza's chronology. Eight or nine days after leaving Apalachee they entered a burned Aute, but did find food to fill their bellies.

The route from Apalachee to Aute was probably southwest through the last part of the Greenville Islands and Swamps area just north and west of modern Lamont. Cabeza tells us that during the first three days the party waded several large lakes (or swamps). In one, on the second day, Indians ambushed the army but were beaten off. Once on the St. Marks Coastal Strip, the going got better in the relatively flat and open country.

This section of the narrative presents an additional problem because we have two different sequences for the discovery of the Magdalena River. According to Cabeza de Vaca's *Naufragios* account, on the second day of their stay in Aute, "The governor asked me to go to discover the sea, given that the Indians said it was near there. Already in this road we had discovered it by means of (*por*) a very great river that we found on it [the road], to which we gave the name Río de la Magdalena."[39] The anonymous "Relation," on the other hand, says, "From here they went to discover the sea and on the road found a river that they named the Magdalena."[40] The so-called "Joint Report" preserved by Oviedo fails to mention this river.[41]

There is no satisfactory way to resolve this discrepancy, especially since the date of the composition of the "Relation" is not known. If it is derived from either the "Joint Report" or the *Naufragios* (see Appendix II), then this difference in sequence is due to a mistake in summation; if it is the source for those texts, then perhaps when Cabeza de Vaca composed the *Naufragios,* he chose to move the river, and possibly increase its size, to make it a "foreshadowing" of the discovery of the sea that he then makes. The implied date, July 22, the feast of St. Mary Magdalene, places the discovery before the arrival at Aute, although only two days after leaving Apalachee, rather too little time for reaching the St. Marks River, the most likely candidate, and much too little to be near the seacoast, unless Narváez's "Apalachee" was much further south than available evidence would suggest.[42] Further, Cabeza de Vaca says that on the second day of march from Apalachee to Aute they were ambushed while crossing a lake (or swamp) but does not say that they found a river on that day's march. Perhaps this river is best considered a product of Cabeza de Vaca's literary imagination rather than an accurately reported fact. Any attempt to use its name for establishing chronology seems pointless.

Whatever the truth about the Magdalena River, the scouting party did find the inlets that marked the entrance to the Gulf of Mexico. They reported back to a camp now racked with illness. The mounted men and those who were well plotted a desertion of their sick comrades, but in the end were persuaded to stay with the main party.

From Aute, the army made its way to the coast about a day's journey further south or southwest. Here they built their boats, with great difficulty. To get food, raiding parties went into Aute—clearly to be understood as a native polity (rather than a town) having a fairly large Indian population. Every third day a horse was sacrificed to give fresh meat to the sick and to those working on the ships. Finally, on September 20, the five barges were finished. Construction had taken forty-seven days.[43]

As with so much else connected with this journey, scholars differ on the location of this final land camp. Some prefer the vague suggestion that it was at an inlet along Apalachee Bay.[44] Davenport has suggested that it had to be "three leagues inland" from the eastern entrance into Ochlockonee Bay or at the mouth of the Ochlockonee River because the next stage of the journey was through swamps and shallow bays (not more than waist deep) from which the open sea could not be seen. A port on Apalachee Bay would have required some open water passage before entering the area behind the barrier islands that demarcate St. George's Sound.[45] Attempts to infer a location from de Soto's reconnaissance of the site do not add any clarity so far as I can see because the approach to Aute (de Soto's Ochete?) was from a different direction, and this part of de Soto's trip is poorly reported except for Garcilaso de la Vega's account, which was written with Cabeza de Vaca's book at hand!

Putting to sea on September 22, the Spaniards rowed and sailed the barges for seven days among inlets where the water was waist deep. Since the barges had barely half a foot of freeboard, it was probably a good thing that the Spaniards had this shallow water to work with until they were able to capture some Indian canoes, from which they made additional gunwales, giving the barges two hands, or about 16 inches of freeboard. This occurred just beyond an island in a strait that led to the open Gulf. They were probably at St. George's Sound.

The argonauts' adventures over the next thirty days included unfriendly encounters with Indians, several periods of thirst, and, finally, anchoring off the mouth of a river whose current was so strong that fresh water was found some distance into the Gulf. The only river capable of that sort of outflow in October is the Mississippi. To this point the five barges were still traveling together, and only a few men had been lost, most notably Teodoro the Greek, who, with a black slave, had gone with Indians into a bay near Mobile, never to return, although his subsequent death among the Indians was reported to de Soto.[46]

From the Mississippi mouth, the party continued further west, eventually separating as ships fell behind because their crews no longer had strength to work the sweeps and because a storm scattered them. In any case, a week after leaving the Mississippi, Cabeza de Vaca's barge was cast on the Island of Malhado. Others of the barges came ashore at points north and south of Cabeza's landing. According to Cabeza's dates, they had been at sea for forty-four days.[47]

Cabeza's landing place is in dispute, although the range of possibilities is fairly limited. Proponents of one of the Louisiana barrier islands have disappeared along with the islands.[48] Three Texas islands remain in contention. From north to south they are: Galveston Island, favored by Clive Hallenbeck, the Velasco Peninsula, said to have once been an island, and favored by Davenport and most of the more recent studies, and finally Matagorda Island, first suggested by Buckingham Smith and still supported.[49] At issue are the dimensions of Malhado as given by Cabeza and the ease of communication from island to mainland in accordance with various parts of his account of the Spaniard's stay on the island.[50]

The rest of the odyssey is not of concern to us. Donald Chipman has concluded that the best study of this part of Cabeza de Vaca's story is not Hallenbeck's, despite his pioneering use of Indian trail routes to lay out the path, but rather the unpublished doctoral dissertation of Alex D. Krieger, which incorporates a good deal of geographic, biological, and ethnographic information not available to Hallenbeck and other early students of the route across Texas and Mexico (if not New Mexico and Arizona).[51]

In conclusion, we may note a number of observations about the historical and ethnographic importance for southeastern history of the Narváez–Cabeza de Vaca expedition. First, Cabeza de Vaca's report, and even more his public silence about certain matters that were only for Emperor Charles V's ears, excited the hopes of persons contemplating joining in the de Soto expedition in 1538. Cabeza even suggested that certain of his own relatives might wish to join the Adelantado, a suggestion taken to mean that riches were assured. A cynic might conclude that Cabeza bore these persons particular animus!

None of the de Soto chronicles and records indicate that Cabeza's knowledge of peninsular Florida was sought by de Soto or his captains. Yet de Soto's practices and his route within the peninsula may indicate that he knew about Narváez's mistakes and put them together with his experiences in Central America and Peru to formulate tactics that assured his army of better logistical support (at the expense of the Indians).

Another de Soto connection was the three-way lawsuit that grew out of Fray Marcos de Niza's and Estebanico's follow-up of Cabeza de Vaca's odyssey. When they reported the discovery of Cibola, the lawyers went to work. Núño de Guzmán and Hernán Cortés each claimed that the new area fell into his conquests, and de Soto's lawyers claimed it as part of

La Florida![52] Like Narváez, de Soto (through his agents) coveted northern Mexico.

De Soto's chroniclers repaid Cabeza de Vaca by supplying data that has ever since been used to interpret the *Naufragios*. But as the reader should be aware by now, much of that cross-interpretation depends on the account of Garcilaso de la Vega, who wrote with a copy of the *Naufragios* at hand and seems to have made an effort to tie his hero to the travels of that earlier hero, Cabeza de Vaca. This "tie-in" makes for good literature, but is poor history and a weak source for ethnohistorical studies.

Curiously, Pedro Menéndez de Avilés seems not to have read either edition of the *Naufragios* and thus seems to have seriously believed that the east coast of La Florida was but a few weeks' march from northern Mexico. Juan Pardo learned the truth in 1566–68 when it took him several months to reach and cross the Appalachian Mountains, still many months' journey from Mexico. This omission in Menéndez de Avilés's investigation (of early 1565) of what was known about La Florida suggests that he was less thorough than he claimed to be (as with so much else that he claimed). Although it is not directly relevant to southeastern history, the influence of Cabeza de Vaca's report on the origins of the Coronado expedition also are well known.

Turning from history to ethnohistory, we have found that Cabeza de Vaca's narrative provides important, if limited evidence on settlement patterns on the western side of Florida from Tampa Bay to the panhandle. First, it is clear that to the eyes of Cabeza de Vaca and his companions, settlement around the northern and western shores of Old Tampa Bay and along the Pinellas Peninsula was quite sparse.[53] Second, the Spaniards found areas of Indian settlement along the major rivers, but not in the sandy wastes and swamps in between. Settlements along the Withlacoochee and Suwannee are indicated, with some villages in the area between, perhaps in the uplands. These settlements were, however, widely separated. Cabeza comments that he and his companions were frequently hungry because the clusters of maize fields along their line of march were usually separated by 7 or 8 leagues (17–25 miles, depending on which league he used) of empty land. That is, the villages were as far as three days' march apart (at an average rate of 7 miles per day).[54] Other clusters of settlements were at Apalachee and at Aute.

A second finding from this study of Cabeza de Vaca's text is that Narváez's "Apalachee" was a small outlying village of that chiefdom well to the east of de Soto's Apalachee (Tallahassee). Its residents effectively shielded the rest of the tribe from the Spaniards by telling them lies about the richness of the country further west and, apparently, by misdirecting them when the Spaniards went out on scouting expeditions. On the other hand, these Apalachee seem to have had some sort of quarrel with the Aute villages; how else to explain directing the Spaniards to them?

Finally, some miscellaneous facts about Indian customs show up for the first time in Cabeza de Vaca's tale. Perhaps most interesting is the incident reported from the second village visited, the first on the western side of Old Tampa Bay. There the Spaniards found human bodies in European merchandise boxes. Already well decomposed, the bodies were covered with painted deerskins. The Spanish priests and other members of the expedition thought this mortuary practice was idolatry and had the bodies and boxes burned. In fact this was probably a variation on the southeastern Indian practice of interring bodies in charnel houses.

Cabeza's other observations are more prosaic. They include the chief borne on the back of a man and preceded by flute players, comments on the bows and arrows of the Indians, and note of the corn, beans, and squash triad that made up the basic vegetable diet of the Indians. Although not specifically noted by Cabeza, his information on when corn was ready for harvest shows that the Indians practiced a double harvest of maize, once in the early spring (late April) and once in the late summer (July).

The omission of more data about what must have been strange and novel customs when Cabeza de Vaca first saw them is probably due to his subsequent life among less sophisticated peoples and the literary form in which he shapes his narrative, a form that required more emphasis on the transcontinental portion of his odyssey than on its initial, Florida stage.

Appendix I: The Landing Place

Of the various proposed landing places of the Narváez expedition, Pensacola Bay and Apalachee Bay may be ruled out. Pensacola Bay was proposed by Andrés Gonzalez de Barcia in his *Ensayo cronológico* of 1723, probably to support Spain's claim to that port in the face of French claims arising from the then just-concluded war of 1719–22 during which the French had seized Pensacola.[55] None of the facts of the journey support this proposed site. Apalachee Bay was proposed by John G. Shea in 1886.[56] The bases for this suggestion were a number of maps discussed as well by Woodbury Lowery in 1901.[57] The argument is that Miruelo's Bay was named in 1528 because that was where Narváez landed.

Equally untenable is Charlotte Harbor, which was first suggested by Le Baron Bradford Prince.[58] According to Prince, the "large bay" Narváez found after a day's march to the north from the landing place was Tampa Bay. Apparently Prince did not consult a map; it is roughly 60 miles from Charlotte Harbor to Tampa Bay, assuming you are a crow flying straight and departing from the northern end of the former! No party of men on foot could have gone that far in one day.

Sarasota Bay, the last of the erroneous proposals, was offered by Clive Hallenbeck in 1940 and has been repeated since by authors who find his paraphrase of and commentary on the *Naufragios* of value. It has even been claimed that his view is that of "the majority of authorities." Robert Weddle says he "prefers" this possibility among the sites south of Tampa, a direction that he believes is indicated by the narrative.[59] This proposed site, like Charlotte Harbor, ignores the considerable difficulties of marching to Tampa Bay from Sarasota Bay—not the least of which is crossing the Manatee River! These proposed landing sites south of Tampa Bay also rest on ignoring or misreading part of Cabeza de Vaca's narrative (see text above).

Such clearly erroneous proposals aside, there remain four proposals for the immediate vicinity of Tampa Bay. Tampa Bay itself was suggested as early as 1851 by Buckingham Smith. Herbert Howe Bancroft gave this suggestion wide circulation in 1886 in *History of Texas*. Elizabeth Scott has recently restated this thesis, identifying the landing site as on the southern end of Pinellas peninsula. Clearwater Bay was first suggested by Buckingham Smith in 1854 and repeated by Fairbanks in 1871. And finally, Woodbury Lowery suggested in 1901, after a review of the opinions of other writers and the accounts, that the most likely site for the landing was inside Johns Pass, Boca Ciega Bay's northern entrance, possibly at St. Clement's Point. This area is just south of Clearwater and 15–16 nautical miles north of the entrances into Tampa Bay. Lowery's landing place is thus a variation on the Smith-Fairbanks proposal. A. D. Phinney's often cited article of 1925 on the Narváez and de Soto landing places supports the Lowery thesis by introducing evidence in the form of shell mounds at sites that Phinney thought corresponded to Cabeza de Vaca's description of the landing site and nearby points.[60] Morris Bishop followed Phinney in his influential if controversial *Odyssey of Cabeza de Vaca,* published in 1933. Swanton claimed to have independently arrived at the same conclusion.[61]

Appendix II: Texts and Translations

Three accounts of the Narváez expedition have survived. The most complete is Alvar Núñez Cabeza de Vaca's *Relation* first published in 1542 at Zamora but popularly known as the *Naufragios* from the title given to it by Andrés Gonzalez Barcía when he published it in 1749. The *Naufragios* were reprinted in 1555, with minor changes, along with Cabeza de Vaca's account of his work in the Río de la Plata. A number of modern Spanish editions exist; the 1986 edition by Favata and Fernández is especially attractive because it indicates the points at which the 1555 edition differs from the 1542 edition and what the changes were.[62]

By general agreement, Fanny Bandelier's 1904 English translation is the preferred text in that language even though it has been criticized as being so literal in places that the sense of the idiomatic expressions is lost. My

own reading of the Spanish text suggests that this criticism of excessive lit-
eralness is made by persons who do not understand the original language.
In fact, she mistranslates a number of passages, sometimes by not being
literal enough![63]

Buckingham Smith's nineteenth-century translations, which continue to
be reprinted, are much less accurate.[64] Cyclone Covey's recent "new" translation, while improved with respect to the idioms, introduces some peculiar
readings that suggest information not carried by the original.[65]

Literary criticism has shown that this account, especially the transcontinental journey section, has many features similar to those found in
romances from the time. The various conversations, the prophesies, the
mentions of storms, and a host of similar details serve to define the literary
theme of the hero and his labors and eventual triumph.[66] The imitation of
such literary conventions does not mean that the account is inaccurate in
the facts that Cabeza presents, but it should put the reader on guard and
certainly helps to explain why the *Naufragios* is less useful to scholars than
is Rodrigo Ranjel's diary of the de Soto expedition, for example. The section of interest here is less "literary" in construction than later sections of
the narrative, but it is not free of such elements.

The second account is the so-called "Joint Report" published by Gonzalo
Fernández de Oviedo in the third edition of his short *Historia General de
las Indias* (1547) but also incorporated into the manuscript for the full *Historia General.*[67] According to Oviedo, the original of the "Joint Report"
was sent to the Audiencia of Santo Domingo but supplemented by him
from conversations with Cabeza de Vaca and from the 1542 edition of the
Naufragios.[68]

As was his custom, Oviedo edited the document and added commentary
appropriate to his own literary and didactic purposes. The first six chapters
of Oviedo's text are regarded as being paraphrases or even copies from the
now lost original. The final chapter was added, Oviedo says, after he talked
to Cabeza de Vaca in 1547; it constitutes a running commentary on certain
aspects of the story. My suspicion is that Oviedo interpolated a good deal
from the *Naufragios* into those first six chapters, especially materials that
identify Cabeza de Vaca's point of view and actions (for example, Cabeza's
protest of Narváez's decision to move inland without having a fixed base
camp). I say this because the third document reads more like the sort of
report that would have been drawn up for official use. It notes the protest,
but does not say who made it nor goes into the details of the arguments
made in the Junta. Some scholars think that the "Joint Report" is similar
to the one that the survivors presented to Viceroy Antonio de Mendoza
and which has not survived, so far as we know. Perhaps the principal value
of the "Joint Report" is its account of the wanderings in Texas of Andrés
Dorante's group of survivors up to the moment they joined Cabeza's party
in 1534.

Three English translations exist. A translation by three different persons edited by Harbert Davenport (one of the three) was published in 1923–24 in the *Southwestern Historical Quarterly*.[69] Davenport relegates Oviedo's commentary to notes and adds his own about route, historiography, and related matters. He also adds notes indicating what the *Naufragios* and the third source, the "Relation," say about particular matters. Like most scholars who have dealt with Cabeza de Vaca's account, Davenport is concerned with where the route lay in Texas and Mexico, not with the Florida and Gulf Coast sections of the journey.

The other two English translations are more accurate and are not elaborately annotated. The first covers only the first six chapters of the "Joint Report." It was included with the 1972 edition of Bandelier's translation.[70] Basil C. Hedrick and Carroll L. Riley published the third English translation in 1974. Their edition is complete (all seven chapters) and also includes the Spanish text.[71]

The third account is the least complete and detailed, but probably the "oldest" or closest to what Cabeza de Vaca wrote out when he first returned to Mexico. Called the "Relation" and first published in 1870 in a defective transcription in the *Colección de Documentos inéditos para la historia de las Indias*, it is attached to a copy of Cabeza de Vaca's instructions as Treasurer of the Río de las Palmas preserved in the Patronato section of the Archive of the Indies, Seville.[72] It ends at the point that Dorante's narrative begins in the "Joint Report."

Davenport believed that the "Relation" was Cabeza's original description of his own role in the expedition and the likely source of both the section of the "Joint Report" (chapters 1–3 in Oviedo's text) and of the *Naufragios* (chapters 1–16) that are nearly the same. Davenport provides translations of those sections that differ from the "Joint Report." A complete, and generally accurate translation is in *Documents Ancillary to the Vaca Journey* (1976), translated by Hedrick and Riley.[73]

Some scholars have tended to dismiss the "Relation" because it seems to be an incomplete fragment, a dismissal that is unwarranted. The prose style strongly suggests that it is a copy of the original report that Cabeza de Vaca drew up upon his return to "civilization," as Davenport suggested. On the other hand, my very quick comparison of the Spanish texts of the "Relation" and the *Naufragios* suggests that the former could also be a rough summary taken from the latter. The sentences of the "Relation" are frequently identical to some in the *Naufragios*, which is evidence for either hypothesis.

NOTES

1. Bernal Diaz and Bartolomé de las Casas as quoted in Davenport, "Expedition," 126, n. 6.

2. Núñez Cabeza de Vaca, *Relation*, 98, suggests that these lands had streams with alluvial gold that his wife, María de Valenzuela, mined during the years he was a prisoner in New Spain. However a check of Smith's source indicates that she "gathered" [*cogido*] thirteen to fourteen thousand pesos de oro, but where they came from is not stated. See Oviedo, *Historia general*, 3: 580.

3. Minutes, writs, copies of orders, etc., Jan. 4–Feb. 23, 1520, *Colección de documentos* (hereafter cited as *DII*), 35: 38–139. See also Ayllón to Charles V, Guaniguanico, Cuba, March 4, 1520, Archivo General de Indias (hereafter cited as AGI), Patronato 178, R. 7.

4. Depositions, etc., 1520, 1529 are in *DII*, 35: 139–46 and *DII*, 27: 301–445; Audiencia to Charles V, Santo Domingo, Aug. 30, 1520, *DII*, 13: 332–48, is a summary of the whole affair; see also Gómara, *Historia general de las Indias* 2: 176, 179. Narváez's resistance is described in Núñez Cabeza de Vaca, *Relation*, 97.

5. Núñez Cabeza de Vaca, *Relation*, 207–11; *DII* 10: 40 ff; for Ayllón's contract terms, see Hoffman, *A New Andalucia*, 34–39, and Asiento, June 12, 1523, *DII*, 14: 504–15 (one of several copies).

6. *DII*, 22: 224–25, 14: 265–69. For notes on his ancestry and the presumed origins of Cabeza de Vaca's name "cow's head," see Núñez Cabeza de Vaca, *Relation*, 233–34, and Núñez Cabeza de Vaca, *Naufragios*, x–xi.

7. For Garay see Lowery, *Spanish Settlements*, 1: 151–53; Oviedo, *Historia General*, 3: 579, confirms that the Río de las Palmas was Narváez's goal.

8. Bancroft, *History of Mexico*, 2: 193–237, and Floyd, *The Columbus Dynasty*, passim.

9. Quoted in Davenport, "Expedition," 139, from Oviedo, *Historia General*, 3: 586. I have revised Davenport's very defective translation.

10. Núñez Cabeza de Vaca, *Relation*, 97, 99.

11. From this point forward, I will cite the Spanish text of Núñez Cabeza de Vaca, *Naufragios* from the Favata and Fernández edition of 1886 and then give the corresponding pages in Bandelier's translation, *Journey of Cabeza de Vaca*. The form will be: *Naufragios*, 7–10 (*Journey*, 3–7).

12. *Naufragios*, 12 (*Journey*, 7–8).

13. Weddle, *Spanish Sea*, 187, 204; cf. Núñez Cabeza de Vaca, *Relation*, 20.

14. The Hedrick-Riley translation of the Vaca summary account incorrectly says that they were aground in one place for twenty-five days. *Documents Ancillary to the Vaca Journey*, 1.

15. *Naufragios*, 13 (*Journey*, 8–9).

16. *Journey*, 8–9. In addition to the authors cited in Appendix I, the reader may wish to compare my route with those of John R. Swanton in the U.S. de Soto Commission's *Final Report*, and of Scott, "Route of the Narváez Expedition." Marrinan, Scarry, and Majors, "Prelude to de Soto," provides a brief overview, using Swanton as their authority for route, discussing the location of Aute from archaeological evidence, and concluding with general considerations about the effects of Narváez's expedition on native Florida cultures.

17. *Naufragios*, 16 (*Journey*, 11).

18. Chaves, *Alonso de Chaves*, 121, no. 9.

19. Cf. Weddle, *Spanish Sea*, 204–5.

20. *Naufragios*, 16 (*Journey*, 11), and 18 (*Journey*, 14).

21. The direction of travel after sighting land is of considerable importance for unraveling the mystery of where Narváez landed. The key to the direction is the phrase "the way of Florida." (*Naufragios*, 13.) Other parts of this narrative indicate that Cabeza de Vaca used a system of directions that included, for westerly directions, the "way of the Palms" (*Naufragios*, 18 [*Journey*, 14])—that is, the Río de las Palmas in northern Mexico—and "the way of Pánuco" (*Naufragios*, 18 [*Journey*, 15]) and, for southerly directions, "towards Florida" (*Naufragios*, 16 [*Journey*, 11]). This (latter) use of this directional phrase, which is exactly the same in Spanish as the phrase translated above ("the way of Florida"), is especially instructive. The text says, "The Governor ordered the brigantine to coast towards Florida in search of the port . . . in case it were not found, [the brigantine was] to cross over to Havana" (*Journey*, 11). By this, a southern voyage is meant.

"La Florida" was the "Cabo de la Florida," now called Cape Sable. That is, from Tuesday to Thursday of holy week, 1528, Narváez's ships sailed *south* along the coast until they met a bay whose entrance was selected as an appropriate place to approach the shore of the mainland, a shore separated from the Gulf of Mexico by barrier islands.

22. *Naufragios*, 144 (*Journey*, 191–92); Buckingham Smith in his translation insisted that Cabeza de Vaca had this direction wrong and that the harbor lay *north* of the landing place (Núñez Cabeza de Vaca, *Relation*, 204). Weddle, *Spanish Sea*, 205, and other proponents of a landing south of Tampa Bay have repeated this error.

23. *Naufragios*, 13 (*Journey*, 8–9).

24. *Naufragios*, 18 (my translation); cf. *Journey*, 15. Jeffrey M. Mitchem found that the eastern side of Pinellas Peninsula was heavily occupied during the Safety Harbor period. The type site for that cultural complex is large and had many burial mounds nearby, suggesting a large native population. (Mitchem to Hoffman, March 22, 1990.) Cabeza de Vaca's comments may thus reflect what the Spaniards expected to find—populations as dense as those in coastal Mexico, perhaps—rather than what they did find. Other explanations—such as the flight of the Indians from fear of being enslaved (because of previous experience), the deliberate leading of the Spaniards to a town other than the Safety Harbor site, or Cabeza de Vaca's literary purposes—are also possible. The significance of this judgment about Tampa Bay for studies of de Soto's route has been overlooked.

25. "Narváez and de Soto," Jeffrey M. Mitchem, "Redefining Safety Harbor," 58–60, 86–88, reviews what is known about the Johns Pass Mound, Narváez Midden, and Jungle Prado Mound, mostly from uncontrolled excavations. I wish to thank Dr. Mitchem for bringing this information to my attention.

26. Milanich, "The Expedition in Florida," 307–8. Milanich's views are based on Vega, *The Florida of the Inca*, 105, where the place of de Soto's crossing is described as a swamp one league wide with a 100-foot channel in the center that had to be crossed on a bridge. Cabeza de Vaca says that his party crossed on rafts, suggesting firm banks and a wide, deep stream. Blake, *Route*, 8–9.

27. Blake, *Route*, 8–9.

28. *Naufragios*, 22 (*Journey*, 20).

29. *Journey*, 21.

30. *Naufragios*, 23–24 (*Journey*, 22–23).

31. Milanich favors a crossing by de Soto along the route of the later Bellamy Road, but other authors give other locations. Milanich, "The Expedition in Florida," 309–10.

32. *Journey*, 23.

33. In the original version of this study, I suggested that after crossing the Suwanee below its junction with the Santa Fe River, the Spaniards were guided northward in or near the lower Suwannee Valley, with perhaps a deliberate passage into the Mallory Swamp courtesy of their guides. This might, at 6–7 miles per day, have put them somewhere near Mayo or even, assuming a much higher rate of travel, as far north as Lee, on the edge of the Madison Hills. Or they may have been on the northeastern edge of San Pedro Bay when they got to "Apalachee." From there they went west and southwest across San Pedro Bay for the first three days—days Cabeza recalls were made difficult by the large "lakes" or swamps that they had to cross and by the ambush that the Indians laid in one swamp on the second day out from Apalachee. Once across San Pedro Bay, they would have been in the St. Marks Coastal Strip, which is relatively flat and open. Somewhat invigorated by the food they had consumed at Apalachee, the army might have made 10 miles a day on this section of the trip. This reconstruction seems less likely in view of what is known about the distribution of Apalachee sites.

For scholarly opinion supporting claims that this "Apalachee" was the same as de Soto's town of the same name, see, for example, Lowery, *Spanish Settlements*, 1: 185; Weddle, *Spanish Sea*, 190–91.

34. Hann, *Apalachee*, 25, and *Naufragios*, 26 (*Journey*, 25–26).

35. *Naufragios*, 25 (*Journey*, 24).

36. Swanton concluded that Narváez averaged about 4 miles per day between the Withlacoochee and the Suwannee, but about 6 miles per day from the landing site to the Withlacoochee and from the Suwannee to "Apalachee." Swanton, *Final Report*, 113–14.

37. Hann, *Apalachee*, 5, and figure 3.1, p. 72.

38. I want to thank the members of Charles Hudson's seminar for suggesting this. Scott, "Route of the Narváez Expedition," 58, places "Apalachee" near Lake Miccosukee, but that seems too far west.

39. *Naufragios*, 31 (*Journey*, 33); Bandelier's translation: "After this the governor entreated me to go in search of the sea, as the Indians said it was so near by and we had, on this march, already suspected its proximity from a great river to which we had given the name the Río de la Magdalena."

40. *DII*, 14: 273, my translation.

41. Oviedo, *Historia General*, 3: 587.

42. Cf. Weddle, *Spanish Sea*, 191.

43. *Naufragios*, 33–36 (*Journey*, 35–40); The "Relation" mistakenly says twenty-five days, *DII*, 14: 273.

44. Lowery, *Spanish Settlements*, 1: 187, n. 1 for opinions.

45. Davenport, "Expedition," 217, n. 1, and Scott, "Route of the Narváez Expedition," 59; Weddle, *Spanish Sea*, 191–92. Jeffrey M. Mitchem suggests that the final camp was on the St. Marks River where several Indian sites contain Spanish items of the correct date (Jeffrey M. Mitchem, "Archaeological and Ethnohistoric

Evidence for the Location of Narváez's *Aute*," unpublished typescript of paper presented at the Fifty-second Annual Meeting of the Florida Academy of Sciences, May 12–14, 1988. Collection of the author). However, these artifacts could also have been traded to the Indians by Spaniards whose voyages are not recorded.

46. Lowery, *Spanish Settlements*, 1: 189.

47. His chronology of events, on the other hand, can be (mis-) read to show fifty-six days. See Davenport, "Expedition," 225–26, n. 14.

48. E.g., Davis, *Spanish Conquest of New Mexico*, 41.

49. Hallenbeck, *Alvar Núñez Cabeza de Vaca*, 119; Davenport, "Expedition," 235, n. 13; and Lowery, *Spanish Settlements*, 1: 191.

50. For a good review of the literature, see Chipman, "Cabeza de Vaca's Route."

51. Krieger, "Un nuevo estudio"; his key findings are published as "The Travels of Alvar Núñez Cabeza."

52. *DII*, 15: 300–408.

53. Mitchem's findings suggest that this Spanish observation was incorrect; the area was in fact heavily populated around Safety Harbor and at points along the eastern side of Pinellas Peninsula. "Redefining Safety Harbor," passim.

54. *Naufragios*, 25 (*Journey*, 24).

55. Barcía Carbillido y Zuñiga, *Chronological History*, 335. Cf. p. 10, where he gives the Narváez story.

56. Shea, "Ancient Florida," 43.

57. Lowery, *Spanish Settlements*, 2: 454.

58. Prince, *Concise History of New Mexico*, 89–91.

59. Hallenbeck, *Alvar Núñez Cabeza de Vaca*, 36; Núñez Cabeza de Vaca, *Naufragios*, 36; and Weddle, *Spanish Sea*, 205.

60. Scott, "Route of the Narváez Expedition," 55, and Phinney, "Narváez and de Soto," 15–16.

61. Bishop, *Odyssey of Cabeza de Vaca*, and Swanton, *Final Report*, 113.

62. *Naufragios*, xiv–xvi.

63. Núñez Cabeza de Vaca, *Journey of Cabeza de Vaca*. Other reprints exist although not always with the pagination of this edition.

64. Cabeza de Vaca, *Relation*.

65. Covey, *Cabeza de Vaca's Adventures*.

66. Bost, "History and Fiction," 81, 106, 124–25.

67. Oviedo, *Historia General*, 3: 582–618.

68. Ibid., 3: 582, 614.

69. Davenport, "Expedition."

70. Theisen, "Oviedo's Version."

71. Oviedo, *Journey of the Vaca Party*.

72. *DII*, 14: 269–79.

73. Hedrick and Riley, trans., *Documents*, 1–15.

The Hernando de Soto Expedition, 1539–1543

Hernando de Soto was born between 1496 and 1500 in the town of Jerez de Badajoz, in Extremadura, a part of Spain that produced more than its share of the Spaniards who explored and conquered the New World. As a teenager he went to Central America as a page for Pedrarias de Avila, who was as autocratic and cruel a master and teacher as de Soto could have had. Before he was twenty de Soto was accomplished in the weaponry of the day, and he was an expert horseman. He participated in the exploration and plundering of Panama and Nicaragua. With Francisco Pizarro, he was one of the leading participants in the conquest of the Incas in 1531–35. Afterwards, when the Pizarros and other conquistadors began fighting among themselves, de Soto decided to take his leave from Peru.[1]

Returning to Spain in 1536, he was a wealthy man, a multimillionaire by modern standards. He married Isabel de Bobadilla, the third daughter of Pedrarias de Avila. But a life of ease was not for de Soto; he wanted to command his share of the New World. He first asked for territory in what is now Ecuador and Colombia, but he was denied. On April 20, 1537, the King granted de Soto an *asiento* to conquer and settle La Florida— North America. He was appointed Governor and Captain-General of La Florida and also Governor of Cuba. Under the terms of the *asiento*, de Soto had four years in which to conquer the Indians of La Florida and to select for his domain two hundred leagues of coast. Once the conquest and pacification was complete, the King would grant him 12 square leagues of land.[2] Alvar Núñez Cabeza de Vaca, one of the few survivors of the Pánfilo de Narváez expedition of 1528, returned to Spain shortly after de Soto received his *asiento* from the King. Narváez had landed at Tampa Bay before continuing north to the chiefdom of Apalachee, where his expedition foundered and then failed. Members of the expedition built crude boats and tried to sail to New Spain (Mexico), but the boats were not seaworthy.

Some sank and others were cast up on the Texas coast. Only Cabeza de Vaca and three others survived many years of captivity among the Indians of the Texas coast before they succeeded in walking to New Spain.

More by his reticence than by what he said, Cabeza de Vaca heightened the expectation in Spain that a new golden land existed in La Florida, waiting to be conquered and exploited. Several Spaniards of the lesser nobility were caught up in the enthusiasm and joined the expedition. De Soto signed on about 650 to 700 people, some half of whom were from Extremadura. Many occupational specialities were represented: sawyer, boatwright, farrier, blacksmith, shoemaker, cooper, tailor, and carpenter, among others. There were at least two women and at least three blacks. De Soto's fleet departed from Spain on Sunday, April 7, 1538. Their first destination was Cuba, where final plans and preparations for the expedition would be made.[3]

Even before he landed in Cuba, de Soto must already have possessed considerable knowledge of the western coast of the Florida peninsula.[4] Alonso de Chaves's *Espejo de Navegantes,* a guide for navigators, was compiled no later than 1527. It shows two harbors on the western coast: the Bahía de Juan Ponce (that is, Charlotte Harbor) to the south and the Bahía Honda (Tampa Bay) to the north. De Soto must also have had benefit of at least some of the knowledge and experience of Cabeza de Vaca. In addition, while in Cuba making preparations for his expedition, de Soto sent northward Juan de Añasco in command of fifty men in a caravel and two pinnaces to explore the harbor where they would make their landing. When he returned to Cuba, Añasco brought four Indians, captured on the coast, who were to serve as guides and interpreters.

De Soto and his army departed from Havana on Sunday, May 18, 1539, with a fleet of five large ships, two caravels, and two pinnaces. They sighted their landfall seven days later, on Sunday, May 25, casting anchor off the coast some 5 leagues south of Tampa Bay. After some initial difficulty in locating the entrance to the bay, the fleet began cautiously sailing inside, with a pinnace piloting each of the large ships. By May 28, all of the ships were safely inside the bay. At first opportunity, some of the men went ashore in boats to take on fresh water and forage for the horses. On May 30 they unloaded the horses and most of the men at Piney Point, thereby lightening the ships. They then proceeded farther inside the bay until they came near the mouth of the Little Manatee River.[5]

De Soto had for his landing place the Indian town of Uzita, on the northern side of the mouth of the Little Manatee River. In small boats, sailors ferried food, clothing, supplies, and equipment to the landing site. They also unloaded a herd of pigs that were to be driven along with the expedition and used as food. The infantry and cavalry who had been put ashore at Piney Point traveled by land to the mouth of the Little Manatee River. The entire army reached the camp at the landing place by June 2. De

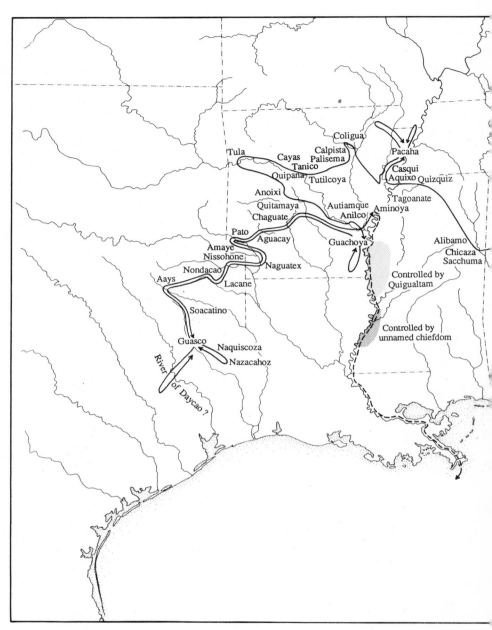

FIGURE I
The Hernando de Soto expedition, 1539–1543

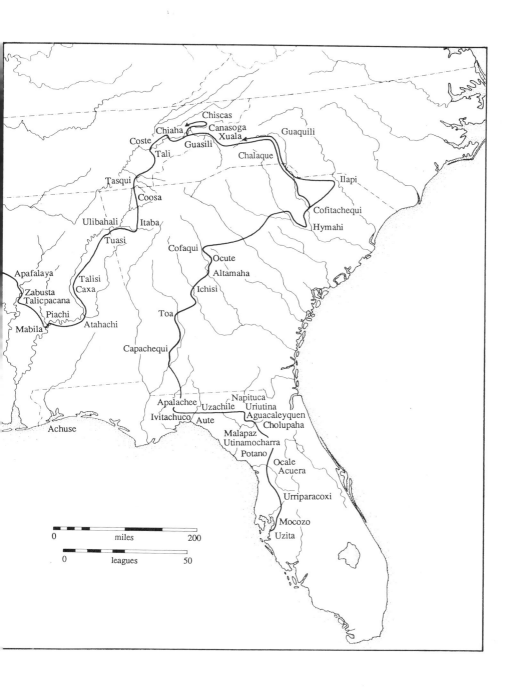

Chiscas
Chiaha
Canasoga
Coste
Guasili
Xuala
Guaquili
Tali
Chalaque
Tasqui
Ilapi
Coosa
Ulibahali
Itaba
Cofitachequi
Hymahi
Tuasi
Cofaqui
Ocute
Apafalaya
Altamaha
Talisi
Caxa
Ichisi
Zabusta
Talicpacana
Piachi
Toa
Mabila
Atahachi
Capachequi
Napituca
Apalachee
Uzachile
Uriutina
Ivitachuco
Aute
Aguacaleyquen
Achuse
Cholupaha
Malapaz
Utinamocharra
Potano
Ocale
Acuera
Urriparacoxi
Mocozo
Uzita

0   miles   200

0   leagues   50

Soto and his soldiers used some of the houses they found at Uzita for residences, and they stored food and supplies in others. Still others were torn down, and the materials were used in the construction of other shelters for the men.

On one of their early forays from Uzita to explore the country and to search for Indians, they encountered a Spaniard, Juan Ortiz, who had been associated with the Narváez expedition. He had fallen into the hands of Indians and had been held captive for about ten years. Ortiz provided de Soto with intelligence about the lay of the land around Tampa Bay, and even more importantly he served as translator from the Indian language he spoke into Spanish. Ortiz spoke only one language (or at most two) among the large number of languages that the expedition would encounter. As they traveled into the interior and encountered other languages, Ortiz depended upon bilingual Indians to translate into the Indian language he spoke, and then he completed the last link in the chain of translation into Spanish. At times there were several links in this chain of translation.

To the Spaniards, the land near Tampa Bay seemed barren, and they immediately began to make preparations to move elsewhere. On June 20, de Soto ordered Baltasar de Gallegos to lead a party of infantry and cavalry east and then northeast to the "province" of Urriparacoxi. Gallegos would seem to have only reached the fringes of the territory of Urriparacoxi, which appears to have been in the area east of the upper Withlacoochee River. Gallegos did encounter some people who were subject to Urriparacoxi, and from them he learned of the existence of a wealthy chiefdom, Ocale, which lay to the north of the point he had reached.

When de Soto was informed of what Gallegos had learned, he ordered forty calvary and sixty infantry to remain at the camp at Uzita. They were to guard supplies as well as the two caravels and two pinnaces. The five large ships had returned to Cuba after everything had been unloaded. On July 15, de Soto and a large contingent of his army set out to rendezvous with Gallegos. As they traveled eastward, they crossed the Alafia River by building two bridges across it. They traveled past several lakes, until on July 18 they came to a stretch of land between the headwaters of the Hillsborough River and the Withlacoochee River where they could find no drinking water. Under a very hot sun, they became so dehydrated one of the men died and others suffered greatly. On July 20, they rendezvoused with Gallegos in the vicinity of the present town of Lacoochee.

De Soto traveled northward, passing by the towns of Vicela and Tocaste. On July 26, the Spaniards came to the river of Ocale—the Withlacoochee. They crossed this river by stretching a rope from side to side at a place where they could wade. Even so, the current was swift, and one of the horses was swept away and drowned. They reached the province of Ocale, but they found less food than they expected.

After exploring the surrounding country, including the "province" of

Acuera, de Soto again began traveling northward toward the chiefdom of Apalachee, which the Indians in and around Ocale had described as being very large, populous, and abounding in corn. De Soto took fifty cavalry and a hundred infantry, leaving the remainder behind at Ocale under the command of Luis de Moscoso. De Soto and his men passed through the towns of Itarraholata, Potano, Utinamocharra, and a place they named Malapaz (that is, "Bad Peace"). This last town was somewhere in the vicinity of present Alachua.

On August 15, they came to the town of Cholupaha, which lay on the south side of the Santa Fe River. Here they were told by an Indian that Apalachee was surrounded by water on all sides, and that this was the reason why the Narváez expedition had failed. With this news, some of the Spaniards wanted to return to Tampa Bay, and a quarrel broke out. In reference to this, they named the Santa Fe River *las Discordias*—the River of Discords.

They built a bridge across the Santa Fe and crossed to the other side, and the next day they arrived at Aguacaleyquen, said to be a moderately large town. From here de Soto sent word southward to Ocale for Moscoso to lead the remainder of the army forward. Moscoso and his men arrived at Aguacaleyquen at some time before September 9.

The entire army departed from Aguacaleyquen on September 9, coming immediately to a stream (perhaps the Ichetucknee River), which they crossed by building a bridge out of pine logs. Evidently this was a small stream. They traveled to Uriutina and the "Village of Many Waters," so called because there were so many bodies of standing water in the area. On September 15, they reached Napituca. Here they fought a battle against a great many Indians who attempted a surprise attack. As the battle proceeded, the Spaniards got the upper hand, and the Indians fled into the water of two small ponds, probably lime sinks, in which they swam out to the middle and treaded water in a vain attempt to escape the weapons of the Spaniards. Many were killed.

On September 23, they marched from Napituca to the "River of the Deer" (the Suwannee). Across this river they built a bridge three large pine trees in length and four in breadth. Crossing the river, they continued on, passing through several towns of the province of Uzachile. They encountered an uninhabited wilderness before coming to Agile, the first town that was subject to Apalachee. Agile was probably located on or near the Aucilla River.

This river, with a swamp on either side, was known as the River of Ivitachuco, named after the town of Ivitachuco, located just west of the river. They built a bridge and crossed to the other side, where they were assaulted by the Indians of Apalachee. This was de Soto's first experience with the chiefdom that had successfully resisted Narváez. From the refuge of the many swamps in their land, the people of Apalachee waged guerrilla warfare against de Soto and his men the entire time they were in Apalachee territory.

After the towns of Ivitachuco and Calahuchi, de Soto and his men arrived at Anhayca, the principal town of Apalachee, on October 6. There they spent the winter of 1539–40. It is now known with virtual certainty that the central towns of Apalachee were located within the city limits of present Tallahassee.[6]

After establishing his camp, de Soto also sent out parties of men to explore the country to the north. These parties may have gone as far as present Decatur, Grady, or Thomas County, Georgia, or even farther. And he sent Juan de Añasco with a party of men to explore south to the Gulf Coast, where they found the remains of the camp where the survivors of the Narváez expedition built the crude boats in which they attempted to sail to Mexico. Then de Soto sent Añasco with a small contingent of cavalry back to Tampa Bay to order the men there to rejoin the others at Apalachee. After Añasco carried this news to Tampa Bay, the men stationed there burned their camp and under the command of Pedro Calderón began the long march northward. Añasco sailed in one of the ships, leading the others northward to Apalachee Bay, presumably intending to land at the place where the Narváez expedition had built their boats. Añasco and the others who went by boat arrived at Apalachee on December 28, a short time after Calderón arrived with the cavalry and infantry.

As soon as the ships arrived, de Soto commanded Francisco Maldonado to take a party of men in the two pinnaces to explore the Gulf Coast. For the next two months, Maldonado coasted along the shore, entering into rivers, creeks, and inlets until he discovered a good port. They called this port Achuse (also Ochuse), and it was very probably Pensacola Bay. Its location was given as 60 leagues from Apalachee Bay. Maldonado also captured an Indian chief from this town whom he took to Apalachee when he returned.[7]

Having completed the reconnaissance, on February 26 de Soto sent Maldonado in the pinnaces to Havana with orders to resupply him at Achuse in the coming summer. If de Soto happened not to meet him there, he was to return to the same place the following summer, and he would surely meet him there at that time. De Soto may also have told Maldonado that if he should have no word from the expedition in six months, he should try to make contact by sailing along the coast from Achuse to the mouth of the Mississippi River. When de Soto departed from Apalachee, he forced the chief of Achuse to go with him. Presumably, this man was to serve as a guide and interpreter when de Soto traveled to Pensacola Bay.

Throughout the winter of 1539–40, the warriors of Apalachee kept up constant guerilla attacks against de Soto's army. De Soto succeeded in capturing several Indians, and it was his practice to interrogate captives about the locations and characteristics of other societies in the vicinity. It so happened that the Spaniards captured two boys sixteen or seventeen years old who had been traveling about with Indian traders. They claimed to possess detailed knowledge of trails in the interior. One of these, a boy whom they named Perico or Pedro, was from "Yupaha," a province to the east. Perico said that this province was governed by a woman to whom her subjects paid tribute, including quantities of gold and other precious substances. Perico appears to have possessed considerable powers of persuasion, and de Soto determined to go in search of "Yupaha," whose actual name was subsequently found to be "Cofitachequi." Later, to their distress, they learned that Perico's knowledge was neither as comprehensive nor as accurate as they wished it to be.

When they departed from Apalachee on March 3, the Spaniards carried enough food to see them across sixty leagues of wilderness.[8] That is, while crossing the Coastal Plain, they did not expect to find adequate stores of food. By the end of the first day of travel they had come to the River of Guacuca, the Ochlockonee, which they forded easily. But the next river they came to, the River of Capachequi (the Flint), was deep, wide, and swift. An advance party may have reached this river on March 5, but the entire expedition reached it on March 6 or 7. They cut down trees, sawed boards, and built a flat boat, which they pulled back and forth across the river by means of a rope. It took them until March 10 to ferry the entire army to the other side.[9]

The next day they came to a village of the chiefdom of Capachequi somewhere east of Chickasawhatchee or Kiokee Creek. It was already dark before they reached the main town of Capachequi, possibly located at a mound site (9DU1) on present-day Magnolia Plantation. This chiefdom had its territory in the Chickasawhatchee Swamp. When the Spaniards reached the principal town, they found that the people had all fled and taken refuge in nearby swamps, in a manner reminiscent of the people of Apalachee. The Spaniards did find supplies of food in Capachequi, and this discovery is presumably the reason why they went to the trouble of crossing the Flint River twice. Had they not been so anxious about finding food, they could have proceeded north without crossing the Flint at all.

After resting, they departed from Capachequi on March 17, and the following day they came to the River of Toa, again the Flint River. They traveled up the western side of the Flint until, on March 21, they came to a place where they determined that they would cross back to the eastern side. Here, a few miles north of present Montezuma, Georgia, after several unsuccessful tries, they built a bridge out of pine poles. On March 22, all had crossed to the eastern side of the river, and they camped, probably near the bridge. Early the next morning they arrived at a village of Toa.[10]

At midnight on the day they reached Toa, de Soto commanded a contingent of about forty cavalry to travel eastward. In a remarkable maneuver, they departed in the dead of night and traveled for eighteen hours, covering

12 leagues, more than twice the distance of an ordinary day's travel. At the end of their travel, they came to the Ocmulgee River, somewhere in the vicinity of old Buzzard's Roost (present Westlake). The next day, on March 25, they came to a village of the chiefdom of Ichisi, situated on an "island" in the Ocmulgee River.

They then traveled up the eastern side of the river, passing through additional villages of Ichisi. They stopped at one of these villages and rested for three days, no doubt waiting for the rest of the expedition to catch up with them. They resumed travel on March 29, rested on March 30, and on March 31 they were ferried to the eastern side of the Ocmulgee River in dugout canoes paddled by people of Ichisi. They arrived at the main town of Ichisi (probably the Lamar Mound site) on this same day.

They departed from Ichisi on April 2, traveling eastward. On April 3, they came to a considerable stream—the Oconee River. Shortly afterward, perhaps the next day, they were ferried across the river in dugout canoes provided by the people of the chiefdom of Altamaha, probably located at the Shinholzer mound site, located about 12 miles southeast of present Milledgeville. The people of Altamaha were subject to Ocute, who was a paramount chief. De Soto sent word that the chief of Ocute should come and meet with him. It soon became clear that the paramount chiefdom of Ocute was engaged in a conflict of long duration with Cofitachequi, the chiefdom that was their destination.

They departed from Altamaha on April 8, and the following day they arrived at the principal town of Ocute. The principal town would seem to have been located at the Shoulderbone mound site, northwest of present Sparta, Georgia, even though preliminary archaeological evidence suggests that this site had a relatively small population at the time of the de Soto expedition. Further research may indicate that the center of the paramount chiefdom was elsewhere, but for now the Shoulderbone site is the best prospect.

De Soto remained in the main town of Ocute for only two days. On April 12, they departed from this town and traveled to Cofaqui, which was probably at the Dyar site, just west of present Greensboro, Georgia. They departed from Cofaqui on or about April 13. While they were there, they realized that Perico knew less about trails in the interior than he had claimed. He told de Soto that from where they were located it was only about four days of travel to Cofitachequi, but the Indians of Ocute denied that this was true, saying that a wilderness lay between them and the people of Cofitachequi, and that if the Spaniards went in that direction they would die from lack of food.

De Soto was not deterred. At the end of the first day of travel, April 13, they camped just beyond present Union Point, Georgia; on April 14, they camped in the vicinity of present Washington; on April 15, they camped southwest of present Lincolnton; and on April 16, they camped on the lower course of the Little River. On April 17, they came to a very large river, the Savannah, at a place that in the nineteenth century was called Pace's Ferry. They describe the river as being divided into two branches, which in fact were two channels on either side of two long and narrow islands. There were flat stones in the water where the ford was located, but the water was deep, coming up to the stirrups and saddlebags of the horses. The footsoldiers formed themselves into a line of forty men tied together, and in this way all reached the opposite side. The current was so swift that several of the pigs were swept away and were lost.

The Indians of Ocute had been correct. In these five days of travel the Spaniards had encountered no people, and therefore they had not been able to obtain fresh supplies of food. Now desperate, they began traveling more rapidly than was their custom. After crossing the river on April 17, they camped near present Edgefield, South Carolina; on April 18, they camped in the vicinity of present Saluda; and on April 19, they came to another very large river—the Saluda—which they crossed, at a ford at Pope's Islands just above the mouth of the Little Saluda River or else just below the mouth of the Little Saluda. On April 21, they came to another very large river, divided into two streams. They had come to the Broad River, which they forded with difficulty at a place where an island divided the river into two streams.

Here, a few miles northwest of present Columbia, their situation was desperate. They found a few hunters' or fishermen's huts, but no permanent settlements were to be seen. De Soto sent out scouts in several directions to look for Indians. In desperation, de Soto ordered his men to kill and butcher some of their precious pigs. Finally, on April 25, Juan de Añasco came back reporting a town—Hymahi or Aymay—to the southeast. The expedition then went to this town, which was located near the junction of the Congaree and Wateree Rivers.[11]

They departed from Hymahi on April 30, heading north. They arrived on May 1 at a point on the Wateree River opposite a town of Cofitachequi. A major town of Cofitachequi was located at the Mulberry or McDowell site, near the mouth of Pine Tree Creek.

They were told that a disease had struck Cofitachequi two years earlier, and perhaps because of this, food was in short supply. De Soto split his forces, sending a large detachment under the command of Baltasar de Gallegos northward to "Ilapi," a secondary center. This appears to have been the same town as the Ylasi of the Pardo expedition, which was located in the vicinity of present Cheraw, South Carolina.[12]

De Soto and the detachment under his command remained in Cofitachequi for a relatively short period of time. They departed on May 13, heading north up the Wateree River. The detachment under Gallegos departed at about the same time from Ylasi, following after de Soto. On May 18 the de Soto detachment reached Guaquili on the upper Catawba

River. Three days later they arrived at Xuala, in the vicinity of present Marion, North Carolina, and the Gallegos detachment arrived there soon afterwards.

The entire army departed from Xuala on May 25 and climbed over a high range of mountains, probably going through Swannanoa Gap. The next day they waded in the waters of an upper tributary of the French Broad River. If not at this point, then certainly later they understood that the waters of the French Broad eventually flowed into the Mississippi River. They then proceeded to follow for a distance a trail which lay along the banks of the river, and on May 29 they came to Guasili, near the mouth of Ivy Creek, a few miles from present Marshall, North Carolina. On June 1, they passed near Conasoga, in the vicinity of present Hot Springs, North Carolina. On June 3, they crossed over to follow the lower course of the Pigeon River for a distance. On June 4, they came to a pine woods near the French Broad River where they were visited by Indians of Chiaha. The next day they reached Chiaha, located on Zimmerman's Island in the French Broad River near present Dandridge, Tennessee. The horses were tired, and the members of the expedition were exhausted after having crossed the mountains. They rested at Chiaha for more than three weeks.

While in Chiaha, de Soto sent two men to the north to investigate the Chiscas, a people who were said to deal in copper, and that could mean gold as well. The Chiscas probably lived on the upper Nolichucky River and in neighboring areas.[13]

Presumably having made plans to later rendezvous with these two men, de Soto and his army took their leave of Chiaha. De Soto and his army departed from Chiaha on June 28, crossing the ford across the French Broad River where they had earlier crossed when going to Chiaha.[14] Perhaps this was an easy crossing, as none of the chroniclers mentions it. Biedma specifically says that upon leaving Chiaha they followed down the banks of the river, perhaps because they expected that the men who remained behind would come downstream in canoes. As they traveled on this day, they passed through five or six villages which lay on the south side of the French Broad River.[15]

In the afternoon, they came to a river—the Little Pigeon River—that had a very swift current and was difficult to cross. They managed to cross this river by positioning their horses in a line, head to tail, all the way across the stream. This line of horses broke the force of the current, so that the infantry and Indian porters could cross the river just downstream, holding onto the horses and their stirrups as they made their way across the river. Once on the other side, they bivouacked in a pine grove near a village.[16]

On June 29, they continued on down the southern side of the French Broad River, passing through a village where they obtained some corn. They bivouacked for the night, probably in the vicinity of present Shooks.[17] On June 30, they forded the French Broad River and passed through a village and then forded the Holston River. They continued on down the west side of the Tennessee River and bivouacked for the night in what is now southwestern Knoxville.

On July 1, they continued traveling down the western bank of the Tennessee River, passing by some islands which were part of the province of Coste. This included Post Oak Island (40KN23). During the course of this day, the chief of Coste came out to meet them, and they spent the night in a town of Coste.[18] On July 2, they continued on and came to the Tennessee River opposite Bussell Island, where the principal town of Coste was located. Here the Tennessee River was broad, swift, and difficult to cross, but Lenoir's Shoal stretched all the way across the river to Bussell Island. The normal depth of the water at this location was 20 inches, but in low water it could be only 12 or 13 inches deep.[19]

The Spaniards remained at Coste for six days. While they were there the two men who had gone to the Chiscas, as well as several who were ill and had been left behind at Chiaha, came down the river in dugout canoes and rejoined them.

On July 9, they departed from Coste, fording the "other branch of the river," that is, the eastern channel of the Little Tennessee River, which ran alongside the island. They then proceeded along the northern bank of the Little Tennessee River, reaching a point where they bivouacked for the night. On the opposite side of the river was the chiefdom of Tali. The river was too large and too swift for them to ford, but the people of Tali were nonetheless afraid that the Spaniards would cross. They loaded their wives, children, and clothing in some dugout canoes, and they attempted to escape downstream along the opposite bank of the river, going down with the current. But the Spaniards turned them back, presumably by shooting at them with their arquebuses and crossbows.

With this, the chief of Tali thought it prudent to establish peaceful relations with the Spaniards, and he provided canoes for them to use in crossing the river. The principal town of Tali was probably at the Tomotley or Toqua site. The Spaniards spent July 10 in Tali. They remained there that night, and they no doubt helped themselves to supplies of food and clothing.[20]

The chief of Tali provided them with porters, and on July 11 the army set out, traveling through the territory of Tali. It is quite likely that they followed a trail paralleling the Tellico River. For the next several days, as they passed through this territory, the people of Tali brought out cooked food for the Spaniards: *mazamorras* (that is, *sofkee*), beans, and other foods. This implies that the Spaniards were traveling through inhabited areas. At the end of the day they bivouacked, perhaps in the general vicinity of present Belltown.

On July 12, they continued, crossing a stream (possibly the upper Tellico River), and they bivouacked for the night, possibly in the vicinity of present

Prospect. They continued on July 13, crossing another stream, possibly Conasauga Creek, and they again bivouacked. They were a few miles from the Hiwassee River. On July 14 they continued on, crossed a large stream, the Hiwassee River, and they slept at Tasqui, located in the general vicinity of present Old Fort or Ocoee.[21]

They continued traveling on July 15, passing through a small village, and camping in the vicinity of present Eton. On July 16, they passed through several more villages and came to the central town of the paramount chiefdom of Coosa. It was located in the intermontane valley of the Coosawattee River, just east of present Carters, Georgia. The location of this town, both with respect to other towns and geographical features, is consistent with accounts written by members of a detachment from the Tristán de Luna colony who were sent to this place in 1560.[22] The power of the paramount chief of Coosa extended to the northeast to Chiaha, and slightly beyond, and to the southwest to Talisi, a town they were to visit after departing from Coosa.[23] The expedition remained in Coosa for just over a month. They departed on August 20, taking as hostage the chief of Coosa, his sister, and some retainers. They also enslaved some of the people of Coosa to serve as laborers and as burden-bearers. At the end of the first day of travel they reached Talimachusy, a large abandoned village, in the vicinity of present Pine Log. On August 21, they traveled through heavy rain, reaching at the end of the day Itaba, which was probably located at the Etowah site. Because the Etowah River was swollen by rain, they had to remain at this place for six days until the water subsided enough for them to cross the river.

On August 30, they forded the river, traveled for a distance, and camped in an oak woods. The next day, August 31, they reached the town of Ulibahali at present Rome. After spending a day at Ulibahali, on September 2, they traveled down the Coosa River to a town where they spent the night. The next day they traveled to a second town, Piachi, further down the river.[24]

After remaining in Piachi for a day, they departed, and at the end of the day on September 5, they bivouacked in the vicinity of present-day Tecumseh, Alabama. On September 6, they reached the town of Tuasi, probably located on Nance's Creek, perhaps at its junction with Terrapin Creek. They remained at Tuasi for six days, departing on September 13 and bivouacking at the end of the day near present Jacksonville, Alabama. On September 14, they camped at an abandoned town whose palisade was still standing. This was probably in the vicinity of present Talladega.

On September 16, they came to a new village situated near a stream, probably on upper Tallaseehatchee Creek.[25] They rested at this village for one day, and the next day they traveled to the main town of Talisi, situated near a large river, the Coosa. The main town of Talisi was in the vicinity of present Childersburg.

On October 5, they departed from Talisi and began traveling down the eastern bank of the Coosa River. At the end of the first day of travel they came to the town of Casiste possibly in the vicinity of present Sylacauga. On October 6, they came to Caxa, perhaps on Hatchet Creek. Caxa was located on the boundary between Talisi and Tascaluza, the next chiefdom they would encounter. On October 7, they bivouacked near the river, with the town of Humati on the opposite side, possibly near the mouth of Shoal Creek. On October 8, they came to Uxapita, probably in the vicinity of present Wetumpka. On October 9, presumably after having forded or having been ferried across the Tallapoosa River, they camped a league or so from a town of Tascaluza.

On this same day, a detachment entered the town of Atahachi, a mound center, where they encountered chief Tascaluza. This town was the same as the Atache of the Luna expedition, which was said to be located near the head of navigation of the Alabama River.[26] This places it somewhere in the vicinity of present Montgomery. De Soto demanded women and slaves from chief Tascaluza, who promised de Soto all that he desired if he would go with him to Mabila, one of his tributary towns.

On October 12, they departed from Atahachi, traveling south of the Alabama River and camping at the end of the day in the vicinity of present St. Clair. On October 13, they reached the town of Piachi (the second town with this name), which was high above the cliff-lined (and rocky) gorge of a river (*un pueblo alto, sobre un barranco de un río, enriscado*). Piachi was somewhere in the vicinity of Durant Bend or Selma.[27] De Soto demanded canoes from the people of Piachi, but they claimed to have none. De Soto and his men had to spend two days building rafts on which to cross to the north side of the Alabama River. Clearly, the people of Piachi were attempting to slow down the progress of the expedition.

The Spaniards completed their crossing of the river on October 16 and bivouacked in a woods on the other side. On October 17, they reached a palisaded village to the west or southwest of present Selma. They spent the night in this village, and rising early the next day, they set out for Mabila. De Soto and an advance party reached the town early in the morning of October 18. The remainder of the army lagged behind looting Indian houses that were scattered about over the countryside.

Mabila was a small, heavily palisaded town, situated on a small plain. When de Soto and a few of his soldiers impetuously entered the town, they were the target of a surprise attack by thousands of the warriors and allies of chief Tascaluza. The battle raged for the entire day. During the course of the battle, the Spaniards lost 22 men, with 148 wounded; seven horses were killed while another 29 were wounded. The number of Indian dead was estimated at 2,500 to 3,000.

The site of Mabila has not been discovered by archaeologists. All that can be said at present is that it appears to have been in the vicinity of the lower Cahaba River, and perhaps it was at the Old Cahawba site (1DS32), on the western side of the mouth of the Cahaba River.[28] Alternately, it could be located on the western side of the Alabama River anywhere from Old Cahawba to about Gees Bend. Since the direction in which they traveled beyond Piachi is not mentioned, it is possible that Mabila lay to the west of the lower Cahaba River, so that a location as far away as northern Marengo County is not out of the question and it could lay up the Cahaba River about as far as present Sprott.[29]

De Soto remained at Mabila for about a month, while his men recovered from their wounds. Presumably from the Indians at Mabila, de Soto learned that ships were waiting for him at Achuse—Pensacola Bay. He attempted to keep this information from his men, because he knew that they were weary and discouraged, and that his expedition could disintegrate. He released the chief of Achuse, who had been traveling with the expedition, and this man probably returned home. The Spaniards estimated that Achuse lay forty leagues to the south, a reasonably accurate estimate of the actual distance.[30]

On November 14, de Soto roused his army, and they departed from Mabila heading north. They possessed only a two-day supply of corn, so they probably traveled rapidly, following a trail that lay on or near present Alabama State Highway 14, skirting the edge of the Fall Line Hills. For three cold and rainy days they traveled through a wilderness before arriving, on November 17, at the Black Warrior River, somewhere east of present Eutaw.

On November 18, they continued their march, crossing several swamps and bad places. They crossed Big Brush Creek and Fivemile Creek before arriving at the town of Talicpacana, probably at the White Mound and village site (1HA7/8). This is the southernmost minor ceremonial center of the Moundville archaeological complex. They remained at this town for several days, sending out parties of cavalry to explore the country. They succeeded in finding several towns to the north. One of these, Moxuliza, had been abandoned by its people, who had fled to the opposite side of the river, taking their corn with them and piling it beneath mats on the river's bank.

De Soto apparently moved his army to Moxuliza (1HA107) where he built a flatboat in secrecy. Early on the morning of November 30, the Spaniards hauled the boat to the river on a sled they had built. They launched it into the river, and a contingent of infantry and cavalry boarded the boat. They swiftly crossed the river and routed the Indians on the other side. On December 1, the entire army traveled to Zabusta, probably at the Moundville site, where they all crossed the river in the flatboat and in some dugout canoes they found there. At the end of the day they came to a town (probably 1TU46/47) where they spent the night. The next day, December 2, they continued to another town, probably the Snow's Bend site (1TU2/3), and here they encountered chief Apafalaya. The town probably also had this same name, as did the chiefdom at large.

De Soto and his men rested for about a week at Apafalaya. Then, on December 9, they set out in search of the next chiefdom, taking the chief of Apafalaya as their guide and interpreter. On their sixth day of travel, after having crossed a wilderness with several swamps and cold rivers, they reached the River of Chicaza, the Tombigbee. There were two routes they could have followed. They could have gone north to cross the Sipsey River near present Moores Bridge, then to about present Millport to cross Luxapallila Creek, and thence to the vicinity of present Columbus. Or they could have gone northwest, following a trail that lay on or near the present Gulf, Mobile, and Ohio Railroad, which would have taken them to the Tombigbee River southwest of present Columbus.

When they reached the Tombigbee River, they found it to be flooded and out of its banks. On the opposite side they could see many Indians who were armed and threatening. Precisely where this encounter occurred is uncertain because the site of the central town of Chicaza has not yet been located. One good possibility is that it was south of Tibbee Creek, where there are a number of mound sites, at least two of which show evidence of protohistoric occupation. Any of the several sites on Magowah and Catalpa Creeks are candidates.[31] If future research reveals that Chicaza was indeed located in this area, travel along a trail north of Luxapallila Creek would most likely put the crossing at present Columbus; whereas, if they took a trail south of Luxapallila Creek the crossing was probably a few miles south of Columbus.

Given the high water in the Tombigbee, by far the easiest crossing would have been the one at present Columbus. At this point, high bluffs lay quite close to the channel of the river on both sides, so in flood conditions the channel would have been narrower here than in adjacent areas.[32]

The Spaniards built a flatboat in which to cross the Tombigbee, and on December 16 or 17 they all made it across without incident, discovering that the Indians retreated from their positions on the other side of the river. When all of the Spaniards had crossed, de Soto set out with a party of cavalry and went to the main town of Chicaza, arriving there late at night. The Spaniards found that the people had fled from their town.

De Soto and his army spent a difficult winter at Chicaza. The winter of 1540–41 was very cold. One snowstorm was so severe that it reminded them of the winters at Burgos, in northern Spain. Their clothing was in bad repair and in short supply, and they did not have adequate shelter. The Chicazas kept up a constant military pressure by waging small guerilla actions, with frequent alarms at night. When the Spaniards ran out to fight, the Chicazas would fade into the darkness. The Chicazas were astute strategists in depriving the Spaniards of their principal military advantage, the mounted lancers, who were ineffective at night.

Eventually the Spaniards captured a man who was close to the chief of Chicaza, and in this way de Soto forced the chief to deal with him. For a time, relations between Spaniards and Chicazas were harmonious. On one occasion, de Soto led a contingent of Spanish soldiers along with a force of Chicazas to punish the Sacchumas (Chakchiumas), who were tributaries of the Chicazas, but who were refusing to pay tribute. The Sacchumas appear to have been located south of the Chicazas, perhaps near present Macon.[33]

In early March 1541, de Soto began making preparations to depart. He commanded the chief to provide him with two hundred burden-bearers, but the Chicazas were openly hostile toward this demand. The expedition was to depart on March 4, but just before dawn of that day several hundred Chicazas attacked the Spaniards, setting fire to their houses. A strong wind fanned the flames rapidly. The attack killed twelve Spaniards and fifty-nine horses, and many Spaniards were wounded. More than three hundred pigs were burned up in their sty.

After the battle, the Spaniards moved a league or so away to a small town, Chicazilla. Here they rested and recovered from their wounds, and they built a forge and retempered their weapons that had been in the fire. They made new lances, saddles, and shields. From information he got from Chicaza informants, de Soto decided upon the route he would follow next. He knew that he would have to cross an uninhabited area—a wilderness—that would require seven to twelve days of travel. The only food the Spaniards would have on this journey was that which they carried with them.

On April 26, they departed from Chicazilla traveling toward the northwest, where they arrived at a town of Alibamu, possibly the Lyon's Bluff site (22OK506). The people had fled, and the Spaniards found very little corn. De Soto sent out scouts, and they came back reporting a strong fortification on a savannah near a small stream with very steep banks. This fort was probably situated on Line Creek, or on one of its tributaries.[34]

De Soto and his men assaulted this fort at a cost of seven or eight killed and twenty-five or twenty-six wounded. They succeeded in killing only a few Alibamus, and they found that the fort contained nothing of value. Like the Chicazas, the Alibamus contrived to deprive the Spaniards of the tactical advantage of their mounted lancers. That is, when pressed they fled to the other side of the steep-sided creek, which the horses were unable to cross.

On April 30, they departed from the fort of Alibamu, presumably continuing in a generally northwestern direction. Their probable course ran near present Houston, Pontotoc, New Albany, and Holly Springs before swinging west, crossing the northern tributaries of Coldwater River.

They reached the first town of the chiefdom of Quizquiz on May 8, taking the people completely by surprise. The people of Quizquiz appear to have had no warning that de Soto and his army were moving about in the country. The first village was probably the Irby site (22DS516), the first habitation they would have encountered in coming down from the high ground on which they had been traveling. From here they went to a second town, probably the Lake Cormorant site (22DS501), and from there to a third town, probably the Norfolk site (22DS513).

The day on which they first saw the Mississippi River is not recorded. It could have been as early as May 9 or 10, but certainly it was before May 21, when they moved to a small savannah near the river and began building four large flatboats in which to make a crossing.[35] These boats were ready by June 18, and early in the morning of June 19 the first contingent of men and horses reached the other side of the river. The Indians put up no resistance. Within a few hours all members of the expedition had been ferried to the western side of the river.

They found themselves to be in the territory of the chiefdom of Aquixo, whose towns were located in the vicinity of present Horseshoe Lake in Crittenden County, Arkansas. Both the chiefdoms of Aquizo and Quizquiz were subject to the paramount chief of Pacaha, whose chiefdom was located farther up the Mississippi River. Some Indians of Aquixo evidently told de Soto that he could obtain gold at Pacaha, and de Soto determined that he would go there.

Perhaps because de Soto learned that Pacaha was at war with Casqui, he decided to visit Casqui first, presumably to see whether he could form an alliance with him. The Spaniards departed from Aquixo on June 21, but they soon came to a river across which they had to build a bridge. This was probably Fifteenmile Bayou. They spent the entire day of June 22 crossing a very large and difficult swamp. In many places they had to travel in water up to their knees, and even up to their waists. They traveled near present Simsboro, Greasy Corner, and Round Pond. On June 23, they reached the first village of Casqui, located on the levee ridges along the eastern side of the St. Francis River. The next day they reached the main town of Casqui—the Parkin site.[36]

With a large force of Casqui warriors as allies, they departed from Casqui on June 28, crossing over a footbridge which the people of Casqui had built for them across Gibson Bayou. The next day they reached the main town of Pacaha (3CT7). It was located quite near the Mississippi River, and it was almost entirely surrounded by a man-made ditch that was connected by water to the Mississippi River.[37]

They remained at Pacaha for about a month. During this time de Soto sent out several expeditions to explore the country. One of these went northwest for eight days, across very swampy terrain, before coming to a small group of Indians whom they believed subsisted solely by hunting and gathering, but who may in fact have been agriculturalists out on a hunt.[38] A second expedition apparently went northeast, returned with a quantity of rock salt as well as with some copper. This expedition may have gone as far as the Campbell site in southeastern Missouri.[39] On July 29, they departed from Pacaha and returned to Casqui. Then they continued southward along the St. Francis River to a place where the people of Casqui ferried them across the river in dugout canoes. Three days later they came to the principal town of the chiefdom of Quiguate. This chiefdom consisted of a concentration of towns in present Lee County.[40]

De Soto learned from the chief of Quiguate that the chiefdom of Coligua was situated in some mountains to the northwest. It seemed to de Soto that their chance of finding gold and silver would be improved if they went to these mountains. For the next seven days, following an indistinct trail, they crossed some very large and difficult swamps, guided by an Indian who knew the way. For four of these seven days, they marched through extensive stretches of water, crossing the swamps that lay along L'Anguille River, Bayou de View and Cache River. The entire area was devoid of human habitation.

On August 30, they came to the River of Coligua, the White River south of present Newport. On September 1, they came to the main town of the chiefdom of Coligua in the vicinity of present Magness and Batesville.[41] They found a quantity of buffalo skins at this place, but the documents do not mention eating buffalo meat or actually seeing buffalo on the hoof. But clearly they had come near what was then the eastern fringe of the habitat of the buffalo.

After resting at Coligua for a few days they set out on September 6 in a generally southwestwardly direction, in search of large populations. On the first night, they probably camped on Departee Creek. The next day they began following a trail that lay on or near present Arkansas State Highway 67, and at the end of the day they reached Calpista, where they found a salt spring from which good salt could be obtained. This was probably the salt spring southwest of present Worden, where a Confederate salt works would later be located.[42] This was the only such salt works to exist in this general vicinity.

On September 8, they arrived at Palisema, where they found only a few scattered houses and very little corn. It was probably located in the vicinity of present Judsonia, on the Little Red River. On September 9, they bivouacked in the vicinity of present Garner. On September 10, they camped at a "water" (*un agua*), perhaps Cypress Bayou. On September 11, they came to Quixila, perhaps near present Vilonia or Hamlet, where they rested for a day. On September 13, they came to Tutilcoya, probably near present Conway. Here they learned that a large society—the Cayas—lay farther up the Arkansas River, which the Spaniards called the River of Cayas.

On September 14, they arrived at a village on the Arkansas River somewhere in the vicinity of Morrilton. On September 15, they bivouacked near a swamp, probably Kuhn Bayou. On September 16, they came to Tanico, a town of Cayas, probably in the vicinity of present Russellville.

They remained at Cayas for about three weeks. It is likely that during this time expeditions went out to explore the country, like the ones sent out from Pacaha. They mention, for example, finding a warm, brackish lake where the Indians extracted salt. Salines do exist in this general area. For example, one existed on the West Fork of Point Remove Creek.

They departed from Tanico on October 5. They traveled up the Arkansas River, passing through a constriction in the Arkansas Valley, entering the Fort Coffee phase area. They camped in the open for two nights, until they arrived at the town of Tula on October 7. Tula was located between present Ozark and Forth Smith. A sharp linguistic boundary lay between Cayas (Tanico) and Tula, and probably a sharp cultural boundary lay there as well.[43]

The people of Tula were buffalo hunters. The Spaniards were given a large quantity of buffalo skins as well as buffalo meat to eat. Also, the Spaniards found the warriors of Tula to be formidable opponents because they would stand against cavalry attacks, defending themselves with long wooden lances. Through their experience in hunting buffalo, horses did not intimidate them as they had intimidated the Indians encountered up to this point.

After resting in Tula, de Soto and his men departed on October 19. They turned to the southeast, traveling for three days through mountains. They traveled past Pisgah Mountain to pick up the valley of the Petit Jean River. In the course of these three days they only encountered a few isolated Indian houses.[44]

On October 22, they came to the first town of Quipana, which lay near a river at the foot of some steep mountains. Quipana lay in the valley of the Fourche la Fave River, surrounded by the Ouachita Mountains. Evidently, they rested for several days in the province of Quipana.

They headed east, probably following a trail that paralleled the river, and then they turned south. On October 31, they came to Quitamaya, which was probably in the vicinity of present Benton. Continuing, on November 2, after two days of travel, they arrived at Autiamque, located in a densely populated savannah. Autiamque was probably located near present Redfield. The town was specifically said to have been located on the River of Cayas—the Arkansas River.

The de Soto expedition spent their third winter, that of 1541–42, in Autiamque. Again, the winter was very cold. For an entire month they were snowbound, venturing outside their camp only to gather firewood. Juan Ortiz, their interpreter, died during the winter, and from this point onward they had to rely upon Indians who had learned some Spanish to serve as the last link in the chain of translation.

On March 6, the expedition set out in search of Anilco.[45] They spent ten days traveling down the south bank of the Arkansas River, visiting several towns along the way. On about March 16, they came to the town of

Ayays, probably in southeastern Jefferson County or northeastern Lincoln County.

They built a flatboat and crossed to the northern bank of the Arkansas River. After three days of travel through swampy country, they came to the town of Tutelpinco, probably in the southeastern corner of present Jefferson County. Tutelpinco was near Bayou Meto, which they crossed with considerable difficulty.

On March 29, they reached the principal town of Anilco, probably at the Menard site in Arkansas County. Anilco was a rich chiefdom, with many towns and fields nearby. It was the most densely populated chiefdom they had encountered, and except for Coosa and Apalachee, the greatest supplies of corn were found here.

From Anilco, de Soto next traveled to Guachoya, situated on the southern side of the Arkansas River. Guachoya appears to have been located near a no longer extant channel connecting Bayou Macon to the Mississippi River. It was a strongly palisaded, compact town. Part of de Soto's army reached Guachoya by dugout canoes, while others crossed the Arkansas River and then marched overland. Guachoya was possibly located east of present McArthur. Guachoya and Anilco were at war with each other, and they spoke different languages.

From Guachoya, de Soto sent a small party of cavalry under the command of Juan de Añasco to explore to the south. They returned after eight days, reporting that they had only been able to travel a total of 14 or 15 leagues because of the great bogs that lay along the waterways. They further reported that they discovered no trails and no people. Apparently, they explored the area along the upper Boef River, Crooked Bayou, and Big Bayou.

This news must have been profoundly depressing for de Soto, whose expedition had been grievously damaged from the battles at Mabila and at Chicaza. He knew at this point that no state-level society existed east of the Mississippi River. West of the Mississippi River the Indians had informed him that a wilderness lay to the north and to the west. And now his own men had come to him with the news that the land to the south was swampy, without trails, and without people. Soon after hearing this news, according to the chroniclers, de Soto fell ill with a fever, and he died on May 21, 1542.

Luis Moscoso de Alvarado succeeded de Soto as captain-general. He wished to conceal news of de Soto's death from the Indians. The Spaniards at first buried de Soto near the gate of the palisade encircling Guachoya. But the Indians noticed loose dirt where the grave had been dug. Under cover of darkness, the Spaniards dug up de Soto's body, wrapped it in shawls weighted with sand, loaded it into a dugout canoe, and took it out into the channel of the Mississippi River, where they cast it overboard. When the Indians asked where de Soto had gone, Moscoso told them that he had ascended into the sky.

Under Moscoso's command, the survivors debated about their best avenue of escape to New Spain (Mexico). Should they go down the river or overland? They decided that they would try to travel overland. On June 5 they departed from Guachoya, probably traveling to the northwest on a trail that lay to the north of Bayou Bartholomew. They passed through several towns of Catalte, a possible chiefdom.[46] In the vicinity of present Pine Bluff they took a westward turn and for six days they passed through an uninhabited wilderness.

On June 20, they came to the first town of Chaguate, a chiefdom that lay on the Ouachita River between present Malvern and Arkadelphia.[47] In the chiefdom of Chaguate, they saw a salt lake that was fed by water from nearby salines, and from this brine the local Indians produced a great quantity of salt. They remained in Chaguate for at least six days. During this time it is quite possible that some members of the expedition explored in the vicinity of present Hot Springs.[48]

From Chaguate they traveled west for three days to the chiefdom of Aguacay, reaching it on July 4. This chiefdom was located along the Little Missouri River and its tributaries. Here the Spaniards observed Indians extracting salt from sand in a vein the color of slate. It reminded them of the way they had seen salt extracted from sand in Cayas.[49]

They wished to continue traveling westward, but the people of Aguacay told them that in order to find large populations of people, they would have to travel southwest and south (*sudueste y sud*).[50] Traveling southward, at the end of the first day of travel they reached a small town subject to Aguacay. This town, located near a salt lake, was probably at 3SV69.[51] The next day they camped between two ridges or hills, in a wooded area with scattered trees, and on the next day they came to Pato, a small town, perhaps located on the lower Little River.

On the following day, they came to the first town of the chiefdom of Amaye in the general vicinity of present Ogden. They were told that Naguatex lay a day and a half away and that their travel would be through an area that was continuously inhabited. They continued on down the eastern side of the Red River and camped in the area that lay between Amaye and Naguatex, in the general vicinity of present Fulton. For their camp they selected a place in a luxuriant grove beside a brook.[52] The Indians in this area organized a determined military resistance against the Spaniards. From incidents that occurred, and from information the Spaniards obtained, these Indians appear to have been organized into a paramount chiefdom. The chief of Naguatex was paramount chief, and his subjects were Amaye and Macanac, the latter being a chiefdom the Spaniards did not visit, but which presumably lay downstream from Naguatex on the Red River.

The central territory of Naguatex lay somewhere between present Fulton, Arkansas, and Shreveport, Louisiana, perhaps in the area of the Spirit Lake Complex, where the densest population appears to have occurred.[53]

The Spaniards asked the Indians whether the river (the Red) could be forded, and the Indians told them that it could be forded in certain places at certain seasons. After searching, the Spaniards did find a place where the river could be forded. The Spaniards moved their camp southward to a town of Naguatex, where they learned that the chief of Naguatex was at a town on the western side of the river.

Just as they were about to cross the Red River, it suddenly rose. This astonished the Spaniards, because a month had passed with no rain locally. Obviously, the river in question was a large one with distant headwaters, and the rise would have been exacerbated by backwater from the Great Raft of the Red River.[54]

After crossing to the other side, they set out from Naguatex, evidently traveling west. In three days they came to a town of Nissohone. It consisted of only four or five houses, and there was very little corn. Nissohone was probably in the vicinity of present Carbondale. The distance between this town and Naguatex implies the existence of an uninhabited area or a buffer zone between the two polities.[55]

From here they went to Lacane, probably located in the Cypress Creek basin. Again the country seemed miserable to the Spaniards. From here they continued on to Nondacao, further still up Cypress Creek, probably located in Titus or Camp County.[56] In several instances the Indians in this area misled or seemed to mislead the Spaniards. Possibly they did so deliberately, but it is clear that the Spaniards were discomforted by having to go in directions they did not wish to follow.[57] They had no choice but to go to places where they could find corn, and even then they found precious little of it.

From Nondacao they traveled for five days before arriving at Aays. Their direction of travel was probably toward the west, and Aays was probably near the forks of the Sabine River, in Rains or Hunt County. The Spaniards learned that in certain seasons buffalo could be hunted near this place. This is consistent with a location on the edge of the Blackland Prairie.

From Aays they traveled to Soacatino. The province of Soacatino was probably located on the upper Neches River.[58] To the Spaniards it seemed to be poor country, and they found very little corn. From here they went to another province, Guasco, whose towns were farther down the Neches River, perhaps as far as San Pedro Creek. Here they appear to have found somewhat more corn than at Soacatino, Aays, and Nondacao. Also, the Indians of Guasco possessed cotton shawls and pieces of turquoise that they had acquired by trade with Indians who came from the west. This implies that Guasco was located near a principal trail to the west.

The Indians in the territory of Soacatino and Guasco hid their corn from the Spaniards. This impeded the Spaniards' rate of travel greatly, because they were constantly having to stop to look for the hidden corn. It is possible, as well, that the Indians of this area stored their corn differently than did the Indians that the Spaniards had previously encountered.

Evidently the people of Guasco told the Spaniards of the existence of some people who had seen other Spaniards. Accordingly they traveled eastward to Naquiscoza.[59] When the Spaniards asked these people whether they had ever seen any Spaniards, they denied having done so. Then the Spaniards tortured some of them. Those who were tortured said that farther on, in the territory of Nazacahoz, Spaniards had come there from the west, and they had then returned in the direction from which they had come. Moscoso then proceeded for two days to Nacazahoz. They captured some women, one of whom said that she had seen Christians before. But she later said that she had lied, and the Spaniards concluded that all such reports about other Spaniards also had been lies. They returned to Guasco, having found very little corn in Nazacahoz.

It is difficult to know what to make of these Indian reports of other Spaniards. Naquiscoza and Nazacahoz were not so very far from where Cabeza de Vaca and his comrades spent many years on the Texas coast.[60] But these reports could also have been an artifact of wishful thinking on the part of the Spaniards, abetted by their extracting information from the Indians through torture.

The people of Guasco told the Spaniards that ten days toward the west lay the River of Daycao, where they sometimes went to kill deer. They said that they had seen people on the other side of this river, but they did not know who they were. Moscoso and his army loaded up as much corn as they could carry, and they headed south and southwest.[61]

If Guasco was in the vicinity of San Pedro Creek, they probably followed a trail which lay on or near Texas State Highway 21. But it is difficult to know how far westward they traveled in what is now the state of Texas. The Gentleman of Elvas says they traveled ten days and arrived at the River of Daycao, where they halted. From here they sent out ten cavalry who crossed the river and searched its banks for people. But Biedma says that they traveled for six days and halted, and from there they sent out cavalry to go as far as they could go in eight or so days to explore the country. Given this travel time, they easily could have reached the Trinity River or the Navasota River, and the detachment of cavalry may even have reached the Brazos River.

The detachment of cavalry happened upon some people living in very small huts. They captured a few of them and took them back to where Moscoso and the others were. These people subsisted solely by hunting and gathering. Beyond the River of Daycao lay the country that Cabeza de Vaca had described, in which the Indians had no settled towns, but wandered about "like Arabs," living on prickly pears, roots, and game. None of the Indians traveling with Moscoso could understand the captives from the River of Daycao. It would seem that they spoke a language other than Caddoan.

If Moscoso and his men continued toward the west, they realized that they would not be able to find the stores of corn on which they depended.

Also, because of the language barrier, they would not be able to obtain intelligence from the Indians. It was already early October, and if they remained for too long where they were, it would begin to rain and snow, and they would not be able to travel. They decided that as quickly as possible they would return to the Mississippi River where they knew they would be able to find food.

Their return trip was more difficult than it otherwise might have been because they had treated the Indians so harshly their first time through, and they had already plundered most of the food the Indians had stored. The Indians were understandably hostile, and they had taken to hiding what little corn they had remaining. Returning on the same trail by which they had come, the Spaniards arrived at the lower Arkansas River in early December 1542. They again crossed the river at Ayays and returned to Anilco. But the people of Anilco had been so devastated and terrified by de Soto's brutal actions when he had launched a surprise terroristic attack against them, they had not planted a crop of corn, and they themselves were reduced to begging the Spaniards for food.

Moscoso would have to take his army elsewhere. The Indians of Anilco told the Spaniards that corn could be obtained from their enemy, Aminoya, at a distance of two days of travel. When the Spaniards arrived at Aminoya, they found two large palisaded towns on level ground, about half a league apart. The Spaniards occupied one of these towns, and they tore down the second to obtain building materials with which to build additional houses. Aminoya could have been located anywhere from about present Deerfield to Old Town in Phillips County.

As soon as they were settled in Aminoya, the Spaniards began building seven keeled boats. During the winter, Moscoso sent a party of men two days' travel upriver to the chiefdom of Tagoanate. This chiefdom probably lay between the vicinity of Clarksdale, Mississippi, and the mouth of the St. Francis River.

They completed building the boats in June 1543. Luckily, when the time came for them to embark, the river rose up to where they had built the boats, so that they did not have to haul them down to the river. The thin planks and short nails they used in building the boats might not have been equal to being moved overland. Because the river was high, the velocity of the current would have been about three to three and a half miles per hour.

On the morning of July 2, they started down the river. In addition to the current, each boat, according to Garcilaso, was propelled by seven pairs of oars manned in turn by all the men, and each had a sail that could be used when the wind was right. On the first day, if they traveled for twelve hours at 4 miles per hour, they would have gone a distance of 48 miles. At the end of the day they passed by the entrance to the stream that ran through the territory of Guachoya. They moored for the night at a point that could not have been far below the mouth of the Arkansas River.

The next day, July 3, they came to Huhasene, a town subject to chief Quigualtam, a powerful chief whose domain lay on the eastern side of the Mississippi River. They pulled ashore and seized a supply of corn from the granaries in this town. They may have traveled no more than about 15 or 20 miles before coming to this place. This would place Huhasene to the north or to the west of present Winterville, Mississippi.

The next morning, July 4, a fleet of a hundred large war canoes of chief Quigualtam began to attack the Spaniards as they sailed down the river. The warriors in the canoes continued to attack all that day and through the night. The Spaniards fled down the river as fast as they could. This fleet of canoes did not cease its attack until noon, on July 5, when they turned around and began paddling back up the river. On this segment of their journey, assuming that the Spaniards put into the river at about eight in the morning on July 4, they traveled continuously for twenty-eight hours. At 4 miles per hour they would have covered 112 miles. Hence, it would seem that the canoes of Quigualtam ceased their attack just above the mouth of the Yazoo River.

But no sooner had this attack ended, when the Spaniards evidently entered a stretch of the river under the dominion of another chief whose name is not given. A second fleet of fifty large canoes began to attack. This attack continued for the remainder of that day and throughout the night, as the Spaniards continued underway through the darkness. This fleet ceased its attack at about ten in the morning of the next day, July 6. Presumably this fleet had reached the southern limit of its territory.

In this second segment of their journey, the Spaniards were underway continuously for some twenty-two hours. If their speed was 4 miles per hour, they would have covered 88 miles, placing them near present Natchez, Mississippi. After this, they were not attacked by any more fleets of canoes, implying that there were no more large chiefdoms between the vicinity of Natchez and the mouth of the Mississippi River.

Twelve days later, Moscoso and his men reached the mouth of the Mississippi River. From Aminoya to the mouth of the river it was about 750 miles. In the time they had available, they could have traveled this distance by averaging no more than about 3.4 miles per hour.

On September 10, 1543, the little fleet entered the mouth of the Pánuco River in what is now the state of Vera Cruz, Mexico. Four years and four months had passed since they had sailed out of the harbor of Havana. From Tampa Bay to Aminoya, where they spent their last winter, they had walked and ridden approximately 3,500 miles. About half of the army had survived this ordeal. Some of these men remained in Mexico, others went to Peru, and still others returned to Spain. The documents are silent on how many of their Indian slaves survived. But it is known that at least one survived, a woman of Coosa who returned to her homeland in 1559–61, while serving as interpreter for the Tristán de Luna expedition.[62]

NOTES

This paper is a synopsis of a ten-year research project to reconstruct the routes of the de Soto, Luna, and Pardo expeditions. An earlier version of this paper was submitted to the National Park Service and published in *De Soto Trail: De Soto National Historic Trail Study.* The general approach and the methods used in this research may be seen in: Hudson, Smith, Hally, Polhemus, and DePratter, "Reply to Boyd and Schroedl"; Hudson, "The Uses of Evidence"; and Hudson, "An Unknown South."

The principal documents useful in reconstructing the route of the de Soto expedition are as follows:

A. Oviedo, *Historia general,* first published in 1851, includes Rodrigo Ranjel's narrative (pp. 153–81). As de Soto's secretary, Ranjel wrote a day-by-day account of their activities, and any reconstruction of the route must begin with this document. Ranjel's original document is not known to have survived, and the degree to which Oviedo modified the text is unknown. A translation into English by Edward Gaylord Bourne is available in Ranjel, *Narratives,* 43–150.

B. *Relacam verdadeira dos trabalhos q ho governador do Fernado de Souto y certos fidalgos portugueses passarom no descobrimeto de provincia de Frolida* [sic], by an anonymous gentleman of Elvas, published in 1557. The best translation is by Robertson, *True Relation.*

C. Luis Hernandez de Biedma, "Relación de la Isla de la Florida." This brief account by the factor for the expedition contains the most consistent references to direction of travel, as well as some information not to be found in the longer accounts by Ranjel and the Gentleman of Elvas. A translation by Buckingham Smith is available in Bourne, *Narratives of the Career of Hernando de Soto.*

D. *La Florida del Inca.* First published in Lisbon in 1605, a facsimile edition, with an introduction and notes by Sylvia Hilton, was published in 1982; an edition using modern typography, also edited by Sylvia Hilton, was published in 1986. This long, grandiose, secondhand account is of almost negligible use in reconstructing the route of the expedition. It has been translated into English as *The Florida of the Inca.*

The principal publications produced by the de Soto-Luna-Pardo project are: DePratter, Hudson, and Smith, "Route of Juan Pardo's Explorations"; Hudson, Smith, and DePratter, "The Hernando de Soto Expedition"; DePratter, Hudson, and Smith, "Hernando de Soto Expedition"; Hudson et al., "Coosa"; Hudson, "De Soto in Arkansas"; Hudson, "Juan Pardo's Excursion"; Hudson, Smith, and DePratter, "Victims of the King Site Massacre"; Hudson, *Juan Pardo Expeditions;* Hudson, "A Spanish-Coosa Alliance"; Hudson, Smith, DePratter, and Kelley, "Tristán de Luna Expedition"; Hudson, Smith, and DePratter, "Hernando de Soto Expedition"; Milanich and Hudson, *Hernando de Soto;* Hudson, "New de Soto Route."

1. Albornoz, *Hernando de Soto,* 13–20, 45–59; Lockhart, *Men of Cajamarca,* 199; Albornoz, *Hernando de Soto,* 45–59; and Swanton, *Final Report,* 65–74.

2. Ibid, 75–82.

3. Avellaneda, *Los Sobrevivientes,* 68. All dates are in the Old "Style" Julian calendar. To convert to "New Style" dates, add ten days.

4. The route of de Soto from his landing place to Apalachee is drawn from Milanich and Hudson, *Hernando de Soto.*

5. A detailed account of their landing at Tampa Bay may be seen in Milanich and Hudson, *Hernando de Soto*, chapter 3.

6. Ewen, "de Soto's First Winter Encampment," 113–18.

7. Detailed evidence for locating Achuse at Pensacola Bay is contained in Hudson, Smith, DePratter, and Kelley, "The Tristán de Luna Expedition," 31–34. Later in the expedition de Soto's men speculated incorrectly that the Alabama River emptied into the Port of Achuse.

8. Unless otherwise noted, the route from Apalachee to Chiaha is drawn from Hudson, Smith, and DePratter, "Hernando de Soto Expedition."

9. This reconstruction of de Soto's route from the Flint to the Congaree River in South Carolina differs in several details from Hudson, Smith, and DePratter, "Hernando de Soto Expedition." The improvements are detailed in Hudson, Worth, and DePratter, "Refinements in de Soto's Route."

10. John Worth, "Mississippian Occupation of the Middle Flint River" (M.A. thesis, University of Georgia, 1988).

11. This same town was visited by Juan Pardo in 1566–68, who called it *Guiomae* or *Emae.* DePratter, Hudson, and Smith, "Juan Pardo's Explorations," 138–39, and DePratter, "Cofitachequi," 134–38.

12. "Ylasi" is the preferred spelling.

13. The route from Chiaha to Mabila is based on DePratter, Hudson, and Smith, "Hernando de Soto Expedition."

14. The route from Chiaha to Tali described herein differs from that set forth in DePratter, Hudson, and Smith, "Hernando de Soto Expedition," and also in an earlier draft of this present paper. I am grateful to Lowell Kirk for spotting several inconsistencies in the earlier draft that led me to this revision.

15. Biedma, "Account," 15, and Ranjel, "Narrative," 108.

16. Ranjel, "Narrative," 109.

17. Ibid.

18. Biedma, "Account," 15, and Ranjel, "Narrative," 109.

19. Long, *Examinations and Surveys*, 29.

20. Ranjel, "Narrative," 111.

21. Ibid.

22. Hudson et al., "Tristán de Luna Expedition," 39–42, and Hudson, "A Spanish-Coosa Alliance."

23. Hudson et al., "Coosa."

24. This second town was probably located at the King Site.

25. This location differs from the one proposed in DePratter, Hudson, and Smith, "Hernando de Soto Expedition," 120. The chiefdom of Talisi comprised some or all of the Kymulga phase sites in this area.

26. Hudson et al., "Tristán de Luna Expedition," 37.

27. The verb *enriscar* ("to find refuge in cliffs") definitely implies the presence of rock. Archaeological research at the Durant Bend site appears to indicate that the site was occupied both too early and too late for it to have been Piachi. Other late prehistoric sites are known to exist near Selma, but little is known of them.

28. Unless otherwise noted, the route from Mabila to the Mississippi River is drawn from Hudson, Smith, and DePratter, "Hernando de Soto Expedition."

29. James Atkinson, personal communication with the author.

30. Hudson, Smith, DePratter, and Kelly, "Tristán de Luna Expedition," 35–36.

31. Atkinson, "The de Soto Expedition," 63.

32. I am grateful to Rufus A. Ward, Jr., for pointing out that this was the place where an engineer appointed by Andrew Jackson suggested that a crossing be located for the road that was to be built connecting Nashville and New Orleans. Major Pitchlynne, a local resident, informed the engineer that the Choctaws crossed the river at this point when the water was high. If de Soto and his army had taken a course south of the Luxapallila, they would have had to ferry themselves across a very wide expanse of flood water. Moreover, a crossing as far south as Nashville Ferry would have taken them in a westerly direction from Mabila, and Biedma says that they went northward from Mabila to Chickasaw.

33. Marshall, personal communication with the author.

34. Ibid.

35. Unless otherwise noted, the remainder of this paper is drawn from Hudson, "De Soto in Arkansas."

36. Morse and Morse, *Central Mississippi Valley,* 292–93.

37. Dan F. Morse, "ASU Spring Break Archaeology Project," 3–4.

38. Morse and Morse, *Central Mississippi Valley,* 313; Morse, "Protohistoric Hunting Sites," 91–93.

39. Morse and Morse, *Central Mississippi Valley,* 312.

40. Quiguate comprised Kent phase archaeological sites. House, "Kent Phase Investigations," 46–60.

41. The Chiefdom of Coligua comprised Greenbier phase archaeological sites. Morse and Morse, *Central Mississippi Valley,* 298–300.

42. Akridge, "De Soto's Route," 7.

43. Hudson, "New de Soto Route."

44. This seems to be the first and only instance in which the Spaniards encountered this settlement pattern, that is, scattered isolated houses at a considerable distance from a population center.

45. Rodrigo Ranjel's narrative ceases at Autiamque. As a consequence, the chronology of events occurring during the remainder of the expedition is less precise than it would have been had the Ranjel narrative been complete.

46. Catalte comprised Tillar phase sites. Marvin D. Jeter, "The Protohistoric 'Tillar Complex' of Southeast Arkansas" (Paper Presented at the Forty-seventh Annual Meeting of the Society for American Archaeology, Minneapolis, April 17, 1982).

47. Early, "Caddoan Settlement Systems," 221–29.

48. Hot springs are mentioned in the outline of the uncompleted or missing chapter of Rodrigo Ranjel's "Narrative," 150.

49. From this point onward to Guasco, this reconstruction differs from Hudson, "De Soto in Arkansas." Frank F. Schambach has suggested that the main town of Aguacay was in the general vicinity of present-day Nashville, Arkansas. See "The End of the Trail," 17–18.

50. Biedma, "Island of Florida," 36.

51. Elvas, *True Relation of the Hardships,* Vol. 2, 238–39. Frank F. Schambach made this site identification. See his "End of the Trail," 239.

52. Schambach, "The End of the Trail," 21–22.

53. This paramount chiefdom comprised Belcher phase sites in the densely populated Great Bend area of the Red River. Cf. Schambach, "Archaeological Background," 91–92. Schambach places the center of population of Naguatex in the vicinity of present Garland City; see "End of the Trail," 20–21.

54. Elvas, *True Relation of the Hardships*, Vol. 2, 245–46. I am indebted to Frank F. Schambach for pointing out the importance of the Great Raft. See his "The End of the Trail."

55. Hudson, "New de Soto Route," and Schambach, "The End of the Trail," 25.

56. Both Nissohone and Lacane were probably Titus focus sites: Wyckoff, *Caddoan Cultural Area*, 174–81. Nondacao could also have been located on the Sabine River.

57. Cf. Biedma, "Account," 36.

58. Soacatino was probably at a Frankston focus site. Cf. Wyckoff, *Caddoan Cultural Area*, 181–85.

59. Naquiscoza and Nazacahoz probably lay in the Angelina River basin.

60. Cabeza de Vaca, *The Journey of Alvar Núñez Cabeza de Vaca*.

61. Biedma, 37. Elvas says they went west.

62. Hudson, "A Spanish-Coosa Alliance," 602.

JOHN E. WORTH

Late Spanish Military Expeditions in the Interior Southeast, 1597–1628

The century following Spain's first major penetration of the interior of La Florida with the 1539–43 expedition of Hernando de Soto witnessed a re-markable transformation of what is now the Southeastern United States. During this time Spain mounted a colonization effort that was to ensure a foothold on the mainland for nearly three hundred years. While these early years were marked by dreams of ultimate domination of all of La Florida, the grip that Spain held on the mainland was in actuality limited primarily to the coastlines, and more particularly the area around St. Augustine. Although the interior beckoned many Spaniards, military exploration of this region was never pursued in a systematic or consistent manner.

After the abortive expeditions of Tristán de Luna (1559–61) and Juan Pardo (1566–68), Spanish penetration of the interior seems to have been largely relegated to the ambitious Franciscan missionaries. By the middle of the seventeenth century, these friars had pushed Spanish influence far to the north of St. Augustine and even farther to the west. At the same time, however, several small-scale military expeditions pushed deep into the interior between 1597 and 1628. These expeditions represented the last of the military exploratory ventures in the interior and as such mark a transitional period in the colonization of La Florida. Exploration and re-connaissance of the deep frontier by well-armed military expeditions was to be replaced by the less costly endeavors of isolated missionaries, whose persistent overtures to the Indians of the interior gradually pushed Span-ish influence farther and farther into the interior. An examination of these last expeditions reveals much regarding Spain's changing military posture in La Florida, and at the same time provides a final glimpse of the Indian societies of the interior before the penetration of the English traders from the north.[1]

Three major exploratory ventures were launched into the interior Southeast during the sixteenth century. The first and most famous is the Hernando de Soto expedition, which set out in 1539. While the details of this adventure are treated elsewhere, it is sufficient to note that the members of the de Soto expedition were the first and last Europeans to witness the vast and powerful paramount chiefdoms of the Indians of the interior Southeast in a largely pristine state, and accounts of this entrada provide a remarkable portrait of living societies that would be irrevocably transformed over the next centuries.[2]

Between 1559 and 1568, the Luna and Pardo expeditions provided a final glimpse of the Indian societies of the interior before their ultimate political collapse in the face of massive demographic decline.[3] This period also marked the establishment of the colonial settlements of St. Augustine and Santa Elena on the Atlantic coast of La Florida. The Pardo expedition was the last major military exploratory venture launched by Spain into the interior Southeast, and it was only with the rapid spread of English traders and colonists after the 1670 foundation of Charles Towne that the window of historical documentation opens once again on a somewhat altered social landscape. Consequently, the processes that transformed these Indian societies remained largely unrecorded by European colonists. While archaeology has been able to make significant contributions toward filling this gap,[4] there were at least seven Spanish expeditions into the interior during this time, and documentation relating to these journeys, though scant, includes valuable information regarding those societies that remained in the deep frontier until the coming of the Carolinians.

Almost thirty years passed after the return of Juan Pardo's expedition before Spaniards once again penetrated the northern interior. This period witnessed many changes in the character of the Spanish presence on the Atlantic coast, including the brief appearance of Jesuit missionaries among the coastal Indians, the abandonment of Santa Elena after Francis Drake's 1586 assault on St. Augustine, and the establishment of the first Franciscan mission province among the Guale Indians of coastal Georgia in 1595. This last event set the stage for more than a century of Franciscan efforts among the Indians of La Florida and presaged the eventual domination of the regular clergy in all subsequent Spanish exploration of the interior.

Military exploration was by no means replaced during these first years of missionization, for only two years passed before newly installed Governor Méndez de Canço ordered Gaspar de Salas, a soldier with long experience in La Florida, to accompany two friars on an exploratory journey into the interior. While the scale of this expedition was in no way comparable to that of de Soto Luna, or Pardo, the very fact that Salas accompanied the friars reveals a military interest in the exploration of the interior.[5]

The 1597 entrada is perhaps the best-documented and certainly the most well known of the four examined in this paper.[6] For this reason, the details of the journey will not be treated in full here. Fray Pedro de Chozas, accompanied by fellow missionary Francisco de Verascola, set out with Salas (as military escort and interpreter) from Tolomato, on the mainland in the Guale mission province opposite Sapelo Island. The expedition included thirty Indians, Christian and pagan, from Tolomato, led by its *cacique*, Don Juan, and loaded with an assortment of trade goods.[7] The party marched for eight days, seven of which were through a *despoblado*, an unoccupied region. (See Figure 1.)[8] The group found no good land until they arrived at the town of Tama, where Salas notes an abundance of food. In addition, Salas and the friars discovered evidence of what they believed was silver and projected that these would be "very rich mines."[9]

Chozas's usual practice was to have the Indian king (*rey*) emerge from the council house (*bohio*), carrying the cross and plant it in the middle of the plaza.[10] At Tama, Chozas entered the council house and displayed the cross before taking the king's seat with his companions at his side. Salas informed the Indians of their intentions, and the Indians promised to return with more people the next day. After sleeping in the king's house, Chozas preached the following day. According to Chozas, the appearance of rain, which soaked the Indian fields, brought on their conversion, and he and his companions were given many gifts.[11] Another day's journey brought the Spaniards to the town of Ocute, where the *cacique* warned them to turn back: "And wanting to pass forward, the *cacique* of the said town of Ocute obstructed them with much fervor and crying with them, saying that if they went forward the Indians would have to kill them, because many seasons before, it is understood, when de Soto passed carrying many people who went on horseback, they killed them, and that they would kill them easier, since they were few. Because of this, they did not pass forward and returned from there."[12] Chozas only notes the hostile intentions in this other land, but relates an incident which suggests that the *cacique* of Tama may have been under external pressure to reject the Spanish overtures.

On their way back, Chozas's party stopped for the night at Tama, and there he would have been scalped had Salas not fired his arquebus. Chozas relates that "the king was moved to such an atrocious crime through having as great prowess in his district to remove [from] the Spaniard the hair that covers his head, through there being an ancient rite in the West to give [the scalp] to he who ran with more quickness, in order to wear as a garter usually, because he won the jewel [from] his opponent."[13] The chief of Tama had arranged a contest between himself and another chief, with Chozas's scalp as the intended prize.[14] The next day Chozas was unable to calm the angry chief, who refused the friar's request for burden-bearers, since Chozas related of his own party that "my people have hidden themselves in the desert."[15] This incident perhaps serves to illustrate the tenuous nature of such conversions, particularly in the deep interior.

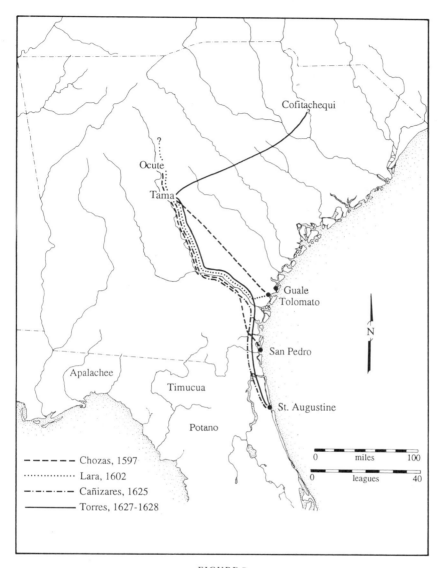

FIGURE I
Late sixteenth- and early seventeenth-century
Spanish expeditions in the Southeast

While the party penetrated no deeper into the interior than Ocute, Salas makes note of another region even farther:

> And likewise they heard the Indians of that town [Ocute] say, and the Salchiches, that across a *sierra* that there was four days journey from there, very high, shining when the sun set like a fire, on the other side of it there were people who wear short hair, and that the pines were found cut with axes, and that it seemed that similar signs could not be but from Spanish people, and the said land seems and is very sufficient for producing whichever kind of grain, even if it be wheat, and many plains and *cabañas*[16] for cattle and rivers of sweet water at stretches, and it seems that if there were someone who knew how to pan gold, it would be gathered in those rivers.[17]

Although Salas's conclusion that these people were Spaniards is almost certainly in error, his description suggests the presence of another Indian province four days from Ocute. Based on the distance and the references to mountains and gold panning, it seems reasonable to locate this province in present-day north Georgia. Chozas and his companions explored no further, however, and the return journey was by a different road (see Figure 1), which traversed a more populous region, eventually bringing the party to the mission of San Pedro on Cumberland Island.[18]

The precise location of the towns of Tama and Ocute are the subject of considerable debate. While it is probable that the towns of the same name were located on the Oconee River within or near the Piedmont physiographical province of northern Georgia when Hernando de Soto visited them in 1540, some scholars place their 1597 location to the south in the forks of the Altamaha, deep within the Coastal Plain.[19] Nevertheless, on the basis of evidence relating to the Chozas expedition and others (discussed below), the northern location seems more probable, with Tama perhaps still located at the Shinholser mound site.[20] Regardless of the specific location of these towns, however, it is clear that Salas and the two friars penetrated deep into the interior. While the ultimate impact of their visit on the Indian inhabitants of these interior provinces is unknown, the intelligence gathered by these explorers had a definite and lasting effect on the Spanish perception of the interior.

Late the following year the Crown requested information regarding Tama in hopes of establishing a settlement, and Governor Méndez's report, dated February 6, 1600, constitutes a major documentary source for the expedition.[21] Within the month, Méndez outlined the needs for a second expedition into the interior, this time with the ambitious goal of ultimately reaching New Mexico. The expedition would have dwarfed that of Juan Pardo, for Méndez requested three hundred foot soldiers along with equipment, weapons, horses, and large quantities of trade goods for the Indians.[22] There is no evidence that this proposed expedition ever went beyond the planning stages, however. The recent English colony at Roanoke may have been a factor in the Crown's decision not to pursue this venture, for in the same letter, Méndez asked for one thousand extra men to comprise an assault force that might oust the English, perhaps reducing a major military exploratory venture to secondary importance. Nevertheless, Governor Méndez's interest in Tama and the interior remained strong.

News of Spaniards in the interior provided the impetus for another exploratory expedition into the interior. In July 1602, Governor Méndez ordered Juan de Lara, a soldier of thirty-four years' experience in La Florida, to investigate these rumors.[23] While Méndez's description of this journey is brief, he does review Spanish contact with these interior Indians, noting:

> I have had very great desires to make an entrada to Tama and Ocute from where I have had news. There are samples of mines and stones from Gaspar de Salas, who entered it with Father Chozas and Father Verascola to the said Tama and Ocute, which are more than fifty leagues from the coast on the mainland. The past days I sent to the said Tama Juan de Lara, a soldier of this presidio, to find out if the news that the Indians of the interior brought me was true, that certain Spaniards had arrived at the said Tama, and they brought horses, and understanding that there might be some scattered people of those that journeyed [?] from New Mexico. [Lara's expedition] was [carried out] with great security and accompanied by the Indians of the province of Guale where the said missionaries were killed. He found the said news not to be true.[24]

This short account is fortunately supplemented by testimony taken in St. Augustine from Lara himself on September 7 of the same year:

> It will have been about two months ago that by order of Governor Gonzalo Méndez de Canço he went to reconnoiter some news that had come through the Indians saying that in the interior there were a quantity of Spaniards, and that he should go from this presidio to the *lengua*[25] and province of Guale and town of Tulafina, and from there he entered the interior carrying with him Indians of the language of Guale. He continued walking about nine days from sunrise to sunset, and it seemed to the witness that he walked up to sixty or seventy leagues. He arrived among Indians that had not seen [the rumored] Spaniards, and they gave him many gifts. He arrived at a *sierra* and at a town which is called Olatama, and from there, which is the capital of the province, he passed twenty leagues to the north.[26] He saw that the land is fertile for whatever cultivation or breeding of cattle, and that there are many large chestnuts like those of Spain and other fruits and many grapes and plums [and] persimmons [of] great quantity. He encountered a river, copious and large, and from there the Indians of the town which is called Olatama [said] that he should not pass from there so that they might not kill him. He turned back and brought some stones so that they might be seen. He gave them to [?] in order to [see] if they were from mines or some metals. He saw that the Indians wore neither gold nor silver nor pearls and that the men walked in hides and the women shawls [*tapadas*] with linen of hemp.[27]

The details of this expedition are remarkably similar to those of Chozas only five years before, and it seems likely that Lara followed nearly the same route as the previous expedition (see Figure 1). In fact, his estimate of the distance to Tama (at the Fall Line of the Oconee River) from Guale is more accurate than that of Salas.[28] Lara also notes that the town of Tama was the political center of a province of the same name, and that the Indians deeper in the interior remained hostile to Spanish entradas.

The contemporary relations of two Franciscan missionaries indicate that the Lara visit only served to confirm Spanish expectations regarding the riches of the interior. Suggesting that the presidio of St. Augustine be moved north into the province of Guale (and nearer to Tama), Fray Francisco de Pareja noted, "I am certain of the entradas of the interior, the one of Fray Fernandez de Chozas and another now this year of 1602. They have found the land to be of better disposition and more population and fertile, and have brought samples of mines and *guitamo real*."[29] Fray Baltasar López further related the information he had acquired from Indians living on the mainland, "having knowledge and news of the interior through being in the same vicinity and road from the *sierras* of Tama where it is known there are mines of gold and silver, and in one of the journeys that I made into the interior I saw some Indians that made use of *chaguales*[30] and beads of gold had from hand to hand from the towns that border with this *sierra*."[31] These accounts indicate that by 1602 the interior, and Tama in particular, was generally perceived to be a well-populated region with an abundance of land and natural resources, including the "mines" Salas described. While Governor Méndez was never able to realize his plans for this region, his successor soon found himself immersed in the legends of the interior.

Within three months of his arrival in St. Augustine as Governor, Pedro de Ybarra wrote to the Crown of his interest in the interior:

> The old soldiers of this presidio have told me of the many riches that there are in the interior, some from having seen it, and that 200 leagues from here are people rich and so civilized that they have their houses of stone. They offered to show it to me and teach the road through where one is able to pass with security. Your Majesty giving me license for it and sending me one hundred arquebusiers that I ask for above and as many again *escupiles*[32] and pikes, I will go to make an entrada with them in order to see what there is, for Your Majesty did not send me here in order that the columns should remain where they are, but rather in order to go forward. But in case I have difficulty [in] what I ask for in this, Your Majesty will be served to give permission so that at least I may send a person of satisfaction to the people in order to make the said entrada for the first time.[33]

While the Crown granted Ybarra permission to explore the interior in November of the same year, a year later the Governor was still waiting for more soldiers to arrive before the expedition could begin.[34]

Though Ybarra met the *cacique* of Tama in person on his visitation of the Guale province in late November 1604, as late as 1607 Governor Ybarra was still waiting for soldiers to pursue his own entrada into the interior.[35]

This year, however, witnessed an event which would shape Spanish policy in La Florida for years to come. The foundation of a permanent English colony at Jamestown marked the first real challenge to Spain's domination of mainland North America since Fort Caroline in 1565, and when news of this town reached the Spanish Crown and St. Augustine, concerns seem to have shifted toward defense.

Before this period, even the continued existence of the Spanish colony at St. Augustine was in some doubt, for despite the wishes of both Governor Ybarra and missionaries in La Florida, King Philip III planned a reduction in military personnel.[36] However, once the decision had been made to maintain the colony, Ybarra's concerns focused on acquiring more soldiers.[37] The proposed minimum of three hundred soldiers could not be met, leaving St. Augustine in a questionable defensive stance. A Royal *Cédula* dated March 15, 1609, reveals the extent of the Crown's concern and established a policy that was to have a significant effect on the role of the military in the exploration of the interior.[38] After this time, soldiers were forbidden to accompany the friars on their entradas into the interior. While the stated concern is the deleterious effect of military force in religious conversions, it seems an unlikely coincidence that such a concern would arise precisely when soldiers were at a premium in the planned defense of St. Augustine from the north.

Just over a month later, Governor Ybarra requested that he be permitted to leave St. Augustine, and he was replaced as Governor in 1610.[39] His plans for the military exploration of the interior, like those of Governor Méndez before him, were never executed. Nearly twenty-five years would pass before Spanish soldiers once again penetrated the interior on an exploratory mission. During this period, however, Franciscan missionaries pushed farther and farther into the interior west of St. Augustine. The early forays of Fray Baltasar López into the Timucua province in 1597 were followed by the establishment of the mission province of Potano to the south in 1606 and in Timucua two years later. By 1616, there were several missions in these provinces, and while the military occasionally entered these established interior provinces, it was the friars who made the initial contacts with interior groups.

After the 1609 *Cédula*, then, exploration of the interior seems to have been relegated to the clergy. Their efforts, however, were apparently confined to the region west of St. Augustine, where the major mission road would later serve as the primary Spanish avenue into the interior. The northern interior, including the province of Tama and others to the north, remained a largely unexplored wilderness, and it is perhaps in part this fact that prompted a brief flurry of military activity in these unconverted provinces during the 1620s.

During this period, rumors of white horsemen in the interior of La Florida created considerable concern among Spanish officials, and five military expeditions were sent into the interior between 1624 and 1628. Documentation regarding the first two of these expeditions is quite limited. On the basis of the report of newly arrived Governor Don Luis de Rojas y Borja, it is apparent that his predecessor, Governor Juan de Salinas, dispatched two small entradas to an undescribed location in the interior during 1624. After conducting a *residencia* of Salinas's term in office, Rojas noted:

> Before I arrived at this government [there was] news through the native Indians that in the interior walked some people, never seen [by] them, on horseback and with some lances.[40] Governor Juan de Salinas, my predecessor, with this news, sent two soldiers [into] the interior to find out what people they were. [They] went and walked 150 leagues, according to what they say. They returned without having seen anything and without bringing more of the relation than was known to be said. They returned through having exhausted the supplies, of food and other kinds, which they carried in order to give to the Indians as barter, which is accustomed, and [for] good passage. Seeing this, the said Governor sent them a second time, and through some disorders of one soldier they returned without having done anything nor even arrived to where [they were] the first time.[41]

The identity of the soldiers making this expedition is unknown, and it is unclear whether any Indians accompanied the Spaniards. The location of their journey is not given, but based on the total distance traveled, they probably ventured some distance inland from the coastal Guale province. In any case, neither expedition was successful, and Salinas's successor, Governor Rojas, was forced to make further inquiries soon after his arrival.

Confronted with these persistent rumors, Governor Rojas immediately began making plans for a larger expedition. While awaiting approval and making preparations for this entrada, Rojas vowed, "Meanwhile I will not stop doing all possible measures and making this investigation in order to advise Your Majesty of the most certain thing."[42] Apparently, Rojas soon dispatched another soldier on a reconnaissance journey, described by Ensign Adrián de Cañizares y Osorio in a later record of his military service:

> [Governor Rojas] ordered that he should go to the discovery of some mines of lead[43] with traces of gold and silver to the province of Tama that is more than one hundred leagues distant from the said presidio. He did this with much care and diligence, bringing an account to the said Governor of what he had ordered, with much risk to his life by all that province of Indians being pagans and very bellicose warriors, and enduring many hardships by walking on foot out and back with weapons shouldered.[44]

Rojas later mentioned this expedition in preface to his report of the subsequent Torres expedition, and noted that the party was forced to return due to lack of "food and sustenance," and was unable to provide a satisfactory report.[45]

Nevertheless, Cañizares evidently penetrated farther into the interior than the two Salinas expeditions, and was the first to reach the province of Tama since Juan de Lara nearly a quarter century before.[46] His account above reveals several things. The legend of mines in the province of Tama was clearly a persistent one, though it is doubtful that Cañizares found any proof since his expedition has long since been forgotten.[47] In addition, Tama remained an unconverted province in 1625, and it is also possible that relations with the Spanish had deteriorated somewhat by this time.[48] Ultimately, the failure of the Cañizares expedition to complete a military reconnaissance of the interior soon prompted another venture even farther to the north.

In 1627, Governor Rojas mounted what was to be Spain's last military exploratory expedition of the interior Southeast. After the unproductive Cañizares expedition, Rojas was urged by the Crown to determine positively whether the English had penetrated the interior from the north.[49] Plans for this expedition dated to early 1625, when Rojas learned of the abortive Salinas expeditions in search of the rumored white horsemen:

> Through the information and relation that the Indians make of these people and through their dress it is held for certain that they are English or Dutch of those that are in Jacan [Jamestown], and the Indians say that they are very white and blond. This and knowing that the English of Jacan continue entering the interior and marrying with Indian women, it is held for certain that they are them. Where these English go is traveling in the direction of New Spain and discovering this land, which gives me concern [that] they should go so near. . . . It is a very certain thing that the fort and population of Jacan continue growing greatly each day with a large number of people, in excess of two thousand men, and with the fortification of the place. The Indians say that these people that they have seen on horseback are about fifty men and in no place have they taken foot and to the appearance [their purpose] is to continue reconnoitering the land in order to enter it.[50]

The Governor outlined his plans for a reconnaissance expedition composed of soldiers and Indians, and indicated that they were not to return until having achieved their mission.[51] This letter was not seen until October 1626, and Rojas was finally given permission to undertake the entrada by Royal *Cédula* in May 1627.

Soon thereafter, the Governor dispatched Ensign Pedro de Torres in command of ten Spanish soldiers and sixty Indians under the trusted *cacique* Don Pedro de Ybarra.[52] The party was sent into the interior twice, for the first attempt, which apparently lasted some three to four months, failed to provide the necessary information.[53] A brief, if somewhat fanciful, description of this initial journey has been discovered in the 1678 service record of one of its participants:

> The said Governor [Don Luis de Rojas y Borja], with news that he had that there were three hills of diamonds in the Province of Cofatachiqui, 200

leagues from this presidio, dispatched a group of infantry to its discovery, and among them the said Ensign [Juan Bauptista Terrazas], and having traveled and been lost during the course of three months through the woods without a guide or a road or sustenance, he obligated the rest of his companions to cast lots in order to eat one of them in order not to die of hunger, and it fell upon the said Ensign, and being [prepared] to kill him, they left off doing it by having found people who guided them to the said province, who came forth from it with news [of the Spaniards] that one of the guides that they took, who fled, gave to them; and because of wars that they were having with other nations they did not let them enter.[54]

Although the above account was penned more than half a century after the Torres expedition, and not by Ensign Terrazas himself, it provides some intriguing bits of information regarding the deep interior in 1627. First, the description of near-starvation during the journey to Cofitachequi forms a remarkable parallel to the progress of the Hernando de Soto expedition across the infamous "Desert of Ocute," suggesting that Torres may have followed a similar route, once again crossing the depopulated region between Tama (visited by Cañizares only two years earlier) and Cofitachequi. Furthermore, the fact that the party was prohibited from entering the province because of wars between Cofitachequi and neighboring provinces might serve as evidence for continuing hostility between the provinces on either side of this persistent buffer zone.

Fortunately, the second journey succeeded in actually entering the province of Cofitachequi, and it is this expedition that provides the basis for Governor Rojas's formal account, the relevant portion of which follows:

The Ensign [Pedro de Torres] with all of the people that he led, having penetrated the interior more than 200 leagues and through detours which the road made more than 300, arrived at a place called Cofitachiqui, which is the farthest where reached Hernando de Soto, he who discovered and conquered these provinces. In that place he was very regaled by the *cacique*, who is very respected by all the remaining *caciques*, and all obey him and recognize vassalage. There were 82 years [since] Hernando de Soto was there, and until this occasion Spaniards have not arrived and they remain sheltered.[55] All that the Indians said of the horsemen that they had seen was not true and was a lie. The telling of [lies] is ordinary among the Indians because they talk each day with the Devil and there are many sorcerers and enchanters. Between the *fiestas* that this principal *cacique*[56] made for the Ensign and the rest of the Spaniards, he showed them some lakes from which come forth rivers where there is a great quantity of pearls.[57] The *cacique* and Indians of that land fish for them and gather them in their shells and wear them strung around the neck and on the arms, although [they are] very poorly treated, for they burn the shells in order to roast what they have within in order to eat. They gather large and small. The Ensign made some Indians of those that he carried with him enter the lakes and rivers and dive so that they might gather from the shells as [the Indians] did, although [they gathered] few through the weather being very cold and the divers not being able to remain in the water nor do what they wished. From the shells that they gathered there was one pearl and two and three in each shell, and although those that he brought here as specimens are minute but very fine, so say the persons who understand it that the Indians say and assure that there are those as thick as garbanzos.[58]

The Torres expedition was the first to visit Cofitachequi since Juan Pardo more than sixty years earlier.[59] Although Torres's account is brief, his description of the *cacique* as preeminent over all other *caciques* in the region suggests that even in 1628 Cofitachequi retained a second tier of chiefly leadership, reminiscent of the paramount chiefdoms witnessed by the early explorers of the Southeast. In addition, the ethnographic details regarding the use of freshwater pearls by the Indians is informative.

The Ensign's report prompted Governor Rojas to request permission from the Crown to send Torres again, this time accompanied by divers and fifty or sixty Spaniards and two hundred Indians to acquire more of these pearls.[60] In August of the following year, Torres presented his report, along with a sample of pearls, in person in Madrid, and was given permission to return to the "fishery of pearls."[61] This venture was apparently never pursued, perhaps due in part to the end of Governor Rojas's term the following year. The Torres expedition was the last to visit Cofitachequi, and it was more than forty years before Carolinians would once again establish European contact with this province.

After the Torres expedition of 1628, Spanish exploratory ventures were left in the hands of the Franciscans, and only five years passed before the foundation of the Apalachee mission province far to the west of St. Augustine. This province would serve as the western terminus of the important mission road, providing St. Augustine with much-needed supplies and Indian labor. The interior of modern north Florida was successfully penetrated, but not by military exploration. The general pattern seems to have been one of clerical exploration and contact with interior Indians, followed by the establishment of permanent missions and mission provinces, and finally followed by the military garrisons placed to defend the Spanish holdings in the interior.

The ultimate task of the military seems to have been the defense of territorial acquisitions, initiated by the friars in the interior, and not the actual exploration itself. This pattern marks an important departure from the early years of Spanish exploration of La Florida, when clergy were brought on massive military ventures only as minor functionaries. The establishment of a permanent Spanish colony on the coast of La Florida does not seem to have been pivotal in this transformation, for the Pardo expedition was one of the first ventures of the newly emplaced Spaniards, and even as late as 1607 there were plans for major military exploration of the interior. What, then, initiated a shift away from such expensive ventures and toward the low-level, low-risk, and far less costly activities of Franciscan missionaries?

The key may be in the establishment of a permanent English colony, Jamestown, on the northern coastline of La Florida. No longer was Spain the only European power on the mainland, and this event was followed almost immediately by a subtle but significant change in perspective. Spanish officials shifted from a more exploratory stance to one increasingly dominated by concerns of defense. The lack of soldiers and supplies took on new importance, increasing the stakes in the already risky venture of dedicating limited military forces to exploratory expeditions that could last for months on end, leaving St. Augustine open to attack. In the end, the maintenance and defense of St. Augustine and the established mission provinces won out over new conquests in the interior. The ambitious plans of Governors Méndez and Ybarra never came to fruition, and the small-scale expeditions of the 1620s consisted of very small contingents of Spanish soldiers in charge of larger forces of Indian allies. These groups were dispatched for reconnaissance only, and even the discovery of freshwater pearls in the north remained unexploited.

Although the southern interior provinces of Potano, Timucua, and Apalachee were brought under Spanish control by Apalachee missionaries, the northern interior remained largely unexplored after 1628. Indeed, it seems no coincidence that this open territory was to be the very region where Carolina traders began their enterprises in the deerskin trade and the Indian slave trade during the 1670s, a venture that would ultimately lead to the downfall of Spanish domination of La Florida. While it is improbable that a concerted effort on the part of the Spanish would have won a lasting control of the interior, the apparent lack of Spanish commitment to the exploration of the northern interior left a vacuum far more easily filled by the English, and perhaps hastened the spread of the English trade network.

The seven expeditions examined in this paper left little in the form of documentary accounts. Their descriptions of the Indian societies of the interior Southeast between 1597 and 1628 offer brief but tantalizing glimpses of cultures experiencing a process of transformation largely beyond the realm of historical scrutiny. Ultimately, these entradas were to be the final contact between Spanish explorers and the Indians of the interior, and as such reflect the end of an era for both parties involved.

NOTES

I gratefully acknowledge the assistance of the staff of the P. K. Yonge Library of Florida History at the University of Florida in Gainesville, where the bulk of the research for this paper was carried out during 1989–90. Archivist Bruce Chappell deserves special mention for his tremendous aid and instruction in Spanish paleography and for helping me find my way through the library's rich documentary collections. In addition, I would like to thank Charles Hudson and Murdo MacLeod for their comments on an earlier version of this paper.

1. An examination of documentary sources from the late sixteenth and early seventeenth centuries reveals that several small expeditions did successfully penetrate the interior after Pardo. While the Chozas expedition of 1597 has already been examined in some detail, two more (Lara in 1602 and Torres in 1628) have been mentioned only in passing in the literature (and accounts from these have never been published, either in transcribed or translated form), and three others (two sent by Salinas in 1624 and Cañizares in 1625) have remained almost completely unknown.

2. See Hudson, "The Hernando de Soto Expedition, 1539–1543," this volume, and Part 3 of this volume.

3. See the introduction, this volume, by Hudson and Tesser; M. T. Smith, *Aboriginal Culture Change*, and also Dobyns, *Their Number*.

4. See M. T. Smith, *Aboriginal Culture Change*.

5. This expedition is known from two primary sources. The first comprises testimony from Gaspar de Salas as related by Governor Méndez de Canço to the King, Feb. 4–6, 1600, Archivo General de Indias, Santo Domingo (hereafter AGI SD) 224, Stetson Collection, P. K. Yonge Library of Florida History, University of Florida, Gainesville. This account is transcribed by Serrano y Sanz, *Documentos históricos*. A later and partially incomplete copy of this testimony is translated by Reding, "Letter of Gonzalo Méndez de Canço." The second source is based on the report of Father Chozas and is included in Fray Alonso de Escobedo's poem "La Florida," the relevant portion of which is transcribed by López, *Relación Histórica*. An imprecise and sometimes inaccurate translation is provided by Covington, *Pirates, Indians, and Spaniards*.

6. This expedition has been noted by several authors, with the most extensive treatment by Geiger, *Franciscan Conquest*. The expedition is mentioned in the introduction to Bolton, *Arredondo's Historical Proof*. In addition, the details of this expedition figure prominently in Lawson, "La Tama." See also Hudson, *Juan Pardo Expeditions*, 184–86.

7. Escobedo, "La Florida," 27. Chozas "loaded them with Castillian blankets, with knives, fish-hooks, and scissors, and with very fine [*muy galanos*] beads of glass, with sickles and with axes [and] chisels" (Escobedo, "La Florida," 27–28). Some of these items undoubtedly reached the interior and may have entered the archaeological record. On August 2 of that year, Don Juan arrived in St. Augustine with three Indians, and during their ten-day stay the *cacique* was rewarded with a shirt and hat "for having gone in the company of the father Fray Pedro de Chozas to Tama, and having returned in his company" (Alvarez de Castrillón, Sept. 14, 1597, AGI SD 231). Another Indian had arrived earlier, on July 19, saying that "father Fray Pedro Fernández de Chozas sent him from Tama, to where he had gone with order of the said General [Méndez] to find out about the disposition of that land, and if they would willingly receive the Spaniards, and if they wanted to be instructed in the [Christian] faith" (Mugado, July 27, 1597, AGI SD 231). This Indian was given a blanket by the Governor for his services. These documents incidentally provide a rough date for the expedition, which seems to have occurred during the summer months.

8. Méndez de Canço, Feb. 4–6, 1600. While Geiger, *Franciscan Conquest*, 83, assumes that Escobedo's description of Chozas's journey (Escobedo, "La Florida," 28) relates to the march inland to Tama, the account undoubtedly refers instead to

the march from St. Augustine to Guale, for Escobedo relates marching to the north northeast for 40 leagues with the sea on their right, crossing marshes on the way.

9. Méndez de Canço, Feb. 4–6, 1600. This report, along with the samples brought back by Salas, formed the basis for a persistent legend about mines at Tama.

10. While the phrase *casa común* could indicate "common house" or "ordinary house," Chozas was more likely referring to a public structure of the town, probably the well-known council house often described by Spaniards. *Bohío* typically translates simply as "hut." This structure is later referred to as the "house frequented by everyone."

11. Escobedo, "La Florida," 29–31.

12. Méndez de Canço, Feb. 4–6, 1600. Chozas apparently uses the name Quaque and lists it as the one kingdom [*reino*] he did not convert. He locates Quaque "farther off from Tama." The *cacique*'s statement that the Indians deeper into the interior killed de Soto's men is clearly erroneous, although it is tempting to suggest that this refers to the tragic surprise attack by the Indians at the town of Mabila in Alabama, which may have involved Indians from as far away as the chiefdom of Coosa, a province that lay directly inland along the path Chozas and his companions had followed from Guale. See Hudson, DePratter, and Smith, "Victims of the King Site Massacre." The chief of Coosa was, after all, the leader behind the planned ambush of Juan Pardo's men only thirty years earlier.

13. Escobedo, "La Florida," 31.

14. While the Spanish text reads *carrera,* or "race," it is possible that the contest was actually a game of chunkey, a traditional game between males, and one that apparently involved a great deal of running and physical activity. See Hudson, *Southeastern Indians,* 423.

15. Escobedo, "La Florida," 32. Many of this group were pagan and may have chosen to remain in the interior. One Indian, who evidently arrived in St. Augustine before Chozas's own return to St. Augustine, might have been one of this group who deserted the expedition (see note 7).

16. While this term can denote "cabins," here it most likely refers to a landscape suitable for domestic animals.

17. Méndez de Canço, Feb. 4–6, 1600.

18. The exact dates of the Chozas expedition are unknown, but the friar had definitely reached Tama by mid-July 1597, from where one of the Indians in his party returned to St. Augustine by July 19 (Mugado, July 27, 1597). His return was prior to August 2, when Don Juan of Tolomato arrived in St. Augustine after the journey (Alvarez de Castillón, September 14, 1597).

19. See Mark Williams, "Growth and Decline of the Oconee Province," this volume. The more southerly location is proposed by Bolton, *Arredondo's Historical Proof,* 16, and Lawson, "La Tama," develops a well-reasoned case for the region of the forks of the Altamaha River.

20. The evidence for the location of the towns or provinces of Tama and Ocute falls into two areas: geography and distances. First, the several descriptions of Tama and Ocute during this period strongly suggest that these provinces were situated at or within the Piedmont. This becomes evident when one considers the fact that the Spanish experience of La Florida was largely restricted to the comparatively level Coastal Plain, in large part characterized by sandy soils and pine barrens. Salas notes that "roundabout the said town and its confines is very good dun colored

land, which when it rains sticks to the feet like clay. It has in places many bare hills where kinds of metallic rock have been seen" (Méndez de Canço, Feb. 4–6, 1600). The land around the town most likely refers to floodplain deposits, which increase in clay content significantly within or just below the Piedmont. The bare hills may very well refer to open farmland in the Piedmont uplands, a phenomenon that archaeologists now recognize to have peaked in the Piedmont region of the Oconee watershed during the late sixteenth and early seventeenth centuries (Kowalewski and Hatch, "The 16th Century Expansion). Salas further relates, "Likewise this witness and the said missionaries have gathered some stones on the said hills and next to copious rivers, in the manner of unrefined [?] crystal, and others of delicate crystal." These crystals almost certainly refer to the numerous outcrops of quartz, often in crystalline form, in the Piedmont.

Furthermore, later descriptions of this region leave little doubt as to their Piedmont association. Governor Méndez (Sept. 22, 1602, AGI SD 224, Lowery Collection, P. K. Yonge Library of Florida History) writes relative to Tama and Ocute that "the said mines are on *tierra firme* where there are hills and high land," and Father Pareja (Sept. 14, 1602, AGI SD 235) refers to a "road from the *sierras* [mountain-ranges] of Tama, where it is known there are mines of gold and silver." Juan de Lara also reports arriving in 1602 at a *sierra* where he found the town of Tama (see below), strongly suggesting its location at the foot of the hilly Piedmont region. M. T. Smith, *Aboriginal Culture Change*, 15–17, reaches a similar conclusion based on the Chozas expedition.

The other line of evidence involves distances. Although Salas and Méndez believed Tama to be located only 50 leagues from St. Augustine, the imperfection of Spanish estimates of distance in La Florida is well known. Better evidence is revealed from the journey that resulted in this estimate. The distance from St. Catherines Island to the forks of the Altamaha river is just over 80 miles, and thus Salas would only have been traveling 10 miles (or under 4 leagues) each day for the journey to last eight days. Furthermore, seven days of this voyage were through an unoccupied region, and it seems doubtful that this entire stretch of the Altamaha was completely abandoned.

The distance to the Shinholser mound site, known to have been occupied at this time, is just over 150 miles, and it seems more likely that this small party traversed this greater distance. Indeed, the 1602 expedition of Juan de Lara places the distance between Guale and Tama at 60 to 70 leagues, closely matching the actual distance of 59 leagues (see note 28). Also, the 1625 Cañizares expedition places Tama some 100 leagues from St. Augustine, a figure that corresponds more closely with this northerly location (see below). In addition, the town of Ocute was only a day's journey farther inland from Tama, and this relationship corresponds with the accounts from de Soto's expedition. Moreover, the route proposed in this paper accounts for currently known archaeological evidence of the distribution of seventeenth-century aboriginal occupation. The *despoblado* through which the party traveled was the interriverine uplands, and the return trip was along the river bottom, where the party would have begun to encounter Indian occupation only a couple of days south of Tama at the Fall Line of the Oconee River (see Figure 1). Hudson (*Pardo Expeditions*, 185) reaches a similar conclusion.

On the basis of this reconstruction, it is suggested that the early seventeenth-century Bell Phase (J. Mark Williams, *Joe Bell Site*) defined by archaeologists for the upper Oconee River corresponds to the provinces of Tama and Ocute, while the Square Ground Lamar region at the forks of the Altamaha (Frankie Snow, "Pine Barrens Lamar") constitutes a portion of the "more populous" region traversed by the Chozas expedition on their return trip.

21. Royal Cedulario, Nov. 9, 1598, AGI SD 2528. The skewed Spanish perception of distances during this period in Florida is revealed by the Crown's estimate of the distance between Tama and New Mexico at only 200 leagues!

22. Gonzalo Méndez de Canço, Feb. 28, 1600, AGI SD 224, Microfilm Collection, P. K. Yonge Library of Florida History. The list of items to be brought from Spain to be traded to the Indians includes "400 axes and four hundred hoes, one hundred sets[?] of butcher knives from Flanders, fifteen hundred *Reales* of large blue beads of glass and two hundred ordinary mirrors, one hundred pairs of scissors. All of this in order to give away to the *caciques* and Indians where they might pass and to serve as gifts for food, because they give it with much pleasure." While these items never reached the interior, they probably reflect a typical assemblage of European items traded to the Indians during this period.

23. The details of this expedition are reviewed by Arnade, *Florida on Trial*, 42; Lawson, "La Tama," 3, makes note of the Lara visit. Hudson, *Juan Pardo Expeditions*, 185, however, finds inconsistencies in Lara's account.

24. Governor Gonzalo Méndez de Canço to the King, Sept. 22, 1602, AGI SD 224. This letter was transcribed by Woodbury Lowery (on microfilm at the P. K. Yonge Library of Florida History) and is now missing from the cited *legajo*. The reference to a journey from New Mexico is not explained.

25. A spit or strip of land, occasionally used in this period in reference to the barrier island chain of the Guale province.

26. The name "Olatama" (Tama) appears to be related to the name Altamaha recorded by the de Soto chroniclers for the same town. Indeed the frequent appearance of *latama* in Spanish accounts may not derive from the Spanish article *la* in front of the name Tama, but may instead reflect the actual pronunciation of the name as Latama. Lara's Olatama appears to support this conclusion, as does the phonetic similarity to the persistent name Altamaha.

27. Excerpt from the testimony of Juan de Lara in "Información de orden de Su Majestad sobre el estado general de las provincias de la Florida y si conviene o no desmantelar el fuerte de San Agustín," Sept. 3–9, 1602, AGI SD 2533. A detailed examination of all the testimony contained in this massive document is provided by Arnade, *Florida on Trial*.

28. The straight-line distance of 59 leagues (156 miles) compares well with Lara's travel distance of 60 to 70 leagues.

29. Francisco de Pareja to the King, Sept. 14, 1602, AGI SD 235. *Guitamo real* was noted by Salas as "an herb [or grass] that the Indians much esteem for medicines with which they cure themselves, and for wounds, that they call *guitamo real*" (Méndez de Canço, Feb. 4–6, 1600). Lawson, "La Tama," 12, suggests that this herb was "button snakeroot" (*Eryngium yuccafolium*).

30. Evidently a type of gorget.

31. Baltasar López to the King, Sept. 14, 1602, AGI SD 235.

32. A type of padded armor.

33. Pedro de Ybarra to the King, Jan. 8, 1604, AGI SD 224. The old soldiers referred to were undoubtedly veterans of the Pardo expedition. The mention of

"houses of stone," while clearly inaccurate, may derive from the legend of the fabulous city of *La Gran Copala* (see Hudson, *Juan Pardo Expeditions*, 194).

34. Royal Cedulario, Nov. 4, 1604, AGI Mexico (hereafter MEX) 1065, Stetson Collection; Pedro de Ybarra to the King, Dec. 26, 1605, AGI SD 224.

35. Serrano y Sanz, *Documentos históricos*, 184; Pedro de Ybarra to the King, May 16, 1607, AGI SD 224.

36. Geiger, *Franciscan Conquest*, 208–9.

37. See, for example, Royal Cédula, Aug. 16, 1608, AGI MEX 1065; Lucas de Soto to the King, Dec. 24, 1608, AGI SD 130; Pedro de Ybarra to the King, Jan. 8, 1609, AGI SD 232; and Ybarra to the King, Jan 16, 1609, AGI SD 224.

38. Royal Cédula, March 15, 1609, AGI MEX 1065. This *Cédula* was drafted in response to an earlier letter from Governor Ybarra to the King (Aug. 22, 1608, AGI SD 224), reporting the dispatch of soldiers to Guale and the need for more in defense of the Potano province. This prompted the placement of restrictions on the use of soldiers in the interior.

39. Pedro de Ybarra, April 31, 1609, AGI SD 224.

40. *lancillas,* the diminutive of *lanzas.*

41. Governor Luis de Rojas y Borja to the King, Jan. 20, 1625, AGI SD 225, Mary L. Ross Papers, Georgia Department of Archives and History, Atlanta. Ross's typed transcription of this document is the only surviving copy; the original is no longer in the cited *legajo* in microform at the P. K. Yonge library of Florida History and may have been lost or stolen in the intervening years. Bolton, *Arredondo's Historical Proof,* 24–25, cites the same letter but only briefly mentions Salinas's expeditions.

42. Rojas y Borja, Jan. 20, 1625.

43. Lead is not mentioned in other documents describing the "mines" at Tama.

44. Adrián de Cañizares y Osorio to the King, Sept. 28, 1635, AGI SD 233. This soldier would later serve as the leader of the military detachment that captured the leaders of the 1656 Timucuan rebellion.

45. Governor Luis de Rojas y Borja to the King, June 30, 1628, AGI SD 225.

46. Presuming the figure of 150 leagues refers to the total distance marched (that is, round trip) by Salinas's men.

47. Such legends may also have been influenced by the stories of *Las Diamantes,* a mountain of gems rumored to exist since the Pardo expedition. See Hudson, *Juan Pardo Expeditions*, 191–97.

48. There is a clear tone of Indian hostility in the Cañizares account, and Rojas's note that the expedition was forced to return due to lack of food suggests that the soldiers were unable to obtain food from the pagan Indians. It is also possible that Cañizares's inability to obtain food was a result of depopulation owing to the effects of epidemic disease sweeping across the interior, though there is no further evidence to support this possibility. Despite this, the later Torres expeditions may well have passed through Tama again on their subsequent journey to Cofitachequi.

49. Royal Cédula, May 3, 1627, AGI SD 225. This document, mentioned by Governor Rojas y Borja and cited by Bolton, is also missing from SD 225. Its general contents may be surmised from the Governor's letter of June 30, 1628.

50. Rojas y Borja, Jan. 20, 1625. While ultimately these rumors were dismissed as lies, the detail of Rojas's information suggests a possible basis in fact. In determining the veracity of the reports, the Spaniards expended much energy over the

course of four years and five reconnaissance expeditions, and one cannot help but wonder whether isolated traders from Virginia did indeed penetrate some distance to the south during the 1620s.

51. Although Bushnell, *The King's Coffer*, 92, suggests that the Torres expedition was specifically sent to locate the pearls noted by the de Soto chroniclers, evidence in Governor Rojas's letters of Jan. 20, 1625, and June 30, 1628, indicates that the pearl fishery was an unanticipated discovery and that Torres was originally sent only to reconnoiter the interior for white horsemen.

52. Rojas y Borja, June 30, 1628. Evidently, this was the only one of the seven expeditions described in this paper to include more than one or two Spanish soldiers. These may have been included to effectively manage the large complement of Indians.

53. This first expedition was evidently dispatched during the late spring or early summer of 1627. The date of their return is fixed by an incident that occurred on the return journey, in which their passage was barred at the coastal mission of San Juan del Puerto, prompting Governor Rojas to send a military detachment to apprehend its rebellious *cacica* in mid-August (Certification by Antonio de Argüelles, Francisco González de Villa Garcia, Francisco García de la Vera, Nicolás Estebes de Carmenatis, Salvador de Cigarroa, Francisco de la Rocha, Juan Sánchez de Urisa, Oct. 20, 1678, AGI SD 234; Order of Don Luis de Rojas y Borja to Alonso de Pastrana, Aug. 17, 1627, AGI SD 232).

54. Argüelles et al., Oct. 20, 1678.

55. This statement is incorrect, since the Pardo expedition passed through Cofitachequi more than sixty years earlier.

56. *cacique mayor*, suggesting a leader among *caciques*.

57. *unas lagunas que dellas salen rios adonde hay grande cantidad de perlas.* Both de Soto and Pardo make note of pearls at Cofitachequi.

58. Rojas y Borja, June 30, 1628.

59. Neither Torres nor Governor Luis de Rojas y Borja made mention of the Pardo expedition, suggesting that documentary accounts were unavailable and recognizing additionally that most, if not all, veterans of the voyage were dead by 1628. Torres noted only that Cofitachequi was the "farthest where Hernando de Soto reached," which may refer to de Soto's progress up the Atlantic seaboard, since the objective of the Torres expedition was to reconnoiter the interior between the English colony and St. Augustine. For a discussion of the important chiefdom of Cofitachequi, see Chester B. DePratter, "The Chiefdom of Cofitachequi," this volume.

60. Rojas y Borja, June 30, 1628.

61. Pedro de Torres to the King, Aug. 1, 1629, AGI SD 225. The Governor was to supply him with "three or four soldiers and two Indians" for his new entrada. The last available record regarding Pedro de Torres places him in Madrid on September 26, awaiting passage to Florida and requesting permission to take one servant (Pedro de Torres to the King, Sept. 26, 1629, AGI SD 27).

The Southeastern Chiefdoms

RANDOLPH J. WIDMER

The Structure of
Southeastern Chiefdoms

When the Spanish explorers of the sixteenth century encountered the native peoples of the southeastern United States, they experienced societies whose political and social organization was markedly different from their own as well as from the state-level societies they had encountered in highland Mexico and Peru. Their predicament, however, was not unique. It had been experienced on numerous occasions by other explorers in various parts of the world. Julius Caesar had encountered comparable societies in Gaul and Germany; Tacitus had encountered them in Britain; and Cook would encounter similar societies in Polynesia. However, in spite of the differences in geography and time, all of these contact situations had one thing in common: people from state-level societies encountered other people who belonged to a type of social organization that in anthropological parlance is called the *chiefdom*. The concept of the chiefdom is increasingly being employed to study early European cultural developments prior to the formation of states. It has been utilized to interpret prehistoric groups in Europe, in the study of Iron Age Roman and Greek trade with protohistoric groups in Europe, and it has been employed for studying the Celts.[1]

Quite possibly, the inability of sixteenth-century Spanish explorers to comprehend the distinctive features of this type of social structure contributed to their failure to successfully colonize the Southeast, even though previously they had enjoyed brilliant successes in Hispañola, New Spain, and Peru. The hacienda system, the principal instrument of colonial expansion in highland Mexico and Peru, could not be established in the sixteenth-century southeastern United States. Although the Spanish were experts in the system, they were unable to find a suitable form of labor for implementing it in the Southeast. This system was labor intensive. It worked best where there were dense, settled peasant populations already governed by an indigenous bureaucratic centralized political system. Such forms simply did not exist in the southeastern United States.

The Spanish had little trouble understanding the economic, political, and bureaucratic workings of the centralized bureaucratic states of Peru and Mexico. Oviedo and Las Casas, for example, comment repeatedly on the similarities of those systems to the Spanish bureaucracy.[2] However, no such easy understanding could be had of the noncentralized polities found throughout the New World, and it was these societies that hindered Spanish colonial efforts. The Spanish eventually dealt with these types of societies through the development of missions and the encomienda systems. Now as then, failure to consider these native southeastern societies in their underlying cultural patterns will seriously hinder our understanding of these societies at the time they were first encountered in the sixteenth century. When these native societies are understood from the perspective of their internal social, economic, and political structure, we can better understand the Spanish contact period in the Southeast.

The chiefdom is a type of society with wide geographic distribution. Chiefdoms, although dwindling in numbers today, were at various times the most common form of society found throughout Europe, Africa, the Americas, Melanesia, Polynesia, the Near East, and Asia. Today these societies are limited to Africa and South America and are rapidly being incorporated into modern nation states. However, to our modern, Western way of thinking they represent a type of society that is very different from our own.

The concept of the chiefdom was originally devised as a societal type to classify a number of similar societies found in South America. Later, it was expanded to characterize societies found in Polynesia, and, as mentioned above, it is currently considered to be applicable on a cross-cultural basis as a general level of sociocultural integration. Various schemes have been developed to further divide chiefdoms into subtypes, either three or two, based on their degree of complexity.[3] A tripartite hierarchical division of chiefdoms specifically developed to describe the variation that exists in the Southeast will be used here: (1) *simple chiefdoms,* incorporating only a few towns and clans or lineages with a minimal development and ranking of chiefs; (2) *intermediate chiefdoms,* with numerous clans or lineages, towns, and chiefs integrated in an elaborate ranking system that has developed through intrinsic growth under the control of a powerful provincial chief, with minimal incorporation of external groups; and (3) *complex paramount chiefdoms,* which politically integrate numerous different social and kin groups. These groups have been brought into the political hegemony of a powerful paramount chief and his supporters through military conquest of foreign provinces, resulting in the incorporation of these groups as low-ranking tributary units with political alliances established through marriage and the placement of the paramount's relatives in positions of authority in the conquered villages.

Chiefdoms are first and foremost kin-based societies. All of their social, political, and economic activities operate within the framework of kinship. The corporate unilineal descent group is the most common form of this kinship system and is probably the type that characterized chiefdoms of the sixteenth-century southeastern United States. These unilineal descent groups were matrilineal in the agriculturally based chiefdoms of the Southeast.[4]

Chiefdoms represent a specific level of sociocultural integration.[5] That is, the chiefdom is a *general type* of society. While such an approach may gloss over subtle differences among societies subsumed within the type, the concept has extraordinary power such that in historical interpretation much can be inferred about a particular chiefdom, even when there is a minimum of actual substantiative data available. This is most useful when dealing with contact situations, be they Spanish or otherwise, where the commentators either do not understand the societies they are involved with, or else provide only incomplete or anecdotal descriptions or accounts. These are exactly the conditions that pertain to the Spanish contact situation in the southeastern United States. Therefore, the use of the chiefdom as a general type of society can provide a model or framework for evaluating and interpreting incomplete, sketchy, historical accounts.

Much of the discussion that follows is theoretical rather than substantive and represents a model, rather than a reconstruction based on primary materials. I believe that this approach is justified not only because of the lack of data but, more important, because of the profound social transformations that were caused by European contact. Although there are clearly historical continuities between the native and postcontact societies, the dramatic effects of disease, depopulation, settlement disruption, slavery, and foreign military conquest would have resulted in new and very different forms of social and political organization that bear little resemblance to their original forms. Because we do not necessarily know a priori which cultural features have changed and which have stayed the same, it is dangerous and inappropriate to use the primary materials alone; it is necessary instead to compare the aboriginal Southeast with similar types of societies elsewhere that have not been so severely disrupted. We should not expect the native precontact societies of the Southeast to have had cultural features identical to their eighteenth-century counterparts. Societies with growing populations have very different social and cultural characteristics than those whose populations are declining. Since we do not have ethnographic data from growing populations in the Southeast it is necessary to utilize models, such as the one presented here, to understand the precontact societal situation.

As there is as yet no consensus among southeastern specialists as to the precise nature of the social structure of the late prehistoric groups, any reconstruction is going to be open to debate. The reconstruction offered here is an attempt at understanding these societies as chiefdoms rather than as specific cultural historical reconstructions. While this deductive approach may be unsettling to some, I believe it provides the most useful approach to understanding these societies.

The unilineal descent group is referred to as the *clan* or *lineage*. The members of a lineage can trace their descent from a known ancestor, whereas the members of a clan believe they are related but cannot trace their descent from a specific known ancestor. Often, lineages are smaller segments of larger clans. In situations where both clans and lineages coexist, the individual lineages that comprise the maximal clan are usually the corporate kin units, with the larger maximal clan having marriage, etiquette, dispute resolving, or other ritual roles and obligations rather than control of property or resources. The maximal clan composed of a number of corporate lineages appears to be the kinship structure most common in the sedentary groups in the Southeast.[6] The lineage is by definition an exogamous social group. That is, one becomes a lineage member by being born into it, and one must obtain one's spouse from outside it. Membership in the unilineal descent group is reckoned through the female line through one's mother or through the male line through one's father. This former type is referred to as a *matrilineal* kinship system (see figure 1), while the latter type is a *patrilineal* kinship system. These unilineal descent groups are *corporate* in nature. That is, not individuals but the kinship group as a whole has rights to access, ownership, and control of resources. Most of the societies in the Southeast during the eighteenth and nineteenth centuries had matrilineal descent, and this descent type more than likely was typical of prehistoric and contact period agricultural chiefdoms. Only the non-agricultural Calusa of south Florida appear to have had patrilineal descent, and this is based largely on a theoretical rather than substantive basis.[7]

The household and its individual family is the basic social and economic unit of a chiefdom and in fact maintains a high degree of autonomy in all of its domestic, subsistence, and economic activities. This is referred to as the *domestic mode of production*.[8] Each household in a chiefdom, except for the household of the chief and his elite relatives, is redundant with every other household in terms of its economic and domestic activities. There is *no* specialization in the tasks of individuals in terms of their everyday activities or livelihood. But, although each household is economically independent, there are certain activities that require resources exceeding those possessed by the individual household unit. These needs are met through the kinship group.

As members of a lineage or clan, individuals have certain rights to use

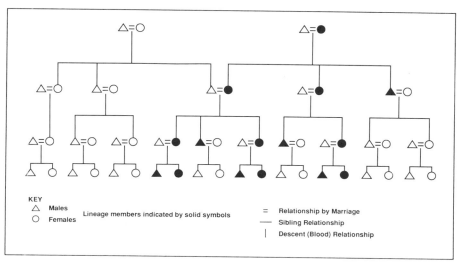

FIGURE I
A matrilineal descent group

lineage resources. These include not only land for growing crops, but also labor for clearing fields and building houses. These tasks are frequently beyond the abilities of individual households. However, the pooled labor and cooperation of kinsmen can mitigate this deficiency. This is a major function of these corporate lineages.

Although each lineage is a discrete social group, the members do not necessarily live in a single physical locale. Since invariably there are numerous villages or hamlets in a chiefdom, it is uncommon for all lineage members to reside in the same settlement. Usually, the members of a lineage live in more than one community within the chiefdom. In such cases, households are organized into smaller segments of the clan or lineage, and each lineage segment will have a lineage head within that village or hamlet to organize local lineage affairs. There are occasions, however, when hamlets or villages essentially comprise a single lineage with their spouses, and the hamlet or village headman is the same as the lineage headman, and is also a chief.

Although kin groups are matrilineal, they are usually headed by a male. However, this man should not be thought of as "father" in kinship terms, but instead as "mother's brother" because a man's children do not belong to his kin group, only the children of his sisters do. That is, a woman's brother usually acts as the figure of authority and leadership in the lineage or clan, acting as a representative for his sister's social position. This results in a number of predicaments associated with marriage and residence patterns in matrilineal kinship systems, because of the desire to keep kin group members together to maintain male political and social control while still observing clan and lineage exogamy which tends to disperse males in matrilineal kinship systems.[9]

A variety of residence patterns are possible in matrilineal kinship systems to resolve this conflict. These include uxorilocal, avunculocal, virilocal, or duolocal residence types. The most obvious of these is uxorilocal residence, where a man moves into the vicinity of his wife's household. This form of residence pattern keeps the women of the lineage together, which facilitates tracing descent, but tends to disperse men of the lineage, thereby undermining male control. In the avunculocal residence pattern, a man lives in the vicinity of his sister. Since a man's children do not belong to his kin group, but instead to those of his wife, the man will reside where the children of *his* kin group reside, namely with their mother who is the man's sister. Not only will a man reside with the children of his kin group but he will also be in physical proximity with the other members, both male and female, adults and children of his clan or lineage. Among the Trobriand Islanders of Papua New Guinea, avunculocal residence is a form of residence pattern but not the most common one and there only practiced when a man is next in line to take control of the lineage. It is also found among the matrilineal Taíno of Hispaniola and among the matrilineal Ashanti of western Africa. Another form of residence pattern in matrilineal societies is virilocal residence, in which a man upon marriage will set up a household in the vicinity of his father even though his father is not a member of his kin group. This pattern is found in the Trobriand Islands and also among the matrilineal Ashanti of west Africa. Duolocal residence, where each spouse remains with their own matrilineal relatives, is another residence type found in matrilineal societies. Among the Ashanti, three different residence types were used: duolocal, avunculocal, or virilocal. Traditionally, Ashanti duolocal residence was practiced in the early years of marriage and then shifted to either virilocal or avunculocal residence. Avunculocal residence appears to be the more common of the two patterns, with virilocal residence restricted primarily to chiefs who wish to keep their sons nearby for political reasons. Within one matrilineal descent society, it is possible to have a number of different residence types to keep male kin together including types where the spouses do not always live together.[10]

This makes it extremely difficult to identify the specific types of residence patterns that existed among the native southeastern groups. It appears that there is more variability in residence type associated with matrilineal societies that have more political complexity, as is seen in the Ashanti example and to a lesser extent among the Trobriand Islanders and the Taíno. This suggests that in matrilineal societies where political authority is important, virilocal and avunculocal residence, which tend to group rather than disperse males, would be found. These are the conditions that prevailed in the aboriginal Southeast where chronic warfare tended to favor these residential forms, particularly the avunculocal form that grouped men of the same corporate group.[11]

Settlement patterns of households in chiefdoms vary considerably. They can be dispersed into hamlets comprising a few households, clustered into large villages, or these patterns can be combined. These differences can be attributed to: (1) the distribution of suitable agricultural lands; (2) the need for defense from external aggression; and (3) transportation costs of moving food resources within the kinship network. These three factors are also found in other types of societies, and therefore do not by themselves define the chiefdom.[12]

The individual household lineage segments and villages do not possess the organizational wherewithal to resolve all of the problems that face multicommunity societies. Therefore, new organizational resources are needed. Since, as emphasized earlier, these are kin-based societies, the basis of these organizational resources must be found within the kinship system. Thus, a new organizational principle, *ranking*, is pressed into service.

Ranking is a type of status differentiation whereby members of a society have distinct, unique social positions. Ranked social positions are not based on individual achievement by lineage members, but instead are determined by the order in which they are born. Ranked social position, in effect, is determined by how closely one is related to the founding ancestor of one's lineage. Figure 2 illustrates how this principle works in a matrilineal descent system. Lineages are also ranked relative to each other. This is usually determined by the generational time depth of the lineages. The lineage with the longest history will have the highest rank followed by the next oldest lineage, and so on to the lineage with the shortest history. Often, new lineages are formed by splitting from existing lineages, and so the order in which the lineages are "born" determines the relative ranks of the lineages.

However, principles other than rank order splits from an original founding ancestor may be responsible for the ranking of the lineages. For example, among the Trobriand Islanders, a matrilineal society, the lineages are ranked, but local tradition has it that the rank of the lineages is based not on any genealogical priority of the lineages but instead on the order in which the lineages arrived on the island. In effect, what happens is that the conical nature of lineages is either replaced by a set of ranked unilineal descent groups that are clans, with totems replacing ancestors, or else it never was present and some principle other than genealogical distance from a founding ancestor is used to rank the lineages.[13]

In effect, it is the crosscutting of these two principles—rank order within the lineage and ranking of lineages with respect to each other—that determine an individual's social position within the chiefdom. In theory, every individual in such a society has a unique social position or rank. The single most important characteristic that distinguishes *ranking* from *social classes* found in state level societies is that ranking *crosscuts* the kinship groups.

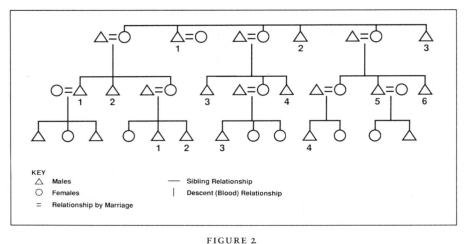

The principle of ranking for males in a matrilineage.
Senior members are to the left; numbers represent rank within generations.

That is, members of the same lineage and even members of the same individual household have differing and unique social positions. But despite his or her rank, every individual who is a lineage member can claim the full benefits of membership in that lineage. It should be emphasized, however, that there is great variation in how these notions of ranking are expressed. Through time these unique distinctions become glossed over. What often happens is that the original, genealogically based connections are lost in history, and only the rank order of the clans or lineages themselves remains.

A ramification of this situation is that only the chiefly "dynasty" and their close kin follow the strict genealogical distance (that is, birth order from the apical ancestor, or founding chief) and have a rank order within their lineage; the rest of the nonchiefly members of lineages or clans do not use internal ranking for social or political purposes. What typically results is that the chiefs of each lineage are ranked relative to each other, but their nonelite members are not internally ranked but instead have the rank of their lineage. The simple and intermediate-level chiefdoms characteristic of many of the chiefdoms of the Southeast at contact had a social structure where ranking was invested in chiefs and elites and not in nonelite individuals.[14]

Some understanding of the dynamics of demographic processes of chiefdoms is necessary if one is to understand how this ranking system works and the basis for its apparent complexity. Typically, chiefdoms are expanding societies that are fueled by systems of food production requiring large amounts of land. In order to increase food production, chiefdoms put more land under cultivation instead of intensifying use of existing units of land by resting the soil for shorter periods or through additional labor or technological inputs such as weeding, terracing, or irrigation. Since an extensive horticultural system requires the clearing of new land, more available labor means more land that can be put into production. This labor is ultimately acquired through increasing population. Thus, in chiefdoms it can be said that food production requires human reproduction.[15]

In a patrilineal descent group, the most rapid way of achieving additional labor is through polygyny. Although the multiple wives cannot themselves be lineage members, for reasons discussed previously, their children are lineage members at birth. Polygyny therefore can result in a dramatic increase in lineage size, although this additional lineage labor cannot be fully realized for warfare, building, and clearing land until the wives' children grow up. Hence there is approximately a generation delay in labor production. Thus, when labor demand is immediate, and especially where it exceeds existing supply, polygyny is not a successful short-term solution to labor demand.

Matrilineal descent systems, on the other hand, are more effective in rapidly adding adult males to the social group, since adult males are recruited through marriage. Their labor, which is essential for clearing land and waging war, becomes immediately available to the social group. Furthermore, males are also added internally through the lineages, since in a matrilineal descent system the children belong to the mother's group. However, potentially fewer males can be added to the group since the number of children produced is limited by the number of females, not the number of males. The addition of more wives in a patrilineage will result in more lineage members, while the addition of more husbands in a matrilineal system will not. In both strategies, the effect on the labor force is the same. The primary difference is that in a matrilineal system, the labor provided by adult males can be added more rapidly to households through marriage alliances whereas a patrilineal system can only add males by the slow process of producing more children.

The relative advantage of a matrilineal or patrilineal descent system appears to be based on the greater need: control over resources such as land or property, which favors patrilineal systems, or need for males to clear land and wage warfare, which favors matrilineal descent.[16] If this set of choices is functionally correlated with descent type, then it would seem that flexibility in recruitment of male labor was a more critical resource to the chiefdoms of the Southeast during the historic period where we have ethnographic descriptions of matrilineal unilineal descent groups, most notably among the Natchez, Creeks, and Cherokees.[17] However, it should be pointed out that detailed information on the matrilineal descent systems for these groups comes from the eighteenth century and later, *after* aboriginal groups of the Southeast suffered devastating population decline through slave raiding and disease. It is unwarranted simply to assume that matrilineality was widespread among the aboriginal groups of the Southeast during the Late Mississippian Period. At least one southeastern chiefdom, the Calusa, had an inheritance rule for succession to chief that was

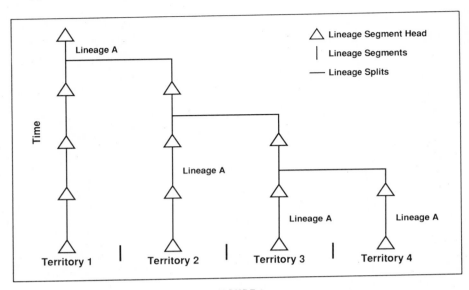

FIGURE 3

Lineage segmentation without the formation of ranked segments

patrilineal, but since there is no ethnohistoric description of their lineage system, it cannot be assumed that theirs was a patrilineal descent system. This issue of descent system will be elaborated in greater detail below.

Chiefdoms are societies capable of rapid population growth, and there is considerable variation in their population size, ranging from as few as one thousand in simple chiefdoms to as many as fifty thousand in complex chiefdoms. This growth, however, cannot usually be absorbed internally within the existing hamlets or villages because of the limitations posed by local resources. Because of this, villages usually fission to form daughter communities.[18]

As time goes on, fissioning results in a number of social outcomes for lineages. At its most basic, as villages or hamlets fission, so do their unilineal kin groups. Two distinct social and political directions can occur. In the first scenario, no new lineages are formed in the fissioning process. Instead, the original lineages are maintained and the divisions are treated merely as territorial segments. (See Figure 3.) This is simply a reproduction of like settlement *and* social units that ultimately results in a number of villages or hamlets clustered together and interacting with one another, primarily through exchange of marriage partners. Under this system, fissioning does not create new social ranks since no *new* lineages are created. The rank of the lineage or clan members is the same as it was prior to the fissioning; only their settlement location has changed. This form of lineage structure was probably the more common form found in simple chiefdoms in the Southeast.

The second potential outcome of the fissioning principle has different political consequences. When a village fissions, lineages also fission, and *new* lineages are formed. While these new lineages are autonomous, they recognize their genealogical connection with the parent lineage and its founding ancestor. Each subsequent split recognizes the rank order of splits that have occurred from this original lineage, and the resulting lineages are referred to as cadet lineages. The descendants of older siblings have higher standing than the descendants of younger siblings. Thus, the order of the fissioning from the initial apical lineage becomes the rank order of the lineages. This results in a conical clan.[19] Robin Fox refers to this method of lineage fissioning as a form of the "drift" method of segmentation and notes that the Nayar of India, a matrilineal society, practice this form of lineage segmentation. This principle of lineage fissioning is also seen in the Konga of Zaire, Africa.[20] A diagram illustrating this principle is presented in Figure 4 utilizing the Nayar example.

As can be seen, each lineage is ranked relative to each other based on how close the lineages are related to the apical ancestor. This type of lineage system is characteristic of some intermediate and complex paramount chiefdoms. Although in intermediate and complex paramount chiefdoms with conical clan or lineage systems there can theoretically be as many distinct ranks as there are individuals, it is impossible in practice to differenti-

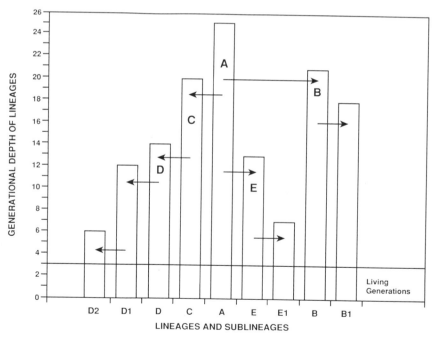

FIGURE 4
Formation of a conical lineage through lineage segmentation

ate and keep track of all of these unique positions. Instead, what develops is a series of *groupings* of elite social positions or ranks. This grouping of ranked individuals can result in serious errors in social misunderstandings by outsiders. For example, European explorers, utilizing their own cultural systems for comparative models of social organization, mistakenly equated these categories of ranking with social classes. Ethnohistorians, historians, or anthropologists who are not familiar with the chiefdom societal type have sometimes uncritically accepted these European categories. The result is that chiefdoms are mistakenly interpreted as states. Such errors have been made in interpreting the social development in the aboriginal Southeast, and they have even made their way into introductory cultural anthropology textbooks.[21]

The early-eighteenth-century Natchez of the lower Mississippi Valley are a case in point. The Natchez were described by Le Page Du Pratz as having four social classes, ranked from high to low: Suns, Nobles, Honored People, and Stinkards.[22] However, since the Natchez had a special rule requiring one to marry beneath one's "social class," this would seem contradictory, since social classes are usually endogamous. But, for the Natchez, these were not social classes. Rather, they were a means of lumping together a number of similarly ranked elite positions to streamline social rank. If this is the case, why is it that these social groupings are created, and why don't they actually represent social classes, particularly since these groupings do represent differential social strata within the society? The reason for the difference is important. These social groupings or classifications have as their basis *kinship and birth order within the unilineal descent group*. Members of the *same* lineage or clan actually have different social positions in these groupings, whereas in a social class system, all members of a lineage or clan would be in the same grouping. One must be aware of this difference to prevent misclassification of the society.

It would be impossible for any individual to remember all the unique social positions that ranking in complex chiefdoms would theoretically produce. Each person in a society of, say, 30,000 would have to be able to rank themselves with respect to the other 29,999 individuals. The use of terminological groupings makes this manageable, but it is notable that the "elite members" of chiefdoms (that is, the high-ranking individuals or high-ranking lineages) do *not* employ such generalizing principles. Among this "elite," the principles of ranking are strongly emphasized because this is where political control and succession to office lie, not among the lower levels of social ranks. Thus it often seems that an emerging "elite" class has formed in these societies, but in fact it has not. The social position of "eliteness" can be directly accountable in terms of the system of ranking, which applies equally to all lineage members of the chiefdom. Chiefdoms are ranked societies, not class societies.[23]

As we have seen, the conical clan results from a ranked series of genealogical splits from a founding lineage. However, these segmentations do not always lead to a ranking of the lineage segments. The reason for this lies in the economic workings of the chiefdom. As Morton Fried has observed, the major process of economic integration in chiefdoms is redistribution, and it is from this process that ranking is financed.[24]

Redistribution is the economic mechanism by which chiefs pool resources in a central location in order to later return them to their constituents in times of need. Elman R. Service's thinking was that regions within chiefdoms would be deficient in one or more basic resources, particularly where environmental diversity was great, and that these inequities could be mitigated through a system of pooling resources in political centers, where they could then be meted out when needed to relieve local resource scarcity. However, this was not spelled out in Sahlin's original treatment of the role of redistribution in chiefdoms, and the function of redistribution has been misinterpreted and even rejected as an important variable in the organization and operation of chiefdom societies.[25]

This is unfortunate. Chiefdoms in the Southeast were redistributive societies, and there is primary documentary evidence of redistribution among the Timucua of Florida in the middle of the sixteenth century. Jacques Le Moyne, an artist who accompanied the Laudonnière expedition to Florida in 1564, recorded an instance of redistribution. The following text is a caption to a drawing by Le Moyne that was engraved by De Bry:

> At a set time every year they gather in all sorts of wild animals, fish, and even crocodiles; these are then put in baskets, and loaded upon a sufficient number of the curly-haired hermaphrodites, who carry them on their shoulders to the storehouse. This supply, however, they do not resort to unless in case of the last necessity. In such event, in order to preclude any dissension, full notice is given to all interested; for they live in the utmost harmony among themselves. The chief, however, is at liberty to take whatever of this supply he may choose.[26]

This is a description of the actual function of redistribution in which pooled resources are provided to members of the chiefdom in times of need. Normally, food needs would be met, but certain disruptions in subsistence yields, due to crop failure caused by drought, disease, unexpected frosts, or spoilage or pillaging of stored food, could be mitigated through chiefly redistribution of these pooled resources. This has been illustrated in Figure 5. These storehouses or granaries would also be utilized to supply the chief and his elite family. In the de Soto and Pardo chronicles, as well as in the reference provided above, there are numerous descriptions of granaries and storehouses under the control of local chiefs. The Gentleman of Elvas, for example, notes that prior to de Soto's arrival in the province of Cofitachequi, a "pestilence" had struck the area: "About the place, from half a league to a league off, were large vacant towns, grown up in grass, that appeared as if no people had lived in them for a long time. The

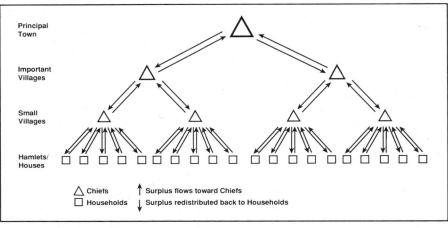

FIGURE 5

Redistribution of surplus in a chiefdom through a hierarchy of chiefs

Indians said that, two years before, there had been a pest in the land, and the inhabitants moved away to other towns."[27]

Although this statement has always been interpreted as an instance of epidemic disease, this need not have been the case, particularly since the main town, which was spared the epidemic, would have had a greater population and density, and thus would have been more vulnerable epidemiologically.[28] It seems more likely that this "pestilence" represents crop failure. The principal town of Cofitachequi was spared because it was a center of redistribution and contained storehouses of food to relieve just such subsistence shortages. This is illustrated in the account of Garcilaso de la Vega:

> She [the chieftainess of Cofitachequi] referred once more to the message delivered by her vassals and declared that the scourge of the previous year had robbed her of the supplies she would like to have had in order to minister to his lordship [de Soto] more adequately, but that she would do all possible in his service. And that he might judge of her sincerity by her actions, she offered him immediately one of two deposits in that town, in each of which were six hundred bushels of corn that had been gathered for the relief of her vassals who had escaped the pestilence. She begged him, however, to agree to leave her the other deposit for her own great need.[29]

Thus, there exist two explanations of the role of this storehouse of food: (1) to redistribute food to members of the chiefdom in time of need, and (2) to draw upon this reserve for the use of the chief and his or her immediate family. There is little doubt that redistribution occurred in the southeastern United States during the sixteenth century. However, the more important question is how does it relate to the development of the political power of chiefs? As the critics of redistribution have rightly pointed out, there is a redundancy of basic economic activities within chiefdoms. There is *no* specialization of resource procurement in local territories within chiefdoms. Local villages and hamlets, if not households themselves, are autonomous producers of all the economic resources they require. Therefore, there is no need for redistribution to meet local inadequacies resulting from specialization or environmental differences. There is, however, as noted above, a real need to mitigate natural and cultural disasters, which can impact local food supply. This is the real *economic* function of redistribution.

It is also the source of the differential power of chiefs. How is it then that a chief comes to possess differential political power? This is the single most important question relating to the operation of chiefdoms. It is necessary to remember that this power always exists within the context of kin-based social relationships. The development of chiefly benefits of power and authority ultimately derive from the outstanding characteristics of the social and economic structure of chiefdoms: ranking and redistribution.

Within a chiefdom, the principle of ranking creates a number of elite social positions in the highest-ranked lineages. These positions are hereditary offices recognized by all individuals in the chiefdom. Yet, there is a difference between social position (prestige) and political power. This has led some researchers, based primarily on the anthropological observation and analysis of the actual political operations of contemporary chiefdoms in Africa, to distinguish two types of chiefs: *titular chiefs* who do not have exclusive control of force but instead maintain traditional ways of life through persuasion, pacification, and generosity, and *strong chiefs* who have coercive authority and complete sovereignty.[30] Paramount chiefs in the Southeast were strong chiefs. Not only did they have prestige, but also political power legitimized by authority, which is usually ideological in nature (that is, the divine right to rule). This is ubiquitous among the complex paramount chiefdoms of Polynesia and is found in the complex chiefdoms of Africa as well.[31] The most common means of deriving this sacred authority is through the deification of the apical ancestor, who is recognized as a god. The lineal descendants are believed to be descended from gods and therefore divine. This system has been documented for the southeastern United States among the eighteenth-century Natchez and the sixteenth-century Calusa.[32] But, while the divine right to rule may legitimize power, it is not the source of this power. Power can only be derived from economic control of the everyday lives of members of the chiefdom.[33] While ranking and divine legitimization of chiefly authority is established through the social and ideological structure of chiefdoms, the basis for power lies in the differential control of wealth derived through redistribution, a larger lineage, and the productive capabilities of multiple wives.

Since the elite derive their basic economic resources from their lower ranked constituents, the latter must get something from the elite. Since the provisioning of elites is somewhat voluntary, what prevents lower ranking individuals from "voting with their feet" and simply moving away and establishing their own lineage? There must be real advantages in putting up with the "cost" of chiefs.

It should be remembered that lower ranking chiefdom members are also kinsmen of elites and chiefs. Therefore, when these kinsmen promote the interests of chiefs it also serves to promote the welfare of individual lineages, villages, and the chiefdom. This is because powerful chiefs have greater effectiveness in resolving internal disputes that individual clans or villages could not resolve on their own. This in turn minimizes feuding, the threat of violence, and migration, all of which will weaken the internal stability of a chiefdom, making it vulnerable to competing chiefdoms. The frequency of these potential disputes increases as a function of the increasing population of the chiefdom.[34] Therefore, internal harmony is maintained by the centralization of the chief's power and the political expansion of the chiefdom, while at the same time a differential advantage is gained over smaller, less centralized competing chiefdoms. However, a balance must be struck between the resources a family produces and the surplus available for chiefs. Since food production depends upon human reproduction in the chiefdom, the more members a family and lineage has, the more *absolute* surplus it can produce, even though *per capita* production remains the same. This can lead to differential power since social debts can be created through redistribution of land, food, and spouses. And in the case of spouses it will also create important social and political alliances.

In Hawaiian chiefdoms, land was managed and distributed by the paramount chief through his elite managers, who were also his brothers.[35] There is no evidence that land was ever under the direct control of a paramount chief in the southeastern United States during the sixteenth century. But it is not necessary to invoke land management and distribution as a source of chiefly power, because such power can be derived in other ways. The most obvious is the differential production made possible by the greater size of the chief's lineage. This will lead to social debt and obligations, and in this way power accrues to the chief.

The founding lineage, which is the chief's lineage, will invariably be located in the best area for economic production, since the oldest lineage will have had first choice of location. All subsequent segmentations will take up residence in increasingly less desirable areas and will therefore not be able to support as many people nor produce as much surplus. This means that the apical lineage will have more people than subsequent lineages and will therefore possess more productive potential. This differential production can be translated into differential power by creating debt through feasting and giftgiving made possible by the greater food surplus and by the large pool of potential wives (the source of production via reproduction) made available to other lineages. Thus, chiefs can internally provide more surplus food, labor, and spouses through their own lineages than other lineages can. In this way chiefs obtain political power through differential access to and control of this wealth.

The leading lineage with its elites can also provide a control mechanism by removing high-ranking brothers from competition for succession to the office of chief. These individuals are made officeholders, and they represent the chief's interests in a number of ways. These offices typically include "war chief," "talking chiefs," "priests," and "craft specialists." The cacique of Tascaluza sent an address to de Soto at Talisi via his son who was probably a "talking chief."[36] Often, such "chiefs" are placed in other villages in the chiefdom in order to protect the interests of the chief and to serve as conduits for redistribution. Secondary political centers are important sources of stored food for redistribution and are drawn upon by the paramount chief's representatives. In the documents of the de Soto expedition there are references to the chief having stores of food in other towns in the provinces of Cofitachequi, Anilco, and Aminoya.[37]

For example, among the Timucua of Florida, the name of one of the villages encountered by de Soto, Urriparacoxi, has been translated as "Village of the War Chief." A similar situation is seen among the eighteenth-century Natchez, where the Great Sun's relatives were chiefs of lesser villages within the chiefdom.[38]

There is a paradox here because high-ranking brothers are often the sons of chiefs rather than the sons of the chief's sister, which would be expected in a matrilineal kinship system. Vernon Knight has analyzed the system of hierarchical inheritance among the contact period groups in the Southeast and has suggested that there is an agnatic component, inheritance through the male line, to the inheritance of elite positions in the chiefdoms of the Southeast.[39] Knight suggests in his scheme that the paramount is produced by a royal matriline and the position inherited from mother's brother to sister's son. There would be a number of ranked positions inherited matrilineally based on the birth order of sisters. This is how the ranking principle would work in a matrilineal system. However, there is also a set of ranked elite positions reckoned genealogically from the children of the *sons* of the paramount. Thus the agnatic inheritance of some social positions serves as a mechanism for maintaining elite status among the sons of chiefs, who do not belong to his lineage. Eventually, through a number of generations the children of both the sons of chiefs and the sons of sisters of chiefs will lose their elite status as their genealogical distance from the paramount line becomes so great that they are no longer classified as elite. In effect, this results in a conical ranking of elites from a single paramount matrilineage or "dynastic" family, with a number of genealogically ranked agnatic and collateral matrilineal elite positions, which through time eventually slough off to commoner status.

Another purpose served by high-ranking elites is to obtain or produce sumptuary or exotic goods for redistribution to lower ranking individuals within the chiefdom, and more importantly, with other chiefdoms. These items become political currency and may almost be as important as food in the political system of precapitalist economies.[40]

The Citico-style gorget is a classic example of this type of sumptuary artifact in the Southeast. This artifact, manufactured from Gulf coast whelk shells, is found associated with burials in nineteen of the twenty-two sixteenth-century archaeological sites in the interior Southeast. This artifact has a distribution that strikingly coincides with the territory of the Coosa chiefdom, one of the most powerful chiefdoms in the sixteenth-century Southeast. In the earlier Mississippian period, marine shell gorgets were primarily associated with high status elite burials. But in the Coosa chiefdom, they are not an elite sumptuary good but instead a symbol of age status.[41] Nonetheless, this is exotic, valuable material that requires external trade to obtain and considerable craft input to produce. Thus, surplus food obtained by the chief through redistribution is not only used by the chief and his family for their support, but is also converted into social currency, such as prestige items, like Citico-style gorgets, to be given to his kin-based constituents.

It is important to remember that the surplus food which the chief receives is, after all, just surplus; it has no value to the producer other than subsistence. If the subsistence need is met through normal production, it has no value at all to the producer. Instead, it only has value to the producer if it can be exchanged for prestige items or can be received in times of crop failure. Thus, the production of surplus by lineage members provides both social benefits and economic security.

Prestige can be achieved not only by producing surplus food but also through military obligations. Chiefs, to be successful, must effectively muster military support from the lineages they control. This is a voluntary activity, but one that is engaged in readily by the members of chiefdoms. Although social status is ultimately fixed through the principle of ranking, one's prestige may be raised through success in military exploits. This explains the occurrence of "status" goods that archaeologists find in mortuary contexts not associated with high-ranked individuals. Vernon Knight has even suggested that important community leadership positions might have been obtained through success in warfare.[42]

One of the most intriguing and difficult problems in chiefdom studies is the question of how complex paramount chiefdoms developed. Simple chiefdoms, and to a lesser extent intermediate chiefdoms with clearly defined lineage links, are relatively stable societies, and their formation is easy to comprehend. In these societies, the principle of rank is clearly established through the genealogical relationships among the cadet lineages. As long as new lineages recognize their kin ties and rank relationships with the lineages from which they emerged, the chiefdom units they constitute will be stable. Internal segmentation does not typically lead to the formation of complex paramount chiefdoms, because the chiefdom becomes larger only through *intrinsic* growth of already existing units. Such chiefdoms could grow to considerable size, with thousands of members in segmented lineages. However, chiefdoms do not exist in a social and demographic vacuum. Neighboring groups are growing as well, and this creates problems.

That is, there will come a time when the ability of a territory to meet the food needs of several contiguous chiefdoms is met, the environment becomes circumscribed, and no more expansion through internal segmentation is possible. When this threshold is reached, intrinsic internal growth cannot be utilized to expand a chief's prestige and wealth. Marriage alliances are one mechanism to incorporate external kin groups into the chiefdom. But there is another mechanism, warfare, which allows chiefdoms to incorporate political units that lie outside the maximal clan or lineage structure of the chiefdom. Through military usurpation, smaller political units can be incorporated into larger political units under the control of the paramount chief, and this is the stuff of which complex chiefdoms are made. While traditionally this has been postulated as a mechanism for the origin of the state, it also seems to have played an important role in the formation of complex paramount chiefdoms as well.[43]

The formation of complex paramount chiefdoms was probably *not* the outcome of intrinsic chiefdom development in the aboriginal southeastern United States, although Cahokia, centered at present-day St. Louis, probably developed in this way. Only in areas of extremely high environmental productivity with no competing groups will such complex paramount chiefdoms develop intrinsically. This appears to have occurred in Hawaii, where initial colonization by a chief was followed by continued expansion of the conical clan as the island was colonized through village fissioning and lineage segmentation. However, because numerous local chiefdoms were scattered throughout the Southeast in relatively close proximity to one another, complex paramount chiefdoms probably developed in the aboriginal Southeast through warfare and usurpation of conquered groups.

Interchiefdom warfare was chronic in the aboriginal Southeast. In the eighteenth century, intergroup warfare was based primarily on retaliation and revenge, and relatively few were killed.[44] However, this does not seem to be the case in the early contact period and before. Among the sixteenth-century Timucua, Le Moyne records that killing, mutilation, and taking of scalps as war trophies were important aspects of Timucua warfare.[45] He also notes that chief Outina marched into battle in a distinctive cross-shaped formation with himself in the middle, and when they broke camp at night they split up into squads of ten men each. He further states that Saturiba, his enemy, did not march into battle in an organized manner, noting that Outina was more powerful and had more warriors and wealth. This cruciform military formation, with the chief in the middle, was also seen by members of the Tristán de Luna expedition in northeastern Georgia. Le Moyne describes the battle between the two chiefdoms as a pitched engagement of massed forces. Although there is no direct evidence of pitched battles in the prehistoric era, Mississippian art and cosmography indicates the importance of warfare.[46] However, this is not the only, or even the more typical, form of warfare in the aboriginal Southeast.

Ethnohistoric sources for the mid-sixteenth century indicate that ambush and raid were the more prevalent forms of warfare, and that they inflicted few casualties.[47] This type of warfare was also the most frequent type encountered by de Soto and Luna. Thus, two distinct forms of warfare appear to have coexisted in the Southeast: the more typical ambush and raid, which usually resulted in few casualties and death, and pitched battles of massed warriors from competing chiefdoms. This latter form has the potential to stimulate the formation of complex paramount chiefdoms, and it provides a mechanism for improving one's social standing irrespective of one's actual rank. Most of the time, however, warfare among chiefdoms would result in a standoff, with little demographic and political impact.

Conquest of one's neighbors through warfare might result in the victors' incorporating the defeated groups into subservient political and economic roles, ultimately producing a landless class, as the lands of the vanquished were taken over by the victors, and leading to the formation of the state.[48] However, this type of conquest warfare could also lead to the development of complex paramount chiefdoms, as can be seen in the Calusa in the middle of the sixteenth century, where the paramount chief, Carlos, extended his political hegemony throughout south Florida and up the Atlantic coast to the St. Augustine area. Carlos was able to do this because the core of the chiefdom, which had developed through intrinsic growth, was centered on the southwest Florida coast with eight times the population of its surrounding neighbors, giving this paramount a military advantage. The difference here is that defeated groups would be treated as lower-ranking lineages or tributaries as they became incorporated into the chiefdom. They would be under the control of the paramount chief's relatives, who would be placed in charge in the villages. In addition, their positions could be reinforced through marriage alliances created by elite persons marrying spouses from conquered groups. These spouses would then function as hostages. Thus, powerful paramounts could emerge through the expansion of the chiefdom by conquering tributaries. In this way, as the amount of absolute surplus increased, so did the wealth of the chief. Also, the relative ranks of individuals in the chiefdom as a whole would rise, since conquered groups are placed at the lowest level.

Complex paramount chiefdoms, therefore, can be formed by military expansion and the incorporation of conquered groups into the chiefdom, as lower-ranked "fictive" kin with surplus amassed through the mechanism of tribute, rather than redistribution. This situation is seen in the large and well-organized chiefdom of Coosa, who along with their Spanish allies, raided the Napochies.[49] Not only was the purpose of this attack to avenge deaths previously inflicted on the Coosa, but more importantly to reestablish through conquest their tributary alliance with the Napochies, which had been broken off. The Napochies quickly sought peace and reaffirmed their tributary relationship once the superior military advantage of the Coosa was displayed. Thus warfare plays an important role in the creation, expansion, and maintenance of complex paramount chiefdoms.

However, this is not the only way in which complex paramount chiefdoms form. They can also come about through disruptions in the structure of the ranked conical clans. Politically, once the lineage links created by the conical clan structure have been severed, for whatever reason, there is potential for usurpation by chiefs who have been placed in secondary political centers. When a powerful paramount dies, other high-ranking chiefs may make claims to the paramountcy even though they have no genealogical "rights" to that position. Competing chiefs can argue or create fictive genealogies with which to establish their authority. Often, this legitimacy is based on the *de facto* demographic strength of the chief and his elite rather than on genealogy and ranking. If the claim cannot be settled, warfare can result, and if it is a military standoff, the chiefdoms remain separate. But, when one is defeated the winner becomes the paramount.[50] De Soto encountered just such a situation when the cacique of Pacaha and the cacique of Casqui argued about their right to paramount rule. They both argued their primacy to de Soto, which was to be recognized by having one of them seated at the place of honor at his table. Both caciques based their claim on their ancestry and rank. They were actually appealing to a higher authority, de Soto, asking him to legitimize their claim. Had the Spaniards become a permanent presence, this could have ended the conflict between these chiefdoms and resulted in a paramountcy. The resulting chiefdom, which would have been populous, would have involved a reordering of the rank relations of existing chiefs and their lineages.

However, it is more likely that friction over chiefly inheritance hindered the formation of complex paramountcies and actually led to the dissolution of existing paramountcies in the Southeast. Instead, an intermediate chiefdom more typically resulted. The formation of a powerful complex paramount chiefdom incorporating numerous different social groups means that the groups involved were already linked through some form kinship or marriage alliance and had roughly equal power. Since both competing chiefs would have had roughly equal power and may not have been able to gain any military or demographic advantage, it would have been difficult for one of these groups to achieve the necessary differential power base to effectively create a powerful paramountcy. It seems that this situation was quite common in the Southeast and was one of the reasons why powerful paramountcies were not more common.

Splitting off of lineages to form new chiefdoms will occur only when there are shifts in the demographic strength of chiefs and their followers. If a potential advantage can be gained because a junior lineage and a number of related lineages are stronger and more numerous than their senior lineage and feel they can split from the chiefdom and attack it, previous kinship and political links will be severed. This is when warfare arises. One of the benefits of the chiefdom is, after all, the resolution of *internal* conflicts that concern rank, authority, and prestige, since these are established by birth right. However, if it happens that ranking cannot be used to regulate social and political relationships and their underlying economic operation, the conflict almost certainly results. This means that complex paramount chiefdoms are inherently fragile and therefore not likely to have occurred everywhere in the Southeast. Only in those areas where the underlying demographic base of the chiefly lineage greatly overwhelms claims to political usurpation through warfare will complex paramount chiefdoms with considerable time depth exist. This is what is seen archaeologically at sites such as Etowah, Moundville, and Lake Jackson. But even at these sites, the political power, without exception, eventually shifts to other areas.

Rather than complex paramount chiefdoms, these societies may have been intermediate chiefdoms that developed their political power internally through intrinsic growth of their lineage units. The tributary nature of complex paramount chiefdoms would require food and perhaps exotic goods from dependent groups, but not the *labor*, manifested in temple mound construction, which would be drawn from local sources. Thus, the impressive size of the temple mounds at these sites do not necessarily indicate the existence of a complex paramount chiefdom. Likewise, the presence of foreign elite paraphernalia and burial offerings does not imply the existence of complex paramount chiefdoms, since these materials may have been obtained through balanced chiefly exchange rather than as tribute.

The simple chiefdom and the intermediate chiefdom based solely on the conical clan system or else the conical system of inheritance that crosscuts ranked clans and lineages seems to be the more typical chiefdom in the Southeast in the sixteenth century. This is mirrored in the type of polities encountered by de Soto. Only the chiefdoms of Coosa in the Tennessee Valley, Cofitachequi in South Carolina, Pacaha in Arkansas, Tascaluza in Alabama, and the Calusa of south Florida, and possibly the Quigualtam in Mississippi seem to represent complex chiefdoms with powerful paramounts that integrated *large* areas and *differing* local polities. Indeed, these should be the principal traits that identify complex chiefdoms and differentiate them from intermediate and simple chiefdoms in the aboriginal Southeast. This is not to suggest that smaller chiefdoms, such as Apalachee and Ocute, were not powerful and had no "paramount" chiefs; it is just that the political structure of these paramountcies was at a lower scale, where the extension of the chief's political domain to social groups outside the provenience of their chiefdom and their territory is minimal.

Ideology is an important component in the political structure of chiefdoms. One mechanism of control that a chief has over his polity is religious. Among the Calusa, Father Rogel specifically noted that only the chief and his priest, not his subjects, possessed esoteric religious knowledge, and it was their duty to perform certain ceremonies to maintain natural harmony. This religious knowledge was privy to the chief and his priests. It was passed down from generation to generation, and this knowledge was necessary to legitimize the chief's position.[51] Chiefs not only have the right to rule through inheritance, but this inheritance is justified and legitimized through religious mythology. The chief's rule is supernaturally sanctioned because he claims that his ancestors are gods. Once again, the use of kinship to establish relationships is seen even in the ideological realm of the culture.[52] This is a general characteristic of chiefdoms. In the southeastern United States the apical ancestor was the sun, and the chiefs were believed to be descended from the sun. Among the Timucua, Le Moyne described how a stag was sacrificed every year to the Sun, with the chief and his priest offering prayers to the Sun. This was done so that the lands would be fruitful.[53]

Although neither Le Moyne nor Rogel states specifically that chiefly and priestly esoteric knowledge was linked with ancestors and ancestor worship, there is a documentary account suggesting that both were commonplace, as is typically the case in chiefdoms throughout the world. During the Luna expedition, the Coosa paramount addressed his warriors before attacking the Napochies by recognizing the bravery and high status of the Spanish, who were allied with them, stating that they were *sons of the Sun and relatives of the gods.*[54] This historical anecdote is extremely important since it clearly notes that the elite, assumed here to include both Coosa chiefs and their close relatives as well as Luna's soldiers, were linked to the supernatural through their ancestors and were directly descended from these deities. In effect, chiefs and their priests are earthly representatives of the supernatural.

Burial patterns of Mississippian sites also conform to expectations that some form of ancestor worship was associated with chiefs. High-status individuals are buried under the floors of elite houses situated on platform mounds. This association of chiefly residence with the dead suggests a functional link of the living and the dead and therefore the importance of ancestors. A continuity through generations might also be inferred from the superimposed burials, which span approximately two hundred years, found at Mound 3 of the Lake Jackson site, the center of a Mississippian chiefdom ancestral to the Apalachee.[55]

A more important issue with respect to the role of ideology in chiefdoms is the extent to which it is important as a source of power and not just a means of legitimizing authority in chiefdoms. There can be little argument that chiefdoms in the Southeast had an ideology that religiously sanctioned the political centrality of chiefs. With respect to simple chiefdoms, the magnitude of food and labor being extracted by the chief for his use is relatively small. Since the economic cost of compliance for a chief's subjects was low, ideology may have been a sufficient mechanism for maintaining economic and political control.[56] This was reinforced internally, since the chief's subjects are kinsmen. Any veneration of the chief and his ancestors as deities served to venerate the lineages of the chiefdom. However, this ideological principle cannot be used among competing chiefs to sanction their authority.

In complex paramount chiefdoms, one chief emerges as the paramount. Since all chiefs have ideological claim to authority through their genealogical links to deified ancestors, this cannot be a mechanism of control to those kin groups that are *external* to the paramount. After all, the paramount's gods are not their own. Only the lineages that directly link to the paramount will ideologically "recognize" the divine legitimization of the paramount. This does not suggest that sanctity of the paramount is unimportant; in fact, it is elaborated above other chiefs. But ideological claims of authority cannot be used as a mechanism or explanation for the incorporation of external tributary polities into the complex chiefdom. However, once they are incorporated, such ideology will be used to validate and justify the tributary relationships that have been created. Complex political systems, as Timothy Earle has argued, developed not out of simple access to a source of power but instead by control of it.[57] Ideology alone cannot create or maintain complex chiefdoms, particularly since all the players for that power have access to approximately equivalent esoteric religious knowledge, and all are descended from divine ancestors. Establishing the validity of ideological claims of legitimacy, which are ultimately based on genealogies, can become strained and unclear when genealogies are deep and links have been severed or become pure fiction. This fact becomes particularly relevant because it is only the elites who have access to this information. This removes the validity of this claim from the perception of the chief's followers. Ideology, therefore, can be used by *any* chief to legitimize his right to rule.

Vernon Knight has analyzed Mississippian religious systems in the Southeast and has identified three *sacra* which operated within them. One of these was the warfare/cosmogony complex. This *sacra* was associated with chiefs/warriors and their high-ranking retainers who were also, of course, close relatives. As such, it was "a type of cult institution having worldwide distribution and always serving to undergird and to sanctify political power by means of supernatural monopolies expressed in exclusive rituals. Typically, the institution is not restricted to the political offices alone, but rather serves to link such offices to a particular descent group among others."[58]

The second cult institution in Knight's scheme is the platform mound cult. This served as a communal or public *sacra*. Unlike the warfare/cosmogony cult, the platform mound cult does not appear to have been associated with chiefly esoteric power. Instead, it functioned as the basic public supernatural sphere in which the entire community participated. This cult institution crosscuts lineage and community ties, and its priests/officers seem to have been determined by merit rather than rank. Its power seems considerable since one of its functions appears to have been renewal rituals and labor organization for mound construction.

The third cult institution proposed by Knight is the temple statuary cult, which he interprets as an ancestor cult. Knight sees this priesthood "as mediating between the chiefly community ritual affairs, yet clearly having exclusive ritual and supernatural prerogatives distinct from both of the former [cults]." This seems a correct interpretation, particularly since the ancestors being attended to are deceased lineage heads of *differential* rank, yet they would be recognized as legitimate deities by all members of the chiefdom.[59]

Knight's analysis rightly separates the chiefly esoteric priesthood from its more public or communal counterparts and clearly demonstrates the role of chiefly religion in validating the power of chiefs. More importantly, it illustrates how potential tensions within the political and social structure of chiefdoms could be mitigated and balanced through the three types of religious cults that relate to different social units. Two of these are kin based, the chiefly cult and the ancestor cults. The temple mound cult appears, however, to crosscut kinship. As such, it is an essential medium of integration in a chiefdom, because it provides an institution that is not based solely in corporate lineage affairs.

The chiefly *sacra*, because of its esoteric nature, cannot be used as a mechanism for *organizational* control and integration since, as mentioned earlier, it is not participated in by the chief's followers. While it may *justify* and *legitimize* the right to rule, it cannot be used to integrate or organize the public by *directly* bringing them into ritual. This, however, is facilitated through the temple cult, since it crosscuts all kinship divisions and because it is a means by which important prestige positions might be obtained through personal achievement rather than the normal ascriptive system of ranking. More importantly, the institution of temple cults would effectively isolate and maintain the extreme sanctity of the chief from more "common" religious affairs.

The fact that the temple cult institutions are powerful and are separated from the chiefly cult questions the warfare/cosmogony cult as a source of power. It does not seem likely that a set of religious institutions with obvious political importance would be tolerated by chiefs since, in effect, those institutions ignore the ranking principle and therefore the importance of the chief. This alone, if Knight is correct, would tend to minimize the importance of religion as a *source* of power for chiefs.

The ancestor cults provide the religious institutions for the lineage units themselves, and it is easy to envision how one of these cults could be "promoted" as the warfare/cosmogony cult. It is more than likely that the chiefly cult is, in most cases, an exaggerated, elaborated, or "promoted" ancestor cult, simply "holier" than the others and restricted to just the elite of the lineage. If this interpretation is accurate, then a hierarchy or ranking of "deities" should exist within the religious systems of southeastern chiefdoms. Unfortunately, there is little direct observation with respect to the structure of the sixteenth-century religious pantheon in the Southeast. The notable exception is Father Rogel's discussion of the Calusa pantheon.[60] This dialogue is important because it is the only religious query of indigenous, sixteenth-century southeastern religion by the clergy specifically for the purpose of understanding the native religion.

The Calusa pantheon included three persons who ruled the world. They were *ranked,* with one being highest, and the second was greater than the third. The supreme deity controlled the weather and other heavenly events. The second ranking deity was linked to political rule, and the third was linked to warfare. Misinterpretation by Rogel can be ruled out, since he used the Christian Trinity for comparison.[61]

In Knight's scheme, all of these deities would be associated with the chiefly cosmogonic *sacra.* More importantly, the deities are specifically identified as *persons.* As such it is reasonable to equate them with ancestors. Furthermore, they are hierarchically ranked in importance just as living individuals are in chiefdoms. What Father Rogel appears to have described were the deities worshiped by or associated with the Calusa paramount chief and his close high-ranking relatives. What we do not know is the totality of the Calusa pantheon as it relates to the ancestor cults and other deities. However, since there is a hierarchical principle operating in the highest *sacra,* then there is little reason to doubt that the principle also existed for nonchiefly ancestor cult institutions. Ranking is a thoroughgoing principle that operated in ideology as well as in everyday life. Ideology, especially ancestor worship, was not a source of power for chiefs, but a means of validating it and the inheritance principle.

A single dominant theme permeates chiefdoms—the principle of ranking. First and foremost, chiefdoms are kin-based ranked societies. Ranking governs every aspect of chiefdom organizational structure: social, economic, political, and ideological. Put another way, it is impossible to conceptualize or understand chiefdoms from *any* perspective without realizing that ranking is central. If this is true, why is it that sixteenth-century Spanish explorers failed to understand this important feature of the social structure of chiefdoms? The reasons are not immediately apparent.

The motives of the sixteenth-century Spanish explorers of the Southeast did not include the production of anthropological treatises. In the pursuance of personal wealth and the furtherance of Spanish interests, the Spanish did not need to understand the kinship structure of the societies they encountered. Kinship relationships and the principles of ranking were not systematically studied by people in the Western world until the nineteenth century. For the Spanish, there was simply no existing framework for comparing Indian societies with their own. But this alone cannot account for the lack of understanding of social structure of these societies.

It is important to remember that chiefdoms were not the societies that the Spanish were interested in discovering. They were looking for states to conquer. The major expeditions into the interior Southeast came after the highly successful conquests of Mexico and Peru, where the Spaniards discovered not only gold and silver, but also peasant communities already under the political control of *bureaucratically* organized political systems. It is a simple matter to usurp such a bureaucracy, leaving the underlying infrastructure intact. These were the types of cultural systems needed for creating haciendas and wealth. The explorers of the Southeast were trying to replicate earlier successes in Mexico and Peru, but the societies they found in the Southeast provided them only with food and human bearers of burden. They found no valuable metals. Had gold or silver been discovered, the native populations might well have been enslaved to mine those metals, just as similar populations were enslaved in Hispañola. The chiefdoms encountered by the Spanish were *not* the societies they wished to find.

The chiefs and their close elite relatives were all the Spaniards saw of the actual social structure. Other individuals were seen as bearers or warriors, but no one acquainted the Spaniards with the kinship system. Unlike states, where one takes over the bureaucracy, all the other institutions remain in place. Deposing a chief in a chiefdom results in an entirely different outcome. The obligations of chiefdom members to their chiefs are limited, and there is an expectation of reciprocal exchange. The chief is not a mere holder of an office, he is a real individual, and he deals with his subjects on a day-to-day, familiar basis. The Spaniards failed to understand the entire nature of family and kin relationships. If the Spaniards had married into the Indians' lineages, and settled in their communities, they might have come to understand this kin-based societal type. But they did not. Even when de Soto and his men wintered over in an Indian town, they remained separate from their hosts. For these reasons none of the Spanish explorers understood the principle of ranking *as an integrating factor.* In spite of this lack of understanding, they did witness and record on numerous occasions the principle of ranking in operation.

The Spanish explorers should not be criticized for this failure of understanding. After all, it was not until the latter half of this century that the chiefdom was recognized as a general cultural type, and it is now the task of anthropologists, ethnohistorians, and archaeologists to correct the deficiencies of these early explorers and to understand and interpret these "strange" societies in light of modern concepts. A surprisingly complete depiction of the structure of the societies encountered by the sixteenth-century explorers can be reconstructed if the anecdotes, observations, and asides (and even the exaggerated if not fictitious accounts of Garcilaso) are utilized within a general comparative framework.

A final caution is necessary. These chiefdoms, being "middle range societies" that lie between simple egalitarian cultures and "civilized" states, have an enormous amount of variability in their internal structure in spite of the basic similarity of this cultural type. For example, not all chiefdoms develop paramountcies, and the reasons why paramountcies develop is still hotly debated.[62] Furthermore, within chiefdoms there is a wide variation in the kinship system, economy, settlement configuration, and principles of inheritance. Differences in all of these cultural features can be seen in the sixteenth-century chiefdoms of the Southeast. The Calusa, for example, were a complex paramountcy but they did not practice agriculture.[63]

The purpose of a general cultural type, such as the chiefdom, is not to force upon a particular society or group a series of specific traits derived from an ideal conceptual formulation. Its strength, particularly with respect to ethnohistory, is that it provides a skeleton or structure that can be utilized to reconstruct particular chiefdoms, and more importantly to analyze and understand their dynamics. The anecdotes and accounts of explorers and castaways, in spite of their biases, misunderstandings, and incompleteness, provide the "flesh" for this general "skeleton." These accounts will not speak for themselves if they stand alone, but when utilized in the context of a general type, they can provide a remarkably "complete" reconstruction of the cultural characteristics of sixteenth-century southeastern aboriginal groups. It is no longer valid nor necessary to project information in the eighteenth century back to the sixteenth century.[64] The devastating changes that befell the aboriginal groups in the Southeast after the initial contact period vitiate the usefulness of ethnohistorical "upstreaming." Instead, ethnographic analogy utilizing cross-cultural general types provides far more powerful tools for understanding the structure and process of sixteenth-century societies in the aboriginal Southeast.

NOTES

1. Oberg, "Types of Social Structure"; Sahlins, *Social Stratification in Polynesia*; Service, *Profiles in Ethnology* and *Primitive Social Organization*. For prehistoric groups in Europe, see Renfrew, *Before Civilization* and *Approaches to Social Archaeology*; and Renfrew and Cherry, *Peer Polity Interaction*. For trade with

protohistoric groups in Europe, see Dyson, *Creation of the Roman Frontier;* Hasel-grove, "Wealth, Prestige, and Power"; Hedeager, "Empire, Frontier, and Barbarian Hinterland"; and Wells, *Culture Contact and Culture Change* and *Farms, Villages, and Cities.* For the Celts, see Crumley, "Social Causes for Population Fissioning."

2. Las Casas, *Historia de las Indias* and Oviedo, *Historia General y Natural de las Indias.*

3. For South American societies, see Oberg, "Types of Social Structure." For Polynesian societies, see Sahlins, *Social Stratification in Polynesia.* For cross-cultural applications, see Service, *Primitive Social Organization.* For chiefdom subtypes, see Sahlins, *Social Stratification in Polynesia;* Taylor, *Some Locational Aspects;* Johnson and Earle, *Evolution of Human Societies;* and Earle, "Evolution of Chiefdoms."

4. Kirchoff, "Principles of Clanship"; Sahlins, *Tribesmen;* and Knight, "Social Organization and the Evolution of Hierarchy."

5. Service, *Primitive Social Organization,* 161–69.

6. Knight, "Hierarchy in Southeastern Chiefdoms," 6.

7. Service, *Primitive Social Organization,* 43. For the Calusa, see Widmer, *Evolution of the Calusa,* 272–73.

8. Sahlins, *Stone Age Economics,* 74–99.

9. Fox, *Kinship and Marriage,* 97–121.

10. Weiner, *The Trobrianders of Papua New Guinea,* 94; Keegan and Mac-lachlan, "Taíno Kinship and Politics," 620; Basehart, "Ashanti," 288; and Fortes, "Kinship and Marriage Among the Ashanti," 262.

11. Keegan and Maclachlan, "Taíno Kinship and Politics," 620–21.

12. Johnson and Earle, *Evolution of Human Societies,* 177–78.

13. Weiner, *The Trobrianders of Papua New Guinea,* 99–103.

14. This is compatible with Vernon Knight's conclusion that clans did not have internal status differences except within the single highest ranking lineage. Knight, "Hierarchy in Southeastern Chiefdoms," 18–20.

15. Goody, *Production and Reproduction.*

16. Julian Steward has suggested that the need for additional males was the reason for matrilineal clans in the American Southwest, and Mary Douglas has argued for its presence in Africa for similar reasons. Steward, "Ecological Aspects of Southwestern Society," 169, and Douglas, "Is Matrilineality Doomed in Africa," 132.

17. Hudson, *Southeastern Indians,* 185–97.

18. Johnson and Earle, *Evolution of Human Societies,* 235–38; Chagnon, "Social Causes," 264–69, and "Genealogy, Solidarity, and Relatedness," 106–7.

19. Kirchhoff, "Principles of Clanship," 5–9; Sahlins, *Social Stratification in Polynesia,* 139–79, and *Tribesmen,* 24–25.

20. Fox, *Kinship and Marriage,* 124–25, and Richards, "Types of Family Structure," 242.

21. Sears, "State in Certain Areas," 109–25, and "The State and Settlement Patterns," 140–52, and Hoebel, *Anthropology,* 405–6.

22. Le Page Du Pratz, *Historie de la Louisiane,* 393–97.

23. Fried, *Evolution of Political Society.*

24. Ibid., 117.

25. Service, *Primitive Social Organization,* 136; Sahlins, *Social Stratification*

in Polynesia, 4–8, and *Stone Age Economics,* 208–9; Peebles and Kus, "Some Archaeological Correlates"; Earle, "Reappraisal of Redistribution," 213–29; and Johnson and Earle, *Evolution of Human Societies,* 208–11.

26. Le Moyne, *Brevis Narratio,* plate 23, translated by W. P. Cumming, "French, Spanish, and English Attempts to Colonize the East Coast," 191.

27. Elvas, *Narratives of the Career of Hernando De Soto,* 63.

28. Dobyns, *Their Numbers Become Thinned,* 262–63.

29. Vega, *Florida of the Inca,* 300.

30. Lowie, *Origin of the State;* Mair, *Primitive Government,* 167–89; Balandier, *Political Anthropology,* 47; and Lowie, *Origin of the State.*

31. Goldman, *Ancient Polynesian Society,* 4, and Mair, *Primitive Government,* 234–35.

32. White, Murdock, and Scaglion, "Natchez Class and Rank," 369–88, and Zubillaga, *Monumenta Antiquae Floridae,* 288–309. Vernon Knight has shown how this religion and ideology operated as cults at three social and political levels within the Mississippian societies of the southeastern United States; see Knight, "Mississippian Religion," 679–82.

33. Earle, "Evolution of Chiefdoms," 86.

34. Netting, "Sacred Power," 240–42.

35. Johnson and Earle, *Evolution of Human Societies,* 234–35.

36. Elvas, *Narratives of the Career of Hernando de Soto,* 80.

37. Ibid., 136–37, 168.

38. Mitchem, *"Ethnohistoric and Archaeological Evidence";* White, Murdock, and Scaglion, "Natchez Class and Rank"; and Widmer, "Social Organization of the Natchez," 5–7.

39. Knight, "Mississippian Religion," 12–13.

40. Helms, *Ancient Panama,* 75–77; Schneider, "Was There a Pre-Capitalist World-System?"

41. Hatch, *Status in Death,* 133; M. T. Smith, *Aboriginal Culture Change,* 107–10, and "Vestiges of the Southern Cult," 145.

42. Hatch, *Status in Death,* 152–54, and Knight, "Mississippian Religion," 680.

43. Carneiro, "Origin of the State."

44. Larson, "Functional Considerations of Warfare," 391, and Hudson, *Southeastern Indians,* 109–10.

45. Le Moyne, *Brevis Narratio,* plate 15.

46. Ibid., plates 13 and 14; Hudson, "A Spanish-Coosa Alliance," 612–13; Knight, "Mississippian Religion"; and Philips and Brown, *Pre-Columbian Shell Engravings.*

47. Le Moyne, *Brevis Narratio,* plate 30.

48. Carneiro, "Origin of the State."

49. Hudson, "Spanish-Coosa Alliance," 623–24.

50. Johnson and Earle, *Evolution of Human Societies,* 234.

51. Zubillaga, *Monumenta Antiquae Floridae,* 282–88.

52. Robert Netting, in a comparative study of African chiefdoms, views sacred power as essential to the formation of institutionalized leadership and centralization typical of paramount chiefdoms. Netting, "Sacred Power," 240–41.

53. Le Moyne, *Brevis Narratio,* plate 35.

54. Hudson, "A Spanish-Coosa Alliance," 617; emphasis added.
55. Jones, "Southern Cult Manifestations."
56. Earle, "Evolution of Chiefdoms," 86.
57. Ibid., 86.
58. Knight, "Mississippi Religion," 680.
59. Ibid., 681.
60. Zubillaga, *Monumenta Antiquae Floridae*, 280–81.
61. Ibid., 280.
62. Earle, "Evolution of Chiefdoms," 86.
63. Widmer, *Evolution of the Calusa*, 1.
64. See, for example, Hudson, *Southeastern Indians*, 11.

JOHN F. SCARRY

The Apalachee Chiefdom:
A Mississippian Society
on the Fringe of the
Mississippian World

When Spanish explorers first entered the interior Southeast, they encountered dozens of politically and economically independent but nonetheless loosely intertwined societies. The native polities exchanged material goods, information, and, probably, people. They formed political and military alliances. Some may even have formed larger, short-term units under the control of a particularly strong polity—what Charles Hudson has called a paramount chiefdom.[1]

The sixteenth-century Southeast was culturally diverse. There were social, political, linguistic, material, and ecological differences among the native polities. There were also similarities. Many societies had comparable subsistence economies and political organizations and shared a set of religious institutions and sacra.[2] We refer to these societies (and their prehistoric predecessors) as the Mississippian chiefdoms. Not all the native polities of the Southeast were Mississippian chiefdoms. The Calusa and the various Timucuan chiefdoms were not, but many of the most important and well documented societies were.[3]

One of the most important Mississippian societies was the Apalachee chiefdom of northwestern Florida. (See Figure 1.) The Apalachee polity was small in modern terms; its territory lay between the Aucilla and Ochlockonee Rivers and measured only 50 kilometers from border to border. Nevertheless, it was economically and politically powerful. Apalachee fields yielded abundant crops and sizeable agricultural surpluses. The Apalachee played a significant role in trade networks that linked many of the southeastern chiefdoms. They were militarily powerful enough to successfully resist two large Spanish expeditions in the sixteenth century.

After Spain established colonies in Florida, the Apalachee remained important and economically powerful. In the seventeenth century, Spanish authorities established missions, a fort, and several ranches in Apalachee territory. The province became a bastion protecting the Spanish capital at St. Augustine from native groups to the north and west. It was also an important breadbasket, exporting grain and other foodstuffs to St. Augustine and Havana.[4]

The Apalachee survived as a recognizable political entity through the end of the seventeenth century, but eventually they succumbed to the onslaught of European military might and Old World diseases. They suffered several devastating epidemics in the seventeenth century (and probably others in the sixteenth century). By 1704, attacks by English colonists and their Creek allies forced the Spaniards to abandon the Apalachee province. When the Spanish withdrew, the Apalachee dispersed. Some went to St. Augustine, some went to the Mobile area, and many were captured and taken north.[5]

The Apalachee are one of the best known of the Mississippian chiefdoms. In the archaeological record we can trace them back to about A.D. 1100, and we can trace their ultimate origins back as far as A.D. 700. In the historical record we have accounts from the sixteenth century, before the massive changes that accompanied (or preceded) European contact in much

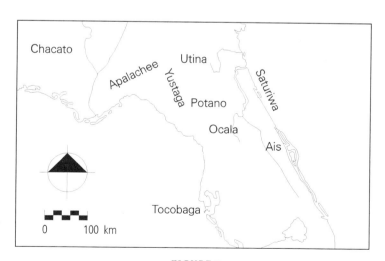

FIGURE I
The Apalachee and their neighbors

of the Southeast. We also have abundant documentary accounts from the seventeenth century, during and after the changes that accompanied their incorporation into the Spanish colonial and mission system.[6]

Our picture of the sixteenth-century Apalachee is based largely on the accounts of the expeditions of Pánfilo de Narváez and Hernando de Soto.[7] Unfortunately, these accounts provide only limited information about the Apalachee. Except for Garcilaso's questionable narrative, the accounts are brief.[8] Furthermore, the interactions between the expeditions and the Apalachee were not amicable, and the chroniclers had little opportunity to observe anything beyond the landscape and the Apalachee's military prowess.

We can augment our picture with accounts from the seventeenth century. There are good descriptions of the seventeenth-century Apalachee.[9] We must be careful, however, when we use later descriptions, since they are from a time when the Apalachee had been incorporated into the Spanish colonial system and changed by over a century of contact with Europeans.

We can also augment our picture with archaeological data from pre- and protohistoric contexts in Apalachee province. Here again we must exercise caution, since there is reason to believe that there were significant changes in Apalachee society in the very late prehistoric period.[10]

In the sixteenth century, the Apalachee territory was bounded by the Aucilla and Ochlockonee rivers and the Gulf of Mexico. (See Figure 1.) The people who lived east of the Aucilla were politically distinct, spoke different languages, had different material cultures, and appear to have had different cult institutions. The area immediately west of the Ochlockonee River was unoccupied in the sixteenth century. The placement of the northern boundary is less precise, but recent archaeological investigations in southwestern Georgia suggest that the territory of the Apalachee did not extend beyond the Ochlockonee River.[11]

These boundaries appear to have changed very little from the initial emergence of the Apalachee chiefdom through the dissolution of the Apalachee as a distinct group. The material culture differences on either side of the Aucilla are evident throughout the period that the Apalachee existed. The area to the west of the Ochlockonee contains very few Mississippian sites. It appears to have always formed a buffer zone between the densely populated Apalachicola River valley and Apalachee province.[12]

The area occupied by the Apalachee was small, but it was very rich. The soils of the northern portion of the territory were fertile, and the flat ridge tops provided locations for extensive agricultural fields. The flat, sandy coastal plain in the southern portion of the territory was lightly occupied. Historically, the Apalachee used it primarily as a source of game and wild plant foods.[13] The many lakes and ponds of the northern portion took the place of the oxbow lakes exploited by Mississippian groups of the interior and provided abundant aquatic resources. To the south, the Gulf of Mexico provided marine resources unavailable to inland peoples. The shell middens of the coastal strand testify to the Apalachee's use of these resources.

The Apalachee exploited their environment using a technology that was limited compared with that of the European invaders of their land. They made no significant use of metal tools in everyday life. Instead, they used stone, wood, bone, and shell. They had no source of energy other than human labor. They had no draft animals, and they did not use the wheel or the plow. Transportation was by foot or canoe, limiting the amount of material they could carry and the rate at which they could transport goods and information.

The economic basis of Apalachee society was cleared-field agriculture. From the accounts of the de Soto expedition we have descriptions of fields that stretched for leagues. The Apalachee use communal labor to clear their fields, burning them in mid-winter.[14] Maize provided the bulk of Apalachee subsistence, but their diet was augmented by other domesticated plant species and wild fruits and nuts.[15] For protein they relied on game obtained when they cleared their fields, on the hunting of large game in uninhabited areas surrounding the central core of their territory, and on the selective exploitation of locally abundant aquatic and marine resources.[16]

Apalachee social structure was based on kinship, not on occupation or residence. Kin group affiliation and inheritance were matrilineal: individuals belonged to the kin-based groups (lineages and clans) to which their mother belonged and males passed on belongings and positions not to their own sons (who belonged to their mothers' families) but to the sons of their sisters. The Apalachee had matrilineal totemic clans and we know that the totems had ritual associations. Social status was also determined, at least in part, by kinship.[17]

Apalachee society was hierarchically structured, both socially and politically. Individuals and groups were ranked, as were political offices. There was a small elite (noble) group and a large commoner group. The differences in social rank affected access to political office, access to certain material goods, access to certain foods, and ritual duties and roles. The Apalachee aristocracy consisted of several kin groups. There were two prominent surnames (Osunaca and Hinachuba) among the seventeenth-century Apalachee elite. Members of those groups occupied high political offices and may have competed for office and other status positions.[18]

The sixteenth-century Apalachee polity was a complex chiefdom. There were political offices that formed at least two administrative levels above the local community. The offices were ranked, and they differed in the amount and extent of political power and authority associated with them. Some of the offices (for example, the office of chief) were inherited, or only a small group of related individuals had access to them. Some chiefs were closely related. The paramount chief exercised authority over the entire polity. The lesser chiefs exercised the same kinds of authority, but the geographic scope of their authority was limited. They presided over villages and districts within the province. Below the chiefs there was a further ranked series of offices. These included the *inija principal,* the *inija,* and the *chacal.*[19]

The Apalachee chiefs received tribute such as agricultural products, bear fat, and skins. They also exercised economic power through their control of community food stores. They had important ritual roles. The paramount chief was linked to a solar divinity. All chiefs were saluted in the same manner in which the ball pole was saluted before the Apalachee ball game was played. The raising of the ball pole was "an elaborate ritual, pregnant with religious symbolism and magical formulas."[20]

While kin group affiliation and access to political office were based on matrilineal descent, there were provisions for the children of male chiefs. They became *usinulos.* This position was politically prominent. It also played a prominent ritual role in the Apalachee ballgame.[21]

There were several distinct hierarchical levels among Apalachee settlements: homesteads, local aggregations of homesteads, larger sites that may have been the towns mentioned in the sixteenth- and seventeenth-century accounts, minor centers with a single earthen mound, and the multimound center at Lake Jackson.[22] To a degree, these reflect the political hierarchy. At the bottom was the individual household. Several households combined to form a district, a community unit. These communities were named entities in the seventeenth century, and we assume that this was the case earlier. Several such communities were under the administrative and political control of a subordinate chief. In the seventeenth century these subordinate chiefs lived at the mission *doctrinas;* in the prehistoric period we assume that they lived at the single mound centers. Finally, the paramount chief presided over the entire chiefdom from the capital: Lake Jackson in the prehistoric period and the town of Anhaica in the sixteenth and seventeenth centuries.

The Apalachee chiefdom resembled other Mississippian societies. The Apalachee raised the same suite of crops as the Mississippian peoples of the interior Southeast. They constructed planned centers with plazas and pyramidal earthen mounds. They had hierarchical social, political, and religious organizations. They shared elements of a regional belief system. They participated in an extensive exchange network in manufactured symbolic items, mundane goods, and localized raw materials.[23]

The Apalachee social structure appears to have followed a general model that characterized societies throughout the Southeast.[24] Like most Mississippian chiefdoms, the Apalachee were matrilineal. Lineages, groups of related individuals, were combined into totemic, exogamous clans. An individual's clan membership was the same as his or her mother's affiliation. The clans in turn belonged to moieties, dual divisions of the society based on kinship and having religious significance. The moieties were ranked; one had higher social status than the other, although these status differences do not appear to have affected access to resources. The clans within the moieties were also ranked. The ranking clan in the higher ranking moiety was the royal clan, and the leading family of the ranking clan was the royal family. Nobility and degree of elite status were based on genealogical proximity to the royal family. Unlike the Polynesian chiefdoms, this conical structure was of limited extent, and beyond a few degrees of kinship from the royal family, an egalitarian clan structure prevailed.

Because clans were exogamous, the elite had to marry commoners. The intermarriage of nobles and commoners provided an organic solidarity to the society. It prohibited the formation of a disconnected elite and the division of the society into sharply contrasting interest groups. There was a limited system of double unilineal inheritance that precluded a total loss of status by children of noble men. The children of male nobles had noble status of a lesser rank. That status decreased by generation, until after a limited number of generations the descendants of noble males were commoners. Among the Apalachee, the position of *usinulo* was occupied by the children of chiefs and had important ritual and political roles and high social status.

Like many of the larger Mississippian societies, the Apalachee polity was a complex chiefdom. There was a paramount chief who had authority over the entire polity. Beneath the paramount were lesser chiefs, whose authority extended over geographically restricted portions of the polity. Under the chiefs there was also a ranked series of offices. One of these was the *inija*. This has obvious parallels to the office of *heniha* in the Muskogean chiefdoms to the north of the Apalachee.[25]

Finally, the Apalachee shared a belief system with Mississippian societies as far away as eastern Oklahoma. Evidence of this shared belief system can be seen in three archaeological complexes found in Mississippian systems across the Southeast: a warfare/cosmogony complex, a platform mound complex, and a temple statuary complex. Each of these complexes consisted of a set of sacra—representational art, artifacts, and icons with conventional supernatural meaning used in ritual activities or displays. The sacra of a given complex were associated with a particular cult institution or set of rituals sharing a general goal, based on similar or related beliefs and supported by the same social group.[26] At least two of these complexes were present in the prehistoric Apalachee chiefdom. The warfare/cosmogony complex can be seen at the Lake Jackson site where a subset of the complex (repoussé copper plates, engraved shell artifacts, and copper and stone celts) was associated with elite individuals who presumably occupied high political positions.[27] The platform mound complex was also unquestionably present in the prehistoric Apalachee chiefdom.

In some respects, the Apalachee differed from most other Mississippian societies. They lived in an environment that was unlike those of most Mississippian societies; they interacted with non-Mississippian groups; and they shared religious institutions with non-Mississippian groups.

Unlike the Mississippian groups of the interior, the Apalachee did not live in a riverine environment. The Apalachee territory contained several small rivers, but these rivers were different from the rivers of the interior, and their relationship to Apalachee settlement and economy was also different. The rivers of Apalachee originate in the Gulf Coastal Plain and do not carry the heavy silt loads of the rivers that originate farther north. For this reason, they do not form natural levees of silt. They are bounded by swamps, not dry, fertile levees. The rivers of Apalachee were not bounded by settlements; rather, the rivers bounded the settlements of the Apalachee. They were transportation routes and sources of aquatic resources, not the providers of the soil of the agricultural fields.[28]

Because Apalachee settlements were located in interriverine areas instead of along natural levees, the Apalachee polity was more compact than most Mississippian polities. Its spatial structure was two-dimensional, not linear as will be seen below.

The Apalachee interacted with groups outside the Mississippian world, groups that did not share the cult institutions and economic basis that linked the Mississippian chiefdoms. This interaction can be seen in the presence of Apalachee ceramic styles in peninsular Florida and along the Gulf Coast of northwestern Florida, and in the Apalachee ball game and its associated rituals, which were shared by Timucuan chiefdoms to the east and south but apparently not by Mississippian chiefdoms to the north.

Over the course of the history of the Apalachee chiefdom, we have identified three sequential phases, what we hope are the archaeological manifestations of a single political entity. The boundaries between the phases mark significant changes in the Apalachee polity and are visible in the archaeological record in changes in material culture and settlement patterns. The three phases are: the Lake Jackson phase (A.D. 1100–1500), the Velda phase (A.D. 1500–1633), and the San Luis phase (A.D. 1633–1704).[29]

The Lake Jackson phase was the earliest recognizable Apalachee polity. There is no evidence of contact between Lake Jackson–phase Apalachee and Europeans. No sixteenth-century European artifacts have been discovered at the Lake Jackson site, the paramount center of the polity, and the Lake Jackson–phase ceramic complex is distinguishable from the later Velda-phase complex seen at the site of the 1540 winter encampment of the de Soto expedition.[30] The late Lake Jackson–phase polity was a complex chiefdom with two administrative levels above the local community. This political hierarchy is evident in settlement patterning. There are four classes of Lake Jackson–phase settlements—homestead, hamlet, single-mound center, and multi-mound center—with a clear qualitative distinction between the mound centers and the smaller residential sites. And status differentiation and political (or religious) offices are evident in mortuary patterning. The elite burials found at the Lake Jackson site by Jones were spatially segregated, were buried with substantial investments of community labor and wealth, and were associated with sacra of the warfare/cosmogony complex and artifacts interpreted as symbols of office and high social status.[31]

The Velda phase was the Apalachee polity encountered by Narváez and de Soto. Like the earlier Lake Jackson–phase polity, it was a complex chiefdom. The earliest accounts describe settlement hierarchies and political relationships of subordination and dominance among communities and elite. Unlike the Lake Jackson–phase chiefdom, the Velda phase was not ruled from the Lake Jackson site; Lake Jackson was abandoned by the sixteenth century, and the capital of the Velda phase was located at Anhaica, some 6 or 7 kilometers south of Lake Jackson. The Velda-phase material culture also differed from that of the Lake Jackson phase. The ceramic complex looked less like those of Middle Mississippian chiefdoms to the northwest and more like those of South Appalachian Mississippian chiefdoms of the Georgia Piedmont.

The San Luis phase was the missionized Apalachee polity of the seventeenth century. It was not a Mississippian chiefdom, although it retained the structural framework of the earlier polities. The San Luis phase was not an independent polity. The San Luis–phase Apalachee were subjects of Spanish Florida. Ultimate political control was exercised by the Spanish governor through his lieutenant at San Luis, and religious control rested in the Franciscan friars at the various *doctrinas*.

Before the emergence of the Lake Jackson–phase Apalachee, northwestern Florida was occupied by Woodland peoples. The Woodland societies were egalitarian tribal systems that lacked the status differentiation and political hierarchies seen in the Apalachee chiefdom. The subsistence economies of the earlier societies also differed from that of the Apalachee. The Woodland peoples grew corn, but it was not the staple for the Apalachee. Instead, the bulk of Woodland diets was provided by wild plants and animals.

The Apalachee chiefdom arose out of changes in subsistence procurement and production, changes in sociopolitical organization, changes in interactions among equivalent polities, and changes in material culture. Production of domesticated plant foods, particularly maize, was intensified. Surpluses were produced, and a system of cleared-field agriculture was adopted. Organizational complexity increased. Formal, permanent political offices appeared, and authority was concentrated in those offices. Officeholders gained control of surplus production. Ascriptive differences in social status arose. A superstructure and body of sacra shared with other Mississippian groups was adopted. Alliances formed between elite groups in different societies. A regional prestige economy associated in part with religious sacra ensued. Relationships of political subordination and dominance emerged. The form and style of ceramic containers changed, and morphological variability increased. A marked similarity in decorative motifs in ceramics prevailed throughout the region.

The emergence of the Apalachee chiefdom was not wholly the result of local, in situ processes. A new population moved into the area, perhaps from the Apalachicola River valley to the west. The emergence of the chiefdom appears to have been a result of demographic forces and the political interaction of competing political segments within the proto-Apalachee chiefdom and between that polity and other, similar polities in the Southeast.[32]

During the period A.D. 500–1000, the initial steps in the emergence of the Apalachee chiefdom took place in the Woodland societies of northwestern Florida. The forces that ultimately produced the Fort Walton Mississippian chiefdoms, including that of the Apalachee, were at work. There was demographic pressure on resources and on the mechanisms of social integration. Within societies, individuals competed for prestige positions, and there was competition and other forms of interaction between societies.

The necessary precursors of Apalachee institutions were also present in the Woodland societies. Woodland people grew maize, albeit not as intensively as it would be grown later. Decision-making positions existed, although their scope and authority were limited compared with that of the chiefs of Apalachee, and they were open to a much larger segment of the population. Woodland period leaders included lineage elders, religious practitioners, and situational leaders (individuals who assumed leadership roles for particular tasks and for limited periods of time).

During the Late Woodland period in the Apalachicola Valley there was an apparent increase in the number of people living in and around the valley. The number of archaeological sites dated to this period increased sharply. If we make the reasonable assumption that the number of sites reflects the number of people, this implies a marked increase in population. The increase was a local one, however, because there were nearby areas (for example, the Tallahassee Hills) where there were very few sites and presumably few people. This suggests that the territory of the Woodland peoples of the Apalachicola was socially bounded or circumscribed. Researchers in other portions of the Southeast have suggested that the Late Woodland period was a time of increasing hostility between groups and forced aggregation of populations. Regardless of its causes, the increase in population in the Apalachicola Valley had predictable consequences. It led to changes in subsistence procurement (how the people obtained their food), information processing (particularly, how the people managed interpersonal and intergroup interactions), and social integration (how the people resolved conflict and coordinated the activities of individuals).

The population increase in the Apalachicola Valley undoubtedly would have increased the labor required to obtain needed food (that is, total subsistence costs). Since food resources are limited, the per unit costs of obtaining food (marginal costs) would also have increased. As local food supplies declined with exploitation and increasing social circumscription reduced the size of the territories available to local groups, the effort required to obtain needed food would have increased. Search and transportation costs would have risen as resources became less available near settlements. For example, the more deer that are harvested from a given territory, the harder they are to find, and the greater the effort needed to kill them. There may also have been increased risks of localized shortfalls, although this seems unlikely.[33]

The changes in subsistence procurement costs resulting from increased population densities undoubtedly altered the relative costs of different foods, since the rates at which costs change are not the same for different resources. If the Woodland peoples of the Apalachicola Valley allocated their efforts in a rational manner (by seeking less costly foods), and if the costs of one procurement strategy rose faster than another, labor would have been shifted to the less expensive strategy. As costs rose, and they must have, the Woodland peoples could have responded in two different ways. They could have expanded into new areas, taking with them their existing procurement system (with its mix of strategies), or they could have altered the allocation of effort to different procurement strategies. Expansion is a less radical change, and I expect that it was tried first. In fact, during the Late Woodland Wakulla phase in the Apalachicola Valley, we see maintenance of an earlier procurement strategy coupled with an expansion into previously underutilized habitats.

The increased population density in the Apalachicola Valley would have made it increasingly harder to integrate the various components of the society (individuals, kin groups, communities) and to make and implement informed decisions at a society level (such as the resolution of conflict within the society and interactions with other societies). Eventually, the workload began to tax existing integrative and decision-making institutions, leading in turn to increasing complexity in the decision-making organization of the society. There are two mechanisms for increasing organizational complexity. Horizontal specialization involves an increase in the number of equivalent decision-making units while vertical specialization involves an increase in the number of hierarchical levels of decision-making units. The hierarchies produced by vertical specialization can be temporary (or sequential), in which case the hierarchical units are situational groupings of lower level units (for example, within a single community the units being integrated might be individual people while at the societal level, the units might be communities rather than people). Alternatively, the hierarchy can be permanent (or simultaneous), in which case the higher units are specialized institutions (chiefs and other decision-makers).[34]

In the Late Woodland period in the Apalachicola Valley we can see evidence of horizontal specialization and the formation of sequential (temporary) hierarchies. The number of communities increased, multiplying the number of decision-making entities at that level of the society.[35] The material culture changes that took place during the Late Woodland (that is, the decreasing complexity of ceramic styles and increasing regional homogeneity in ceramic styles) suggest an increase in the strength of linkages among equivalent settlement units. This is the kind of stylistic change that could be expected if there was an increase in the importance of integrative mechanisms involving the elaboration of sequential hierarchies such as clans and sodalities that crosscut residence.[36]

Thus, in the initial response to the stresses of the Woodland period in the Apalachicola Valley, earlier subsistence procurement systems expanded and the egalitarian institutions of social integration and decision making were strengthened. We see the results of these processes in the Wakulla phase. It is evident that this response was not successful. Subsistence costs continued to rise, and relative costs continued to diverge as the intensity of exploitation within the valley stayed high, new areas being exploited proved less productive, and social competition among individuals and groups produced increased demands for surplus production. The effectiveness of tribal mechanisms of social integration decreased in the face of increasing competition within the society, and sequential hierarchies proved ineffective in dealing with external sources of information.

As the costs of maintaining the earlier subsistence procurement strategy increased, as cost disparities among resources increased, and as demand increased, the peoples of the Wakulla phase altered their subsistence system. They shifted resources (labor) to the production of maize. Cleared-field agriculture has high initial costs (for example, field clearance, planting, and cultivation), and at low levels of production it is not as cost efficient as strategies that focus on abundant wild resources. But the costs of cleared-field agriculture increase more slowly than those of strategies based on wild foods, thus making agriculture more amenable to intensification. Increased agricultural yields are also possible without dramatic territorial increases. Eventually, demand and the costs of alternative resources increased to the point where the high initial costs of maize agriculture were no longer a barrier. At that point, land clearance began.

The increased costs of maintaining social integration taxed the tribal institutions of the Wakulla phase. Eventually, the workload involved in maintaining social integration and making decisions threatened to exceed the capabilities of horizontally specialized tribal institutions and ritual. Eventually higher level decision-making offices and social integrators emerged. In a sense, such positions already existed in the form of religious functionaries and lineage and community headmen. As they exist in tribal societies, these offices have limited abilities to make and carry out decisions and to integrate large numbers of people. The scope of their authority is limited to certain aspects of community life or to certain geographical or demographic subunits of the society, or they are handicapped by the lack of formal authority associated with their office.

The mechanisms by which formal, permanent political offices appeared in the Woodland societies of the Southeast is unclear, but appear they did. With their appearance, the essential infrastructural and structural features of what we know as the Mississippian chiefdoms were in place. Perhaps the scope of authority of existing religious functionaries was expanded to include secular areas of responsibility. More likely, existing kin group leaders or bigmen were able to expand the scope of their authority and establish distinctions in status and associated decision-making powers that lasted beyond the tenure of a single individual. If lineages or other local kin groupings controlled the means of production through control of agricultural fields, and competitive feasting and other social uses of food surpluses provided an avenue for the acquisition of political authority and decision-making office, then differences in productive capacities could have produced permanent differences in status among lineages and clans. Furthermore, if clans and other kin groupings had particular ritual roles and consequent, albeit situational, differences in status and authority, sanctification of status differentiation and political office and the addition of ideological power to the emerging chiefly office would have been likely.[37]

Gregory Johnson has argued that once simultaneous hierarchies with their permanent decision-making positions emerge, ascriptive status differentiation and hereditary offices are a logical if not inevitable result.[38] In kin-based societies, inheritance of political office solves some problems that might otherwise affect a chief's ability to make decisions. It reduces problems associated with the recruitment of new leaders, because there is an existing pool of recognized candidates among the relatives of the incumbent. It lessens problems associated with the training of new leaders, since candidates for office can observe leaders in action and learn necessary skills from an early age. It lessens problems associated with transitions from one chief to another by reducing the number of competitors for the office. It also reduces the likelihood that competition among candidates would involve large segments of the society by confining such competition to a single kin group. Ascriptive status differentiation, particularly if it links rulers to the supernatural world, also increases a ruler's ability to carry out decisions once they are made.

The emergence of the Lake Jackson phase followed the appearance of simple chiefdoms in the Apalachicola Valley. New people moved into the Apalachee territory in the Tallahassee Hills. The Woodland population of the area was small compared with the Apalachicola Valley, and it seems unlikely that they could have supported the in situ development of the

Lake Jackson phase. Instead, what seems to have happened is that one of the riverine chiefdoms in the Apalachicola or Chattahoochee Valley segmented, and part of the population moved to the Tallahassee Hills.[39]

Areas peripheral to the Apalachicola Valley that were intensively used by the Wakulla phase were abandoned by the Cayson phase peoples. This would have effectively raised the population density of the valley. This in turn would have increased the costs of social integration. Segmentation into two roughly equivalent political units is one solution to the political problems caused by population increase, and it appears to be a not uncommon phenomenon in chiefly societies. If there is more than one potential claimant to high office, if territory is available, and if there are followers for both claimants, then fissioning is feasible. Archaeological data (in the form of stylistic relationships of ceramic assemblages) suggest that the Lake Jackson phase was closely linked to the Apalachicola Valley chiefdom. Since the Apalachicola Valley was not abandoned, we can assume that the polity fissioned. The material culture of the Lake Jackson phase and the Cayson and Sneads phases of the Apalachicola Valley are very similar, but there was an uninhabited buffer zone between them, suggesting that they did not constitute a single system.[40]

The Apalachee chiefdom continued to evolve after it became established in the Tallahassee Hills. Change occurred in the Apalachee ceramic assemblage and in high status goods found with elite burials.[41] Population appears to have increased during the prehistoric period, followed by population loss and relocation in the post-Contact period. Centers were abandoned. Coupled with a general fluidity in settlement location there was a decided shift southward in the seventeenth century. Archaeological data also suggest that there may have been changes in the sizes of communities in the seventeenth century. Finally, there were political changes. The chiefdom went through periods of gradual change and it experienced periods of rapid and dramatic change. During the life of the Lake Jackson phase, there seems to have been a gradual increase in the centralization of political authority. This was followed by the abandonment of political centers and political decentralization in the Velda phase. At the end of the Velda phase, the Apalachee lost their independence.[42]

These changes were the products of internal structural conflicts, of personal actions and desires, and external influences. There was not a single, simple cause for political change, nor was there a single, simple process of political change.

The Lake Jackson phase appears to have been a time of significant population growth. Such growth would have produced the same stresses that it did earlier in the Apalachicola Valley. It would have led to increased information, integrative workloads, and organizational and managerial stress. It would have taxed the abilities of the Lake Jackson phase chiefs to maintain their positions and political unity.

Perhaps the most important result of these forces was the transformation of the political structure of the early Lake Jackson–phase chiefdom. Unlike the earlier Apalachicola Valley chiefdom, the Lake Jackson–phase polity did not segment. Instead, it underwent further vertical specialization within its political hierarchy leading to the formation of two distinct tiers of decision-making offices. This involved two processes, the multiplication of local chiefs (horizontal specialization) and the separation of the paramount chief from the local chiefs (vertical specialization). Unfortunately, the sequence and mechanisms by which these processes occurred are not known.

The differences in the evolutionary trajectories followed by the Apalachicola Valley chiefdoms and the Lake Jackson phase chiefdom were profound and affected the later evolution of both systems. Three major factors produced these differences. First, there does not appear to have been suitable vacant land around the Lake Jackson phase, lessening the opportunities for fissioning. Second, the Lake Jackson phase territory was much more productive than the Apalachicola Valley and was capable of supporting larger populations and producing larger surpluses. Third, the geographic structure of the Lake Jackson phase was unlike that of the Apalachicola Valley chiefdoms. The latter were linear systems, constrained by the distribution of alluvial soils in the valley. This limited the amount of productive land near any single settlement and the chief's ability to extract surpluses from the local support base. It also increased the distances between a chief and at least some subordinates. This would have made it harder for the chief to monitor potential rivals and thus would have made secession easier. The Lake Jackson phase was a spatially compact system. This served to concentrate productive soils, population, and potential rivals closer to the chief and reduce the ability of subordinates to successfully secede.

We can see archaeological evidence of political change in the Lake Jackson phase chiefdom at the Lake Jackson site itself. Burials from Mound 3 at the Lake Jackson site show evidence of change in the prestige goods buried with the high-status individuals found there.[43] The range and nature of the accompaniments suggest that the people buried in Mound 3 had very high social status and may have been the rulers of the Lake Jackson polity. Three trends can be seen in the burial accompaniments: the more recent burials contained more copper objects than the earlier burials, the more recent burials contained objects not found in earlier burials (copper celts, engraved shell, copper headdress ornaments), and the more recent burials contain both celts and copper plates while these artifacts had complementary distributions in the earlier burials. The increasing concentration of exotic status symbols in the more recent burials suggests that there was an increase in the chief's ability to acquire and retain exotic (and therefore valuable) materials, that there was inflation in the absolute value of exotica, and that there was a concentration of status in the person of the chief, assuming that we are correct in tying these symbols to authority. The association of copper plates and celts may reflect a consolidation of offices in the person of the paramount chief. In other Mississippian chiefdoms these artifacts appear to have been tied to different offices, and they may have been tied to different cult institutions.[44]

The transition from the Lake Jackson phase to the Velda phase was marked by major changes in material culture, settlement, and political structure. The material culture changes were perhaps the most dramatic that took place during the life of the Apalachee chiefdom. Changes occurred in vessel form, decorative techniques, and decorative motifs. The ceramic changes show new or markedly strengthened links to the chiefdoms of the Georgia Piedmont, while many features that evidenced links to chiefdoms to the west disappeared. The paramount center at Lake Jackson was abandoned, and so too was the minor center at the Velda site. The capital moved to Anhaica. The mounds of Lake Jackson were abandoned, and we have no evidence that new mounds took their place at Anhaica. These changes may reflect a change in the ruling line, perhaps with new symbols of chiefly authority, perhaps with a diminution of the sacra associated with the old line, and perhaps with new external links.[45]

The transition did not involve a loss of complexity, however. The Velda-phase polity was a complex chiefdom, as the Lake Jackson phase had been. The transition appears to have been more a rebellion than a revolution.

During the Velda phase the Apalachee chiefdom continued to change. We can assume that there was at least some demographic stress following the intrusions of Narváez and de Soto, with attendant settlement shifts and population declines in the sixteenth century.[46] There were further material culture changes (for example, an increase in the frequency of Lamar Complicated Stamped pottery) that reflect increasing interaction with the chiefdoms of the Georgia Piedmont. There were probably changes in the Apalachee world view resulting from the initial contact with Europeans and the failures of the visitors to support the elite. The failure of the elite to defeat the intruders or to counter the subsequent epidemics of European diseases, together with an increasing geographic separation of paramount and subordinate chiefs, would have provided the seeds of political change, the political change that led to the San Luis phase.

The transition from the Velda phase to the San Luis phase was less apparent in the archaeological record than the earlier change from the Lake Jackson phase to the Velda phase, but it was much more dramatic in a political and cultural sense. There was political change that featured significant decentralization of power and ultimately a loss of independence. There were changes in settlement patterns associated with the establishment of missions and a *presidio*.

The political change began with competition among the Apalachee elite for political power and position that led some to request the presence of missionaries in the province. Most likely, this reflects the effort of one political faction to gain external allies for internal political maneuverings. Similar native political strategies among the Calusa led them to invite the

Jesuits to send missionaries in the sixteenth century.[47] The Spaniards did not immediately send the requested friars, citing an inability of the Apalachee chiefs to control those opposed to the missionaries.[48] Probably, the people they were unable to control were their rivals among the elite, not their subjects. Perhaps the sacred status of the reigning faction had weakened, causing it to look for new sources of legitimation, and opening the door for rivals.

The political change resulted in the establishment of a chain of missions, rejection of much of the native belief system, imposition of Spanish military and secular authority, subordination of the chiefly elite, and a loss of independence. The Apalachee went from being a powerful independent chiefdom to being a quasi-feudal province under the authority of the King's governor.

Associated with these political changes were changes in settlement patterns, religion, and economics. The Spaniards built a *presidio* at San Luis and caused the capital of the province to move there. They built *doctrinas* and established *visitas*. These may have been at the sites of Apalachee communities, but the numbers of people living at these sites appear to have increased. Many of the Apalachee continued to live in individual homesteads, but there was increasing nucleation around the Spanish centers, which is reflected in the general shift of sites toward the south, nearer the missions, and a general increase in the mean size of sites. The conversion of the Apalachee (at least nominally) to Catholicism signaled their entrance into the European world system and the western economy. By the second half of the seventeenth century, a money economy was established in Apalachee.

Despite the many changes it underwent during its lifetime, the Apalachee chiefdom was quite stable compared with other Mississippian chiefdoms. This stability can be seen in political organization, subsistence economy, and polity boundaries. We see no evidence of the dramatic collapses that can be seen in other parts of the Southeast. The Apalachee polity was a complex chiefdom at least by the end of the thirteenth century and it retained the organizational structure of a complex chiefdom through the end of the seventeenth century.[49] During that span, it survived dramatic transitions. At the end of the Lake Jackson phase, it survived the political disruption associated with the abandonment of the Lake Jackson center. During the Velda phase it survived the Narváez and de Soto entradas and the shocks associated with them. It survived the loss of independence that came with the imposition of Spanish political, military, and religious authority at the beginning of the San Luis phase.

The bases of this stability lay in the legitimation of chiefly authority and status and in the political and natural geography of Apalachee province. Ideological legitimation of chiefly authority and status lent supernatural authority to the ruling chief and provided a source of ideological power. It also sanctified the existing social order and status differentiation and the positions of the elite. The geography of Apalachee province allowed the paramount chief to monitor subordinate chiefs, control potential rivals, and play a major role in the regional elite networks.

We know that the Apalachee elite used ideological manipulation to strengthen their positions both in the society as a whole and within the elite segment of the society. The Mississippian warfare/cosmogony cult was very important in Lake Jackson–phase political and religious life. This is evident from the elite burials in Mound 3. The assemblage of sacra recovered from the mound is one of the largest ever found in the Southeast. The exotic raw materials and manufactured items that comprise this assemblage were obtained through ties linking the Apalachee elite (or at least the paramount) to the elite of other Mississippian polities. Judging from similar exchange systems that operated in sixteenth-century Panama, those links could be controlled by the paramount. To the extent that these symbols were used to bolster claims to authority and office, control of the symbols would have been equivalent to control of the lesser elite who needed them.[50]

We also know that the Apalachee elite had important religious roles. In the ball game, which was very important to the Apalachee, they had to perform certain rituals in order to insure success in the game.

Ideological manipulation was the first foundation of Apalachee political stability. It was an important source of legitimacy for rulers, as ideological power can be as potent as economic or physical power in a chiefly society.[51] Ideological manipulation, however, cannot have been the sole basis for the long-term stability of the Apalachee chiefdom. Other Mississippian chiefdoms shared cult institutions with the Apalachee, and presumably their rulers were capable of manipulating ideology, as were the Apalachee chiefs. Furthermore, ideological manipulation was not the exclusive tool of paramount chiefs and their rightful heirs. Aspiring nobles outside the royal family or even ambitious commoners can use ideology to justify usurpation. What made the Apalachee different from other Mississippian chiefdoms was not the ideological basis for the Apalachee political order, it was the Apalachee territory.

The Apalachee territory was the second and more important basis of political stability. It was very productive and supported both a large total population and high population densities. It yielded substantial agricultural surpluses in historic times, and we can assume that it yielded similar surpluses in prehistoric times as well. Access to marine shell, both from the nearby coast and from other native polities in south Florida allowed the Apalachee elite to trade for exotic status symbols and sacra with the elite of other systems. Possession of these symbols would have increased the status of the highest Apalachee elite. This in turn would have given them greater command of local surpluses. Their control of surplus would have allowed them to increase the production of locally manufactured status goods. With more local status goods (for example, shell beads) they would have been able to obtain more exotic goods. This would have increased status differ-

entiation within Apalachee society. To the extent that the paramount chief
controlled local surpluses and status goods and the supply of exotic status
goods, it would also have increased status differentiation among the elite
of Apalachee society.

A productive environment was an important source of political and economic power, but the Apalachee were not alone in having a productive environment. Other Mississippian chiefdoms occupied productive environments and had high population densities. The key feature of the Apalachee
environment was its spatial structure. The Apalachee polity was a spatially
compact system. This allowed the concentration of population and productive capability near the elite centers (and the ruling elite). The resulting
lack of geographic separation between the paramount chief and the subordinate elite concentrated military strength and increased internal control
and external security. It allowed the paramount to monitor subordinates.
It allowed greater rates of tribute extraction. All these things increased the
security of the paramount and lessened the ability of subordinates to rebel.

Control of exotic materials, together with spatial proximity, allowed
the paramount to influence the strategies of subordinate elite. Elites, including subordinate elites, work to maintain or increase their status and
political authority and power. To accomplish this, subordinates can follow two different strategies. They can follow a development strategy by
retaining tribute extracted from areas under their control, establish a local
power base, establish alliances with other elite, and form their own political faction. If successful, they can aspire to the position of paramount.
Alternatively, they can follow a dependency strategy by currying favor with
the paramount, supporting the established authority in internal disputes
and external conflicts, and relying on that authority to bolster their own
status and position.[52] I believe that for much of its history, the Apalachee
elite followed this latter strategy.

The arrival of European explorers, colonists, and diseases disrupted this
pattern. The impacts of the sixteenth-century entradas upon the political
and social fabric of the Apalachee weakened the control of the established
authorities. This, then, allowed lesser elite to pursue development strategies and to advance their own causes. They sought external support and
were, for a time, successful. The most successful of the Apalachee elite of
the 1600s were those most distant from the capital at Anhaica. By the end
of the seventeenth century, the greatest of the Apalachee chiefs came not
from the capital at San Luis, but from Ivitachuco, the easternmost mission
village.[53]

The Apalachee chiefdom was one of the important native societies in
the sixteenth-century Southeast. It was both militarily and economically
powerful. Its reputation extended for hundreds of miles beyond its own
boundaries. To the Spaniards who first entered the Southeast in the sixteenth century, the Apalachee chiefdom was a place where they hoped to
find riches, or at least food to sustain themselves. It proved to be a for-

midable obstacle to the two expeditions that entered its territory. To the Spanish colonists and missionaries of the seventeenth century, the Apalachee polity was a fertile ground for converts. It was a breadbasket capable of supplying St. Augustine with food and other supplies. It was a source of labor. It was also a bulwark against the potentially hostile native groups in the interior and the definitely hostile English colonists.

To contemporary scholars, the Apalachee chiefdom is still important, although the Apalachee themselves are no more. Through study of the Apalachee, we can examine the emergence and evolution of a Mississippian chiefdom with a thoroughness that can be duplicated for few other systems. The combination of archaeological data and sixteenth- and seventeenth-century documents make possible a detailed picture of the Apalachee chiefdom. They also allow us to examine the interaction of European and native cultures from initial contact, before the massive changes of the sixteenth century, through the seventeenth century, when the Apalachee were converted to Catholicism and incorporated into the Spanish colonial system.

The Apalachee chiefdom was a product of demographic and social forces that operated within and among the earlier Woodland societies of northwestern Florida. The emergence of an agricultural subsistence economy, permanent political hierarchies, and institutionalized social inequality were linked, and together they shaped the Apalachee polity. The subsequent political evolution of the Apalachee was driven by internal structural conflicts, the political geography of the polity, and interactions (military, economic, social, and political) with other societies. With the coming of Europeans in the sixteenth century, the world of the Apalachee changed and so probably did the Apalachee world view. The Europeans introduced new complications and forces into the world of the Apalachee. The Apalachee sought to use those complications and forces for their own social and political ends. Together the Europeans and the Apalachee wrought dramatic changes in the Apalachee chiefdom.[54]

NOTES

1. Two excellent overviews of the native peoples of the Southeast are the classic Swanton, *Indians of the Southeastern United States,* and the more recent Hudson, *Southeastern Indians.*

A discussion of these paramount chiefdoms focusing on the sixteenth-century Coosa polity can be found in Hudson, Smith, Hally, Polhemus, and DePratter, "Coosa."

2. Knight, "Mississippian Religion," 685. This article presents an encapsulated description of Mississippian religious institutions derived from Knight's dissertation research.

3. There are several definitions of Mississippian in widespread use today. They differ in emphasis, and there is not a perfect overlap in the societies that they subsume. For the most part, however, the late prehistoric societies of the interior

Southeast were Mississippian by all of the definitions. Perhaps the most widely cited definitions are found in J. B. Griffin, "Changing Concepts," 63; Peebles and Kus, "Archaeological Correlates," 435; and Smith, "Mississippian Patterns," 64–67. For the Calusa see Marquardt, "Calusa Social Formation," and Widmer, *Evolution of the Calusa*. For the Timucua, see Deagan, "Cultures in Transition," and Milanich, "The Western Timucua."

4. Specific discussions of the economic status and role of Apalachee Province in the seventeenth century are to be found in Hann, *Apalachee*, 126–59; and Matter, "Seventeenth-Century Florida Missions."

5. The ultimate demise of the Apalachee has received considerable attention from historians. Among the works focusing on the destruction of the Apalachee people are Boyd, "Fort San Luis"; Bushnell, "Patricio de Hinachuba"; Covington, "Apalachee Indians Move West" and "Apalachee Indians," 366–84; and Hann, *Apalachee*.

6. The details of the archeology of the Apalachee and their evolution may be found in Scarry, "Fort Walton Development"; John F. Scarry, "Stability and Change in the Apalachee Chiefdom: Centralization, Decentralization and Social Reproduction," typescript, Florida Bureau of Archaeological Research, 1988; John F. Scarry, "A Provisional Chronological Sequence for Apalachee Province," typescript, Florida Bureau of Archaeological Research, 1989; J. F. Scarry, "Mississippian Emergence," 1123–238; and J. F. Scarry, "Fall of Apalachee."

The sixteenth-century accounts of the Apalachee are derived from the accounts of the expeditions headed by Pánfilo de Narváez and Hernando de Soto. For the Narváez expedition, see de Vaca, *Journey;* and John H. Hann, "Translation of the Florida Section of the Alvar Núñez Cabeza de Vaca" (typescript, Florida Bureau of Archaeological Research, 1988). For the de Soto expedition, see Vega, *The Florida of the Inca*, 175–263; John H. Hann, "Translation of Luys Hernández de Biedma's Report of the Outcome of the Journey that Hernando de Soto Made and of the Characteristics of the Land through which He Traveled," typescript, Florida Bureau of Archaeological Research, 1988; John H. Hann, "Translation of the Fidalgo de Elvas's Relation of the de Soto Expedition," typescript, Florida Bureau of Archaeological Research, 1988; John H. Hann, "Translation of The Florida of the Inca: History of the Adelantado, Hernando de Soto, Governor and Capitán General of the Kingdom of Florida," typescript, Florida Bureau of Archaeological Research, 1988; John H. Hann, "Translation of the Narrative about the de Soto Expedition Written by Gonzalo Fernández de Oviedo and Based on the Diary of Rodrigo Ranjel, de Soto's Private Secretary," typescript, Florida Bureau of Archaeological Research, 1988; and R. Ranjel, "A Narrative of de Soto's Expedition."

The record from the seventeenth century is quite rich and it continues to grow as more documents are translated. Among the more significant translations of seventeenth-century documents relating to the Apalachee are those found in Boyd, "Fort San Luis"; Calderón, *A 17th Century Letter;* Hann, "Governor Rebolledo's 1657 Visitation," and *Apalachee*, 328–53.

7. Hann, "Biedma's Report," "Elvas' Relation," "Florida of the Inca," "Translation of the Florida Section," and "Narrative about the de Soto Expedition." I have relied on Hann's translations rather than the more commonly used translations of Buckingham Smith, John and Jeannette Varner, and Fanny Bandelier because Hann has avoided paraphrasing and attempting to infer what the chroniclers intended to say.

8. See Henige, "Context, Content," for an analysis of the reliability of Garcilaso's account.

9. See, for example, Boyd, "Fort San Luis"; Bushnell, "That Demonic Game" and "Patricio de Hinachuba"; Hann, *Apalachee;* and Pearson, "Spanish-Indian Relations." These are not the only excellent sources of data on the seventeenth-century Apalachee, but they provide a good overall picture. In particular, John Hann's volume provides a comprehensive view of the Apalachee during the Mission period.

10. See J. F. Scarry, "Stability and Change in the Apalachee Chiefdom" and "Fall of Apalachee," 179–85, for analyses of the political changes in the Apalachee chiefdom during the late prehistoric period. See M. F. Smith and Scarry, "Apalachee Settlement Distribution," 359–62, and Marion F. Smith, Jr., and John F. Scarry, "A Disquieting Synthesis of Apalachee Fort Walton: Micro-scales for Mississippian Research" (Paper presented at the Fifty-fourth Annual Meeting of the Society for American Archaeology, Atlanta, Ga., 1989) for discussions of demographic changes.

11. Karl T. Steinen, "Ochlockonee River Weeden Island Project" (typescript, Department of Sociology and Anthropology, West Georgia College, 1988), 59.

12. Scarry, *Fort Walton Development,* 357, 382, 388.

13. Hann, *Apalachee,* 131; Claudine Payne, "Farmsteads and Districts: A Model of Fort Walton Settlement Patterns in the Tallahassee Hills" (Paper presented at the Thirty-ninth Annual Southeastern Archaeological Conference, Memphis, Tenn., 1982).

14. de la Vega, *Florida of the Inca,* 182. Calderón, *A 17th Century Letter,* 127; Hann, *Apalachee,* 127.

15. Michelle M. Alexander, "Paleoethnobotany of the Fort Walton Indians: High Ridge, Velda, and Lake Jackson Sites" (M.A. thesis, Florida State University, 1984), 116–21; C. Margaret Scarry, "A Descriptive Report on Plant Remains from the Mission Sites 8Jel and 8Je2," typescript, Florida Bureau of Archaeological Research, 1986, "Preliminary Examination of Plant Remains," 252, "Plant Remains from the San Luis Mission Church," and "Plant Production and Procurement," 289–91.

16. Calderón, *Letter,* 127.

17. Bushnell, "Demonic Game," 13, and Hann, *Apalachee,* 77.

18. Knight, "Hierarchy in Southeastern Chiefdoms," 16; J. F. Scarry, "Fall of Apalachee," 185; and Scarry, "Native Lords of Apalachee," 173–74.

19. Hann, *Apalachee,* 106, 401, 404, and J. F. Scarry, "Native Lords of Apalachee," 167–72.

20. Hann, *Apalachee,* 260, 79.

21. Ibid., 104; Knight, "Hierarchy in Southeastern Chiefdoms"; and Scarry, "Native Lords of Apalachee," 170–71.

22. Stephen C. Bryne, "Apalachee Settlement Patterns" (M.A. thesis, Florida State University, 1986), 114–17; Payne, "Farmsteads and Districts"; M. F. Smith and Scarry, "Apalachee Settlement Distribution," 360; and M. F. Smith and Scarry, "Apalachee Fort Walton."

23. An overall description of the Fort Walton Mississippian societies, which includes the Apalachee, can be found in Scarry, "Fort Walton Development." More narrowly focussed descriptions of prehistoric and protohistoric Apalachee society can be found in Scarry, "Stability and Change" Scarry, "Mississippian Emergence";

Scarry, "Rise, Transformation, and Fall of Apalachee," 178–85; and Scarry, "Native Lords of Apalachee," 164–79.

24. Much of the following discussion is drawn from Knight, "Hierarchy in Southeastern Chiefdoms." In addition to his fascinating and provocative discussion of general aspects of the social organization of Mississippian societies, Knight presents an excellent analysis of Apalachee social organization.

25. Hann, *Apalachee*, 107.

26. Knight, "Mississippian Religion," 677–82.

27. Jones, "Southern Cult Manifestations," 12–20.

28. Gary Shapiro, "Rivers as Centers, Rivers as Boundaries: Florida Variations on a Mississippian Theme" (Paper presented at the Fifty-first Annual Meeting of the Society for American Archaeology, New Orleans, La., 1986).

29. These phases were originally defined in Scarry, "Fort Walton Development," 379–99. A more recent discussion of the phases and the chronological framework of Apalachee prehistory is contained in Scarry, "Chronological Sequence for Apalachee Province." Claudine Payne has recently revised the Apalachee chronology, see Payne, "Structure and Development at the Lake Jackson Site" (Paper presented at the Forty-eighth Annual Southeastern Archaeological Conference, Jackson, Miss., 1991).

30. Payne, "Lake Jackson Site." The Apalachee ceramic complex is discussed in detail in Scarry, "Fort Walton Ceramic Typology."

31. Jones, "Southern Cult Manifestations," 10–19; J. F. Scarry, "Native Lords of Apalachee"; and "Mound 3 and the Political Structure of the Lake Jackson Chiefdom" (Paper presented at the Forty-eighth Annual Southeastern Archaeological Conference, Jackson, Miss., 1991).

32. J. F. Scarry, "Mississippian Emergence." Knight has recently proposed an elegant alternative to this model that incorporates a mechanism for the introduction of people into the Late Woodland groups of the Tallahassee Hills, the emergence of political complexity, and the construction of monumental earthen mounds. See Vernon J. Knight, Jr., "Lake Jackson, and Speculations on a Demographic Paradox" (Paper presented at the Forty-eighth Annual Southeastern Archaeological Conference, Jackson, Miss., 1991).

33. See Earle, "Model of Subsistence Change," 25–26, for a detailed presentation of arguments relating procurement costs to subsistence change. See C. M. Scarry, "Change in Plant Procurement," 113–30, and "Agricultural Risk," for discussions of risk in subsistence procurement in the late prehistoric Southeast.

34. Much of my thinking concerning the role of information processing in the evolution of the Apalachee chiefdom is based on a model presented by Gregory Johnson. See Johnson, "Decision-making Organizations." For a discussion of the distinctions between sequential and simultaneous hierarchies and how they relate to social structure in human societies, see G. Johnson, "Organizational Structure."

35. See N. M. White, *Archaeological Survey at Lake Seminole.*

36. The arguments relating material culture change and the strengthening of such social linkages can be found in Braun and Plog, " 'Tribal' Social Networks."

37. See C. M. Scarry, "Agricultural Risk," for a discussion of the possible impact of competition among individuals on subsistence and political evolution in the Southeast.

38. G. Johnson, "Decision-making Organization," 101.

39. For discussions of the Woodland population of the Tallahassee Hills area, see J. F. Scarry, "Mississippian Emergence," 234–35, and Tesar, *Leon County,* 597–606.

40. James Knight has recently proposed an alternative mechanism for the emergence of the Lake Jackson chiefdom that appeals to social mechanisms of kinship, marriage, and alliance and provides an explanation for how people from the Apalachicola Valley could move to the Tallahassee Hills and how the movement of relatively few people could have triggered the emergence of the Lake Jackson chiefdom. See Knight, "Lake Jackson."

41. See J. F. Scarry, "Fort Walton Ceramic Typology," 207–31, for a discussion of the changes in the Apalachee ceramics, and Scarry, "Fall of Apalachee," 181, for a discussion of the changes in high status goods.

42. M. F. Smith and Scarry, "Apalachee Settlement Distribution" and "Apalachee Fort Walton."

43. Jones, "Southern Cult Manifestations," 37–40; B. Calvin Jones, "High Status Burials in Mound 3 at Florida's Lake Jackson Complex: Stability and Change in Fort Walton Culture" (Paper presented at the Forty-eighth Annual Southeastern Archaeological Conference, Jackson, Miss., 1991); J. F. Scarry, "Fall of Apalachee," 181–83.

44. Brown, "Dimensions of Status," 101; Peebles, "Moundville and Surrounding Sites," 85–87.

45. J. F. Scarry, "Fort Walton Ceramic Typology," "Apalachee Chiefdom," and "Fall of Apalachee," 179–85.

46. M. F. Smith and Scarry, "Apalachee Settlement Distribution," and "Apalachee Fort Walton."

47. Marotti, "Juan Baptista de Segura," 273–74.

48. Hann, *Apalachee,* 12.

49. J. F. Scarry, "Native Lords of Apalachee."

50. See Helms, *Ancient Panama,* 75–92, 172–83.

51. For an extensive treatise on forms of power, including ideological power, see Boulding, *Three Faces of Power.*

52. Paynter, "Surplus Flow," presents a lengthy discussion of dependency and development strategies in the context of eighteenth- and nineteenth-century New England.

53. Bushnell, "Patricio de Hinachuba," 1.

54. For a general discussion of non-European world views and their impact on the initial interactions between Europeans and Native Americans, see Helms, *Ulysses' Sail.* For a discussion of the impact of Europeans on the Apalachee world view, see Marrinan, Scarry, and Majors, "Prelude to De Soto," 78–79.

MARK WILLIAMS

Growth and Decline of the Oconee Province

The Oconee Province, a prehistoric Mississippian polity in the Oconee River valley of northern Georgia, was first recorded in 1981 by Marvin Smith and Stephen Kowalewski. Shortly after that, Charles Hudson, Marvin Smith, and Chester DePratter suggested that the Oconee Province, so designated, could be identified with the towns of Altamaha, Ocute, and Cofaqui as described in the accounts of the expedition of Hernando de Soto, who had visited them in the spring of 1540. Hudson and his colleagues believed that the paramount chief in the area was Ocute and thus rechristened the Oconee Province the Province of Ocute.[1]

I accept that the piedmont portion of the Oconee Valley was the location of these three towns, as well as the presumed location of the unvisited town of the Indian known as Patofa. For reasons outlined elsewhere, I believe, however, that Cofaqui, not Ocute, was the paramount chief in the valley in 1540, and I also believe that the Shoulderbone site (9Hk1) was the location of Cofaqui's center.[2] Without further detailing the specifics here, and in order to separate the ambiguous question of specific site attribution from the archaeological reality of the province, I choose to refer to it in this paper by the more generic phrase *Oconee Province* rather than the *Ocute Province*.

It is clear that in the spring of 1540, all the towns in the Oconee Valley were allied or combined into a single political unit, regardless of which chief was in charge at that time. It is also certain that several known mound centers were occupied at that time and likely did represent some of the towns visited by de Soto, although to date, no specific artifacts from the de Soto expedition have been recovered archaeologically from the Oconee Valley. The purpose of this paper is to discuss the growth, consolidation, and decline of the Oconee Province, particularly as one of the better documented examples of how such chiefdom societies formed in the southeastern United States during the Mississippian period.

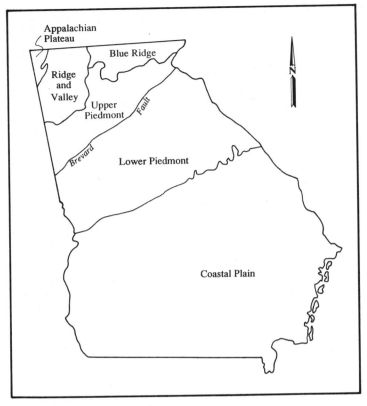

FIGURE I
Georgia's topographic regions

Georgia is divided into four major physiographic/topographic zones: the Blue Ridge mountains in the north, the Piedmont in the north center, the Coastal Plain in the south, and the Ridge and Valley in the northwest. (See figure 1.) The Brevard Fault is a major northeast-southwest trending ridge and valley running through the upper part of the Piedmont. The Oconee River, like the Ocmulgee River and the Flint River, begins on the southeastern slopes of the Brevard Fault and courses some 150 kilometers (95 miles) across the Piedmont to the Fall Line. From there it continues for another 130 kilometers (80 miles) to the southeast where it joins with the Ocmulgee River to become the Altamaha River, which in turn empties into the Atlantic Ocean after another 145 kilometers (90 miles). The portion of the Oconee River forming the Oconee Province, as now defined, is some 95 kilometers (60 miles) in length, beginning several miles below Athens and continuing to just below Milledgeville on the Fall Line. (See figure 2.)

In this section the river basin ranges in width from 55 to 70 kilometers

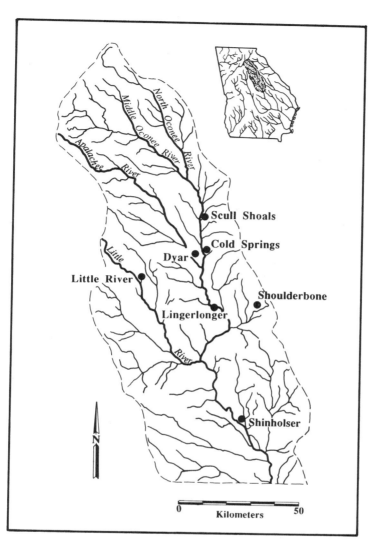

FIGURE 2
The Oconee province

(35 to 45 miles) and is remarkably varied in form. The uplands are moderately steep and well drained. There are hundreds of smaller streams that flow into the Oconee River in this stretch. In some sections, particularly in the south, the river crosses huge granite outcrops and is confined to narrow, shoaly gorges. In other stretches, the river has a wide flood plain and has deposited large amounts of rich sedimentary soil. There are two major expanses of this rich soil in this section of the river. The first, as might be expected, is located immediately south of the Fall Line where the river becomes wider and more sinuous as it enters the relatively flat Coastal Plain. The second area is just northwest of Greensboro in the upper part of the Oconee Province. While both the rich river bottoms and the shoals were used extensively by the Mississippian Indians of the Oconee Province, they were, of course, used differently—the bottoms were used for agriculture and the shoals were used for fishing.[3]

After de Soto, few records of European visits to the Indians of the Piedmont portion of the Oconee Valley are available, although a few may have taken place.[4] The best data we have for the Oconee Valley Indians, from 1540 up to the time they left in about the year 1650, is archaeological. The same is obviously true for the pre–de Soto period. Thus, in order to assess the current state of knowledge about the Oconee Province, a review of the available archaeological data is essential. It should be stated here, however, that much additional archaeological survey is necessary, particularly in the southern part of the Province area. Future work may well change some of the interpretations discussed in this paper.

In the last ten years there have been many archaeological research projects conducted in the Oconee Valley. Almost all these grew out of the massive amount of data derived from the Wallace Reservoir (now Lake Oconee) project conducted by the University of Georgia in the heart of the Oconee Province. The dam and hydroelectric facility for this 17,000-acre lake is located just below the largest shoals in the province in the northeastern corner of Hancock County. The initial archaeological survey projects for this reservoir began in 1973. The excavations of thirty sites began in 1977 and continued until the lake was filled in 1979.[5]

In the years following the completion of the data recovery portion of the Wallace Reservoir project, several reports were written on various aspects of the excavations. Those that involved the Mississippian portion of the sequence included the Dyar site, the Joe Bell site (9Mg28), the Punk Rock Shelter (9Pm211), 9Ge153, 9Ge175, 9Pm220, 9Pm260, and Cold Springs (9Ge10).[6] These excavations provided the data for the initial chronological segmentation of the Mississippian period in the valley.[7] They also provide a strong indication of the diversity of site types during the Mississippian period. Along with the excavation of these sites, a renewed effort was made to survey completely the stripped reservoir area. In this manner, more than eight hundred small to medium sized Mississippian sites were located within the area to be flooded.[8]

While a massive quantity of data relevant to the Mississippian sites in the valley was gathered in the Wallace project, these data were limited to the extent that this area represented only a small fraction of the area presumably included within the Oconee Province. Work outside the Reservoir area is needed, and the lack of data from Lake Sinclair immediately south of Lake Oconee is a very large handicap. This slightly smaller hydroelectric dam and lake were completed in 1951, and virtually no archaeological surveys or excavations were completed before presumably hundreds of Mississippian sites were flooded.

The first project of importance after the Wallace project was that of Daniel Elliott. He established two important points with his survey near Finch's store, north of Greensboro and east of Lake Oconee.[9] First, he showed that the best areas in which to conduct large-area controlled surveys were those areas recently cleared of pine trees by pulp wood companies. These areas range up to one thousand acres and admirably provide samples of sites from specific areas. The second point he made clear was that large numbers of small Mississippian sites are located away from the Oconee River. This was quite surprising, because at the time of his work most local researchers assumed that most of the Mississippian sites would have occurred near the river itself. In the years since Elliott's work, several of these pine tree clear-cut surveys have been conducted.[10] Virtually all of these were volunteer projects that, for simple logistical reasons, had been conducted in the areas north of Lake Oconee near Athens. Collectively, these surveys provide important information on the distribution of sites in the northern portion of the Oconee Province. Unfortunately, we have almost no similar survey data from the central and southern parts of the province, while data from the north is quite uneven in extent.

The next major project, conducted by the LAMAR Institute, consisted of fieldwork on the Mississippian period mound centers in the province. As stated earlier, at the time of the Smith and Kowalewski formulation, the Dyar site was the only one of the six mound centers discussed that had received any excavations. Mark Williams led excavations at the Scull Shoals site in 1983 and 1985; Williams and Gary Shapiro conducted excavations at the Little River site in 1984 and 1987; Williams led excavations at the Shinholser site in 1985 and 1987; Williams supervised research at the Shoulderbone site in 1986; and Williams and Shapiro conducted test excavations at the Lingerlonger site in 1986.[11] All these excavations have led to substantial changes in our understanding of the Oconee Province.[12] (For example, the Lingerlonger site [9Ge35] was found to be not a Mississippian site, but a Woodland site.)

James Hatch of Pennsylvania State University joined the Oconee Valley research effort in 1987. Since that time he has conducted total excavations of three small late-Mississippian period homesteads in the north-central part of the province. His work at these homesteads has greatly amplified our understanding of these small homestead sites within the Oconee Province.[13]

Besides the above data, some useful information has come from Cultural Resource Management surveys and excavations at various parts of the province. These include several surveys in the Oconee National Forest, again in the northern and central parts of the province. Also of some importance are the excavations of Dennis Blanton. He conducted excavations on a small village or homestead of the late sixteenth century in southern Hancock County, somewhat into the lower portion of the province as defined.[14]

It should be clear from this brief discussion that the data from the Oconee Province are decidedly uneven in distribution. We have little or no survey data from the south, and the number of excavated sites there is only a small fraction of those in the north. Obviously, more work in the south is necessary before we can develop a complete picture of the Oconee Province.

The Oconee Province did not exist in a cultural vacuum. As did all Mississippian chiefdoms, it had active and complex social and political relationships with other chiefdoms, at both the local and the paramount levels. Further, the relative political and military strengths and weaknesses of these other chiefdoms varied a great deal from the beginning to the end of the Mississippian period. While it is not possible here to completely review the other Mississippian chiefdoms that the Oconee people may have interacted with from beginning to end, a few must be mentioned. (See figure 3.)

The first of these were the Indians who lived in the Savannah Valley just to the east of the Oconee Valley. These people built several mound centers in that valley, but all were abandoned by A.D. 1450. The fate of the Savannah Valley Indians is not completely certain, but many likely moved west into the Oconee Valley. Some may even have moved east into the central South Carolina chiefdom on the Wateree River, but this is less clear.[15]

To the immediate southwest of the Oconee Province was a cluster of mound centers and sites on the Ocmulgee River, at and just below the Fall Line.[16] This has been identified with the Province of Ichisi of the de Soto chroniclers.[17] The relations with this smaller chiefdom are poorly understood, although in 1540 it may well have been subordinate to the much larger Oconee Province.

To the west of the Ocmulgee River was the Toa chiefdom on the Flint River, also at and just below the Fall Line. While the existence of this chiefdom would have been known to the Oconee chiefs, their relations with

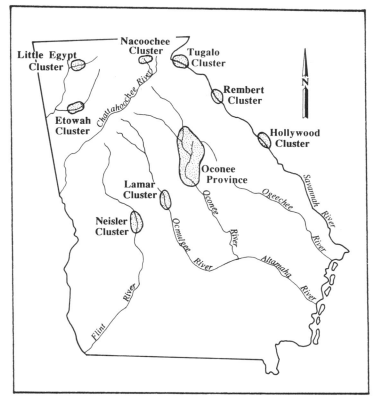

FIGURE 3
The Oconee province and its neighbors

them were probably more indirect than with the Ichisi chiefdom on the Ocmulgee River.[18]

To the northwest, there appear to have been no chiefdoms near the Oconee Valley for most of the Mississippian period. The Chattahoochee Valley in that area has very little flood plain soil and never was a Mississippian core area. Beyond it, however, the powerful chiefdom of Coosa was present in 1540.[19] At earlier times the Etowah site, also located northwest of the Chattahoochee River, represented an obviously powerful if somewhat distant neighbor to the Oconee people.

To the north, a small chiefdom centered on the Nacoochee site near the headwaters of the Chattahoochee; it was a minor neighbor of the Oconee Province. This small group has not been studied recently and deserves more study before we can even speculate about any potential political alliances they may have had with the Oconee or other groups.[20]

Finally, there was a small, but persistent, chiefdom near the headwaters of the Savannah River, just below where it (as the Chattooga River) cuts at right angles through the Brevard Fault. The rapid drop of the river in this stretch created a local environmental analogue to the Fall Line and provided the types of soils favored by Mississippian farmers. Centered on the Tugalo site (9St1), this small chiefdom must have interacted with the Oconee Province, at least its northern members, and may have been considered a part of the Oconee paramountcy in 1540. Because de Soto did not go near it, however, we do not know what its political affiliations were.[21]

During the Middle Woodland period, at about A.D. 150, the Oconee Valley was well populated. There are at least three mound centers known from that time: Cold Springs, Little River, and Lingerlonger.[22] It is interesting that two of these sites were later reoccupied during the Mississippian period. At least one small site of this period has been excavated in the Oconee Valley—the Cane Island site located in the lower portion of the Wallace Reservoir, near the Lingerlonger site.[23] Corn was probably not an important part of the diet of the people, although a single cupule was located in the Cane Island excavations.

The Late Woodland period presents a very different story, however. During the Wallace Reservoir excavations, archaeologists attempted to define Late Woodland sites by using ceramic types (such as Napier Complicated Stamped) that had been defined by Robert Wauchope as indicative of that period.[24] But it is clear that Napier, while present in some areas in Late Woodland times, is not a significant Late Woodland marker over the whole state. In fact, no single ceramic type or decorative style is characteristic of Late Woodland over all Georgia. In Middle Woodland times, it appears that there was relative similarity in the ceramics over a large area, while in Late Woodland times, several small regional ceramic traditions developed. By Late Mississippian times the ceramics were again relatively similar over a very large area.

Within the area of the Oconee Province, it is now becoming apparent that the predominant ceramic type for the Late Woodland period was not Napier Complicated Stamped, but a simple stamped ware, probably identical to the type Vining Stamped.[25] This type was long misidentified as an Early Woodland ceramic type, and such it may be in some other areas. But for the lower piedmont area in central and east-central Georgia, it is predominantly a Late Woodland ware. The distribution of this ceramic type is just beginning to be recognized, but we do know that it occurs on many small sites and some larger sites, particularly in Morgan and Putnam counties within the Oconee Valley. There are no known mound sites associated with this material. Given the knowledge that corn agriculture was widely adopted elsewhere in the Southeast in the Late Woodland/Early Mississippian period, the following scenario seems quite likely.

The small Vining sites probably represent the remains of homestead-based corn farmers. The larger Vining sites may represent the beginnings of village life, but most of these sites probably will turn out to be reoccupied small homesteads. There is no real evidence of political centralization—that is, there are no mounds. Many, perhaps most, of the Vining sites are in upland settings away from the large floodplains of the Oconee River itself. This upland, perhaps swidden (slash and burn), agriculture is apparently part of a dispersed settlement pattern. As Williams and Shapiro have suggested for a later period, such a pattern is to be found in a system where warfare and raiding is not well developed.[26] Little more can be said about the Oconee Late Woodland patterns until more field research is conducted, however.

By about A.D. 1100 or a little later, the settlement pattern in the Oconee Valley began changing and the ceramics of the valley changed to predominantly complicated stamped wares. The small homesteads associated with the Late Woodland period were abandoned and occupation began to be more associated with the immediate valley of the Oconee River. Nucleation began.

Data on the sequence of the mound centers can now be summarized. The first site of note is Cold Springs (9Ge10) site. As mentioned earlier this had been a mound center during Middle Woodland times and was reoccupied. It was located near the center of the largest area of rich flood plain soil along the entire length of the Piedmont Oconee. This was ideal land for growing corn.

At about A.D. 1200, the Indians apparently moved their village across the river to the Dyar site (9Ge5), which shared the same environmental advantage. This may have been occasioned by a slight change in the river channel, but this is uncertain. For a time, Dyar was the only Mississippian mound center in the valley. This site was abandoned, and two more mound sites were built during the Savannah period, probably around A.D. 1275. (See figure 4.)

One of these, the Scull Shoals site (9Ge4), was only 16 kilometers (10 miles) north of Dyar. It is likely that the inhabitants of the Dyar site may have relocated slightly to the north because of local depletion of firewood, game, and other resources, or because of problems with sanitation or vermin.[27]

The Shinholser site (9B11) was established at the same time, but 90 kilometers (55 miles) to the south of Scull Shoals.[28] This is just below the Fall Line on the Georgia Coastal Plain, where the Oconee River begins to meander within a 5 kilometer- (3 mile-) wide floodplain. The ecological advantages of life along the Fall Line have been outlined by many researchers who have recognized the easy access to forested uplands, ideal farming soils, and the shoals fishery. Shinholser and Scull Shoals were probably independent simple chiefdom centers at that time. They would certainly have been aware of each other and may have fought one another. That

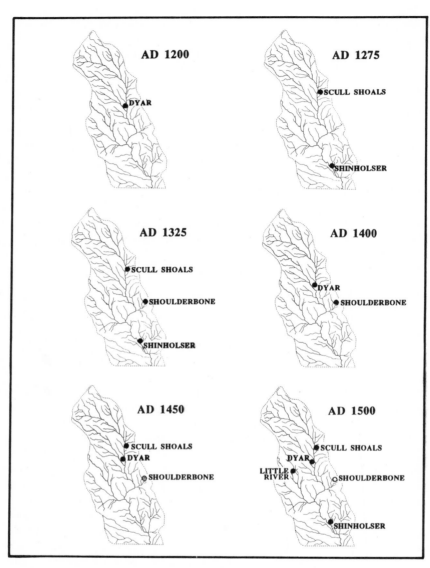

FIGURE 4
The Oconee province, A.D. 1200–1500

FIGURE 5
Medlin copper plate, Shinholser site

the Indians at the Shinholser site participated in Mississippian ceremonial/ religious activities is demonstrated by the discovery of the Medlin copper plate from Mound B there. (See figure 5.)

For the first two centuries of Mississippian life in the valley, the location of mound centers was thus determined with reference to their "ideal" environmental settings. This situation changed dramatically with the founding of the Shoulderbone site around A.D. 1325.[29] Shoulderbone (9Hk1) was situated on an upland ridge adjacent to a small creek, which, itself, was a minor tributary to another creek that eventually flowed west into the Oconee River. The site is about 13 kilometers (8 miles) east of the main river channel and in an area with practically no flood plain soil.

The environmental characteristics traditionally favored by Mississippian peoples across the Southeast, therefore, are not found at Shoulderbone, and an extraenvironmental explanation of its location must be discovered. Besides its unusual environmental setting, there are three more remarkable facts about the site's placement. First, it was placed precisely 47 kilometers (29 miles) equidistant from both Scull Shoals and Shinholser, the other two mound sites occupied when it was settled. Second, it was located on an important historic trail that provided east-west communication outside the valley, and third, it was placed at the Oconee Valley's easternmost edge.[30]

The exact mechanism that led to the equal spacing of Shoulderbone with respect to Scull Shoals and Shinholser is uncertain. Possibilities include the placement of a new chiefdom so as either to avoid conflict with or to maximize access to both Shinholser and Scull Shoals. It seems likely, however, that its eastern Oconee Valley orientation along a trail to the Savannah Valley was related to its interaction, whether in warfare or trade, with the chiefdoms located in that valley.

There is no clear evidence that the three Oconee Valley towns were integrated into a single chiefdom—the Oconee Province—at this period either. The even spacing is, of course, intriguing, but the distance between them is more than a day's travel and return, and they all appear to be of roughly equal size. Shoulderbone might briefly have been the "disembedded capital" of a paramount chiefdom, but this is difficult to test.

The Shoulderbone site was palisaded, showing that there was potential conflict with somebody. Was the conflict with towns within the Oconee Valley or with towns in the Savannah Valley 100 kilometers (60 miles) to the east? If it was the latter, then its effective functional relationship to these Savannah Valley groups was to provide border protection of the bulk of the people in the Oconee Valley.

By A.D. 1400 Shinholser and Scull Shoals were abandoned, Dyar was reoccupied, Shoulderbone was at its pinnacle, and the Lamar period was well under way. (See figure 4.) Because of their close proximity to one another, Dyar and Shoulderbone probably had an amicable relationship. The abandonment of Shinholser and the accompanying peak development of Shoulderbone may imply that there was a movement of the valley population from south to northeast by this time period. It is also quite interesting that just when Shoulderbone was at its peak, the Savannah Valley populations were rapidly disappearing. It is likely that many of the people migrated east and west from the Savannah Valley.

By A.D. 1450, the Shoulderbone site began to be abandoned, following the complete loss of the Savannah Valley population. At the same time, the Scull Shoals site was reoccupied without the abandonment of the Dyar site. (See figure 4.) This was the first time that both Dyar and Scull Shoals were occupied at the same time. These two sites occupy the same core chiefdom territory, and one of the sites was probably a tributary to the other, although which one is unknown.[31]

Also around A.D. 1450, farmsteads, at least in the upper part of the Oconee Province, appear in great numbers along the river channel and reappear in the uplands away from the river. This represents the beginning of a rural expansion that found its extreme expression a century or more later.[32] This rural expansion and the development of an uninhabited buffer zone to the east probably provides the best evidence for potential political integration of all the mound sites in the valley. More survey data from the south is needed to test this rural expansion pattern hypothesis and its implications, however.

By A.D. 1500, Shinholser had been reoccupied, Shoulderbone was barely continuing its existence with a very small population, probably as a chiefly compound, and hundreds of small sites dotted the landscape.[33] (See figure 4.) Also, a new mound center, Little River (9Mg46), was founded at this time. Like Shoulderbone before it, Little River was situated in an unlikely environmental setting, but this time on the western side of the Oconee Valley rather than on its eastern side.

The western orientation of the Little River site likely reflects the abandonment of the Savannah Valley to the east and the development of the paramount chiefdom of Coosa to the northwest. The unusual placement of the Little River site on the western edge of the valley may be related to Coosa's growing power and, therefore, reflect the same settlement process that led, two hundred years earlier, to the settlement of the Shoulderbone site on the eastern side of the valley.[34]

There is no direct archaeological evidence that de Soto ever visited the Oconee Province. Fifteen years of work have yet to locate the first Spanish artifact of the period. On the other hand, he was in the valley for only a short period of time. The elusive cannon he left at Ocute, wherever that was, remains to be located. By A.D. 1550, all the mound centers were beginning to lose their population, and by about A.D. 1580, the mounds were no longer in use.[35] We do know that the Scull Shoals and Shinholser sites still retained small, perhaps tribally organized, populations at that late date.

Even if the de Soto expedition had minimal effects on the Oconee Province, the same cannot be said for the settlement of St. Augustine, Florida, in 1565. The Indians in the interior of the South, the Oconee Province included, probably saw the Spanish there as merely the latest in a long series of major regional power centers, and many of them began to move south along the Oconee River and into Florida.[36]

Disease was not an immediate factor in reducing the populations of the Oconee Valley area. The evidence is clear that, at least for the northern part of the province, the population continued to increase until almost 1600.[37] What did happen after the mid-sixteenth century was a dispersal of much of the valley population away from the now abandoned centers into individual farmsteads in the uplands away from the river. In effect, the process of decentralization (presumably brought about by the chiefdom consolidation and resulting peace within the valley after A.D. 1450) continued after the entire chiefdom collapsed as a political entity and system. This political collapse, represented by the abandonment of the mound centers, is most closely tied to the growth of St. Augustine as a power center.[38]

The Shinholser site has a large component dating to the 1580s a few hundred yards to the south of the then totally abandoned mound area. This

FIGURE 6
Pottery vessels, Joe Bell site

may represent a refugee camp of people moving south. Frankie Snow has located several sites in the lower Oconee River area, near its junction with the Ocmulgee River and well south of the traditional Oconee Province area, that were occupied after the 1580s by people from upstream.[39] John Worth has recently documented ceramics from north-central Florida that were derived from the interior south.[40] Clearly, some of the former residents of the Oconee Province and other areas were moving to Florida and coming under Spanish rule and power. Which survivor groups of the collapsed Oconee Province went to Florida and which stayed home in small farmsteads under a loose, nonchiefdom-based confederation is uncertain. But many did stay, and some did go south toward the Spanish.

Those that stayed in the Oconee Province after the 1580 period continued for the most part to live in individual homesteads. Many of these were clustered around the springheads of small streams, with individual houses some 400 to 500 meters (1300–1600 feet) apart. It is likely that these springhead settlements represented kinship-related settlement clusters. Individual houses were probably not used for more than ten to twenty years, and perhaps less. At least one larger site of the early seventeenth-century upper Oconee Valley has been excavated—the Joe Bell site (9Mg28) in the Wallace Reservoir.[41] The most interesting aspect of this site was a 15 meter (50 feet) diameter, round "council house." This sort of structure became very common later in northern Florida and in the Creek towns in the lower Chattahoochee Valley. The implication for the Oconee Valley is that while a chiefdom structure was likely absent after 1580 in the valley, some lower-order political integration was still present. Some of the varieties of pottery vessels made by the Indians who lived at the Joe Bell site are shown in figure 6.

By 1630, things again changed for these people. Apparently disease finally made inroads into the valley, and the population began to decline rapidly. Indians from farther north and northeast of the Oconee Valley were supplied with arms from the Virginia settlers, and the Indian slave trade began in earnest by 1660 or earlier. It is possible, in fact likely, that some of the late survivors of the Oconee Province were victims of slave raids. Such raids probably provided the final impetus for the remaining survivors to leave for good. They probably joined the exodus of other central Georgia groups to the lower Chattahoochee River, where they were integrated into the growing Creek Confederacy. No specific sites in that area have yet been identified with Oconee Valley ceramics, however. By 1670 at the latest, the year Charleston was founded, the Oconee Province area was completely abandoned. No future permanent Indian settlements were made there as the Georgia colony expanded into the valley by the middle of the eighteenth century. The long history of the Oconee Province was over.

NOTES

The growth and consolidation sections of this paper are slightly modified versions of portions of another paper by the author and the late Gary Shapiro. Without Gary's aid, intellect, and friendship, the data as presented and interpreted here would not have been a reality.

1. M. T. Smith and Kowalewski, "Identification of a Prehistoric Province." Hudson, Smith, and DePratter, "de Soto Expedition: From Apalachee to Chiaha."

2. Williams, "The Hernando de Soto Expedition."

3. Gary Shapiro has carefully documented the varied uses of these two areas and has shown how their relative linear relationships to one another in the Georgia piedmont differs from the adjacent relationship between levees and oxbow-lake farming and fishing areas in the Mississippi Valley. Shapiro, "Site Variability," 1–316, and "Bottomlands and Rapids," 147–62.

4. See John E. Worth, "Late Spanish Military Expeditions in the Interior Southeast, 1597–1628," this volume. Sam Lawson has, in my opinion, built a strong case that at the time of the 1597 visit of the Spaniard Chosas to Tama, it may have been further south in the vicinity of the junction of the Oconee and Ocmulgee rivers; see Lawson, "La Tama."

5. See Chester B. DePratter, "The 1974–75 Archaeological Survey in the Wallace

Reservoir, Greene, Hancock, Morgan, and Putnam Counties, Georgia" (Department of Anthropology, University of Georgia, 1976), 1–393. Mimeographed.

6. See M. T. Smith, "Dyar Site, 9Ge5"; Williams, "Joe Bell Site," 1–574; and *Excavation at 9Pm211*, 1–12; Smith, Hally, and Shapiro, "Ogeltree Site, 9Ge153"; Shapiro, "Site 9Ge175"; Rudolph and Hally, "Site 9Pm220"; Manning, "Archaeological Investigations"; and Fish and Jefferies, "Site Plan at Cold Springs."

7. M. T. Smith, "Dyar Site, 9Ge5."

8. James Rudolph and Dennis Blanton conducted an initial examination of the distribution of these sites; Rudolph and Blanton, "Mississippian Settlement."

9. Elliott, "Finch's Survey."

10. Jennifer A. Freer, "Archaeological Settlement Patterns in Oglethorpe County, Georgia" (M.A. thesis, University of Georgia, 1989); Dennis Blanton, personal communication with the author; Jerald Ledbetter, personal communication with the author; and Stephen Kowalewski, personal communication with the author.

11. Williams, "Scull Shoals Mounds"; Williams, "Scull Shoals Revisited"; Gary Shapiro and Mark Williams, "Archaeological Excavations at the Little River Site" (Paper presented at the Forty-sixth Annual Southeastern Archaeological Conference, Pensacola, Fla., Nov. 10, 1984); Mark Williams and Gary Shapiro, "Shoulderbone was a Fourteenth Century Frontier Town" (Paper presented at the Forty-eighth Annual Southeastern Archaeological Conference, Nashville, Tenn., Nov. 7, 1986); Williams and Shapiro, *Little River;* Williams, *Shinholser Site;* Williams, *Shoulderbone Mounds* and *Lingerlonger Mound.*

12. Mark Williams and Gary Shapiro, "The Changing Contexts of Oconee Valley Political Power" (Paper presented at the Forty-ninth Annual Southeastern Archaeological Conference, Charleston, S.C., Nov. 13, 1987); Williams and Shapiro, *Lamar Archaeology*, 1–263.

13. James W. Hatch, "Upland Lamar Farmsteads in the Ocute Province: The Penn State Archaeological Program in Piedmont Georgia" (Paper presented at the Forty-ninth Annual Southeastern Archaeological Conference, Charleston, S.C., Nov. 14, 1987); James W. Hatch, "Lamar Period Farmsteads in Piedmont Georgia" (Paper presented at the Fifty-fourth Annual Meeting of the Society for American Archaeology, Atlanta, Ga., Apr. 7, 1989); and James W. Hatch, "New Excavations at the Carroll Site" (Paper presented at the meeting of the Northeast Georgia Chapter of the Society for Georgia Archaeology, Athens, Ga., July 23, 1989).

14. Blanton, *Archaeological Data Recovery.*

15. Anderson, Hally, and Rudolph, "Mississippian Occupation."

16. A. R. Kelly, "Archaeological Excavations at Macon"; H. G. Smith, *Lamar Site Materials;* Williams, "Stubbs Mound in Central Georgia Prehistory" (M.A. thesis, Florida State University, 1975); and Mark Williams, Don Evans, and Bruce Dod, "The Bullard Site; Twenty-Four Mounds in the Georgia Swamp" (Paper presented at the Fiftieth Annual Southeastern Archaeological Conference, New Orleans, La., Oct. 22, 1988).

17. Hudson, Smith, and DePratter, "de Soto Expedition: From Apalachee to Chiaha."

18. John E. Worth, "Mississippian Occupation of the Flint River" (M.A. thesis, University of Georgia, 1988).

19. Hudson et al., "Coosa," 723–37.

20. Heye, Hodge, Pepper, "Nacoochee Mound."

21. Williams and Branch, "Tugalo Site."

22. Fish and Jefferies, "Site Plan at Cold Springs," 61–73; and Williams, *Linger-longer Mound,* 1–23.

23. W. Dean Wood, "An Analysis of Two Early Woodland Households from the Cane Island Site, 9Pm209" (M.A. thesis, University of Georgia, 1979).

24. Wauchope, "Archaeological Survey."

25. Daniel T. Elliott and Jack T. Wyann, "The Vining Revival: A Late Simple Stamped Phase in the Central Georgia Piedmont" (Paper presented at the Fiftieth Annual Southeastern Archaeological Conference, New Orleans, La., Oct. 21, 1988).

26. Mark Williams and Gary Shapiro, "Extra Environmental Factors of Settlement Location: The Little River Site in the Oconee Province" (Paper presented at the Fiftieth Annual Meeting of the Society for American Archaeology, Denver, Co., May 4, 1985).

27. M. Williams, "Scull Shoals Mounds," 1–62, and "Scull Shoals Revisited"; Williams and Shapiro, "Paired Towns," 163–74.

28. Williams and Shapiro, *Lamar Archaeology.*

29. Mark Williams and Gary Shapiro, "Shoulderbone Was a Fourteenth Century Frontier Town" (Paper presented at the Forty-eighth Annual Southeastern Archaeological Conference, Nashville, Tenn., Nov. 7, 1986); and Williams, *Shoulderbone Mounds.*

30. B. D. Smith, *Mississippian Settlement Patterns;* Shapiro, "Site Variability in the Oconee Province"; and Mark Williams and Gary Shapiro, "Extra Environmental Factors of Settlement Location: The Little River Site in the Oconee Province" (Paper presented at the Fiftieth Annual Meeting of the Society for American Archaeology, Denver, Co., May 4, 1985).

31. Anderson, Hally, and Rudolph, "Mississippian Occupation," 32–51; Rudolph and Hally, *Beaverdam Creek Site;* and Anderson and Schuldenrein, *Prehistoric Human Ecology.*

32. Rudolph and Blanton, "Mississippian Settlement," 14–37.

33. Mark Williams, "Chiefly Compounds" (Paper presented at the Annual Meeting of the Society for American Archaeology, Apr. 17, 1989, Atlanta, Ga.) and Stephen A. Kowalewski, "A Conceptual Framework for Social Evolution" (Paper presented at the Forty-eighth Annual Southeastern Archaeological Conference, Nashville, Tenn., Nov. 7, 1986).

34. Hudson et al., "Coosa."

35. Williams, "Indians along the Oconee," 27–39.

36. M. T. Smith, *Aboriginal Culture Change;* M. Williams, "Early History of the Indians," 1–23; and Mark Williams and Marvin T. Smith, "Power and Migration" (Paper presented at the Fifty-first Annual Southeastern Archaeological Conference, Tampa, Fla., Nov. 10, 1989).

37. Stephen A. Kowalewski and James W. Hatch, "The Sixteenth Century Expansion of Settlement in the Upper Oconee Watershed, Georgia" (Paper presented at the Fiftieth Annual Southeastern Archaeological Conference, New Orleans, La., Oct. 22, 1988).

38. Mark Williams and Marvin T. Smith, "Power and Migration" (Paper presented at the Fifty-first Annual Southeastern Archaeological Conference, Tampa, Fla., Nov. 10, 1989).

39. Frankie Snow, personal communication with the author.

40. John E. Worth, "Extralocal Shell-Tempered Ceramics in the Timucua Mission Province" (Paper presented at the Fifty-first Annual Southeastern Archaeological Conference, Tampa, Fla., Nov. 10, 1989).

41. M. Williams, "Joe Bell Site."

The Chiefdom of Cofitachequi

During the summer of 1670, Henry Woodward made a trek inland from the newly founded English colony at Charles Towne to the Indian town of Cofitachequi. Although Woodward did not leave a narrative account of this expedition, we have available several contemporary sources that provide some details of his visit. In order to reach Cofitachequi, Woodward traveled fourteen days to the northwest from Charles Towne, stopping to seek peace with chiefs or "Petty Cassekas" that he encountered along the way. Woodward referred to the chief of Cofitachequi as the "Emperor," and there were reported to be "100 bowmen in his towne." Woodward convinced the "Emperor" to visit the English settlement, and after a delay caused by an attack on Charles Towne shipping by several Spanish vessels, the "Emperor" and his entourage arrived there for a state visit in mid-September 1670. A Spanish account of about the same period states that the Carolina coast to the south of Charles Towne was subject to the mico, or chief, of "Cafatache," or Cofitachequi.[1]

Following this interaction with the English, the chief of Cofitachequi apparently endured only a brief relationship with these newly arrived settlers. During the spring of 1672, the Emperor was again in Charles Towne for unspecified purposes.[2] As historian Steve Baker indicated, there is only one documentary reference to Cofitachequi in the Carolina archives for the years following 1672. That reference, dated 1681, makes only passing mention of Cofitachequi.[3] By the time that John Lawson traveled up the Wateree–Catawba River valley in 1701, the area formerly occupied by the Emperor Cofitachequi and his subjects was occupied by a new group of people known as the Congaree. The main Congaree town consisted of about a dozen houses with additional small "plantations" scattered up and down the river.[4] Clearly, the people of Cofitachequi abandoned their homeland shortly after 1672.

The history of the Cofitachequi would be truly enigmatic if we had only these few passing references to the history of this powerful Indian

society that lived in interior South Carolina. But there had been many
Europeans at Cofitachequi prior to Woodward's visit. Hernando de Soto
and his followers were there in 1540, and they may have been preceded by
members of the 1526 Ayllón expedition.[5] Spanish Captain Juan Pardo and
his force of 125 soldiers visited Cofitachequi in 1566 during their attempt
to open an overland route to Mexico from the Atlantic coast. In 1568,
Pardo established a small fort there, leaving a contingent of 30 soldiers in
an outpost that was overrun by the local Indians within a year.[6] Another
small Spanish expedition traveled through the region in 1627–28, and the
only Indian placename mentioned in accounts of this expedition is Cofitachequi.[7] Clearly Cofitachequi was an important place throughout the early
historic period. For the time before the Spanish arrival in the Southeast,
we must turn to archaeology for answers to our questions concerning the
origin and development of the chiefdom of Cofitachequi.

Due to newly accumulated historical and archaeological evidence, there
are a number of intriguing questions relating to Cofitachequi that can
be answered more clearly now than in the past. First, who were these
Indians of Cofitachequi and what were their origins? Where were their
villages located, and how extensive was the territory controlled by their
chief? What was the impact of the several sixteenth- and early seventeenth-
century Spanish expeditions that visited the chiefdom? What happened to
the peoples of Cofitachequi in the decade following Woodward's visit?

At the present time, all of the hard evidence for the location of the town
and chiefdom of Cofitachequi comes from documentary sources. Although
Cofitachequi may be identical with the province of Duhare described by
survivors of the 1526 Ayllón expedition, or with the province of Chiquola
(Chicora) described by the French in 1562–64, there is simply not enough
evidence to convincingly argue the case one way or the other. We are left
to begin this discussion with the evidence provided by the 1539–43 de Soto
expedition.[8]

Hernando de Soto was a seasoned conquistador who had served in
the conquest of Panama, Nicaragua, and Peru prior to his arrival in "La
Florida." In 1536, he was appointed Governor of Cuba, and he acquired the
right to explore the Gulf of Mexico coastline previously assigned to Pánfilo de Narváez and the south Atlantic coastal region previously assigned
to Lucas Vásquez de Ayllón.[9] In May 1539, de Soto arrived in Tampa Bay
on Florida's Gulf Coast with an army of about 625 soldiers and 250 horses.
The gulf coast was fairly well mapped by that time, and de Soto's plan for
exploration of "La Florida" involved travel in land parallel to the coast
while maintaining close contact with his ships, which were intended for
use in resupply.[10] While he was still at Tampa Bay, de Soto sent his ships
back to Cuba to obtain supplies as he prepared to march north.[11]

The army fought its way north through peninsular Florida, arriving at
Apalachee at present-day Tallahassee in October 1539.[12] De Soto immedi-

ately made contact with his supply fleet in the Gulf of Mexico; he then sent his ships west along the coast to find a suitable port for the next rendezvous. While the ships were absent on their westward voyage, soldiers captured a young boy in the vicinity of Apalachee, and information he provided led to a dramatic change in de Soto's plans. This boy, named Perico, claimed to have traveled throughout "La Florida" with traders, and he described a place called Yupaha where a women chieftainess ruled over a territory rich in gold, silver, and pearls.[13] Yupaha turned out to be another name for Cofitachequi.

Based on the information provided by this boy, de Soto turned north, away from the Gulf Coast in quest of Yupaha. He traveled across what is today Georgia, arriving on the banks of a river at Ocute in early April 1540.[14] Upon arriving in Ocute, de Soto enquired about Yupaha or Cofitachequi. He was told that Cofitachequi was located farther to the east, across a wilderness that contained neither trails, Indian towns, nor food supplies.[15] The Indians of Ocute described another large and populous province called Coosa located inland to the northwest, but de Soto was not to be deflected from his quest for Cofitachequi and its chieftainess.[16] He gathered together supplies and bearers for a trek across the wilderness that lay between Ocute and Cofitachequi, and in mid-April he departed from Cofaqui heading east with the trading boy, Perico, as his guide. Perico soon lost his way and claimed to be possessed by the Devil; an exorcism was held and Perico recovered, but the expedition was by then lost in an uninhabited region without trails. The expedition spent ten days crossing this wilderness, finally reaching a small hamlet, called Aymay (or Hymahi), that provided enough corn to temporarily supply the starving expeditionaries with food. Cofitachequi was reported to be only two days' journey from Aymay.[17]

After only a brief rest, de Soto and a small contingent moved upstream toward Cofitachequi, soon reaching the riverbank opposite its main town. De Soto was greeted there by the woman chief who crossed the river in canoes specially outfitted for her use. The available de Soto expedition accounts are not clear on who this woman chief was. Elvas and Ranjel both say she was the ruler of the chiefdom, while Biedma says they were greeted first by the chieftainess's niece and then by the chieftainess herself. Garcilaso says they met the chieftainess's daughter, who had recently inherited the position from her mother, who remained hidden in the woods. Whomever the Spaniards met, she welcomed them to her territory and presented de Soto with a string of pearls. Soon thereafter, the army was ferried across the river, and the soldiers were housed in half of the houses in the town of Cofitachequi.[18]

De Soto immediately began questioning the chieftainess and her subjects about the gold they were reported to possess. The chieftainess had samples of all of the metals and precious minerals found in her territory brought before de Soto for inspection, but they were only copper, mica, and pearls, and not the gold and silver the Spaniards sought. The chieftainess then offered to allow the Spaniards to inspect the contents of her temples that contained many pearls and other objects of interest.[19]

In the temple of Cofitachequi, de Soto found more than 200 pounds of pearls and an abundance of deerskins. He also found a variety of European items including a knife or dirk, glass beads, rosaries, and Biscayan axes.[20] All members of the expedition agreed that these materials must have originated from Ayllón's 1526 expedition to the nearby Atlantic coast. In the temple of Talimeco, an abandoned town located a league from Cofitachequi, de Soto entered another temple located atop a high mound. Inside the temple was a vast array of captured weaponry and tribute items, including an abundance of mica and copper, as well as innumerable pearls.[21]

While at Cofitachequi, de Soto sent about half of his army to the town of Ilapi, because the chieftainess had a large supply of corn stored there. Only Garcilaso provides any information on where Ilapi was located relative to Cofitachequi; he says it was located 12 leagues distant, but he does not provide a direction of travel to get there.[22]

Food supplies were soon exhausted at Cofitachequi, so de Soto enquired about neighboring chiefdoms. He was told about Chiaha, subject to Coosa, and located twelve days' travel distant through the mountains.[23] On May 13, 1540, de Soto departed from Cofitachequi, taking with him the chieftainess to assure his safe passage on the way to Chiaha.

Biedma says that de Soto departed from Cofitachequi traveling to the north.[24] Along the way the army passed through Chalaque and Guaquili before arriving at Xuala. Word was sent to the soldiers at Ilapi, and they caught up with the army a few days after it had arrived at Xuala. Xuala was a large town and chiefdom located at the eastern margin of the Appalachians. During their stay there, the Spaniards were treated well and supplied with an abundance of food. Garcilaso says that Xuala "belonged" to the chieftainess, but that it was a separate province. Elvas says that her territory extended to Guaxule, the next town along the trail beyond Xuala on the way to Chiaha.[25] A full discussion of the extent of the chieftainess's territory will be provided later in this paper.

On the way to Guaxule, five days' travel through the mountains from Xuala, the chieftainess escaped, taking with her a box of the finest pearls removed from her temple.[26] Spanish deserters who caught up to the army at Chiaha reported that the chieftainess and a Spanish slave were living together as man and wife at Xuala and were to return to Cofitachequi. Although this account may well be true, it could just as well have been the creation of envious soldiers who themselves had wanted to remain behind in Cofitachequi.[27]

The de Soto expedition passed through Chiaha and Coosa and ultimately explored most of what is today the southeastern United States. De

Soto died on the banks of the Mississippi River in 1542, and the surviving members of the expedition ultimately reached Mexico in September 1543.[28]

It was only twenty-six years after de Soto's departure that another Spanish expedition traveled to Cofitachequi. Captain Juan Pardo led a force into the interior from Santa Elena located near present-day Beaufort, South Carolina.[29] At that time, Santa Elena was the Spanish capital of La Florida. Pardo's mission centered on plotting an overland route by which treasure obtained from Central America could be safely transported to Santa Elena for shipment to Spain. Pardo's secondary missions were to pacify interior Indians and obtain foodstuffs to supplement the limited supplies at Santa Elena and St. Augustine.[30]

Pardo entered the interior with 125 soldiers on December 1, 1566. He had with him an interpreter, survivor of the 1562 French outpost at Port Royal Sound (also near Beaufort), and he was led by Indian guides. On this first expedition, Pardo made it as far as the eastern foothills of the Appalachian Mountains where he found a town called Joara, the same town as de Soto's Xuala. At that point, the trail became impassable due to snow, so Pardo established a fort at Joara and left 30 soldiers there under the command of Sergeant Moyano. Pardo then returned to the coast with the remainder of his small force. He traveled back to Santa Elena by a different route than the one he used going inland, and he stopped at a town called Guatari (the Wateree River probably takes its name from this town) on the way home.[31] He spent about two weeks at Guatari, and when he left, he left behind his chaplain, Sebastian Montero, and four soldiers in a mission station.[32]

On September 1, 1567, Pardo set off into the interior again, this time with 120 soldiers. He headed inland across 40 leagues of coastal plain, passing through several small towns along the way. (See figure 1.) On September 8, Pardo arrived at Guiomae, which was the same town as de Soto's Aymay or Hymahi. From there, the expedition traveled north along a river to reach Cofitachequi, which was also called Canos in the Pardo accounts. At Cofitachequi, the Pardo expedition accounts note that the terrain changed from low and swampy to higher with deep valleys, abundant stone, and red soil. Clearly, Cofitachequi was at or near the Fall Line. From Cofitachequi, Pardo moved on upriver through Tagaya, Tagaya the Lesser, Gueza (cf. the modern placename Waxhaw), Aracuchi, and Otari; these towns were spaced about one or two days' travel apart. After then passing through Quinahaqui and Guaquiri, Pardo reached Joara where he had left Sergeant Moyano, but he found that Moyano was not there. Moyano had already gone north into the mountains, attacking village after village, and finally arriving at Chiaha, another place that de Soto had visited a quarter of a century earlier.[33]

Pardo continued on from Joara after a brief stopover, and on October 7 he arrived at Chiaha where he was greeted by Moyano and his men. The reunited forces then proceeded farther inland in their quest for Mexico, but

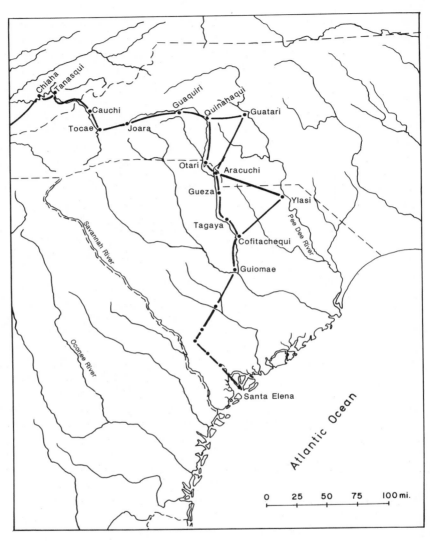

FIGURE I
Route of the Juan Pardo expedition, 1566–1568

threat of attack by a large force of Indians soon forced them to turn back. As they retired toward the coast, Pardo established several small forts to protect the passage that he had explored; forts with garrisons of fifteen to thirty men were built at Chiaha, Cauchi, and Joara.[34]

From Joara, Pardo traveled to some potential mining locations that Moyano may have collected information on during his time there. The expedition visited several "crystal" mines in the vicinity of Yssa (southeast of Joara), staking claims in the name of the Spanish crown. Continuing on, Pardo then passed through Guatari, where he picked up his chaplain and established another of his forts before moving on to Aracuchi. At Aracuchi, Pardo decided to divide his force, sending half on to Cofitachequi, while the other half traveled to Ylasi. Ylasi is clearly the same town as de Soto's Ilapi.[35]

On January 23, 1568, the two forces were reunited at Cofitachequi. At Cofitachequi, Pardo obtained a good supply of corn, which he ordered moved downstream to Guiomae in canoes. From Guiomae, the expedition moved across the coastal plain, gathering corn along the way for the resupply of Santa Elena. Once back on the coast, Pardo built another fort at Orista (near present-day Beaufort), and he sent a contingent of thirty men back to Cofitachequi to build and man a fort there. The remainder of his party arrived back at Santa Elena on the afternoon of March 2, 1568.[36]

Before moving on to discussion of other European visitors to Cofitachequi, it should be pointed out that the Pardo expedition accounts are extremely important in trying to reconstruct a map of sixteenth-century explorations in the interior. The long Bandera account, written by the official Pardo expedition scribe, provides an abundance of information on distances and directions of travel between Indian towns, in many cases on a day-by-day basis.[37] Because Pardo frequently made side trips and then returned to the main trail that he was following, we have triangulation points and measurements that are useful in plotting town locations accurately. Equally important is the fact that Pardo visited many of the same towns that de Soto visited. Thus, the Pardo accounts can be used to locate accurately such places as Cofitachequi, Ylasi, Joara, and Chiaha that would be located with far less accuracy using the de Soto accounts alone.[38]

The next European expeditions that provide information relating to the region surrounding Cofitachequi arrived in the first decade of the seventeenth century. In 1605 and 1609, Captain Francisco Fernandez de Ecija was dispatched from St. Augustine to search along the Atlantic coast for signs of a reported English colony. In August 1605, Ecija's ship entered the mouth of the Jordan River (the Santee); from there he tried to sail upstream, but the current was too swift. Stopping in the harbor, he enquired about Indians in the interior. He was told that Indians from the interior brought skins, copper, and other metals to the coast to trade for fish, salt, and shellfish. The copper was said to come from a town called Xoada located near a high range of mountains. Xoada is probably the same as Pardo's Joara and de Soto's Xuala.[39]

Ecija took several Indians from the mouth of the Jordan back to St. Augustine for questioning. One of the captives said that he had been as far inland as Guatari (a place previously visited by Pardo), and he provided a list of places that lay between the mouth of the Jordan and Guatari. Among the towns he listed was Lasi, probably identical to Pardo's Ylasi and de Soto's Ilapi.[40] Other towns listed by the captive could not be identified with placenames listed by either Pardo or de Soto, perhaps because neither of those expeditions spent much time inland in the area around Ylasi.

Ecija returned to the mouth of the Jordan in 1609, again in search of an English settlement thought to be farther north along the coast. Despite the fact that Jamestown had been settled by then, Ecija found no sign of that colony. His account of a second stopover in the mouth of the Jordan provides no additional information on Indian town locations in the interior.[41] Neither of Ecija's accounts provides any mention of Cofitachequi, possibly because Ylasi and the other towns located on the Pee Dee River were no longer subject to Cofitachequi early in the seventeenth century.

The final Spanish expedition known to have reached Cofitachequi arrived in 1627–28. Sometime in 1627, the Governor of Florida dispatched an expedition from St. Augustine to investigate reports that there were mounted Europeans roving about in the interior. Ten Spanish soldiers and sixty Indians under the command of Pedro de Torres spent four months in the interior searching for these intruders. Torres returned to St. Augustine and reported his failure to find any sign of Europeans.[42]

The Governor was not satisfied by this report, however, so sometime late in 1627 or early in 1628, Torres and his small force were once again sent into the interior. Available documents do not say how long Torres was gone on this second trip, but he is reported to have traveled more than 200 leagues in his search. Torres and his men reached Cofitachequi where "he was well entertained . . . by the chief, who is highly respected by the rest of the chiefs, who all obey him and acknowledge vassalage to him."[43] It is worth emphasizing here that the only named place in the available summaries of Torres's expeditions is Cofitachequi.

In the years following Torres's journeys to Cofitachequi, there were no other Spanish expeditions into the interior, or at least none are known from documents studied and published to date. Accounts describing additional expeditions may still await discovery in archives located in Spain, Cuba, Mexico, or other former Spanish colonies.

By 1670, Spanish withdrawal southward to St. Augustine was well underway. Santa Elena had been abandoned in 1587, and all of the coastal Georgia missions were abandoned by 1686. The English settlement at Jamestown was founded in the lower reaches of Chesapeake Bay in 1607, and another English settlement of coastal North Carolina was attempted as early as the

1660s. Charles Towne was settled in the late spring of 1670, and only a few months later Henry Woodward traveled to Cofitachequi. Within little more than a decade after Woodward's visit, Cofitachequi was gone.

Given the documentary information summarized in the preceding section of this paper, any proposed location for the chiefdom of Cofitachequi must mesh with descriptive details contained in available documents. A number of those details can be summarized as follows. Cofitachequi was located to the east of a large uninhabited buffer zone nine or ten days' travel or about 150 miles across.[44] The archaeological remains of the chiefdom of Ocute must be present to the west of the same wilderness.[45] The remains of the Cofitachequi chiefdom should be composed of a major town or center located on a river with other large towns nearby.[46] One of the towns (Talimeco), about a league from the main town, should be on high terrain overlooking "the gorge" of the river and contain a high mound.[47]

Upstream from Cofitachequi should be remains of towns occupied by the Waxhaw, the Sugeree, and the Catawba or Issa.[48] There must also be another river to the east of the river on which Cofitachequi was located, since both de Soto and Pardo sent contingents to the town of Ilapi or Ylasi located on that second river. The seacoast should be about 30 leagues (about 104 miles) distant from Cofitachequi if we accept Biedma's estimate.[49]

Remains of the main town of Cofitachequi should be extensive, because de Soto's army of more than six hundred men was housed in half of the town's houses.[50] Although there is no mention of mounds in any of the descriptions of Cofitachequi, the main town did contain a large temple, and such temples were typically located atop mounds.[51] And, finally, if the chiefdom of Cofitachequi observed by de Soto and Pardo in the sixteenth century and by Woodward in the late seventeenth century were indeed the same place, then archaeological remains of the chiefdom must span the interval between 1540 and 1670.

Sources of information regarding the placement of Cofitachequi include the accounts of the de Soto, Pardo, Torres, Ecija, and Woodward expeditions as previously discussed. Until recently, the four accounts describing the de Soto expedition were the most reliable sources for plotting the distribution of Indian societies in the interior Southeast. Although the information in those de Soto expedition accounts is often general in nature and sometimes conflicting, taken together that information does allow reconstruction of the route followed.[52] Details contained in the three brief Pardo expedition accounts, as well as those of Torres and Ecija, supplement information found in the de Soto narratives.

Despite the fact that there were many attempts to trace de Soto's route prior to and following the work of the United States de Soto Expedition Commission, it is the work of this commission that has remained the standard reference on de Soto's route until very recently.[53] The Commission was created by Congress in 1935 to trace de Soto's route as part of the commemoration of the expedition's four hundredth anniversary. The Commission was composed of John Swanton, an eminent ethnohistorian from the Bureau of American Ethnology at the Smithsonian Institution, and six other members, but it is clear that Swanton was the Commission's most active and most influential member. Appointment to the de Soto Expedition Commission allowed Swanton to continue research on a topic that had interested him for more than twenty years. As Chairman of the Commission, Swanton took the opportunity to travel along his proposed route, visiting with historians and archaeologists as well as viewing the landscape of the region.[54]

As a result of the exhaustive research that went into the Commission's report, that volume has stood as a nearly unimpeachable reference on the route taken by de Soto and his followers. The Commission's report differs from most of its predecessors in that it carefully plots the movements of the expedition along the entire route followed. Most other previous reconstructions traced only portions of the route or were presented as route lines on maps without reference to daily movements.

In more recent times, the Commission's reconstructed route has come under increasing scrutiny for several reasons.[55] First, several of the sites identified by the Commission as locations of sixteenth-century towns were collected or excavated by archaeologists and found to be either too early or too late to have been visited by de Soto.[56] Second, we now know much more about the distribution of archaeological sites across the region than was known in Swanton's time, and we are therefore better able to match concentrations of sixteenth-century archaeological sites with places where the Spaniards encountered concentrations of people. Also, we can match areas lacking archaeological sites with the uninhabited buffer zones or "deserts" crossed by the expedition.[57]

Third, we have additional primary documents, particularly the long Bandera account describing the Pardo expedition, that contribute significantly to our ability to pinpoint towns and provinces visited by de Soto. Fourth, we know that there were two league measures in use in sixteenth-century La Florida and that it is likely that travel estimates in both the de Soto and Pardo accounts were in "common" leagues of 3.46 miles rather than "legal" leagues of 2.63 miles.[58] Swanton and the de Soto Expedition Commission accepted the "legal" league as the standard used by these expeditions. And finally, we now have far better topographic maps of the Southeast than were available to Swanton and his colleagues. These maps have proved to be a critical resource in plotting the expedition's route across the southeastern landscape.

Using the information and resources then available to them, Swanton and the de Soto Expedition Commission placed the main town of Cofitachequi on the Savannah River below Augusta at Silver Bluff. The Commission's report summarizes the arguments for placing Cofitachequi on the Savannah rather than on the Broad or Congaree in South Carolina, and those arguments do not need to be repeated here.[59]

Problems with placement of Cofitachequi on the Savannah River were apparent to Swanton from the very beginning. For instance, Swanton was aware of the fact that the Pardo expedition accounts place the Waxhaw, Esaw (Catawba), Sugeree, and other Siouan groups in close proximity to Cofitachequi. If Cofitachequi were on the Savannah River, then these other groups must also have been on or near the Savannah in the sixteenth century. But in 1670, when Charles Towne was settled, each of those groups was clearly located on the upper Wateree–Catawba River drainage. In order to compensate for this inconsistency, Swanton was forced to conclude that there was a general northeastward migration of Siouan groups from the Savannah River drainage to the Wateree–Catawba River drainage in the century following Pardo's expedition.[60]

Another example of problems relating to placement of Cofitachequi on the Savannah River concerns another Indian group, the Westo. From Spanish and English accounts of the 1660s and 1670s, it is clear that the Westo were settled near the Fall Line on the Savannah River by the 1660s. It is equally clear from Henry Woodward's 1670s visits to the Cofitachequi and the Westo that these town groups were not neighbors.[61] So how did Swanton deal with this problem? He proposed another relocation, this time suggesting that Cofitachequi must have moved upstream along the Savannah River from their sixteenth-century Fall Line location to make way for the arrival of the hostile and aggressive Westo in the mid-seventeenth century.[62]

There are several points that can be made which clearly illustrate the inaccuracy of these movements proposed by Swanton and the de Soto Expedition Commission. First, we have an increasing body of archaeological knowledge that allows us to plot the distribution of major Indian settlements in the sixteenth century, and by the same means we can identify areas devoid of Indian occupation during that period. This newly available archaeological data demonstrates that the Savannah River valley, extending from the coast nearly to the Blue Ridge province, was unoccupied between about A.D. 1450 and 1660. Thus, it is clear that neither the chiefdom of Cofitachequi nor its Siouan neighbors ever occupied the Savannah River valley, despite Swanton's arguments to the contrary.[63]

Second, we now have available Bandera's detailed account of Pardo's second expedition into the interior, which provides travel distances and directions from Santa Elena to Cofitachequi and beyond. This document, taken in conjunction with the other Pardo expedition accounts, makes it clear that Cofitachequi was located on the Wateree River near Camden, South Carolina.[64] This Pardo expedition placement of Cofitachequi is supported by information contained in the de Soto expedition accounts.[65] (Placement of Cofitachequi and its neighbors, based on tracing the de Soto and Pardo routes, is given in figure 1.)

Although Hudson and his colleagues have provided the most thorough documentation for de Soto's and Pardo's travels in South Carolina, historians Mary Ross, Steven Baker, and Michael Gannon each previously placed Cofitachequi in central South Carolina.[66] Ross, drawing on the three shorter Pardo accounts, placed Cofitachequi on the Congaree River near present-day Columbia. Baker, using the de Soto, Pardo, and Woodward accounts, argued for the placement of the chiefdom's main town on the upper reaches of the Santee River, approximately 30–35 miles south of Camden. Gannon, using the longer, detailed Bandera account of the Pardo expedition, placed Cofitachequi in the vicinity of Columbia, South Carolina. These three placements of Cofitachequi vary from one another, and none traces daily movements of the de Soto or the Pardo expedition.

If we accept the placement of Cofitachequi on the Wateree River, then the next question to ask is: Does the available archaeological evidence support that placement? We can begin answering this question by looking at the distribution of major archaeological sites (that is, those with platform mounds) over an area including eastern Georgia and all of South Carolina. (See figures 2–5.)[67]

Mound sites that were occupied about A.D. 1250–1300 are distributed across the landscape with most major river systems containing one or more mound centers. (See figure 2.) Excavations in mounds at these sites typically show evidence of ceremonial structures covered by later platform mounds. This construction sequence has been interpreted to be a reflection of increasing sociopolitical complexity where tribal level societies were gradually developing into chiefdoms ruled by powerful chiefs.[68]

In the interval between about A.D. 1400–50, many of the same sites occupied earlier continued to be occupied, and some new mound centers were settled for the first time. (See figure 3.) The known site distribution is still rather even across the landscape, with each major river valley containing one or more major centers. Our current understanding of polities in existence at this time is not well developed, but David Hally and James Rudolph have provided preliminary polity boundaries for the Savannah River and areas to the west.[69]

At some time shortly after A.D. 1450, a dramatic series of changes occurred in the distribution of centers with mounds. (See figure 4.) The most dramatic shift in site distribution occurred in the Savannah River valley, which had been a major focus of regional occupation in the preceding centuries. The upper reaches of the Savannah River drainage continued to be occupied, but the remainder of the valley all of the way to the coast was abandoned. To the east in South Carolina, both the Broad and Saluda River valleys also were abandoned at this time. The Scott's Lake Mound Site on

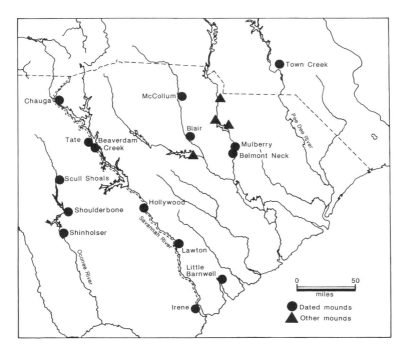

FIGURE 2
Mississippian mound sites, 1400–1450

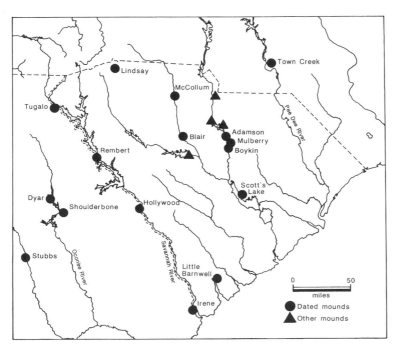

FIGURE 3
Mississippian mound sites after 1450

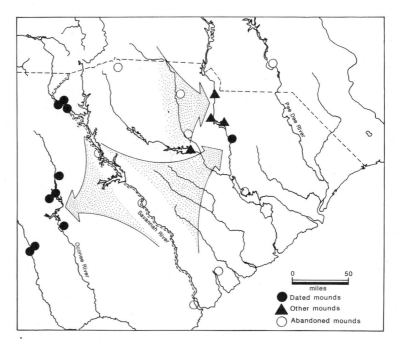

FIGURE 4
Abandonment of the Savannah River

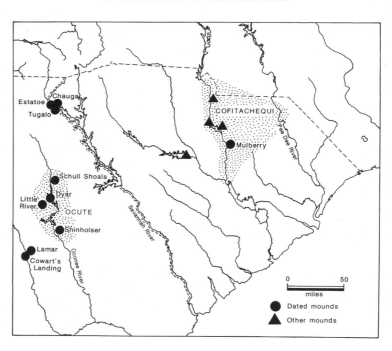

FIGURE 5
Cofitachequi and Ocute

the upper reaches of the Santee River was also abandoned, and no other mound center seems to have developed in its vicinity to take its place.[70]

Following this series of movements and abandonments, the lower Wateree River valley was clearly the focus of occupation to the east of the Savannah River. (See figure 5.) The lower Wateree Valley site cluster undoubtedly represents the archaeological remains of the chiefdom of Cofitachequi, whereas the Oconee River cluster contains the remains of the Ocute chiefdom.[71]

How does the Wateree Valley location for Cofitachequi fit with the locational criteria listed at the beginning of this section? Clearly the necessary buffer zone of an appropriate width exists between the Wateree and Oconee rivers. The Wateree Valley contains several mound sites, but at present only one, the Mulberry site, is known to have been occupied during an appropriate time interval to have been seen by de Soto and those who came after him. In the early historic period, the Waxhaw, Sugeree, and Catawba were located up the Wateree–Catawba Valley from the Camden area where the Mulberry site is located, just as we would expect from the historical accounts. The distance from the seacoast, approximately one hundred miles, fits with Biedma's estimate. At present, there is no other known locality that fits these conditions as well as the Wateree Valley.

Of the several mound sites located in the lower Wateree River valley, only the Mulberry site (38KE12) can be shown to have been occupied during the sixteenth century. (See figure 5.) The site was first recorded in the early nineteenth century, and since then there have been several testing and mapping projects conducted there. Despite this research, little is known about the site and its multiple occupations.[72]

The site originally had at least three mounds. The largest mound, Mound A, was approximately 9–10 feet (2.75–3.05 meters) high when it was first described. This mound is located adjacent to the present channel of the Wateree River and more than three-quarters of it has been eroded away in the past century and a half. Mound B, located approximately 50 meters east of the riverbank, was also originally about 12–15 feet (3.7–4.6 meters) high. A smaller mound, two feet (0.6 meters) high and located near Mound B, was destroyed in 1953.[73]

The occupation of the Mulberry site spans the interval between A.D. 1250 and the latter part of the seventeenth century.[74] Occupation spans for the various parts of the site are not completely known at present, but some estimates can be made. Village occupation apparently began at about A.D. 1250 along the riverbank, with construction of Mound A atop village deposits by about A.D. 1300–50. Given presently available data, an abandonment date for Mound A cannot be determined. Mound B was begun about A.D. 1450–1500 and may have been used for 75–100 years. Burials excavated by A. R. Kelly date to the A.D. 1400–50 era, but it is not known at present if they were from house floors, a mortuary, or a cemetery.[75] Village debris dating to the later portion of the site's occupation extends inland away from the river for a distance of at least 250 meters. Total size of the village area has not been fully determined due to the presence of a thick alluvial layer that covers much of the site.

Clearly the Mulberry site is large enough to have been the main town of Cofitachequi, and its occupation spans the appropriate time interval for it to have been visited by de Soto, Pardo, and Woodward. There is no other large site anywhere in the vicinity that can be shown to have been occupied during the mid-sixteenth century. Despite the fact that excavations have been conducted on both the land portion of the site and in adjacent portions of the Wateree River and Big Pine Tree Creek, no sixteenth- or seventeenth-century European artifacts have been recovered. While at first glance this would seem to be an argument against the Mulberry site being Cofitachequi, the lack of European artifacts is probably a factor of their distribution. Only limited excavations have been conducted in the contact period portion of the site, and in none of these areas have any burials been excavated. We know from excavations elsewhere in the region that European trade items appear most commonly in association with burials, so the lack of European artifacts is, at least in part, probably due to a lack of data from burials. Present evidence makes the Mulberry site the most likely candidate for Cofitachequi despite the lack of European artifactual evidence from the contact period.

If Mulberry is indeed Cofitachequi, then the Adamson site, 38KE11, is the most likely candidate for the location of de Soto's Talimeco. Adamson is located about 6.4 kilometers (a little more than a league) upstream from the Mulberry site, and it has two mounds, including one located directly adjacent to a former channel of the river. These characteristics fit with the descriptions provided by the de Soto chroniclers for Talimeco. Although the Adamson site appears to date mainly to the A.D. 1250–1400 interval, there is some indication of later use. There is a strong possibility that the temple atop the large mound on this site was maintained long after the surrounding village was abandoned, and that it was this temple that was entered by de Soto in 1540.[76]

The next question to be answered concerns the extent of the territory included in the chiefdom of Cofitachequi. Although the available documentary information is not as complete on this subject as we might like, there are some inferences that can be made from that which is available.

John Swanton, working in the first half of the twentieth century, did not have benefit of recent theoretical work on the concept of the chiefdom, and he generally argued against evidence for any degree of advanced levels of sociopolitical complexity among southeastern Indian groups. That problem, compounded by the fact that Swanton and the de Soto Expedition Commission placed Cofitachequi on the Savannah River rather than the

Wateree, makes most of what Swanton had to say on the subject useless today. More recently, Steven Baker, Charles Hudson and his colleagues, and David Anderson have been the primary investigators concerned with the extent of this chiefdom.

Baker indicates the greatest extent for the chiefdom, and his map shows Cofitachequi extending from the mouth of the Ogeechee River on the Georgia coast inland to include most of the Savannah River valley, the Congaree, Wateree, Santee, and Black River valleys in South Carolina, the Broad and Saluda River valleys except for their headwaters, and that portion of the Pee Dee River drainage immediately to the north and south of the North Carolina–South Carolina state line.[77]

In papers detailing the exploration routes of Hernando de Soto and Juan Pardo, Hudson and his colleagues provide no estimate of the extent of the chiefdom of Cofitachequi, concentrating instead on plotting exploration routes followed by those expeditions.[78] Chester DePratter, however, has argued that this chiefdom may have been 200 miles (320 kilometers) across, stretching from central South Carolina to the vicinity of Asheville, North Carolina.[79] Charles Hudson also proposes an extensive area for the chiefdom of Cofitachequi, although he does not include as broad a territory as Baker does. Hudson's boundary for the chiefdom includes "Indians all the way from the mouths of the Santee and Pee Dee Rivers on the coast of South Carolina to the upper reaches of the Catawba River on the eastern edge of the Blue Ridge Mountains."[80] Elsewhere Hudson also includes "the Peedee [sic] River up to the narrows of the Yadkin."[81] The map accompanying each of Hudson's papers incorrectly shows Cofitachequi extending inland along the Broad and Saluda rivers to the mountains rather than along the Wateree-Catawba drainage as described in the text of his papers; this discrepancy is clearly a drafting error.[82]

David Anderson indicates a different, but still extensive, set of boundaries for Cofitachequi. Anderson's Cofitachequi includes a large portion of the South Carolina coast extending from the mouth of the Edisto River north to the North Carolina border, and then inland to include the entire Pee Dee–Yadkin River drainage, the Santee and Catawba River valleys, and the lower portion of the Broad River.[83]

Each of these disparate sets of boundaries is based primarily on interpretation of information contained in the de Soto and Pardo expedition accounts. Review of these documents suggests that the boundaries of Cofitachequi may not be nearly so extensive as indicated in the previously cited papers. If the main town of Cofitachequi was located on the Wateree River near Camden, South Carolina, then clearly the lower portion of the Wateree Valley must be included within the boundaries of the chiefdom. When de Soto reached the town of Aymay at the junction of the Wateree and Congaree Rivers, it was there that he first learned that he was in the territory of Cofitachequi, and it is certain that the chiefdom extended downstream to this small town.[84]

Baker, Hudson, and Anderson each extend the boundaries of Cofitachequi down the Santee River to include large portions of coast and coastal plain South Carolina. Baker places the center of the chiefdom on the upper Santee River just below the junction of the Wateree and Congaree Rivers, so it is logical that Baker would include the Santee within his proposed boundaries.[85] His reasons for including the central portion of the Pee Dee River valley within the Cofitachequi chiefdom are unstated. Hudson and his colleagues place the Indian town of Ylasi (Ilapi) on that stretch of river, but Baker locates Ylasi near Camden on the Wateree River.[86] In drawing his boundary for the chiefdom, Hudson draws primarily on the list of chiefs who came to visit Juan Pardo as he traveled through the interior in 1566–68. The fact that Hudson would use Pardo era data to construct boundaries for Cofitachequi is perplexing, because elsewhere he argues that Cofitachequi entered a period of rapid decline after de Soto's 1540 passage and by the time of Pardo's arrival Cofitachequi did not, in Hudson's estimation, possess a paramount chief.[87]

For piedmont areas, none of these authors provides good information on why most included areas on their maps were seen as part of Cofitachequi. Anderson simply provides territorial limits without any justification in his text, although he does cite Elvas as his primary source. Baker includes the Congaree, Broad, and Saluda River valleys within the limits of his "Greater Chiefdom," but he admits that "occupation [of these river valleys] is not documented but these areas were almost certainly within the territory of the chiefdom." [88] The error in Hudson's maps showing territorial limits in the Piedmont has already been identified above.

So, what were the limits of the chiefdom of Cofitachequi? Before answering, we must pinpoint the time of which we are asking the question. Do we mean in 1540 when de Soto visited the chiefdom or 1566–68 when Pardo was there? Or are we referring to 1670 when Woodward was there? Or were the territorial limits consistent through time? If we accept Hudson's argument that the chiefdom had undergone severe declines in both population and the degree of political centralization by 1566, then Cofitachequi must have been more extensive in 1540 than at any subsequent time.[89]

Presumably it is these maximum territorial limits that Hudson plotted on his maps. Anderson dates his map showing the extent of Cofitachequi and other chiefdoms in the region at 1540, so presumably he is using the de Soto and earlier accounts for his boundaries. Baker proposes great loss of life through epidemic prior to the arrival of de Soto, but he saw Cofitachequi continuing as a powerful chiefdom up to the late seventeenth century, when Woodward traveled there. It is clear, however, that Baker's boundary for the chiefdom would also be applicable to the 1540 era.[90]

Just what do the de Soto accounts have to say concerning the territorial limits of Cofitachequi? That information is not, of course, as clear as we would like, and that which is available is subject to various interpretations. Not one of the four extant de Soto expedition accounts provides a clear statement concerning the extent of the chiefdom. De Soto and his men visited only a narrow strand of terrain that wound its way through the region, so speculations by the chroniclers on the region's larger territorial limits and political structure must have been based on information supplied by the Indians. Clearly interpreters must have garbled some information, and we know that local chiefs also supplied misinformation just to convince the expedition to move on to the next chiefdom.[91]

Several examples of either misinformation or misunderstanding of conversation by de Soto and his men at Cofitachequi can be identified. The Gentleman of Elvas says he was told that the sea was two days' travel distance from Cofitachequi, but that straight line distance is actually more than 100 miles, and clearly even more than that by trail or by water. Another example is the fact that the expeditionaries never knew if they were dealing with the chieftainess of Cofitachequi, or both the chieftainess and her niece, or with the chieftainess's daughter. There can be no doubt that part of this problem relates to failure of the Spanish to comprehend the kinship system of these Indians. Nonetheless, translation difficulties may have further confused the issue.[92]

A final and more critical problem of misinformation concerns the epidemic said to have swept through Cofitachequi prior to de Soto's arrival. Neither Ranjel nor Biedma mentions the supposed epidemic, but Elvas provides a number of details.[93] He states that there were several abandoned towns, grown up in grass, in the immediate vicinity of the main town of Cofitachequi. According to Elvas, the Indians said that these towns had been abandoned due to an epidemic that had struck two years earlier. Garcilaso, describing the same series of events, says that an epidemic had struck the chiefdom during the previous year, causing many deaths and the abandonment of a number of towns. He further states that only the main town of Cofitachequi had been spared from the ravages of the epidemic. Elsewhere in his account, Garcilaso cites Alonso de Carmona, who accompanied de Soto, as saying that in Talimeco the Spaniards found four large houses containing bodies of those who died as a result of the epidemic.[94]

These are the sources on which George Milner, J. Leitch Wright, Henry Dobyns, Charles Hudson, and Marvin Smith base their conclusion that Cofitachequi had been devastated by an epidemic prior to de Soto's arrival.[95] I feel that there are alternate explanations that can be provided for the details of this "epidemic" as noted in the accounts above.

Garcilaso says that the main town of Cofitachequi "had been free" of the epidemic, and Elvas seems to make the same point when he says that the inhabitants of the "nearby towns" had moved away due to the epidemic. If there had indeed been an epidemic in the chiefdom of Cofitachequi, the main town surely would not have been spared devastation when all neighboring towns were depopulated. Perhaps there was no pre-1540 epidemic at Cofitachequi.

Archaeology provides an alternate explanation for the descriptions of abandoned towns provided by Elvas and Garcilaso. Upon arrival at the main town of Cofitachequi in May 1540, the expedition found corn to be in short supply because the new crop had just been planted. Half of the expedition was dispatched to Ylasi to use corn stored there, and undoubtedly search parties were dispatched into the countryside surrounding the town of Cofitachequi to seek corn stored in other towns. These search parties would have reported the existence of the vacant towns.

We know from archaeological survey and historical documents that the area around present-day Camden, South Carolina, contained a number of large mound sites situated along the Wateree River.[96] Some of those mounds have not yet been relocated, but the ones that have (with the exception of the Mulberry site, 38KE12) all date to about A.D. 1200–1450. This includes the Adamson Mound (38KE11), Boykin Mound (38KE8), and Belmont Neck Mound (38KE6). These three mound sites are all located within 5 miles (about a league and a half) of the Mulberry site (38KE12, the most likely candidate for the main town of Cofitachequi), and these sites may well be the large vacant towns mentioned by Elvas and Garcilaso. Elvas notes that the vacant towns were grown up in grass, and it appeared as if they had been unoccupied for a long time, clearly suggesting that they had been abandoned for more than the one or two years since the supposed epidemic had driven away the towns' inhabitants.[97] I propose that these nearby mound sites, abandoned long before de Soto arrived in the Wateree Valley, were the abandoned towns referred to in the expedition accounts.

In a discussion of the supposed epidemic at Cofitachequi, Charles Hudson refers to many deserted towns and "several buildings . . . piled full of corpses" as evidence for the supposed Cofitachequi epidemic.[98] Buildings full of corpses would indeed be good evidence of a recent epidemic if the Spaniards truly saw such mortuaries, but there is evidence that they never saw such piles of epidemic-related corpses. The Alonso de Carmona account quoted by Garcilaso provides the only reference to houses filled with the bodies of epidemic victims. If such buildings truly existed, it seems that one of the other chroniclers would have mentioned them. Raiding parties would have scoured the region around Cofitachequi for food supplies to feed the army and its horses, and these foraging parties would have visited all of the towns affected. Garcilaso says that de Soto's men paused in some houses in Talimeco, one of the abandoned towns, before entering the temple there, but he makes no mention of those houses containing bodies.[99]

It seems far more likely that instead of describing houses full of epidemic victims, Carmona was reporting on the fact that the Talimeco temple contained bodies of past rulers of the chiefdom, and he was mistakenly identifying those bodies as victims of "the pestilence." Clearly, the temple at Talimeco contained bodies of past chiefs and not just defleshed bones stored in baskets or other containers as we know occurred elsewhere in the Southeast.[100] Probably, the interior of the Talimeco temple looked much like the coastal North Carolina temple depicted by John White in the 1580s, showing extended bodies laid out shoulder to shoulder, and it was likely this sort of arrangement of bodies within a high status mortuary that Carmona was trying to describe.[101] It is possible that Carmona never entered the Talimeco temple and that he based his description on hearsay, because he suggests that there was some secrecy involved in the visit to the Talimeco temple, and it may have been entered by only de Soto and his lieutenants.[102] If that were indeed the case, then the remainder of the army would have known about the temple's contents through second- or third-hand accounts.

I have attempted to show to this point that there may not have been a devastating epidemic at Cofitachequi prior to de Soto's arrival. We know that de Soto had some trouble understanding the Indians at Cofitachequi. We know that there were abandoned towns around Cofitachequi that could have been abandoned decades before de Soto's arrival, and there is at least some doubt that the expedition saw houses full of epidemic victims. I would argue that the evidence for the supposed epidemic is weak.

The importance of this argument is that if there was not an epidemic just prior to 1540, how does that affect our interpretation of the later history of the chiefdom of Cofitachequi? Charles Hudson argues for a marked decline in the fortunes of Cofitachequi between 1540 and 1566–68, based on the fact that Juan de la Bandera does not mention the presence of a paramount chief at Cofitachequi during Pardo's visit.[103] At the same time, it is clear from Bandera's account that a great many chiefs traveled great distances to come to Cofitachequi to visit Pardo. If, as Hudson argues, Cofitachequi was no longer the great center or power that it had formerly been, why did so many chiefs come from so far to be there when Pardo arrived in 1567? Why did Pedro de Torres, who visited Cofitachequi sixty years after Pardo, describe the chief there as "highly respected by the rest of the chiefs, who all obey him and acknowledge vassalage to him?"[104] How is it that the "Emperor" found by Woodward at Cofitachequi still ruled a vast territory with many chiefs subject to him? Clearly Cofitachequi was not totally decimated by the 1538 or 1539 epidemic, if there ever was such an epidemic.

The de Soto accounts do not provide much information concerning the towns subject to the chieftainess of Cofitachequi. Aymay or Hymahi was the first place that de Soto reached after crossing the wilderness between the chiefdoms of Ocute and Cofitachequi.[105] None of the expedition accounts specifically states that Aymay was part of the chiefdom of Cofitachequi except Garcilaso. Ranjel and Elvas, however, both describe a situation where an Indian of Aymay had to be burned to death before directions to the main town of Cofitachequi could be obtained from other captives; clearly there was some sense of loyalty involved in this episode, and it is likely, therefore, that Aymay was part of Cofitachequi. The Pardo expedition accounts do not provide any information on the affiliation of this town, which was called Guiomae by Bandera.[106]

For towns to the south and east of Aymay, neither the de Soto nor Pardo accounts provides any clear clues to the extent of the chiefdom in that direction. While it is possible that the territory of Cofitachequi extended down the Santee River from Aymay, there is no good evidence in sixteenth-century documents to support such a possibility. There is, however, the late seventeenth-century account of Bishop Calderon, who states that the Indians around Port Royal Sound on the coast south of Charles Towne were subject to the Mico of "Cofatache" or Cofitachequi. The Bishop did not visit this part of the coast, and the source of his information is unknown. If Cofitachequi indeed controlled any portion of the coast, it is odd that no contemporary English document mentions that fact.[107]

Upstream from Cofitachequi, there is seemingly conflicting evidence for the extent of the chiefdom. Ranjel and the Gentleman of Elvas clearly state that the chieftainess of Cofitachequi was taken as hostage by de Soto and forced to accompany the expeditionaries as they traveled north and west toward the mountains through her territory, and that her presence led to various services being provided at towns along the way. Garcilaso clearly states that the chieftainess was left behind in her capital. Biedma makes no mention of the fate of the chieftainess. Given the relative unreliability of Garcilaso compared to Ranjel and Elvas, it seems likely, as is generally accepted, that the chieftainess was indeed kidnapped and forced to accompany the expedition, and her presence may have helped de Soto obtain goods and services at some points along the way.[108]

The fact that de Soto and his men were treated well by the Indians whom they visited between Cofitachequi and Guaxule, located in the Appalachian mountains, has led some researchers to conclude that the intervening towns were subject to the chieftainess. But the evidence from the de Soto accounts is not so clear-cut.

The first place visited by de Soto after his departure from Cofitachequi was Chalaque, which is variously described in the expedition chronicles as a "province," a "territory," and "some small settlements."[109] This province may not have been a chiefdom, because Ranjel says that de Soto was unable to locate the village of the chief there. Elvas described Chalaque as having the least maize of any of the places de Soto visited in Florida, and the people there lived by hunting and gathering.[110] Even the powerful chieftainess of Cofitachequi was of no assistance in either locating the main town of the province or obtaining more than turkeys and a few deerskins as gifts for de Soto. As John Swanton indicates in the de Soto Expedition Commission Report, the name Chalaque was a Creek word meaning "people of a different speech," and it is likely that the expedition had entered a region occupied by tribal-level Catawban speakers after having passed through Muskogean territories. Location of this linguistic boundary just south of the South Carolina–North Carolina state line is confirmed by information in the Pardo expedition accounts.[111]

The next place visited by de Soto also presents problems regarding its affiliation with the chieftainess as well as its level of sociopolitical organization. The town (or province?) of Guaquili, located a few days beyond Chalaque, is mentioned by Ranjel but not by the other three chroniclers. Ranjel mentions neither a chief nor a principal town there, but he does say that the Indians provided de Soto with a limited quantity of corn, roasted "fowls," dogs, and tamemes or bearers. Neither the role of the chieftainess in obtaining these supplies nor the size or extent of Guaquili is provided by Ranjel.[112]

After passing through Chalaque and Guaquili in a trip that took about ten days (including a two- or three-day stopover at Chalaque), the expedition arrived at Xuala on May 21, 1540. At Xuala, according to Ranjel, de Soto found a chief who provided the expedition with abundant supplies and bearers. But Biedma says only that Xuala had "a thin population," and Elvas says that they found little grain there. Garcilaso, on the other hand, says that Xuala contained great quantities of corn and all of the other vegetables of Florida. Garcilaso says that the expedition rested in Xuala for fifteen days, but Elvas places their stay at two days, and Ranjel says four days. Clearly there are major discrepancies in the accounts pertaining to Xuala.[113]

From Xuala de Soto moved on to Guaxule, a place with little maize. The chieftainess escaped from her captors between Xuala and Guaxule, and Elvas indicates that Guaxule was at the "farthest limit of her territories." Garcilaso also implies that the chieftainess's territory extended to Guaxule.[114]

This problem can be summarized as follows. Some of the de Soto expedition narratives imply that the territory between Cofitachequi and Guaxule was controlled by the chieftainess of Cofitachequi, but some of the related information in those accounts is conflicting. When traveling from Cofitachequi to Xuala, a trip of several days on the road, the Spaniards encountered only two towns and neither was well populated nor contained an abundance of foodstuffs. The fact that there were no other towns present in the area is clearly indicated by the fact that the army's campsites for this segment of the expedition were consistently placed in swamps, plains, or woods, with no reference to nearby Indian habitations. Even having the chieftainess as hostage did not bring de Soto abundant supplies along this part of the route. Clearly two towns in a distance of more than 150 miles does not mesh with what we know of town spacing within chiefdoms from the remainder of the Southeast.[115]

We can look at the Pardo expedition accounts for additional information on the distribution of towns in this region, since both de Soto and Pardo followed the same trails through this part of the interior. When Pardo departed from Cofitachequi (or Canos as he also called it), he also moved north where he found several towns called Tagaya, Tagaya the Lesser, Gueza, Aracuhi, and Otari in the first 60 miles of his travels. Beyond Otari, Pardo encountered only two additional towns in an area that took him five or six days to cross on his way to Joara or Xuala. One of those towns was Guaquiri, clearly identical with de Soto's Guaquili. As was the case with the de Soto expedition, Pardo and his men were forced to camp in the open along this part of their route due to the absence of Indian towns.[116]

Based on the information in the accounts of these two expeditions, I would argue that both de Soto and Pardo traveled through many towns between Cofitachequi and the present-day North Carolina–South Carolina line where Pardo found Otari. These towns, including Tagaya, Tagaya the Lesser, Gueza, and perhaps Otari, within three to four days' travel from Cofitachequi, would have been subject to the chieftainess of Cofitachequi and would have been the places where she ordered the Indians to carry the Spaniards' burdens as was described by Elvas.[117] At about the present North Carolina–South Carolina state line, there was the previously discussed linguistic boundary with Muskogean languages spoken to the south and Siouan spoken to the north. Beyond that line was a vast, sparsely occupied territory that stretched along the Catawba River the one hundred or so miles to Xuala. Within that distance, de Soto encountered only Chalaque and Guaquili (discussed above), and Pardo found Quinahaqui and Guaquiri. All available information on these places indicates that they were small, isolated settlements.

While it is possible that the chiefdom of Cofitachequi extended west to Xuala or Guaxule as described by Elvas and Garcilaso, it seems far more likely that it extended only as far north as the linguistic boundary at the present state line. (See figure 5.) This interpretation is consistent with what is known of the archaeology of the upper Wateree–Catawba River valley. Beyond that point there were only a few small towns that probably were tribal level peoples not subject to anyone. The affiliation of the Yssa (Issa or Catawba) that Pardo found to the west of the Wateree–Catawba River is not known.[118]

Downstream from Cofitachequi there is even less firm evidence for the extent of the chiefdom. If Aymay or Guiomae were indeed subject to Cofitachequi, as the documents seem to indicate, there do not seem to be too many other towns in that direction. The absence of sixteenth-century mound sites in the upper Santee River valley would also seem to indicate that there were no large population centers there. Any attempt to extend the limits of Cofitachequi even farther south and southeast to the coast is pure speculation that counters the sparse evidence available.

To the east of Cofitachequi, it is clear that Ilapi (of de Soto) and Ylasi (of

Pardo) was part of the chiefdom of Cofitachequi. Both de Soto and Pardo sent contingents there to gather corn supplies belonging to Cofitachequi. Distances and directions provided in the de Soto and Pardo expedition accounts, as well as evidence in the Ecija accounts, clearly indicate that Ylasi was located on the Pee Dee River in the vicinity of present-day Cheraw, South Carolina. Extent of this territory upstream or downstream from Cheraw cannot be determined from the documents.[119]

To the west, Cofitachequi was bounded by the vast uninhabited buffer that extended all of the way to the Oconee River valley in Georgia. Large sites that had formerly existed in the adjacent Broad River valley were abandoned by about A.D. 1450.

The preceding discussion of Cofitachequi's boundaries is based on information from the de Soto and Pardo accounts and therefore is applicable only to the mid-sixteenth century. Unfortunately, the seventeenth- and eighteenth-century accounts of Torres and Woodward, respectively, do not provide us with any clear information regarding boundaries at the time of their visits. Given my arguments against a pre-1540 epidemic at Cofitachequi and the likely continuation of chiefdom status for this polity throughout the sixteenth and most of the seventeenth century, I feel that it is unlikely that the restricted boundaries that I have defined for the chiefdom changed markedly during the period in question. In other words, the "Emperor" of Cofitachequi who entertained Henry Woodward in 1670 must have ruled over most, if not all, of the same territory that was controlled by the "Lady" of Cofitachequi when de Soto passed through the region 130 years earlier.

In 1670, the English settled Charles Towne on the South Carolina coast, and the chief of Cofitachequi visited there on at least two occasions. Within only a few years of Charles Towne's founding, the chiefdom of Cofitachequi ceased to exist. Its people had left their homeland, abandoning their sacred mounds and the graves of their ancestors. The region in which Cofitachequi existed and flourished for at least two centuries had entered a new era that was to be dominated by the persistent expansion of the English settlement on the nearby coast.

NOTES

This paper is a revised version of DePratter, "Cofitachequi."

1. Cheves, "The Shaftesbury Papers," 186–87, 194, 201, 249; Wenhold, "A 17th Century Letter of Gabriel Diaz Vara Calderon."
2. Cheves, "Shaftesbury Papers," 388, and Waddell, *Indians of the South Carolina Lowcountry*, 236.
3. Steven Baker, "Cofitachequi: Fair Province of Carolina" (M.A. thesis, University of South Carolina, 1974), 52.
4. Lefler, *A New Voyage to Carolina*, 34.

5. Swanton, *Early History of the Creek Indians,* 31; Quattlebaum, *Land Called Chicora;* Quinn, *North America,* 143–44; and P. Hoffman, *A New Andalucia.*

6. Juan de la Bandera, "Proceedings of the Account which Captain Juan Pardo Gave of the Entrance which He Made into the Land of the Floridas" (Archivo General de Indias, Santo Domingo 224, 1569). Photostats of the original and a translation believed to be by Herbert E. Ketcham are in the Spanish Archives collection of the North Carolina State Archives, Raleigh, N.C. A more recent transcription and translation by Hoffman, "Bandera Relation," has been published in Hudson's *Juan Pardo Expeditions.* The other three Pardo expedition accounts are in Ketcham, "Spanish Chronicles."

7. Don Luis de Rojas y Borja to the King of Spain, June 30, 1628. Photostats of the original and a translation by Mary Ross are in the Mary Ross Papers, Georgia State Archives, Atlanta.

8. Swanton, *Early History of the Creek Indians,* 31–48, 219; Quattlebaum, *Land Called Chicora,* 14, 106; Baker, "Cofitachequi," 73; and Bennett, *Three Voyages,* 29–30.

9. Swanton, *Final Report,* 65–74, 76.

10. Weddle, *Spanish Sea,* and Elvas, "True Relation," 62.

11. Elvas, "True Relation," 34, and Ranjel, "Narrative," 62.

12. Ewen, "The Discovery of de Soto's First Winter Encampment."

13. Elvas, "True Relation," 47–48, 51; Ranjel, "Narrative," 81.

14. Hudson, Smith, and DePratter, "de Soto Expedition: From Apalachee to Chiaha," 70.

15. Elvas, "True Relation," 59; Ranjel, "Narrative," 89–91; Biedma, "Conquest of Florida," 11; and Vega, *Florida of the Inca,* 276.

16. Hudson et al., "Coosa: A Chiefdom in the Sixteenth Century."

17. Elvas, "True Relation," 59–63; Ranjel, "Narrative," 91–96; and Biedma, *Conquest of Florida,* 11–13.

18. Elvas, "True Relation," 64–65; Ranjel, "Narrative," 98–99; and Biedma, *Conquest of Florida,* 13.

19. Vega, *Florida of the Inca,* 310–11; Elvas, "True Relation," 66; and Ranjel, "Narrative," 101.

20. Elvas, "True Relation," 67; Ranjel, "Narrative," 100; and Biedma, *Conquest of Florida,* 14.

21. Ranjel, "Narrative," 101–2, and Vega, *Florida of the Inca,* 314–24.

22. Ranjel, "Narrative," 100, and Vega, *Florida of the Inca,* 325.

23. Elvas, "True Relation," 68.

24. Biedma, *Conquest of Florida,* 14.

25. Ranjel, "Narrative," 102–3; Vega, *Florida of the Inca,* 326–28, 330; and Elvas, "True Relation," 71.

26. Elvas, "True Relation," 71, and Ranjel, "Narrative," 105.

27. Elvas, "True Relation," 72, 68.

28. Hudson, DePratter, and Smith, "Hernando de Soto's Expedition through the Southern United States."

29. Stanley South, "The Discovery of Santa Elena," South Carolina Institute of Archaeology and Anthropology Research Manuscript Series, 65 (1980).

30. Hoffman, "Bandera Relation," 256–57.

31. Ibid., 258–59, and Ketcham, "Spanish Chronicles," 69–71.

32. Gannon, "Sebastian Montero," 343–46.

33. Hoffman, "Bandera Relation," 264–65; Ketcham, "Spanish Chronicles," 72–73, 75–77, 80, 87–88.

34. Hoffman, "Bandera Relation," 274–78; Ketcham, "Spanish Chronicles," 74; DePratter and Smith, "Sixteenth Century European Trade"; and DePratter, "Explorations in the Interior South Carolina."

35. Hoffman, "Bandera Relation," 278–87.

36. Ibid., 288–95.

37. Ibid.

38. Hudson, "Uses of Evidence," 3–4.

39. Hann, "Ecija Voyages of 1605 and 1609," 1–10.

40. Ibid., 10.

41. Ibid., 17–61.

42. Rojas y Borja to the King, trans. by Mary Ross.

43. Ibid.

44. Elvas, "True Relation," 61, and Biedma, *Conquest of Florida*, 11.

45. Elvas, "True Relation," 60, and Ranjel, "Narrative," 91.

46. Elvas, "True Relation," 64–66; Ranjel, "Narrative," 99; Biedma, *Conquest of Florida*, 13; Ketcham, "Spanish Chronicles," 70, 79; and Vega, *Florida of the Inca*, 298.

47. Ranjel, "Narrative," 101, and Vega, *Florida of the Inca*, 314.

48. Hoffman, "Bandera Relation," 260–62, 281–88; Ketcham, "Spanish Chronicles," 79; and Hudson, *Juan Pardo Expeditions*, 33–35.

49. Ranjel, "Narrative," 100; Hoffman, "Bandera Relation," 287–88; Vega, *Florida of the Inca*, 325–28; Biedma, *Conquest of Florida*, 14; and Ketcham, 79.

50. Biedma, *Conquest of Florida*, 13, and Vega, *Florida of the Inca*, 303.

51. Chester B. DePratter, "Early Historic Chiefdoms," 139–41.

52. Hudson, "Unknown South" and "Uses of Evidence."

53. Swanton, *Final Report*; Brain, "Update of de Soto Studies," xi–lvi.

54. Sturtevant, "Foreword," v–vi; and Swanton, *Creek Indians*, "De Soto's Line of March," and "Ethnological Value of the de Soto Narratives."

55. Brain, "Update of de Soto Studies."

56. DeJarnette and Hansen, "Childersburg Site," 60–61; Scurry, Joseph, and Hamer, "Silver Bluff Plantation," 6–7; and M. T. Smith, "Route of de Soto."

57. DePratter, "Early Historic Chiefdoms"; Brain, "Update of de Soto Studies," "Introduction"; Hudson, "Uses of Evidence," 28–33; Hudson, Smith, and DePratter, "de Soto Expedition: Apalachee to Chiaha"; and Hudson et al., "Coosa."

58. DePratter, Hudson, and Smith, "Route of Juan Pardo's Explorations"; Chardon, "Elusive Spanish League"; Hudson and Smith, "Reply to Eubanks."

59. Swanton, *Final Report*, 180–85; Milling, *Red Carolinians*, 65.

60. Swanton, "Early History of the Eastern Siouan Tribes," 371–81; Swanton, *Indians of the Southeastern United States*, 30, 67, 104, 206.

61. Cheves, "Shaftesbury Papers," 186, 191, 194, 220, 316, 456–62.

62. Swanton, *Early History of Creek Indians*, 220.

63. The archaeological evidence for this temporary abandonment of the Savannah River has been presented in detail in the following sources: David J. Hally, Charles Hudson, and Chester DePratter, "The Protohistoric along the Savannah River" (Paper delivered at the Forty-first Annual Southeastern Archaeological Con-

ference, Birmingham, Ala., 1985); Anderson, Hally, and Rudolph, "Mississippian Occupation"; and David Anderson, "Political Change in Chiefdom Societies." For a contrary view, see Eubanks, "Studying de Soto's Route."

64. Hoffman, "Bandera Relation"; Ketcham, "Spanish Chronicles"; DePratter, Hudson, and Smith, "Route of Juan Pardo's Explorations"; and DePratter, "Explorations in Interior South Carolina."

65. Hudson, Smith, and DePratter, "de Soto Expedition: From Apalachee to Chiaha"; Hudson, Worth, and DePratter, "Refinement in de Soto's Route."

66. Ross, "With Pardo and Moyano," 273; Baker, "Cofitachequi," 91; Gannon, "Sebastian Montero," 347; Gannon, *Cross in the Sand*, 30–33.

67. Information on the dating of sites illustrated in figures 2 and 3 is derived from several published and manuscript sources as well as reexamination of archaeological collections stored at the South Carolina Institute of Archaeology and Anthropology. For complete references on sources, see DePratter, "Cofitachequi," 140–41.

68. Chester DePratter, "Sixteenth and Seventeenth Century Chiefdoms in the Southeastern United States" (typescript, University of Georgia Laboratory of Archaeology, Athens, Ga., 1977), 91–94; DePratter, "Early Historic Chiefdoms," 163–65; Rudolph, "Earthlodges and Platform Mounds"; Anderson, "Political Change in Chiefdom Societies," 589–90.

69. Hally and Rudolph, "Mississippian Period Archaeology."

70. Hally and Rudolph, "Mississippian Period Archaeology," 63–80; Anderson, "Political Change," 451–64; Ryan, "Test Excavations at McCollum Site," 104–10; George Teague, "Excavations at the Blair Mound" (typescript, South Carolina Institute of Archaeology and Anthropology, Columbia, S.C., n.d.); and Ferguson, "Exploratory Archaeology."

71. Smith and Kowalewski, "Tentative Identification," 1–13.

72. C. Thomas, "Mound Explorations"; Ferguson, "Mulberry Plantation" and "Archaeological Investigations"; Stuart, "Post-Archaic Occupation of Central South Carolina"; Carl Merry, "An Archaeological Boundary Model for the Mulberry Site" (M.A. thesis, University of South Carolina, 1982); Merry and Pekrul, "Excavations at Mulberry Site"; Kenneth Sassaman, "Stratigraphic Description and Interpretation of the Mulberry Mound Site (38KE12), Kershaw County, South Carolina" (M.A. thesis, University of South Carolina, 1984); Paula Sutton, "Soil Coring at the Mulberry Mound Site, South Carolina" (M.A. thesis, University of South Carolina, 1984); DePratter, "1985 Archaeological Field School"; Kimberly Grimes, "Dietary Choices at the Mulberry Site" (M.A. thesis, University of South Carolina, 1986); and Christopher Judge, "Aboriginal Pottery Vessel Function in South Appalachian Mississippian Society: A Case Study from the Mulberry Site (38KE12)" (M.A. thesis, University of South Carolina, 1987).

73. Squier and Davis, "Ancient Monuments," 107; Thomas, "Mound Explorations," 327; and Stuart, "Post-Archaic Occupation," 99.

74. Chester DePratter and Christopher Judge, "A Late Prehistoric/Early Historic Period Ceramic Sequence for the Wateree Valley, South Carolina" (typescript, South Carolina Institute of Archaeology and Anthropology, Columbia, S.C., 1986).

75. Ferguson, "Archaeological Investigations at the Mulberry Site," 83–87.

76. Squier and Davis, "Ancient Monuments," 106–7; Stuart, "Post-Archaic Occupation," 59–84; and DePratter, "Adamson Site," 37.

77. Baker, "Cofitachequi," map facing page 1.

78. DePratter, Hudson, and Smith, "Juan Pardo's Explorations," and Hudson, Smith, and DePratter, "de Soto Expedition: From Apalachee to Chiaha."

79. DePratter, "Early Historic Chiefdoms," 20–21.

80. Hudson, "Social History of the Cherokees," 139–41, "Unknown South," and *Juan Pardo Expeditions*, 68–73.

81. Hudson, "Unknown South," 18.

82. Hudson, "Social History of the Cherokees," figure 1, 140; Hudson, "Unknown South," figures 2, 15.

83. David Anderson, "Stability and Change in Chiefdom Level Societies: An Examination of Mississippian Political Evolution on the South Atlantic Slope" (Paper delivered at the Forty-third Annual Southeastern Archaeological Conference, Nashville, Tenn., 1986), figure 2.

84. Hudson, Smith, and DePratter, "de Soto Expedition: From Apalachee to Chiaha," 72; Hudson, Worth, and DePratter, "Refinement in de Soto's Route," 103; and DePratter, Hudson, and Smith, "Juan Pardo's Explorations," 137–38.

85. Baker, "Cofitachequi," 91, 94, iv–4, v–15, 16.

86. DePratter, Hudson, and Smith, "Juan Pardo's Explorations," 155–56; Hudson, Smith, DePratter, "de Soto Expedition: From Apalachee to Chiaha," 73; Baker, "Cofitachequi," v–17.

87. Hudson, "Unknown South," 18, and "Genesis of Georgia's Indians," 31.

88. Anderson, "Stability and Change," 6, "Mississippian Political Evolution," and "Chiefdom Level Societies," 52–54; Baker, "Cofitachequi," 144.

89. Hudson, "Genesis of Georgia's Indians," 31. See also Baker, "Cofitachequi," 100–101; Milner, "Epidemic Disease," 43–44; and Wright, *The Only Land They Knew*, 51.

90. Hudson, "Social History of the Cherokees," figures 1, 140; Hudson, "Unknown South," figure 2; Anderson, "Stability and Change, 12"; and Baker, "Cofitachequi," 100–101.

91. Biedma, *Conquest of Florida*, 13; Vega, *Florida of the Inca*, 422.

92. For estimates of distance to the coast, see Elvas, "True Relation," 66, and Biedma, *Conquest of Florida*, 14. For references to the chieftainess, see Elvas, "True Relation," 65; Ranjel, "Narrative," 98–99; Biedma, *Conquest of Florida*, 13; and Vega, *Florida of the Inca*, 304.

93. Elvas, "True Relation," 66.

94. Vega, *Florida of the Inca*, 298, 325.

95. Milner, "Epidemic Disease," 43–44; Wright, *Only Land They Knew*, 44; Hudson, "Genesis of Georgia's Indians," 31; M. T. Smith, *Aboriginal Culture Change*, 57, 59; and Dobyns, *Their Number Become Thinned*, 262–63, 267–68.

96. Stuart, "Post-Archaic Occupation"; Ferguson, "Archaeological Investigations at the Mulberry Site"; and Squier and Davis, "Ancient Monuments," 105–8.

97. Elvas, "True Relation," 66.

98. Hudson, "Genesis of Georgia's Indians," 31.

99. Vega, *Florida of the Inca*, 325, 315.

100. Ranjel, "Narrative," 100; Biedma, *Conquest of Florida*, 14; Vega, *Florida of the Inca*, 319; and DePratter, "Early Historic Chiefdoms," 119–34.

101. Lorant, *The New World*, 201.

102. Ranjel, "Narrative," 101.

103. Hudson, "Genesis of Georgia's Indians," 31.

104. Rojas y Borja to the King, June 30, 1628.

105. Elvas, "True Relation," 63; Ranjel, "Narrative," 96–97; and Biedma, *Conquest of Florida,* 13.

106. Vega, *Florida of the Inca,* 294; Ranjel, "Narrative," 97; Elvas, "True Relation," 63; Hoffman, "Bandera Relation," 259, 288–89; and Ketcham, "Spanish Chronicles," 79.

107. Wenhold, "17th Century Letter," 10–11.

108. Elvas, "True Relation," 70; Ranjel, "Narrative," 105; and Vega, *Florida of the Inca,* 325, 328.

109. Elvas, "True Relation," 70; Ranjel, "Narrative," 102; and Vega, *Florida of the Inca,* 325, 328.

110. Ranjel, "Narrative," 102; Elvas, "True Relation," 70–71.

111. Elvas, "True Relation," 70–71; Swanton, *Final Report,* 50, 53; Ketcham, "Spanish Chronicles," 79; and Hudson, Smith, and DePratter, "de Soto Expedition: From Apalachee to Chiaha," 73.

112. Ranjel, "Narrative," 103.

113. Ranjel, "Narrative," 103–4; Biedma, *Conquest of Florida,* 15; Elvas, "True Relation," 71; and Vega, *Florida of the Inca,* 330–31.

114. Elvas, "True Relation," 71–72; Biedma, *Conquest of Florida,* 15; Ranjel, "Narrative," 105; and Vega, *Florida of the Inca,* 332.

115. Ranjel, "Narrative," 102–3; see papers on chiefdoms in Smith, *Mississippian Settlement* for comparison of settlement distributions.

116. Hoffman, "Bandera Relation," 261–64; Ketcham, "Spanish Chronicles," 70, 79–80; and DePratter, Hudson, and Smith, "Juan Pardo's Explorations," 140–42.

117. Elvas, "True Relation," 70.

118. Janet Levy, J. Allen May, and David G. Moore, "From Ysa to Joara: Cultural Diversity in the 15th and 16th Century Catawba Valley" (Paper presented at the Fifty-fourth Annual Meeting of the Society for American Archaeology, Atlanta Ga., 1989).

119. Hoffman, "Bandera Relation," 260.

DAVID J. HALLY

The Chiefdom of Coosa

At the time of initial Spanish contact in the middle of the sixteenth century, the paramount chiefdom of Coosa was one of the largest and most powerful polities of its kind in the southeastern United States. Today, scholars can pinpoint the geographical location of Coosa's capital and several of its component chiefdoms and can identify their counterparts in the archaeological record. Furthermore, decades of archaeological research have produced great quantities of information pertaining to the way of life of the Coosa people. With these developments, we may begin to fully appreciate the cultural achievements of these people who figured so prominently in the early Spanish explorations of the interior southeastern United States.

Ethnohistoric information on the paramount chiefdom of Coosa is contained in documents of three Spanish expeditions that traveled through all or part of the paramount chiefdom: Hernando de Soto in A.D. 1540, Tristán de Luna in A.D. 1560, and Juan Pardo in A.D. 1567.[1] The major sources of archaeological information are from University of Georgia excavations at the Potts Tract, Little Egypt, King, and Leake sites in northwestern Georgia; Tennessee Valley Authority excavations at the Rymer, Mouse Creek, Ledford Island, Hiwassee Island, Dallas, Hixon, and Citico (40MR7) sites in eastern Tennessee; and excavations by the University of Tennessee at the Toqua site in eastern Tennessee. While all of these sites had mid-sixteenth-century occupations, the majority of archaeological information from the Dallas culture sites that has been used in writing this paper is derived from fifteenth-century components.[2]

The sixteenth-century Spanish used the name *Coça* [hereafter anglicized as "Coosa"] to refer to three different sociopolitical entities. They used it to refer to a single town that served as the capital of a large province. They used it to refer to a group of towns located along the Coosawattee River in northwest Georgia that had the town of Coosa as its capital, here referred to as the chiefdom of Coosa. Finally, they used it to refer to several groups of towns distributed within a territory in Tennessee, Georgia, and Alabama that acknowledged the chief of the chiefdom of Coosa as their overlord. This will be referred to as the paramount chiefdom of Coosa or simply Coosa. The Spanish seem to have used the term "province" in reference to both the chiefdom and the paramount chiefdom. We will look at all three of these entities during the course of this paper.

There is no need to review the historical and archaeological evidence upon which the location and geographical configuration of the paramount chiefdom of Coosa is based. This evidence has been presented in detail elsewhere.[3] The de Soto expedition entered the territory of the paramount chiefdom at the town of Chiaha, located on Zimmerman's Island in the French Broad River in eastern Tennessee. (See figure 1.) From there, the expedition traveled generally in a southwest direction reaching the chiefdom and town of Coosa after twelve days of travel and reaching Talisi, the last town to acknowledge the dominion of Coosa, after twelve additional days of travel. The chiefdom of Coosa was located on the Coosawattee River in northwest Georgia and its capital was the Little Egypt (9MU102) archaeological site located at Carters Dam. Talisi was located in the vicinity of Childersburg, Alabama.

All of the towns visited by the de Soto and Luna expeditions in the Coosa domain were located within a relatively narrow geographic zone that stretched for almost 400 kilometers along the Great Valley, adjacent to the hills and mountains of the Blue Ridge and Piedmont physiographic provinces. Whether Coosa had additional subject towns or chiefdoms situated outside of this zone to the northwest or southeast is not known. The Spanish sources mention none, and, as we shall see, archaeology may be incapable of providing a definitive answer.

Within this zone, archaeologists recognize three distinct cultures: Lamar, Dallas, and Mouse Creek. Lamar is restricted to the Coosa River drainage and can be divided into three regional variants or phases on the basis of ceramic criteria: Barnett, Brewster, and Kyumulga. (See figure 2.) There has been considerable disagreement among archaeologists over the temporal and spatial distributions of Dallas and Mouse Creek cultures. All would agree that Mouse Creek culture is present along the Hiwassee River and that Dallas culture is found along the Tennessee River north of the mouth of the Hiwassee River. Less consensus exists concerning whether Mouse Creek culture or Dallas culture, or both, are present on the Tennessee River in the Chattanooga area.[4]

With few exceptions, archaeologists have generally viewed Lamar culture as being quite different from Dallas and Mouse Creek cultures.[5] This perception is based almost entirely on the ceramic evidence. Lamar culture is characterized by grit- or sand-tempered pottery, the pottery types Lamar Incised and Lamar Complicated Stamped, and the carinate bowl and jar with outflaring, thickened, and pinched rim. Dallas and Mouse Creek ceramic assemblages are characterized by shell tempering, plain or

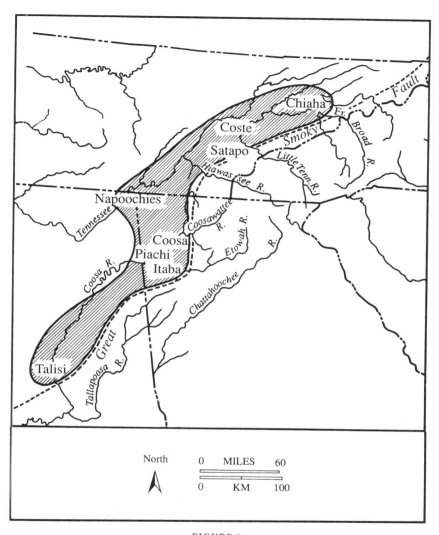

FIGURE I
The territory subject to the paramount chiefdom of Coosa

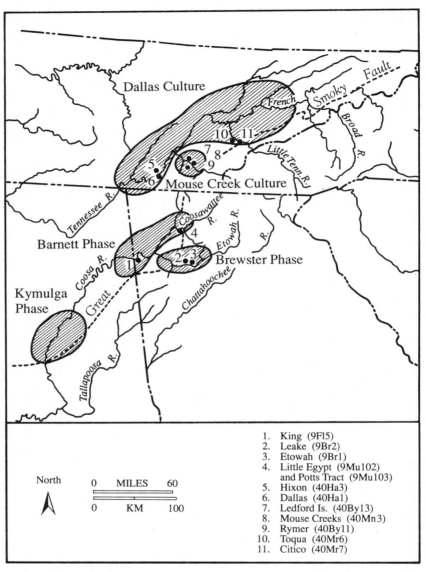

North

0   MILES   60

0   KM   100

1. King (9Fl5)
2. Leake (9Br2)
3. Etowah (9Br1)
4. Little Egypt (9Mu102)
    and Potts Tract (9Mu103)
5. Hixon (40Ha3)
6. Dallas (40Ha1)
7. Ledford Is. (40By13)
8. Mouse Creeks (40Mn3)
9. Rymer (40By11)
10. Toqua (40Mr6)
11. Citico (40Mr7)

FIGURE 2
Archaeological cultures and phases and important sites

cordmarked vessel surfaces, and a jar with handles and incised decoration. These differences are lessened to some extent, however, by the fact that shell tempering and jars with handles and incised decoration are common in Barnett phase and by the fact that Lamar Incised and Lamar Complicated Stamped in both shell and grit tempered forms do occur in Mouse Creek and late Dallas ceramic assemblages. Beyond the realm of ceramics, the three cultures are overwhelmingly similar, a fact that will be amply documented later in this chapter.

Plant and animal remains have been systematically recovered and analyzed from only two sites, Little Egypt and Toqua. The following observations, therefore, relate directly to these sites, but presumably are generally applicable to all three archaeological cultures. Horticulture must have been practiced throughout the entire region of the Coosa paramount chiefdom. Large habitation sites are located in the valleys of major rivers and are frequently adjacent to larger sections of floodplain. While some sort of slash and burn cultivation cannot be ruled out for adjacent upland areas, it appears likely that the great majority of food was grown in these floodplain fields.

Carbonized plant remains from Little Egypt and Toqua indicate that maize was the primary crop and that beans, squash, gourd, sunflower, and *Iva annua* (sumpweed) were also cultivated. To judge by their frequency in the archaeobotanical samples, wild plant foods were also important elements of the aboriginal diet. Hickory nut is predominant in most samples, but acorn, walnut, and butternut are also present. Seeds from a number of grasses and shrubs (for example, chenopod, smartweed, bearsfoot, ragweed, and poke) are present in analyzed samples, but their low frequency indicates they had minor, if any, dietary importance. Wild fruits are somewhat better represented and include persimmon, honey locust, may pop, grape, and plum. Persimmon is so common that we must conclude that it was harvested and consumed in relatively large quantities.[6]

The meat diet at Little Egypt and Toqua was dominated by mammals, of which white-tailed deer and black bear were far and away the most important. Other mammals represented in faunal samples from Little Egypt and Toqua include raccoon, cottontail rabbit, beaver, opossum, and several squirrel species. Turkey and passenger pigeon were the most important birds, with turkey being second to white-tailed deer and black bear in overall dietary importance.[7]

Fish appear to have been a relatively unimportant dietary element, accounting for only 12–14 percent of the minimum number of individuals in the samples from Toqua and Little Egypt. The most important species at both sites were sucker, drum, and catfish in that order. The former two may have constituted important seasonal additions to the diet. Both are easily captured at the time of spawning in the spring, a time of year when few other wild food species are available and stores of cultivated plants would have been running low. Fish in general may be underrepresented in the samples due to methods of processing. That is, if fish were filleted on the banks of streams where they were caught, few of their bones would have been deposited in large settlements such as Little Egypt and Toqua.

Reptiles were also relatively unimportant in the diet. Snake bones occur with sufficient frequency to indicate that they were being eaten, but they are outnumbered by turtles. Box turtle and aquatic species occur with approximately equal frequency at Little Egypt, while the former dominates the samples from Toqua.

Overall, maize, beans, squash, and white-tailed deer were probably the mainstays of the diet. Black bear and several of the smaller mammal species probably supplemented this diet throughout the year, although they may have been most important in the fall. Nuts, which can be stored for long periods of time, probably provided an important supplement throughout much of the year. Seasonally important foods probably included fish, turkey, and the various fruits.

Bioarchaeological data from burials at Etowah, King, Toqua, and the Mouse Creek sites indicate that the populations of at least some chiefdoms in the Coosa domain were experiencing a rather high level of nutritional stress.[8] Most researchers attribute this to the heavy dependence on maize that gave rise to protein deficiency and iron deficiency anemia. Evidence to support this interpretation is found in the high level of infant mortality and the high frequency of pathologies such as porotic hyperostosis, growth arrest lines, enamel hypoplasis, and dental caries that are characteristic of many of the skeletal populations. Not all communities, however, were experiencing similar dietary deficiencies. Comparison of the incidence of porotic hyperostosis, enamel hypoplasis, and dental caries and cortical bone thickness in Etowah and King site skeletal samples indicates that individuals in the latter community were eating a greater variety of gathered foodstuffs and a greater amount of protein than was the case at Etowah.[9]

The effects of dietary deficiencies would have been compounded by infectious diseases that were probably endemic to the large sedentary populations characteristic of the period.[10] These are evidenced by the common occurrence of periosteal lesions on long bones in several skeletal samples. If the bioarchaeological evidence from Etowah, Toqua, and the Mouse Creek sites is reliable, somewhere around a third of the population was dying during the first five years of life, probably in conjunction with weaning. At that time, infants were subjected to a variety of stresses, including loss of nutrients and immunity provided by mother's milk and exposure to pathogens in the environment.

With mortality rates as low as 6 percent, the second decade seems to have been one of the healthiest periods of life. Adult mortality peaks in the third decade and can probably be attributed in large part to the stresses incident to childbirth, warfare, and hunting. Average life expectancy at birth appears not to have exceeded twenty-six years.[11]

A great deal of settlement pattern data is available from surveys of the Little Tennessee, Hiwassee, Coosawattee, Etowah, and Coosa Rivers and excavations at the Toqua, Mouse Creek, Ledford Island, Rymer, Little Egypt, and King sites. This data indicates that a rather uniform settlement pattern existed throughout at least the Tennessee and Georgia portions of the Coosa paramount chiefdom.[12]

Most, if not all, people lived in towns ranging in size between 1 and 6 hectares.[13] The layout of towns seems to have followed a regular pattern. At the center of each was a public area consisting of a plaza containing one or more clusters of burials. A single large posthole, measuring 1 meter in diameter and 2 meters deep, was located at the approximate center of King site plaza and settlement. (See figure 3.) Large ground-level structures, measuring 15 square meters, are associated with the plazas at King and Ledford Island. At King, the structure is located within the plaza but near its northern end, while at Ledford Island, it is on the northern edge of the plaza. Platform mounds with multiple structures on their summits occurred on the edges of the plaza at Toqua and Little Egypt. (See figure 4.) Burials were clustered in two locations on the northeast and southwest sides of the plaza at Ledford Island. In the excavated portion of the King site, four burial clusters occurred: two on the east side of the plaza, one in the large public building, and one immediately north of it.[14]

Domestic habitation zones containing domestic structures and burials are known to surround the public zone at Toqua, Ledford Island, Little Egypt, and King. The King site had a defensive perimeter consisting of a ditch and palisade, while Toqua and Ledford Island were enclosed by palisades only. Bastions along the palisade are present at Toqua and possibly at King.[15]

Almost without exception towns are located on the floodplain and adjacent terraces of major rivers. The known exception, 9PA39, is located five kilometers up a small stream tributary to the Etowah River in northwestern Georgia. Possibly, some people resided in scattered small hamlets or farmsteads, but the existence of such settlements remains to be demonstrated. Little upland survey has been conducted in the region, so that it is not known whether such sites exist in the hills surrounding the river valleys. Few sites smaller than 1 hectare have been found in surveyed river valleys: four along the Little Tennessee River and one along the Etowah River.[16] Since little is known about the artifactual content of such sites, it is not known whether they represent permanently occupied settlements or special activity sites. Flint quarries, fishing stations, and hunting camps are almost certainly part of the settlement system.

We can assume that people inhabiting the large towns of northwest

FIGURE 3
Map of the King site settlement

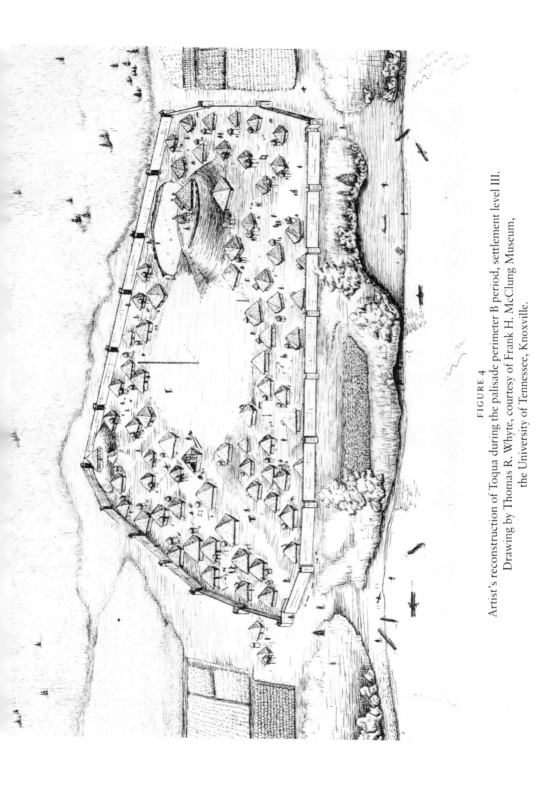

FIGURE 4

Artist's reconstruction of Toqua during the palisade perimeter B period, settlement level III. Drawing by Thomas R. Whyte, courtesy of Frank H. McClung Museum, the University of Tennessee, Knoxville.

Georgia and eastern Tennessee were organized at the most basic level into households; that is, groups of people who habitually resided together and prepared and consumed food together in and around one or more adjacent structures. Members of such groups were probably related to one another by blood and marriage, although this aspect of the household cannot be readily recognized in the archaeological record and is not an essential element in defining the household. Households can be identified at several sites: Toqua, Mouse Creek, Ledford Island, Rymer, Little Egypt, and King. Again, considerable uniformity is evident throughout the Georgia and Tennessee portions of the Coosa domain.

The most common and the most substantially built structure throughout the area is square in floor plan and ranges between 5 and 10 meters on a side, with an average of 6.5 meters. (See figure 5.) These structures were set in a shallow basin of approximately half a meter depth and had earth banked against at least the lower portion of their exterior walls. The latter were constructed of individually set vertical posts and covered with thatch, bark, or possibly clay. Roofs were evidently peaked and covered with thatch. The central portion of the roof, adjacent to the smoke hole, was frequently daubed with clay, presumably to prevent sparks from the hearth from setting the roof on fire. Entrance was typically gained through a narrow passage, measuring approximately 1 meter long and half a meter wide, and constructed of boards set on end in two parallel trenches. These were located near the center of an exterior wall in structures at Toqua, and near the end (corner) of an exterior wall in the Mouse Creek and Lamar culture structures.[17]

A prepared clay hearth is located in the center of the structure and is often accompanied by a section of fired floor surface. The latter may measure 1–2 meters across and apparently was used in food preparation.[18] Four large posts were set around the hearth forming a square measuring 2–3 meters on a side. These served as interior roof supports. The floor space circumscribed by these posts is usually free of occupation debris, in contrast to the zone between the posts and the exterior walls. The former has been identified as the "public" area of the house, with the latter as the "private" area.[19] At least some steps in food preparation took place within the central or public zone. The outer or private zone of floor space is typically divided into several compartments by wattle and daub partition walls. Ethnohistoric documentation suggests that benches or beds occupied some of these compartments. Concentrations of tools and work debris indicate that other compartments were the scene of various activities such as flint knapping and bone tool manufacture. Compartments located at the corner of structures may have served as storage areas. Human burials are typically located in the outer zone, but in at least one case, Structure 2 at Little Egypt, they were placed adjacent to the central hearth.[20]

Several kinds of evidence indicate that these structures were domestic in nature and served as the primary residence for household members during

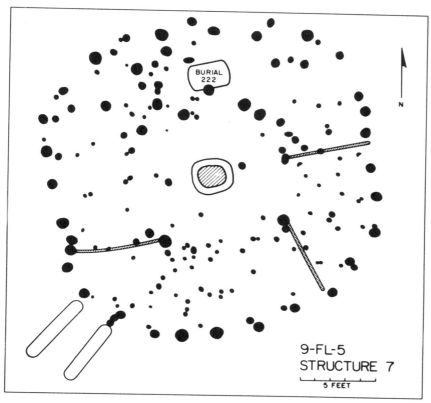

BURIAL
222

9-FL-5
STRUCTURE 7

5 FEET

FIGURE 5
Architectural features of a typical King site domestic structure

at least the colder portion of the year. Artifacts recovered from excavated floors indicate that a variety of activities took place within them, including food preparation, food storage, flint knapping, bone tool manufacture, and stone pipe manufacture. With their subterranean floors and earth embanked walls, these structures would have been well suited for occupancy during the colder seasons of the year. Carbonized plant material recovered from structures at Little Egypt indicates that they were occupied at least during the fall and winter and may have been partially abandoned during the summer.[21]

At the Toqua and King sites, structures with depressed floors typically faced a small open area that may have served as an outdoor activity area. A second type of structure occurs with some frequency in these open areas at the two sites. It consists of a rectangular posthole pattern measuring approximately 5 meters by 3 meters. In Figure 3, an especially clear example can be seen in the courtyard between structures 2 and 23. Human burials typically occur in the area outlined by posts, and at Toqua, fired soil features are also present. Possibly the posts may have supported a raised corn crib. The existence of hearth-like fired features suggests that whatever was supported by the posts was sufficiently high off the ground to allow people to stand and work beneath it. There is no evidence for ground level walls, and it is therefore possible that the lower portion of the structure served as an open shed where people conducted domestic chores.[22] This interpretation may be taken further by suggesting that these sheds were the summer counterpart of the depressed floor structures. The practice of burying the dead in both kinds of structures is consistent with this interpretation.

The published maps of the three Mouse Creek phase sites—Rymer, Mouse Creek, and Ledford Island—on the Hiwassee River show posthole patterns and burial distributions that resemble the pattern described above for King and Toqua. However, these patterns have been interpreted differently. Lynne Sullivan believes that the rectangular area directly in front of the depressed floor structures was roofed over and that burials were placed around the margins of this roofed area. She also identifies the depressed floor structure as a winter dwelling, and the flimsier structure as a summer dwelling.[23]

The combination of depressed floor structure, courtyard, and open shed is repeated numerous times at King, Toqua, and the Mouse Creek phase sites leading some to suggest that it represents the basic household unit in the respective communities. This interpretation is supported by the presence of human burials that may represent deceased household members beneath the floors of the two kinds of structure. The number of burials recovered from depressed-floor structures ranges between zero and eighteen; for the shed-like structures, the range is zero to nine. Both sexes and a wide age range are generally represented in the burials associated with individual structures. In one King site structure, several individuals had molar teeth with an extra cusp, an inherited trait known as Carabelli's cusp, that suggests they may have been genetically related. Clusters of burials of all ages and sexes and associated with domestic structures are also reported for Dallas culture sites.[24]

There are several instances at the King and Toqua sites of two or more depressed-floor structures being arranged around a single courtyard. Especially clear examples are represented by structures 2, 4, and 9, and structures 7 and 23 at the King site (see figure 3) and structures 2, 4, 32, and 33 at Toqua. It is possible that these arrangements represent extended-family households, each depressed-floor structure being occupied by a group of people roughly corresponding to a nuclear family. This reconstruction is given some support by ethnohistoric evidence. Among eighteenth-century Creeks, matrilocal, extended-family households were common, and there was a tendency for household structures to be arranged in a square around a small courtyard.[25]

Depressed-floor structures frequently show evidence of rebuilding. This varies from little more than the addition of a layer of puddled clay to the hearth to the dismantling and rebuilding of the entire superstructure. At the King site as many as five hearth stages have been recorded in one structure, and some structures have been completely rebuilt two or three times. It is not known why the decision to rebuild was made, but the fact that it occurs indicates that some structures were utilized over a period of several decades. The continued use of house sites suggests that they had some emotional/symbolic value to the people occupying them.

Structures with one or more rebuilding stages were probably occupied longer, in general, than those with only one construction stage. The validity of this relationship is supported by the fact that the King site structures with the most building stages also tend to contain the most burials. The King site structures with the most building stages and burials tend to have the largest floor area and tend to be located closest to the plaza. A similar set of relationships may exist at Toqua and Mouse Creek sites. Polhemus reports that the largest structures tend to occur nearest the plaza at Toqua, and Sullivan reports a tendency for larger Mouse Creek structures to have more burials.[26]

There is a model of domestic household growth that can account for all of these relationships. The larger and older structures located on the edge of the plaza were the residences of members of the senior line in each extended family. Through time, as these families grew and daughters established their own families, new depressed-floor structures were constructed adjacent to that of the parents, but in a less prestigious location and of smaller size. In several instances (for example, structures 3, 4, and 7 in figure 3), these latter structures are literally wedged into small spaces between the structure of the senior family line and the palisade.[27]

The size of twenty-three large habitation sites located on the Upper Coosa, Lower Etowah, Lower Coosawattee, Hiwassee, and Little Tennessee Rivers varies between 1 hectare and 5.6 hectares and averages 2.8 hectares. The size of the population residing at these sites can be estimated using estimates of the number of contemporary habitation structures per site and the average number of structure occupants. Dividing the area excavated at King, Mouse Creek, Rymer, and Ledford Island sites by the number of depressed-floor structures recorded in that area yields an average figure of 470 square meters of site space per habitation structure. Dividing this figure into the estimated site area for all twenty-three sites yields a range of 21 to 119 domestic structures per site, with an average of 59 structures per site. The floor space of 47 depressed-floor structures mapped at King, Mouse Creek, Rymer, and Ledford Island averages 61 square meters. Depending upon the formula for estimating household size from dwelling space, the average depressed-floor structure at each of these sites would have been occupied by 5.9 or 11.0 people. Using the smaller figure, the resident population of the twenty-three sites ranges between 124 and 702, and averages

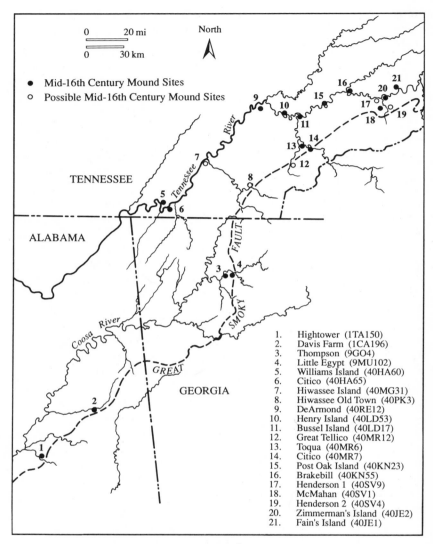

FIGURE 6
Distribution of middle sixteenth-century platform mounds

350. With the larger figure, population ranges between 253 and 1309, and averages 652. Using burial data, population estimates were made for Ledford Island, Rymer, and Toqua sites that are comparable to those made with site size data.[28]

At least a dozen sites located within the area of the Coosa paramount chiefdom had platform mounds dating to the sixteenth century. (See figure 6.) Five of these—Citico (40HA65), Williams Island, Hiwassee Island, Bussell Island, and Citico (40MR7)—had two mounds, while Little Egypt (9MU102) and Chilhowee (40BT7) may have had three mounds. Plowing has greatly reduced the height of many mounds to 1 meter or less, but it seems likely that most were 3–4 meters tall. The tallest recorded mounds, approaching 8 meters, are at Toqua and Citico (40HA65).[29]

Only two platform mounds have been extensively excavated by professional archaeologists and described in print: Mound A at Toqua and Mound A at Little Egypt. The former was constructed in sixteen stages, and at its maximum it had basal dimensions of 52 meters and 48 meters and a height of 7.3 meters. The last intact construction stage (stage H) was number 11 and is unlikely to have been in use at the time of de Soto. Its summit architecture conforms to a pattern that is present throughout all earlier construction stages and apparently in the subsequent stage I. It seems unlikely, therefore, that the terminal stage would have been significantly different.[30]

Two square structures, measuring 11 square meters and 7 square meters, are located on the western half of the Stage H summit. (See figure 7.) The larger structure has a clay embankment around the lower portion of its walls and is joined by a wall-trench passageway to the smaller structure. No embankment was recorded for the smaller structure, but in earlier construction stages, this building had an embankment. The smaller building has been identified as a domestic habitation structure on the basis of its size, smaller proportion of public to private floor space (less than 32 percent), and the absence of interior elaboration such as raised clay platforms and benches. In contrast, the larger structure is inferred to have been used for activities of a public nature. Each of these structures is paired with a shed-like structure on the eastern half of the mound summit. The larger of these, opposite the larger earth embanked structure, contained a number of high-status burials and fired surface areas.[31]

Mound A at Little Egypt measures 61 meters by 40 meters at the base and was at least 3 meters tall. The last intact summit (stage 3) dates to the fifteenth-century Little Egypt phase and is followed by at least two Barnett-phase construction stages. Within the excavated portion of this summit, there was a single structure measuring 10 square meters and having 36 percent public floor space. There was sufficient space available in the unexcavated portions of the summit for a second smaller domestic structure and two shed-like structures.[32]

In addition to the probable similarity in summit architecture, both

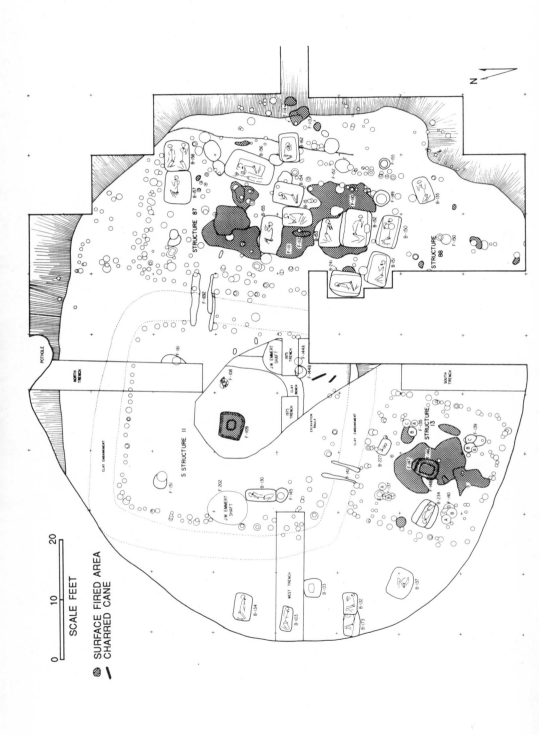

SCALE FEET

● SURFACE FIRED AREA

╱ CHARRED CANE

mounds are similar in having a large structure located on a terrace next to the mound—structure 1 at Little Egypt and structure 3 at Toqua. The presence of abundant domestic debris on the floors of these structures suggests that they served as habitation for high-ranking households.

Plaza area architecture at the King site conforms in several respects to the Toqua mound summit pattern.[33] Structure 17 is a large building measuring 14.5 square meters located in the northeast corner of the plaza. (See figure 3.) Immediately to the west is structure 16, which in size (6 square meters) resembles the domestic structures at the site and may have served as the residence of the town headman. A posthole pattern lying immediately north of structures 16 and 17 suggests a large rectangular shed measuring 18 meters by 7.5 meters. Eleven burials containing high-status grave goods are located within this latter feature. This same pattern may be represented at Ledford Island by features 36 and 47 and a cluster of postholes and burials located immediately in front of them.[34]

Information on status differentiation is available from a number of sites located within the domain of Coosa. Mortuary practices have been analyzed for the King site, the Mouse Creek culture sites, and several Dallas culture sites. Bioarchaeological analyses have been conducted on skeletal material from these same sites as well as from Etowah.[35]

The mortuary data indicates that status differentiation was characteristic of all of the societies represented by these sites. Burials differ with respect to where they are placed (in the domestic habitation zone, in the plaza, in or near the mounds), the size and shape of the pit in which they are placed, and the kinds of artifacts that accompany them. Typically, less than 50 percent of burials are accompanied by grave goods. The great majority of grave goods are made of local materials, and they functioned as subsistence and domestic articles prior to their interment. A few types of grave goods were made of exotic (nonlocal) materials, required exceptional craftsmanship to make, or have obvious supralocal symbolic significance. These are generally identified by archaeologists as markers of high status.

Mound sites and nonmound sites present different pictures of the status system. At the King site, a small number of males, thirty years of age and older, are buried with a rather consistent group of items: a large bipointed flint blade, a flint worker's kit, and a cluster of triangular points. With only one exception, these individuals also have the only examples of iron tools, conch shell cups, ground stone discoidals, embossed copper pendants, and spatulate celts. Much the same situation occurs at Ledford Island, except that the variety of grave goods is smaller and some individuals are younger than adult.[36] At both King and Ledford Island, half or more of the individuals with these kinds of grave goods are buried in the plaza and plaza area structures. At King, most of the remainder are buried in two large, multistage domestic structures (structures 1 and 15) located on the northeast edge of the plaza.

Given the age, sex, and plaza associations of these burials, it is likely that they represent one or a small number of achieved high-status positions in the two communities. Their association with structures 1 and 15 at the King site supports the identification of these structures on architectural grounds as belonging to high-status households.

No burials were found in good Barnett-phase context in the mounds at Little Egypt. There is considerable data on mortuary practices available from Dallas culture mound sites along the Tennessee and Little Tennessee Rivers, but its relevance to the present discussion is questionable since much of it pertains to the fourteenth and fifteenth centuries.

As at the King site, large bipointed flint blades, flint worker kits, and clusters of triangular points occurred together in association with adult males in the village zone at Dallas sites. Presumably, this combination of attributes was the result of achieved status here as well. The preeminent status in Dallas society is represented by a small number of adult male, adult female, and subadult burials located in mounds and accompanied by a variety of artifacts of exotic material and fine craftsmanship, including copper earspools and headdresses, painted and modeled pottery, and conch shell cups. Possibly, these individuals inherited their high-status positions and represent the chief and members of his descent group.[37]

Bioarchaeological evidence tends to support the existence of an inherited elite stratum at Dallas mound centers. Adult males buried in mounds appear to have been subject to less physiological stress than their village counterparts. They were significantly taller, they manifest fewer growth arrest lines formed in the 0–8 year range, and they have thinner-walled leg bones. The former may reflect a lower incidence of disease, a higher nutritional level, or both. Cortical bone thickness appears to vary directly with the level of physical activity, and in this case suggests that males buried in mounds were less physically active than those buried in the village. In contrast to the mound situation, males interred adjacent to mounds had the highest cortical bone thickness. Artifact associations and burial location indicate that these individuals had achieved high status in Dallas society. Their greater cortical bone thickness suggests that they achieved their status through physically demanding tasks.[38]

Trace element analyses of zinc, copper, manganese, strontium, and vanadium indicate that individuals buried in mounds enjoyed a more varied and protein-rich diet than those buried in the village. These findings are supported by zooarchaeological evidence showing that the occupants of Mound A and high-status village areas at Toqua had access to more meaty portions of large mammals such as white-tailed deer and bear. Furthermore, the incidence of porotic hyperostosis at Toqua is higher among village burials, indicating greater incidence of iron deficiency anemia in that segment of the population.[39]

At several Dallas sites, males buried in close proximity to mounds differed from males buried elsewhere in the village: they had richer grave goods; they were taller; and they had greater cortical bone thickness. These individuals may have had higher status than other nonmound-burial males, and their status positions may have been attained through achievement or through a combination of achievement and ascription. They may have been, for example, the heads of junior lineages in a ramage system where lineages were ranked with respect to their genealogical proximity to the chief's lineage.[40]

The available evidence indicates that social systems in the Coosa paramount chiefdom were characterized by status hierarchies incorporating both achieved and ascribed ranks. The highest positions were inherited and probably included the political leaders of the various chiefdoms and their immediate kinsmen. Below this level were men of intermediate rank who probably achieved their positions through hard work and skill, but who also may have enjoyed easier access to those positions through birth. These men are represented archaeologically by individuals who were buried in or close to the plazas of nonmound sites or in close proximity to mounds. Grave goods appropriate to their status may have included large bipointed blades, clusters of projectile points, flint worker kits, spatulate celts, ground stone discoidals, and even conch shell cups and embossed copper ornaments. These men probably functioned as town headmen and lineage heads.[41]

Platform mounds were likely a central element in the political organization of Mississippian chiefdoms in the southeastern United States. Ethnohistorical evidence indicates that they played a major functional and symbolic role in the institution of the chieftainship, and that they served as a focus of administrative and ritual activity for each chiefdom. The exalted status of the chief was symbolized by the location of his residence on top of the mound. His divine nature was validated by the bones of his ancestors stored in the mortuary temple located on top of the mound. Succession to the office of chief may have been symbolized by the addition of mound stages and rebuilding of summit structures. A number of the duties that the chief had as head of the state religion were carried out on the mound or in temple structures on its summit. In short, platform mounds were necessary for the chief to properly carry out his role as political and religious leader, and they served to legitimize and sanctify the office of chief and the incumbent's claim to that position.

Available archaeological evidence from the Coosa River and Tennessee River drainages tends to support this view. Where there has been sufficient excavation, mound summits usually contain structures that could have served as domestic habitations and others that could have served ritual purposes. Burials containing quantities of exotic and finely crafted artifacts occur in these mounds. Mounds were erected in a number of stages, each involving the addition of a mantle of fill, and summit structures were frequently constructed directly above architecturally similar buildings on earlier summits.

The spatial distribution of mound sites and large villages provides considerable insight into the geographical and organizational nature of the paramount chiefdom of Coosa and the polities constituting it. In areas where there has been site survey and where sites can be dated to the mid-sixteenth century with some degree of confidence, large villages and mound sites tend to occur in clusters. Seven easily discernible clusters are located on the Little Tennessee River, the Hiwassee River, the Tennessee River near Chattanooga, the Coosawatee River, the lower Etowah River, the upper Coosa River, and the middle Coosa River.[42] (See figure 8.) Additional clusters probably exist on Cholccolocco Creek in eastern Alabama and in several locations along the Tennessee River above Chattanooga.

Clusters consist of between four and seven large sites greater than one hectare in size. With the exception of the Childersburg cluster, sites are strung out in a linear fashion along rivers. The maximum distances across clusters range between 11 and 24 kilometers, while the minimum distances separating neighboring clusters—Little Tennessee, Chattanooga, Carters, and Childersburg—are known to contain one or more sites with platform mounds, and there is a strong likelihood that the others did as well.

Some have argued that these site clusters represent chiefdoms; that is, the site clusters represent politically integrated societies that had centralized administrative hierarchies and were largely politically autonomous.[43] This argument is based on the following evidence:

1. Sites with platform mounds served as the administrative center for each site cluster.

2. The number of large village sites in each site cluster—approximately six—is the optimal number of units for a single-level administrative hierarchy to administer.[44]

3. Site clusters are small enough in spatial extent that travel time from the administrative center to any component town was less than one day, thus allowing chiefs to exercise direct control over their inhabitants.[45]

4. The distance between administrative centers—that is, sites known or believed to have mounds—in different site clusters usually exceeds 30 kilometers and would have made it difficult for chiefs to exercise direct control over the inhabitants of neighboring site clusters.

5. The areas between site clusters were largely uninhabited and may have served as military buffer zones and game reservoirs.

6. A similar spatial pattern, with administrative centers spaced 40 kilometers or more apart, is characteristic of complex prestate societies throughout the world.[46]

The de Soto narratives refer to at least five "provinces" that were under some form of control by the chief of Coosa. They were spread out over a

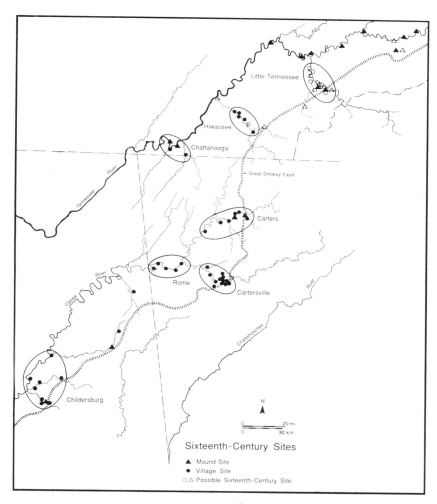

FIGURE 8
Mid-sixteenth-century archaeological sites and site clusters
in the paramount chiefdom of Coosa

distance of twenty-four travel days with the province of Coosa itself located at the approximate midpoint. Each province consisted of multiple towns, and each had a capital town where the chief resided. Provinces were separated from one another by uninhabited territories that required several days to traverse.[47]

The provinces referred to in the expedition narratives are almost certainly equivalent to the site clusters of the archaeological record. At least some of the seven site clusters can be identified with specific named provinces: Carters with Coosa; Cartersville with Itaba; the Rome cluster with Ulibahali; and the Childersburg cluster with Talisi. When Elvas describes Coosa as being "thickly settled in numerous and large towns with fields between, extending from one to another," he is probably speaking of Little Egypt and the six large sites that are strung out below it along the Coosawattee River for a distance of 19 kilometers.[48] In this sense, Coosa was a chiefdom consisting of approximately seven large towns with its capital at the multimound Little Egypt site. A secondary center probably existed at the single mound Thompson site, located 8.5 kilometers downstream from Little Egypt. The total population of this chiefdom would have been 2,850 using Raoul Naroll's formula, or 5,400 using Sherburne Cook's formula.

At various times during the late prehistoric period, some if not all of the chiefdoms represented by these site clusters probably were politically independent polities. In A.D. 1540, they were politically subordinate to the chief of the Coosa chiefdom. The nature of this relationship is not altogether clear from either the ethnohistoric or the archaeological evidence. Chiefs of subordinated chiefdoms acknowledged "being subject to" the chief of Coosa. They paid tribute to him several times a year, and they entered into military alliances with him against common enemies. Whether he actually governed the populace of subordinate chiefdoms is not known, however.[49]

The domain of the paramount chiefdom cannot be established using archaeological evidence alone. There is considerable uniformity in material culture throughout the region of the paramount chiefdom, but this uniformity extends in some cases well beyond the presumed limits of Coosa. Depressed-floor domestic structures with wall-trench entrance passages, for example, are found throughout northern Georgia and probably over much of western North and South Carolina. There is, on the other hand, little uniformity in ceramic styles within the domain of Coosa. The pottery of Lamar and Dallas cultures differs in numerous and fundamental ways, and even the Lamar ceramics of the northwest Georgia and eastern Alabama site clusters are recognizably distinct from one another.

There is no evidence of a settlement hierarchy of the kind that might be expected to characterize a paramount chiefdom. The Carters site cluster, the supposed chiefdom of Coosa, may have one or two more large habitation sites than the other clusters, but it is not distinctive in other ways. It is not the only cluster containing more than one site with mounds and sites with multiple mounds. The mounds at the Little Egypt site are smaller than those at Toqua and Citico (40MR7) on the Little Tennessee River and at Citico (40HA65) on the Tennessee River. No burials with mortuary features indicative of inherited rank, much less exalted status, have been reported from Little Egypt, although they may exist in unexcavated portions of the mounds.

The only archaeological phenomenon that might be indicative of the paramountcy is the rattlesnake gorget. These have been found buried with women and subadults at several of the excavated sites in the region. Their known spatial distribution conforms quite closely to that of the paramount chiefdom as reconstructed by Charles Hudson and his colleagues. They may be symbolic representations of the paramount chief and identity markers for those people under his control.[50]

The lack of archaeological evidence for the paramount chiefdom of Coosa is not surprising. It is unlikely that the polity was in existence for very long prior to A.D. 1540, and prior to its formation, the component chiefdoms may have been politically independent or part of other paramount chiefdoms. Prior to A.D. 1400, most of northwest Georgia must have been under the control of a chiefdom centered at the Etowah site. Given the distances separating the Carters site cluster from other site clusters and the existence of uninhabited territories between site clusters, the paramount chiefdom must have been very weakly integrated. The chief of Coosa probably had little interest in or control over the day-to-day affairs of subordinate chiefdoms. As a political phenomenon, the paramountcy probably existed primarily as a set of relationships between the chief of Coosa and the leaders of the chiefdoms subordinate to him, and these relationships may have been primarily symbolic.

Spanish contact in the mid-sixteenth century had a devastating effect on aboriginal society in the Coosa region. Communities continued to be occupied for a number of years following de Soto, as is indicated by the presence of burials with European iron artifacts at several sites.[51] By 1560, however, the chiefdom and paramount chiefdom of Coosa were clearly in decline. In that year, members of the Luna expedition found the town and chiefdom of Coosa much reduced in size: "It did not have above thirty houses, or a few more. There were seven little hamlets in its district, five of them smaller and two larger than Coosa itself." So great was the contrast between the Coosa chiefdom of A.D. 1540 and 1560 that "those they had brought along as guides, being people who had been there before, declared that they must have been bewitched when this country seemed to them so rich and populated as they had stated."[52] The decline in size and power of the paramountcy is evidenced by the fact that Luna's men were enlisted to aid the chief of Coosa in subjugating a group of towns on the Tennessee River, known collectively as the Napochies, that had broken away from the paramount chiefdom. Evidently, the paramountcy persisted in some form up to at least 1567, for in that year Juan Pardo's expedition was threatened with attack by the combined forces of several chiefs including the chief of Coosa, who was their leader.

Old World epidemic diseases are generally believed to have greatly reduced the native population within a few decades of A.D. 1540. Mass burials, in which three or more bodies were interred in a single pit, have been documented for several sites within the Coosa domain and may be a result of epidemics. Little evidence of epidemic disease, however, has been found in the large burial population from the King site.[53]

The upper Coosa River drainage in Georgia was abandoned during the latter half of the sixteenth century. The process evidently involved population reduction, population consolidation into a smaller number of communities, and the progressive relocation of settlements southward along the Coosa Valley.[54] Postcontact developments along the Tennessee River drainage are not as well known. Toqua appears to have been abandoned during the latter part of the sixteenth century, but other sites evidence occupation well into the seventeenth century.[55] Archaeologists in the region are divided over the question of the historical relationship between Dallas culture and eighteenth-century Overhill Cherokee culture; some argue that the latter developed out of the former, and others that the Overhill Cherokee were recent migrants into a region that had been largely abandoned by its former inhabitants.[56]

Within a few decades following Spanish contact, the paramount chiefdom of Coosa ceased to exist, its population was decimated and scattered, and much of its culture was transformed beyond recognition. Were it not for the few brief passages in the de Soto narratives and the archaeological evidence provided by such sites as Little Egypt, Toqua, and King, the former existence of this society would be unknown to us today. Fortunately, through the collaborative efforts of ethnohistorians and archaeologists, we have begun to learn a great deal about Coosa; and since these efforts have only recently begun, we can anticipate learning a great deal more.

NOTES

1. Hudson et al., "Coosa"; Hudson, "A Spanish-Coosa Alliance"; and DePratter, Hudson, and Smith, "Route of Juan Pardo's Explorations."

2. Hally, "Potts' Tract Site," "Little Egypt Site, 1969 Season," "Little Egypt Site, 1970–72 Seasons," and "Plan of the King Site"; Garrow and Smith, "The King Site (9FL5) Excavations, April 1971 through August 1973: Collected Papers," typescript, Department of Anthropology and Linguistics, University of Georgia, 1973; Patricia Kelly, "The Architecture of the King Site" (M.A. thesis, University of Georgia, 1988); Marvin T. Smith, "Mississippian Settlement in Eastern Tennessee: The View from the Chickamauga Reservoir" (Paper delivered at the Fiftieth Annual Southeastern Archaeological Conference, New Orleans, La., 1988); Sullivan, "Late

Mississippian Village"; Lewis and Kneberg, *Hiwassee Island;* James W. Hatch, "Social Dimensions of Dallas Mortuary Patterns" (M.A. thesis, Pennsylvania State University, 1974); and Polhemus, *"Toqua Site."*

3. DePratter, Hudson, and Smith, "Juan Pardo's Explorations"; Hudson et al., "Coosa"; and Hudson, Smith, Hally, Polhemus, and DePratter, "Reply to Boyd and Schroedl."

4. Hally and Langford, *Mississippi Period Archaeology;* Knight, Cole, and Walling, *Coosa and Tallapoosa;* Garrow, "Mouse Creek 'Focus' "; Lewis and Kneberg, *Hiwassee Island;* Schroedl, *Overhill Cherokee Archaeology;* Sullivan, "Late Mississippian Village."

5. Garrow, "Mouse Creek 'Focus.' "

6. Hally, "Plant Preservation"; and Shea, Polhemus, and Chapman, "The Paleoethnobotany of the Toqua Site."

7. Roth, "Analysis of Faunal Remains"; Bogan and Polhemus, "Faunal Analysis."

8. Blakely and Detweiller-Blakely, "Impact of European Diseases"; D. Boyd, "Comparison of Mouse Creek Phase to Dallas"; A. B. Brown, "Diet and Nutritional Stress"; Detweiler-Blakely, "Stress and Battle Casualties"; Hatch, Willey, and Hunt, "Status-Related Stress"; Kestle, "Subsistence and Sex Roles"; and Parham, "Toqua Skeletal Biology."

9. Blakely, "Life Cycle"; Brown, "Diet and Nutritional Stress"; Detweiler-Blakely, "Stress and Battlefield Casualties"; and Parham and Scott, "Porotic Hyperostosis," 45.

10. Blakely, "Life Cycle"; Boyd, "Comparison of Skeletal Remains;" Hatch, Willey, and Hunt, "Status-Related Stress;" Parham, "Toqua Skeletal Biology."

11. Blakely, "Life Cycle," 28–31; Boyd, "Comparison of Skeletal Remains," 110; and Parham, "Skeletal Biology," 443, table 7.6.

12. Kimball, *1977 Archaeological Survey;* Marvin Smith, "Mississippian Settlement in Eastern Tennessee: The View from the Chickamauga Reservoir" (Paper delivered at the Fiftieth Annual Southeastern Archaeological Conference, New Orleans, La., October 23, 1988); James B. Langford, Jr., and Marvin T. Smith, "Recent Investigations in the Core of the Coosa Province"; Polhemus, *Toqua Site;* Sullivan, "Late Mississippian Village"; Hally, "Little Egypt Site, 1970–72 Seasons"; and Hally, "Plan of the King Site."

13. Hally, Smith, and Langford, "The Archaeological Reality"; Polhemus, *Toqua Site,* 1240–42.

14. Hally, "Plan of the King Site"; Sullivan, "Late Mississippian Village"; Polhemus, *Toqua Site;* and Hally, "Little Egypt Site, 1970–72 Seasons."

15. Hally, "Plan of the King Site"; Polhemus, *Toqua Site;* and Sullivan, "Late Mississippian Village."

16. Kimbal, *1977 Archaeological Survey,* table 71, 297–310; Hally and Langford, *Mississippi Period Archaeology,* 76.

17. Hally, "Plan of the King Site," 11–12; Polhemus, *Toqua Site,* 236–40; Sullivan, "The Mouse Creek Phase Household," 21–22.

18. Hally, "Domestic Architecture," 46.

19. Polhemus, *Toqua Site,* 236–37.

20. Garrow and Smith, "King Site Excavations," 16–17; Hally, "Domestic Architecture," 47–48; and Polhemus, *Toqua Site,* 284–85.

21. Garrow and Smith, "King Site (9FL5) Excavations," 13–17; Hally, "Little Egypt Site, 1970–72 Seasons," 93–393; and Polhemus, *Toqua Site*, 258–59, 284–85; and Hally, "Plant Preservation," 735–36.

22. Polhemus, *Toqua Site*, 241.

23. Sullivan, "Mouse Creek Phase Household," 23–24.

24. Polhemus, *Toqua Site*, 1242–43; Sullivan, "Mouse Creek Phase Household," 24; Tally, "King Site Burial Population," 75; and Scott and Polhemus, "Mortuary Patterning," 399.

25. Polhemus, *Toqua Site*, figure 3.5, 64; and Swanton, *Indians of the Southeastern United States*, 172–74.

26. P. Kelly, "Architecture of the King Site," 79–81; Polhemus, *Toqua Site*, 1221; and Sullivan, "Mouse Creek Phase Household," 25.

27. Kelly, "Architecture of the King Site," 92–94.

28. Cook, *Prehistoric Demography*, 16; Naroll, "Floor Area and Settlement Population," 587–89; D. Boyd, "Comparison of Skeletal Remains"; and Parham, "Toqua Skeletal Biology," 453.

29. Hally, Smith, and Langford, "de Soto's Coosa," 10, and Polhemus, *Toqua Site*, figure 13.5, 1249.

30. Polhemus, *Toqua Site*, 97, 117.

31. Ibid., 143.

32. Hally, "Little Egypt Site, 1970–72 Seasons," 516.

33. Hally, "Plan of the King Site," 15.

34. Sullivan, "Mouse Creek Phase Household," figure 4, 20.

35. Ernest W. Seckinger, Jr., "Social Complexity During the Mississippian Period in Northwest Georgia" (M.A. thesis, University of Georgia, 1977); Sullivan, "Late Mississippian Village"; Hatch, "Dallas Mortuary Patterns"; Hatch, "Citico Site"; Hatch and Willey, "Stature and Status in Dallas Society"; Hatch and Geidel, "Status and Diet in Prehistoric Tennessee"; Hatch, Willey, and Hunt, "Status-Related Stress"; and Scott and Polhemus, "Mortuary Patterning."

36. Sullivan, "Late Mississippian Village," 367–69.

37. Hatch, "Dallas Mortuary Patterns," 120, 130–34.

38. Hatch and Willey, "Stature and Status," 113–22, and Hatch, Willey, and Hunt, "Status-Related Stress," 60.

39. Hatch and Geidel, "Status and Diet in Prehistoric Tennessee," 58; Bogan and Polhemus, "Faunal Analysis," 987; and Parham and Scott, "Porotic Hyperostosis," 497.

40. Hatch and Willey, "Stature and Status in Dallas Society," 122–23; Hatch, Willey, and Hunt, "Status-Related Stress," 60.

41. Blakely, "Life Cycle," 31–32; Hatch and Willey, "Stature and Status in Dallas Society," 122–23; Hatch, Willey, and Hunt, "Status-Related Stress," 60–61; Scott and Polhemus, "Mortuary Patterning," 399.

42. Hally, Smith, and Langford, "de Soto's Coosa," 6–7.

43. Ibid., 11–13.

44. G. A. Johnson, "Organizational Structure and Scaler Stress," 410–12.

45. Cherry, "Power in Space," 166; Johnson, "Uruk Administration," 116; Renfrew, "Trade as Action," 14.

46. Renfrew, "Trade as Action," 13–18.

47. Hally, Smith, and Langford, "de Soto's Coosa," 2; Hudson et al., "Coosa," 723, 729.

48. Elvas, *Narratives of de Soto*, 76.

49. Swanton, *Creek Indians*, 232, 239; DePratter, Hudson, and Smith, "Juan Pardo's Explorations," 149.

50. Hudson et al., "Coosa," 732–33.

51. Smith, *Aboriginal Culture Change*, 45–52.

52. Swanton, *Creek Indians*, 231.

53. Smith, *Aboriginal Culture Change*, 61–62, and Blakely and Detweiler-Blakely, "Impact of European Diseases," 73.

54. Smith, *Aboriginal Culture Change*, 75–77.

55. Richard R. Polhemus, "The Early Historic Period," and Smith, *Aboriginal Culture Change*, 45–52.

56. Schroedl, *Overhill Cherokee Archaeology*, 533, and Lewis and Kneberg, *Hiwassee Island*, 10–20.

Structural Change

MARVIN T. SMITH

Aboriginal Depopulation in the Postcontact Southeast

From 1539–43, the expedition led by Hernando de Soto explored much of the interior of the southern United States. De Soto and his followers were the first Europeans to encounter the large Indian chiefdoms that existed in the interior South, and they were also virtually the last to see them. Within the few decades after the survivors of de Soto's army made their way down the Mississippi River to the Gulf of Mexico and New Spain, these southern chiefdoms collapsed in terms of both population and social structure. In part, their collapse was caused by the economic and social impact of the de Soto expedition, but even more by the introduction of germs and viruses for which the Indians had no natural immunity.

In 1559–61, members of the Tristán de Luna expedition visited some of the towns de Soto had visited in Alabama and Georgia, and in 1566–68, Juan Pardo visited some of the towns de Soto had visited in South Carolina, North Carolina, and Tennessee. In both cases, these Spanish explorers found the Indians reduced in numbers and perhaps in social complexity. Beyond these two expeditions, with negligible exceptions, it was over a hundred years before Europeans again visited the places where de Soto had been. When they did, they found far smaller populations of Indians, and nowhere did they find the large, bellicose chiefdoms that de Soto had encountered.

De Soto was not the first European to attempt to explore and colonize the Southeast. Before de Soto landed in Florida, there had already been three attempts to explore and to establish colonies: Juan Ponce de León on the western coast of Florida in 1521, Lucas Vásquez de Ayllón on the South Carolina or Georgia coast in 1526, and Pánfilo de Narváez in Florida in 1528. All of these attempts failed, but each may have contributed to the collapse of native society by introducing European and/or African disease.[1]

The effects of the introduction of new diseases from Europe and Africa by the conquistadores and their armies has been the subject of much scholarly debate. Pioneering work by Henry Dobyns, Carl Sauer, Alfred Crosby, and Sherburne Cook and Woodrow Borah focused on Central and South America, the Caribbean, and California. This work has been followed by studies of the effects on the southeastern United States. There have been two contrasting interpretations of the effects of disease. Earlier researchers, such as A. L. Kroeber and James Mooney, based their aboriginal population estimates on early observations by Europeans, but these observations often were a century or more after initial contact. These early estimates did not consider the effects of disease.[2]

The other interpretation, best elaborated by Henry Dobyns, stresses the great loss of life that took place when Europeans and Africans brought new pathogens into the New World. The Indians had no natural immunity to diseases that had evolved among Old World populations, and they died in great numbers. Dobyns argues for a depopulation ratio of as much as 20 to 1. That is, there were twenty times more Indians alive in 1492 than after European diseases struck, and the aboriginal populations reached very low points before they began to recover. Dobyns takes a radical stance in arguing that there were large pandemics that swept across the New World among these "virgin soil" populations. Thus, a smallpox epidemic documented in Mexico might be expected to have spread across North America. He constructs a model of wave after wave of disease decimating aboriginal populations during the sixteenth and seventeenth centuries. His research has stirred up great controversy, and his methodology has been questioned on several levels. His use of documents has been questioned and his methods of estimating population from historical records and using a carrying capacity model have also been criticized. Nonetheless Dobyns alerts us to the proposition that epidemics of smallpox, measles, influenza, bubonic plague, diphtheria, typhus, cholera, scarlet fever, and other diseases swept through the Southeast.[3]

There is no doubt that Europeans in direct contact with Indians helped spread disease. Figures of population decline from areas in direct contact with Europeans are shocking in their enormity. For example, the Arawaks of Santo Domingo numbered an estimated one million in 1492, but according to Oviedo, by 1548 only about five hundred survived. Indians in the Valley of Mexico were decimated by a smallpox epidemic started by a single infected Spaniard in 1519. More directly, Ponce de León's colonizing venture of 1521 on the Gulf coast of Florida ended in failure, but significantly, many people died of disease and may have transmitted this illness to the Indians, and similarly, the Ayllón expedition of 1526 may have introduced disease to the Atlantic coast.[4]

The chroniclers of the de Soto expedition of 1540 describe an epidemic that struck Cofitachequi just prior to the arrival of de Soto. Garcilaso reports that hundreds of bodies were stacked up in four of the houses, and Elvas reports that several towns were depopulated, and survivors had moved to other towns. Some researchers believe that this is evidence for an early European epidemic, while others question this interpretation.[5] Evidence from the Luna expedition of 1560 suggests that Coosa had lost some of its former glory, although its towns were still where de Soto encountered them.[6]

In 1587, the Englishman Thomas Hariot reported on the effects of European disease on Indians on the coast of present North Carolina. "Within a few days after our departure from everies such townes, that people began to die very fast, and many in short space."[7] If such rapid decimation of aboriginal population were caused by only a few of the many sixteenth-century contacts, the loss of life was still staggering.

During the seventeenth century, Spanish missionaries to the Florida Indians kept good records of aboriginal depopulation. Historian John Hann estimates a population of some 25,000 Apalachee Indians in the early seventeenth century, which is close to estimates of 30,000 made by friars in 1608 and 1617. Estimates made in 1638 numbered over 16,000, while in 1676 only 5,000 Indians were left according to the Lenten census, an enumeration made for the church. Hann believes that this figure is low. He accepts as a good indicator the 1703–4 estimate of 8,000 that was made just before the missions were destroyed. Hann also notes that there is "surprisingly little documentary evidence" about the disease epidemics. There are only three definite references to epidemics among the Apalachee: a 1655 smallpox epidemic, a 1693 epidemic, and a 1703 epidemic. He believes that many of the epidemics that struck the Timucua area of Florida probably spread to the Apalachee. Additional epidemics around 1613 and 1617 killed half of the Timucua. A 1649–50 epidemic (which Dobyns believes was yellow fever), a 1659 epidemic of measles, and a 1672 outbreak of disease in Timucua may have caused further Apalachee depopulation.[8]

Later eighteenth-century accounts show that disease caused further depopulation. According to the historian James Merrell, "The smallpox epidemic that struck the Southeast in 1738 killed one of every two Cherokees, and it may have been equally lethal among Catawbas." Another outbreak of smallpox in 1759 reduced the Catawba warriors from around 200–500 to a mere 50–150. The most ambitious effort at documenting southeastern Indian population by region has been carried out by historian Peter Wood for the period 1685–1790. Wood notes that population had been declining in some areas, particularly along the coast, for nearly two centuries prior to his late seventeenth-century estimates based on historic sources. He further estimates that in the period 1685–1730, the Native American population of the Southeast was reduced by two-thirds from around 200,000 to fewer than 67,000, and he blames this decline on epidemic disease. A recent study of the Cherokee by Russell Thornton also documents population changes.[9]

In recent years, archaeologists have attempted to detect evidence of depopulation in the archaeological record. In an influential article, George Milner set forth the basic archaeological approach to the question of epidemic depopulation. He notes that mass and multiple burials and unusual population curves could be evidence of epidemics. Population curves show the frequency of different age segments of a population. They should demonstrate the effects of disease on normally healthy population segments, such as young men. Contrary to Dobyns, Milner suggests that disease epidemics might have been restricted to specific aboriginal political units, and might not have spread unless carried by traders or refugees, but he concludes that epidemic disease had severely altered the population of the Southeast prior to A.D. 1700. Ann Ramenofsky and Marvin Smith have used archaeological data from the Southeast in attempts to measure depopulation. Ramenofsky concludes that there is evidence of depopulation during the sixteenth century in the lower Mississippi Valley, and Smith argues that although evidence is weak, depopulation occurred at the same time in the Alabama/Georgia/Tennessee area.[10]

The most obvious approach to the epidemic disease problem would be to look for direct skeletal evidence in aboriginal burials. Unfortunately, epidemics are usually quick killers, and seldom leave any evidence on the skeleton. Nevertheless, smallpox and measles have been known to affect bone. Survivors of epidemics may show various signs of illness, such as Harris lines or enamel hypoplasias. Harris lines are areas of interrupted growth that can be detected on skeletal elements, while enamel hypoplasias are similar interrupted growth lines that can be seen on teeth. The problem is that these are general symptoms of stress, and cannot be correlated with any specific disease. Famine, for example, might also cause such responses.[11]

Milner suggests that mass or multiple burials could indicate deaths due to an epidemic. In 1698, the Frenchman St. Cosme reported on the Arkansas of the Mississippi Valley, "Not a month had elapsed since they had rid themselves of smallpox, which had carried off most of them. In the village are now nothing but graves, in which they were buried two together, and we estimated that not a hundred men were left."[12]

Marvin Smith studied the incidence of mass and multiple burials from sites in the province of Coosa. Such burials have been noted in middle sixteenth- and early seventeenth-century contexts. Unfortunately, comparative data from the immediate precontact period are not available for comparison. At the Toqua site in eastern Tennessee, mass burials of up to five individuals have been reported, and a mass grave was also reported from the King site in Georgia.[13] A more recent reinterpretation of the King site burials will be discussed below.

George Milner advocates the analysis of population curves to determine the presence of European disease epidemics. The idea is that disease is hardest on the very young and very old, and consequently these age groups would be disproportionately represented in an epidemic mortuary series. Normally healthy young adults and adolescents might also show increased mortality. Unfortunately, there have been few skeletal series subjected to such analysis. One such data set, that from the King site in northern Georgia, has yielded conflicting results.[14]

To one who is not a physical anthropologist, the conflicting interpretations of such specialists seem confusing. The interpretations of the data from the burials at the King site offer a good example. Excavations by Patrick Garrow and David Hally at the King site, an early sixteenth-century village located near present Rome, Georgia, have provided as many as 222 burials. This is one of the largest sixteenth-century populations to be excavated in the Southeast, and the largest investigated by physical anthropologists. The question of European disease was a consideration from the beginning.[15]

The first study of the King site skeletal series was conducted by Lucy Tally, a graduate student at the University of Georgia. Tally selected for analysis a sample of 109 burials from the best preserved portion of the site. She reported an "abnormally high" mortality rate for the 18–30 age group. Although she discusses death during childbirth as possibly accounting for some of the mortality, the deaths among the males were not so easily explained. She concluded that the advent of European diseases, such as smallpox, measles, or mumps, would be a plausible explanation for the unusual mortality rate.[16]

A second study by Gary Funkhouser selected a sample of 127 individuals of the 222 excavated for analysis. Using a life table analysis procedure, Funkhouser found that a slightly different percentage (18 percent) had died between the ages of 18 and 30 years. He concluded that this was not an unusual number, and found it comparable to other prehistoric populations. He found little evidence of an epidemic.[17]

The most recent analysis by Robert Blakely and his associates suggests that there is little evidence of epidemic disease at the King site in their sample of 189 individuals. However, they caution that evidence of an epidemic can be easily hidden in large skeletal populations of individuals from sites occupied for long periods. Finding evidence of a brief epidemic episode in a site occupied for generations is extremely difficult.[18] Nevertheless, it appears that a few such instances may already have been located. Jeffrey Mitchem and Dale Hutchinson, in their preliminary report on excavations at the Tatham Mound in Florida, note that seventy-four primary burials were made at approximately the same time, and they suggest that a disease epidemic was the possible cause.[19]

One indication of population loss is a decrease in the absolute number of sites occupied during a given interval of time. But for this to work, out-migration must be taken into account.[20] Using a carefully controlled sample of archaeological sites from Georgia and Alabama, it is possible to demon-

strate a decrease in the number of sites occupied during the period 1540–
1670. For example, within the portion of the province of Coosa located
on the upper Coosa River of Georgia and Alabama (see figure 1) north of
Woods Island, there are twenty-three mid-sixteenth-century villages and
two smaller sites that can be dated by means of diagnostic European artifacts found on the sites or by comparison of aboriginal ceramics with those
of sites with European artifacts. Following this period, there was a dramatic decrease in population: only one late sixteenth-century village, three
or four early seventeenth-century villages, and thirteen possible hamlets in
the Weiss Reservoir area; three mid-seventeenth-century villages and four
hamlets in the Gadsden, Alabama area; and one late seventeenth-century
village of Woods Island are known.[21]

Within a sample of sites from the Wallace Reservoir on the Oconee River
in the Georgia piedmont, there are 101 Dyar phase sites (early sixteenth-
century) compared to only 63 Bell phase sites (ca. 1580–1630), although
multicomponent sites (that is, sites that were occupied more than one time)
have been removed from the sample. More archaeological data from other
regions are needed to corroborate these findings.[22]

The size of an archaeological site is a recognized means of estimating
population size. Unfortunately, site size can be very difficult to determine
for any given time period. Our data range from excavated town plans, such
as that for the King site in northwestern Georgia, to crude estimates of the
size of artifact scatters seen in plowed fields.[23] When sites are occupied and
abandoned several times in their lifespan, it is very difficult to determine
the size at a particular time. Only through carefully controlled surface collections or extensive excavation can such estimates be made. In spite of all
the problems, attempts have been made to determine changes in site sizes
for two areas, the Coosa paramount chiefdom and a sample of sites in the
province of Ocute.

In the province of Coosa, sixteenth-century sites averaged 29,700 square
meters. The one known late sixteenth-century village is over twice as large
as this average, and even early seventeenth-century sites (mean size 7.3
hectares), middle seventeenth-century sites (3.2 hectares), and the one late
seventeenth-century site (10.7 hectares) are larger on average if the sizes
recorded in the Alabama State Archaeological Site Files are accurate. (It
should be noted that some are particularly suspicious, while some of the
sites had multiple occupations and the size of the historic period component is unknown.) While the number of sites was declining dramatically,
the available data appear to indicate that site size in Coosa was increasing.
This may simply indicate that several former towns were joining together
in an attempt to maintain a size. Perhaps more likely, the recorded sizes do
not indicate the true area occupied at the period under study. The quality
of the data is such that decrease in site size cannot be ruled out.[24]

A sample of single component (occupied only during one period) sites

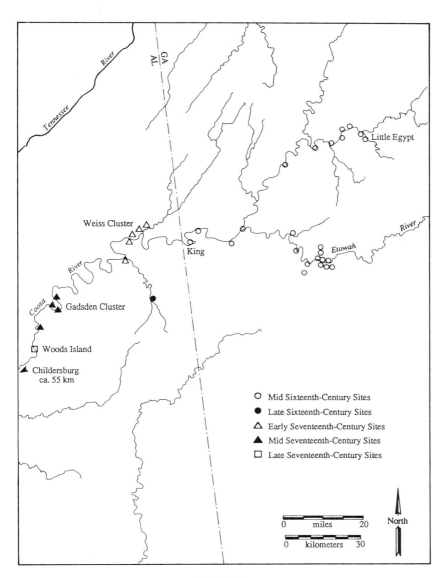

FIGURE I
Map of Coosa towns

in the Wallace Reservoir on the Oconee River in central Georgia showed a drop in average size from 6,807 square meters during the Dyar phase (sixteenth-century) to 4,648 square meters in the Bell phase (seventeenth-century). These figures are skewed by the presence of many small sites, but perhaps more telling is the fact that there were fifteen Dyar phase sites with areas of over 10,000 square meters, but only five Bell phase sites of this size.[25]

There is now good historical and archaeological evidence of the direct devastation of aboriginal populations of the Southeast as a consequence of warfare between Europeans and Indians. Narratives of the de Soto expedition provide numerous accounts of armed conflict with the Indians of La Florida. For example, the Battle of Mabila killed some 2,500 Indians, while the Battle of the Ponds in Napituca, the guerilla warfare in Apalachee and Chickasaw, and the destruction of Anilco accounted for numerous others. Lesser incidents of violence by members of the de Soto expedition may have been so common as to go unrecorded by the chroniclers.[26]

Archaeological evidence for trauma inflicted by Europeans is becoming more and more common. Within the last few years, analysis of the skeletal population from the King site has produced strong evidence of a massacre of Indians by Europeans in the mid-sixteenth century. Not only were metal weapons used in the trauma, but the pattern of wounds suggests that they were inflicted by Europeans.[27]

Recent excavations at the Tatham Mound in Florida have also produced evidence of trauma with metal weapons. At least two human bones found in the Tatham Mound show evidence of having been cut by metal tools. These traumas are believed to have been inflicted during contact with the Narváez or de Soto expeditions.[28]

Such warfare must have killed numerous Indians, but perhaps more importantly, it must have had secondary effects. De Soto's theft of stored food from the Indians probably caused direct starvation. Battle casualties and disease victims were obviously unable to maintain their customary planting and harvesting schedule, thus leading to more starvation. Those weakened by wounds and famine were more susceptible to new disease. Working together, these three factors in depopulation—disease, military conflict with Spaniards, and starvation—could have resulted in massive depopulation in the immediate aftermath of the de Soto expedition.[29]

Three major responses to depopulation can be seen in the archaeological and historical record: displacement, dispersion, and stability. There are varying degrees of each, and it is possible to see one response giving way to another.

Probably the most common response to severe depopulation brought about by European disease epidemics, warfare, and famine was to flee the area. According to the Gentleman of Elvas, survivors of an epidemic in some of the towns of Cofitachequi fled, and Cakchiquel Mayas of Guatemala noted that half of their people fled after an epidemic in 1520–21. James Merrell describes movements of Catawbas after a 1759 smallpox epidemic. One need not believe in the germ theory of disease to know to flee a place where many people have died.[30]

Probably the best documented archaeological evidence of population displacement during the early historic period in the interior Southeast comes from the Coosa River drainage of northwestern Georgia and northeastern Alabama. (See figure 1.) Following European contact, towns of this area apparently migrated farther downstream every thirty or forty years. Northwestern Georgia was abandoned by the last quarter of the sixteenth century. Then a cluster of towns appeared in the Weiss Reservoir area of northern Alabama by the early seventeenth century, and by ca. 1630, the inhabitants of this group of towns apparently moved south again to the Gadsden, Alabama, area. Finally, most of the known archaeological population of the late seventeenth century is located on Woods Island, still farther south, and by the eighteenth century, the principal archaeological sites are located near present Childersburg, Alabama.[31]

The archaeological evidence suggesting gradual movement downstream is confirmed when the sixteenth-century locations of towns mentioned by de Soto and Luna are contrasted with eighteenth-century locations from contemporary maps. For example, Coosa was located at the Little Egypt site in 1540 and 1560, but by the early eighteenth century, it had moved over 140 miles downstream to the Childersburg site. Luna's Apica of 1560 was located near present Rome, Georgia, but it had moved to the Bead Field site near Childersburg by the early eighteenth century.[32]

Other areas show evidence of population displacement. Eastern Tennessee shows little evidence of occupation during the middle of the seventeenth century. The Hiwassee River appears to have been abandoned in the sixteenth century, and there is little evidence of early seventeenth-century occupation on the Little Tennessee River. It can be historically documented that several Tennessee towns visited by de Soto moved to the area of the junction of the Coosa and Tallapoosa rivers in Alabama by the early eighteenth century. The Overhill Cherokee soon moved in and occupied the area that had been vacated.[33]

The middle Mississippi Valley was depopulated some time after the de Soto entrada, and by the late seventeenth century, only a few towns near the mouth of the Arkansas River were occupied. On the eastern side of the Mississippi, the Yazoo basin was largely depopulated about the same time. By the end of the seventeenth century, populations had almost totally abandoned the Yazoo basin, generally moving south, although a few small towns continued to occupy the Yazoo bluffs. This pattern of a few small towns was in sharp contrast to the earlier settlement pattern of the more numerous and larger towns scattered throughout the basin during the Wasp Lake and Emerald Phases.[34]

Both Mabila and Talisi, frequently mentioned in the de Soto expedition narratives, are virtually absent from the Luna narratives of only twenty years later. Mabila was burned by de Soto, so its disappearance is not hard to understand, but the fate of Talisi cannot so easily be explained.[35]

Another response to depopulation appears to have been population dispersion. This process is best documented in the Wallace Reservoir of the Oconee River. Following contact with the de Soto expedition in 1540, all mound centers on the Oconee appear to have been abandoned by 1600, if not earlier. European trade goods are virtually unknown in the Mound centers (one nondiagnostic glass bead from Scull Shoals village and a glass bead reported to have been found at the Dyar Mound are exceptions), except for the Shinholser Mound site, which has a major seventeenth-century occupation and is believed to be the town of Altamaha. (This seventeenth-century occupation is to one side of the mound complex, and it appears that the mounds were not in use during this period.) With the large centers abandoned, the population moved into small villages, such as the Joe Bell site. No large villages are known from the seventeenth century, and it appears that many people moved into the uplands. A movement toward utilizing the interfluvial uplands began prehistorically, but seems to have accelerated during the Bell phase. Hundreds of isolated farmsteads have been documented in this area. Thus it appears that following Spanish contact, populations dispersed and many people moved into the uplands, but they did not flee the area. However, by the middle of the seventeenth century, the area appears to have been totally abandoned. It is believed that the survivors moved in with missionized Indians on the coast of Georgia.[36]

Other groups seem to have lost their centrality as their mound centers were abandoned. Groups in the Moundville area, believed to be the Apafalaya Province mentioned in the de Soto narratives, appear to have survived in the area as a variant of the Alabama River Phase. Burial practices shifted to urn burial, there was little evidence of social stratification based on grave goods, settlement patterning lost any semblance of hierarchy, and villages were the norm. This area does not show rapid displacement nor dispersion, but appears to demonstrate an intermediate response. This area was later abandoned, and these people may have become one of the sources of population for the central Mississippi Choctaw of the eighteenth century.[37]

Finally, some groups may have been able to sustain themselves in their homeland. Chester DePratter argues that Cofitachequi was able to maintain its importance from the de Soto period to the 1680s, and it is assumed that they did not change location during this time. Although archaeological evidence is weak, what little there is does not conflict with DePratter's interpretation, and it is theoretically possible that Cofitachequi survived depopulation by disease to remain an important political and population center in the Carolina piedmont. It is not known whether moundbuilding continued, or exactly what powers the late seventeenth-century "emperor" actually had. Further archaeological research should help to clarify this situation. But one suspects that if Cofitachequi was able to maintain its importance and population, it did so by incorporating other population remnants from the piedmont. It should be noted that Cofitachequi already controlled the important Fall Line ecotone, an area which appears to have been receiving numerous refugees following European contact.[38]

Other areas may have managed to maintain populations in place without dispersing. Archaeological evidence suggests that the Fall Line area of the Chattahoochee River maintained a continuous but declining population throughout the sixteenth and seventeenth centuries and into the eighteenth. The province of Ichisi, located on the Fall Line of the Ocmulgee River near present Macon, Georgia, may have remained intact. There is some evidence of seventeenth-century ceramics at the Lamar site, believed to be the main town of Ichisi visited by de Soto, and there are also late seventeenth-century/early eighteenth-century European artifacts from the site. Thus there may be population continuity at the Lamar site. The name Ichisi was later picked up by the English and applied to the Ochesee Creeks.[39]

The Shine II Phase inhabitants of the Lower Tallapoosa River may have maintained their population in place following the de Soto and Luna entradas, to enter history in the eighteenth century as the Tallapoosa division of the Upper Creeks. Again, the favored Fall Line location may have had an important effect on their stability.

The Natchez have also been touted as a group who remained in their territory following European contact, although at a reduced scale.[40] But it is equally clear that many of the Natchez towns were made up of refugees of other groups. Shortly after sustained French contact in the early eighteenth century, the Natchez were dispersed, and portions joined the Overhill Cherokee, the Upper Creeks, and the Chickasaw. Their political continuity was destroyed.

But perhaps the most compelling argument for relative stability of location is the case of the Florida Indians. The Apalachees and many of the Timucuan chiefdoms appear to have stayed in their homelands. Indeed, recent excavations in the Timucuan area of north central Florida have demonstrated that seventeenth-century missions were often founded on sixteenth-century town locations.[41]

Henry Dobyns has estimated that there were 722,000 Timucuan-speaking Indians in Florida prior to 1519. This figure represents the population of over a third of the area of the modern state. The methods for obtaining this extraordinarily high figure have been severely criticized, and we need not enter this debate. But it might prove useful to examine some figures obtained from recent studies of the Coosa chiefdom.[42] An estimate of eleven people per household, based on average roofed areas known from excavations of many houses in the region, can be derived by using a procedure advocated by prehistoric demographer Sherburne Cook. The number of houses in each town was estimated based on the amount of space per house known from large excavated portions of several towns in the study area and on the size of each town site. With these data, Hally and his colleagues were able to estimate the population of the paramount chiefdom of Coosa. While the paramount chiefdom of Coosa did not control as much territory as all the Timucuan speakers in Florida, it was arguably one of the most highly organized chiefdoms in the interior Southeast east of the Mississippi River. Using known village sizes when possible and substituting average village populations for sites that are not accurately measured, an estimate of 30,200 can be advanced for the paramount chiefdom of Coosa. Clearly, this figure is significantly lower than Dobyns's figure, and it should serve as an independent means of assessing Dobyns's methodology.

George Milner points out that the population estimates for the Cahokia mound center located in the American Bottoms near St. Louis, the largest prehistoric town in North America, range from 25,500 to an "absurdly high" 42,780. He points out that the Timucua had no towns like Cahokia, and thus he, too, questions Dobyns's figures.[43]

If the average size of a Coosa town was around 600 inhabitants of all ages and sexes, then de Soto's force of 600 soldiers, plus numerous native bearers, must have been formidable. It is little wonder that the Indians launched few frontal attacks against de Soto's army. It must have taken an elaborate plan and unusual cooperation to organize the battle of Mabila.

But how does this estimate of 30,000 Coosa Indians fit with other historical data? Apalachee in the early seventeenth century is said to have had 30,000 people, and this number is believed to represent a significant decline from de Soto's day.[44] It is hard to believe that seventeenth-century Apalachee had the same population as sixteenth-century Coosa, especially when the size of their territories are compared. Thus, the estimate of 30,000 Coosa may be far too conservative. It seems unlikely that the sites of many other towns of Coosa will be discovered, and at only approximately 600 people per town, a few more towns would not greatly increase the population estimate. It also seems unlikely that many Coosa Indians lived outside of the large towns. Currently, there is almost no evidence of settlement in isolated farmsteads in the Coosa area. Perhaps part of the problem lies in the method of calculating the number of people based on roofed area. We have used only the winter houses to estimate population; perhaps we should have used both winter and summer house area to derive population estimates. Summer houses are smaller than the winter structures, so the estimate would be less than twice the 30,000. Perhaps we could arrive at a figure of 45,000 to 50,000 if we also used summer house area, but this would imply very large households of more than eleven people. Clearly more research is needed.

Figures from Coosa can also be used to assess Dobyns's overall depopulation ratio of 20 to 1. In 1715, a census of fifteen Abihka towns yielded 502 men and a total population of 1,773. This figure probably includes Coosa towns.[45] If we look at the proposed sixteenth-century populations of the Carters cluster (eight sites of Coosa) and the Rome Cluster (five sites including the sixteenth-century Abihka), we obtain a population estimate of 8,886 people for the early to mid-sixteenth century. If we add in the four sites of the Cartersville cluster, none of which are later seen in the historical record and presumably were absorbed by the Coosa and/or Abihka, then the total jumps to 11,947. Many of the named towns located in eastern Tennessee can be shown to have moved to the lower Tallapoosa or the Chattahoochee, and are therefore not included in the eighteenth-century Coosa/Abihka cluster of towns in the Childersburg, Alabama, area.[46] Dividing 11,947 by 1,773, a depopulation ratio of 6.47 to 1 is obtained. This is a far cry from Dobyns's ratio of 20:1, but some discussion is in order. First, Dobyns would argue that using a mid-sixteenth-century estimate instead of a pre-1520 estimate does not allow for the possibility of the early pandemics that he advocates. Also, the 1715 census may not represent the population nadir. It was simply a convenient number that could be obtained. It was selected because it gave a total population estimate without having to add more possibility of error by being forced to extrapolate the total population from a warrior count. By the early eighteenth century, Coosa/Abihka's population may already have been on the rebound, as suggested by the later 1832 census figure of 3,792, which includes the "entire Coosa connection."[47] It should be possible to estimate population from archaeological remains over several different time intervals, and this method should be preferred to that which compares archaeologically derived population estimates with historically documented population estimates.

In calculating a depopulation ratio from strictly archaeological data, one method would be to compare the area occupied by sixteenth-century towns in a sample of the Coosa area with the archaeologically derived population nadir, that is, the period in the study area that shows the least occupied area. There were some 52 hectares of occupied area in northwestern Georgia during the sixteenth century, but by the late seventeenth century, there was only one large site of 10.7 hectares. (I have chosen to ignore the one identified late sixteenth-century site size of 7.2 hectares as the true nadir, since I expect that more late sixteenth-century sites will be found.) Thus, 52 divided by 10.7 gives a depopulation ratio of 4.86 to 1, or even less than the figure obtained above using a combination of archaeological data and historical data. There are obvious problems with this latter approach. For example, it assumes that settlement density remains constant, that there were as many people living on a hectare of land in 1680 as there were in 1550. It is virtually certain that settlement had changed by this time to a more dispersed pattern. There were probably many less people per hectare of village area in 1680 than there were in 1550. Nevertheless, these two depopulation ratios calculated for the Georgia-Alabama area provide a sharp contrast to Dobyns's ratio of 20 to 1.

Archaeologists and historians tend to research the largest, most important towns and societies. This procedure often overlooks small population groups in many areas. But it is precisely these small groups that were the first to disappear after disease and famine struck. The refugees of the small groups would amalgamate with larger groups, seemingly bolstering their populations. Thus, by studying the large groups, there is a tendency to not detect the true depopulation rates that occurred. In this way, population estimates for the larger groups may remain relatively constant, while in fact hundreds were actually dying of disease. For example, the Huron of Canada, Seneca Iroquois of New York, and the Susquehannock of Pennsylvania do not seem to lose population during the seventeenth century, but in fact they were absorbing many other groups that eventually disappeared. The entire Ohio Valley was quickly emptied of people. The same scenario can be documented for Apalachee in the seventeenth century.[48] The Apalachee absorbed population groups from southern Georgia, and groups such as the Upper Creeks, Choctaw, and Catawbas of the eighteenth century are known to have been taking in refugees. Population decline must be studied within large regions to truly understand the process. We must remember that even large, important groups such as the Cofitachequis and Natchez disappeared, but perhaps more important in the total scheme of things, many unnamed groups were destroyed before they could even enter the light of history.

Epidemic disease led to the demise of chiefdom level organization, and a kind of political decentralization occurred in the Southeast. The loss of chiefdom organization can be seen in the loss of monumental architecture, the loss of hierarchical settlement patterns, the end of part-time craft specialization, and the end of elaborate burial rituals signifying ascribed status.[49]

The construction of mounds was an important activity among the protohistoric groups of the Southeast. The numerous temple mounds served as platforms for chiefly residences and mortuary temples. Presence of the mounds serves as testimony to the coercive power of the chiefs to mobilize labor for large construction projects. From evidence provided by datable European artifacts associated with mound sites, it can be argued that mound building ceased in much of the interior of the Southeast by the end of the sixteenth century.[50]

With the end of mound construction, hierarchical ordering of towns and villages also disappears. The sixteenth-century chiefdom of Ocute in piedmont Georgia appears to have consisted of one site with three mounds, two sites with two mounds, two sites with one mound, and hundreds of villages, hamlets, and special purpose sites.[51] By the early seventeenth century, all of the mound sites were abandoned. Evidence from the Coosa Province of Tennessee, Georgia, and Alabama also indicates that elaborate site hierarchies disappeared by the beginning of the seventeenth century. The core of the Coosa Province consists of eight archaeological sites located along the Coosawattee River. The capital (the Little Egypt site) had two or three mounds; the Thompson site, believed to be a secondary administrative center, had one mound; and six other large villages had no mounds. This pattern ceased when northwestern Georgia was abandoned prior to the end of the sixteenth century.[52]

The Mississippian elite of the interior probably supported part-time craft specialization. Such specialized objects as shell gorgets and native copper ornaments can be demonstrated to have ceased being produced no later than the first third of the seventeenth century, again suggesting political collapse.

Settlement pattern changes also took place. There was a general trend from compact, round, or nearly square towns to long, linear arrangements of more dispersed households. The elaborate fortifications known archaeologically and historically in the sixteenth century were no longer constructed by the early seventeenth century.[53]

The loss of aboriginal markers of high status can also be documented by comparing grave lot and site specific associations of such artifacts with datable European trade goods. Such markers as embossed native copper and spatulate stone celts disappear by the first third of the seventeenth century, suggesting that the loss of these artifacts signaled the demise of the aboriginal status categories. Chiefly organization gave way to less centralized organization.[54]

Special areas reserved for burial of the elite also disappear. Prehistorically, the ruling elite were buried in a special area, such as in a mortuary temple on a mound. With the end of mound building, there is no evidence of special segregation of elite burials. At later seventeenth-century sites individuals with grave goods, usually European artifacts, appear to be interred "randomly" around the village. No burial cluster in or near any particular house appears to show exalted status, although more-extensive excavations of these sites may change this interpretation.

All this disruption caused many populations to move to new locations. The possibility of people fleeing diseased areas during the sixteenth century has already been mentioned, but other movements are known to have taken place, probably as the result of changes in the balance of power, and later as the result of the Spanish mission system of the late sixteenth and seventeenth centuries and the English slave trade of the late seventeenth century.

Archaeological evidence suggests possible areas of migration during the seventeenth century that need to be tested through future research. Groups from northwestern Georgia apparently moved down the Coosa River; Little Tennessee River and Hiwassee River groups may have moved to the main Tennessee River valley; the Napochies in the Chattanooga area apparently moved to the north side of the river, then later moved downriver to the southwest; Oconee River groups may have concentrated on the Fall Line or moved to Spanish missions on the coast; and Alabama River Phase groups reoccupied the upper Alabama River.[55]

By the late seventeenth and early eighteenth centuries, historical documentation is again available to help us locate aboriginal groups. Eastern Tennessee groups appeared on the Fall Line area of the Coosa and Tallapoosa rivers. Chattahoochee River and Tennessee groups occupied the Fall Line area of the Ocmulgee River. Groups were appearing on the long-abandoned middle Savannah River near the Fall Line. The Fall Line areas of the Wateree River and Oconee Rivers were documented as important centers, and the Fall Line of the Chattahoochee River was reoccupied by groups following the Yamasee War of 1715.[56]

Major chiefdoms, such as the Coosa, Ocute, and Ichisi documented by de Soto, had virtually disappeared or had become relatively minor towns (or groups of towns) in the Creek Confederacy by the eighteenth century. Thus, northwestern Georgia and much of eastern Tennessee were depopulated, allowing the movement of Cherokee-speaking people into the area during the late seventeenth, eighteenth, and nineteenth centuries.[57]

By the end of the seventeenth century, the complex, highly centralized, multilevel chiefdoms described by members of the Hernando de Soto expedition had collapsed. In their place were new societies made up of the refugees of these chiefdoms. These groups lived in relatively small villages, often in locations far removed from their sixteenth-century homelands. Probably as an adaptation to incursions of armed Indians participating in the English slave trade, many of these small-town Indians banded together into confederacies for mutual protection. The so-called Creek Confederacy eventually evolved from these alliances. The small groups documented so well during the eighteenth century by English and French explorers were a pale remnant of the grand chiefdoms visited by the Spaniards in the sixteenth century. To properly understand the social history of the Southeastern Indian, it is necessary to study this process of collapse. The social history of the southeastern Indians, as we have come to know them, is indeed complex, much more so than we have previously thought.

NOTES

1. Dobyns, *Their Number Become Thinned.*

2. Dobyns, "Andean Epidemic History" and "Estimating Aboriginal American Population"; Sauer, *Sixteenth Century North America;* Crosby, *Columbian Exchange;* Cook and Borah, *Indian Population.* For the Southeast, see Milner, "Epidemic Disease"; Dobyns, *Their Number Become Thinned;* Ramenofsky, *Vec-*

tors of Death; M. T. Smith, *Aboriginal Culture Change;* Kroeber, *Native North America;* Mooney, "Aboriginal Population."

3. Dobyns, *Their Number Become Thinned;* Henige, "Primary Source"; Milanich, "Review of *Their Number Become Thinned*"; Storey, "Review of *Their Number Become Thinned*."

4. For Arawaks and Mexico, see Crosby, *Columbian Exchange,* 45, 48–49; for Ayllon, see Hudson, "An Unknown South: The World of Sixteenth-Century Southeastern Indians," paper presented at the Chancellor's symposium, University of Mississippi (1980).

5. Researchers stressing epidemic interpretation include Milner, "Epidemic Disease"; Hudson, "Unknown South"; and Dobyns, *Their Number Become Thinned.* Researchers questioning the epidemic interpretation include Chester B. DePratter, "The Chiefdom of Cofitachequi" this volume, and Randolph J. Widmer, "The Structure of Southeastern Chiefdoms" this volume.

6. Hudson, Smith, DePratter, and Kelly, "The Tristán de Luna Expedition," 31–45.

7. Crosby, *Columbian Exchange,* 40.

8. Hann, *Apalachee,* 163–67.

9. Merrell, *Indians' New World,* 136, 195.

10. Milner, "Epidemic Disease"; Ramenofsky, *Vectors of Death;* and Smith, *Aboriginal Culture Change.*

11. Blakely, "Life Cycle"; Blakely and Detweiler-Blakely, "Impact of European Diseases," 70; and Milner, "Epidemic Disease," 49.

12. Milner, "Epidemic Disease," 45.

13. M. T. Smith, *Aboriginal Culture Change,* 61–63, and Polhemus, *Toqua,* 401, 424.

14. Milner, "Epidemic Disease," 45.

15. Tally, "King Site Burial Population"; Hally, "Plan of the King Site"; Gary Funkhouser, "Paleodemography of the King Site" (M.A. thesis, University of Georgia, 1978).

16. Tally, "King Site Burial Population." 75.

17. Funkhouser, "Paleodemography."

18. Blakely, "Life Cycle," and Blakely and Detweiler-Blakely, "Impact of European Diseases," 72.

19. Mitchem and Hutchinson, "Archaeological Research at the Tatham Mound," 67.

20. Both Ramenofsky and Smith advocate a regional approach to control for such out-migration. Ramenofsky, *Vectors of Death,* and M. T. Smith, *Aboriginal Culture Change.*

21. M. T. Smith, "Wake of de Soto."

22. M. T. Smith, *Aboriginal Culture Change,* 74.

23. Hassan, *Demographic Archaeology;* Ramenofsky, *Vectors of Death,* 15–17; and Hally, "Archaeology and Settlement Plan."

24. Sixteenth-century average site size is based on figures in Hally, Smith, and Langford, "de Soto's Coosa, 126–27." Other figures from M. T. Smith, "Wake of de Soto," 36, 39, 40, 43.

25. M. T. Smith, *Aboriginal Culture Change,* 70.

26. Hudson, DePratter, and Smith, "Victims of the King Site Massacre," 130.

27. Mathews, "The Massacre"; Hudson, DePratter, Smith, "Victims of the King Site Massacre," 117.

28. Mitchem and Hutchinson, "Archaeological Research of the Tatham Mound," 66–67.

29. Milner, "Epidemic Disease," 47.

30. For Cofitachequi, see Elvas, *Narratives of de Soto* (Gainesville, Fla.: Palmetto Books, 1968), 63; Milner, "Epidemic Disease," 43. For the Maya, see Crosby, *Columbian Exchange*, 58. For the Catawbas, see Merrell, *Indians' New World*, 195.

31. M. T. Smith, *Aboriginal Culture Change* and "Wake of de Soto," 34–44.

32. For reconstruction of de Soto's route, see DePratter, Hudson, and Smith, "de Soto Expedition." For discussion of archaeological population movements, see M. T. Smith, *Aboriginal Culture Change*, 75–84, "Indian Responses," and "Aboriginal Population Movements."

33. M. T. Smith, "Aboriginal Population Movements," 22–25.

34. Morse and Morse, *Central Mississippi Valley*, 314–15; Brain, "Late Prehistoric Settlement Patterning," 358.

35. Hudson et al., "The Tristan de Luna Expedition."

36. On the disappearance of mound centers, see M. T. Smith, *Aboriginal Culture Change*, 89–94. Williams, *Shinholser Site*, 202, and "Joe Bell Site." For dispersion into the uplands, see Steve Kowalewski and James Hatch, "The Sixteenth-Century Expansion of Settlement."

37. Curren, *Protohistoric Period;* Patricia Galloway, "Confederacy as a Solution to Chiefdom Dissolution," this volume.

38. DePratter, "Cofitachequi."

39. Knight and Mistovich, *Walter F. George Lake.* Information on Lamar ceramics provided by David Hally, oral communication. For European artifacts at Lamar, see H. G. Smith, *Lamar Site (9Bi7) Materials,* 71–86.

40. Brain, "Prehistoric Settlement Patterning," 360, 362.

41. Jerald T. Milanich, "Franciscan Missions and Native Peoples in Spanish Florida," this volume.

42. Dobyns, *Their Number Become Thinned,* 294. For criticism of Dobyns, see Milanich, "Review of Dobyns" and Storey, "Review of Dobyns." For recent studies of Coosa, see Hally, Smith, and Langford, "de Soto's Coosa."

43. George R. Milner, "Population Dynamics and Archaeological Interpretation" (Paper presented at the annual Midwest Archaeological Conference, University of Illinois Urbana-Champaign, 1988).

44. Hann, *Apalachee,* 164.

45. Swanton, *Creek Indians,* 431.

46. M. T. Smith, "Aboriginal Population Movements," 26–30.

47. Swanton, *Creek Indians,* 431.

48. Hann, *Apalachee,* 33–35, 191–92.

49. These are the correlates of chiefdoms proposed by anthropologists Chris Peebles and Susan Kus; Peebles and Kus, "Some Archaeological Correlates."

50. M. T. Smith, *Aboriginal Culture Change,* 93–94.

51. Mark Williams and Gary Shapiro, "The Changing Contexts of Political Power in the Oconee Valley" (Paper presented at the Forty-fourth annual Southeastern Archaeological Conference, Charleston, S.C., 1987).

52. Hally, Smith, and Langford, "de Soto's Coosa," 128–30.

53. M. T. Smith, *Aboriginal Culture Change*, 108–12, 95–97.

54. Ibid., 98–103.

55. Ibid., and "Aboriginal Population Movements."

56. M. T. Smith, *Aboriginal Culture Change* and "Aboriginal Population Movements"; and Knight and Mistovich, *Walter F. George Lake.*

57. M. T. Smith, *Aboriginal Culture Change.*

Franciscan Missions and Native Peoples in Spanish Florida

[O]f the seventeen years that I have been in this land I have spent all of them among the Indians. And, thus, because I know them from such experience and from knowing the language of this province of Timucua and from having made expeditions into the hinterland [northern Florida], I am aware of their capacity and customs. . . . they come to Mass very willingly and take part in the chanted divine services and some already know how to read and to write.—*Letter of Father Baltasar López of the San Pedro mission on Cumberland Island, Georgia, September 15, 1602*[1]

Few people realize that San Antonio, San Diego, and San Francisco were Florida Spanish-Indian mission settlements that existed 150 years before missions with the same names were established in California and Texas. In 1584, only two decades after the founding of St. Augustine, Spanish Franciscan friars came to La Florida to build missions among the aboriginal peoples. They followed an earlier attempt by Jesuits to missionize coastal native peoples in peninsular Florida and along the Atlantic as far north as Chesapeake Bay. Priests also had accompanied Hernando de Soto and Juan Pardo in their expeditions of conquest and discovery into the Southeast and they had been members of the Tristán de Luna attempt to found a colony at Pensacola Bay in 1559.[2]

By 1602 a chain of Franciscan missions had been established along the Atlantic Coast from St. Augustine northward almost to South Carolina. A second string of missions stretched from St. Augustine westward across northern Florida, reaching the Apalachicola River by 1635. Attempts were made at various times to place missions in central and southern Florida, but these were short-lived.[3]

At the height of its development in the late seventeenth century, the Franciscan mission system included 40 churches and 52 missionaries.[4] Many more missions were established, but most were short-lived. Some were abandoned or destroyed as a result of rebellions, while others moved to new locations, sometimes more than once. John Hann has carefully examined the documentary record and can account for the presence of more than 130 separate mission locations in La Florida, most of which were in north and northwest Florida.[5]

The Franciscan missions were the primary focus of Hispanic–Native American interaction in La Florida in the late sixteenth and seventeenth centuries following the attempts by Pánfilo de Narváez, Hernando de Soto, Juan Pardo, and others to explore and establish settlements in the southeastern United States. The missions were an important link in the expansion of Spain's empire northward from the Caribbean into eastern North America beginning in the sixteenth century. Pedro Menéndez, founder of St. Augustine, saw the missions as an integral part of his plan for colonizing La Florida.[6] Establishing missions—first Jesuit, then Franciscan—accomplished several goals. First, the indigenous peoples of La Florida could be brought to Catholicism, and it was hoped that they would abandon their native "pagan" beliefs that were thought by the priests to be associated with the devil.[7] Second, missionizing the native peoples transformed them from possible military opponents into allies. It was more expedient to use missionaries to control the people of La Florida than to establish forts and try to accomplish the task by military might. That rebellions did occur indicates that conversion did not always make lifelong allies. Lastly, the mission system was intertwined with Spanish ranches for which missionized natives could serve as laborers and transporters of food and goods to St. Augustine for use there or for export. La Florida was a relatively poor colony, and one way a profit could be turned was through the ranches. Missionized Indians also served as laborers for military and civic projects in St. Augustine.[8]

The final destruction of the Florida missions in 1702–4 by English armies from the Carolinas, aided by their Indian allies, severely weakened Spain's hold on her Florida colony. Eventually Florida was ceded to the United States, ending nearly three hundred years of Spanish rule. In time, memories of the missions faded, and the wooden buildings and fields became overgrown and were lost. Only the documents stored in Spanish archives could give testimony to what had been.

Today there is renewed interest in our nation's Hispanic past and in the native peoples of the seventeenth century, and investigations are now underway at several mission locations in north Florida and on the Georgia coast. Historians and archaeologists from a number of institutions are working to locate and reconstruct the mission system, its nature and context within the Florida colony, and its interactions with the native populations. The last decade has seen a tremendous increase in scholarship on these and related topics.[9]

Just as the narratives of the Hernando de Soto expedition provide important information on the state of the indigenous cultures of the southern United States during the period 1539–43, so do accounts and archaeological data from the mission settlements provide perspectives on the native societies during the late sixteenth and seventeenth centuries, the period during which many missionized groups such as the Guale, Apalachee, and Timucua became extinct or nearly so. Comparisons of geographical and other data from the period of the early Spanish explorers with information gleaned from mission period documents yield important perspectives on cultural, demographic, and settlement pattern changes. The story of the missions, then, is also the story of the native peoples they served.

The earliest La Florida missions were those established between 1567 and 1572 by the Jesuits at the garrison outposts established by Pedro Menéndez at Tequesta in the Miami area and among the Calusa south of Fort Myers on the southwest Florida Gulf coast. Both the Tequesta and the Calusa had been encountered by Juan Ponce de León on his first voyage to Florida in 1513. Jesuits also visited other Florida garrison outposts, and they attempted to establish missions on the Atlantic coast as far as Virginia. These early missions were not successful. Native populations were apparently scattered, and in places like the Atlantic coast, they did not live year-round in their villages, but moved inland as necessary to grow crops and gather food. The Calusa and Tequesta, and possibly the Tocobaga, among whom Menéndez also established a garrison, and who lived on the north end of Tampa Bay, were not farmers at all.[10]

Several Jesuits were killed by the Indians, and there were frequent disagreements between soldiers and friars at some outposts. The initial successes the Jesuits had enjoyed in Brazil would not be duplicated in Florida, and it was decided that the Jesuit friars, never more than a handful, would be withdrawn.[11] Afterwards, Pedro Menéndez quickly made arrangements for the Franciscan order to provide missionary friars to his colony, and in 1573 the first Franciscans reached Santa Elena, the Spanish settlement on Parris Island, South Carolina. By 1578 a friar had been assigned to St. Augustine, where, like his counterpart at Santa Elena, he served as chaplain to the garrisoned soldiers. The extent of missionary activities among the native peoples near Santa Elena and St. Augustine, if any, is unknown.[12]

Doctrinas, missions with churches and resident friars who could instruct the native peoples in religious doctrine, were needed in Florida if the colony was to be successful. The region from Santa Elena to St. Augustine needed to be missionized, which would help assure safe passage and communication by the Spaniards between the two coastal settlements, and missions were needed in the interior of northern Florida in the regions where native allies were sought and where Spanish farms could be established. A group of eight Franciscans sailed from Spain in May 1584, led by Father Alonso de Reinoso, who, perhaps, had been with the small group of Franciscans who arrived at Santa Elena in 1573. But some of the Franciscans never arrived in Florida, and one left soon after arriving. Possibly one of the friars who came with Reinoso was Baltasar López, whose 1602 letter quoted at the beginning of this chapter states he had been in Florida seventeen years by that date.[13]

In 1587, Reinoso brought twelve additional Franciscan friars to Florida, but five years later only five remained. Another group of twelve friars arrived in Florida in 1595, and missionary efforts began in earnest. By the next year nine missions were established: Nombre de Dios (a Timucuan mission on the north side of St. Augustine), San Juan de Puerto (another Timucuan mission, located on Fort George Island just north of the mouth of the St. Johns River), San Pedro (a Timucuan mission on the southern end of Cumberland Island, Georgia), Ibi (in southeast Georgia near the coast, also Timucuan), Asao (a Guale mission on the Altamaha River in Georgia, probably near its mouth; later Asao came to refer to St. Simons Island), Tolomato (Guale, on the Georgia mainland north of the Altamaha River), Tupique (Guale, on the Georgia mainland north of Tolomato), Ospo (in northern Guale), and St. Catherines Island (Guale, probably the northernmost mission at the time; the town of Santa Elena, further north, had been abandoned in 1587). Father Baltasar López also visited Timucua, 50 leagues inland from Cumberland Island. Timucua was the major town of the northern Utina and was probably located in present-day southwest Columbia County, Florida, site of the later San Martín de Timucua mission.[14]

In September 1597, the Guale peoples of the Georgia coast revolted in response to Franciscan missionary activities, which included attempts to alter marriage and inheritance patterns. Five Franciscans were killed in the rebellion, and all of the Guale missions were destroyed. In October and early November, a Spanish military force sailed northward from St. Augustine and destroyed abandoned villages and stored crops.[15]

The documentary record for the Guale missions in the first years following the rebellion is sketchy. It seems clear, however, that during the two decades after the rebellion, missions were rebuilt in Guale, often on the sea islands, and the chain from St. Catherines Island to St. Augustine was reestablished. During the period from 1606 to 1616, it is also known that the Franciscans began for the first time to build *doctrinas* among the inland Timucuan peoples in northern Florida. These latter missions were placed among the Potano and the northern Utina, two Timucuan groups, near or on trails that crossed the region. The westernmost of the northern Utina missions was San Juan de Guacara near the Suwannee River. ("Guacara" is the Timucuan word for that river.) Others included Santa Cruz de Tarihica, San Martín de Timucua, Santa Fé de Teleco (in present-day northwest Alachua County), and San Francisco de Potano (near present-day Gainesville). At least one mission was located in southern Georgia and another, San Antonio de Enacape, was on the St. Johns River, probably at the famed Mount Royal archaeological site.[16]

Gradually the inland mission chain moved westward. By 1620, several missions had been established among the Yustega, a Timucuan group living between the Suwannee and the Aucilla River. Beginning in 1633 missions were established for the first time among the Apalachee west of the Aucilla. Over the next few years perhaps more than a dozen Apalachee missions would be built.[17]

A list of missions made in 1655 and two lists compiled in 1675 give the names of thirty-eight, thirty-seven, and thirty-eight missions, respectively, for Guale, the coastal Timucuans from St. Augustine northward to Cumberland Island, the inland Timucuans, and the Apalachee. The latter two 1675 lists also provide data on distances between and among the missions at that time, giving modern researchers an important clue to the geography of the missions, especially those in interior Florida.[18]

By the mid-seventeenth century the mission system was well established. The Spaniards routinely referred to various provinces that correlated roughly with geographical areas and native linguistic groups. The Georgia coast north of Cumberland Island was *Guale; Mocama* was the Timucuan coastal region from Cumberland south to St. Augustine (by the late seventeenth century, the term "Mocama" fell into disuse and that region was generally included as part of Guale); the coastal region south of St. Augustine was often called *La Costa* (the coast); the St. Johns River was the home of the *Agua Dulce* (freshwater) Timucuans; *Timucua* was the interior of northern Florida east of the Aucilla River; and *Apalachee* was the populous province west of that same river. These were the major regions of Spanish-Indian interaction. (See figure 1.)

Although the mission system was well established by 1655, it was not static. New missions were attempted in the southern interior of Florida as well as in coastal regions. We still have much to learn about these missions. As John Hann has demonstrated, although the focus has been on the more numerous missions in the northern portion of La Florida, there is a rich documentary record for the late seventeenth-century Franciscan efforts to establish a Hispanic presence among the Calusa on the southwest Florida coast.[19]

A major effect on the northern missions was the continued depopulation of native peoples, a trend begun at the time of first European contact. The mission Indians, like their ancestors in the sixteenth century, were devastated by epidemics. Rebellions leading to Spanish retribution also contributed to the turmoil. The year 1656 seems to have been pivotal in the history of the missions. A rebellion broke out among the mission Indians in

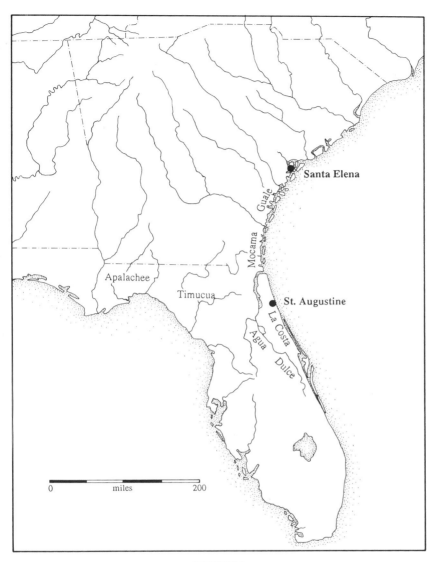

FIGURE I
Locations of native provinces and Spanish settlements

Timucua, and as a result, many of the Timucuan missions were abandoned or moved.

The Timucuan rebellion occurred during a decade of epidemics that "killed uncounted thousands" of natives between 1649–59. To put down the rebellion, which lasted about eight months, and to punish its leaders, Spanish soldiers executed eleven native chiefs. Disease, military retribution, and relocation together must have devastated the already dwindling Timucuan population. Writing in 1657, Governor Rebolledo noted that the Indians of Guale and Timucua were few in number "because they have been wiped out with the sickness of the plague (*peste*) and smallpox which have overtaken them in the past years." In 1659 Governor Francisco de Corcoles y Martínez reported that ten thousand Indians had died of a measles epidemic.[20]

Rather than being a golden age of the missions, then, the mid-seventeenth century marked the demise of most of the Timucua and the Guale. Some of the missions that existed previously in Timucua and were abandoned in the 1656 rebellion apparently were not rebuilt. Others were rebuilt or moved, and new ones were established. It appears that the Timucuan missions spread out along the trail between Apalachee and the St. Johns River. In this fashion, mission villagers could be used to help transport food from Apalachee, the Spaniards' breadbasket, to St. Augustine. In order to assure an adequate number of natives to support the post-rebellion missions, Indians from within and outside the mission provinces had to be enticed or moved to the Timucuan missions. For instance, the mission of Santa Fé, which was located just south of the Santa Fé River in northwesternmost Alachua County, was repopulated by northern Utina Arapaja (perhaps from northern Hamilton or Madison county) in 1657 and by Yustega in 1659. Shortly after this time, some of the coastal missions north of St. Augustine were probably repopulated by Muskhogean-speaking peoples from the interior of Georgia.[21]

This mid-seventeenth-century break in the mission system and population replacement in Guale and Timucua is reflected in the archaeological record as well as the documentary history of those provinces. At the mission villages in Timucua, the indigenous styles of pottery gradually disappear and are replaced by types more common to interior Georgia and/or northwest Florida, perhaps a reflection of the replacement of the Potano, northern Utina, and others with native peoples brought in from other locations.

Archaeological surveys by the Florida Museum of Natural History have located several mission sites in western Timucua, including the mission now identified as San Martín de Timucua, as well as Santa Fé and an unidentified mission located west of Lake City, possibly the pre-1656 location of Santa Cruz. A fourth probable mission location has also been found

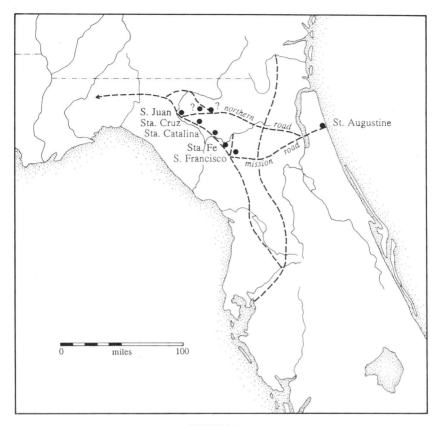

FIGURE 2
Trails across northern Florida with locations of
early seventeenth-century missions

further west, closer to Live Oak. The latter two missions are very near
U.S. Highway 90, believed to be an old trail across present-day northern
Columbia and Suwannee counties (near present-day Lake City and Live
Oak), and the one probably taken by the Hernando de Soto expedition in
1539. (See figure 2.) This old trail runs parallel to, but well north of, the
later mission road, along which the majority of the missions in the two
1675 lists were situated. The northern route was probably still part of the
major east-west trail early in the mission period. After the 1656 rebellion
in Timucua, when many of the missions were abandoned or moved, the
ones on this northern portion of the trail either were not rebuilt or were
moved south. From that time on, the southern trail from Apalachee to St.
Augustine across present-day lower Columbia and Suwannee counties was

the main trail, and some of the northerly missions were moved and reestablished along it. New missions were also built on the southerly trail. (See figure 3.) It is these new and rebuilt missions that appear on the 1675 lists.[22]

That the southern trail was not the main trail early in the mission period is supported by a 1597 document that describes the location of the future site of the San Martín mission, at present-day Ichetucknee Springs in southwest Columbia County. The mission has been located and is almost directly on the southern mission trail. Yet the 1597 document describes its location as "off the beaten path (*desviado*)" from St. Augustine.[23]

Archaeological evidence for the destruction of the missions in 1656 comes both from San Martín and from the Santa Fé mission. The Spanish pottery recovered suggests that both locales were occupied in the first half of the seventeenth century only. Santa Fé is known to have been occupied in later times, but as yet, the portion of the site that was reoccupied has not been pinpointed. On the other hand, the mission of San Francisco de Potano, excavated in the 1960s, yielded an assemblage of aboriginal pottery thought to date from the last half of the seventeenth century. Perhaps the excavated portion of the site was associated with a mission which was rebuilt after the rebellion.[24]

Although the number of missions in 1675 was reduced to the number that had existed in 1655, the Spaniards were not able to maintain the system. The reason was not continued depopulation, but raids by the English who were colonizing the eastern seaboard and developing a lucrative trade in deerskins and Indian slaves, and posing a threat to Spain's La Florida colony. In 1670, the English founded Charles Towne. In that same year, the Treaty of Madrid was signed between Britain and Spain, giving each the right to lands in the West Indies and America that they controlled at the time. The land from the Carolinas to St. Augustine, largely the provinces of Guale and Mocama, was an area of contention, setting the stage for military encounters between the two colonies, encounters that would lead to the destruction and abandonment of both the coastal and interior mission systems.[25]

The first military action was a raid by the Spaniards that did not succeed in assaulting Charles Towne, but destroyed Port Royal. Fearing English retribution, the Spaniards constructed a stone castillo in St. Augustine and put a military garrison at Santa Catalina, the northernmost mission settlement in Guale. For three decades, from the early 1670s into the early 1700s, an "undeclared war was waged."[26] English retaliation at first took the form of small raids into Guale. Then, in 1680, English soldiers, often in league with Indian allies, began to move southward. In that year the mission on Jekyll Island was attacked, as was the mission and garrison on St. Catherines Island. The missions and garrison were withdrawn and moved further south to Sapelo Island. But the harassing raids, some by English-inspired pirates, continued. By 1686, all of the missions in Guale

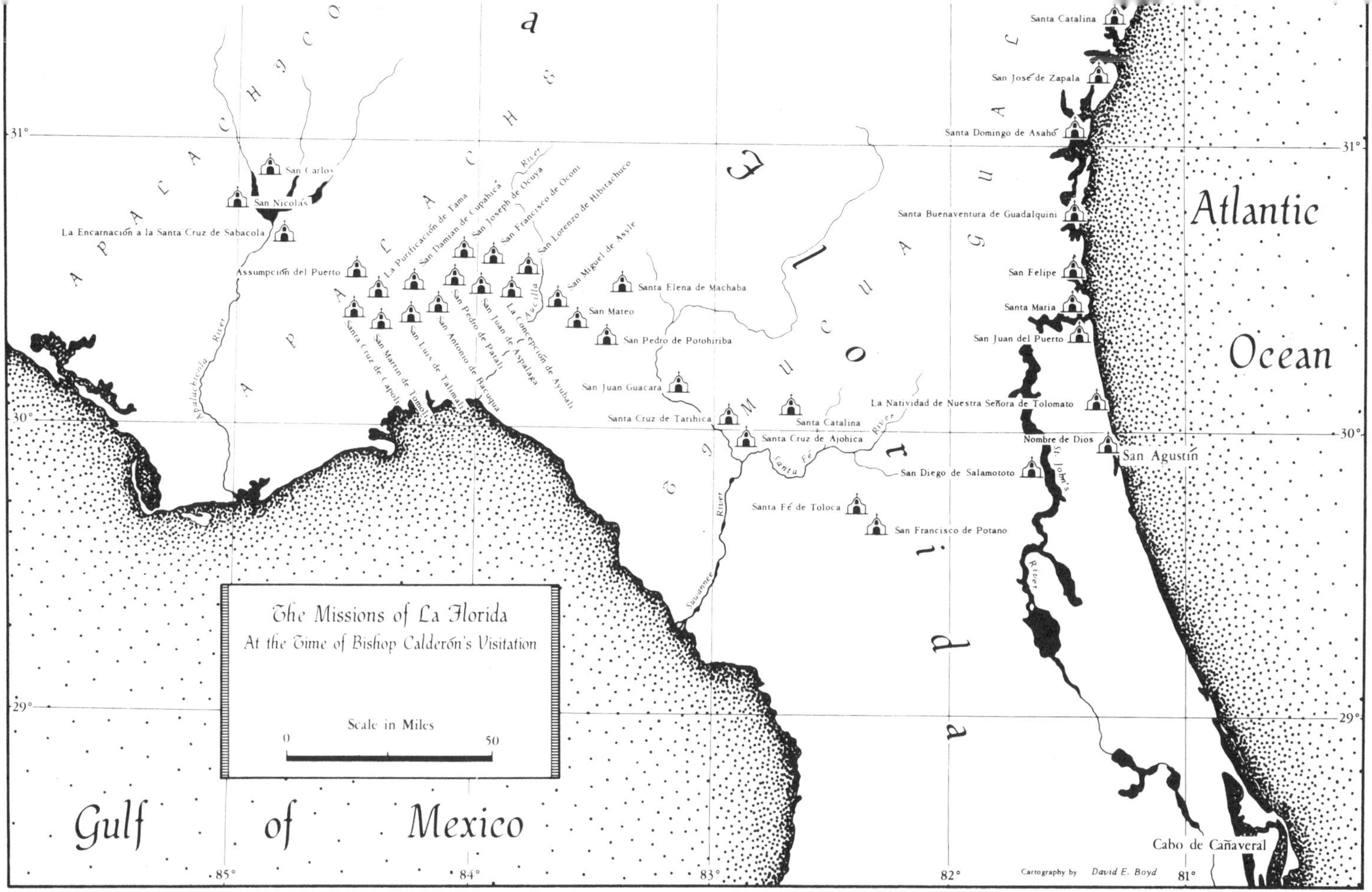

FIGURE 3

Locations of the missions, 1674–75

The Missions of La Florida

At the Time of Bishop Calderón's Visitation

Scale in Miles

Cartography by   David E. Boyd

Atlantic

Ocean

Florida

Gulf of Mexico

Santa Catalina
San José de Zapala
Santa Domingo de Asabó
Santa Buenaventura de Guadalquini
San Felipe
Santa María
San Juan del Puerto
La Natividad de Nuestra Señora de Tolomato
Nombre de Dios
San Agustín
St. John's River
San Diego de Salamototo
San Francisco de Potano
Santa Catalina
Santa Cruz de Ajohica
Santa Fé de Toloca
San Juan de Guacara
Santa Cruz de Tarihica
San Pedro de Potohiriba
Santa Elena de Machaba
San Mateo
San Miguel de Asyle
San Lorenzo de Ibitachuco
San Francisco de Oconi
La Concepción de Ayubali
San Juan de Aspalaga
San Pedro de Patali
San Antonio de Bacuqua
San Luis de Talimali
La Purificación de Tama
San Damián de Cupaica
San Joseph de Ocuya
San Martín de Tomoli
Santa Cruz de Capoli
Assumpción del Puerto
La Encarnación a la Santa Cruz de Sabacola
San Nicolás
San Carlos

Suwannee River
Santa Fé River
Apalachicola River

Cabo de Cañaveral

and northern Mocama—the entire Georgia coast—had been withdrawn. The embattled people moved ever closer to St. Augustine and the seeming protection of the castillo. By 1686, the northernmost Spanish outpost and missions were on Amelia Island. Many of the missionized Indians—including Yamasee from the Guale missions—fled the coast, and others sought refuge among the English. Still others were moved southward, repopulating the Mocama missions north of St. Augustine.[27]

In early 1685, Yamasee allies of the English marched into Timucua and destroyed the mission of Santa Catalina de Afuica, probably one of the missions established after the 1656 rebellion near the mission road in present-day southern Suwannee County. Sometime between that raid and 1690, the mission of San Juan de Guacara on the Suwannee River in western Suwannee County (its post-1656 location) was also destroyed. These raids not only destroyed the buildings and villages of the missions, but decimated the Indian inhabitants, some of whom were killed while others were taken back to the Carolinas to be sold as slaves.[28]

The raids into Timucua continued into the new century. San Pedro y San Pablo de Potohiriba (in present-day Madison County west of the Suwannee County) and Santa Fé were attacked in 1702. The Apalachicola Indians who raided Santa Fé had been armed by the English. They were repulsed by the Spanish garrison stationed at Santa Fé, but in an ill-advised retaliatory skirmish against the attackers, ten Christian Indians were killed.[29]

The Spanish governor of Florida, Don Joseph de Zuñiga y Zerda, wrote his sovereign in September of that year, relating what had occurred. Governor Zuñiga's letter tells us a great deal about the physical nature of the Santa Fé mission: "On Saturday, the 20th of May of this year 1702, they entered in the dawn watch and burned and devastated the village of Santa Fé . . . , attacking the convent with many firearms and arrows and burning the church. . . . Finally, the fight having lasted for more than three hours, our force repulsed them, after the hasty strengthening of an indefensible stockade which served as a fence to the gate of the convent." [30]

In November 1702, English attackers led by Carolinian Governor James Moore sailed southward from Port Royal, landing on the northern end of Amelia Island and then marching southward, destroying the missions. They continued southward, routing the Spanish soldiers at San Juan del Puerto on Fort George Island and taking the missions that lay between them and their goal, St. Augustine.[31]

Apalachee would be next. An initial raid in 1703 destroyed at least one mission. Then, in early and mid-1704, two more military campaigns were waged that effectively wiped out the Apalachee missions, enslaving or scattering the missions' villagers. In 1706 and 1707 additional raids into Timucua completed the destruction. By 1708 the Florida missions were destroyed, and as many as ten thousand to twelve thousand Christian Indians had been taken as slaves. Those few hundred remaining villagers were removed to the vicinity of St. Augustine, where mission villages were established.[32]

During the period shortly before and after 1720, Franciscan missionaries returned to the field in Florida, serving eleven towns, probably all composed of Creeks, Yamasees, or remnant Apalachees. Apparently these missionary efforts continued into the mid-eighteenth century, although little research has been done on them relative to the earlier missions. However, it is clear enough that the mission system in Apalachee, Guale, and Timucua ended with the raids of 1702–4.[33]

Although the missions themselves have disappeared, they have left a legacy on the landscape in the form of place names, some of which date back to the time of Hernando de Soto. Some are indigenous names, while others are names assigned by the Spaniards. In both instances, the names have at times been altered by the tongues of the later Miccosuki and Seminole inhabitants of northern Florida and still later by American colonists. For instance, the Indian town of Asile of de Soto's era is clearly associated with the seventeenth-century mission of San Miguel de Asile and our twentieth-century Aucilla River. In Timucua, San Juan de Guacara was corrupted into San Juan-ee and gave its name to the Suwannee River. San Francisco de Potano likewise has yielded San Felasco Hammock, and San Pedro y San Pablo de Potohiriba lives on in Lake Sampala. In Guale, Santa Catalina de Guale still lives in St. Catherines Island, as does Santa María in St. Marys, Georgia, and San José de Zapala in Sapelo Island. Names like Apalachee, Aspalaga, Oconee, Altamaha, Saint Simons, and Santa Fé all date from the time of the missions or before.

What were the missions like and how did the Christianized Indians live? How did the missions transform the lives of the native peoples they served? One might think that the more than a century-long history of the Florida Franciscan missions would have left modern researchers with an excellent documentary record to be mined for information about the mission system and the lives of the Guale, Timucuan, and Apalachee aborigines. Unfortunately, this is not the case. Historians have found that the surviving documents are often heavy with official business and very light on descriptions of everyday life. Tens of thousands of pages have been read and reread to find the smallest pieces of data.

In the past, historical research often studied the events surrounding the establishment, functioning, and destruction of the missions. However, for the last decade, historians and anthropologists have been collaborating and refocusing their attention on the native peoples within the mission system and their interaction with the Spaniards. The result is significant new information, much of which is still being digested and synthesized. New data from documents and from recently located and excavated mission sites are opening new vistas of understanding.

The missions were not randomly situated on the landscape of La Florida.

They were placed where the native populations were within reasonable distances of St. Augustine. Successful missions systems existed in Apalachee, Guale, and Timucua, reflecting the relative density of population compared to southern Florida. Also, all the successful missions were founded among agricultural populations, like those of northern Florida and coastal Georgia. Attempts to establish missions in southern Florida among non-agriculturists, such as the Calusa of the southwest coast, never succeeded. Stable, sedentary farming societies apparently were easier to missionize. They also could provide agricultural products for the Spaniards' use.

The Spaniards never established missions in the piedmont of Alabama or Georgia where there were very large, sedentary agricultural populations. In 1597, a Spanish expedition, including two Franciscan missionaries, visited Tama, one such native province in the Georgia piedmont, and described it as a good place for missions and a Spanish settlement. Why were no missions ever founded in Tama or elsewhere in the piedmont? One reason was financial. The Spanish crown could not afford the cost of establishing settlement, and the missionaries were apparently unwilling to live so far from St. Augustine without military protection. The distance from St. Augustine to Tama, for example, was eight days by foot. Without a Spanish settlement or garrison, priests in Tama would have been far from supply lines and protection. When the Franciscans were considering establishing missions in Apalachee in 1608, it was noted that they would not have any nearby support if needed, and because of the distance from St. Augustine, supplies (mainly food) could not easily reach them. It was not until after 1633 that Franciscans entered Apalachee on a full-time basis. By then the chain of missions across Timucua had reached the eastern edge of the province of Apalachee.[34]

The earliest missions in interior La Florida were located in Timucua in north Florida, and all seem to have been established adjacent to existing native villages, probably major villages. Many of these locales correlate with villages visited by the Hernando de Soto expedition in 1539. Thus, the seventeenth-century mission station of Santa Ana just west of present-day Gainesville is probably at the location of the village of Utinamocharra where de Soto stopped; Santa Fé was at or very near Cholupaha; San Martín at Aquacaleyquen; an unidentified mission (perhaps Santa Cruz de Tarihica) at Uriutina; and San Miguel de Asile was at Asile. Apparently the populations had not shifted or disappeared between 1539 and the early seventeenth century.

In time, especially after the 1656 rebellion, missions were moved and new ones established. The Timucuan missions were placed on or very near the main (southern) east-west trail or, as in Apalachee, along trails that intersected it. These post-1656 missions were not necessarily built at established native villages. Missions were occasionally moved because the inhabitants had used up the nearby easily obtainable wood supplies (used as fuel and for construction) and because the nearby fields had lost fertility. And, as with the post-1656 Timucuan missions, they were also moved to locations where the native villagers could better satisfy the labor needs of the Spanish.[35]

The *doctrinas* had resident missionary priests who administered to the native peoples residing at the mission villages. But these villagers were only a part of the total number of Indians served by any one mission. Documents frequently refer to surrounding districts containing one to eight satellite villages, whose inhabitants participated in many aspects of mission life and were served by the doctrina's friar. For instance, in 1602 it was reported that the mission of San Juan de Puerto on Fort George Island (north of present-day Jacksonville) had the following outlying villages (subject to it): Vera Cruz (½ league away), Arratobo (2½ leagues distant), Niojo (5 leagues), Potaya (4 leagues), San Mateo (2 leagues), San Pablo (1½ leagues), Hica-charico (1 league), Chinisca (1½ leagues), and Caraby (¼ league). If this is the legal league of 2.6 miles, the satellite villages ranged from a little more than half a mile to 13 miles away. It is no wonder priests complained when they had to administer last rites to a villager in a satellite village, since the person could die before they arrived.[36]

The presence of satellite villages surrounding a *doctrina* is also well documented for Apalachee and Timucua. The number of satellite villages in Timucua gradually declined, but not so in Apalachee. Probably, this reflects the declining native population in Timucua, while the larger population in Apalachee had apparently stabilized during the last half of the seventeenth century, but perhaps only because non-Apalachees were being incorporated into the Apalachee missions.[37]

Archaeological surveys attempting to locate the satellite villages around the Santa Fé mission in Timucua have shown that the presence of clusters of villages within a locality (over several square miles) also occurred in the pre-Columbian era. Likewise, a review of Apalachee site patterning has shown similar clusters for sites in that province on the eve of the mission period. Detailed reconstruction of old trails in north Florida, including those to and from Santa Fé, has demonstrated that during the mission period, the satellite villages near that mission are arranged linearly along the trails leading to the mission, rather than in an annular cluster as in pre-Columbian times. This change to a linear distribution was probably an artifact of the mission system and allowed easy access by Spaniards to the villages.[38]

No single detailed description of a *doctrina*/mission complex exists in the historical documents. Perhaps our best depiction is a 1691 map sent by the governor of Florida to the king of Spain. (See figure 4.) The map or plan is labelled as follows: "Palisade made on the island of Santa Maria and place of Santa Catalina in the Province of Guale; three varas of height with bastions to fire arms; the bastions have earth ramps to half their height; there is a moat; and within it are the church, the Convento of the Doc-

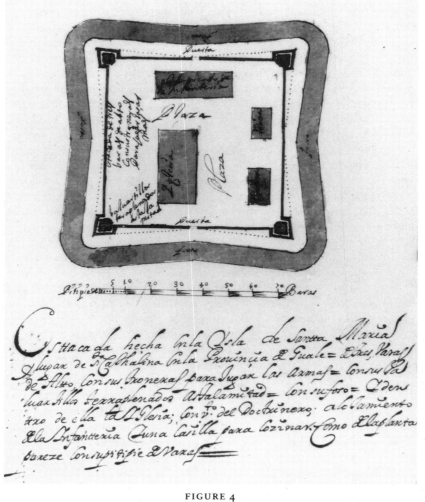

FIGURE 4
The 1691 plan of the Santa Catalina mission on Amelia Island, Florida

trina, barracks for the infantry, and a small house for cooking. The plan has a scale in varas."[39] The map purportedly shows the Santa Catalina mission and garrison complex built on Santa María (Amelia Island) after it was moved from St. Catherines Island, Georgia, in the early 1680s and reestablished on Amelia Island in 1686. However, from other documents and archaeological research carried out at the site, we know that this palisade was never built. The map represents a template, one apparently based on the mission of Santa Catalina on St. Catherines Island, Georgia, which has been the subject of long-term archaeological investigations. The general plan of the palisade or stockade and its surrounding moat are very similar to the 1689 map of the Spanish fort built in Apalachicola, and both maps appear to have been drawn by the same hand.[40]

Although the 1691 map does not show a real mission complex, it does identify the buildings that were part of a doctrina. The rectangular church (with long axis running north to south) had plazas on its north and east sides. Across the eastern plaza were two smaller rectangular buildings, the larger of which was the *convento* or residence for the missionary friars, and the smaller the *cocina* or cookhouse. Both were also oriented north to south and the *cocina* was in line with and north of the *convento*. The garrison house was oriented east to west across the plaza north of the church. At St. Catherines, Georgia, a church, *cocina,* and *convento* have been identified with approximately this same orientation.[41]

Various documents, such as that cited above describing the Santa Fé mission, mention *conventos* and churches at *doctrinas,* and those missions probably had kitchens as well. Archaeological investigations in Apalachee, Guale, and Timucua have revealed complexes of rectangular mission buildings of varying sizes at a number of *doctrinas*. At each site, the church is thought to be the largest building (averaging about 60 by 35 feet), and none contains many artifacts beyond building materials. Many more artifacts are present in the other buildings, especially the *cocinas*. Archaeological investigations and documents also indicate that fences or walls were used to delineate areas within the mission complex, surrounding, for instance, the church and the *convento*.[42]

At some of the *doctrinas,* archaeologists have found the mission cemetery, or *campo santo,* in which the Christian natives were interred, generally extended on their backs in individual graves with arms folded on chests and, at times, with hands clasped. Some burials were wrapped in shrouds. The cemeteries are generally located near (within 150 feet) the churches. Investigations at Santa Fé suggest that a wall or fence surrounded the cemetery. At some missions, such as Santa Catalina, Georgia, and San Martín, interments were made in the floor of the church itself, a pattern also found in some Apalachee missions.

The orientation of the cemetery and burials at individual sites is the same as that of the church and other buildings. Rarely is this orientation

FIGURE 5
Wattle and daub construction

north to south. Instead, the orientation is well off north, often about 45 degrees east of north. This orientation, which might be called the "Spanish slant," is also reflected in the positioning of the Spanish colonial land grants demarcated on maps of northern Florida.

Church building materials varied.[43] Some had vertical board walls, while other walls were made of wattle and daub. (See figure 5.) Still others apparently had no walls at all, but were open, pavillion-like structures. One hypothesis is that at a *doctrina,* an open, pavillion-like structure might be built first to serve as a church. Interments were made in and near the earth floor of the open structure. Later, a second, more substantial church might be constructed, with burials continuing to be made in the consecrated ground of the pavillion as well as in the new church. Eventually, the support posts and roof of the pavillion disappeared, leaving only large postmolds like those found around the burial areas at the Santa Catalina mission on Amelia Island and at Santa Fé.[44]

Individual churches were built by the mission villagers, supervised by the Spanish priests. In 1630, one friar begged the king to order St. Augustine officials to increase the number of nails allowed the missions so that churches could be built. The king was also asked to authorize the loan of carpentry tools from St. Augustine to the mission.[45]

Roofs of churches, like those of the other buildings, were of palm thatch. Like churches, the walls of *conventos* were either wattle and daub or board, and the *cocinas* probably the same. At least some of the churches were elaborate, with bell towers and possibly sanctuaries. San Pedro on Cumberland Island was noted as having an especially elaborate church.[46]

One or more Indian villages were situated at each *doctrina*. At the Baptizing Spring site (perhaps the pre-1656 mission of San Juan de Guacara), and at San Martín de Timucua as well as at Santa Fé, the houses of the villagers were probably situated across the plazas from the churches and other buildings. At Baptizing Spring and Santa Fé, both early missions, the villages were crescent-shaped, as were some pre-Columbian villages in northern Florida. However, by the time of the later missions, such as San Luís in Apalachee, villages were apparently arranged on a grid pattern, reflecting Spanish influence. (See figure 6.) Early missions that served Christianized indigenous peoples may have been quite different in plan and structures than later missions that served populations of people born within the mission context.[47]

What was life like for the native peoples who lived at the missions or in nearby satellite villages? Documentary descriptions and emerging archaeological data suggest several ways in which aboriginal society was transformed. First, the mission priests sought to Christianize the natives, to instruct them in the Catholic faith. In so doing, the priests also sought to acquaint Indians with many aspects of Hispanic culture, including new crops, the Spanish language, and objects of Spanish material culture. To do this, the priests had to convince the villagers that behaviors deemed as pagan or in conflict with Christian teachings had to change. Finally, Christian Indians provided a labor force for the Spanish governmental officials and military, including labor for ranches and the transport of food to St. Augustine. Let us look at examples of these transformations, beginning with the efforts to Christianize the native populations.

As mentioned above, we might expect mission efforts to evolve through time. Initially, the priests worked to make first-generation converts; later, children were born into Christian families and grew up within the mission system. At least partially, this seems to have been the case. Father Francisco Pareja, writing just prior to 1620, noted that Catholicism had so effectively vanquished many of the native, "pagan" superstitions that the mission Indians "do not even remember them; so much so that the younger generation [who grew up under the missions] derides and laughs" at the older generation, who occasionally still practiced the old ways.[48] At the same time, new converts were continually being missionized, especially as Guale and Timucua were being repopulated by people who moved there

FIGURE 6
Artist's reconstruction of San Luís de Talimali

from elsewhere. In 1677, "heathen" Indians were reported to be living in Guale and Mocama; these were probably people from the interior of Georgia who had moved to the coast.[49] The process of bringing these people to Christianity may not have been very different from the friars' task when they first entered the Florida mission field.

To gain the attention of potential converts, chiefs who visited Spanish officials in St. Augustine were given presents. In one five-week period in 1597, 517 pounds of flour, clothing, a spade or hoe, and hatchets or axes were given to such visitors. The clothing included shoes, material for suits, calico, woolen cloth, silk thread, and taffeta from China. Priests and government officials knew that European goods were an important stimulus to cause native peoples to request that they be served by missions. The Indians who were a part of the expedition to Tama in 1597 handed out Spanish blankets, knives, fishhooks, scissors, glass beads, hatchets, and sickles to the local natives. The message was, "live as Christians under our aegis and you, too, could have access to such items." Creating in the Indians a desire for and a reliance on goods controlled by the Spanish was a not-so-subtle way to exert power.[50]

The priests worked diligently to convince native leaders to commit to missionization and influence their followers to do likewise. Throughout the seventeenth century, the friars and Spanish officials continued to work through the indigenous sociopolitical system with its hereditary chiefly positions and hierarchy of social ranks. The governors of Florida sent officials to visit the missions and to adjudicate disputes relating to inheritance and chiefly power; they inevitably supported the native system, except where it was in their best interests to interfere.[51]

But while the Spanish church and governmental officials supported village chiefs, they severely undermined the authority of the intervillage head chiefs that existed prior to the European presence. The king of Spain, through his representatives, replaced the traditional heads of chiefdoms. But even so, the villagers themselves still recognized that some village chiefs were more important than others.[52] Loyal native leaders were rewarded with gifts. One, Don Juan of San Pedro on Cumberland Island, served so well that he was given two hundred ducats.[53]

The education of mission Indians included religious teachings through the medium of the native languages and, in some instances, instruction in learning to read and write Spanish. As *catecumenos,* the instructees learned the catechism and other information before attending their first baptism and becoming *cristianos;* some eventually became *muy españolado.* As Christians, they received a Christian name, and male leaders were awarded the honorific *Don.*[54] In 1677–78, Spanish officials visiting the missions of Apalachee and Timucua gave orders for the establishment of schools for the instruction of children. The teachers, selected by the local head military official, were to be supported by the community.[55]

As Christians, the mission Indians knew how to sing mass and partici-
pate in morning and evening prayers. Some served the priests at Mass. The
Christian Indians also celebrated the appropriate festivals and feast days.
Apparently at some missions, the villagers became so *muy españolados*
that they took part in religious cofraternities like those present in Catholic
communities in the Old World. In every sense, they *were* Catholics.[56]

Christian life at the missions was probably quite similar to that described by Custos Benavides for the western United States Pecos missions:
"More than twenty Indians . . . live with [the priest] in the *convento*. They
take turns relieving one another as porters, sacristans, cooks, bell-ringers,
gardeners, waiters and at other tasks. . . . In the evening they say their
prayers. . . . In every pueblo . . . a friar . . . has schools for the teaching of
prayer, choir, playing musical instruments, and other useful things."[57] The
mission gardens contained imported species such as watermelons, peaches,
figs, hazelnuts, and oranges, as well as local crops. Wheat grown at the
inland ranches has now been identified at several mission sites. Extra crops
were cultivated for the support of the mission friars. Missions also kept
livestock, including chickens, hogs, cattle, and horses.[58] At one mission,
the villagers had access to wine, which normally was discouraged.[59] However, the mission Indians were never totally Hispanicized; their everyday
life was a mixture of indigenous elements melded with select aspects of
Spanish life, adjusted to New World conditions.

As Maynard Geiger has noted, "Spiritual ideas were conveyed by . . .
architecture, painting, statuary, [and] the symbolism of the liturgy."[60] Similarly, ideas about Hispanic culture were also conveyed to the mission populations, including ideas about food, clothing, material items, and acceptable behavior. Indigenous cultural elements that were viewed by the friars
as "morally dangerous and detrimental" were discarded.[61] Those aboriginal beliefs and practices that were viewed as superstitions or that involved
prayers to powers other than those associated with Christianity (and thus
were associated with the "Devil's arts") were to be ignored. "Signs of
birds and animals, none of it is to be believed," wrote Francisco Pareja.[62]
Abortion, certain sexual practices, and polygamy were eradicated.[63]

Native symbols were also destroyed when they were thought to conflict with Christian ones. When Father Martín Prieto began his missionary
work among the Timucua, he burned twelve wooden "idols" in the plaza
of the main town (later San Martín) and then traveled to four other towns
where he destroyed six in each.[64]

Much has been written about the southeastern ball game and the efforts
by the friars to ban it, both in Apalachee and in Timucua, because of its
association with non-Christian elements.[65] Although some Christian Apalachee and Timucuans readily admitted that it should be banned, others
were not so sure. The native peoples did not always agree with the friars on
what was to be deemed "morally dangerous and detrimental." One of the

leaders of the 1597 Guale revolt noted, "They [the friars] prohibit us . . . our dances, banquets, feasts, celebrations, games and war. . . . [They] prosecute our old men, calling them wizards."[66] But in the missions, old ways had to give way to new, or so the missionaries wished.

Prior to European contact, the payment of tribute, especially goods and foods to supreme chiefs, as well as labor for chiefly projects, was common among the people of the Apalachee and Timucuan chiefdoms. Although the indigenous chiefs who received such tribute did not survive into the mission period, a system of labor tribute continued, often organized through village chiefs and with the Spanish as recipients.

Mission Indians were required to serve as burden bearers to transport foodstuffs and other supplies from Apalachee and Timucua to the Gulf coast, where they could be shipped to St. Augustine, or to transport the supplies overland, across the main east-west road to St. Augustine. Another route was along the Wacissa River to the Suwannee River and then up the Suwannee to near Santa Fé, where the overland trail could be reached and where, at times, the Santa Fé chief provided horses for transport.[67] The Indians were also used as laborers on the cattle ranches and farms of interior north Florida and as laborers for the fields that provided food for the St. Augustine garrison.[68] Understandably, the Indians often complained about not being paid.

The mission Indians were required to maintain the road to St. Augustine, clearing brush and repairing crossings. People from the village at Salamototo complained about having to provide ferry service across the St. Johns River, a task that often kept them away from home for several days in bad weather. In Guale, similar ferry service was required of the mission villagers to allow passage between the barrier islands.[69]

Undoubtedly, the Christian Indians also served the friars and the Spanish soldiers stationed at the mission garrisons, tending gardens and providing them with maize, fish, and other food. They also bartered food and labor, receiving goods and, at times, money in exchange.[70] In 1677, the villagers of San Juan de Aspalaga complained to Spanish officials that seven or eight years earlier their chief, now deceased, had traded one hundred *arrobas* of beans and maize to a Spaniard for half their worth in money plus a horse, but no payment had been forthcoming. On another occasion the villagers had traded maize for blankets, but they had not received payment.[71]

Soldiers stationed at the garrison at Santa Catalina in Guale were provided food, cacina (a tea), and fishing lines by the villagers. Deerskins must also have been an item traded by the Indians to the Spaniards. A government official decreed that any villager who allowed a nonlocal Indian to stay at his village for more than a few days without Spanish permission would be required to pay a twelve deerskin fine to the provincial garrison head, who was to use it for "pious works."[72]

Quite likely these hides entered the Spanish trade network. In June 1677, raiders (pirates, perhaps) entered the port of Saint Marks, which served the interior Apalachee missions and farms. The raiders stole a frigate and goods belonging to soldiers. Included were a quantity of deerskins and "amber" (probably ambergris).[73] Apparently, Spanish soldiers stationed at the inland garrisons sought to parlay their positions into a profit, using valued items that could be obtained from the Indians. In a colony as poor as Florida, the Christian Indians, controlled by the mission system, represented one of the few resources that could provide a profit. Certainly, the missions sought to better the life of the native inhabitants, but the system also provided a means of support for Spanish economic initiatives.

The Spanish crown and its representatives sought to change the Apalachee, Guale, Timucua, and other native groups from indigenous societies into a population that was not only *not* detrimental to the La Florida colony, but also an aid to Spanish colonial interests. The most expedient way to do this was through the mission system, by turning the native peoples into native Catholics who participated in and were dependent on the Spanish empire. Essentially the mission villagers provided a labor force for the colony.

A review of the various aspects of mission life suggests how this was accomplished. First, the culture contact situation between Spaniard and Indian heavily favored the former over the latter. The Franciscans entered the La Florida mission field more than seventy years after Juan Ponce de León's initial voyage along Florida's coast. The first inland Timucuan mission was founded nearly seventy years after Hernando de Soto's army had marched through the province.[74] By the time of the missions, depopulation and culture change had been ongoing for several generations. As Henry Dobyns has noted, epidemics "made inoperative many conventional understandings evolved by large populations," and led to many affected native groups questioning "their respective visions of the fundamental postulate of ethnic superiority."[75] Traditional lifestyles present during the late pre-Columbian period in northern Florida and on the coast of Georgia were being changed, and traditional values were altered. We would also expect that the definition of sumptuary craft items by the late pre-Columbian chiefdoms shifted as political structures were realigned, elites died, and craftspersons became fewer as a part of the ongoing cultural changes. Spanish ideology and material culture were substituted for some correlates in native culture, a process made easier by the effects of depopulation.[76]

The Spanish monarchs and colonial governmental officials replaced traditional intervillage chiefs. Soldiers and priests offered native villagers access to valued European-derived goods, including crops, that replaced or supplemented aboriginal ones. Agriculturists may have been sought as converts not only because of their sedentism, but because they could be coerced into farming for the Spanish. And the missionized villagers also could provide other goods to the Spanish.[77]

Thus, by converting the native peoples to Catholicism—and subjecting them to Spanish ideology, aspects of Spanish material culture, and the colonial economic system—the missions made the villagers participants in Spain's New World empire and assigned them the task of producing for the La Florida colony. Florida was the northernmost colony in the Spanish empire, and the Franciscan missions were on the very fringes of that realm. Even so, the interactions between Spaniard and Indian that were played out at those remote missions for more than a century were a part of similar events taking place throughout the New World, events that changed our world forever.[78]

NOTES

1. I am grateful to John Hann for providing me with this translated document, which is filed at the University of Florida in the P. K. Yonge Library of Florida History's Stetson Collection as "Santo Domingo 235, Relación de fray Baltasar López." Dr. Hann, a consummate scholar, has been selfless in his sharing of new information on the Florida missions with me and my students.

2. Documents and historical studies of the Jesuits in Florida are found in Alegre, *Historia;* Lewis and Loomie, *Spanish Jesuit Missions;* and Felix Zubillaga, *Monumenta Antiquae Floride.* For information on Catholic priests with the Hernando de Soto expedition, see Swanton, *Final Report.* For Juan Pardo's expedition, see DePratter, Hudson, and Smith, "Route of Juan Pardo's Explorations," and Hudson, *Juan Pardo Expeditions.* For de Luna, see Hoffman, "Chicora Legend," and Hudson, Smith, DePratter, and Kelley, "Tristán de Luna Expedition."

3. The best overview of the missions is Gannon, *Cross in the Sand.*

4. Ibid., 69.

5. Hann, "Spanish Florida Missions." This figure includes *doctrinas* and *visitas* with churches.

6. Lyon, *Enterprise of Florida,* 196–97.

7. For examples of some aboriginal practices viewed as "pagan" by the Franciscans, see Milanich and Sturtevant, *Francisco Pareja's 1613 Confessionario,* 23–39. Pedro Menéndez's *asiento* (charter) for the La Florida colony required him to take priests so that "the preaching of the Gospel might take place in the said land, and in order that the Indians might be converted to our Holy Catholic faith and to the obedience of His Majesty." See Lyon, *Enterprise of Florida,* 215.

8. See Bushnell, "Ruling 'the Republic of Indians,' " for an excellent overview of the authority relationships among and within the Spanish military and friars and the native societies and chiefs.

9. Recent studies include Bushnell, "The Menéndez-Marquez Cattle Barony," "That Demonic Game," "Patricio de Hinachuba," "Santa María in the Written Record," and "Ruling the 'Republic of Indians' "; Deagan, "Cultures in Transition"; Hann, "Church Furnishings," "Demographic Patterns," "Alonso de Leturiondo's Memorial," "Governor Rebolledo's 1657 Visitation," *Apalachee,* and "Spanish Florida Missions"; Larson, "Historic Guale Indians"; Loucks, "Political and Economic Interactions"; Milanich, "Western Timucua"; Milanich and

Johnson, "Santa Fé"; Milanich and Saunders, "Spanish Castillo"; Saunders, "Excavations at 8Na41"; Shapiro, "Archaeology at San Luís"; Thomas, *Archaeology of Mission Santa Catalina;* Weisman, "Excavations at Fig Springs." See Marrinan, "Spanish Missions of Florida," for a summary of mission archaeology.

10. Gannon, *Cross in the Sand,* 32–34. Background on the Calusa, Tequesta, and Tocobaga can be found in Milanich and Fairbanks, *Florida Archaeology,* 230–37, 241–50.

11. See Hemming, *Red Gold,* for the story of the early Jesuit mission effort in Brazil.

12. Fathers Francisco del Castillo and Alonso Cavezas served Santa Elena and St. Augustine, respectively; see, Geiger, *Biographical Dictionary,* 8, 41–42.

13. Ibid., 68, 91–92, for information on López and Reinoso (Geiger says Father López arrived in Florida in 1587, two years later than indicated by the information in the letter); Geiger, *Franciscan Conquest,* 46–47.

14. Geiger, *Franciscan Conquest,* 53–64, and *Biographical Dictionary,* 120; Luís Oré, *Martyrs of Florida,* 66–86. See Hann, "Spanish Florida Missions," for locational data on the missions. The San Martín mission has been the recent focus of an archaeological study, see Weisman, "Excavations at Fig Springs."

15. The events of the rebellion and its aftermath can be found in Geiger, *Franciscan Conquest,* 86–115.

16. Geiger, *Biographical Dictionary,* 123–24; Hann, "Spanish Florida Missions."

17. Hann, *Apalachee,* 27–69.

18. Geiger, *Biographical Dictionary,* 125–31.

19. Hann, *Missions to the Calusa.*

20. Hann, "Governor Rebolledo's 1657 Visitation," 84, 111, 133–34, and *Apalachee,* 22–23. Quotes are from Hann, *Apalachee,* 22, and "Governor Rebolledo's 1657 Visitation," 111.

21. Hann, "Spanish Florida Missions," 497; Geiger, *Biographical Dictionary,* 129. Yamasee may be derived from Tama, a region in interior Georgia. Perhaps people from Tama began to repopulate the Guale missions.

22. Weisman, "Excavations at Fig Springs," 1. As John Hann has pointed out, six of the twelve western Timucuan missions on the 1655 list do not reappear in the documentary record after that time: Hann, "Western Timucua and its Missions," typescript on file, Florida Bureau of Archaeological Research (Tallahassee, Fla., 1989), 31.

23. Weisman, "Excavations at Fig Springs," 34–38, and Hann, "Western Timucua," 20.

24. Weisman, "Excavations at Fig Springs," 33; Milanich and Johnson, "Santa Fé," 7; Milanich, "Excavations at the Richardson Site," 58; and Symes and Stephens, "Fox Pond Site."

25. Bolton and Ross, *The Debatable Land,* and Thomas, "Archaeology of Mission Santa Catalina," 56.

26. Arnade, *Siege of St. Augustine,* 1.

27. Thomas, "Archaeology of Mission Santa Catalina," 56–57, and Gannon, *Cross in the Sand,* 71–72.

28. Boyd, Smith, and Griffin, *Here They Once Stood,* 8, 11, and Gannon, *Cross in the Sand,* 72.

29. Boyd, Smith, and Griffin, *Here They Once Stood*, 11–12, 36–37.

30. Ibid., 37. As indicated by this example, the translated documents often are as important for their descriptive information of the physical appearance of the missions as for the historical events they recount.

31. See Arnade, *Siege of St. Augustine,* for an excellent account of Moore's raid and the subsequent siege of St. Augustine, which continued to late December 1702.

32. Boyd, Smith, and Griffin, *Here They Once Stood,* contains many of the documents describing the events in Apalachee. Also see Jones, "Colonel James Moore," 25–33, and Gannon, *Cross in the Sand,* 76.

33. Gannon, *Cross in the Sand,* 31. For information on the later missions, see Hann, "St. Augustine's Fallout," 180–200.

34. Geiger, *Franciscan Conquest,* 82–86, 127–29; Oré, *Martyrs of Florida,* 118. On the trip to Tama one of the priests barely escaped being scalped. Tama was described in glowing terms—a fertile land perfect for a Spanish settlement—and Governor Canzo asked to be allowed to put a settlement there, but the king never acquiesced.

35. See Hann, "Governor Rebolledo's 1657 Visitation," 90–91, for an example from Apalachee.

36. Geiger, *Biographical Dictionary,* 121.

37. Hann, "Governor Rebolledo's 1657 Visitation," 104–5, and *Apalachee,* 28, 30, 160–74, 354–55.

38. Frank J. Keel, "Research on the de Soto Expedition in Northwest Florida," field report on file, Florida Museum of Natural History (Gainesville, Fla., 1989). Kenneth W. Johnson, "Settlement Systems in North Central Florida" (Paper presented at the Forty-fourth Annual Southeastern Archaeological Conference, Charleston, S.C., 1987).

39. Milanich and Saunders, "Spanish Castillo," 2–4; Saunders, "Excavations at 8Na41," figs. 5, 27; translation by Bruce S. Chappell, archivist, P. K. Yonge Library of Florida History, University of Florida, Gainesville.

40. Bushnell, "Santa María," 10–11; Thomas, *Archaeology of Mission Santa Catalina.* The map is illustrated in Hann, *Apalachee,* 204.

41. Thomas, *Archaeology of Mission Santa Catalina,* 115.

42. Jones and Shapiro, "Nine Mission Sites," 491–509; Milanich and Johnson, "Santa Fé," 7–8, figs. 1–2; Morrell and Jones, "San Juan de Aspalaga," 25–43. See especially Thomas, *Archaeology of Mission Santa Catalina,* 81–107.

43. Thomas, *Archaeology of Mission Santa Catalina,* 77.

44. Milanich and Johnson, "Santa Fé," 7; Saunders, "Excavations at 8Na41," 6.

45. John H. Hann, "The Fray Alonso de Jesus Petition of 1630," typescript research report on file, Florida Bureau of Archaeological Research (Tallahassee, Fla., 1988), 6.

46. Bushnell, "Santa María," 2.

47. Loucks, "Political and Economic Interactions," 149, 322; Weisman, "Excavations at Fig Springs," 29–30; Milanich and Johnson, "Santa Fé," 7, fig. 2; Shapiro, "Archaeology at San Luís," 47.

48. Geiger, *Franciscan Conquest,* 254.

49. John H. Hann, "The 1677–1678 Visitations of Guale, Apalachee, and Timuqua," typescript research report on file, Florida Bureau of Archaeological Research (Tallahassee, Fla., 1988), 18.

50. Geiger, *Franciscan Conquest*, 78–79, 82–83; Hann, "De Soto, Dobyns, and Demography," 19.

51. Examples of the Spanish officials supporting the political status quo can be found in Hann, "Visitations and Revolts in Florida," passim.

52. Milanich, "Western Timucua," 67; Hann, *Apalachee*, 99.

53. This was a considerable sum, considering the governor's salary was 2000 ducats per year. It was estimated that each friar's upkeep cost 1535 reales per year, or about 140 ducats; Geiger, *Franciscan Conquest*, 80, 164, 187.

54. Ibid., 29, 148, 258.

55. Hann, "Visitations and Revolts in Florida," 50–51, 53, 56, 72, 82; but it is not known if the schools were established.

56. Oré, *Martyrs of Florida*, 104–5, and Geiger, *Franciscan Conquests*, 29, 254, 258.

57. Quoted in Kessell, *Kiva, Cross, and Crown*, 129–31.

58. Deagan, "Fig Springs," 39; Geiger, *Franciscan Conquest*, 242; Hann, "Visitations and Revolts in Florida," 48, 60–61, and "Fray Alonso de Jesus," 4; Reitz, "Zooarchaeological Evidence," 543–54; and Ruhl, "Spanish Mission Paleoethnobotany," 555–80.

59. Hann, "Visitations and Revolts in Florida," 89.

60. Geiger, *Franciscan Conquest*, 29–30.

61. Ibid., 30.

62. Milanich and Sturtevant, *Francisco Pareja's 1613 Confessionario*, 25.

63. Geiger, *Franciscan Conquest*, 88; Milanich and Sturtevant, *Francisco Pareja's 1613 Confessionario*, 23–39.

64. Oré, *Martyrs of Florida*, 114–15.

65. Bushnell, "Demonic Game;" Hann, "Visitations and Revolts in Florida," 3, 7, 39–40, 90–91.

66. Geiger, *Franciscan Conquest*, 90.

67. Hann, *Apalachee*, 89, and "Visitations and Revolts in Florida," 95.

68. Hann, "Visitations and Revolts in Florida," 8, 96, and Milanich, "Western Timucua," 65.

69. Hann, *Apalachee*, 105, and "Visitations and Revolts in Florida," 119–20.

70. For example, see Hann, "Governor Rebolledo's 1675 Visitation," 89.

71. Hann, "Visitations and Revolts in Florida," 60–61.

72. Ibid., 12–13, 51, 56, 72.

73. Ibid., 75.

74. Martín Prieto, who founded the first Franciscan mission among the Timucua in 1606, reported that the cacique of Santa Ana, a village just south of the San Francisco mission, still remembered the cruelties shown by Hernando de Soto, who had taken him captive when the chief was a boy; Oré, *Martyrs of Florida*, 113.

75. Dobyns, *Their Number Become Thinned*, 10.

76. M. T. Smith, *Aboriginal Culture Change*, 98–112, and Dobyns, *Their Number Become Thinned*, 331–32.

77. An excellent discussion of the role of the seventeenth-century Spanish and their mission Apalachee subjects in stimulating the deerskin trade with interior, proto-Creek peoples is Waselkov, "Seventeenth Century Trade," 117–33. As historians and archaeologists refocus their research questions regarding Spanish-Indian

interaction, it is likely that many more such studies examining the economic aspects of the La Florida colony will appear.

78. Since this chapter went to press several important mission studies have become available. Weisman, *Franciscan Frontier,* reports on extensive excavations at the San Martín mission in Timucua believed to date from the period before the 1656 Timucuan Rebellion, while the main post-1656 Apalachee mission-garrison village is reported in McEwan, "San Luis de Talimai." An account of the rebellion itself and the subsequent reorganization of the missions is Worth, "The Timucuan Missions." Johnson, "The Utina and the Potano Peoples," includes a detailed study of the trail systems that connected the missions in Timucua and a report of excavations at several mission sites. Sixteen articles on archaeological, biological, and historical aspects of La Florida are contained in McEwan, *The Missions of Spanish Florida.*

JOEL W. MARTIN

Southeastern Indians and the English Trade in Skins and Slaves

In depicting the colonial encounter of native peoples of eastern North America with the English, it is all too tempting to reduce to an overly simplified narrative what was actually an extraordinarily complex and regionally varied history. It would be comforting to historians facing this diversity if research revealed a coherent theory or model that applied universally to all times and places. This would make southeastern contact history easy to explicate and present. Unfortunately, given the complexity of southeastern Indian experiences, even the best of theories and models cannot be made to fit all cases.

Economic dependency theory, for instance, has been shown by ethnohistorian Richard White to be extremely useful in interpreting the trade experiences of eighteenth-century Choctaws.[1] Using the theory, White interprets the ways in which Choctaws became dependent upon trade, trapped in debt, and vulnerable to colonizers' exploitation. Although White does not attempt or even recommend it, the same theory that he has applied so carefully to the Choctaws could be effectively applied to other southeastern groups. Careful use of dependency theory might provide a useful framework for showing how southeastern Indians participated in the world system, and it might account for why the English prevailed over the Spanish in the region. The portrayal of contact that would emerge, however, might be incomplete. At the least, the portrayal of contact created through a faithful usage of dependency theory would shed little direct light upon the experience of groups who never traded extensively with the French or English, groups such as the Apalachees of Florida. More importantly, the portrayal would leave far too undeveloped the ways generations of southeastern Indians resisted, undermined, and countered the forces, trends, and practices that produce economic dependency.[2]

If dependency theory holds intriguing promise but entails inevitable problems for scholars of southeastern contact history, the latter might turn instead to the model proposed by James Merrell. Unlike White, Merrell does not employ a formal analytic theory. Nonetheless, he does encourage his colleagues to envisage contact history as manifesting a definite pattern or sequence. Based on his study of the Catawbas, Merrell concludes that "for American Indians a new order arrived in three distinct yet overlapping stages. First, alien microbes killed vast numbers of natives, sometimes before the victims had seen a European or African face. Next came traders who exchanged European technology for American Indians' products and brought these peoples into the developing world market. In time traders gave way to settlers eager to develop the land according to their own lights."[3] Although his summary seems sound enough when applied to the Catawbas, Merrell does not restrict its application only to that piedmont population, and implies that it accurately summarizes the experience of "American Indians." He is, in short, offering not just a case study, but a general model for the contact experience in eastern North America.

As persuasive as Merrell's model may be, it, like dependency theory, obscures the complexity and variety of Native American–European encounters in the Southeast.[4] The diversity of experiences lived and the range of options pursued by southeastern Indians in the early historical period are too rich to be represented by any single model, narrative, or theory. This will be demonstrated by exploring and comparing the regional context, growth, character, and impact of the English trading regime on Catawbas, Creeks, Apalachees, Choctaws, and other native groups.

Perhaps the most important force that makes the southeastern experience different from other regions in eastern North America was the early, powerful, and persistent presence of the Spanish. The Spanish brought diseases to the Southeast more than a century before the English successfully entered the region. This meant that in most areas of the region demographic collapse and the inauguration of English trade did not "overlap" in any significant manner, and in some sections probably not at all. Rather, most native groups that survived the plagues of the late sixteenth century and early seventeenth century had several generations to recover, reorganize, and reorient themselves before they had to deal with English traders. They had time to adjust to diminished populations, to create appropriate kinds of polities, to rebalance subsistence strategies, to alter or innovate upon ceremonial life, to expand and amend mythologies and symbology, to adjust to the novel presence of Europeans in their midst or as neighbors, in sum, to learn how to live their lives in new ways. In contrast, New England Indians enjoyed no such respite, and faced English traders even as their societies continued to reel under demographic devastation. Virginia Indians likewise faced a compressed contact history in which disease, trade, and settlers came almost all at once, an overwhelming experience that almost immediately prompted a great revolt, the Powhatan rebellion of 1622.[5]

When English traders finally did arrive in the Southeast in 1670, after the founding of Charles Towne, they entered a region in which native peoples had already weathered the horrors of disease-spawned holocausts. Moreover, these were peoples who had gained some experience with Europeans or European goods. Their ancestors had faced Spanish conquistadors. Timucua, Apalachee, and Guale Indians living in Florida and Georgia had intimate knowledge of the Spanish traders from Apalachee who penetrated the interior, bringing iron goods, brass ornaments, glass beads, and other products to the Lower Creeks to exchange for deerskins, furs, and food. Spanish missionaries also made sporadic but unsuccessful ventures into the piedmont.[6]

The Indians of the interior South were apparently exposed to English goods before the English themselves arrived. Although the English had no sustained forms of contact with most inhabitants of the interior regions of the Southeast before 1670, some English goods reached the peoples of the interior. In the precontact and protohistoric periods, an indigenous exchange network had moved exotic materials over considerable distances, linking regional centers, and enabling their elites to signify and convey status.[7] Exchanged materials included marine shell and copper; unusual lithic materials such as quartz, mica, pyrite, and gelena; and other distinctive or symbolically valuable substances. During the period after the founding of Virginia (1607) but before the founding of Carolina, these well-established pasts and exchange practices enabled piedmont peoples such as the Tutelos, Occaneechees, Tuscaroras, and Catawbas to bring English goods to interior groups, including Cherokees, Creeks, Alabamas, and Choctaws. By 1673, even Chickasaws along the Mississippi possessed "guns, axes, hoes, knives, beads, and double glass bottles," manufactures that may have been of English or Spanish provenience and were probably brought to the region by native middlemen.[8]

Given these preludes to trade and the long duration of Spanish occupation in Florida, it makes little sense to describe the southeastern Indians that English traders encountered in the late seventeenth century as "aboriginal." Rather, these peoples consisted of postcontact communities that had already weathered demographic crises, recreated themselves politically, innovated culturally, and gained varying degrees of knowledge of Europeans and some of their goods. They were New World peoples who had already changed in response to contact. This certainly did not mean that they would avoid the perils involved in trading with the English, but it did mean that they faced these perils from a different and stronger position than did peoples in regions where contact history was more compressed.

As native middlemen disseminated goods to interior peoples, they achieved a powerful, but very precarious and short-lived position in the southeastern trade network. Perhaps realizing that their power was based upon nothing more than an accident of geography, the Occaneechees, Tuscaroras, and Catawbas tried to prevent direct contacts between Virginia's traders and more distant groups. Their efforts ultimately failed, for English traders were loathe to share their profits, and they were willing and able to travel hundreds of miles to reach new consumers. In 1676, Virginians led by Nathaniel Bacon attacked and defeated the Occaneechees, opening up the trade route for English packhorsemen, and in 1711, the Tuscaroras were devastated in a war with the English. Although the Catawbas also fought the English (in 1715 they joined other southeastern groups assaulting Carolina), they at least fared a bit better than some others. As they lost their status as middlemen, they shifted to providing English caravans with food and lodging as they made their way to Cherokee country.[9]

Though Virginia's commerce to the interior never directly involved the majority of southeastern Indians, it did demonstrate what a successful commerce entailed, and it anticipated the particular features and perils that would characterize the English trading regime wherever it would later take hold. First, a successful trade venture relied upon a critical number of Anglo-Americans who possessed frontier experience and knowledge of native inhabitants and the land. Because military men had experienced and surveyed the land (and encountered, "treated" with, and formed allies among southeastern Indian groups), they figured prominently in all frontier trade ventures.[10]

Second, the Virginian experience showed that frontier knowledge had to be articulated with capital. Trade required extensive investments in goods, labor, and means of transport. Further, commerce relied heavily upon obtaining, circulating, and floating credit. Traders obtained goods from London merchants, and distributed goods to factors, hirelings, and clerks, who in turn gave the goods to southeastern Indian hunters. Thus, the line of credit extended from the warehouses of London to the woods of Virginia. To get the business off the ground in the first place required someone in the middle with enough wealth to inspire the confidence of London houses and suppliers. The only colonists able to do this were the substantial planters and merchants who already possessed land, mercantile businesses, and slaves. Thus the early deerskin commerce depended upon and helped enlarge the fortunes of many of Virginia's and Carolina's "first families."[11]

Third, a successful trade obviously required the services of a good number of native hunters. The enterprise presupposed the existence of a native group that had not been destroyed by the diseases of early contact nor dispossessed of their hunting grounds. Because local or coastal populations were almost always terribly reduced in numbers and power by the spread of diseases and the massive intercultural violence that accompanied colonization, traders invariably had to travel to interior regions beyond the limits of the colony to find strong trading partners. Virginia traders diligently sought trade with the Cherokees. Later, after Carolina was founded, English traders would cultivate trade with other strong interior groups and try to fend off the commercial advances of the Spanish and French.[12]

This introduces a fourth feature of the deerskin commerce, its connection with regional politics and imperial contests. Exchange followed and cemented the forming of alliances, "bonds of peace" between the colony and its native trading partners.[13] In the 1630s, when Virginians Henry Fleet and William Claiborne bartered furs with Chesapeake peoples, they traded with those groups—Patawomekes, Accomacs, and Accohannocs—who had served as Virginia's allies in the Second Powhatan War (1622–32). The connection between commerce and politics remained strong throughout the history of the deerskin trade. Exchange articulated in its very fiber a political relationship that both partners sought to turn to their advantage against rival native groups and competing European powers.[14]

As exchange and imperial contests involved southeastern Indians in new kinds of power struggles, it also involved them in new forms of slavery, both as suppliers of slaves and as slaves themselves. Well before Europeans arrived, native peoples had held captives of war as servants. The vanquished survivors lived as marginal members of the victor's society; some were abused, some adopted, some killed. After the English arrived, native people found a new use for the subjugated, and the subjugated found themselves facing an unprecedented destiny: war captives were sold for great profit to tobacco planters. Raiding enemy villages to obtain captives appeared a quicker and more profitable way to obtain manufactured goods than hunting deer. On the Virginia market, a child was worth more than her weight in deerskins; a single adult slave was equal in value to the leather produced in two years of hunting. Armed by traders, native allies of Virginia did not hesitate to raid the villages of their enemies, kill the men, and capture the women and children. By the latter half of the seventeenth century, if not before, slavery was big business in Virginia, an important part of the English trading regime.[15]

By the middle of the seventeenth century, the Virginia trade was thriving and possessed a form that would characterize subsequent trading experiences. Trains of packhorses regularly journeyed from Virginia deep into the backcountry, carrying cloth and other manufactured goods into the southeastern interior, and conveying leather and slaves out. By 1670, the network extended even farther away to the Savannah River, where traders from Virginia had located and armed a group of native people known as the Westoes. Employing the latter as slave catchers, the Virginians sent waves of terror far into the interior of the Southeast, affecting peoples that the English had yet to meet face-to-face. Among peoples such as the Yamasees and Creeks, rumors spread that cannibals were about in the land. As they listened to and spread these stories, southeastern Indians were evidently bracing themselves for encounters with new kinds of people, unnatural powers, and novel dangers.

Because many interior southeastern Indians first encountered Spanish and English goods from native traders, an extra layer of mediation separated these peoples from the Europeans and delayed the time when they would become enmeshed in imperial politics and market economics. Initially, this buffer enabled them to assimilate more fully the novel goods within traditional patterns and expectations. During the seventeenth century, southeastern Indians carefully turned new materials and technologies to time-honored purposes. European glass aided divination, and jagged shards could be used for arrowheads; imported beads provided additional bright colors to traditional motifs; iron celts displaced stone tools; lead balls were flattened into medallions.[16]

Yet, if distance cushioned "contact," this fact was probably unappreciated by southeastern Indians in the interior, particularly by those who found themselves attacked by Virginia's slave-catching allies. It is much more likely that the Yamasees, Chickasaws, Choctaws, Creeks, and Cherokees were painfully vulnerable to what they experienced. They must have heard stories about "the blond men," the "Virginians," but they could not establish direct contact with them. The Westoes seriously threatened southeastern peoples, including Yamasees and eastern Creek towns, and there was no available counterforce for the latter to tap. Although southeastern Indians found themselves in a situation of considerable terror, the Spanish officials of La Florida made it illegal to sell guns to non-Spanish subjects.[17]

The founding of South Carolina, a coastal colony located hundreds of miles to the south of Virginia, gave southeastern Indians a highly valued and extremely timely opportunity to trade for the arms they desperately needed to protect themselves from and empower themselves against other groups. From the very beginning of Carolina, there was never any question that Carolinians and southeastern Indians would engage in a vigorous deerskin trade. Before the colony itself was established, seafaring scouting expeditions out of Barbados, such as the one led by Robert Sandford in 1666, had contacted coastal communities, exchanged interpreters, and initiated a small trade. By March 1670, when a longboat landed near a village of Sewee Indians, both Sewees and English knew what goods the other had to offer. An English captain described the first encounter thusly: "As we drew up to ye shore A good number of Indians . . . ran up to ye middle in mire and watter to carry us a shoare where when we came they gaue us ye stroaking Complimt of ye country and brought deare skins some raw some drest to trade with us for which we gaue them kniues beads and tobacco and glad they were of ye Market."[18]

Carolina's Barbadian-bred founders quickly and aggressively expanded their influence in the Southeast. Charleston planters armed the Savannahs and waged war against the Westoes, virtually annihilating them in 1680 and thus removing the chief obstacle to trade with the great interior peoples: the Creeks, the Cherokees, the Choctaws, and the Chickasaws. With similar independence, planters of the Goose Creek area boldly ignored proprietary rules limiting the extent of the trade to the vicinity of the English settlement. Not content with planting and cattle raising, they sent their agents hundreds of miles inland to establish contact with Cherokees, Creeks, and Chickasaws.[19]

The Goose Creek planters forged a strong and direct trade with the interior groups. They directed a large caravan of goods to Coweta as early as 1685, and guided native burdeners carrying hundreds of pounds of deerskins back to Charleston. By 1690, Carolina planters virtually monopolized the southeastern deerskin trade. In a few more years, Charleston merchants used their command of the credit system to gain control over the trade, and they transformed the trade into one of the young colony's great mercantile interests. In 1708, an official remarked on its rising importance, noting that the interior Southeastern Indians "are great hunters and warriours and consume great quantity of English goods."[20] Except for brief war-related interruptions, Carolina would remain overwhelmingly the most important player in southeastern commerce until the American Revolution.

The deerskin trade provided Carolina with a badly needed export commodity. In the reports of colonial officials, "buck and doe skins" were considered as important as the colony's other products: rice, beef, pitch, and tar. By involving thousands of native consumers in Carolina's commerce, the trade enabled Charleston merchants to import far more goods than English subjects alone could have consumed, thus strengthening mercantile and shipping interests. Finally, using the profits gained in trade, many colonists invested heavily in plantation slavery and increased the production of staple crops such as rice.[21]

Within the realm of imperial politics, the trade provided colonists with a means to spread English culture and combat the influence of European rivals, beginning with Spanish Florida. While the English relied upon trade to mold and transform native cultures, the Spanish deployed the mission system. The mission system was initially most successful with the Guale Indians of the Georgia coast and the inhabitants of the provinces of Apalachee and Timucua, places where missions were supported or accompanied by other colonial institutions such as the army, the crown, and the regular church. During the seventeenth century, the mission system extended its reach westward and southward to incorporate Apalachees and Calusas respectively. Franciscan friars built an impressive network of churches, chapels, and mission stations to serve thousands of southeastern Indian converts. Nevertheless, as successful as the mission system was as a frontier institution of the Spanish empire, it was unable to extend its direct influence into interior piedmont regions of the Southeast. In a sense, the mission system was too organized, required too much state support, and was intended to institute too many fundamental changes in native life to be spread easily and securely to regions beyond Spanish control.[22]

In contrast, the English trading regime expanded most successfully when it was least regulated; the trade seemingly required no fundamental changes in Indian life; and traders could thrive in places far removed from colonial control and population centers.[23] The English trading regime was able to penetrate the interior Southeast with incredible rapidity and comprehensiveness. Unlike Spanish missionaries, traders did not directly oppose southeastern Indian religions, dances, or games; nor did traders force southeastern Indians to provide labor for building, ranching, and mission projects; nor did traders interfere with basic seasonal rhythms and subsistence strategies of native cultures. Quite to the contrary, traders encouraged the traditional and very important indigenous practice of hunting deer. English or Scottish resident traders, most of them with Native American wives and offspring, connected themselves to the existing culture instead of proscribing or attacking it.

The match between the trade and the indigenous cultures initially gave the deerskin trade a quite benign appearance to its southeastern Indian participants. Because the trade meshed so well with their ordinary practices, because it harmonized with indigenous lifestyles, southeastern Indians found it difficult to prevent the trade from expanding and involving them more deeply in a market system that they could not control. This made it possible for the trade to shift almost imperceptibly from a useful form of intercultural interaction that benefitted both sides into a form of colonial exploitation that increasingly worked against the Creeks, the Choctaws, the Cherokees, and other southeastern peoples. Yet such a shift would not fully take place for several generations, not till the latter part of the eighteenth century.[24]

Throughout the last decades of the seventeenth and the first several decades of the eighteenth centuries, the trade seemed safe, and it made good sense to southeastern hunters. Thanks to the favorable deer/hunter ratio, interior hunters had little reason to worry about depleting the deer population. The supply of deer seemed inexhaustible.[25] As European newcomers placed a premium on deerskins, southeastern Indians readily and successfully intensified their hunting of deer. In exchange for skins, furs, tallow, oils, honey, horses, and slaves, southeastern Indians obtained a wide variety of goods, some necessities, some near necessities, and some outright luxuries. Among the most important necessities were the "powder, bullets and shot" that southeastern Indian men used to hunt deer and defend themselves.[26] Interior groups appreciated the English willingness to sell munitions; trade with the English seemed the best way to gain an advantage over or at least maintain parity with their traditional enemies.

As important as munitions were, by far the most important trade item consumed by southeastern Indians was cloth. A comfortable and colorful substitute for leatherware, clothing was consumed in great quantity, diverse fabrics, and manifold styles. As Carolina's Governor Nathaniel Johnson reported, southeastern Indians purchased noteworthy quantities of "English cottons, broad cloths of several colours, blue and redd beads of several collours, sorts and sizes, axes, hoes, faulchions."[27] Bright red or blue woolen leggings and skirts were extremely popular trade goods, but southeastern Indians also bought blankets, shirts, belts, hats, overcoats, ear bobs, ostrich feathers, ribbons, combs, and mirrors.

By trading with the English, southeastern Indian peoples gained access to a world of novel, practical, beautiful, and destructive goods and materials produced or gathered in every corner of the globe. Southeastern Indians enjoyed this access and were loathe to have it cut off. Nevertheless, their reliance on it left them open to the colonists' influence and coercion. Because the English dominated manufacture and the market, they could manipulate the trade to advance their own political purposes. Trade, like war, provided the English of Carolina with the means to secure and increase the fruits of colonial conquest. Indeed, in the colonial setting, trade went hand in hand with war.

The English constantly pursued profits and greater control over Carolina's territory and the entire Southeast. In pursuing these goals, Carolinians did not hesitate to encourage rivalries and conflicts between native peoples. The Goose Creek men sowed war, arming Savannahs against Westoes (1680); Yamasees against the peoples of Spanish Guale and Timucua (1680–90); Yamasees and Creeks against Apalachees (1702–4); Creeks against Chatot (1706); Yamasees, Chickasaws, and Creeks against Choctaws (1690–1710); Yamasees and Creeks against Tuscaroras (1711–12). Through these and subsequent wars, South Carolina wrecked Spain's mission system in Florida, deepened divisions between native groups, squelched anti-colonial revolts, and gained for itself thousands of Native American slaves.[28]

The Apalachees paid the heaviest price. Firmly allied with and successfully missionized by the Spanish, the Apalachees did not have access to English goods or firearms. They became prime targets of Carolina officials eager to extinguish Spanish influence in the Southeast and obtain native slaves for English plantations. In 1704, Colonel James Moore led a force of fifty English soldiers and one thousand warriors (drawn from the Yamasees, Apalachicolas, and Creeks) on a ruthless slave raid. The invaders leveled fourteen mission villages, killed hundreds of Apalachees, and brought a thousand men, women, and children into captivity.[29]

As it had served Virginia, slavery provided early Carolina with cheap labor and marketable exports that were eagerly sought by planters in Barbados and as far away as New England. But Native American slavery was not destined for a lasting career in Carolina. Native Americans were still terribly vulnerable to European and African diseases, inexperienced in plantation agriculture, and prone to try to run away to their kinsmen and kinswomen in the interior. The supply of captives was finite and the costs of perpetual war too great, even for the English. In 1708, Governor Nathaniel Johnson informed the Board of Trade: "That which has been a considerable (though unavoidable) hindrance to the greater encrease of our trade is the great duty on goods both imported and exported occasioned by the debts of the country is involved in by the late expedition in the time of Governor Moore against St. Augustine."[30] Carolina's economy was still trying to recover from the tremendous debts incurred during prior military campaigns.

Additionally, colonial officials also began to fear that their policy of promoting conflicts among southeastern Indians might backfire and evoke a widespread rebellion. As early as 1705, Governor Moore was warned by the Cherokees to desist from the "trade of Indians or slave making" and return to "the trade for skins and furs."[31] However, Moore and Carolina did not heed the warning, and in 1715, the Creeks and Yamasees grew so "Dissatisfied with the Traders" that they determined to "fall on the Settlement." They almost destroyed Carolina.[32] After this nearly fatal rebellion, which historians have named "the Yamasee War," English planters considered it far wiser to meet the colony's labor needs by importing African slaves from the Caribbean and West Africa. In doing so, Carolina planters obtained laborers who were aliens to the land and hence less able to run away. Moreover, African laborers were experienced in plantation agriculture and less vulnerable than southeastern Indians to malaria, dengue fever, and yellow fever.[33]

As Native American slavery declined, the stronger groups of southeastern Indians steadily shifted their energies from hunting for human captives to hunting for deerskins, producing ever more skins for trade. Between 1699 and 1715, an average of 54,000 deerskins were sent annually to England from Charleston. In 1707, the total numbered more than 120,000; in 1748, the number was 160,000.[34]

After its founding in 1733, Georgia successfully diverted a substantial portion of the deerskin trade away from its elder sister colony. In 1735, Georgia Governor General James Oglethorpe built "a handsome fort" that "drew the traders to settle the town of Augusta." By 1740, Augusta encompassed "several warehouses, thoroughly well furnished with goods for the Indian trade, and five large boats . . . which can carry nine or ten thousand weight of deerskins each, making four or five voyages at least in a year. . . . The traders, packhorsemen, servants, townsmen, and others . . . are moderately computed to be six hundred white men, who live by their trade, carrying upon packhorses all kinds of proper English goods; for which the Indians pay in deerskins, beaver, and other furs; each Indian hunter is reckoned to get three hundred weight of deerskins in a year."[35] At first, these deerskins were transhipped to London via Charleston. However, with the rapid development of Savannah and Sunbury, Georgia established direct links to London, and by the 1760s exported almost as many deerskins as Carolina.[36]

Although the English in Carolina and Georgia dominated the deerskin trade for much of the eighteenth century, during the first half of the century they faced important and annoying competition from the French of Louisiana. From 1699 to 1763, the French offered a significant outlet for the deerskins of interior peoples. The French presence especially benefited the Choctaws and Creeks. Enjoying access to both the English and French, Choctaws and Creeks were somewhat immunized from the pernicious control of either. Unlike the Catawbas and Cherokees, the Choctaws and Creeks could continue to obtain large supplies of manufactured goods, but simultaneously postpone the practice of overhunting deer and delay the moment when they would have to cede land to pay debts. Rather than having to rely too heavily upon the hunt to provide materials to exchange with the English or French, Choctaws and Creeks could rely upon diplomacy and play-off politics to gain goods that came in the form of gifts. As long as the French were a viable presence in the Southeast, interior peoples could avoid economic dependency and the dispossession that inevitably followed.

The French provided the Choctaws, their main allies in the region, with gifts that annually equalled the value of thousands of deerskins, and it was these gifts more than anything else that kept the French-Choctaw alliance alive. The French also gave sizable gifts to the Alabamas. At annual conferences in Mobile and through the officers at Fort Toulouse, the French provided the chiefs of the Alabamas with "knives, hatchets, swords, pipes, kettles, looking-glasses, needles, scissors, beads, vermillion, blue paint, red caps, white blankets, Limbourg and Alaigne cloths, trade shirts and stockings."[37] If the gifts stopped, the French knew the Alabamas would abandon them. As the French Commissary General in Mobile wrote in 1717: "All the chiefs of the Indians, even those remote from these posts, ordinarily go to [the forts] to see the commandants, with the expectation of receiving some presents from these officers. That is what keeps these nations on our side. Deprived of these little attentions, they are less disposed in our favor. That makes them think that the French are beggars and slaves, just as the English, who heap presents upon them, have insinuated to them."[38]

This remained true a dozen years later, as the Governor of Louisiana recognized in 1730: "One is certain to be loved by them as long as one gives them what they wish, and in proportion as they feel that we need them they increase and multiply their needs so that the English, and we, are the dupes of these Indians who are less dupes than we are." And two dozen years later still, the French were giving generous gifts to keep the

Alabamas loyal, but now, ironically, the French themselves "were under the necessity of purchasing from [English] Traders the very presents" they gave away. In 1733, Jean Baptiste Le Moyne (Sieur de Bienville) bitterly described "the insolence with which [Southeastern Indians] pretended to consider as tribute the presents which the King is so kind to grant them." The French never successfully extricated themselves from the expense of giving gifts, and indeed, it seems that the more they gave, the larger became their partners' expectations.[39]

Fearing French influence, English colonists in Carolina and Georgia had no choice but also to give generous gifts to interior peoples. This practice first became significant after 1715. After the Yamasee War, Carolina colonists desired to renew trade with interior peoples. They invited the latter to visit Charleston and receive gifts. In May 1713, several headmen of the Creeks traveled to Charleston where they met with the Governor. In a careful negotiation, they determined the exchange rate of skins for English goods and reestablished a full trade, including guns, powder, pistols, flints, and bullets. While in Charleston, the headmen enjoyed the hospitality of the government. Upon their departure, the board in charge of the Indian trade gave each of "the Head Men . . . a Bottle Wine and three dozen pipes." The Board also ordered that "the Guns of the Head Men . . . now in Charles Town . . . be mended at the Charge of the Trade, according to the Desire of the Head Men."[40] Thus began a practice of officially sponsored gift exchange that would grow far larger than any Englishman ever anticipated.

In subsequent years, it became an annual practice for the headmen of the Creeks to travel to Charleston to discuss trade and politics, and to receive gifts. These annual "talks" grew into a major event, with ever larger numbers of chiefs participating, expecting finer and more diverse gifts. By 1732, it was common for "all the Talapoosa chiefs and other neighboring round about" to leave every fall "with the English traders in order to go and get some presents in Carolina." In 1749, James Adair encountered "a considerable body of Muskohge head-men, returning home with presents from Charles Town." By 1753, the Creeks considered it "a Practice of an old Standing to come hither [to Charleston] to see our Friends the English, and to renew our Treaties with them." The mounting expense of these regular visits prompted Carolina to petition the Crown for help, arguing "that in order to keep up a good Understanding with several Nations of Indians, and to prevent the influence of the French and Spaniards, that Province has been at a charge in Treaties and presents amounting generally to about Fifteen hundred Pounds Sterling Pr. Annum."[41] The King agreed to provide three thousand pounds sterling for presents to be obtained in England and distributed from Carolina and Georgia.

During the 1750s, as competition and conflict between the English and the French increased, so did Carolina's and Louisiana's "Indian Expenses."

From the simple bestowal of a bottle of wine and some dozen pipes to a few headmen, English gift giving had evolved into a very large, expensive and unwieldy annual distribution of goods and hospitality.[42]

During the 1750s, but also in previous decades, the Creeks and Choctaws benefited greatly by playing the English and the French off against one another. If one European power did not satisfy their needs, they threatened to turn to the other. In 1755, for example, after failing to gain concessions from the English, many of the Creek headmen, including Malatchi, the powerful chief of the Cowetas, went to Mobile to hear what kind of trade and presents the French offered. The Choctaws were equally adept at using this strategy. Though allied with the French, Choctaws regularly threatened to switch their loyalties to the English, because the English promised them "considerable presents."[43]

If they courted the Choctaws and held the Creeks with gifts, the English also tried to win the affection of interior groups by offering favorable prices in the regular trade.[44] In his 1772 tour of the Creeks' country, David Taitt, an English agent, encountered a village leader who wistfully recalled the days when French competition inspired the English to offer good prices for hunters' skins. In those days, the English had "sold Stroud and duffle Blankets at Six pound leather each and every thing else in proportion, and took their buck Skins at five pounds and doe at three."[45]

By 1772, such favorable terms were only memories. After their defeat in 1763 in the Great War for Empire, the French departed the Southeast, leaving interior groups with no recourse but to trade almost entirely with the English. Though the trade was nominally divided between Carolina, Georgia, and Florida, this division did not constitute a form of competition that worked to the favor of the Choctaws and Creeks. Rather like the Catawbas of 1700, the Creeks and Choctaws now found themselves surrounded on all sides by English colonists, forts, soldiers, and settlers. Just as the Catawbas had had to learn the perils of total reliance upon the English for manufactured goods, so now the Creeks, Choctaws, and Cherokees, the last strong southeastern Indian groups, would learn the same lesson.

Signs of this new reluctance to provide gifts surfaced immediately after the English took over West Florida in 1763. Hundreds of Creek and Choctaw Indians accustomed to enjoying hospitality assumed the new commander would keep his "house constantly open to them, giving them victuals whenever they ask it, and the government making them annually considerable presents." For his part, the commander, Major Robert Farmar, bitterly complained that this was a "vile custom," a "most disagreeable custom," and assumed that it was one introduced by the French.[46]

At a conference held in Mobile in 1765, Farmar and Governor George Johnstone suggested that the Creeks cede land to help the English raise the food needed to feed native visitors. At the next conference, held this time in Pensacola, the English again demanded land cessions. The Creeks continued to demand presents. Clearly, there was a serious gap between Creek expectations and English intentions.[47]

If gift giving was being abandoned in West Florida, a colony most vulnerable to attack, it was rapidly dying in the older and stronger colonies of Georgia and South Carolina. After 1763, these latter colonies relied less upon persuasion and gifts to establish peace and encourage commerce, and turned increasingly to harsher measures, including outright coercion. Unlike the infant and isolated colony of West Florida, which routinely devoted 20 percent of its budget for "Indian Expenses," Georgia and South Carolina gradually phased out the practice of gift giving. Rather than give presents, these colonies, especially Georgia, turned to a strategy of debt collection to obtain what they wanted most: southeastern Indians' land.[48]

After the French departed, the deerskin trade fell under the almost complete control of a few traders living on the border of South Carolina and Georgia, at Silver Bluff and Augusta. Located at Silver Bluff, George Galphin "possessed the most extensive trade, connections and influence, amongst the South and South-West Indian tribes, particularly with the Muskogees and Chactaws."[49] Through his network of hirelings, clerks and traders, Galphin engrossed a substantial percentage of the leather production of interior peoples. From Silver Bluff, his packhorsemen drove pack trains of one hundred "good size, well-made, hard-hoofed, handsome, strong and fit" Cherokee packhorses to the interior of Creek country. Moving at a cruel pace, whipping the horses till they nearly dropped, Galphin's packhorsemen, some of whom were African Americans, raced westward, determined to reach Creek hunters before any of Galphin's competitors.[50]

Galphin's traders included many of the most ruthless and exploitative men in the Southeast, and they routinely used illegal means to cheat the Creeks. The most common strategem involved alcohol. Taitt, writing in 1772, witnessed how a trader, Francis Lewis, "met with the Indians (last night as they came into town [Tuckabatchee] with their Skins from hunting) and Supplyed them plentifully with rum on purpose to get what skins they had brought in, and deprive the other Trader of any part of them."[51] The Tuckabatchee Indians lost their skins, and the town's resident trader was left without any means of covering the cost of credit already extended to the hunters.

Another, slightly more complicated version of this scheme made use of the trader's Native American wife: "This man makes it a Common practice to give Rum to his wench for her to purchase back the goods from the Indians, which he has before sold or Trusted them with, so that he is Obliged to fitt them out a Second time on Credit, which greatly increases their Debts to his Employer, but is a great profit to himself as the Skins that he purchases with Rum or goods bought with it he Claims as his own; this I have been informed is a common practice with hirelings in this Country."[52]

Francis Lewis was only one of many hirelings of George Galphin, and

Galphin was but one of several licensed and countless unlicensed traders of the mid-eighteenth century. Together, they directed what amounted to a river of alcohol into Creek and Choctaw country. They did this so that they could, at very low cost, dramatically increase the flow of skins, manufactures, horses, and other commodities passing through their hands. James Adair, a veteran trader, described the practices of his less honorable colleagues: "Many Traders licenced and unlicenced . . . have made a constant Practice of [carrying] very little Goods, but chiefly, and for the most part intierly Rum from Augusta, from whence as soon as the Indian Hunters are expected in from their Hunts, they set out with small or large Quantities of that bewitching Liquor according to their Ability. Then some of the Rum Traders place themselves near the Towns, in the way of the Hunters returning home with their deer Skins. The poor Indians . . . are unable to resist the Bait; and when Drunk are easily cheated." [53] In his report on the trade, Edmond Atkin related how rum merchants tracked hunters into the woods to ply them with rum. The celebrating hunters quickly found themselves stripped of "the fruit of three or four Months Toil . . . without the means of buying the necessary Clothing for themselves or their Families. . . . Their Domestick and inward Quiet being broke, Reflection sours them, and disposes them for Mischief." [54] Like so many officials before him, Atkin urged that the state step in to regulate the trade more closely lest abused southeastern Indians strike back.

While creating a state of economic dependency and debt among the Creeks and Choctaws, rum traders made enormous profits. Moreover, the rum traders' practices served as the precondition for the next level of exploitation. Having used rum to create debt, they now sought to exploit debt to gain land. Galphin and the merchants of Augusta exercised considerable power in determining prices and arranging for the payment of southeastern Indians' debts. In 1772 it was these traders, the "Augusta rum traders," who insisted that the Cherokees and Creeks cede land. This cession was the first of many to come as a result of the market's shift toward monopoly, and it served as a precedent for subsequent cessions. [55]

Another cost of the rum trade, internal conflict, occurred at the village level. After consuming alcohol, men were prone to violence. Alcohol explosively touched off conflicts that otherwise might have remained suppressed. As the English agent reported in 1772, "The Abeckas desired that no more than ten Keggs of Rum might be brought to each Town by their Traders and the Tallapuses desired only four, as some of their men had been lately killed in Rum drinking and others greatly burnt." Fatal fights between men frequently erupted and disrupted village life. [56]

As the Creeks and Choctaws lost control of the deerskin trade, they were also facing an ecological crisis much like the one the Yamasees and Catawbas had faced generations earlier. The deer population could withstand only so much pressure before yields would drop, and the drop could be dramatic. This fact had already been demonstrated time after time, first in Virginia, then in Carolina, most recently in the Cherokee country, and now in the hunting grounds of the Choctaws and Creeks. At the end of the seventeenth century, Virginia's deer population was in such critical condition that the government established a closed season. By the middle of the eighteenth century, deer were becoming scarce in Catawba and Cherokee country.[57] During the second half of the eighteenth century, Creek hunters, as William Bartram noted, began to find "deer and bear to be scarce and difficult to procure." In response, many Creeks, taking advantage of the sparsely settled frontier to the south, migrated to Florida where game remained plentiful and a hunter could "enjoy a superabundance of the necessaries and conveniences of life."[58] Most Creek and Choctaw hunters, however, did not have this option. In order to continue harvesting the same number of deer, they had to extend the season and range of their hunt. Their prolonged absence undermined traditional village life, but even more disturbing was a trend that prevailed among young men. No longer content to stay with their clans in winter hunting camps, they roamed far and wide over the countryside seeking deer to kill, and increasingly, horses to steal. Needless to say, these practices brought them into violent conflict with neighboring southeastern Indians and Georgia settlers.

In the mid 1760s, conflicts over hunting lands erupted between Creeks and Choctaws, and these conflicts escalated quickly into a serious war between the two groups. This war, which caused the deaths of hundreds on both sides, was the direct result of economic pressures caused by the deerskin trade. It was also abetted by the English.[59]

If Choctaw-Creek war weakened both combatants and left the English unscathed, it did not fundamentally alter the history of the deerskin trade. Nor did it lessen the economic distress suffered by Creeks and Choctaws alike. At most, the conflict temporarily relieved some of the pressure upon the deer population in contested borderlands. During times of war, as a Cherokee leader in 1752 complained, it was virtually impossible to "hunt in Safety and get Skins."[60] During the Choctaw-Creek war, hunting slowed, but did not cease. In 1774, William Bartram observed a band of forty Creek warriors "destined against the Chactaws of West Florida." Though prepared to fight, they claimed that "the principal object of this expedition was hunting on the plentiful borders of the Chactaws."[61]

The future of the deerskin trade was not bright. Locked into an economic relationship that increasingly worked against their interests, Creeks and Choctaws were discovering what their true position was in the world market. It was to be a very bitter lesson. They were learning and would continue to learn that they were extremely vulnerable, economically dependent, and now destined to lose much of what they had heretofore preserved so remarkably, creatively, and energetically. For the first time, their contact experience came to resemble that of other southeastern Indians. For the first time, their economic relations with Europeans became destructive to both economic and village life. This destructive shift is best understood by using the concepts and perspective developed within dependency theory.

In terms of dependency or world-systems theory, Carolina merchants occupied the position of what has been termed the "core," and interior southeastern Indians occupied the position of the "periphery." Like other peoples on the "periphery," southeastern Indians received but could not extend credit. With the decline of the practice of gift giving, Choctaws, Chickasaws, Cherokees, and Creeks could not avoid going into debt if they were to obtain arms, cloth, and consume goods. Unlike the merchants of Carolina, who could quickly diversify in response to market forces by literally plowing the profits made in the deerskin trade into plantation slavery and staple crop production, southeastern Indian hunters possessed few economic options, no liquidity, no capital, and no control over credit. They could not afford to let the deerskin trade languish or they would lose access to necessities such as clothing and weaponry. In the words of one midcentury observer, commercial hunting provided "the only means the Indians have to get everything else they stand in need of." [62] Southeastern Indians were bound to a dominant staple export and were increasingly encumbered by debt.

Although the Creeks, Choctaws, and Cherokees had avoided the perils of trading with the English longer and more successfully than any other southeastern Indians, they could no longer do so. They were now economically vulnerable, and in the late eighteenth and early nineteenth centuries they would have to pay a very heavy price. Suffering military defeats and removal, yielding most of their land and losing political independence to invading Anglo-American settlers, their final experiences of contact in the Southeast came to resemble the much earlier experiences of the Apalachees, Yamasees, and Catawbas. That this resemblance finally came to pass supports the work of ethnohistorians (such as Richard White and James Merrell) who have attempted to identify common patterns that characterized the contact experiences of southeastern Indians. Yet the fact that the similarity of outcomes only came about after several generations of successful resistance by interior peoples should caution historians to avoid oversimplifying the history of contact in the Southeast. Irreducible to a single theory or model, this history was always richly varied, contradictory, and complex, and its complete telling will require the labors of a great many more scholars.

NOTES

1. White, *Roots of Dependency,* 69–96.
2. This is the fundamental criticism that has been directed at dependency theory wherever it has been used by scholars. Dependency theory, despite its usefulness,

commonly fails to appreciate the complex ways people resist the power of the market. For critical appraisals of Immanuel Wallerstein's ideas, see Garst, "Wallerstein and His Critics"; and especially, Nash, "World Capitalistic System." Classic formulations of the theory include Frank, *Capitalism and Underdevelopment,* and Wallerstein, *The Modern World System.* See also Anders, "Theories of Underdevelopment."

3. Merrell, *Indians' New World,* 529.

4. See Merrill, *Indians' New World,* 539 n. 11.

5. The intensity of the overlap in New England leads ethnohistorian Neal Salisbury to consider diseases and trade as components of the first phase of contact. In his model, disease and trade are followed by a second phase, settlement; Salisbury, *Manitou and Providence,* 12.

6. Waselkov, "Seventeenth Century Trade."

7. On the southeastern communication network and the traders' use of existing trails, see Meyer, *Ancient Trails;* Goad, "Exchange Networks"; Tanner, "Land and Water Communication"; Goodwin, *Cherokees in Transition,* 88; and Turnbaugh, "Wide-Area Connections."

8. Marquette made this observation near Chickasaw Bluffs; Gilmary, *Discovery and Exploration,* 44. On southeastern Indians as middlemen, see Hudson, *Catawba Nation;* Merrell, " 'Our Bond of Peace' "; Goodwin, *Cherokees in Transition,* 94.

9. As William Byrd lamented in 1728, the Virginians failed to locate "a shorter cut to carry on so profitable a Trade" (William Byrd [1728], quoted in Hudson, *Catawba Nation,* 38). The Spanish also had to rely upon native middlemen. During the latter half of the seventeenth century, the Apalachees acted as middlemen between the Spanish and Apalachicolas (Waselkov, "Seventeenth-Century Trade," 118–19).

10. Fausz, "Patterns of Anglo-Indian Aggression," and Wright, *The Only Land They Knew,* 95–96, 106–9.

11. "If the Masons, Lees, Claibornes, Byrds, and Fleets [in Virginia] gained their start in part through trafficking with the Indians, the same was true of the Moores, Middletons, Wraggs, and Grimkes in Carolina" (Wright, *The Only Land They Knew,* 109–10).

12. Fausz, "Patterns of Anglo-Indian Aggression," 227. See also his article, "Fighting 'Fire' With Firearms," and "Powhatan Uprising."

13. John Banister to Dr. Robert Morison, April 6, 1679, in Ewan and Ewan, *John Banister,* 42.

14. See Fausz, "Patterns of Anglo-Indian Aggression," 225–26, 247–53. James H. Merrell explores the changing meaning of the "bond of peace" for Carolina tribes in his article, " 'Our Bond of Peace'." See also Charles Hudson (*Catawba Nation,* chapt. 3) who reflects on the dialectical relationship between trade and politics.

15. Wood, "Indian Servitude," 407–9; Merrell, *The Indians' New World,* 36. See also Perdue, *Cherokee Society.*

16. Smith, *Aboriginal Culture Change,* 27, 119–22, and "Aboriginal Depopulation in the Postcontact Southeast" (this volume), and Merrell, "Indians' New World," 549. Other peoples also absorbed novelty within tradition; see Miller and Hamell, "Indian-White Contact"; Sahlins, *Islands of History,* 140; and especially Lederman, "Changing Times."

17. "The Indians call the English 'blond men' to distinguish them from the

French and Spanish" (Bernard-Bossu, *Travels*, 138). Historians have long debated the origins and identity of the Westoes; see Wright, *The Only Land They Knew*, 105–7; Hudson, *The Catawba*, 32–33; Smith, *Aboriginal Culture Change*, 132–35. Spain's policy banning the sale of firearms to southeastern Indians would later cause many to flee from Florida. In 1704, for instance, hundreds of Chatot Indians fled Spanish Pensacola and sought refuge in French Mobile. When Commandant Bienville asked them "why they left the Spaniards," the Chatot replied that the Spanish "did not give them any guns, but that the French gave them to all of their allies" (quoted in Swanton, *Creek Indians*, 123). Also see the legend near Pensacola on the map reproduced in ibid., plate 3, in pocket of back cover. For discussion of the Spanish policy against distributing guns to Indians, see Larson, "Guale Indians," 135–36; and TePaske, "Indian Policy on the Gulf Coast," 13–24. Waselkov argues that despite the official ban firearms were sold to Florida Indians "in quantity" ("Seventeenth-Century Trade," 120).

18. Cheeves, *Shaftsbury Papers*, 165–66; Swanton, *Creek Indians*, 66.

19. Rivers, *History of South Carolina*, 53–59; Wright, *The Only Land They Knew*, 102–25; Hudson, *Catawba Nation*, 39–51. The best history of this commerce remains Crane's *Southern Frontier*, esp. 21–69; 108–85. See also Coker and Watson, *Indian Traders*; Goodwin, *Cherokees in Transition*; Merrell, " 'Our Bond of Peace' "; and Hatley, "Dividing Paths," 101–56, 472–84, 631–43.

20. N. Johnson, "Report of the Governor and Council," 35; Cockran, *Creek Frontier*, 50–51. The influx of Carolina traders spelled destruction for the southeastern middlemen, the Occanecees, Catawbas, and Tuscaroras. See Hudson, *Catawba Nation*, 38–40; Wright, *The Only Land They Knew*, 102–25; Crane, *Southern Frontier*, 119–22.

21. N. Johnson, "Report of the Governor and Council," 33; "An Interview with James Freeman," in *The Colonial South Carolina Scene*, 53; Crane, *Southern Frontier*, 120–23; Wright, *The Only Land They Knew*, 108, 110.

22. See Jerald T. Milanich, "Franciscan Missions and Native Peoples in Spanish Florida" (this volume); Gannon, *The Cross in the Sand*; Bushnell, "That Demonic Game," and "Ruling 'the Republic of Indians.' "

23. The contrasts between the Spanish and English approaches were noted by French officials eager to emulate the English model. In 1730, Philibert Ory, the French Comptroller General of Louisiana, urged Périer, the Governor of Louisiana, not to imitate the Spaniards, but "to follow the example of the English, who apply themselves only to causing the Indians to find profit in the trading that they carry on with them" (Ory to Périer, Nov. 1, 1730, *Mississippi Provincial Archives: French Dominion* [hereafter *MPA: FD*], 4: 48).

24. Ray, "Indians as Consumers"; Jennings, *Ambiguous Iroquois Empire*, 58–83. Compare Miller and Hamell, "Indian-White Contact." For a provocative and interdisciplinary discussion of the symbolic character of consumption, see McCracken, *Culture and Consumption*.

25. The size of deer herds awed early colonists in Carolina; Crane, *Southern Frontier*, 111.

26. N. Johnson, "Report of the Governor and Council," 36.

27. Ibid.; Braund, "Mutual Convenience-Mutual Dependence," 139–42.

28. Wright, *The Only Land They Knew*, 105–23; Waddell, *Indians*, 3–12; White, *Roots of Dependency*, 35; and Wood, "Indian Servitude in the Southeast."

29. Approximately thirteen hundred more voluntarily marched to New Windsor on the Savannah River where they remained until 1715. Swanton, *Creek Indians*, 121–22; Hann, *Apalachee*, 264–83.

30. Johnson, "Report of the Governor and Council," 34.

31. "Documents of 1705," 904.

32. April 12, 1715, MacDowell, *Journals* (hereafter *JCIT*), 65; Swanton, *Creek Indians*, 97–101; Wright, *The Only Land They Knew*, 121–25; Crane, *Southern Frontier*, 162–86.

33. Wood, *Black Majority*, 37–42, "Changing Population," and "Indian Servitude."

34. L. R. Smith, "British-Indian Trade," 70; De Vorsey, "Colonial Georgia Backcountry," 11.

35. "Province of Georgia."

36. Wright, *Creeks and Seminoles*, 59.

37. Hamilton, *Colonial Mobile*, 203–4; Bienville and Salmon to Maurepas, April 5, 1734, *MPA: FD*, 3: 652. Richard White estimates that in the 1730s annual French gifts were worth "8,500 to 25,000 deer." French giving remained at high levels until 1763; White, *Roots of Dependency*, 67, 63. See also Galloway, " 'The Chief Who is Your Father'."

38. Hubert to the Council, October 26, 1717, *MPA: FD*, 2: 250–51.

39. Périer to Maurepas, Apr. 1, 1730, *MPA: FD*, 4: 31; Jacobs, *Indians of the Southern Colonial Frontier*, 12; from De Bienville, May 15, 1733, *MPA: FD*, 1: 193; Périer and Salmon to Maurepas, Dec. 5, 1731, *MPA: FD*, 4: 91; Ory to Périer, Nov. 1, 1730, *MPA: FD*, 4: 46; Hubert to the Council, Oct. 26, 1717, *MPA: FD*, 2: 249–50.

40. Board of Commissioners to Capt. Charlesworth Glover, June 3, 1713, *JCIT*, 281–82.

41. Crémont to Salmon, August 18, 1732, *MPA: FD*, 4: 122; Adair, *History of the American Indians*, 296–97; McDowell, *Documents Relating to Indian Affairs*, 411; and Jacobs, *Indians of the Southern Colonial Frontier*, 31.

42. Jacobs, *Indians of the Southern Colonial Frontier*, 27; McDowell, *Documents Relating to Indian Affairs*, 401–13. The irrationality of the system troubled the British, but they found no good alternative for distributing presents in Charleston, and did not dare abandon the practice. See Jacobs, *Indians of the Southern Colonial Frontier*, 27–33.

43. King's Paper, May 29, 1738, *MPA: FD*, 1: 368; McDowell, "Journal of an Indian Trader," 57–60.

44. The fear of the French prompted Edmond Atkin to write his plan for regulating the deerskin trade; Jacobs, *Indians of the Southern Colonial Frontier*, 4, 7–13.

45. Taitt, "Journal," 532. The figure "five pounds" for a buckskin was an exaggeration. In 1718, Carolina officials considered a heavy skin to be any "raw" skin that weighed more than two pounds or any "drest" skin that weighed more than one pound (*JCIT*, 269). Most raw skins probably weighed about two-and-a-half pounds on average, and that is a "generous estimate" (White, *Roots of Dependency*, 67).

46. "I have had five hundred a day during the congress to entertain in this manner, and now that the main body is gone, I must have twenty or thirty that dine every

day in the house and must have Indian corn to carry to their camp for their children" (Farmar to the secretary of war, January 24, 1764, *MPA: English Dominion 1763–1766*, 1: 7–17).

47. Johnson, *British West Florida*, 39–43.

48. Johnson, *British West Florida*, 21 n. 50.

49. Bartram, *Travels*, 258.

50. Adair, *History of the American Indians*, 230; Bartram, *Travels*, 350–51; "Dannll. Pepper to Governor Lyttelton," 354; Willis, "Anthropology and Negroes," 48–49; Porter, *Negro on the American Frontier*, 47, 50, 58, 61, 172–73; Wright, *Creeks and Seminoles*, 57, 94, and *The Only Land They Knew*, 269, 270; Wood, *Black Majority*, 115; and Littlefield, *Africans and Creeks*, 40–47.

51. Taitt, "Journal," 505.

52. Ibid.

53. Adair, *History of the American Indians*, 35.

54. Quoted in Jacobs, *Indians of the Southern Colonial Frontier*, 35.

55. Bartram, *Travels*, 53–62, and Taitt, "Journal," 507, 513, 524–25. The traders gained over one million acres above the Little River for Georgia in the Second Treaty of Augusta, 1773. A map representing this and other cessions is provided in Cashin, "'But Brothers, It Is Our Land'," 243; see also Pickett, *History of Alabama*, 328–29.

56. Taitt, "Journal," 553.

57. Merrell, *Indians' New World*, 137–38; Cowdrey, *This Land, This South*, 56–58; and Goodwin, *Cherokee in Transition*, 132–44.

58. Bartram, *Travels*, 181–82, 165, 170, 172.

59. Governor Johnstone confessed: "The present Rupture is very fortunate for us more specially as it has been effected without giving them the least possibility of thinking we had any share in it. It was undoubtedly our interest to foment the dispute between these Nations. . . . I am of the opinion we should now feed the war" (quoted in White, *Roots of Dependency*, 77). The Choctaw-Creek war probably diverted the Creeks from waging war on their English neighbors to the east. In 1772 a Creek chief "observed that they were already at war with the Choctaws and thought these Sufficient without falling out with the white people." Another chief, Effatiskiniha, startled David Taitt by declaring that he purposely promoted war with the Choctaws in order to avoid war with the English. Since his town was on the eastern border of Creek country and most vulnerable to English attack, he "made war on purpose to keep his Young people from falling out with the English and as soon as his Nation makes peace with the Chactaws he will Spoil it again as he knows they must be at war with some body" (Taitt, "Journal," 553–54).

60. "Talk of the Cherokee Emperor," 256. Because of these hostilities with the Cherokees, the Creeks at Coweta also lost "their Winter Hunts" ("Second Journal of Thomas Bosomworth," 321). See also White, *Roots of Dependency*, 77.

61. Bartram, *Travels*, 215–16.

62. Jacobs, *Indians of the Southern Colonial Frontier*, 11.

The Formation of New Societies

JOHN H. HANN

The Apalachee of the Historic Era

On June 25, 1528, trail-worn forces led by Pánfilo de Narváez burst upon the Apalachee world, capturing the women and children of a village "of forty small and well sheltered houses." The Spaniards met no resistance, as all the men were away from the village. Most likely, the Apalachee had no warning of the approach of these strangers from another world. The lands through which Narváez had been traveling held enemies of the Apalachee. The Apalachee men would hardly have left homes undefended had they been aware of the approach of strangers carrying fearsome weapons such as they had never seen before.

The first encounter of those two worlds was a brief one. After two days, the village *cacique* (chief) and his men came back and approached peacefully to ask that their women and children be released. Narváez complied, but then seized the cacique as a hostage. The next day a force of two hundred natives began hostilities that would continue intermittently for the rest of the twenty-six days that Narváez spent in the settlement while his men reconnoitered the countryside. Although the land provided ample supplies of food, the region was a bitter disappointment to Narváez's hopes of finding a second Mexico there. The cacique whom Narváez held hostage, and Indians whom he captured before reaching Apalachee, told him that further on he would find fewer people with less food and vast uninhabited areas of woods, ponds, and swamps. His disappointment was so great, and harassment by the natives so discomforting, that he abandoned the enterprise.[1]

Despite Narváez's disillusionment, the Apalachee's territory might be considered a land most favored by nature for its combination of rich upland soils, lowland aquatic resources, and relative proximity to estuarine resources as well. The province was bounded on the east and west by the Aucilla and Ochlockonee Rivers.[2] In historic times the Apalachee lived in the southern part of the fertile uplands between those two rivers, not far from the Cody Scarp, a sudden rise from coastal lowlands that runs east-west across north Florida about 30 kilometers (20 miles) from the coast. Many of the later Apalachee missions lay close to this scarp, enabling the inhabitants to exploit both the good upland soils and the aquatic resources of the lowlands.[3]

A third river, the St. Marks, divided Apalachee physiographically into eastern and western halves that were somewhat isolated from one another by the swampy St. Marks Valley lowlands. Garcilaso described that divide vividly as an arroyo with much water and thick woods on either side, which made passage very difficult. Even beyond it, he noted, there was another five miles without any planted fields or settlement. In mission times, this physical separation of the upland soils into two distinct territories may have provided a basis for the east-west political subdivision of two constellations of settlements grouped respectively around two preeminent villages, San Luis and Ivitachuco.[4]

Late prehistoric Apalachee, with its major Lake Jackson mound center and other mound complexes, heavy dependence on agriculture for subsistence, and participation in the "Southern Cult" ceremonialism, is recognized as having been a Mississippian-type culture similar to those found throughout much of the Southeast. But Apalachee's distribution of good farming soils dictated a settlement pattern distinct from the most common Mississippian adaptation. Villages and farmsteads were located in river bottomlands in most Mississippian societies. Bottomlands provided the most suitable soils for maize and their nearby oxbow lakes were excellent sources of fish at a season when it was most difficult to procure deer, the most important source of animal protein. Originating from lowland swamps or underground springs, Florida's rivers (except the Apalachicola) do not carry silt or mineral nutrients to enrich their bottomlands, which are among the poorest microenvironments for growing crops. This unsuitability of floodplains for agriculture induced the Apalachee and others who faced similar conditions to locate in areas between the rivers that held better soils. Thus, rivers in Florida served more often as boundaries between polities than as the heart of the polity, as they were in most Mississippian societies.[5]

On this resource base and Mississippian adaptation, Apalachee farmers and hunters developed a powerful, prosperous, and apparently secure chiefdom whose reputation had reached deep into south Florida when Narváez and de Soto landed there in the second quarter of the sixteenth century. The Apalachee chiefdom in Mississippian and early historic times is considered to have been a complex one with an elaborate ruling hierarchy and a clear distinction between elite and commoners. As this phase of Apalachee culture is discussed elsewhere (see John Scarry, "The Apalachee Chiefdom," this volume), there is no need to go into it here except to note that some development led the Apalachee to abandon the Lake Jackson complex in the late prehistoric period, and possibly as early as A.D. 1450. De Soto found the Apalachee already living south of the major lakes, where they were to be located in mission times as well.[6]

Whatever disruptions may have occasioned abandonment of the Lake Jackson site, Apalachee is believed to have remained a unified, powerful chiefdom when Narváez and de Soto arrived within its borders just eleven years apart. The Fidalgo de Elvas identified the chief of the settlement named Anhayca Apalache as "lord of all that land and province" and the other leading village, Ivitachuco, as "subject to Palache."[7] Although de Soto was able to entrench himself in the head chief's village, the chroniclers commented repeatedly on the persistence and ferocity of the Apalachee attacks throughout the five months that the Spanish wintered in their land. None of the Apalachee broke ranks to come to terms with the intruders. De Soto's followers were impressed by the natives' pride in being known as Apalachee. And natives of faraway settlements perceived the Apalachee as a homogeneous regional unit, referring to them as Apalachee rather than as Ivitichuco, Anhayca, or Uzela.[8] At the end of the sixteenth century, so great was the Spaniards' perception of Apalachee power that the province was referred to at times as "Great Apalachee," and its boundaries were expanded to include much of the hinterland west of the coastal plain as far north as South Carolina. On a lesser scale Garcilaso remarked that five days were needed to leave the province of Apalachee and come to the boundary of another named Altapaha in central Georgia's Oconee valley.[9]

Despite de Soto's five months in Apalachee, the chroniclers give surprisingly little specific information about the head chief's power, the settlement pattern, or the size of the population. The Fidalgo observed "that the land was heavily settled" once they passed Ivitachuco and that de Soto's six hundred men were able to be lodged round about the main settlement of Anhayca, which Garcilaso described as having 250 houses. Both Garcilaso and the Fidalgo noted that there were other villages scattered around the main one at distances of half a league, a league, or more. Garcilaso recorded further that there were a great number of dwellings "which were sprinkled about and not arranged as a town."[10] The de Soto narratives say nothing explicitly about the nature of the overlordship wielded by Anhayca's chief and give no indication of his being treated with the pomp and circumstance that would show clearly that he held a position high above that of the other chiefs. Throughout the seventeenth century, Ivitachuco's chief held the position of preeminence, such as it was, though the heir to Anhayca at San Luis enjoyed a special status higher than that of the chiefs of the rest of the villages. Consideration of Ivitachuco as head peace town and of Anhayca as head war town provides an explanation for their chiefs' alternation in leadership. If the institution of war and peace towns prevailed, de Soto's arrival, in precipitating war, would make Anhayca's chief

lord of the land for the duration of the invaders' presence. That peace negotiations took place at Ivitachuco in 1608 and that Ivitachuco was spared in
the 1704 Anglo-Creek assault on the province may have significance in this
respect, but the deference shown to Ivitachuco is also susceptible to other
explanations.[11]

The earliest rough estimates of the Apalachee population, dating from
the early seventeenth century, place the population between thirty and
thirty-four thousand. The population probably was considerably higher
before the first contacts with Europeans eventually unleashed devastating
epidemics.[12] De Soto's prolonged stay there would have provided ample opportunity for such a catastrophe. Once the Spanish established themselves
at St. Augustine, occasions for such contagion multiplied. But it cannot be
assumed (as Henry Dobyns does) that every contagion that appeared in
St. Augustine or Havana spread inexorably northward, westward, southward.[13] A remark by Florida's governor in 1657 implies that Apalachee
had been spared much of the impact of earlier epidemics. Even though
Apalachee was affected by the mid-1650s epidemics of which he spoke,
the governor remarked that even then the loss had been less drastic in
Apalachee than in Guale and Timucua.[14] Population lists for the three provinces in 1675 support a similar conclusion. The figures suggest that survival
was proportionate to a settlement's distance from St. Augustine, with the
Suwannee serving as a major barrier to the spread of the epidemics. San
Luis de Talimali alone had more people in 1675 than all of Western Timucua, which had only a little over 1,330 people. The vast majority of those
Western Timucuans were Yustagans living west of the Suwannee.[15] This
is all the more surprising in view of Apalachee's occasional direct contact
with Havana as a source of contagion.

Except for Escalante de Fontaneda's memoir, neither Spanish nor French
sources have anything more of value to say about Apalachee for the rest of
the sixteenth century. French sources from the 1560s, in portraying Apalachee as located in the southern Appalachian mountains, seem to have been
responsible for that mountain chain having been named for the Apalachee,
whose territory was so distant from those mountains. René Laudonnière
so identified the mountains as early as the 1560s. Jacques Le Moyne's map
depicted Apalatci as well within the mountains at the head of a fictitious,
lengthy northwestern tributary to the St. Johns River. Le Moyne labeled
the mountains "Apalatci Mountains." A curious, seventeenth-century account by a French Huguenot minister, which allegedly reflects conditions
five hundred years earlier, also extended Apalachee into the mountains,
although the people to whom he applied the name Appalachites seem to
have been Cherokee.[16] Fontaneda, who spent a long captivity among south
Florida Indians, referred to the Apalachee as the best Indians of Florida
among those with whom he had become acquainted, and he observed that
"by sending them cloth by an experienced and capable linguist their friend-

ship may be easily won."[17] It is not clear what characteristic or characteristics Fontaneda had in mind in making that tribute, but it may have been an allusion to their sedentary way of life, which made them good prospects for missionization.

Neither Pedro Menéndez de Avilés nor his successors through the rest of the sixteenth century tried to contact the Apalachee, although they sent expeditions into the interior farther north. Narváez and de Soto had established that tales of Apalachee gold, as related by south Florida's natives, were unfounded. The markedly hostile reception the Apalachee gave those two adventurers was doubtless a major reason for the long hiatus in Spanish contact. Despite Apalachee's relative proximity to Pensacola Bay by sea and its reputation for abundance of food, Tristán de Luna apparently gave no thought to seeking the food he needed in that direction.

Unfortunately, we know very little from historical sources about developments in Apalachee and in the remainder of interior Florida to the east of Apalachee during the second half of the sixteenth century and even back to the abandonment of the Lake Jackson Mounds around 1450 or soon thereafter. Archaeologists conjecture that the appearance of Lamar-like ceramics signifies a disruption of the alliance and trading systems of the earlier mound-building period. Pottery in earlier mounds suggests greater interaction with the Middle Mississippi cultures to the west. Although the ceramics at the Martin site (site of de Soto's 1539–40 winter camp) are basically those of a Late Fort Walton settlement, the presence of small amounts of Lamar pottery establishes that complicated stamped ceramics had reached Apalachee by 1539. With the passage of time, Lamar ceramics would become steadily more prominent through the early and late mission periods between 1633 and 1704.[18] At present one can only speculate about the reason for these ceramic changes, which appear among the Yustaga and Utina as well. As Shapiro has noted, archaeologists like Louis Tesar suggest an immigration of people from Lamar areas of central Georgia but broad shifts in regional trade relationships or political alliance might just as easily account for the introduction of new pottery styles. Unfortunately, there are few data yet available to help resolve the problem.[19]

Early in the seventeenth century, for reasons not specified, the Apalachee were one of a number of groups in the Florida and Georgia hinterland who began to express interest in giving obedience to Spain's monarch and in being Christianized.[20] Potano's cacique appears to have made the first move. Early in the latter half of the 1590s, he sent word that he was ready to live in peace with the Spaniards. In 1597, Potano's chief joined the chief of Timucua (Utina) and the chieftainess of Aguera in rendering obedience to the Spanish monarch for the first time. Until then, Potano's war with the Spaniards had prevented that chief and his people from living a settled village life. And the chief of Timucua, as the governor put it, had until then refused to come, despite the many times he had been summoned either by

petitions or by threats.[21] Fray Baltasar López appears to have been working at the village of the head chief of Timucua for some weeks, when the
chief's brother and his entourage of nineteen *mandadores* and leading men
arrived at St. Augustine on July 20, 1597, to render obedience and to receive gifts.[22] Fray Martín Prieto began formal missionization of the Potano
in 1607. Although Timucua's head chief himself held off accepting baptism for some time, Fray Prieto seems to have established a rapport with
him rather quickly, which permitted other friars to begin Christianization of the province before the chief himself was baptized in 1609. Prieto's
knowledge of a change of attitude among some of the Apalachee, and his
conviction that chronic hostilities between Apalachee and the Timucua of
Utina and Yustaga were an obstacle to the friars' work in Utina, led Prieto
on a mission to the Apalachee village of Ivitachuco to work out a treaty of
peace between the Apalachee and the Timucua.

Upon his arrival, accompanied by Timucua's head chief and 150 warriors
drawn from Potano and Utina, Prieto found Apalachee's entire population
assembled at Ivitachuco under some seventy chiefs. He estimated the crowd
at more than thirty thousand people. Prieto's mission received a friendly
reception. Ivitachuco's head chief, identified as then the most important of
the Apalachee chiefs, spoke at great length in favor of peace. Subsequently,
peace negotiations were carried out successfully in a meeting of chiefs of
the two peoples presided over by Prieto. After a feast, the assembled Apalachee chieftains appointed the cacique of Inihayca to visit the governor at
St. Augustine. In his account of these events, the governor identified the
chief of Inihayca as a brother of the chief of Ivitachuco.[23]

Some might see Prieto's role in this affair and in the initiation of the conversion of Utina as conforming to a thesis advanced by Ramón Gutiérrez
about the conversion of the Pueblos of New Mexico. Gutiérrez maintains
that the friars sought to step into the shoes of the native leaders, or as
John Kessell expressed it, Gutiérrez "details 'how the Spanish conquest
weakened the native hierarchy of power and authority, allowing a group
of charismatic Franciscans assisted by fierce soldiers to seize control over
the native religio-political apparatus.'" Kessell continues: "The seemingly
magical friars sought to usurp not only the role of the cacique, or inside
chief, who controlled the law and the sacred in Pueblo society, but also
the functions of war and hunt chiefs, rain chiefs and medicine men."[24]
Although Prieto does especially fit the image of the friar as charismatic
leader, the friars' missionary approach to the natives of the Florida hinterland contrasts in many ways with the forceful one used among Spanish
Florida's coastal peoples and above all with the approach used with the
Pueblos and other natives of the Southwest. With the inland Timucua and
the Apalachee, the friars began their work unaccompanied by soldiers and
at the invitation of some among the natives rather than by thrusting themselves in uninvited. No large herds of cattle, horses, or sheep trailed the

friars who established the beachheads in Potano, Utina, Yustaga, and Apalachee to impress the natives with their control over the animal kingdom, in contrast again to the Southwest. In the Southwest, Franciscans and Jesuits brought ample resources in cattle and other supplies to convince natives to accept their tutelage and to agree to live at sites chosen by the religious, where they in effect dominated various categories of chiefs in their control of the new settlement.[25] Hogs and chickens became available rather quickly, and eventually cattle and horses also became available, but those at the missions were owned and controlled largely by the natives rather than by friars. None of the Florida missions is known to have become an economic enterprise in the manner of the typical California mission or the Tupi-Guarani missions of the Parana and Paraguay basins.[26] The *repartimiento* labor draft (a system of forced paid labor for a specified time, developed to extract labor deemed necessary for the common good from natives culturally unaccustomed to providing it voluntarily or consistently) was the sole formalized exploitative Spanish institution introduced into hinterland Florida.

In Florida, the padre was doubtless still a force to be reckoned with, who had considerable power and influence once the natives had accepted baptism, but he was not in control in the sense that he was in the Southwest.[27] In Florida, the friar had to rely more on persuasion and exhortation than was the case in other parts where "conquest" preceded conversion. In Apalachee, this was true particularly of the early years of the mission effort. Governors eventually stationed soldiers at San Luis, headquarters mission for the province, but initially the friars objected to their introduction and tried to convince the crown to remove them or to keep their numbers to an absolute minimum.[28] The reduction system does not seem to have been used in the inland missions of Timucua or Apalachee. Instead, friars began their work in existing settlements. Movement of villages, in the instances when it was recorded, was dictated by civil authorities to suit their needs and wishes, or by the needs and wishes of the natives themselves.[29] In interior Florida, consequently, the early conversions were much more a voluntary phenomenon than seems to have been the case in many other mission provinces. As a result of this, religious acculturation of many among the Apalachee after three-quarters of a century or less of missionization was far more profound than that which occurred in the Southwest over a similar span of time.

Although Prieto reported in 1608 that half or more of Apalachee's people desired to become Christian, the Spanish established no permanent presence there for another twenty-five years. Friars visited the province intermittently down to 1612 at least, and probably thereafter, although on a reduced scale. Supply problems because of the distance of Apalachee from St. Augustine, the need for friars in the closer burgeoning Utina missions, opposition to the friars' presence by some elements among the Apalachee, and the unruliness of some natives described as not obeying their chiefs well, all moved the Franciscans and the governors of the 1612–17 period to defer establishment of a permanent mission among the Apalachee. Additionally, the friars suspected the motives of some of the chiefs who were anxious for the friars to come, remarking that "the chiefs would like to gain control over their Indians" with the aid of the Spanish authorities.[30] Decline in chiefly power from what it had been earlier is reflected in a governor's statement that in Apalachee, chiefs were not given much respect, and that for this reason the friars had twice been forced to leave during the 1608–12 period.[31] Four years later a Franciscan visitor noted another cause for hostility toward the friars' presence: "In Apalachee the priests . . . are not able to have peace with the Indians, for there is much for which they should be taken to task; for instance, the extirpation of their immoral practices, which are of the worst kind."[32]

No direct evidence indicates "immoral practices" among the Apalachee, other than the ball game, scalping, recourse to the shaman-healer, and certain dances. Analogous information about other Florida tribes suggests that those "immoral practices" mainly involved sexual mores or native religious practices or both. Efforts to prohibit polygamy and casual sexual unions and native dances that the friars considered obscene were major sources of friction between friars and natives. The Guale rebellion of 1597, in which five friars were killed, was sparked by a friar's attempt to deprive the heir to a major chieftainship of his right of succession because he would not abandon his polygynous habits after having been baptized. A friar's condemnation of polygyny and adultery touched off the Chacato revolt in 1675.[33] Father Rogel's experience among the Calusa in the 1560s shows that conflict over sexual mores was a significant problem there as well. But it is not known to have been an issue in the Apalachee revolt of 1647, although it may well have been one.

Elimination of polygyny was a particularly delicate issue, as polygyny was associated with the leadership class and one of their forms of conspicuous consumption that distinguished them as a class, and, among the Calusa at least, a form of political bonding that helped hold the chiefdom together. Tributary and allied settlements were expected to provide one of their daughters for the ruling head chief, and in some cases, for the heir-apparent as well, soon after he reached puberty. Even among tribes where the practice is not known to have been so formalized as among the Calusa, it doubtless served the process of political bonding.[34]

Elimination of native religious practices in the sense of physical destruction of idols and temples may not have been too serious a problem when friars were invited in by tribal leaders who served as head shamans as well as caciques. In Lake Jackson Mound times, the Apalachee paramount is believed to have been head priest and cacique, using control of prominent posts of religious leadership as a prop for political legitimacy. Because of the failure of the traditional religious practices to protect the natives from the devastating impact of new diseases introduced by Europeans, such practices may have lost their value as props. This may have made rulers jettison them for the sake of the interests that led them to establish ties with the Spanish.

For Apalachee, we do not know what the situation was during the early days of the mission effort, but it may have been analogous to that of Utina. Even before the head chief of Utina had himself become a Christian, he asked the friars to visit all his towns and to destroy all the idols the places contained. About this process, Fray Prieto reported that, starting with the chiefdom's head village, "we burned twelve images in the center of the plaza; then we went to four other places and in each one of them we burned six images. I addressed the Indians and the cacique took my hand and told them definitively that throughout his territory they should leave their pagan superstitions and that all should prepare to be instructed and become Christians."[35] With that example before them, the elements among the Apalachee who received the friars warmly during the 1608–12 period may well have made the preliminary move toward religious acculturation at that time. When friars informed the friendly leaders in 1612 that the friars whom they had asked for on a permanent basis would not be available for some time, the Indians insisted that the friars set up crosses before leaving and indicate sites where the natives might build churches so that they would be ready when friars should become available.[36]

Presumably, transitory contacts with the Apalachee continued until the launching of the formal mission effort in 1633. After the installation of each new governor, it is likely that some of the major chiefs visited St. Augustine to renew pledges of allegiance and to receive the traditional gifts. That the two friars who launched the mission in 1633 were described as knowing the language like natives indicates that they had probably spent time in the province. The same conclusion is suggested by a 1630 report that Florida held twenty thousand baptized Indians and more than fifty thousand catechumens, not yet baptized, but catechized. So great a disparity, and the number of catechumens by itself, indicates that a considerable portion of them were Apalachee or even Tama. The spread of Timucua missions to Yustaga on the border of Apalachee would have facilitated such contacts. The San Juan de Guacara mission on the Suwannee was established as early as 1612. The move into Yustaga, which began at the Suwannee, may have followed soon thereafter. San Pedro de Potohiriba, easternmost of the Yustaga missions, was in existence prior to 1630.[37] Such contact is reflected in the observation that Timucua Alta (Utina and Yustaga) and Apalachee were primary sources of maize for St. Augustine since 1625. The prospect that Apalachee would solve St. Augustine's chronic shortages of food and labor was an important consideration in the launching of the permanent mission effort there.[38]

Fray Pedro Muñoz, one of two friars who initiated the mission effort in 1633, appears to have been an excellent choice. Presumably he was young, having arrived in Florida only in 1626. During the 1657 visitation, when the governor encouraged natives to criticize the friars in Apalachee in order to undermine the friars' efforts to thwart his policy of expanding the Spanish military presence in Apalachee, Muñoz was one of two friars singled out by the natives for praise. Ivitachuco's chief spoke of Muñoz as having cate-chized them with great love, in contrast to resorting to the whip for which other friars were criticized. Such was the esteem in which Muñoz was held that one of Ivitachuco's leading men adopted the name Pedro Muñoz.[39]

Nothing is known of the circumstances that surrounded the arrival of Muñoz and his companion or the ones in which they worked during the years immediately following. With the exception of 1655–57, the first forty years of Apalachee's mission period are a great void in which information about the province, its people, and progress of the mission effort is scant. Documents available do not indicate the village or villages in which the two friars began their work, although it is likely they began in the two prin-cipal villages of Ivitachuco and Inihayca. The first report on the progress of the conversions in 1635 claimed five thousand baptisms out of an alleged population of thirty-four thousand. In 1639, the governor reported over one thousand baptisms for Apalachee, remarking that conversions were increasing there more rapidly than elsewhere. There were still only two friars in the province in that year.[40]

In about 1638, the first five or six soldiers joined the friars. They seem to have served mainly as fiscal agents and factors for the governors. That small a number could hardly have provided much protection for the friars had there been serious trouble. It is not known whether the soldiers had a permanent domicile in the province during the first years after their arrival. They spent at least part of their time visiting various villages to assemble foodstuffs or other items to send to the governor. While traveling thus, sol-diers were lodged and fed in the village's principal council house, as any other guest or traveller would have been.[41]

Dispatch of the first soldiers probably was timed to coincide with the opening of a port in Apalachee so that supplies for the missions might be brought in by sea and foodstuffs sent to St. Augustine in the same manner. Apalachee's distance from St. Augustine made overland transport of such goods on the backs of Indians very onerous. In the late 1620s, friars asked for horses to carry supplies to the missions of Western Timucua in order to ease the burden on the natives.[42] As early as 1637, Governor Horruy-tiner commented that the mission effort in Apalachee could not survive or progress unless a suitable port was found there. He sent pilots overland to take soundings, using local canoes to search for a feasible landing place. In April of 1639, a frigate made the first run from St. Augustine to the Apa-lachee coast in less than thirteen days.[43] That development assured a rapid transformation of Apalachee society with the influx of more friars and soldiers, and Apalachee's integration within a world economy as Apalachee produce helped sustain the settlement at St. Augustine, which protected the passage of the treasure on which Spain depended for its economic survival. Apalachee would also help victual the fleets assembled at Havana.[44]

With that problem resolved, the mission effort expanded considerably in the early 1640s with the dispatch of additional friars. In mid-1643, the governor reported optimistically that conversions in Apalachee were increasing rapidly. Before 1647, the number of friars had risen to eight, and eight of the major village chieftains had become Christians, allowing establishment of missions in their villages.[45]

The governor under whom the Apalachee port had been opened had ambitious plans for development of the province as a trading entrepôt. As part of that plan, he contacted some of the province's un-Christianized neighbors in an effort to bring peace to the region and thereby expand the potential for trade. In 1639, he ended the state of war between the Apalachee and neighboring Chacato, Apalachicola, and Amacano (Yamasee), but was less successful with a nomadic group of Yuchi known as Chisca. The governor described the Chisca as especially warlike and as wandering freely through the entire area then comprising Spanish Florida.[46] There is no indication what role, if any, the Apalachee played in the negotiations, or about how they reacted to the constraints of this general peace.

Peace with those neighbors may not have pleased all Apalachee. To a considerable extent, the warriors' ethos was geared to chronic raiding against enemy tribes. The exploits performed and the scalps taken provided status, and the warriors gained wealth at times from the booty or slaves they captured. Traders may have been discontented by competition from the governor's soldier–trading agents or from some of the more mercenary friars. In the 1657 visitation, friars were accused of employing natives as packbearers for such trade without concern for the natives' welfare.[47]

In 1645 a new governor, Benito Ruiz de Salazar y Vallecilla, dramatically increased the Spanish presence, curbing further the natives' former independence of action. He placed the first deputy-governor in Apalachee, visited the province and the neighboring Chacato and Apalachicola himself, and established a large wheat and cattle hacienda on Apalachee's eastern border, on lands belonging to the Yustaga town of Asile, which was only two and one-half miles from Ivitachuco. This intensification of the Spanish presence occurred under the first two of a quartet of governors attacked by the friars in scathing terms:

> Unbounded greed has been the lodestone that has guided the wills of the governors Damián de Vega, Benito Ruiz de Salazar, and Nicolas Ponce, predecessors of don Diego de Rebolledo, and the target at which they have aimed in placing a lieutenant and soldiers in the province of Apalachee; the objective was none other than their private interest and convenience, without heeding

those pertaining to the service of your majesty and the welfare of the Indians. The one in particular about whom this can be said, more than about his predecessor, is Governor Benito Ruiz. For, that he had soldiery in the aforesaid province was (as is evident) in order to have people there for the utility and work of the hacienda, which he had on the lands of the chiefdom of Asile (alongside those of Apalachee) to the injury and loss of the Indians and very much against the will of the cacique, who, to the degree that he tolerated it, did so because he saw that it was done with the powerful arm of the governor.[48]

The evil criticized by the Florida friars was only part of a general deterioration in the quality of Spanish officials assigned to the least desirable positions in a decaying imperial structure.[49] Among the new friars were some who began to curb or prohibit the natives' dances and other practices, such as the Apalachees' ball game, which some friars felt to be incompatible with Christian morals.

The almost immediate consequence of this expanded Spanish presence, and the demands it entailed for more labor by the natives and for abandonment of more of the natives' ways, was the Apalachee revolt of 1647. Despite the opening of a port at St. Marks, increasingly heavy demands were being made on the natives to transport goods to and from St. Augustine for the missions, the soldiers, the governor's new hacienda, the governors' and friars' trading activities. Insurgent Apalachee and their Chisca allies killed three of the friars along with the governor's deputy and the deputy's family. They torched seven of the eight churches along with the mission crosses. The soldiers escaped, probably because they were outside of the province tending to wheat plantings on the governor's hacienda. The remaining friars were protected by loyal Christians and then probably sought refuge in neighboring Timucua. The revolt eliminated the Spanish presence in the province in a manner similar to the later Pueblo revolt of New Mexico, although with a smaller loss of life than the latter.

On learning of this debacle, the authorities at St. Augustine hastily dispatched thirty-one soldiers, who recruited five hundred Timucua as allies. Before this force could reach Apalachee, a much larger rebel force engaged them in a day-long struggle that ended with the withdrawal of the rebels. Having exhausted their shot, the Spaniards made no attempt to pursue them. Instead they withdrew to St. Augustine, believing that forces would have to be recruited in Cuba to restore a Spanish presence and that a permanent garrison of thirty to forty soldiers might be needed to maintain calm in the province.

While plans were being made to raise a larger force to regain Apalachee, an acting governor hastened to Western Timucua with a few soldiers to see what might be done in conjunction with loyal Timucua to contain any new rebel forays into Timucua.[50] On reaching the frontier, he learned that the rebels had become disheartened by their casualties and the rapidity of the Spanish response. The rebels had counted on the labor demands of planting time to prevent Spanish recruitment of allies among the Timucua and on having time to consolidate support among the Christian Apalachee and to form alliances with other non-Christian provinces to resist reassertion of Spanish control. Emboldened by this intelligence, the acting governor crossed secretly into Apalachee with twenty-one soldiers and sixty Timucua. Supported by loyal Apalachee Christians, within a month he persuaded the rebels, both Christian and non-Christian, to surrender and hand over their leaders for trial. Twelve of the rebels considered most guilty were executed in Apalachee and twenty-six others were sentenced to forced labor in the royal works. The rest received a general pardon in return for the province's acceptance, for the first time, of the obligation of providing quotas of laborers under the *repartimiento* to be employed on Spanish building projects and on the farms of soldiers with families.[51]

Nothing concrete is known about the mechanisms used to overcome rebel resistance or the identity of the native protagonists or the interests that they represented. In the postmortems, Spaniards mentioned no single incident that served to trigger the revolt, like that in the Guale revolt of 1597. Friars pointed to fears aroused by the beginning of Spanish settlement and farming activity and to increasing demands for labor brought about by such developments. Royal officials and soldiers, who were the targets of the friars' charges, made similar accusations against friars and spoke additionally of abusive treatment of the natives by some of the friars, particularly the treatment of native leaders. They also indicted the friars for their outlawing of many native practices such as their ball game, dances, and recourse to the shaman for healing. A decline in the volume of gifts distributed by Spanish authorities added to the dissatisfaction. Labor demands arising from Governor Ruiz de Salazar's hacienda and the fears it generated were indicated as major native grievances. There is no direct expression of the native point of view as to the causes for the revolt. But a nativist reaction is suggested in the burning of the churches and crosses and killing of the friars. The loyalty of some among the Apalachee suggests, in addition to the hold of the new religion, that there were natives who had benefited from trade with the Spaniards.

If Spanish officials are to be believed, support for the rebellion collapsed as quickly as it had arisen. Collapse of the uprising, they noted, had rekindled Christian fervor among the faithful and moved many of the non-Christians to seek baptism. The officials remarked that the people were now raising crosses everywhere with the same joy and enthusiasm with which they had burned them shortly before. Within a year of the start of the revolt, the seven burned churches reportedly had been rebuilt.[52]

The change of heart seems to have been genuine. Just three years later, when an interim governor was installed with whom the friars had considerable influence, the friars convinced him to withdraw his deputy and soldiers from the province. Although unrest reappeared in the province in

1656, when arbitrary orders by a new governor precipitated a serious revolt in Timucua, Apalachee remained at peace. After crushing the revolt in Timucua, the governor courted the Apalachee, forbidding friars to prohibit the native ball game or approved native dances, or to inflict punishment on Indians who were members of the leadership elite.[53]

Although the governor's hand in Apalachee was strengthened in the aftermath of the 1647 revolt and although the province might be viewed as one that had been subdued by force, that attitude does not seem to have prevailed. Friars still spoke of the province as one that had not been conquered except by the gospel.[54]

By the early 1670s Apalachee would be spoken of as thoroughly Christianized, and it was well on the way to becoming part of the Spanish world while retaining an identity of its own. The encounter phase between Apalachee and Spaniard had ended.[55]

The Christianized Apalachee of 1670 had become something quite different from what they had been when Narváez and de Soto gave them their first glimpses of the Spanish world more than a century earlier. They were equally well on their way toward becoming greatly different than they had been when friars first began formal work among them in the 1630s. That chiefs had requested friars at the beginning of the seventeenth century suggests significant changes in their culture and values by then. But continuity as well as change characterized the process, even though the dominant trend over the long term favored change. Nonetheless, the Apalachee's relative isolation, strong sense of their own identity, and sedentary agriculturally based society permitted more continuity than was the case, for example, among peoples living to the north of them, whom we know collectively as the Creek.

Whatever disruptions were occasioned by Narváez and de Soto's visits, Apalachee seems to have fared better than the ancestors of many of the peoples who were part of the Creek Confederacy in the eighteenth century. Until the disasters of 1702–4, the Apalachee remained relatively secure and united in their traditional homeland. Nevertheless, when the missions were destroyed in 1704, the ordinary Apalachee male in particular was being drawn increasingly into a Spanish-designed labor system that would soon have transformed him into the equivalent of a European peasant and that was drawing increasing numbers of Apalachee males outside of their homeland as contract workers, ranch foremen, personal servants, and the like. This process was very destructive to tribal and clan organizational patterns. Yet, even in exile, the element that migrated to Mobile (which comprised some of the most acculturated of Apalachee's natives) maintained their separate identity as Apalachee for more than a century despite their steadily shrinking numbers. Of their descendents a century after the exodus of 1704, two American observers of the Apalachee community on the Red River remarked: "No nation have been more highly esteemed by the French inhabitants; no complaints against them ever heard"; and, "These Indians appear to be rapidly advancing toward civilization; they possess horses, cattle and hogs; dress better than Indians generally do, and seem to derive a considerable portion of their support from the cultivation of the earth." [56]

Religious belief and practice were undoubtedly the fields in which Apalachee culture was transformed most drastically. French accounts attest to the advanced religious acculturation of the migrants to Mobile in 1704. Various French authorities remarked on the Apalachee's insistence on being furnished with a priest, noting that they threatened to return to Spanish territory if this demand were not met. Penicault observed that the Apalachee conducted divine services like the Catholics of France, hearing Mass reverently and singing the psalms in Latin. [57] Mission-era Spanish records give no indication that Apalachee sought to retain aboriginal religious practices after becoming Christians, except for those related to the playing of the ball game and recourse to the shaman as healer. Defenders of the ball game maintained that the game itself and the ceremonies associated with it had lost their religious connotation. The ball game manuscript reveals that some practices such as "sleeping the ball" (a vigil consisting of a round of ceremonies designed to enhance the chances of victory) on the night before a game had been "baptized" in the sense of being held in the church, where the friar permitted that to be done. In the latter half of the 1670s, playing the game was banned throughout Florida for its violence and social evils as well as for the religious purposes it once had served. [58] There is no record of the Apalachee's having practiced the Green Corn ceremony or busk. Conceivably, it was superseded by Iberian celebrations held during the summer such as the *Fiestas Juaninas,* which were being celebrated at Cupaica during the final assault on the missions in mid-1704, which led to abandonment of Apalachee by the remnant of its inhabitants. [59] The *Fiestas Juaninas* were celebrations held in honor of four saints, the Apostles John, Peter, and Paul, and the Franciscan, St. Anthony, whose feasts fell in June around the time of the summer solstice. The feast of St. Peter and Paul on June 24 was a holy day of obligation for the Catholic natives of Spanish Florida. [60] The feast of St. Louis is another possibility. Penicault noted that feast day (August 25) was the principal festival of the Apalachee at Mobile and that they solemnized the occasion with special religious ceremonies followed by secular festivities to which they invited both the neighboring Indians and the French. They regaled their guests with plenty of meat and other foodstuffs, and after an evening service of Vespers and Benediction of the Blessed Sacrament, they held a dance at which everyone— men, women, and children—wore masks. There is no indication whether the masks were of a native or European type. [61]

For many among ordinary Apalachee, adoption of European dress was more gradual than the acceptance of European religious practices, possibly because cloth was not available in sufficient quantity. But there is no doubt that Spanish contact influenced the natives' dress significantly by at least the end of the mission period. As late as the mid-1670s, authorities commented on the brevity of the everyday Apalachee attire, noting that men often wore only a deerskin breechclout and, if anything more, an unlined coat of serge or a blanket, and that the women wore only a knee-length skirt made of palm leaves or a shoulder-to-ankles tunic woven from the same material. The skirt was aboriginal, the tunic a European introduction apparently. Bishop Calderón boasted that, during his 1675 visit to the missions, he had persuaded 4,081 women in Apalachee, whom he encountered naked from the waist up, to don the longer version of those two garments.[62]

Cloth began to reach the missions in some quantity soon thereafter, if not earlier. In reporting progress on the building of a fort at St. Marks in 1680, Governor Pablo de Hita Salazar remarked that goods such as cloth provided the best means of paying the rotating work crews, who put in eight days at a time, observing that "Clothing is what passes for money here." Clothing was involved in a number of unpaid debt claims presented during the 1695 visitation.[63] A turn-of-the-century document shows a five-hundred-yard bolt of cloth being used to purchase a variety of items, from maize and beans to tallow and chickens, bearing out Governor Hita Salazar's remark. On the other hand, St. Augustine's pastor, writing circa 1700, noted that the Apalachee, in going to war, "dress themselves elaborately, after their usage, painted all over with red ochre and with their heads full of multicolored feathers."[64] Also, testimony given in a 1695 counterfeiting case involving two young Apalachee from San Luis suggests that to the inhabitants of St. Augustine, something in the dress, speech, demeanor, or appearance of the Indians made them easily identifiable as Apalachee.[65] However, a French observer described the Apalachee who migrated to Mobile in 1704 as dressing in the European fashion, with the women in cloaks and skirts of silk stuff and the men in cloth overcoats. This was their Sunday church dress of course, but the remark by that observer and by others that there was nothing uncivilized about the Apalachee, except their hybrid language of Spanish and Apalachee, implies that they dressed in the European fashion for workdays as well. In commenting on the Apalachee's dress, Penicault noted that their women's bareheadedness was their only departure from European custom. He described the women's hair as long and black, woven into one or two plaits hanging down their backs after the fashion of Spanish girls. If their hair was very long, it was folded up to the middle of their backs and tied with a ribbon.[66] Although men wore long hair before they became Christians, the friars required them to cut their hair in the Spanish style when they were baptized.

By the end of the mission period, the Apalachee had adopted the work ethic, if it was not already part of their ethos prior to that. Speaking of the Indians of Spanish Florida in general, Bishop Calderón noted, "They are stout and rarely does one find a small one, very half-hearted and phleg-matic towards work, although clever and ready to learn any skill that they see performed, and great carpenters."[67] Various French observers of those who migrated to Mobile commented on their being reliable, hard-working, and industrious people, characteristics confirmed by an American observer a century later, as noted above. The English spoke similarly about those who accompanied Colonel Moore to South Carolina in the wake of his 1704 attack on the Apalachee missions.[68]

As to war practices, there is evidence of both continuity and change. As the Spanish did not make firearms readily available, the bow and arrow and the hatchet remained the Apalachee's principal weapons. There is no mention of the Apalachee's use of the war club, known to have been used by Timucua and Guale in the sixteenth century (at least). Of the Apala-chee who had acquired firearms, a Spaniard remarked circa 1700: "And today they use firearms as do the Spaniards, and, in Apalache, they main-tain their arms as well as do the best trained officers." The same Spaniard attested to the survival of scalping, noting that they used their hatchets "to remove the scalps of those whom they kill and they carry it to the council house on a pine branch as an indication of their victory. There they hang it up and they dance the war-dance for many days."[69] But some among the more Hispanicized leaders had abandoned scalping a generation earlier. In a 1677 campaign against the Chisca of West Florida by warriors from San Luis and Cupaica, the native leaders resisted pressure from their men to allow scalping of the slain enemy.[70] A major reason for survival of scalping was its place in the warrior ethos. The taking and display of scalps was a primary means of advancing in rank and achieving status as a warrior. In re-newing the Spanish prohibition of the practice in 1701, Florida's governor ordered his deputy in Apalachee not to permit practices such as "dancing with scalps in the council houses, that they should avail themselves of other means and identification to point out as *norocos* and *tascayas* those who have taken them in legitimate war . . . giving them to understand . . . in a manner acceptable to the natives, so that they do not persist in practicing such a diabolical custom born of, and developed in, their primitive pagan-ism."[71] Survival of the lineage obligation to avenge a member who was killed was vigorously attested to: "They are so bloodthirsty that, if some Indian from their village is killed by one from another, they do not rest until they revenge the killing either on the one who did it or on someone else from his village." But some had also learned to seek redress through the Spanish legal process.[72]

In the matter of language, there is evidence for both continuity and change. The French indicated that Apalachee who migrated to Mobile interspersed a considerable amount of Spanish with their native tongue. A number of Apalachee leaders were literate. The prestige arising from acquisition of such exotic knowledge was doubtless one of the factors that moved Apalachee leaders to accept Spanish sovereignty voluntarily. The royal interpreter at San Luis and various parish interpreters were literate natives.[73] On being Christianized, Apalachee adopted Spanish first names, but except for a few highly acculturated leaders, they clung to native surnames to a much greater degree than did the Guale and Timucua. Even late in the mission period, a few individuals were being identified by completely native names.[74]

We know nothing directly about the Apalachee's pre-Christian sexual mores. However much they may have differed from Christian ideals, such as monogamous marriage, records do not indicate that Christian rules posed any serious problem or that those rules were observed any more loosely than they were by European Christians. But traditionalism survived, little challenged, apparently, in the maintenance of matrilineal lines of descent and matrilocality. An indication of change, however, is the volume of complaint by Apalachee wives in 1694 about the absence of and lack of support from husbands who were away from home working for long periods. The want that they complained of suggests that lineage acceptance of responsibility was declining and fathers were coming to be expected more to support their families and to remain at home.[75]

Since the Apalachee were sedentary agriculturalists at contact, missionization did not change this aspect of their lifestyle abruptly as it did for hunter-gatherers or people less dependent on agriculture. However, the Apalachee were introduced to many new cultigens—such as wheat, peaches, and watermelons—to aviculture, and to animal husbandry. Raising of chickens and hogs began early in the mission period, if not before. Cattle and horses were slower to arrive. But by the late mission period there were communal herds and cattle owned by individual Indians as well. Nothing is known of the mechanism by which chickens, hogs, cattle, and horses were introduced. Introduction of wheat dates from the abandonment of Governor Ruiz de Salazar's hacienda on Apalachee's eastern border. Iron tools such as the axe and digging hoe replaced ones made of stone and shell, but it is not known whether they were supplied in sufficient abundance to eliminate the aboriginal tools. Planting of maize and beans probably increased in scale as the Apalachee began to supply those commodities—along with chickens, hogs, and hams, lard, tallow, and hides—to St. Augustine and Havana.[76] In this fashion, the "Apalachee participated in the world economy," providing produce to the settlements that protected the silver and gold on which Spain depended for its economic survival.[77] There is no evidence of a massive slaughter of deer and other fauna for skins to supply European markets, such as occurred among the Creek and other Indians in contact with the English and French in the eighteenth century. However, Apalachee men were being drawn into a wage economy far from their native villages on a more or less long-term basis. Introduction of the repartimiento in the late 1640s had acquainted them with such labor on a compulsory, short-term, rotating basis. A resort to counterfeiting by two young Apalachee from San Luis attests to their familiarity with a monetary economy.[78]

By the late mission period, spinning of cotton into thread had been introduced, but not weaving, despite numerous requests by friars that natives from Tlascala or Campeche be sent to Florida to instruct its natives. Knapping of gunflints from indigenous mineral, either for Spaniards or for personal use, was a home industry that developed out of existing skills.[79] Knapping was applied to imported bottle glass to produce arrowheads and pendants. Production of cordage and rigging for ships and of saddlebags and other items of leather were other Apalachee cottage industries.[80] In their production of the ceramics known as Colono-Ware, primarily for the use of Europeans, Apalachee potters added to their repertoire. Apalachee Colono-Wares were produced using such traditional aboriginal techniques as the coil technique and tempering with sand, grog, and fine grit, but incorporating unmistakable European features such as brimmed plates with foot-ring bases or pitchers and storage vessels with large, thick loop handles. An augur survey and test pits on the native side of the village of San Luis de Talimali revealed only minor amounts of Colono-Ware sherds as compared with the quantities found in areas of Spanish occupation in association with Spanish pottery.[81] As no mission-era native dwellings have been excavated, at San Luis or at other mission sites, it cannot be said definitively that Colono-Ware did not enjoy wide acceptance among the natives, but available evidence points in that direction.

The Apalachee's dispersed pattern of settlement and the number of missions and settlements remained virtually unchanged throughout the mission period, in contrast to Guale and Timucua where population attrition or other factors led to the disappearance of some missions and to considerable consolidation of missions and villages. The Apalachee pattern consisted of ten principal villages with head chiefs, which became mission centers, and more than thirty satellite villages, each of which had their own chiefs but were under the jurisdiction of a principal village. Smaller chiefless hamlets and isolated farmsteads also dotted the countryside, forming a pattern of dense settlement first reported in de Soto's time. Chiefs of satellite settlements inherited their positions just as did chiefs of principal villages.[82] An eleventh Apalachee mission village named Santa Cruz de Capoli, first mentioned only in the 1670s, may have been created factitiously to serve Spanish communications purposes. Capoli was located on the edge of the St. Marks valley, filling a gap on the more southerly of the Spanish trails through Apalachee.

An influx of non-Apalachee into the province may weakly mirror the process that created the diversity which characterized the Creek Confederacy of the eighteenth century. By the 1670s, Tama-Yamasee, Chacato, Chine, and Tocobaga were living in the province in their own villages. All but the Tocobaga's village became missions.[83]

All eleven of the missions inhabited by Apalachee, and two of the three missions inhabited by non-Apalachee immigrants, survived until the end of the mission era, as did the village of the heathen Tocobaga as well.[84] Survival also of most, if not all, the satellites is indicated in a remark that "In 1705 Spanish officials reported to the crown that the English in general and Moore in particular had destroyed 32 Apalachee villages and at least five missions." A change that the Spanish presence introduced was that villages needed permission from the governor or his deputy to move the site of their village.[85]

By asking for friars and pledging obedience to Spain's monarch and his governor, the Apalachee lost their sovereignty, but this probably changed their real political status very little until the 1640s, when the first deputy-governor arrived. For ordinary Indians, except for being subject to serve in labor details ordered by Spanish authorities, even this political change was not of great significance. Spaniards governed the province through established native leaders, and except for the 1647 rebellion, they do not seem to have interfered with the normal pattern of succession or to have deposed any legitimately constituted chiefs. There is no indication how native leaders interpreted the consequences of their pledge of allegiance to the monarch as their "great chief," except for the bestowal of the native title, "war captain," on the governor's deputy in Apalachee.[86]

Initially, the leaders' perception of benefits to be achieved by making that pledge of allegiance must have been sufficiently attractive to more than balance the loss of sovereignty. Such benefits would include exotic goods (distributed by the governor as gifts) that enhanced the prestige and power of the leaders to whom they were given, serving the same function as had the Southern Cult paraphernalia in an earlier age. Social distinctions between the chiefly class and ordinary Indians were preserved and, if anything, reinforced by the Spanish presence. In 1657, only Ivitachuco's chief bore the noble title "don." By the 1680s all the legitimate Apalachee chiefs bore the title.

The monarch's failure to provide adequately for defense of the province, and the arrogance with which some Spaniards treated the natives, led many of the Apalachee to abandon their allegiance to the monarch during the crisis of 1704. Among those completely free to choose the direction of their move, the east-west division of the province appeared once more. Ivitachuco's leader and people, remaining loyal to the king, moved eastward to supposedly more secure Spanish territory. Most of San Luis and Cupaica's people moved westward to Mobile and French protection.[87]

At the time of the missions' destruction in 1704, the Apalachee were a far different people than they had been at contact or early in the seventeenth century. In addition to introducing the Catholic faith, the missions promoted other forms of acculturation. Yet compared with the Creek in the eighteenth century, the Apalachee give the appearance in their material culture of having maintained great continuity through that period of subjection to European influences. But in comparing acculturation of the Apalachee at the time of their dispersal as a nation with that of the Creek or the Choctaw even a half century later, one must keep in mind that with respect to ideas, Spanish influence on the missionized native was more intense than that of the French and English upon the natives with whom they formed alliances or traded over a similar span of time. This was true above all for the men, many of whom worked at St. Augustine for protracted periods or served alongside Spanish soldiers on various expeditions, not to mention their daily contact with friars living in their midst. The intensity of the contact and fraternization of Apalachee and Spaniard probably produced a much greater understanding of one another's institutions than was the case elsewhere. Their two worlds were no longer so distant.

Among all the native institutions, the council house seems to have been the greatest center of continuity and the element most resistant to change. Contrary to what one might expect, once Christianity had taken hold, the council house remained far and away the most impressive structure in the communities, dwarfing the church. The council house's importance throughout Spanish Florida is reflected in its being the one structure for which there are relatively detailed descriptions from multiple sources. The best overall description is that of Bishop Calderón in 1675. Speaking of Spanish Florida in general, he described them as "round structures made of wood covered with straw (paxa) with a large opening at the top, and the most, capable of holding two and three thousand persons." He portrayed their interiors as furnished all around the inside of the outside wall with niches or compartments called barbacoas, which served as beds and seats for caciques and leading men and as lodging for soldiers and travellers. "In them," he concluded, "they hold their dances and celebrations around a large bonfire, which they make in the middle of it."[88] Other sources reveal that it remained the seat of native governance and place of interface between native leaders and Spanish authorities. A friar noted that a distinct order governed the arrangement and occupation of some of the seats, "with the one belonging to the principal chief being the best and the highest." It was to be approached "only with the great respect and fear with which we are taught to approach our sacred things." Special seats adjoining it were assigned to individual leading men, while the common people took any of the remaining seats as they pleased. The head chief held court from his seat early in the morning. The leaders in attendance would salute him ceremoniously and then discuss village business. Brewing and consumption of cacina was reserved to the council house. Until the banning of the ball game, the council house sheltered many of the pregame ceremonies. But

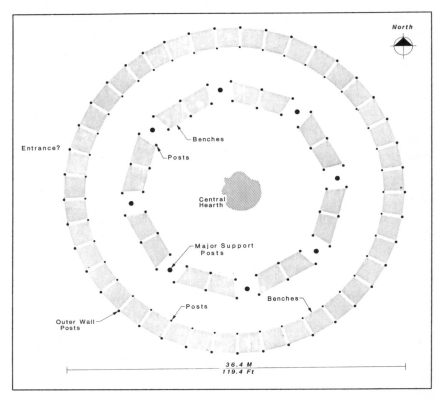

FIGURE I
Apalachee council house at San Luís de Talimali

aside from ceremonies associated with the ball game, there is no evidence that the Apalachee structure housed other religious rituals such as those practiced in the Pueblos' kiva, unless one interprets the banned dances, which friars considered obscene, to have included something similar to the kachina. Meals were also prepared and served in the council house, but generally, smaller fires in front of the individual benches were used rather than the large fire in the open center space. Jonathan Dickinson's reference to this structure as the "Indian war house" attests to another of the building's functions, planning for war and celebrating of victories with displays of scalps and holding of war dances.[89]

Excavations at the site of the San Luis council house have confirmed the importance of the structure and the traditionalism that governed its successive rebuildings. The San Luis structure conforms well to the image portrayed by Bishop Calderón. It proved to be a very large, perfectly circular structure about 120 feet in diameter. Support posts alone numbered 136, a massive amount of lumber to prepare and move by means of a simple technology. That this structure, first built in 1656, was twice rebuilt before 1704 attests to its continued importance to the community. Its only known rival for size is the council house excavated at the Irene Mound site. It had a similar diameter.[90] The very few nails used in constructing the San Luis council house attests to maintenance of traditional methods, whatever may have been the reason. The one apparent concession to European technology was use of imported tools to square off the bottoms of posts. That this adherence to tradition may have been deliberate is suggested by an anecdote in the ball game manuscript. Its author, Fray Juan de Paiva, noted that the ball pole had to be raised with wild grape vines, "and not with anything else, even when they might have ropes." This was adhered to in commemoration of the feats of one of the mythic founders of the game. Roof rafters were supported by eight massive posts, which framed a twenty-meter diameter open space where the dances were held. Replication of the pattern of eight major support posts in a number of eighteenth-century Cherokee council houses in the Overhill territory suggests that a traditional plan may have prevailed over a wide area, particularly as the Cherokee structures were considerably smaller. Interestingly, the octagonal pattern recurs later in Benjamin Hawkins's description of a Creek rotunda, with the difference that the eight posts of Hawkins's structure constituted an outer row of 12-foot-high posts of a 30-foot diameter structure.[91]

Until the Carolinian attacks of 1702–4 that destroyed the missions, the Apalachee had shown considerable resilience to the inroads of disease compared with the other missionized natives of Spanish Florida. In 1675, San Luis alone had more people than all the Timucuan missions westward of San Diego de Salamatoto on the St. Johns River.[92] Had Florida remained under Spanish control, and had it not been for the catastrophe of 1704, the Apalachee might well have survived into modern times as a distinct people. They seem to have had a sense of their own identity together with the adaptability to make that survival possible in a manner similar to the Cherokee. Had they done so, they would have been classed with the Five Civilized Tribes as a Sixth Civilized Tribe. The continued stature of the Apalachee even after their dispersal is reflected in the account of a 1717 visit to St. Augustine of 157 Indians from the Creek country and among them 25 caciques and *micos*. Of those 25 leaders, 4 were singled out as the most important: "Ysipacafe, *usinjulo* and *mico*, heir of the great chiefdom of the province of Cabetta [Coweta], whom all those nations and vassals hold in the same esteem and veneration as we Spaniards hold the prince our lord; . . . Chislacaliche, . . . cacique of the province of the Uchises; . . . Adrian Christian . . . cacique of the Apalachee, all with their batons (*bastones*) that his lordship had given and sent to them earlier, and . . . Tatepique, cacique of the Province of the Talapuses."[93]

NOTES

I am indebted to Bonnie McEwan, particularly in calling my attention to published reports on council house excavations at the Irene Mound site and Chota-Tanasee and for answering my questions about the excavations at San Luis. I am indebted also to John Scarry for suggestions about my allusions to the prehistoric Apalachee.

1. Oviedo, *Historia general*, 1: 585.

2. Some authorities place the western boundary at the Apalachicola or at the Little River at least. A case can be made for the Little River in particular, as the Cupaica mission was located about a mile west of the Ochlockonee late in the seventeenth century.

3. Shapiro, "Archaeology at San Luis," 10–13.

4. Ibid., 15, and Vega, *Florida of the Inca*, 182–83.

5. Shapiro, "Archaeology at San Luis," 12–15.

6. John Scarry, "Rise, Transformation, and Fall," 178–79; Shapiro, "Archaeology at San Luis," 4–5.

7. Scarry, "Rise, Transformation, and Fall," 179, 183–84, and Elvas, *True Relation*, 67.

8. Hann, *Apalachee*, 6–7; Oviedo, *Historia general*, 1: 534; Elvas, "True Relation," 67, 68, 71; and Vega, *Florida of the Inca*, 173, 175, 181–85, 203–10.

9. Joan Baptista de Capilla to the King, St. Augustine, Nov. 4, 1609, AGI, SD 224 Woodbury Lowery Collection (hereinafter WLC) reel 3, of the Florida State University Library copy; Cumming, *Southeast in Early Maps*, 10; Hoffman, *A New Andalucia*, 92; and Vega, *Florida of the Inca*, 267.

10. Elvas, "True Relation," and Vega, *Florida of the Inca*, 184.

11. Hann, *Apalachee*, 98–100, 388, and Oré, *Martyrs of Florida*, 116–17. The most detailed of the accounts, that by Garcilaso, is badly garbled at this point. Garcilaso spent the better part of nine chapters on Ivitachuco, but he placed it in Utina Province and confused it with Utina's Napetuca and Yustaga's Uzachile, whose chief was then the paramount for Utina and Yustaga. Consequently, where Garcilaso goes beyond the other accounts, it is impossible to discern how much of what he says about his Ivitachuco pertains to the real Ivitachuco rather than to Uzachile and Napetuca. See Hann, "De Soto, Dobyns, and Demography," 4–6.

12. [Friar] to the King, St. Augustine, Feb. 2, 1635, AGI, SD 225, WLC, reel 4; Oré, *Martyrs of Florida*, 116; and Milanich and Fairbanks, *Florida Archaeology*, 227.

13. Dobyns, *Their Number Become Thinned*, 12, 13–14, 24–25, 259, 263, 264–65, 283–84.

14. Diego de Rebolledo to the Franciscans, St. Augustine, Aug. 5, 1657, in Hann, "Governor Rebolledo's 1657 Visitation," 109–15.

15. Pablo de Hita Salazar to the Queen, St. Augustine, Aug. 24, 1675. AGI, SD 839, Stetson Collection of the P. K. Yonge Library of Florida History of the University of Florida (hereinafter SC).

16. Laudonnière, *Three Voyages*, 116; Lorant, *The New World*, 34–35; and Rochefort, *History of the Caribby-Islands*, 204–48.

17. Fontaneda, *Memoir*, 38.

18. Charles R. Ewen, personal communication to author, July 2, 1989; Scarry, "Rise, Transformation and Fall," 183–84, and personal communication to author, July 2, 1989.

19. Shapiro, "Archaeology at San Luis," 4; Tesar, *Leon County*, 166–206.

20. Baltasar López to the King, St. Augustine, Sept. 15, 1602, and Francisco de Pareja to the King, St. Augustine, Sept. 14, 1602, AGI, SD 235, SC; and Pareja and Alonso de Penaranda to the King, St. Augustine, Nov. 6, 1607, AGI SD 224, SC.

21. Francisco Machado to Gonzalo Méndez de Canzo, St. Augustine, 1597, AGI, SD 231, WLC, reel 2; Méndez de Canzo to the King, St. Augustine, Apr. 24, 1601, AGI, SD 235, SC; and Swanton, *Early History*, 336.

22. López to the King, Sept. 15, 1602; Machado to Méndez de Canzo, 1597.

23. Oré, *Martyrs of Florida*, 112–17; and Pedro de Ibarra to the King, St. Augustine, Sept. 1, 1609, AGI, SD 128, SC.

24. Ramón A. Gutiérrez, "When Jesus Came, the Corn Mothers Went Away: Conquest and Christianization of the Pueblo Indians" (Paper presented at a Columbus quincentenary forum at the National Museum of American History, Washington, D.C., April 29, 1989); Kessell, "Spaniards and Pueblos," 127–38.

25. Hornbeck, "Economic Growth," 423–34; Luis de Horruytiner to the King, St. Augustine, Nov. 15, 1633, AGI, SD 233, SC; Kessell, "Spaniards and Pueblos," 128–29; and López to the King, Sept. 15, 1602, AGI, SD 235, SC.

26. Hann, "Alonso de Leturiondo's Memorial," 177–79.

27. Castillo, "Native Response," 377–84; Gutiérrez, "When Jesus Came"; and Kessell, "Spaniards and Pueblos," 128.

28. Francisco de San Antonio et al. to the King, St. Augustine, Sept. 10, 1657, in Hann, "Visitations and Revolts in Florida."

29. Hann, "Demographic Patterns and Changes," 371–72.

30. Lorenzo Martínez to the King, St. Augustine, Sept. 14, 1612, AGI SD 232, SC; and Pareja et al. to the King, St. Augustine, Jan. 17, 1617, AGI, SD 235, WLC, reel 3.

31. Juan Fernández de Olivera to the King, St. Augustine, Oct. 13, 1612, AGI, SD 229, WLC, reel 3.

32. Oré, *Martyrs of Florida*, 118.

33. Ibid., 73–74; Hann, "Florida's Terra Incognita," 65–67; and "Visitations and Revolts in Florida."

34. Juan Rogel to Jerónimo Ruiz del Portillo, Havana, Apr. 25, 1568, in Hann, *Missions to the Calusa*, 244–46, 268, and in Zubillaga, *Monumenta Antiquae Floridae*, 272–311.

35. Oré, *Martyrs of Florida*, 114–15.

36. Martínez to the King, Sept. 14, 1612.

37. Alonso de Jesus to Luis de Rojas y Borja, n.d., AGI, SD 235, microfilm 28K, reel 36 of the P. K. Yonge Library of Florida History of the University of Florida (Letters and dispatches of ecclesiastical persons of Florida). Although the letter bears no date, it is accompanied by a notification dated March 2, 1630, convoking an *acuerdo* of the treasury officials at St. Augustine. Alonso de Jesus, "Memorial to the King," 1630, AGI, Mexico, leg. 302 (transcription furnished by Eugene Lyon).

38. Bushnell, "That Demonic Game," 2, 4; Luis de Horruytiner to the King,

St. Augustine, Nov. 15, 1633, AGI, SD 233, SC; Francisco Menéndez Márquez and Pedro Benedit Horruytiner to the King, St. Augustine, July 27, 1647, AGI, SD 235, Jeannette Thurber Connor Collection (hereinafter JTCC), reel 4; and Damián de Vega Castro y Pardo to the King, St. Augustine, Aug. 12, 1639, AGI, SD 225, SC.

39. Hann, "Governor Rebolledo's 1657 Visitation," 100–101.

40. [Friar] to the King, Feb. 2, 1635, and Vega Castro y Pardo to the King, Aug. 12, 1639.

41. Hann, "Governor Rebolledo's 1657 Visitation," passim; Rebolledo to the King, St. Augustine, Sept. 18, 1657, in Serrano y Sanz, *Documentos históricos*, 202–5; and San Antonio et al. to the King, Sept. 10, 1657.

42. Jesus to Rojas y Borja, n.d.

43. Luis de Horruytiner to the King, St. Augustine, June 24, 1637, AGI, SD 225, SC; Vega Castro y Pardo to the King, St. Augustine, July 9, 1643, AGI, SD 224.

44. Shapiro, "Archaeology at San Luis," 8.

45. Vega Castro y Pardo to the King, July 9, 1643; Royal Officials to the King, St. Augustine, Mar. 18, 1647, AGI, SD 229, SC.

46. Vega Castro y Pardo to the King, July 9, 1643.

47. Hann, "Governor Rebolledo's 1657 Visitation," 87.

48. San Antonio et al. to the King, Sept. 10, 1657.

49. Elizabeth A. H. John remarked on the same phenomenon among New Mexico's governors during this period; John, *Storms Brewed*, 83–90.

50. Governor Ruiz de Salazar had been suspended prior to the revolt for non-fulfillment of a promise to build a ship for the royal service, which he had made at the time of his nomination to the governorship.

51. Francisco Menéndez Márquez to the King, St. Augustine, Feb. 8, 1648, JTCC, reel 3; Menéndez Márquez and Horruytiner to the King, July 27, 1647; Royal Officials to the King, Mar. 18, 1647, and St. Augustine, May 22, 1647, AGI, SD 229 and 235, JTCC, reel 3; Benito Ruiz de Salazar y Vallecilla to the King, St. Augustine, May 22, 1647, JTCC, reel 3.

52. Menéndez Márquez to the King, St. Augustine, Feb. 8, 1648; Pedro Moreno Ponce de León to the King, St. Augustine, July 9, 1648, and July 21, 1648, AGI, SD 235, WLC, reel 3; Francisco Pérez to the King, St. Augustine, 1646, AGI, SD 235, WLC, reel 3; Royal Officials to the King, Mar. 18, 1647, and May 22, 1647.

53. Hann, "Governor Rebolledo's 1657 Visitation," 89.

54. Juan Gómez de Engraba to Francisco Martínez, St. Augustine, Apr. 4, 1657, in Hann, "Governor Rebolledo's 1657 Visitation," 128–29.

55. Domingo de Leturiondo to the King, St. Augustine, Dec. 30, 1672 (extracts) AGI, SD 848, WLC, reel 4.

56. Hann, *Apalachee*, 146–47; Donald G. Hunter, "The Apalachee on Red River, 1763–1834: an Ethnohistory and Summary of Archaeological Testing at the Zimmerman Hill Site, Rapides Parish, Louisiana" (submitted to *Louisiana Archaeology*, November 1988), 12–13.

57. Higginbotham, *Old Mobile*, 193; Rowland and Sanders, *Mississippi Provincial Archives: French Dominion* [hereafter *MPA: FD*], 2, 482; and *MPA: FD*, 3: 303; McWilliams, *Fleur de Lys and Calumet*, 134.

58. Hann, *Apalachee*, 338–50.

59. Boyd, Smith, and Griffin, *Here They Once Stood*, 50.

60. Antonio G. Leon, trans., "Synod of the Diocese of Santiago de Cuba, Jamaica, Habana, and Florida, Bishop Juan García de Palacios, 1682," typescript in the possession of the writer, n.d.

61. McWilliams, *Fleur de Lys and Calumet*, 133–35.

62. Gabriel Días Vara Calderón to the Queen, Havana, 1675, AGI, SD 151 (microfilm copy furnished by William H. Marquardt).

63. Hita Salazar to the King, St. Augustine, Dec. 7, 1680, AGI, SD 226, SC; Joachín de Florencia, "General Visitation that the Captain Joachín de Florencia . . . Made of the Provinces of (illegible) Apalachee and Timucua . . . 1694–1695," in Hann, "Visitations and Revolts," passim.

64. Manuel Solana, "Memorandum and Accounting for 500 Yards of Jerqueta," San Luis, n.d. (Boyd, Smith, and Griffin, *Here They Once Stood*, 46–48), and Hann, "Alonso de Leturiondo's Memorial," 200.

65. Hann, "Apalachee Counterfeiters," 54, 55, 56.

66. Alonso de Jesus, "Memorial to the King," 1630, AGI, Mexico, leg. 302 (transcription furnished by Eugene Lyon); McWilliams, *Fleur de Lys and Calumet*, 134–35.

67. Días Vara Calderón to the Queen, 1675.

68. *MPA: FD*, 3:482–84, 536, and Salley, *British Public Office*, 5:208.

69. Hann, "Alonso de Leturiondo's Memorial," 199.

70. Juan Fernández de Florencia to Hita Salazar, San Luis, Aug. 30, 1678, AGI, SD 226, reel 4.

71. Joseph de Zúñiga y Zerda to Manuel Solana, St. Augustine, Mar. 14, 1701, in Boyd, Smith, and Griffin, *Here They Once Stood*, 35–36. *Tascaya* is the native name for an entry-level warrior. *Noroco* was an intermediate rank, achieved apparently by killing three people.

72. Hann, "Alonso de Leturiondo's Memorial," 199–200, and *Apalachee*, 297–301.

73. McWilliams, *Fleur de Lys and Calumet*, 135; Boyd, Smith, and Griffin, *Here They Once Stood*, 24–29; Chiefs of Apalachee to the King, San Luis de Abalachi, 21st Day of the Moon that is called January, 1688, trans. from Apalachee to Spanish by Fray Marcelo de San Joseph, AGI, SD 839, SC; Hann, "Visitations and Revolts," and "Governor Rebolledo's 1657 Visitation," 87, 91, and *Apalachee*, 352; Domingo de Leturiondo, "Visitation of the Provinces of Thimuqua and Apalachee . . . 1677 . . . 1678," in Hann, "Visitations and Revolts."

74. Hann, *Apalachee*, 365–69.

75. Hann, "Visitations and Revolts," and *Apalachee*, 103–4, 259–60; Domingo de Leturiondo, "Visitation of the Provinces."

76. Hann, *Apalachee*, 133–38, 239–42.

77. Shapiro, "Archaeology at San Luis," 8.

78. Hann, "Visitations and Revolts," passim; Hann, "Apalachee Counterfeiters," passim.

79. Boyd, Smith, and Griffin, *Here They Once Stood*, 41–42; Hann, *Apalachee*, 243; Brown, *Firearms*, 118; and Shapiro and Hann, "Council Houses of Spanish Florida," 523.

80. Florencia, "General Visitation"; Antonio Matheos, Testimony from the record of the *residencia*, 1687–1688, AGI, Escribania de Camara, leg. 156C, pieza

25 (E. 20), folios 50–116, SC. Examples of arrowheads and pendants have been found at the San Luis site.

81. Vernon, "Apalachee Colono-Ware," 76–82.

82. Hann, *Apalachee*, 24–26, 339, "Demographic Patterns," 385–88, 392, "Governor Rebolledo's 1657 Visitation," 86–101, and "Twilight of the Mocamo," 4, 12–22, and "Visitations and Revolts."

83. Días Vara Calderón to the Queen, 1675; Florencia, "General Visitation"; Hita Salazar to the Queen, Aug. 24, 1675; Domingo de Leturiondo, "Visitation of the Provinces."

84. Hann, *Apalachee*, 68–69.

85. Quoted in Brown, *Firearms in Colonial America*, 167. See Florencia, "General Visitation," and Hann, "Governor Rebolledo's 1657 Visitation," 90–91.

86. Chiefs of Apalachee to the King, 21st Day of the Moon that is called January, 1688; Fernández de Florencia to Hita Salazar, Aug. 30, 1678.

87. Hann, *Apalachee*, 284–86, 305.

88. Días Vara Calderón to the Queen, 1675. The native (probably Arawak) term *barbacoas* suggests a grill or latticework platform. *Barbacoa* was used elsewhere for seat, a platform for smoking meat or fish, and the bed frame of reed bars in natives' houses.

89. Hann, *Apalachee*, 340–42; Hann, "Visitations and Revolts"; Laudonnière, *Three Voyages*, 14; Méndez de Canzo to the King, St. Augustine, Sept. 22, 1602, AGI, SD 224, JTCC, reel 2; Swanton, *Early History*, 62; Domingo de Leturiondo, "Visitation of the Provinces"; Méndez de Canzo to the King, Sept. 22, 1602; Hann, "Governor Rebolledo's 1657 Visitation," 90; Shapiro, "Inside the Apalachee Council House at San Luis" (Paper presented at the Forty-fourth Annual Southeastern Archaeological Conference, Charleston, S.C., Nov. 12, 1987); Andrews and Andrews, *Jonathan Dickinson's Journal*, 65; and Hann, "Alonso de Leturiondo's Memorial," 199.

90. Shapiro, "Inside the Apalachee Council House," 4, 6, 9, 12, 13, and Caldwell and McCann, *Irene Mound Site*, 30.

91. Hann, *Apalachee*, 337–38; Schroedl, *Overhill Cherokee Archaeology, Report of Investigations* 38 (Tennessee Valley Authority, Publications in Anthropology 42), 229–31; Shapiro, "Inside the Apalachee Council House," 4, 6, 11; Hawkins, *Sketch of the Creek Country*, 71.

92. Hita Salazar to the Queen, Aug. 24, 1675.

93. Juan de Ayala y Escobar to the King, St. Augustine, Apr. 18, 1717, AGI, SD 843, SC. "Beloved son" is the meaning of the term *usinjulo*, bestowed on a son of the cacique. Among the Apalachee the term was spelled *usinulo*.

HELEN C. ROUNTREE
AND E. RANDOLPH TURNER III

On the Fringe of the Southeast: The Powhatan Paramount Chiefdom in Virginia

The Powhatans in Virginia both resemble and contrast with the Mississippian chiefdoms of the Southeast. Their way of life was much like that of such people as the Coosa and Cofitachequi. People lived together in towns governed by chiefs (who could be male or female) and practiced an economy based upon a mixture of horticulture, foraging, and fishing. Chiefs and priests were people set apart from ordinary folk, as in the Mississippian societies. However, the Powhatans did not build mounds, and their high-status luxury items were less elaborate, consisting principally of shell beads and rather simple copper ornaments. They spoke an Algonquian language, so that their linguistic relatives lived mainly to the north. They also were dwellers on the coastal plain, while most Mississippian chiefdoms were to be found at or above the Fall Line.[1]

Although the Powhatans were immediately accessible from the Atlantic, their portion of the coast was the mid-Atlantic, which Europeans did not seriously attempt to colonize until relatively late. The Spanish began visiting Powhatan territory in about 1560, and then only rarely; the first permanent settlement was the English one at Jamestown in 1607. Thereafter the Powhatans were in continual contact with aliens, and the records of that contact are reasonably good. Unlike the Mississippian chiefdoms, the Powhatan paramount chiefdom first emerged in the sixteenth century and was at its height in 1607. It began to decay soon after the English arrived, not as a consequence of English fur trading and slaving (those became a major issue after 1670), but because of English farming of tobacco as a cash crop, which demanded huge amounts of Indian land. Thus the trajectory of the Powhatan paramount chiefdom was a shorter one than is found elsewhere, covering only about a century, and it was also a later one, which allowed it to be recorded by eyewitnesses.

Most Mississippian chiefdoms were located along rivers, often near the Fall Line, in either the Piedmont or the Ridge and Valley provinces. Both provinces in Virginia have mature forest of deciduous trees, producing large quantities of leaves and mast that fertilize soil and feed animals and people. From North Carolina through Louisiana, most of the coastal plain is either pinelands or flat, poorly drained land, both of which were unattractive to Indian farmers. In Virginia the case is different. Only in the southeastern part of the Virginia coastal plain is the land so flat as to be poorly drained. In addition, because of more northerly latitude (37°–38°), the deciduous forest zone covers the coastal plain as well as the piedmont and mountains. Thus, in 1607, chiefdoms existed on the coastal plain (Powhatans) and may have extended into the piedmont (Monacans and Mannahoacs).[2]

For riverine horticulturists, the Virginia coastal plain is exceedingly rich because it is gently rolling to nearly flat country cut through by the Chesapeake Bay and four large rivers, each river with its numerous tributaries, all within an eighty-mile distance from north to south and a hundred-mile distance from east to west. The rivers, actually tidal estuaries, become freshwater streams well below the Fall Line. In places, they and some of their tributaries meander across floodplains, where some of the most naturally fertile soils in the state are to be found. An optimal place for Late Woodland Indians to live in Virginia, and the location of the densest Indian occupation in 1607, was the inner coastal plain. There the people had easy access to rich, flat lands for raising crops to feed themselves in summer and early fall; deciduous forest around them for nut gathering and hunting in the fall, winter, and early spring; runs of anadromous fish in the spring; and large expanses of freshwater marsh producing aquatic tubers like *tuckahoe* (arrow arum) in the early summer before the crops came in.[3]

Yet riches like these would not have been enough in themselves to cause the rise of chiefdoms, unless the population had grown decidedly dense. There is archaeological evidence of steady population growth throughout the Woodland period, resulting in enough pressure to explain, in part, the rise of chiefdoms and then a paramount chief in the region. One of us (Turner) thinks that such growth could have led to a chiefdom, particularly when such growth is examined along with the archaeologically and historically documented patterns of trade and exchange.[4] The other (Rountree) thinks that a chiefdom would have arisen through external, especially military, pressures added to population growth to produce such a development in this lavishly rich region, which does not lend itself to the economic specialization that is frequently seen as a cause of political evolution.[5]

Trade in luxury goods may have contributed to the rise of chiefs, who came to control most of the goods. The available (though limited) archaeological evidence and historical sources tell us that *Busycon* (whelk) and other shells from saltier waters were being traded inland, and pearls from freshwater mussels were being traded coastward. Native copper was being imported from the west. Powdered antimony was being mined near the Potomac River and traded elsewhere. Puccoon (*Lithospermum caroliniense*), the source of a red pigment, came from pine barrens south of the James River. More mundane trade items observed by the English included dried oysters and cakes of deer suet.[6]

Still another impetus to the formation of chiefdoms may have been warfare. The archaeological record in Virginia tells us little here. But when the English arrived, the Powhatans were in a state of enmity with the piedmont Siouans and with Iroquoians called Massawomecks who came down the Potomac River to conduct attacks. The major Indian-versus-Indian military frontier was the Fall Line, and it is not surprising that the English heard in 1607 that the paramount chief had originally come from a town near the falls of the James River. Perhaps earlier simple chiefdoms had first formed there, too.

Chiefdoms and the paramount chiefdom in Virginia were not exclusively linear affairs. Chiefdoms tended to be organized within the drainage basins of streams—for example, the Cuttatawomens along the short Corrotoman River and its tributaries. Where a major river was narrow enough (apparently one half mile or less), then chiefdoms had territory on both sides—for example, the Weyanocks on both banks of a limited stretch of the James. Where the neck of land between rivers was narrow enough (less than 10 miles), a chiefdom would occupy the land clear across the neck— for example, the Pissasecks on the Northern Neck. The paramountcy grew out of the man Powhatan's inheritance of six tribes or petty chiefdoms; three (Powhatan, Arrohateck, and Appamattuck) were on the James River and three (Pamunkey, Mattaponi, and Youghtanund) on the adjacent York River, stretching some distance below the Fall Line, though all clustered within the inner coastal plain. (See figure 1.) The exact date of his inheritance is uncertain but was probably somewhere in the mid-sixteenth century.

Spanish records tell us little about political relations on the Virginia coastal plain in the 1560s and 1570s. Accounts stemming from the short-lived 1570 Spanish *Ajacán* mission in coastal Virginia (see below) indicate the presence of incipient chiefdoms with inherited positions of leadership, polygyny in chiefly families, and a high population density compared to that of other adjacent areas with which the Spanish were familiar. English accounts of the 1580s along the North Carolina coast indicate the existence of a series of small, independent chiefdoms attempting to expand their range of jurisdiction through alliances and warfare. This is precisely the situation Powhatan encountered when he inherited his six territories.

FIGURE I

The Powhatan chiefdom in 1607

Through warfare or threat thereof, Powhatan expanded his inheritance by 1607 into a paramount chiefdom comprising about thirty former tribes or petty chiefdoms. This paramountcy encompassed some 13,000 persons inhabiting slightly less than 6,500 square miles of Virginia coastal plain.[7]

Europeans began to visit the mid-Atlantic coast in the mid-sixteenth century. The earliest possibility is an unidentified, possibly English, ship, whose cabin boy later reported to the Spanish that in 1546 the ship had entered "a very good bay . . . in 37°." Over thirty canoes of Indians had come out to trade with the strangers. The next visit was by the Spanish ship that picked up a man named Don Luis in 1559 or 1560 at an unidentified spot "in" or "near" the Chesapeake Bay region (*Ajacán*). Whether Don Luis went willingly is arguable. The man soon made it known that he was the "brother of a principal chief of that region." When he returned as the guide and interpreter for a Spanish Jesuit mission in 1570, he had the ships debark on a creek in his home territory. The creek was present-day College Creek, so the territory was Paspahegh—not in the nucleus of Powhatan's paramountcy or even very near it. Don Luis had a younger brother ruling a town or towns in the "interior," and he had an uncle and a brother living near the debarkation site. This uncle was later a major target of Spanish revenge. Don Luis later went to live with an uncle (probably another uncle) a day and a half away from the Jesuits' mission, which in turn was less than a day's journey from the debarkation place, across the Lower Peninsula on the York River. The mission site was in what was later to be known as Chiskiack territory, but the Spanish records say nothing about the Indians there having any connection whatever with Don Luis's people. It sounds as though Don Luis's relatives were all in or near Paspahegh, which in 1607 included land on both sides of the mouth of Chickahominy River.[8]

When Don Luis subsequently had the Jesuits killed, one Spanish boy from Santa Elena, Alonso de Lara, was spared by a "brother" (possibly a cousin) of Don Luis. The boy eventually settled with another chief, apparently unrelated to Don Luis but on friendly terms with his family, for Don Luis asked him for corn. This ruler was "a leading chief" who apparently lived at the end of the Lower Peninsula, at what was later recorded as Kecoughtan. We know from later English writings that the Kecoughtans were forcibly incorporated into Powhatan's growing organization around 1596 or 1597.[9]

Thus the records connected with the Spanish Jesuit mission in Virginia indicate only that the Paspaheghs and the Kecoughtans were friendly, that Paspahegh settlements were ruled by several members of a single family (Don Luis's), and that while Paspahegh relations with their Chiskiack neighbors to the north may not have been friendly, they were at least not hostile. Their relations with their neighbors on the west, the Chickahominies, were at least friendly, for the latter were apparently not attacked by any Spaniards as the Paspaheghs were, but they nevertheless preserved a hatred of all things Spanish as late as 1614. There is no mention in the early sources of a powerful and ambitious chief (Powhatan) far up the James River.[10]

In 1584, an English ship may have visited the Chesapeake region, though the records about it are vague. Then, in 1586, a party of Englishmen from the colony being established on Roanoke Island, in the Carolina sounds, spent part of the winter of 1585–86 with the Chesapeake chiefdom and also heard from Indians nearer their colony about the richness of the lands to the north. When the Roanoke colony "disappeared" after 1586, some of the refugees may have made for Chesapeake territory, where they knew they had friends. Unfortunately, the Chesapeakes—and any refugees still surviving with them—were wiped out when Powhatan conquered their territory around 1607. Efforts by the Jamestown colonists to hear news of refugees came to naught. The only recorded meeting of people that may indicate the fate of at least some Roanoke colonists is the 1607 sighting of a blond boy of about ten with a "reasonable white skinne" at Arrohateck, part of Powhatan's original inheritance. The skills of the available interpreters were apparently too poor for the English to discern the boy's origins.[11]

European visits after 1586 were apt to turn out violently. In 1588, a Spanish ship sailed up the Chesapeake Bay. At the mouth of the Potomac River, its crew seized a boy, who subsequently died of grief; another boy, seized somewhere on the Eastern Shore, lived to reach Santo Domingo and died there. We know no other details of the expedition. But a possible byproduct of the Indians' initial hospitality may have been Mosco, whom John Smith met in 1608 at or near Wiccocomico and took for a Frenchman's son because of his heavy dark beard. In July 1603, an English ship captained by Bartholomew Gilbert put into a bay that was possibly the Chesapeake, and a party that went ashore for fresh water was attacked immediately. At about the same time, a ship that may have been a companion vessel captained by Samuel Mace visited the Rappahannock Indians on the Rappahannock River. As the Indians told it later, they made the strangers welcome, and then the strangers suddenly attacked them. They were still angry in 1607, when John Smith was brought to their capital town as a captive for them to examine. The attackers may also have taken prisoners among the Rappahannocks, as judged from the fact that some mid-Atlantic Indians ended up in England, where they gave a canoeing demonstration on the Thames River in 1603.[12]

In the years during which Powhatan was expanding his dominions, the Algonquian speakers of Virginia were being raided by several Indian enemies. Some of these were piedmont Siouans, who were apparently long-term enemies. The Spanish heard that their war parties came down the rivers every summer; the English later heard them described as inveterate enemies. Adding to the threat from the west were Iroquoian speakers who tortured captives to terrify their enemies, and of whom many of the Algonquian speakers lived in mortal dread. These were the Massawomecks, who came down the Susquehanna and Potomac Rivers to fight in the Chesapeake region. Their identity in modern terms is shadowy, though they may have been Eries.[13]

In late sixteenth-century Virginia, there may have been a further disruption of Indian life caused by epidemics of European diseases. The evidence for them is ambiguous, but they may have occurred. The Spanish Jesuits heard in 1570 that the region around their mission had suffered for six years from "famine and death" caused by a drought.[14] Disease may or may not have been involved; starvation certainly was. In 1608 Powhatan himself told John Smith that he had "seene the death of all [his] people thrice."[15] That could be the statement of an old man who had outlived the older generations, or it could be a reference to periods of famine or disease. More to the point is the story that the Accomac chief on the Eastern Shore told John Smith in 1608. Two children had died; their parents in their hysterical grief had had them exhumed to look at them again. The bodies were in such a wonderful state of preservation that many people gathered to see them, and most of those people subsequently died. We also know that European diseases often afflicted the Indians visited by the Roanoke colonists; those Indians were in contact with the Chesapeakes and others in the lower James River basin.[16]

But archaeologists in Virginia have found no mass burials indicative of rapid death. This contrasts with one recent argument that population densities in precontact Tidewater Virginia and Maryland may have been fairly high, from 4.9 to 6.8 per square kilometer.[17] For the area occupied by Powhatan's polity, this would have resulted in a sixteenth-century population of 80,000 to 110,000 people. Such a high estimate is totally unsupported by regional archaeological research; there is simply no evidence for it. Similarly, with the Powhatans numbering about 13,000 or perhaps slightly more by 1607, it is most unlikely that such presumed native depopulation would have gone totally unnoticed either archaeologically or through surviving historical accounts. Moreover, the Powhatans of 1607 and after said nothing to any Englishman about their own population having once been larger. All available evidence, archaeological and historical, shows gradual but consistent population increases over time in coastal Virginia, culminating in the Powhatan paramountcy by 1607. While loss of life due to European diseases may have occurred during the sixteenth century, there is no firm evidence whatever to indicate that it was substantial.

Thanks to the lateness of the emergence of the paramount chiefdom in Virginia, we have English accounts of how and when it happened. The pattern may have been similar to that of the earlier Mississippian chiefdoms, about which we have no records.

By the time Powhatan came on the scene, most of the tribes in the Chesapeake region had probably become chiefdoms, the main exception being the Chickahominies, with their council of elders. Powhatan himself inherited six tribes or petty chiefdoms in inner coastal plain portions of the James and York River basins.[18] There is no record of how these six came to be amalgamated in the first place, for Powhatan never mentioned anything about his elders in the presence of Englishmen. During the mid to late 1500s, Powhatan substantially expanded his holdings, first downriver along the James and the York rivers. His methods were either intimidation or outright conquest. He had reached Kecoughtan in 1596 or 1597; he conquered the Chesapeakes, whom he considered deadly enemies, sometime around 1607.[19] He probably began fairly early to pressure the Rappahannock River peoples to join him. Those that had villages south of the river moved them to the north bank (shown on Captain John Smith's 1612 map of the region) as a defense against Powhatan, but in time they apparently joined. The chiefdoms on the south bank of the Potomac and the chiefdoms of the lower Eastern Shore were also tenuous members of Powhatan's organization by 1607. They would remember their recent autonomy, and they would be hard for Powhatan to keep in line due to their distance from him by water. Thus by 1608, Powhatan could claim to rule (by influence, at least) all of the Virginia coastal plain peoples from the James River north to the Potomac River, and they apparently agreed, at least in the hearing of Englishmen. The one exception were the Chickahominies, with whom Powhatan had a military alliance.[20]

This process of political development and expansion can be seen archaeologically, particularly through an examination of regional ceramic traditions.[21] For the latter part of the Middle Woodland period (ca. A.D. 200–900), the Virginia coastal plain is characterized by the presence of shell-tempered ceramics known as Mockley Ware, a coastal plain ware that is remarkably widespread and homogeneous from Delaware to southern Virginia. However, that homogeneity changed during the Late Woodland period (ca. A.D. 900–1600), by the end of which there were numerous distinct wares that strongly suggest increased territoriality. This picture conforms with historical accounts of the expansion of the Powhatan paramount chiefdom outside its core area by the late 1500s. The archaeological evidence on warfare reinforces this scenario. For the Middle Woodland period there are no known examples of fortified settlements. In contrast, excavations in coastal Virginia, though admittedly limited in scope, still show palisaded settlements becoming increasingly common by the end of the Late Woodland period. These have been found so far in the territories of such groups as the Patawomeck, upriver Cuttatawomen, Chickahominy, Weyanock, and Chesapeake.

By 1607 about 40 percent of the people aligned with the Powhatan paramount chiefdom were to be found in three areas, which represented only five out of the approximately thirty district chiefdoms within the paramountcy.[22] As shown below, these five, densely populated groups correspond geographically to the distribution of certain Late Woodland period ceramic types, even after the establishment of the paramount chiefdom.

Over much of coastal Virginia, the Middle Woodland period Mockley Ware was replaced during the Late Woodland by another shell-tempered ware known as Townsend. By the end of the Late Woodland period, though, other wares had arisen in certain places, and the areas in which Townsend Ware could still be found to the general exclusion of other contemporaneous wares consist as follows: the core region of the paramountcy in the upper York River basin, and territory eastward along the York River, south to portions of the James River basin, north to portions of the Rappahannock River, and across the Chesapeake Bay to the Eastern Shore. The two most populous groups in the paramountcy were characterized by Townsend Ware at the time of European contact. They include the Pamunkeys in the York River inner coastal plain and their neighbors the Chickahominies in the James River inner coastal plain, each with an estimated population of 1,500 persons.

Not surprisingly, the distribution of other major Late Woodland period wares is restricted (with one exception noted below) to two other densely populated areas in coastal Virginia, both of which were among the last locales to be aligned with the paramount chiefdom. This is clearly in contrast to the more uniform distribution of a single ware over the region earlier.

In southeastern Virginia, a very distinct shell-tempered ware known as Roanoke appeared at the end of the Late Woodland period. Named after Roanoke Island, the ware is found in coastal North Carolina and up into Virginia, being common in the lower reaches of the James River and eastward to the Atlantic Ocean. This is precisely the location of the adjoining Nansemond and Chesapeake chiefdoms, with an estimated total population in 1607 of 1,275 persons.

Another distinct Late Woodland period ware occurs in the inner coastal plain of the Potomac River and, to a lesser extent, the Rappahannock River. Known as Potomac Creek, this sand- or crushed quartz–tempered ware is particularly characteristic of sites identified as being in the Patawomeck chiefdom, with an estimated population of 850 persons. The origins of Potomac Creek Ware are to the west above the Fall Line along the Potomac River.

One final sand- or crushed quartz–tempered ceramic ware, Cashie/ Gaston, must be mentioned. It was first defined for the Roanoke Rapids area of North Carolina and was subsequently shown to be found in the inner coastal plain of North Carolina and in adjacent areas of southern Virginia, an area that was inhabited by such Iroquoian groups as the Tuscaroras, Nottoways, and Meherrins. Recently, it has been recognized as being present in considerable amounts in the inner coastal plain of the

James River basin on Late Woodland sites associated with such groups as the Powhatans, Appamattucks, Arrohatecks, and Weyanocks. All but the Weyanocks were among Powhatan's original inheritances. We interpret the presence of this ware among Virginia Algonquian groups as a result of close ties, especially through trade, with groups farther south. Historical sources indicate that the Weyanocks may have been middlemen in this trade.[23] The chronic war the Algonquians fought with the Siouan Monacans and Mannahoacs to the west of the Fall Line must have strengthened such ties. Before European contact, trade also would have been critical in ensuring a regular source of copper as Powhatan expanded his dominions. (The copper was to be used in validating Powhatan's status.) Apparently the Patawomecks maintained a similar position on the Potomac River to the north (their name has even been interpreted as meaning "trading center"), which in conjunction with their large population helps to explain why they were always able to remain semi-independent of Powhatan.[24]

Archaeological evidence thus supports the view of several major developments in coastal Virginia by the end of the Late Woodland period: increased territoriality, intensive warfare, and more visible trade alliances. Associated with all of this was a rising population in the region, especially in areas of high resource potential, such as the inner coastal plain, and in restricted locales farther east, such as the Nansemond/Chesapeake area, where the diversity of resources in some ways duplicated areas further inland. It was in this atmosphere of competition that Powhatan faced the challenge of strengthening his inherited territories through expansion.

Historical accounts note several methods by which Powhatan consolidated his hold over his dominions. Of particular significance was his use of a three-tiered government. Below the paramount chief were the district chiefs, and below them were chiefs of individual villages. Apparently, some formerly autonomous chiefs were retained as district chiefs if they were loyal enough. In other cases, Powhatan appointed his relatives as new district chiefs. He placed a son at his hometown of Powhatan at the falls of the James, a son at Kecoughtan after it was conquered, and another son in Quiyoughcohannock after the district chief there committed an act of disloyalty. It was also a standard practice to place siblings (who were heirs in the Powhatan chiefly matrilineal system) as rulers of subordinate units. Powhatan had his brothers rule Pamunkey, his richest territory, and three known district chiefs had their brothers or sisters rule satellite villages.[25]

It was also common for Virginia chiefs to have multiple wives, and sometimes these were women from long distances away. Powhatan had a great many wives (said to number over a hundred) during his life, and he seems to have employed a revolving-door policy. When he discarded one and wanted to replace her, he went to one or another district, had the marriageable women form a line, and took his pick.[26] He could therefore have had in-law relations with all of his subject districts. Information on individual wives of chiefs is harder to come by. Iopassus (Japazaws) ruled a satellite town for his brother, the chief of Patawomeck, and one of his two wives came from a town a day's walk away. And Powhatan gave in marriage a young daughter of his to a "great king" who lived three days' journey from Powhatan's 1614 capital on the Pamunkey River.[27]

Powhatan and his subordinate chiefs were firmly in alliance with the priests in their society. Both priests and outstanding warriors served as councillors, but the priests' words carried more weight, presumably because of their ability as seers. Priests were allowed to marry, and one very high-standing priest had married Matachanna, a daughter of Powhatan himself.[28] This priest, named Uttamatomakkin, served as Powhatan's ambassador to King James when Pocahontas and her retinue went to England at the expense of the Virginia Company of London in 1616–17.

Another way of increasing his hold over his dominions, new and old, was for Powhatan to move his capital to a central location. He had grown up at the falls of the James, and his richest country, containing the region's holiest temples, was Pamunkey Neck, made by the division of the York River into two streams.[29] But even Pamunkey would not have been central once Powhatan added the Eastern Shore and the Northern Neck to his dominions. For maximum accessibility by land or water, he apparently chose Werowocomoco on the lower York River, and that is where the English found him.

The difference in status between a chief and a commoner was considerable among the Powhatan Indians. Chiefs, and also priests, were regarded as being semidivine. Even so, the paramount chief himself was normally addressed to his face by his personal name rather than a title. All chiefs, including Powhatan, could and apparently did do ordinary labor on most days; Powhatan is recorded as being proud of his abilities in that regard. Chiefs could have many wives, and they unilaterally set the amount of bridewealth they would pay. Even if their wives had produced sons born at exactly the same moment, it did not matter, for chiefly positions were passed on in a system of lateral matrilinealty. Each male chief had presumably inherited from his mother; his heirs were his brothers in order of age, his sisters in order of age, and then the sons and daughters of the eldest sister, or next eldest if the eldest had no children. Thus Powhatan's heirs in 1607 were his next younger brother, Opitchapam, then the younger Opechancanough, then the youngest brother Kekataugh, then the elder of Powhatan's two sisters, then the younger, then the daughter of the eldest sister, and then the daughter of the younger sister.[30]

The paramount chief, and perhaps also the district chiefs, had corn fields planted for them annually, the populations of whole towns turning out for the work. Powhatan also claimed much tribute from his people, having the "refusal" of 80 percent of their goods. However, the things he actually took and stored in his temples were mainly beads, copper, pearls, puccoon, and dressed deerskins. He had a monopoly on copper coming in from westerly sources, and after Jamestown was founded, he managed to gain a near monopoly on traded or stolen English tools and weapons.[31]

Powhatan and his district chiefs were said to have life-or-death power over their people.[32] However, it is likely that they only had such power in cases of offenses committed against themselves personally. They presided over some criminal executions, which were carried out in front of their houses, but the English writers say nothing about whether they themselves handed down the verdict.[33] Priests were key figures in identifying criminals. Very high-ranking priests might preside at executions themselves, with chiefs attending. The paramount chief had the right to "levy" men for war, sending emissaries out to "impress" warriors, but they also sometimes had to pay copper to the men's district chiefs for the privilege of using that labor.[34]

Numerous other characteristics in Powhatan society emphasized the distinctions in rank and the power that attached to the position of chief. These included variations in dress related to rank, obeisance postures while in the presence of chiefs, the use of attendants/servants by chiefs, and a bodyguard for the paramount chief. Even in death, such distinctions were retained, with the bodies of chiefs being preserved and placed along with a variety of rank-denoting objects in temples to which only chiefs and priests had access.[35]

The English originally settled in Virginia to look for treasure and a northwest passage to the Pacific. They found neither. But when the nature of the colony changed, around 1610, to a family oriented farming community, the Powhatans began to be seriously threatened. The English had settled on an island in the paramount chief's heartland; now they would want ever more land.[36]

Initially the English hoped to convert the Powhatans to English religion and culture so that they would join the English community in Virginia. They rapidly found that the Indians nearest them grew hostile toward the colonists' preaching and demands for corn (the colony being poorly supplied in its early years). The Indians farther away were moderately willing to be detached from Powhatan's overlordship, but they were not interested in changing their lifeways. Thus we see the Potomac River tribes occasionally helping the English, remaining neutral in the Great Attack of 1622, and continuing their traditional culture. We also see the Accomacs of the lower Eastern Shore accepting English settlers among themselves by 1621, selling almost all their land to Englishmen by 1640, and yet holding on to most of their old ways. Copper, however, ceased to validate chiefly status, because of a glut of it from English sources.

When the English in Virginia turned to raising tobacco as a cash crop, around 1617, the doom of the Powhatans was sealed. England had a larger population than did the Powhatans; many of those Englishmen were eager to gain land (a limited commodity in England), raise profitable crops, buy more land, and eventually rise into the gentry. A full-fledged boom was on in Virginia by 1618, lasting until 1630 and after, and the cash crop fever persisted for several decades longer.[37] English farming settlements, initially called "hundreds," spread out along the James River and then began to cross the lower York River. Indian resistance was halted by the capture and marriage of Pocahontas, which resulted in a treaty; Indian leadership was also shifting from Powhatan, who had become feeble, to his successors, especially his second younger brother, Opechancanough. Those successors managed to stanch the flow of Englishmen across the York River by their Great Attack of 1622, but the resulting war of attrition waged against the colonists gained the Indians nothing, and more Englishmen came to replace those who were killed. The James and York River chiefdoms were the main participants in the Great Attack; the others were neutral. After an official peace in 1632, English tobacco farmers began blanketing the Eastern Shore and later the lower Middle Peninsula. They finished taking over the lower James basin and began laying claims to prime farmlands on the Rappahannock and Potomac and in Pamunkey Neck, where the Powhatan stronghold and holiest temple still lay. In 1644, Opechancanough led his people to war again. Once more it was the James and York River chiefdoms that did the fighting, but now the more distant chiefdoms were siding with the English. This time the war only lasted two years, ending with Opechancanough's death in a Jamestown prison cell. The treaty of 1646 supposedly guaranteed that Englishmen would stay out of Virginia north of the York River, but the Governor gave permission for settlement there in 1649, and by 1670 nearly all of the coastal plain was in the hands of English planters. Not surprisingly, in 1649 the records show the last appearance of a paramount chief on the Virginia mainland. A different paramount chief, formerly under Powhatan and his successors, retained some power on the Virginia Eastern Shore for a few decades more.[38]

The Powhatans did not fit into the English economic world. Aside from a stubbornness naturally engendered by having had their lands taken away from them, they were not generally amenable to moving into English communities and living by English rules. They had traditionally lived in towns, but their subsistence practices had dictated two major times of year—winter and early summer—in which to live mainly on wild foods, so that both town life and mobile foraging were normal for them. They were also accustomed to a division of labor in which women farmed and gathered, and men hunted and fished. Indian men in particular were not enthusiastic about becoming farm laborers, and few of them took such jobs.[39] Meanwhile, the English colony could tap a tremendous pool of English people too poor to pay their passage who were eager to come to the New World, work for their benefactors for seven years, and then strike out to make their own fortunes as planters. Thus, Powhatan Indians never became a major source of labor in the Virginia colony, and Africans did not either, until the importation of English indentured servants slacked off later in the century.

Powhatans who clung to their old way of life therefore fitted nowhere into the English scheme of things, especially after their first great resistance effort of 1622. The two sides knew that they were direct competitors for land. Immediately after episodes of Indian resistance, the English attempted to exterminate the Indians; at other times, they tried merely to push them off the land.

Later in the century, when the deerskin trade and slaving raids became important to English Virginians, the Powhatans were not much involved. Most of them still lived in the inner coastal plain, where the deer had long been badly depleted by Indians and English alike.[40] By the 1670s, when most surviving Powhatan communities were near the Fall Line, their populations were too small for any deerskin production of theirs to be noted in English records. As for their forming a pool of potential slaves, their small populations only made them worthwhile for English raiding when English paranoia against all Indians was high, as in Bacon's Rebellion (1676). Until that time they and most other Indians were specifically protected from slavery by Virginia law. They may themselves have participated in slaving raids against other Indians to the southwest after 1676, but the records do not tell us clearly.[41]

Thus by 1670, when the Charles Towne colony was founded and the Virginia English began to become heavily involved in exploiting other southeastern Indian groups, the Powhatans had been through a long process of population loss and political devolution. They were not important players in the new English schemes to make money, schemes that caused such havoc in Indian life elsewhere. For the Powhatans, the threat of losing their land and their autonomy had already become a reality.

The ecological situation in Virginia favored chiefdoms, particularly in the coastal plain. The greater richness of the coastal plain, especially its inner half, allowed for the development first of simple chiefdoms and then, in the late sixteenth century, a paramount chiefdom. Such a polity came centuries later than its Mississippian counterparts, perhaps because the internal and external pressures that can cause consolidation also came late, or only indirectly, because of the distance between the Virginia peoples and the nearest Mississippian center.

Because of their coastal location, the Powhatans were easily accessible to Europeans but their location in the mid-Atlantic region caused them to be contacted later than Indian groups to both the north and the south. They were never under heavy colonization pressure from the Spanish; they never met an explorer as brutal as de Soto. For them, contacts with aliens and their diseases were delayed. The contacts that took place may or may not have spurred the formation of a Powhatan paramountcy; with the Mississippian chiefdoms, European contacts either caused or sped their decline.

When the English decided to colonize the Chesapeake Bay area, the Powhatans were accessible and immediately affected. The English, unlike the Spanish, had little interest in missionizing Indians; but like the Spanish, they wanted to tap Indian labor if they could do so. But soon after the founding of the Jamestown colony, tobacco was discovered as a valuable cash crop. A boom ensued, and hordes of ambitious Englishmen poured into Virginia to make their fortunes. The Powhatans, who were not much interested in such farming, were crowded off their lands. When they resisted, the English fought them. Within four decades of the founding of Jamestown, the Powhatans had lost much of their heartland and most of their people, and their paramount chief's position was almost extinct. It had lasted for less than a century.

The trajectory of the Powhatans' grand political organization is therefore shorter than that of the Mississippian chiefdoms, which began around 1200 and ended, for some of them, after 1700. It is also an apparently more spectacular trajectory because it was so much better recorded. But whatever the superficial differences, instructive though they can be, the story in all places must have been much the same. Native peoples with sophisticated political organizations were unable to withstand the onslaughts of diseases and the ways of doing business that the hordes of aliens brought with them.

NOTES

1. In fact, if it were not for the English accounts of their paramountcy, there would be scarcely any archaeological information to tell us of chiefdoms of any kind in eastern Virginia. See Turner, "Archaeological Identification of Chiefdoms."

2. Englishmen speaking of "kings" among them may or may not have been accurate. It is more likely that there were tribes or simple chiefdoms loosely aligned with one another and clustering in groups named "Monacan" and "Mannahoac." See J. Smith, "A Map of Virginia," 165, 238, and "The Generall Historie of Virginia," 175–77, 184–85. For the most recent summary of what is known about the Siouans of the Virginia piedmont, see Jeffrey L. Hantman, "Between Powhatan and Quirank."

3. The analysis upon which this conclusion is based is Helen C. Rountree, "A Guide to the Late Woodland Indians' Use of Ecological Zones in the Chesapeake Region," typescript in author's possession.

4. Turner, "Evolution of Rank Societies," and "Socio-Political Organization," 209–11. Stephen R. Potter agrees: "Chicacoan Settlement Patterns."

5. Rountree, *Powhatan Indians of Virginia*, 32, 55, 93, 106, and Service, *Primitive Social Organization*, 135–39.

6. Rountree, *Powhatan Indians of Virginia*, 56–57.

7. Feest, "Algonquian Population Estimates"; Turner, "Powhatan Territorial Boundaries."

8. Lewis and Loomie, *Spanish Jesuit Missions*, 13, 15–18, 38, 42, 44, 52, 108; see also Quinn, *England and the Discovery of America*, 190. For a more recent account of the mission, see M. Gradie, "Spanish Jesuits."

9. Lewis and Loomie, *Spanish Jesuit Missions*, 46, 49, 52, 108–9, and Strachey, *Historie of Travell*, 68.

10. Hamor, *Present State of Virginia*, 10.

11. Quinn, *England and Discovery of America*, 255 and chapt. 17, *Set Fair for Roanoke*, 42, 345ff, and *Roanoke Voyages*, 106, 110, 244–47, 257–58; Hulton, *America 1585*, 86; Rountree, *Pocahontas's People*, 34–39; and Percy, "Observations," 140.

12. Lewis and Loomie, *Spanish Jesuit Missions*, 56; Smith, "Generall Historie," 173; Canner, "A Relation," 17: 329–35. Quinn says the bay was Delaware Bay: *Set Fair for Roanoke*, 355–56. Quinn, *England and Discovery of America*, 428–29, and chapt. 16; Smith, "True Relation," 51; and Wingfield, "Discourse," 227.

13. Lewis and Loomie, *Spanish Jesuit Missions*, 161; Smith, "True Relation," 55, 67, and "Map of Virginia," 165–66 and 229–31; Knowles, "The Torture," 219; Spelman, "Relation of Virginea," cxiv; Smith, "Virginia Discouered"; Strachey, *Historie of Travell*, 35; Hoffman, "Ancient Tribes," 195–206; Brasser, "Coastal Algonquians," 68; and Dobyns, *Their Number Became Thinned*, essays 1, 2, 6, 7.

14. According to the Quiros and Segura account, there were "six years of famine and death, which has brought it about that there is much less population than usual. Since many have died and many also have moved to other regions to ease their hunger, there remain but few of the tribe, whose leaders say that they wish to die where their fathers have died, although they have no maize, and have not found wild fruit, which they are accustomed to eat. Neither roots nor anything else can be had, save for a small amount obtained with great labor from the soil, which is very parched" (in Lewis and Loomie, *Spanish Jesuit Missions*, 89).

15. Smith, "Map of Virginia," 247.

16. Smith, "Map of Virginia," 225, and Hariot, *New Found Land of Virginia*, 28. In possible support of ties between the lower James River people and the Carolina Sound tribes, there is a Spanish blue tubular bead, common as trade goods before the 1560s, which was found in the 1930s on Jamestown Island (Marvin T. Smith, personal communication to Rountree, 1989). Jamestown is at the northern extremity of the region in which the Carolinian Roanoke ware is found. The first Spanish expedition to meet any Algonquian-speaking Indians was the one in 1559 or 1560 that may have entered the Chesapeake Bay or may only have sailed along the coast near Cape Henry. That expedition picked up a young man, later called Don Luis, who was apparently from the chiefdom (later recorded as Paspahegh) that controlled Jamestown Island. The bead at Jamestown may have come from that Spanish expedition, either by direct trade from a ship in the James River or by indirect trade through Indian channels from Carolina. (Rountree is cautious—and Turner is skeptical—about this connection.)

17. Dobyns, *Their Number Become Thinned*, 44n.

18. Smith, "Map of Virginia," 173, and Strachey, *Historie of Travell*, 57.

19. Strachey, *Historie of Travell,* 57 (copied in part from Smith, "Map of Virginia," 173), 68, and 104–5; and Archer, "Relatyon of the Discovery of Our River," 85. One of us, Rountree, thinks the date of the Chesapeakes' demise was in 1608 (Rountree, *Pocahontas's People,* 22–23, 46).

20. Smith, "Map of Virginia," 148, and Strachey, *Historie of Travell,* 49, 68–69.

21. For further details of this discussion, see E. Randolph Turner III, "Protohistoric Interactions."

22. For the derivation of figures presented here, see Turner, "Powhatan Territorial Boundaries."

23. Strachey, *Historie of Travell,* 56–57. Strachey's wording is "Weionock (a servaunt in whom Powhatan reposed much trust) . . . could repeat many wordes of their [the "Anoeg"] language which he had learned amongst them, in his imployment thither for his king, and whence he often retourned full of Presents to Powhatan." Rountree interprets "Weionock" as the district chief of Weyanock (in the European sense of calling a nobleman by the name in his title, for example, "Norfolk" for the Duke of Norfolk); a retinue from among his subjects would have accompanied him. Turner, on the other hand, thinks "Weionock" may be the personal name of some other individual of uncertain tribal origin, although no Virginia Algonquian personal name resembling "Weionock" was recorded anywhere else.

24. Potter, "European Effects," 151–54. Rountree, *Pocahontas's People,* chaps. 3 and 4.

25. Strachey, *Historie of Travell,* pp. 63–69. On Powhatan's siblings, see Strachey, *Historie of Travell,* 69. On district chiefs' siblings, Ibid., 63, 64–65, and Smith, "Generall Historie," 291.

26. Strachey, *Historie of Travell,* 61–62; Spelman, "Relation of Virginea," cvii–cviii.

27. Spelman, "Relation of Virginea," cviii, and Hamor, *Present State of Virginia,* 41–42.

28. Strachey, *Historie of Travell,* 104 (copied with additions from Smith, "Map of Virginia," 165), and Purchas, *Pilgrimes,* 955.

29. Powhatan temples were multiroomed longhouses that served as places of worship, storage, and sepulchers for chiefs. They were usually built outside of towns. Although they were not placed on artificially raised earth mounds, the holiest temples were on some very high hills overlooking the Pamunkey River.

30. Strachey, *Historie of Travell,* 56, 61–62, 77; Smith, "Generall Historie," 151, and "Map of Virginia," 174. Smith recorded only the personal names of Powhatan's brothers; beyond them in line to the chieftainship we know only that there were "two sisters, and their two daughters" ("Map of Virginia," 247).

31. Spelman, "Relation of Virginea," cxii; Strachey, *Historie of Travell,* 87 and 107; and Smith, "Map of Virginia," 174. For a discussion of collection, storage, and redistribution of tribute among the Powhatans, see Rountree, *Powhatan Indians of Virginia,* 109–11.

32. Smith, "Map of Virginia," 175, and Strachey, *Historie of Travell,* 60.

33. Spelman, "Relation of Virginea," cx–cxi. The crimes were infanticide, accessory to infanticide, and theft from a fellow villager.

34. Smith, "Map of Virginia," 160; Purchas, *Pilgrimes,* 955; and Strachey, *Historie of Travell,* 69, 104, 107.

35. For detailed descriptions of specific traits characterizing the Powhatan polity as a chiefdom, see Turner, "Powhatan Socio-Political Organization," chapt. 2, and Rountree, *Powhatan Indians of Virginia,* chapt. 6.

36. For an overview of the Powhatans in this period, see Turner, "Powhatan Socio-Political Organization"; for a detailed version, see Rountree, *Pocahontas's People,* chapts. 1–6. For a more detailed view of Powhatan-English *aims* in dealing with one another, see Rountree, "Powhatans and the English."

37. Morgan, "First American Boom."

38. The female chief of Pamunkey tried in 1677 to reestablish a small paramountcy with herself as head; the organization did not last long (see McCartney, "Cockacoeske"). The claim of a continuing paramountcy on Virginia's Eastern Shore is Rountree's, not Turner's, and is based on county records and Robert Beverley's *History and Present State of Virginia,* 232–33, which refer repeatedly to "emperors/empresses" and "great kings" over other Virginia Eastern Shore tribes. This paramountcy, if such it was, dates at least from 1621 (Pory, in Smith, *Generall Historie,* 291).

39. Few Indians appear in the detailed muster rolls of the 1620s; see Jester and Hiden, *Adventurers of Purse and Person.* For later in the century, see Rountree, *Pocahontas's People,* chapt. 6.

40. Many Virginia records were destroyed in the Civil War and by negligence at other times, but the surviving records (colonial laws, some county records) show no large-scale southern trade needing regulation until 1661 (Hening, *Statutes at Large,* 2: 20). The first mention in the records of a trade in deerskins was in 1663 (Ibid., 2: 185), and then it was illegal to export the skins from Virginia for years to come.

41. The first mention of an Indian slave comes from 1651 (Northampton County, Deeds, Wills, Etc. 4: 34ro), and references are very sparse thereafter. That some enslaving of Indians went on is indicated by the fact that in 1670 a law had to be passed making servants entering Virginia by land just that, servants and not slaves (Hening, *Statutes at Large,* 2: 283). It became legal to enslave Indians taken as prisoners of war from Bacon's Rebellion onward, but the first reference to Indian slaves sold by Indians comes from 1682 (Ibid., 2: 491).

The Formation of the Creeks

The Creeks formed one of the most populous and important aboriginal groups in the colonial history of the South. But anyone who would speak of "the Creeks," or especially of Creek origins, must choose his words with care. "Creek" has meant many different things. The word can refer to a language, a people, a tribe, a nation, or a confederacy. Too often it is used to refer to some unspecified combination of these. One cannot get around this issue of names. To do so results in confusing, contradictory usages where the distinction between Creek and non-Creek can become meaningless. Creek history touches upon so many different native peoples that John R. Swanton found it impossible to discuss the topic without surveying virtually the whole of southeastern ethnohistory.[1]

Conventional wisdom tells us to resist at the outset any temptation to think of the Creeks as a single people or single ethnic group. It is true that, as a group, they are sometimes called one of the "Five Civilized Tribes." It is also true that a sense of common ethnicity is a prominent factor in their later history. Nonetheless, for the period that concerns us at the moment, we will be mistaken if we think of them as a "tribe" in the normal sense. At the time the Creeks became important to Europeans, they were neither an ethnic group nor a linguistic community. Instead they were a territorial assemblage of many small groups. These were groups with diverse cultural and linguistic backgrounds. Some were more or less long established in the Georgia–East Alabama area, particularly those who spoke the Muskogee and Hitchiti languages. Others were relative newcomers to this area, and these included Yuchis, Alibamos, Shawnees, Natchez, and Chickasaws, representing a hodgepodge of southeastern language groups.

The "glue" that held them together at the end of the eighteenth century was a common political organization. This fact gives us a point of reference that is both concrete and specific. When I speak of Creeks and Creek origins I will be referring ultimately to that *organization*. Without arranging our discussion around this political anchor point, the Creeks might truly be said to have as many different "origins" as there were ethnic components in the Creek melting pot. Albert S. Gatschet, writing in the nineteenth century, correctly understood not just the form, but also the purpose of this entity. I believe we can profit from his definition: "The Creek confederacy . . . was a purely political organization connecting the various and disparate elements, which composed it, for common action against external aggression. It had no direct influence on the *social* organization of the tribes, and the most appropriate term for this . . . is that of war-confederacy, war-league or symmachy."[2]

We are virtually forced by custom to acquiesce in the term "Creek Confederacy," for it now carries the weight of repetition in published work. But, as Gatschet sensed, "confederacy" may be the wrong word. It implies a parity among member groups who ally themselves for a common cause, but in fact Creek towns were never perceived as equal in importance. It is best to think of the Creeks as having a core and a periphery. The core consisted of certain larger, indigenous, conservative towns, most of whom spoke the Muskogee language. These enjoyed a special stature and required from others a certain ceremonial deference. The periphery consisted of various "daughter" towns of lesser rank split off from the core towns, plus attached refugee groups and adopted communities. Much of the cultural and linguistic diversity of the Confederacy was found among these peripheral and non-Muskogee groups, whom Bartram classed as "stinkards," in the same manner as the Natchez labeled people lacking noble lineage or those belonging to groups of adopted foreigners.[3]

Later Creek tradition supplies us with the names of the four Creek "foundation towns"—Tukabatchee, Abihka, Kasihta, and Coweta. All four spoke the Muskogee language, leaving no doubt that in the minds of the Creeks the core was predominantly Muskogee. Tradition also affirms that Coosa held a special prominence among the Upper Creeks and that Apalachicola, a Hitchiti-speaking town, had a similar prominence as a "big town" among the Lower Creeks.

We need not place too much stock in these statements as reflections of historical fact. They may be simply statements of prestige relationships, and they are probably of no great antiquity. There is no evidence, for example, that any of the four "foundation towns" were particularly important at the time of the Spanish explorations in the sixteenth century. Abihka (the Apica of Luna's expedition) was then of no evident importance, being one of many towns subject to Coosa. Likewise Kasihta, if this was de Soto's Casiste (as I think likely), was merely one of the towns subject to the minor chiefdom of Talisi. Coweta and Tukabatchee are not mentioned at all in the sixteenth-century accounts.

One need not go so far as to say that all Creek folklore is irrelevant to their actual history. Some legends discuss the origin of intertown alliances that were quite real and a matter of everyday political existence, so it would be a mistake to treat them as pure fantasies. Instead it may be useful to think of these tales as a sort of folk encyclopedia of information, orally transmitted and fostered. And the type of information contained in this encyclopedia is not history but *status relationships*. For example, prominent Muskogee origin myths portray the origin of the Creeks as arising out of an alliance between Muskogee-speaking towns from the west (Kasihta and Coweta) and an autochthonous Hitchiti-speaking town on a river to the east (Apalachicola). At some level this may be close to the truth, as I will show presently.

What matter to us here are the circumstances and timing of the regional alliances involved in the coalescence of the Creek polity. At the height of Alexander McGillivray's influence in the last quarter of the eighteenth century, the Creek Nation was governed by assembly. Its primary organ of governance was the National Council, presided over by a National Chief. Delegate chiefs from each town were summoned to meetings of the Council, at which policy was decided by consensus.

At the local level the basic unit of governance was the town or *talwa*. Each talwa could act independently of the National Council and was essentially a free agent in both civil matters and matters of war. Talwas were administered by a town chief, various other officials, and a town council. Certainly the National Council was modeled on the pattern of the local town councils.

Our first question, then, concerns the antiquity of coordinated political behavior among the constituent core towns in the form of a centralized council. For the moment a short answer to this question may be given. There is no documentary evidence of any such political centralization prior to the eighteenth century. With that in mind, we can turn our attention to related questions about antecedent political formations in the area and what bearing those might have had on the eventual shape of Creek government. Such questions can be approached from a combined archaeological and ethnohistorical perspective. The main concern of this paper will be along those lines; my desire is to portray in broad strokes the background conditions out of which the Creeks emerged as a political force in the eighteenth century. As to the particular historical events in the eighteenth century Southeast that precipitated the collectivization of the Creek towns, that story will be left for others to tell, although I will not refrain from a few modest suggestions.

Much published scholarship about the formation of the Creek Confederacy flatly contradicts my thesis that it was an eighteenth-century phenomenon. It says instead that the Confederacy existed in some form prior to the arrival of Europeans in the interior Southeast, thus giving the Creek political organization a much greater antiquity than I would allow it. This idea is firmly rooted in the work of John Swanton of the Bureau of American Ethnology. Swanton maintained that position early in his professional career, and a number of scholars have accepted the antiquity of the Confederacy on Swanton's authority.

Prominent among earlier historians of the Creeks who followed Swanton's lead in this matter are Angie Debo and David Corkran. Among more recent writers, we find Michael Green reiterating that the Confederacy originated before de Soto and, indeed, even speculating about the functions of the National Council prior to the early eighteenth century. But in diametric opposition to this we have the opinion of Verner Crane, who pictured the formation of the Confederacy as a native reaction in the wake of the Yamasee War of 1715–16.[4]

What was behind Swanton's insistence that the Confederacy was as early as he said it was? There were, I believe, two prominent reasons. One was that he took Creek origin myths quite seriously as being distorted cultural memories of actual historical events. Second, and this is related to the first, he recognized in the sixteenth-century Spanish narratives various Muskogee place names identical or similar to those of later Creek towns, confirming to his satisfaction a continuity of general location for the Creeks between the sixteenth and eighteenth centuries. For Swanton, this meant that the events described in the migration legends, including the alliance of the core towns of the Confederacy, must have taken place at an even earlier time.

We must understand that at the period Swanton was writing, there was nothing particularly implausible about the story line of Creek migration legends. These differed from town to town, but in general they spoke of a migration from somewhere west of the Mississippi River. During the migration, some of the towns became allies or friends and exchanged medicines. They conquered the former inhabitants and in so doing established a new homeland for themselves in the east.[5]

This supposed invasion of the Gulf region by Muskogean peoples, moreover, seemed to square quite well both with the evidence of linguistic distributions and with what little was known of the archaeology. Swanton believed that the original, displaced inhabitants were Siouan (for example, Catawba), Choctaw, Natchez, and Chitimacha. The Creeks, for their part, were descendants of the great prehistoric "corn states," the town-dwelling mound builders of the Midwest. All this was presented as relatively straightforward and sufficiently obvious to the observer familiar with the tribes in question. As to the potential of archaeology to further clarify these issues, Swanton judged any such attempt as "well-nigh hopeless."[6]

So, if during the sixteenth century de Soto, Luna, and Pardo visited identifiable Muskogee towns in the interior Southeast, some evidently in the same place they were to be found some two centuries later, it could only mean that the great migration had already been accomplished at that time. And if that were true, the alliances among the Kasihta, Coweta, Chickasaw, Coosa, Abihka, Tukabatchee, Apalachicola, and others spoken of in the origin myths would also have been in place at the time of European contact.

Swanton adduced further corroborative evidence of the existence of the Confederacy in some form at this time. First, he believed that the Cofita-chequi of de Soto and Pardo's time was identical with the later Kasihta. If correct, this meant that at least two of the Creek towns prominent in the origin myths and in the Confederacy (the other being Coosa) were also prominent regional capitals in the sixteenth century. Also, he considered the Ulibahali of the de Soto and Luna narratives identical with the later Creek town of Holiwahali. That was important because the name of that town, which translates "to share out or divide war," was, according to Hawkins, an explicit reference to the right of Holiwahali to declare war within the Confederacy. Therefore the appearance of the name in 1540 would indicate the existence of the Confederacy at that date.[7]

Today, with the benefit of more than a half-century of additional research, virtually every aspect of Swanton's reconstruction may be called into question. First, in regard to Swanton's acceptance of Creek mythology as grounded in fact, few present-day ethnohistorians would so casually accept such oral history as evidence of remote factual events in the absence of independent verification. Moreover, it is now recognized that these texts have little to do with "history" in the Western sense. One of the main purposes of these migration stories was to spell out *relationships* of a social and ceremonial nature in a symbolic language. In other words these native "histories" were conceived not as linear narratives of past events but rather as charters establishing the status of the local group in a present and continually unfolding social environment.[8]

As to the reality of a prehistoric Muskogean invasion of the Gulf country, the archaeological evidence for it has never appeared. It is true that prior to the 1960s, North American archaeologists flirted with the notion of a "Mississippian radiation" out of the Central Mississippi Valley. That notion was indeed influenced by Swanton's interpretations of Creek migration myths, as Bruce Smith has pointed out.[9] But the weight of archaeological evidence has come down in favor of local, in-place cultural evolution in most regions during late prehistory. Migration is now seen by most archaeologists as having played only a minor role in the development of the cultural geography of the Southeast as first encountered by Europeans.

Some of Swanton's reasoning in regard to town identifications is also subject to question, and this extends even to his key evidence for the antiquity of the Confederacy. Indeed his two central conclusions in this regard—that de Soto's Cofitachequi and Ulibahali were to be equated respectively with the later Creek towns of Kasihta and Holiwahali—were seen as tenuous even in his own day.

Swanton might have been justified in the linguistic manipulation necessary to derive Ulibahali from Muskogee Holiwahali, were it not for the fact that Albert Gatschet had already pointed out a much more straightforward solution. The name Ulibahali was claimed by Gatschet to be directly from the Alabama/Koasati language, where it means "town downstream" (oli + bahali). But this solution would leave no clear historic Creek descendant for Ulibahali and no de Soto–era counterpart to Holiwahali. Moreover, Swanton thought it "unlikely that any Alabama other than the Tawasa were on the Tallapoosa River in de Soto's time." So Swanton dismissed Gatschet's translation.[10]

A more serious linguistic contortion was necessary to derive the name Cofitachequi from Kasihta. We may note that this equation was rejected by Crane, on the grounds that Gascoyne's map of 1685 placed Cofitachequi clearly in South Carolina at a time when Kasihta was just as surely on the Chattahoochee River in Alabama.[11]

Such instances as these may be attributed to Swanton's passion to tidy up loose ends; to complete the total picture of southeastern ethnohistory by establishing later historic connections for all native groups mentioned in the sixteenth-century narratives. If today we see him as overzealous in that mission, we cannot fault the calling. All told, however, there simply is no reliable evidence to even hint at the existence of some form of Creek Confederacy during the sixteenth century. Even the traditional place of its ancient formation, at Ocmulgee Old Fields near Macon, Georgia, has been recently called into question as a misinterpretation of Creek folklore.[12]

If Creek folklore and place names are not to be trusted as a reliable guide to their early history, can archaeology serve in that capacity? Such an approach would entail connecting historic Creek groups to patterns of archaeological remains, and then tracing those patterns backwards in time, a method known as the "direct historical approach."[13] But as simple as it may sound, the establishment of such histories for the Creeks has proven extraordinarily difficult.

It has been known for a long time that the Creeks were preceded in their area by the much more complex social formations we call Mississippian. These Mississippian societies developed and flourished in the Southeast roughly between A.D. 1000 and A.D. 1550. If historic Creek could be linked up with prehistoric Mississippian in an unbroken sequence, an obvious task would be to explain how the antecedent Mississippian cultures "devolved"—became simpler—in the course of being transformed into Creek culture.

The first detailed attempt to establish the immediate prehistoric background to Creek culture took place in the context of Depression-era archaeological work in the area of Macon, Georgia. Historic Creek material culture was defined on the basis of excavations at the Trading Post, a fortified structure at Ocmulgee Old Fields. At the same time, local Late Mississippian culture was first defined at the nearby Lamar site. Primarily on the basis of similarities in pottery, Charles Fairbanks argued for a direct connection between the two; that is, Lamar was ancestral to the Ocmulgee Old Fields complex.[14] Nonetheless he could not demonstrate this stratigraphically, and to further confuse matters, Lamar also could be shown to be closely related to historic Cherokee material culture. The case made by Fairbanks remained inconclusive, and through the 1970s it remained a subject of dispute.[15]

A great deal has been learned recently through excavations in the Coosa, Tallapoosa, and Chattahoochee River valleys. This has particularly shed light on the seventeenth century, the period roughly intermediate between Lamar and Historic Creek, as these were originally defined. For all these areas it may now be said with some certainty that the local variations of Historic Creek material culture are continuous with earlier South Appalachian Mississippian cultures. We can now say, more specifically, that the westernmost Lamar cultures are the ancestral population out of which sprang the nucleus of the later Creeks. These "Western Lamar" cultures, which were in existence in the time of de Soto, had in common a material culture showing strong connections with non-Lamar Mississippian cultures to the north and west. The most obvious index of this is the prominence of shell-tempered pottery—an introduced trait—in all of these culture complexes.

Having established these regional continuities through archaeological research, the "direct historical approach" allows us to suggest linguistic correlations for the Western Lamar area. Muskogee was probably spoken prehistorically on the Coosa and Tallapoosa Rivers, while Hitchiti was spoken on the Chattahoochee.[16]

We have been able to produce reasonably detailed cultural chronologies for several areas culminating in the archaeological cultures associated with Historic Creek core towns. I harbor no illusions that these area chronologies are the final word on the subject; on the contrary I feel sure that they will be refined. But in the meantime, with a skeletal framework in place, it is permissible to begin speaking of stages of cultural development leading up to the formation of the Creek Confederacy in the eighteenth century. Combining archaeological with ethnohistorical information, this is a story of collapse, subsequent coalescence, and political centralization.

I will not dwell at length on the organization of Mississippian chiefdoms in this area. That subject has already been dealt with in detail by my colleagues in other papers in this volume. My commentary here will amount to certain amendments to their presentations that pertain in a special way to the emergence of Creek political organization.

I am particularly concerned here with Mississippian cultures in three regions: the Upper/Middle Coosa, the Lower Tallapoosa, and the Lower Chattahoochee river valleys, these being the regions in which we may trace direct development from Mississippian Lamar to Historic Creek material culture. Of the three, the sixteenth-century chiefdom of Coosa centered on the Upper Coosa River drainage is of distinct interest as perhaps the dominant political force in this part of the Southeast at the time of de Soto's entrada. Because we have eyewitness accounts as well as archaeological information about this Mississippian chiefdom, its organization and extent can be reconstructed in some detail.[17]

Unfortunately we face a deficit in historical documentation of Mississippian chiefdoms on the Lower Tallapoosa and Upper Chattahoochee Rivers, two areas central to the problem of Creek origins. The former locality has not been unambiguously identified in the narratives concerning de Soto and Luna, and for the latter there are simply no eyewitness accounts. Here we have to rely solely on the archaeology. The pertinent Late Mississippian culture on the Lower Tallapoosa River is called the Shine II phase, and that of the Lower Chattahoochee is called the Stewart phase.

Very little is really known about the Shine II phase, despite its recent appearance in discussions about de Soto's route through what is now Alabama. Excavations have been performed at two sites, Jere Shine and Kulumi, sufficient to verify the existence of the phase and to characterize its material culture in a preliminary way. Neither of these excavations has been reported. There are no radiocarbon dates for the phase, but based on pottery comparisons with the neighboring Chattahoochee area I have estimated a duration of about A.D. 1400–1550.[18]

Despite the fact that so little excavation has been done, the magnitude and general character of Shine II–phase settlements are known from the results of systematic survey. The type site, Jere Shine (1Mt6), is apparently the largest settlement and had several mounds. We are not sure of its size during the Shine II phase, because it also has an extensive earlier Mississippian component (designated Shine I phase), and some or all of the mounds may have been built during this earlier period. Other than Jere Shine there are four more Shine II–phase sites with mounds, all appearing to be small villages. They are crowded along the Lower Tallapoosa River in a stretch of less than 40 kilometers. Dispersed across the valley floor are numerous smaller sites of the same period, presumably Shine II–phase farmsteads.[19]

There is nothing to indicate any great degree of political centralization in the Shine II phase, even if we assume that the multiple-mound Jere Shine site was a fully functioning center at that time.[20] These sites may well have been a single, simple chiefdom during the Shine II phase, and if so, this chiefdom was very similar to the component chiefdoms incorporated by the paramount chiefdom of Coosa to the north.[21] In fact, the recent reconstruction of Coosa opens up as a distinct possibility that the Shine chiefdom was incorporated at some point into a similar larger polity, perhaps one centered on the Chattahoochee River some 90 kilometers to the east.

Stewart-phase sites on the Lower Chattahoochee River were, I believe,

occupied largely by Hitchiti-speaking peoples at the time of first European contact, based on ceramic continuities with later Lower Creek sites
in the same area. These Stewart-phase sites constitute, by any measure, a
greater entity than Shine II. By using the term Stewart, I am adopting Frank
Schnell's new nomenclature for Lamar on the Lower Chattahoochee. Formerly these sites were incorporated into the broadly defined Bull Creek
phase. Bull Creek now has been plausibly subdivided on ceramic evidence
into two parts: Bull Creek (A.D. 1400–75) and Stewart (A.D. 1475–1550).[22]

It is difficult to know with any certainty how many of the eight mound
and village sites formerly assigned to the Bull Creek phase have Stewart-
phase components according to the newer criteria, but from the collections
so far reported it appears that at least some of them do have assemblages
conforming to the Stewart phase. Like the Shine phase, this was also a
farmstead-based settlement system, and dozens of small sites of the period
dot the valley floor in a corridor about 160 kilometers in length.[23]

It is especially important that the large, multiple-mound ceremonial center at Rood's Landing was functioning at this time. Joseph Caldwell's excavations on the top of Mound A, the largest of the eight mounds at Rood's
Landing, revealed three large public buildings assignable to the Stewart
phase.[24] Wood from a preserved wall post from Structure 1 on this mound
has been radiocarbon dated to 260 ± 70 B.P., corrected to A.D. 1530–
1610 ± 70 [MASCA] (BETA-2271). Very little excavation has been conducted at this site, and we lack information on other mounds possibly in
use at this time. Probably most of them were built during the preceding
Rood phase between about A.D. 1100 and 1400.

At its height, the Rood's Landing site was the center of a paramount
chiefdom incorporating a number of smaller mound centers.[25] However, the
evidence from Rood's Landing and the nearby Singer-Moye site, another
large center abandoned about A.D. 1400, suggests some decline in this
hierarchy by Stewart-phase times. Hence it is difficult to judge the relative
complexity of the Late Mississippian polity or polities in this region. I cannot rule out the possibility that an extensive two-tiered polity similar to the
Coosa chiefdom was functioning in Stewart-phase times, though at a less
centralized level than previously. But it seems more likely that by this time
the prior hegemony had disintegrated and the region was controlled by
some number of simpler Mississippian chiefdoms.

In sum, the immediate Mississippian background in the Creek core
area involves several Western Lamar archaeological cultures. Political complexity was evidently different from region to region. Moreover, while
political centralization may have been on the upswing in the Coosa chiefdom, it may have been on the wane on the Chattahoochee, and even the
little Shine II–phase chiefdom on the Tallapoosa probably was more centralized at an earlier time. The broader frame seems to capture the inherent
volatility and fragility of Mississippian polities, all undergoing cycles of

growth and decline. It was into this landscape of constant political flux that Spaniards marched in the sixteenth century.[26]

It is precisely because of this roller-coaster instability in Mississippian political formations that the effects of Spanish contact are hard to determine. For while some polities were robust and expanding at the time of first contact, others were deteriorating. Moreover, some of the larger southeastern chiefdoms may have gone into decline in a coordinated manner just prior to European contact. Christopher Peebles has argued that the legitimacy of the Moundville aristocracy rested on access to prestige goods, and that an external disruption in the traffic of such goods helped to precipitate a Moundville decline between A.D. 1400 and 1500.[27] If he is correct, then one might expect the same disruption to have affected the other larger Mississippian polities in the region—Wilbanks, Rood, and Lake Jackson. Each of these hierarchical systems was undoubtedly as dependent as Moundville on prestige goods, and all appear to have been in a downhill slide during roughly A.D. 1400–1500, a few decades preceding the Spanish entradas.

And yet none of these former giants had entirely collapsed at the time of the Spanish entradas in the sixteenth century. All remained as weakened but still viable chiefdoms, as both the narratives of the conquest and the archaeology attest. And so when we find evidence of truly precipitous collapse during the sixteenth century, we might then look to European-induced causes. Teasing out the contributory factors in each local situation may be a difficult problem, but there is little point to approaching it as a debate between two absolutes: internal collapse versus European disruption. We might a priori expect to identify a combination of both in some instances.

We are fortunate to have Marvin Smith's detailed study of the disintegration of the Coosa chiefdom. In that study, summarized in his paper in this volume, he finds a number of archaeological correlates he believes are ultimately attributable to the European invasions of the sixteenth century. According to Smith's reconstruction, most of these correlates are related to disease-induced population decline, although disease and demographic responses are quite difficult to assess in any direct way.[28]

For the core of the Coosa chiefdom in the period postdating 1540, Smith found that the number of sites shrank from a minimum of five towns to one or two towns between 1540 and 1740. There was also a change in average town size, as there were fewer large, compact towns and more linear, dispersed settlements through time. There was wholesale movement of people out of the area hardest hit by direct Spanish presence. The Coosawattee River area at the headwaters of the Coosa drainage, formerly the nucleus and capital of the paramount chiefdom, was entirely vacated by the end of the sixteenth century. Other correlates included a cessation of native copperwork, shell engraving, and mound building in the period immediately following contact.

For the Lower Tallapoosa and Lower Chattahoochee River regions, we do not yet possess the degree of chronological precision that Smith has achieved for the Coosa Valley. This fact must temper any conclusions to be drawn, but for the moment it appears that the Lower Tallapoosa and Upper Chattahoochee River regions have postcontact histories paralleling the Coosa situation in some respects and deviating from it in others.

For the Lower Tallapoosa region, archaeological evidence of potentially European-induced population decline is ambiguous at best. In fact, because of our poor chronological control at present, any account we might give verges on speculation. It is, however, apparent that the largest of the Shine II–phase sites, the multiple-mound Jere Shine site near Montgomery, Alabama, was abandoned at some point during the Shine II phase, while other Shine II–phase mound sites farther to the east continued to be occupied into the succeeding Atasi phase. The total abandonment of the largest mound center must surely be interpreted as evidence of a decline of the Shine chiefdom, but the problem is that we are not at all sure as to the timing of this abandonment. It may well have been a prehistoric phenomenon having nothing to do with European contact, since many of the artifacts we have come to recognize as sixteenth-century horizon markers are so far missing from that site.

In short, Shine II–phase political organization may have been already in decline at the time of Spanish contact, with the population reoriented around the three easternmost Shine II mound centers (Kulumi, Atasi, and Tukabatchee), since all three of the latter continued to be occupied through the Colonial period. Certain other of Smith's criteria of chiefdom disintegration in the Coosa region do seem to apply here, however. Large-scale mound construction does seem to disappear with the Shine II phase, and native copperwork and shell engraving may have been curtailed as well (although again reliable data are wanting).

For the Lower Chattahoochee, the evidence for a postcontact population collapse is even more dramatic than it is for the Coosa region. Systematic surveys in the Chattahoochee Valley show a reduction in site frequency of 90 percent between the Stewart phase (pre-1550) and the subsequent Abercrombie phase (ca. A.D. 1550–1650).[29] It is difficult to attribute this to anything other than epidemic disease, even though we know of no sixteenth-century European expeditions that passed directly through this region. The dense swath of Stewart-phase Lamar occupation throughout the valley simply vanished, leaving, it seems, just two Abercrombie-phase towns, one on either side of the river south of present Columbus, Georgia. Interestingly, both of these compact Abercrombie towns had large platform mounds and may have functioned as mound centers until well into the seventeenth century, a phenomenon not yet documented in the Coosa or Tallapoosa regions.

Clearly the regions under consideration were affected in different ways by the sixteenth-century European intrusions. A hallmark of the period was the uprooting and relocation of people, sometimes far from their point of origin.[30] As certain areas became attractive for resettlement during the seventeenth century, they actually enjoyed flourishing populations, while other regions saw diminishment or abandonment.

One such area was the Lower Tallapoosa Valley. During the Atasi phase (ca. 1600–1715), settlements grew in both size and number from the preceding period. The Tukabatchee site, for example, appears to have blossomed from a small Shine II–phase Mississippian mound center to an expansive Atasi-phase village covering an area four or five times greater than before. The Atasi-phase village at Tukabatchee had reached its maximum extent by the middle of the seventeenth century. At the same time, several new Atasi-phase settlements, some quite large, were established on the north bank of the Lower Tallapoosa.[31]

Another area of coalescence was the Middle Coosa Valley to the north, particularly along eastern tributaries of the Coosa River in southern Talladega County, Alabama. Here there were several large, late Kymulga-phase (ca. A.D. 1500–1650) villages. Despite their showing evidence of contact with sixteenth-century Spanish expeditions, these towns clearly prospered well into the seventeenth century.[32] Following Marvin Smith's reading of the evidence, this area's population was augmented further during the seventeenth century by remnants of the Coosa chiefdom migrating downriver from their former hearth on the Upper Coosa River.[33]

The same trend may be seen on the Lower Chattahoochee, if perhaps somewhat delayed in that area due to the catastrophic losses of the late sixteenth century. I have noted that the two remaining Abercrombie-phase settlements probably were stable political and population centers during the first half of the seventeenth century. By the first part of the succeeding Blackmon phase (ca. A.D. 1650–1715), a number of large, new villages were established nearby, and the regional population rebounded substantially from the Abercrombie decline.[34]

In all three of these regions, seventeenth-century population stability and growth were prelude to truly remarkable population growths, undoubtedly due in part to the steady influx of refugees, during the eighteenth century. Although no accurate demographic measures have been attempted, soaring populations are plainly manifested in archaeological site frequencies.[35]

A pertinent question is: Why did these areas and not others experience coalescence in the aftermath of sixteenth-century European disruption? One suggestion has been that such areas were only indirectly affected by Spanish expeditions, and that they therefore became disease-free refuges during the turmoil that ensued.[36] This would at first seem plausible, but the Abercrombie-phase population collapse in the Chattahoochee Valley contradicts it, for it indicates that such marginal areas *were* affected, and affected profoundly.

Perhaps no simple or straightforward answer to this question can be found. The interior native Southeast between about 1560 and 1650 must have been a cauldron of demographic instability, political volatility, and social fragmentation. Without documentary records, we can only guess at the complexities involved. We only perceive the most obvious effects: regional abandonment, population decline, long-distance movement, and coalescence. But the three regions I have discussed that experienced co-alescences during the seventeenth century—the Middle Coosa, the Lower Tallapoosa, and the Lower Chattahoochee valleys—had commonalities that may have importance for our understanding of later events (even if we may not be able to explain these commonalities).

In each of these regions there are clear signs of cultural, social, and political continuity from the sixteenth through the seventeenth centuries, showing some degree of resiliance of the local chiefdoms to the onslaught of European disease (even if, as was the case on the Chattahoochee, most of the local population disappeared). This was not merely a continuity of people living in the same area, but more importantly, a long-term stability in certain *towns* as political centers. It seems no accident that such mound centers as Hightower Village in the Middle Coosa region, Tukabatchee on the Lower Tallapoosa, and Abercrombie on the Lower Chattahoochee sur-vived and perhaps even prospered from the late sixteenth century well into the seventeenth. The apparent stability of these political centers *as places* indicates some degree of endurance and continuity of the old chiefly mode of government in each area. Probably there was no time during which these polities lost a basic hierarchical structure subordinating the surviving towns to a single, chiefly center. It might be useful to think of these early seventeenth-century polities as being centralized to about the same degree as the historic Natchez described by the French.

This, it seems to me, is essential to understanding the situation as the Spaniards and Englishmen re-encountered it in the late seventeenth century. Misplaced talk of Creeks and of the possibility of a Creek Confederacy on this time level is not only inaccurate, it also diverts attention from the politi-cal formations actually functioning at this time. During the seventeenth century and the early years of the eighteenth, the largest native political unit in existence anywhere in the interior was still the provincial polity known to the Spaniards as *provincias* or provinces. Each had a head town, a "great chief," and several tributary or subsidiary towns. The provincial polity as a definite mode of political organization was alive and well even after the later establishment of alliances on a broader scale, a point that tends to be submerged in accounts of Creek political organization.

Seventeenth-century annexations of refugee groups by Muskogees and Hitchitis were accomplished not by a nascent Creek Confederacy but by regional polities, which were not yet mutually allied at the close of the century. These were the Tukabatchee polity on the Tallapoosa River, the

Abihka polity on the Middle Coosa River, and the Apalachicola polity on the Chattahoochee River, the latter known by the English as the Cowetas. Here are the three coalescent districts we have identified as nodes of stability through the seventeenth century, now identified by name as the result of re-established contact by European nations. Each one was in a very real sense descended from a corresponding Mississippian chiefdom extant in the sixteenth century.

Revisionist accounts of Creek history have lately portrayed the origin of the Confederacy as a late seventeenth-century phenomenon. Such a view would credit the introduction of guns, the rise of slave raiding, and the associated increase in intertribal warfare as primary catalysts for the banding together of disparate peoples into transient leagues of common protection.[37] I do not doubt that these documented events were increasingly disruptive to native peoples during this period. It is beyond question that such factors lay behind the relocation of many groups into the later Creek territory.

Where I part company with these portrayals is in their failure to acknowledge the existence of chiefdom-like political formations throughout the seventeenth century in a few coalescent zones I have identified. It is essentially a matter of how we interpret the substance of the initial alliances. These were not, in my opinion, leagues of common protection formed of independent towns joined, so to speak, out of thin air and of the exigencies of the moment. Rather, they were annexations of immigrant towns, joined to preexisting town clusters that were already politically centralized. These polities were the stable nucleii toward which the disrupted remnant peoples of the late seventeenth century gravitated. Moreover, the annexation of foreign groups up until the eighteenth century had little apparent effect on the political organization of these independent Muskogee and Hitchiti polities. It was not the influx of refugees but other events that precipitated the broader alliances so obvious to later observers.

Those political transformations that occurred during the eighteenth century are in every case accountable in terms of outside stimuli, namely various crises resulting from the European colonial presence. The historically documented Creek Confederacy gradually stabilized following the Yamasee War in 1715–16 in direct response to European pressure. The nature of that confederacy, and especially its development during the eighteenth century, is not well interpreted in existing scholarly literature.

The problem is due to a general failure to understand that above the level of the town (*talwa*), Creek military and civil alliances were predominantly conditional. Several layers of successively more inclusive political integration generally came into existence on a temporary basis, always metered in appropriate response to an outside challenge judged to be of greater or lesser magnitude. This was true to a large degree even at the height of the

Confederacy at the time of McGillivray, in the last quarter of the eighteenth century.

The levels of aggregation most frequently seen among the Creeks can be described as follows, beginning with the lower orders of inclusiveness.

The most permanent and stable low-level political unit was called in the Muskogee language the talwa, or town, the governmental counterpart to the aggregated group of kinsmen known in Muskogee as an *idalwa*. A talwa was physically manifested in a "square ground town," the nucleus of which was a complex of public buildings and ceremonial facilities. Talwas were mutually independent to the degree that they could dissent and abstain from the action of any larger body, a condition that prevailed from the period of seventeenth-century provincial organization onward.

Above the talwa was the provincial "town moiety" level of organization, consisting of a group of towns belonging to the same town moiety (white or red) within the provincial polity.[38] Apparently this level of organization did not often come into play in important political affairs. At least its operation is only very occasionally hinted at in the documents, as for example when the Acorn Whistler, a Tallapoosa "White King," claimed to "command seven towns" among the larger Tallapoosa group, when treating with Governor Glen in 1752. This apparently refers only to the "white" towns among the Tallapoosa, which were independently at war, under Acorn Whistler, with the Choctaws and Chickasaws at this date.[39]

Above the town moiety was the province, which, because of its greater political potential, more often appears in dealings with powerful European colonies. As stated earlier, several relatively stable provinces headed by "great chiefs" existed independently at the turn of the eighteenth century, representing the most inclusive native political organizations then in existence. Provincial affairs were directed by a head chief, such as the influential Emperor Brimms of the Coweta (Apalachicola) polity; and for the Tallapoosa polity, in succession Tixana, Old Brackett (Ispocogi Miko of Tukabatchee), Olassee King, Gun Merchant, Mad Dog (Efau Hadjo), and Opothleyaholo. At about the same level of organization were certain groups recognized as semi-independent "tribes" in the later years of the eighteenth century, primarily the Seminoles of Florida, and the Alibamo towns on the upper Alabama River.

Provincial polity organization was influential in political affairs involving trade relations during the first part of the eighteenth century, but toward mid-century this level began to be gradually eclipsed in importance by a slightly more inclusive level of alliance, the "division." Upper and Lower town divisions arose, together constituting the "Nation" as the Confederacy began to jell in response to territorial disputes with the Europeans and the constant threat of war. In the case of the Upper division, this involved a gradual political amalgamation of the Tallapoosa towns and the Abihka

388 ✤ VERNON JAMES KNIGHT, JR.

towns, somewhat obscurely augmented by the Alibamo towns. Assemblies of one or the other division could separately adjudicate certain disputes, as for example when the assembled Lower towns settled a Spanish-Seminole quarrel with the Governor of East Florida in 1771.[40]

Finally there was the "Nation," the so-called Confederacy itself. Despite the fact that this supreme political organization, comprising all the Creek talwas, seldom acted on any affairs other than land disputes and cessions, its affairs take up much space in accounts of Creek history, precisely because the subject of land encroachment was the key point of European-Indian contention during the period of its existence. At least at certain points, the Nation was presided over by a provisionally instituted office of national chief, beginning with those of the Brimms dynasty, and later by Alexander McGillivray and the Little Prince.

During McGillivray's tenure (1783–93) at the height of the Confederacy's ability to control the balance of power in the South, the national council nevertheless met only "under conditions of extraordinary emergency."[41] McGillivray was able, however, to institute assemblies of the separate divisions on a regular annual basis, to discuss the business of the Nation. This can be considered an exception to the contingent basis of high-level Creek government, although it should be remembered that these were years of virtually incessant crisis due to Georgian encroachment on the eastern Creek frontier and the constant threat of military invasion from that quarter. In the years following McGillivray's death, Indian agent Benjamin Hawkins tried fervently to institute Creek national government on a more permanent basis, but that effort was ultimately unsuccessful due to growing internal factionalism among the talwas.[42]

The Creek Nation, a politico-military alliance network, thus arose as a progressive accretion of alliances among previously independent provincial polities. It occurred in basically three stages following European first contact with Mississippian chiefdoms. First was the incorporation of former remnant tribes, as talwas, on a provincial basis by the independent polities known as the Abihkas, Tallapoosas, and Cowetas (or Apalachicolas). Each foreign element adopted aspects of provincial Muskogee political organization, including the square ground organization of the talwa and an assigned place in the town moiety system of intertalwa social organization. Next was the gradual eclipse of the provincial polities by a broader divisional political network. Thus the Abihka towns began to act in concert with the Tallapoosa towns during the eighteenth century, later to be more formally joined by the Alibamo towns, to constitute what was occasionally called the Upper Nation, and later the Upper division of the Creek Nation. Last to emerge, largely due to the influence of Emperor Brimms of Coweta among the Upper towns at the time of the Yamasee War, was an alliance between the two main divisions, henceforth the Creek Nation, to be put on a more fully institutionalized political basis by Alexander McGillivray after 1783.

As a further footnote to the interpretation of Creek government as a scaled hierarchy of potential, impermanent aggregations of talwas organized on a contingent basis in response to crises of greater or lesser importance, it might be added that a still higher level of cooperative alliance came into play on some occasions. There were instances of international alliances of Indian tribes involving the Creeks. One was the somewhat abortive general alliance of the southern Indians with the British during the American Revolution. McGillivray claimed that it was his service in this cause that later allowed his personal ascendancy in Creek politics. Another was the Shawnee prophet movement, again abetted by the British, which helped to trigger the Red Stick War of 1813–14. The Creek Nation as a whole was not unanimous in support of either of these general Indian uprisings, but these examples, among others, show that certain Creek leadership was not disinclined to assist in causes and politics of continental scope.[43]

Now I have left until last an important question, perhaps because it is the most difficult one to answer. Namely, what were the common grounds that made possible what I have described as a "contingent" political formation? For to make this claim presumes that the elements which came together had some preexisting conceptual basis for doing so, and I have denied all along that there was any overarching social or political formation that would fill this bill during the formative years of Creek development. Can we identify social and cultural means in other domains that might have served as bridges crosscutting political alignments?

We might begin with common language—Muskogee. By the time of the Yamasee War in the early eighteenth century, important "core" towns of each political province spoke Muskogee. Even in the former Apalachicola polity, which I have argued was traditionally made up of Hitchiti speakers, the Muskogee towns of Coweta and Kasihta had by that time eclipsed Apalachicola in importance. And so there was a linguistic basis for a sense of common ethnicity.

There were further networks of a social nature linking towns and people across political lines, and these I believe must have had some importance too. I think here particularly of the clan system, which made it possible for a person to find "relatives" and thus hospitality in just about any inhabited place. But there were other mechanisms as well. Thomas Nairne in 1708 mentioned seemingly odd correspondences in town names incorporating nearly the entire native Southeast and crosscutting linguistic boundaries, and cartographic evidence of the period confirms it, yet we know little of the meaning of these correspondences.[44]

We do know that native southeastern greeting rituals among chiefs were more than just expressions of friendship or occasions to give gifts and promise peace. They were also, symbolically at least, ritual *adoptions*.[45] Such, for example, was the Calumet Ceremony, which was used throughout Eastern North America to establish fictive kinship among the members of different villages who might otherwise be enemies, and thus perpetuate alliances on a broad scale."[46] The notion that one chief (and hence that chief's town) could ceremonially "adopt" another by a ritual laying down of arms is one that seems well worth exploring as a possible basis for the annexations that so frequently occurred. It is indeed the laying down of arms that is prominently featured in the Kasihta migration myth ratifying their union with Apalachicola.[47] We find the same theme in a traditional account of the adoption of Shawnee by the Tallapoosas, where the compact was confirmed by an offering of symbolic weaponry. These included calumet pipes (symbolic arrow/spearthrowers), a ceremonial war club, and "Tukabatchee Plates" (symbolic war axes).[48] Further explorations into these and related topics will continue to improve our grasp of one of the most important native phenomena in the history of the early Southeast.

NOTES

A portion of this paper is revised from the author's technical report, *Tukabatchee*.

1. Swanton, *Creek Indians*, 9ff. For a recent perspective on the English appellation "Creek" and its colonial significance, see Martin, *Sacred Revolt*, 6–13.

2. Gatschet, *Migration Legend*, 168.

3. Bartram, *Travels of William Bartram*, 292–94, and Swanton, *Indian Tribes of the Lower Mississippi Valley*, 334–36.

4. Debo, *Road to Disappearance*, 4; Corkran, *Creek Frontier*, 44; Green, *Politics of Indian Removal*, 12–13; and Crane, *Southern Frontier*, 254.

5. John R. Swanton, "Social Organization and Social Usages," 33–75.

6. Swanton, "Aboriginal Culture," 724–26.

7. Swanton, "De Soto's Line of March," 153, 156, "Social Organization and Social Usages," 310, and *Creek Indians*, 254, 257.

8. See Knight, "Mississippian Ritual," 38–39.

9. B. D. Smith, "Mississippian Expansion," 23–25.

10. Gatschet, *Migration Legend*, 85n., and Swanton, *Creek Indians*, 254.

11. Swanton, "De Soto's Line of March," 153, and *Early Creek Indians*, 216–17; and Crane, *Southern Frontier*, 13n.

12. Schnell, "Beginning of the 'Creeks'," 24–29. For the traditional view, see Harris, *Here the Creeks Sat Down*, 27–29.

13. Steward, "Direct Historical Approach."

14. Fairbanks, "Creek and Pre-Creek," 298–99, and "Origin of Creek Pottery."

15. Sears, "Creek and Cherokee Culture." See also Russell, "Lamar and the Creeks, An Old Controversy Revisited," and Penman, "The Lamar Phase in Central Georgia."

16. Vernon J. Knight, Jr., "Ocmulgee Fields Culture and the Historical Development of Creek Ceramics" (Paper presented at the Ocmulgee National Monument Fiftieth Anniversary Conference, Macon, Ga., Dec. 13, 1986).

17. David J. Hally, Marvin T. Smith, and James B. Langford, Jr., "The Archaeological Reality of de Soto's Coosa" (Paper presented at the Fifty-fourth Annual Meeting of the Society for American Archaeology, Atlanta, Ga., Apr. 6, 1989), and Hudson et al., "Coosa."

18. Knight, *Tukabatchee*, 9–10.

19. Gregory A. Waselkov, "Lower Tallapoosa Cultural Resources Survey, Phase I Report," typescript, Department of Sociology and Anthropology, Auburn University, 1981; and Knight, "Alabama's de Soto Mapping Project."

20. Knight, *Tukabatchee*, 173.

21. See Hally, Smith, and Langford, "The Archaeological Reality of de Soto's Coosa," 124–31.

22. Williams and Shapiro, *Lamar Archaeology*, 35.

23. Knight, "Alabama's de Soto Mapping Project," 32.

24. Caldwell, "Investigations at Rood's Landing," 27–30.

25. Scarry and Payne, "Mississippian Polities," 86–87.

26. See DePratter, "Early Historic Chiefdoms," 204–11, and Anderson, "Political Change in Chiefdom Societies," 630–33.

27. Peebles, "Paradise Lost, Strayed, and Stolen," 30–31.

28. M. T. Smith, *Aboriginal Culture Change*.

29. Knight and Mistovich, *Walter F. George Lake*, 225, 231–32.

30. M. T. Smith, "Aboriginal Population Movements."

31. Knight, *Tukabatchee*, 56.

32. Knight, *East Alabama Archaeological Survey*, 12–13, and Richard Walling and Robert C. Wilson, "Archaeological Test Excavations, The Hightower Village Site, 1Ta150" (Paper presented at the Twentieth Annual Meeting of the Southern Anthropological Society, Memphis, Tenn., 1985).

33. M. T. Smith, *Aboriginal Culture Change*, 76–77.

34. Knight and Mistovich, *Walter F. George Lake*, 225–26, 231–32, and Mistovich and Knight, *Excavations at Four Sites*.

35. Waselkov, "Lower Tallapoosa Survey"; Knight and Mistovich, *Walter F. George Lake*, 228, 231–32; and Knight, Cole, and Walling, *Coosa and Tallapoosa*, 38.

36. See, for example, M. T. Smith, *Aboriginal Culture Change*, 139–40.

37. Waselkov and Cottier, "Eastern Muskogean Ethnicity," 148, and M. T. Smith, *Aboriginal Culture Change*, 129–42.

38. I use the term "town moiety" for the dual organization of Creek towns, as it conventionally appears in the work of John R. Swanton and others. (See the Works Cited for a list of Swanton's works.) This is, however, technically inaccurate, as these divisions did not function as exogamous categories.

39. "Talk of the Acorn Whistler to Governor Glen" [1752], in McDowell, *Documents Relating to Indian Affairs*, 228–31.

40. Doster, *The Creek Indians*, 1:57.

41. Ibid., 1:122.

42. Hawkins, "Sketch of the Creek Country," 67–68.

43. O'Donnell, *Southern Indians*, 80–108; Doster, *Creek Indians*, 1:83; and Nunez, "Creek Nativism," 1–47, 131–75, 292–301.

44. Nairne, *Nairne's Muskhogean Journals*, 60.

45. Lankford, "Saying Hello to the Timucua," 16–17.

46. Robert L. Hall, "Calumet Ceremonialism, Xipe Worship, and the Mechanisms of Long-Distance Trade" (Paper presented at the Eighty-first Annual Meeting of the American Anthropological Association, Washington, D.C., Dec. 3, 1982), 3.

47. Gatschet, *Migration Legend*, 250.

48. I. W. Brown, "The Calumet Ceremony," 312–14; Knight, *Tukabatchee*, 174.

PATRICIA GALLOWAY

Confederacy as a Solution to Chiefdom Dissolution: Historical Evidence in the Choctaw Case

My study of the origins of the Choctaw people has led to the conclusion that the Choctaws of the eighteenth century were the inheritors of a multi-ethnic protohistoric confederacy. It was *multiethnic* because to a group indigenous to the Mississippi region it added other groups originating from the Moundville chiefdom of north central Alabama and Plaquemine culture groups from the region west of the Pearl River. The confederation was born in the *protohistoric* period, A.D. 1540–1700, from the interaction of two phenomena: the natural cycle of chiefdom development and devolution and the unnatural chaos created by introduced epidemic disease in the beginning of the sixteenth century. These upheavals led to the gathering together of remnants of fragmented groups into a *confederacy*, a series of autonomous villages articulated as a tribal organization, but its motley origins account for its failure to be a "pure" representative of that type.

The steps that lead to this conclusion are complex, and the research is not yet complete. I have decided, therefore, to take the reader "behind the scenes" of this work-in-progress to demonstrate just how such research proceeds. First, however, I outline the major points being pursued:

1. Examination of archaeological and documentary evidence suggests that as has been argued theoretically, there was cyclic development within the tribe-to-chiefdom continuum in the Southeast, and that at time of contact there was at least one devolved chiefdom in the area that could have supplied population to a new tribal confederacy.

2. Investigation of previous historical demographic work for the re-

gion offers strong arguments that so-called "virgin soil epidemics" in the area may have effectively reduced still-functioning chiefdoms to a seriously disrupted condition either during or after first contact, while having considerably less effect upon the devolved population.

3. Close reading of both documentary and traditional evidence for the geographical origin of the Choctaw suggests multiple locations of origin for the postulated constituent peoples, and these locations are compatible with the evidence in points 1 and 2, above.

4. Documentary and archaeological study shows that during the colonial period, Choctaw culture exhibited a patterned variety compatible with a composition by constituent peoples.

5. Case studies of the Choctaw confederacy in operation during the eighteenth century showed that the centripetal forces derived from the common ground of large ethnic patterns and similar historical situation balanced the centrifugal forces derived from the adherence after confederation to political and lineage attachments dating from before confederation. This balancing of tendencies created a social form, confederation, whose stability depended upon outside pressure to maintain a large population agglomeration in alliance on land that had been poorly suited to the communications and subsistence needs of the more complex chiefdoms from which the populations had originally come.

When I began my work, the conventional wisdom held that the Choctaws had always lived in their east Mississippi homeland; this long-unexamined assertion rested upon the early twentieth-century work on the Choctaws by John R. Swanton.[1] Swanton's work had been carried out under then accepted conventions of ethnographic research that assumed that all Indian groups bore essentially the same culture in the nineteenth century as they had for hundreds of years before and that North American Indians had not inhabited the continent for very long. Beginning in the 1930s, however, archaeology in the region had begun to show, first, that there was a much greater time depth to the native cultures of the region and, second, that there had been dramatic culture change over that period.

Beginning my study of the Choctaws with the French documentary sources of the eighteenth century, I realized that even those sources were in several instances dramatically at variance with the picture Swanton had painted on the basis of mostly late nineteenth-century sources. Furthermore, recent archaeological work has brought together several strands of evidence to suggest that the very pottery type that had been identified with the historic Choctaws since the 1930s (because it was found on nineteenth-century sites) had in fact very little time depth and was probably attributable to material culture adaptations of the eighteenth century. This conclusion exploded the notion that we knew anything about the earlier "Choctaws," even where they had lived, and increased archaeological survey in the region of the east-central Mississippi "homeland" demonstrated fairly conclusively that there was in fact a rather dramatic gap in settlement in most of the region from the late Woodland to the historic period. If the Choctaws had not lived in the later homeland in prehistory, where had they come from?[2]

The fact that the homeland region was unpopulated during the last phase of prehistory did not mean that there were no people living anywhere nearby. Large groupings of population clearly were to be found on the Black Warrior River and in the upper reaches of the Mobile-Tensaw delta; smaller but still important populations lived on the middle and upper Tombigbee and on the lower Pearl, while at least one similar group may have lived in the Pascagoula delta. If any of these peoples had had reason to move, then they might have chosen east-central Mississippi. But since intact Mississippian mound-building cultures could not have subsisted on the poor upland soils and narrow floodplains of that area, it would have to have been a forced choice.[3]

Most of these groups were organized at some point as chiefdoms. This form of sociopolitical organization, which is organized hierarchically through a system of ranked kinship groups, is placed by anthropological theoreticians somewhere between tribal organization, which is generally egalitarian, and the truly stratified societies of states.[4] The important thing about the chiefdoms of southeastern North America is that they apparently never crossed the threshold to state organization. If chiefdoms fail to develop into states, they still do not seem to remain stable; archaeological evidence in North America suggests that many of the chiefdoms of the late prehistoric Mississippian culture simply went to pieces mysteriously, leading some archaeologists to propose a "Mississippian Decline," an unspecified cultural exhaustion, to account for it.

But anthropological theorists have developed an explanation of a certain kind of developmental sequence that seems germane to this problem. Jonathan Friedman has argued that human groups exhibiting steady population growth will develop from tribe to chiefdom to state if steady intensification of food production is feasible, but that if ecological constraints limit the food supply in a given physical setting, the group will reach some maximal level of organizational complexity, after which it will collapse and disperse when supplies are no longer sufficient for continued growth, dropping back to a less complex level of organization. This phenomenon is a cyclic one if the group is constrained to one geographical location, and the process will repeat itself. Friedman's argument seems quite applicable to the late prehistoric chiefdoms of the Southeast, but except for the work of Christopher Peebles it has not been used extensively, nor have its postulates been adapted to the conditions prevailing in the Mississippian development of maize agriculture in the ecologically constrained river floodplain setting characteristic of this culture.[5]

If, as Friedman has argued, such a development can cycle through the tribe to chiefdom continuum, then we should be able to see several stages of this cycle in existence at one time, since population growth and environmental setting will inevitably vary from one place to the next. The segmentary tribe is characterized by autonomous villages led by "big-men" whose entrepreneurship organizes constituencies for demonstrations of conspicuous consumption; limited connections beyond the village are maintained through a shared culture and infrequent pan-tribal ceremonialism. The complex chiefdom at the other end of the continuum consists of one major center with ceremonial structures, several minor centers, and surrounding villages and hamlets; it demonstrates a full hierarchical organization based upon ranked lineages. Halfway between these two is what has been called a "simple chiefdom," consisting of villages and hamlets organized around a single center where the functions of lineage authority are localized.[6]

Archaeological evidence certainly allows the argument that all three of these social forms were in existence concurrently in the late prehistoric period, but just as chiefdoms did not develop to the organizational level of states in the Southeast, it is probable that groups settled along minor river systems on the Gulf Coastal Plain would not develop to the full chiefdom level of integration in the first place, except under very exceptional conditions.[7] Hence, it seems likely that only in areas where chiefdoms had preceded less complex organization can we argue that the proposed devolution had taken place. For the region in question, developments in several areas seem to fit these requirements: the Black Warrior Valley, the lower Yazoo Basin, and the Natchez Bluffs.

But exactly how did this devolution take place? Peebles and Kus have argued that an indispensable ingredient facilitating the high degree of population concentration exhibited by the floodplain agriculturists of the Mississippian adaptation was the increase in information-processing efficiency provided by the increase in social integration represented by chiefdom organization. When this organization was damaged or lost, the same population would no longer be able to support itself on the circumscribed resources of the floodplain, and the population would be forced to disperse. The point to be made here is that chiefdom organization could be destroyed from within—that is, it could collapse when the land could no longer bear the degree of intensive agriculture required to produce surpluses for the external prestige-goods trade that was the visible sign of chiefdom institutions' value to the community. In other words, a time would come when the community could no longer afford the overhead of the chiefly apparatus.[8]

When environmental constraints began to be felt in this way, it is likely that junior lineages and perhaps factions based at minor ceremonial centers would pull away, at first simply by withdrawing their contributions to the upkeep of the central ceremonial site and then by actual physical movement. Peebles's long-term work on the Moundville site and its environs has demonstrated patterns that certainly look something like this. A similar situation seems to emerge in the work of Jeffrey Brain and his coworkers on the population agglomerations and movements of the lower Yazoo Basin and the Natchez Bluffs region. Craig Sheldon has argued that some of the late prehistoric populations of the Alabama-Mobile confluence delta and the middle Tombigbee may have come out of the Black Warrior Valley, while Brain has shown that the population movements in his regions of interest also demonstrate movement from greater to less complex social organization. Thus we have what looks like devolution in regions bracketing the Choctaw "homeland" at a time when the area itself seems to have been relatively devoid of settlement. Yet it may be that all this devolution cannot be accounted for by "natural" environmental constraints.[9]

There has been widespread acceptance in the past ten years of the notion that the native population of the Southeast was seriously depleted by a series of pandemic episodes stemming from the wildfire spread of introduced European disease after 1492.[10] Some researchers have gone so far as to see this fact as a handy *deus ex machina* to provide a unitary explanation for the decline of chiefdoms and the ease with which Europeans swashbuckled their way across the Southeast in the seventeenth and eighteenth centuries.[11] Yet it is not easy to pinpoint any specific disease episodes in the deep interior as far west as the Alabama-Mississippi region, since there is no documentary evidence referring to them.

Ignoring for a moment any specific temporal sequences, we can first consider what catastrophic epidemics would do to native societies of different degrees of organization. The diseases that the Europeans brought to the New World were the diseases of civilization, of cities, of large numbers of people living together.[12] Because of this, they were also diseases that thrived among such population agglomerations as the states of the New World, the Aztec and the Inca, where they were able to spread rapidly; that were reasonably deadly among the less thickly populated chiefdoms of North America; and that were least likely to cause widespread mortality where populations were dispersed and large meetings of groups of people occurred rarely.

When these diseases did take hold, they most frequently killed the very old and the very young. By taking the very old they took the traditions of the society and, where religion and kinship and the arts of prophecy had come into the hands of specialists, a good deal of the culture that made it what it was. By taking the very young they took the society's hope for the future and thus doubtless a good deal of its vitality. But both of these effects would strike hardest where there was most to lose: chiefdoms would suffer more than segmentary tribes. Chiefdoms would lose their organization, and we have seen that this would mean their destruction. On the other hand, segmentary tribes or the remnants of devolved chiefdoms would suffer far less, since they retained the web of tradition at a lower

TABLE I

Probable Disease Epidemics in Florida, 1512–1672

Date	Disease	Probability	Mortality
1513–14	Malaria?	Likely	Unknown
1519–24	Smallpox	Nearly certain	50–75%
1528	Measles or typhoid	Nearly certain	About 50%
1535–39	Unidentified*	Documented	High
1545–48	Bubonic plague*	Nearly certain	About 12.5%
1549	Typhus	Very probable	Perhaps 10%
1550	Mumps	Possible	Unknown
1559	Influenza	Nearly certain	About 20%
1564–70	Syphilis	Documented	Severe
1585–86	Unidentified	Documented	Severe
1586	Vectored fever	Probable	15–20%
1596	Measles*	Documented	About 25%
1613–17	Bubonic plague*	Documented	50%
1649	Yellow fever	Documented	About 33%
1653–	Smallpox	Documented	Unknown
1659	Measles	Documented	Unknown
1672	Influenza?	Documented	Unknown

From Smith, after Dobyns, *Their Number Became Thinned.*
*Probable source in Mesoamerica.

level of distributed expertise and since their dispersed settlement pattern and infrequent gatherings would not favor the spread of disease.

It is impossible to prove that such epidemics reached the interior before actual contact with Europeans took place, but some researchers have suggested that the spread of disease overland from Mexico or by water from the Caribbean islands was not only possible but probable. Table 1 is a list of diseases for which Henry Dobyns and Marvin Smith feel there is at least fairly good evidence from peninsular Florida; only one of the early episodes is "documented," and this 1535–39 episode refers to the evidence of disease that one chronicle of the de Soto expedition reported in the vicinity of Cofitachequi east of the Appalachians and credited to infection from the failed Ayllón settlement. Of the others, Henry Dobyns thinks that the 1513–14 fevers came from the Spaniards in the Carribbean and the 1519–24 smallpox from a documented outbreak in Hispaniola. These are the only episodes thus far identified for the period before the de Soto expedition, and I can see no evidence in the reports of that expedition that indicates results of pandemic disease anywhere between the Appalachians and the Mississippi. Thus it seems unlikely that by 1540 European disease had yet seriously touched the peoples who would become constituents of the Choctaw confederacy.[13]

That is not to say that disease could not have affected the peoples along the Gulf coast. The Piñeda and Narváez expeditions that touched there in 1519 and 1528 were doubtless only emblematic of other coasting voyages that have not been recorded, and we know that not only were some of Narváez's men ill (though probably due to bad nutrition rather than communicable disease), but more importantly, the sick men were specifically attacked by the Indians, suggesting that they may have seen and learned to fear illness among the intruders. Disease-carrying voyages touching the coast must have infected any people they contacted, but we have no records to rely upon.

With the relatively elaborate documentation the de Soto expedition received, that situation changed. Not only did de Soto and his men probably bring along at least the common cold and probably also tuberculosis, they also brought along and left behind a truly remarkable disease vector in the shape of their ever-growing herd of pigs. These pigs may have carried a wide variety of endemic ailments communicable to humans, and they were also capable of infecting the deer and turkeys so crucial to the southeastern Indian's food supply.[14] If natives of the deep interior had escaped contagion before, it is unlikely that they remained free of it after de Soto passed through. But all these arguments about disease in the interior must be proved out through reference to archaeological evidence that is as yet insufficient.

I believe that the "native" core of the emerging Choctaw tribe was made up of people who had never been part of a multilevel chiefdom, possibly the people who had built the Nanih Waiyah mound on the headwaters of the Pearl River but never settled thickly around it—the people who shared the "prairie" culture of groups that would emerge as Chakchiumas and Chickasaws.[15] If these people were reached at all by disease at an early date, it probably did not affect them substantially. They were then joined by people from the east who had not been badly affected either—the remnants of the devolved Moundville chiefdom, who had moved down to the mouth of the Black Warrior before the coming of Europeans, then on down the Tombigbee, and then in the seventeenth century were pushed westward into what were probably their former hunting grounds by the pressure of European-allied Indians. From the southwest came people related to the Natchez, perhaps the remnants of a great chiefdom on the lower Pearl.[16] The two incoming groups settled respectively the eastern and southern part of the "homeland" area that had not been settled before because it was poorly suited to the floodplain agriculture of the Mississippian adaptation.

To describe the companion roles of devolution and disease in the formation of the Choctaw confederacy, it is necessary to show that chiefdoms actually did devolve, disease actually had its effects differentially in the region, and the timing of both was such as to make the foregoing scenario credible.

The details of the rise of Moundville have been dealt with at length by

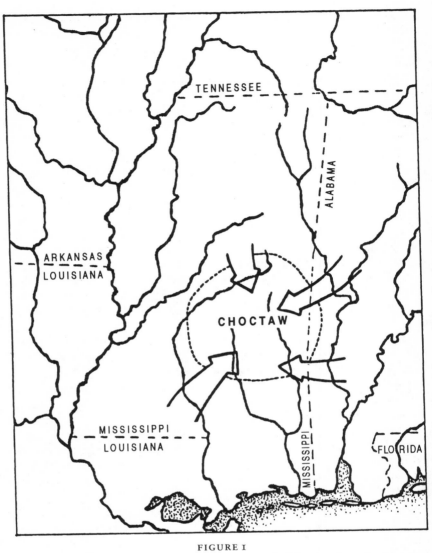

FIGURE I

Hypothesized population movements into the Choctaw homeland
in the late sixteenth and seventeenth centuries

Peebles and his research team, but the fall of Moundville has been less fully treated.[17] The gist of the argument is this: archaeological evidence shows that concurrent with a transition from the Moundville III phase (in which a multilevel chiefdom organization was spatially organized for optimum access to the center) to the Alabama River phase (in which autonomous villages were spaced equidistantly along the Black Warrior River), there was a gradual disappearance from elite burials of fancy external trade goods, then a disappearance of the elite burials altogether. Several possible causes for this effect have been adduced by Peebles, with the caveat that more than one may have been at work: collapse of Moundville's trading partners, interception of Moundville's external trade by others, population growth beyond the capacity to produce a surplus, or the effects of the global cooling of the Little Ice Age.[18] This process was not affected by the presence of European intruders and indeed was completed or nearly so by the time Columbus made landfall.

Much depends upon the dating of the Moundville III to Alabama River cultural sequence, since the burial urns characteristic of the Alabama River phase on the Alabama and lower Tombigbee rivers are thought by some to reflect the results of contagion episodes, and because these episodes are seen as following the traversal of the area by the de Soto expedition, cultural devolution is seen as postdating that expedition as well. This hypothesis requires the corollary assertion that at least the Moundville of the Moundville III phase was still in business when de Soto crossed the Southeast, and he managed somehow to miss even news of it while passing very nearby or he actually visited it and no one bothered to note the impressive cluster of mounds on the site.[19]

It is hardly likely that after having spilled so much ink in describing the impressiveness of the relatively unimportant sites that have been identified with the Coosa and Tascaluca chiefdoms, not one chronicler of the de Soto expedition had more than a few words to spare for a Moundville still at the height of its glory or even somewhat on the wane.[20] Far more likely, when the chroniclers spoke of the Pafalaya "province" (though since no centralized rule was even hinted at, the expression must have been intended to indicate cultural similarity rather than political unity) as a series of empty villages, they were referring to the Alabama River phase villages that Peebles thinks dotted the Black Warrior at the time—or that they missed the Black Warrior altogether.

The assumption that burial urns are somehow linked to contagion episodes reflects one serious misconception in the notion that the lengthy processing of bodies to remove their flesh for interment in urns is something that could have been carried out in the midst of dire contagion. A cursory study of mortuary customs worldwide suggests rather the opposite: secondary processing reflects not hasty desperation but a deliberative tradition rooted in the firm conviction of continuity. And we know that episodes of serious contagion are represented historically rather by mass flesh burials or indeed by lack of any burial at all. Hence the kind of burial population we would expect to see as a result of disease would be either a mass of burials showing unusual age distribution or a great hiatus in the incidence of burial.[21]

What happened to the people of the Pearl River we can only know by archaeology, since no recorded visit was made there in the sixteenth century. And what we know is based so far upon very slim evidence, evidence from controlled surface collections from one important multiple mound site, Pearl Mounds, that probably served a supralocal purpose as a stop on the path from the Natchez region to the Mobile delta. This site is clearly linked in its pottery tradition to the Plaquemine culture of the Natchez Bluffs region, and this accounts for the building of so many mounds. But the pottery types of the latest phase of the Natchez Bluffs—those that define the culture of the historic Natchez Indians and that begin to develop very late in the prehistoric sequence—are missing from this site, suggesting that it had ceased to be occupied by the sixteenth century or thereabouts. We have no excavated features from this site, so we cannot say anything about its mortuary evidence. But some analogies may perhaps be drawn from what is known of parallel developments in the Natchez Bluffs.[22]

Developments there are clearly seen as the end of a long cultural trajectory, and they amounted to population movement, amalgamation, and reorganization. Toward the end of the prehistoric period the greatest of the mound sites in the region, located near the Mississippi River itself, were abandoned, and populations moved and built new mound sites on the region's inner routes: the Natchez Trace and Mississippi River tributaries.[23] Even later than this, many of these mound sites were abandoned, leading to the speculation that population losses had been sustained. Also during this terminal prehistoric period, additional populations were amalgamated with those that were already in place, populations that had migrated in from regions to the north and perhaps to the northwest. The conclusion of researchers is that what was reflected here was an initial "natural" decline followed by definite damage and reorganization as a result of disease.[24]

If this is a valid parallel, this important site on the lower Pearl River may have been related to the flowering of culture of the Plaquemine tradition, and it may have held sway in the region, dominating at least one and possibly several single-mound sites and several Plaquemine-related hamlets and farmsteads known from the east side of the river. This site may have lost importance as the centers of the Natchez Bluffs region declined, but almost certainly it was touched by contagion from exploratory coastwise landings beginning in 1519, and whatever population still remained in the area dispersed to the east and eventually to the northeast to become a part of the emerging Choctaw confederacy.

Having established that populations were available through both chiefdom decline and the aftermath of epidemic disease in the region in question, and having suggested a scenario for their inclusion in an emerging confederation, it is necessary to demonstrate that peoples from such historical backgrounds did in fact amalgamate within some believable time frame. This argument is strengthened if groups constituting the Choctaw can be shown to have come from places where these two processes were active. Such locational evidence comes from two sources: European documents and maps.

The two earliest Spanish maps reflecting interior exploration show so confused a notion of the hydrography and topography of the interior that only external evidence has permitted scholars to match the place names to those of historic tribes. It is the earlier map (*Mapa del Golfo y Costa de la Nueva España*), attributed to the specific evidence of the Hernando de Soto expedition, that seems the more accurate, and had the cartographer not assumed that the Rio de Flores emptied directly into the Gulf of Mexico, but had joined it instead to the next westward Rio de los Angeles, a fair representation of the Tombigbee/Alabama system would have been achieved, the Mississippi would have fallen into place as the Rio del Espiritu Santo, and the Pafalaya, Swanton's erstwhile Choctaws, would have landed neatly in Kemper County, Mississippi. But the "de Soto" map, by Alonso de Santa Cruz, is selective in its representation of place names, and the royal cartographer's successor, in describing the geography of the Southeast, enumerated the rivers as portrayed on the map, but mentioned no inland place names because, he claimed, too little was known about the geography of the interior.[25]

Because there was such a serious temporal gap between the observations upon which the early Spanish and the first French maps of the interior are based, and because during that hiatus native groups suffered the ravages of European epidemic disease, it is not surprising (if not very helpful for the purpose at hand) that they bear little resemblance to one another. The Spanish maps had little opportunity to improve over time, since they were essentially based upon the one deep penetration of the interior by de Soto's expedition. The French and British maps began with the Spanish information as a given, even though the situation had changed drastically; but because the exploration on which they were based was ongoing, they quickly showed radical changes reflecting the changes that actually had taken place. Yet the explorers, apparently unaware that these changes had occurred, continually railed against their predecessors for inaccuracy when they failed to find on the ground what the maps and historical narratives said should be there. Most of the time, what they failed to find was some named tribal group.

There is little doubt that at least something of the drastic locational changes of the protohistoric period must be reflected in the maps, but it is dangerous to generalize on the basis of them alone. Although the early

Spanish maps are so confused hydrographically, they are still used comparatively to suggest gross population movements. Taken on its face, both map and narrative evidence suggest that the Alabama shifted from north central Mississippi to the Alabama River between 1541 and 1700. Such evidence does indicate a real cultural link, but addition of the archaeological record reveals that the documentary evidence probably records a shift in nomenclature rather than population.[26]

Similar facts may also be reflected in early French maps. The most relevant example here is the Delisle manuscript map of 1701, which shows the Choctaw villages crowded around the Black Warrior River.[27] This "error" was quickly corrected in the Delisles' succeeding maps, but until an unequivocal source for the original piece of information is found, one must wonder whether some genuine Indian tradition had not reached the French to the effect that Choctaws had lived on the Black Warrior, since they were still disputing ownership of the Black Warrior Valley with the Alabamas in the nineteenth century.

Changes developing over a chronological sequence of maps are not always in the direction of increasing accuracy. Thus the Black Warrior River was so called by the Delisles from 1718 because someone, perhaps their source Le Maire, thought that was where de Soto had met Tascalusa. What may be its real name is preserved briefly on Delisle 1701 and 1703 as "les Aepaetaniche," where it is used to label the Coosa River.[28] Then the name is found on British maps as the name of the Black Warrior: Pedegoe, Pedoge, and Patagahatche. It may be no accident that some of the eastern Choctaw were known by the cognate term "Ayepategoula" ("Ayepat-people"), and this would fit well with the Delisles' 1701 nomenclature. But this name was all but submerged when they became the "Eastern Party" known to the French and English.[29] As to "Tascalusa," that name had disappeared entirely as the name of a people by the eighteenth century and is preserved only as a place name. The "Pafalaya" province and its accompanying town names were never used on European maps or documents reflecting new exploration after the seventeenth century.

Except for the narratives of the de Soto expedition, some of whose evidence has already been summarized, documentary evidence is sparse for the earliest period, a problem complicated by the fact that the name "Choctaw" does not even appear in the documents until 1675. The expedition of Tristán de Luna, coming barely twenty years after de Soto's, expected to find the interior of the Alabama-Georgia area just as de Soto had left it. Instead, they encountered the relatively small population of the Nanipacana, living in the Mobile delta region.[30] Other parties found the Escambia River deserted, and the final push to locate the Coosa chiefdom, guided by some de Soto veterans, found only a few small villages.[31] In 1566–68, Juan Pardo was sent inland from the new Spanish settlement at Santa Elena to establish Indian alliances and a link with Mexico. He was forced to turn back just beyond the Appalachians, but he learned that Coosa was the most important polity in the region, and Tascalusa was to be found beyond it.[32] Both expeditions apparently saw drastic population reductions, but it is not possible to determine how serious they were or whether mortality or population movement was the cause.

Bishop Calderón's 1674–75 pastoral visit to the Indian missions of Florida yielded a report to his queen enumerating the Indian provinces and missions, most of which he visited. He probably did not visit the unconverted Indians beyond the Apalachee province, but his report of the Choctaw, the first to mention that name, stated that they had 107 villages located 70 leagues from the Tawasa, or Upper Creeks. Of the Tawasa villages that Calderón listed, only a few can be recognized as related to the Alabamas (Muklasha, Pacana, Tawasa), and the Alabama themselves were not named, although they were certainly there. Calderón mentioned that the Mobilians were neighbors of the Choctaw, on an island near Espíritu Santo harbor (here identifying Mobile Bay). It is hard to judge the value of this information, although it is known that trade was being carried on with tribes to the west through Christianized Indians. The number of the Choctaw villages seems high, but it may include more groups than the French later included under the name, and it may indicate that after the disasters of the preceding century, the Choctaw had coalesced in their refuge area and were enjoying a thriving population.[33]

The French attempt at settlement of the Gulf Coast under Cavelier de La Salle in 1685–86 gave rise to considerable Spanish panic. In 1686, Marcos Delgado was sent westward to the Mississippi to establish a link with Mexico. Arriving among the Creeks (Tawasa) on the Alabama River, he heard of hostilities with the Mobilians to the west. Emissaries brought back chiefs of the Mobilian, Tohome, Ysachi, Yagusta, Canuca, and Guassa, five of whom he reported had fled from the English to the north or northeast. These men regretted that their crops had been too poor to provision his expedition, as they were subsisting on shellfish themselves, and beyond their lands the Choctaw, described as a large and dangerous nation, were hostile. At this news, Delgado gave up the journey and sent a letter to Mexico instead, but claimed that he had brought four villages of "Tawasa" into Spanish alliance: Muklasa, Alabama, Pacana, and Koasati.[34]

From Mexico, Enriquez Barroto and Antonio Romero sailed to look for La Salle in the same year. At Pensacola Bay, Pensacola Indians complained of dangerous wars with the Mobilians, whom they described as three strong villages of bellicose Indians located on Mobile Bay. Taking the Pensacolas' advice, Barroto sailed only a short way into Mobile Bay—from which vantage he saw numerous fires at night—and then continued on to the west.[35]

The fuller early French material offers a considerable amount of information as conveyed by the Indians themselves, but events preceding the late seventeenth century are invariably eclipsed by the intolerable pressure of slave raiding being carried out by English-allied Indians, especially the Chickasaws and Creeks. The worst of this slaving went on between 1698, when Thomas Welch established the Upper Path of the Carolina traders all the way to the Mississippi, and 1715, when the Yamasee War turned English attention elsewhere. The Choctaws welcomed the French because they offered firearms that could be used against the raiders.[36]

The Choctaw villagers of Chickasawhay specifically stated that they and the Conchas had fled westward to escape the persecutions of slave-raiding Indians allied with the English, and their close ties with the tribes of the Mobile delta, about which more will be said shortly, emphasize that link. The chief of the eastern village of Scanapa said that his old village had been destroyed, the men killed, and the women and children enslaved. Although Iberville observed numerous Indian sites abandoned due to disease on the lower Pascagoula in 1699, his brother Bienville reported that the abandoned sites of the Mobile delta were due to Alabama and Upper Creek wars on the inhabitants. From the French colonial beginnings, correspondence repeatedly reported (in 1706, 1708, 1709, 1712, and 1715) major raids on the Choctaws from the east. This pressure had surely pushed the Mobilians and Tohomes west of the lower Tombigbee, and it may have pushed some of their population to move westward and join the Choctaws prior to French contact, quite possibly at the Chickasawhays villages.[37]

Perhaps the most direct evidence of Choctaw origin to the northeast of their modern homeland is to be found in their claim to the Black Warrior Valley as late as 1816, when they ceded it by the Treaty of Fort St. Stephens.[38]

As to origins in other directions, there is some scant place name evidence to suggest the amalgamation of population remnants: specifically, the three towns of Yazoo, Abeka, and Ibitoupougoula, which are listed by Régis du Roullet as proper names with no meaning, and which are the names of other tribes, two from the Yazoo Basin and one from the Coosa River to the east.[39]

The hearsay of documentary testimony, however, can offer only an incomplete argument. More compelling evidence can perhaps be found in the patterns of culture, recorded unintentionally in document and artifact, that signalize ethnic identity.

The accepted wisdom in contemporary archaeology is that it is dangerous to attempt to identify ethnicity on the basis of archaeological evidence, just as it is dangerous to do so on the basis of linguistic evidence. Certainly it would be folly to attempt to identify ethnic groups on the basis of archaeology alone. In the case at hand, however, there is a variety of evidence to be considered.

The French documents offer a multitude of telling details, most of them drawn not only from French observation but from Choctaw explanation as well. Because of the observers' ethnocentricity and our own, this evidence must be used with care. The French terminology (for example, "race," "tribe," "caste") cannot be understood in its modern anthropological sense, but must be reinterpreted; certainly it indicates distinctions of some kind, but distinctions whose observation was conditioned by the French colonial experience.

For all Swanton's assertions about the existence of clans among the Choctaws before the nineteenth century, for example, there is nothing in the historical record to support it.[40] Considerable emphasis seems to have been placed instead upon the moieties, the Inholahta and Imoklasha. What I want to suggest here is that the moieties were in fact artifacts of the joining of two groups, the "original" simple chiefdom population that inhabited the "homeland" and the refugees from demographic disaster elsewhere, in much the same way as the Natchez handled incorporation of external groups by bringing them into their system as "stinkards." Among the Choctaws it was the moiety system that supported the integration of peoples into the confederacy.

The two moieties, or tribal halves, were traditionally ranked, according to several statements from Choctaw leaders.[41] The Inholahta was senior, or "elder brother," to the Imoklasha. But what is perhaps more significant, the Inholahta moiety was in its turn ranked junior to the Alabama tribe. In the light of this evidence, it is worth considering a passage from a 1708 letter of Thomas Nairne, Carolina Indian Commissioner:

Sir that at once you may have a notion of ye Indian Governmt and ye progression of on Village out of another, I'le Illustrate by an Example,

```
              C
      _____

  1                              2
      _____

      A        B     D    E
```

Suppose 1:2: to be a river, A: a populous flowrishing Town on ye river side, straightened for planting ground. Upon some disgust, or other reason 2 leading men lead out Colonies of 30 or 40 fameilies Each and sattle 2 new Villages B: C: Bechancing to florish and increase much, out of it by the same means arise D & E. Now the Villages D & E will respect A and all call it their grand father, B their father C their Elder Brother and these names continue by Tradition to be given them. According to these relations they'le give the Chiefs of these Villages respect and precidency in their Town houses. . . . If ye removeall be but a small way, they continue one nation . . . but if . . . they remove a great way they by degrees alter their Language & become an other people.[42]

The archaeological evidence suggests a long-term, large-scale analogy for this scheme: the Alabama of the Coosa-Talapoosa forks region were felt to be the "purest," original representative of the devolved Moundville chiefdom; the Inholahta Choctaw (Burial Urn groups from the Mobile River) a later separated group; and the Imoklasha Choctaw, the central Tombigbee people of the prairie related to the Chickasaws and Chakchiumas. This brings us to explore how these named moieties related to other tribal groups near the Choctaw.

We should begin with the Alabama, senior to the senior Choctaw moiety. There was strong and high-level marriage alliance between the Alabamas and certain groups of the Choctaws, most notably those who made up the easternmost groups, which seem to have been dominated by the Inholahta moiety.[43] These marriage alliances were made by an "export" of women, an unusual proceeding in societies where the usual practice was for the man to marry into his wife's household. What was accomplished by such a proceeding, however, was the creation of a situation in which a child still recognized as having the ethnic identity of his mother (and therefore the allied tribe) would grow up and gain rank within another tribe. Hence we have repeated statements about a certain rank enjoyed in one group by a man of another: Alibamon Mingo being considered a chief among the Alabamas and Alabama chief Tamatlemingo's "Choctaw" son being accorded all the respect of the nephew of a chief (the war chief of the Yanabés) among the Choctaws.[44]

There seems to have been a similar situation of marriage alliances between a faction of the western Choctaws and the Chickasaws. Much of the attachment of Red Shoe and his moiety allies of the Imoklasha for that tribe was cemented by marriage alliances. Ties were so close that just prior to the first Chickasaw war in 1736, the chief of the Ackia village group of the Chickasaws was proposing to settle among the Choctaws as a dependent village group to Couëchitto, Red Shoe's village.[45]

The function of the "divisions" observed within the tribe by Europeans is less clear. They were real enough: three relatively stable subgroupings of villages can be shown to have had political significance from 1702 to 1830. But they were not, or at least not solely, ethnic divisions. Quite obviously there was a physiographic mapping for them, but this also is only the obvious. The divisions were too complex to be accounted for by ethnic or physiographic factors alone, and several villages were recorded as belonging to different divisions at different times.

There were some very real cultural differences among the divisions, but these differences generally offset the eastern and western against the southern or Sixtowns. Certainly this seemed to be the case with language differences; the Sixtowns people were said to speak with a peculiar accent as late as the nineteenth century.[46] There is other, indirect evidence. When the western Choctaws went to visit the Chickasaws, no mention was made of any linguistic problems, whereas when the Alabama chief Tamatlémingo came to speak before an assembly of Choctaws dominated by western and Sixtowns people, he apologized for his rusty Choctaw.[47] Sumptuary habits seem to have varied from north to south as well: the dress and hair style distinctiveness of the Sixtowns people are cited in the literature. Choctaw incorporation of the scattered late Plaquemine populations in the Leaf River drainage and on the lower Pearl would explain much in this connection, since the Plaquemine peoples, including the Natchez and Taensa, spoke a distantly removed Western Muskogean language and were otherwise culturally distinct from the peoples of the Tombigbee/Alabama.

The divisions showed a clearer political focus than the moieties, and this was particularly evident in the matter of alliances. The Mobile River tribes, Tohome, Naniaba, and Mobilian, maintained links with the Chickasawhays. Between them, these groups and the Chickasawhays seem to have controlled the overland route of trade goods transport to the villages of Yowani and Chickasawhay during the French colonial period. Further, Lusser's census of 1730 listed these Mobile River groups as "Choctaws settled on the Mobile River."[48]

Scantier evidence suggests that there were at least tenuous links between the Choctaws of the south and the Choctaw speakers further south along the Pascagoula and Pearl rivers: the Pascagoulas and the Acolapissas. Iberville received his first detailed description of the Choctaws and their numbers from the Pascagoulas, whose chiefs offered escort to seek them.[49]

There is even less to go on in the case of the Natchez. Yet the most telling item is a very strong one: a map legend dating from Régis du Roullet's 1730 reconnaissance of the Pearl River. Across the Pearl, in a straight line with Natchez and the Mobile delta, is the line "Chemin des Natchez pratiqué par les Chactas" (road to the Natchez used by the Choctaws).[50] This road was seen crossing the Pearl by Régis, and he described it as a sunken path. The intensity of contact implied by that worn road perhaps explains the unwillingness of the French colonists to believe that at least the western Choctaws were not involved in the Natchez revolt.

Archaeology can give us one kind of evidence: patterned affinities. An archaeological culture is defined as a recurring set of styles, forms, and usages. When other evidence suggests that nonmaterial patterns are to be attached to these material patterns, as when a culture survives to be identified locationally as a living population having a name for itself, then something can be said about ethnicity, but not before.

The historic locations of the three divisions place them on three watersheds: the eastern Choctaws on tributaries to the Tombigbee; the western Choctaws on the Pearl and its northern tributaries; and the Chickasawhays and Sixtowns on the upper reaches of the Pascagoula River system. This would be an expected distribution of population archaeologically, since the Choctaws were practicing some floodplain agriculture. To the extent that survey has been carried out, the settlement pattern does not seem to exhibit any major concentration of population at any distance from a considerable stream. What is interesting is the documentary assertion of the divisional adherence to different watersheds. If the divisions originally had any ethnic differentiation, then this would make it very easy to identify such variance, since material culture would be expected to vary somewhat from one watershed to the other.[51]

Although the archaeological evidence is so far limited to surface survey and very little excavation, there seems to be some differentiation in ceramic tradition observed from one area to another. The Plaquemine pottery tradition is indigenous to the area between the Mississippi and the Pearl. It has a straight-line *in situ* development beginning with the Coles Creek tradition, moving through the Plaquemine, and flowering finally as the Natchezan in the historic period. The distinctive curvilinear multiline decorative motifs of late Plaquemine pottery bear a strong resemblance to some early types of Choctaw pottery before the combing technique was adopted, and its influence continued to be felt in some of the combed motifs. The Plaquemine influence seems particularly strong in the southern area, where not only the distinctive curvilinear incising occurs, but where other Natchez Bluffs area types—variants on Plaquemine Brushed and some of the Mazique Incised varieties—are also found, along with what appears to be genuine Fatherland Incised pottery, the marked Natchez type.[52] If the Choctaws incorporated late Plaquemine populations from loci like the Leaf River or the Pearl Mounds site, then this is just the distribution one would expect to find.

There is also evidence that the makers of Choctaw pottery had connections to the Alabama River tradition. Some of the rectilinear motifs as well as the less formal free-hand curvilinear patterns owe more to the Alabama River tradition than to the Natchezan.[53] This influence is most clearcut in the east of the Choctaw area, particularly in the region occupied by the eastern division and to a lesser extent among the Chickasawhays. This is all of the ceramic evidence we have to date, but it agrees completely with what was shown above about external alliances and affinities.

The Choctaw mortuary practice was the one cultural element that was remarked upon by all European observers: the body was scaffolded with food offerings until the flesh rotted; men belonging to a special class of "bone-pickers" then came to scrape the bones clean of the last remnants of flesh, after which the relatives and friends would hold a mourning feast; the bones would be bundled and enclosed in a basket or other container in a charnel house; at intervals the collective contents of the charnel house would be buried in a mound.[54] This was not an unusual practice for the Southeast, or indeed for North America; various of the elements of the Choctaw ceremonies can be matched all over the continent.

It is when we examine the elements of the Choctaw ritual structurally and compare them with similar practices of neighboring tribes that we see that the Choctaw mortuary program was by way of being a common denominator for other ceremonies across the Southeast. Victor Rogers's comparative research has shown that the Choctaw mortuary program shares many elements with those of the other tribes of the region.[55]

The clearest parallels can be sought in the practices of the "Choctaw-like" tribes found around the lower Mississippi in 1700: the Bayougoulas, the Oumas, and the Acolapissas. All three of these tribes were speakers of a language indistinguishable from Choctaw, and all three practiced scaffolding, secondary processing of the remains, and bundling in a charnel house.[56]

The Chickasaws, however close their relationship with the Choctaws may be alleged to have been, seem at first glance to have had a radically different burial custom. The dead were buried sitting up (which with the settling of earth became flexed) within the houses they had occupied, and from all evidences the houses continued to be occupied after the burial. All persons were treated the same in death; the only differentiation was in accompaniment with grave goods, since the Chickasaws included the decedent's most precious possessions with him in the grave. There were, however, circumstances under which the Chickasaw practice was identical with the Choctaw, and that was when someone died or was killed far from home. When that occurred, the decedent was scaffolded and his bones later collected for bundle burial at home. The archaeological evidence offers plentiful examples of both types of burial among the Chickasaws.[57]

In strong contrast stands the Natchez burial practice, often taken as representative of practice in a functioning Mississippian chiefdom.[58] Natchez ritual was different in detail if not in structure for elite and common classes. The common classes were treated in death precisely as the Choctaws were, except there is no report of a cadre of morticians. For the elite, on the other hand, things were rather different. First, they were buried in the earth, often under the floors of their houses or of the temple. Second, they were buried along with the retainers who were sacrificed at the time of their funerals. Third, they did not stay buried; after a time sufficient to allow for the rotting of the flesh, the bones were dug up, bundled, and enclosed in a basket or casket, to be kept in the temple. There is no statement whether the temple was also emptied periodically.[59]

The Creeks buried in much the same way as the Chickasaws, including the exceptional scaffolding and bundling, with the single difference that apparently the relatives of a dead person of the elite abandoned the house under which he was buried. This would tally with the Natchez practice of sometimes burning the house in which a particularly high-ranking person had lived.[60]

Put into context, then, the Choctaw burial program no longer seems a gruesome oddity but simply a tradition that survived an unusually long time. (See table 2.) In structure it replicates that of the Natchez common burial, almost as though the Choctaws adopted the common burial for

TABLE 2
Historic Burial Programs

Tribe	Secondary Processing	Social Differentiation	Retainer Sacrifice	Ossuary	Secondary Burial
Natchez	Y/N	Y	Y	Y	Y/N
Bayougoula	Y	Y	Y	Y	Y
Ouma	Y	Y	Y	Y	Y
Acolapissa	Y	N	N	Y	Y
Choctaw	Y	N	N	Y	Y
Creek	Y/N	N	N	N	Y/N
Chickasaw	Y/N	N	N	N	Y/N

everyone, while the Chickasaws adopted an attenuated version of the elite burial for everyone. Common is the operative word here, for these are basically egalitarian rites, although the mourning for persons of rank among the Choctaws dictated compulsory attendance by all the peers of the deceased. Differentiation in mortuary program is the hallmark of social differentiation, and by and large it marked ranked chiefdoms: the Natchez, Moundville, and the rest.[61] We would expect an undifferentiated program in the wake of the demise of chiefdoms, but what we would not expect is that the part of the program chosen would not be a simplified one.

This was perhaps a development begun by the post-Moundville people whose mortuary arrangements have proved nearly as interesting as the Choctaws'. For the Burial Urn or Alabama River groups, it was a gradual process, for these peoples initially seemed to choose burial program almost randomly, alternating flesh and secondary burials in the same vicinity. Over time, secondary burials grew in favor, and among groups on the Tombigbee, burial mounds even began to be made to hold them.[62] Unfortunately we do not know with certainty what burial program the Alabamas (as distinct from the Creeks) and the Chakchiumas followed, although it seems likely that they would be as much like that of the Choctaws as their common cultural heritage suggests.

Even if we agree that the Choctaws were a protohistoric, multiethnic confederacy, there is still a lot to be said about how that confederacy worked and why it was a viable response to the demographic alterations of the colonial period. The confederacy as a social form could be operated either as a segmentary tribe or as a more integrated polity, as the occasion allowed or demanded, and because of this it had enough flexibility to balance the tension between centralizing and decentralizing tendencies.

The centralizing tendencies were what brought the Choctaw together in the first place, and their survival until the present day demonstrates that these tendencies were obviously the stronger. Aside from the common stress of disease, an external pressure, that has already been mentioned, there were many internal factors that tended to draw these western Muskogeans together.

The first was a location that was peripheral to all of them and home to only a few. East central Mississippi had not been settled by the Mississippian chiefdoms because there was too little in the way of floodplain resources concentrated in one area; although there was obviously enough to support the large population that the Choctaws later gathered there, the population concentration and arrangement necessary for a chiefdom to maintain the communications essential to orderly, centralized functioning were impossible. Hence, not only did the confederation structure prove a flexible one for dealing with subsequent stresses, but in the region in question, it was the only structure that could hold the Choctaws together.

East central Mississippi became a refuge location in the wake of the shocks of European contact in the sixteenth century. Areas where no one had lived must have seemed safer to Indian populations than those where bodies lay unburied and towns abandoned. East central Mississippi was about as far from each of the major centers of prehistoric population as one could get; thus it was far from where disease had raged. It was far from surviving Indian populations, too—not only from major population concentrations, but also from the main hunting areas of those concentrations. The only one that could have impinged upon it in this way, the Bottle Creek polity, apparently was more oriented toward the marine resources of the Mobile delta and bay than toward upland hunting.[63] And during the sixteenth century, east central Mississippi was far from whites, as well. The French had not yet begun their push into the Mississippi Valley, and the Spaniards, after the failures of de Soto and Luna, seemed satisfied to develop their colonies slowly to the east and to the west.

The constituent peoples of the Choctaw participated in a common ethnic heritage that must have formed an immediate bond among them. All of them were speakers of western Muskogean languages, the central locus of which was apparently around the Mobile River, so that the Choctaw-related Mobilians lent their name to the koiné that apparently developed to facilitate trade.[64] These peoples would also have shared common traditions and beliefs, as Swanton's studies of their nineteenth-century descendants' oral tradition suggests. Finally, they shared with all Indians of the continent a common culture shock brought on by the debilitating effects of disease and the failure of native ideologies.

Not all of the centralizing mechanisms were preexisting, however, except as the way they were supposed to function was known. I refer here to the tribal sodalities that plainly had to be constructed during the formation of the confederacy. The moieties were perhaps most important and easiest to construct. In any dual division like the Choctaws', where the moieties serve the function of assuring exogamy, they set up an opposition between eligible and ineligible marriage partners. When a confederacy is being made up of diverse elements—and specifically in this case of a core group and incomers—an exogamous moiety arrangement is the quickest way to cement the groups together: in the first generation everyone will have a "foreign" son-in-law in the house, but by the third generation or so "foreign" will have become simply "marriageable." Or as Thomas Nairne observed, "establishing a Custome of not marrying in the same name or fameily seems at first to have been a politick contrivance to encrease Freindship and keep peace." [65]

The physiographic features of east central Mississippi dictated that three watersheds would share the population of the Choctaws, and the exigencies of communication and transportation meant that the political divisions that developed would map closely onto these physiographic divisions. The division was thus in a sense a sort of "subtribal" sodality that served to integrate the village groupings along one watershed.

There may have been other sodality-like groupings that cut across the Choctaw tribe. The argument for classical clans during the European colonial period is not based upon adequate evidence. Certainly there were strong lineages, but the evidence we see suggests that these lineages tended to cluster in a single locality rather than spreading out through the tribe, as was the case with Creek or Chickasaw clans. Swanton has also suggested that there were some sort of warrior classes, and if the fact that men who had not made a kill in battle were known as "stinkards" is indicative, there may have been some such notion, but it does not seem to have been a very systematic one. [66]

Yet in spite of the strength of the centralizing tendencies, there were certainly others to oppose them. Some were tendencies that spelled the intrinsic weakness of chiefdoms and would always be present in societies that had not built a state infrastructure; others stemmed from the specific history of these people joining together in this confederacy at this time.

Problems of the latter kind arose in conjunction with the constituent divisions' behavior toward external allies. External intertribal alliances were most frequently formed with ethnic groups genealogically or geographically related to the several divisions. Generally this would not present a problem, but inevitably a situation would arise when two external allies were themselves in conflict. One obvious source of friction could arise when the hunting grounds of two external allies bordered on one another. With separate Choctaw groups pledged to support conflicting allies, there was ample opportunity for internal strife among Choctaws.

The ambition of individuals to build personal power could also lead to decentralizing pressures. The literature on acculturation speaks of individuals who took it upon themselves to "broker" intercultural exchange; these individuals functioned within their social groups much like the "big-men," who had fostered exchange also with external groups. Anthropologists have argued that in theory big-men are a decentralizing force because they focus the tribe's energies around individual allegiance rather than institutional allegiance. Thus the big-man will foster factionalism within the larger tribe; he needs it to function at all. In a situation where a tribe is made up of several confederated groups, it is likely that the factions in question will arise around lineages that were once of greater significance before the confederation.[67]

In the case of the Choctaws during the colonial period, several case studies can establish this phenomenon beyond a doubt. The lifetimes of the men in question spanned the whole of the colonial period, and the activities of these big-men were apparent from the time of earliest contact with the French.

Alibamon Mingo was a chief of the eastern Choctaws, following Choucououlacta as chief of the Conchas and then rising through his own merit to become chief of the entire eastern division, eventually becoming spokesman for the whole nation by 1765.[68] Alibamon Mingo, true to his name (and perhaps to his breeding—note the remarks above about marriage alliances), wished at one point in the 1730s to establish for his people a position of neutrality that would allow them to play the French off against the English, as the Alabamas were doing in the environs of Fort Toulouse. To that end, he threw in with Red Shoe at this early period, when neither of them had a very large reputation or following, and for a short time he succeeded in establishing English trade among the eastern Choctaws. Later, however, it became obvious to him that in the long run the French would be more reliable (and perhaps less demanding) trading partners. He renounced the alliance almost entirely and turned on Red Shoe. Drafted rather reluctantly at first as leader of the pro-French faction in the Choctaw civil war, he attempted to keep Choctaws from getting killed as long as possible. But once fighting broke out in earnest, he was keen to see justice done and saw to it that at the end the most rebellious villages and faction chiefs were destroyed. After the civil war, Alibamon Mingo became a sort of grey eminence for his nation; in negotiations with the English after the cession of the French colony, his remarks were full of the irony, wisdom, and shrewdness to be expected of an elder statesman.

While Alibamon Mingo was clearly a white, or peace, chief, Red Shoe was just the opposite: a red, war chief. His rise was that of a self-made man, and more than any of the other men discussed here, he seems to have needed the broker's role to rise to prominence. As already mentioned, he was instrumental in establishing the early beginnings of an English trade for the western division, to whose chieftainship he seems to have acceded by the late 1730s after he made a name for himself in the Natchez wars (this too under European conditions). His following clearly consisted of his relatives and in-laws, and Indian spokesmen repeatedly emphasized that fact in a derogatory way. Yet he was able to manipulate the French and defy tradition to become permanent war chief of the nation and to receive a French medal. Apparently, he was able to kindle a great deal of enthusiasm among the younger men, but his personal magnetism was obviously the source of most of his power, since his faction and its influence seems to have fallen apart after his death, even before the conclusion of the civil war that was precipitated by his death.[69]

Fanimingo Tchaa, a chief of Seneacha, was more or less destined to be a broker; his name tells us that he served as fanimingo (foreign minister), perhaps to the nation, which meant in the Muskogean tradition that he had to serve the interests of external allies in the councils of his own people. He proved to be an inveterate dealer with the English, making several attempts not only to bring them to his village but to persuade them to set up warehouses, yet he held a French medal and received the corresponding presents as well, and did so concurrently for some time. There was no contradiction in this, since it was part of the duty of the fanimingo to receive presents from allies and then to take their part. Speeches by this man were, accordingly, ambivalent in their allegiance. In the end he died for his allegiance to English trade goods. Having brought English traders to his village at the height of the Choctaw civil war, he attacked pro-French Choctaws who had come to raid the Sixtowns and lost his life.[70]

Of these three men, it was the peace chief, Alibamon Mingo, who was figuratively as well as literally the survivor. Like the Choctaws as a whole, he learned to get along in the face of changing conditions and to take advantage of the traditional forms of sociopolitical organization to strengthen his position. Once past the turbulence of his younger years, he was the model of a peace chief, which meant that he was the model of a southeastern Indian male as well: strong, deliberative, and gracious to all. And once he rose to this eminence, he disappeared into the role, whether because he really did take advantage of it to seek his privacy or because European observers did not know how to distinguish the man from the role, we will never know. What we do know is that he was the architect of the period of Choctaw consolidation following the civil war and probably continued to be so as he guided policy in dealing with the English on favorable terms for the Choctaw.

It seems to me impossible to say anything significant about colonial period Choctaw history without dragging in the civil war. The war, which saw factions breaking apart on lines very strongly influenced by the moiety divisions, expressed what I believe was the fundamental fault line of multiethnicity that lay in the origins of the confederacy.

NOTES

The thesis argued in this paper is developed at greater length and detail in my volume entitled *Choctaw Genesis, 1500–1700*, forthcoming from the University of Nebraska Press.

1. See Swanton, *Social and Ceremonial Life of the Choctaw.*

2. See Parker, "Investigations at 1Su7"; Blitz, *Mississippi Choctaw Indians;* and Galloway, "Chickachae Combed Ceramics."

3. For the subsistence requirements of Mississippian agriculturists, see B. D. Smith, "Variation in Mississippian Settlement Patterns," 480–83, and for the limits on Mississippian settlement of the coastal plain, see Larson, *Aboriginal Subsistence,* 56–65.

4. Morton Fried, *Evolution of Political Society,* 109–84, and Service, *Primitive Social Organization,* 133–69.

5. Jonathan Friedman, "Tribes, States, and Transformations." The model has been applied to the data for the Moundville chiefdom in Christopher Peebles, "Paradise Lost, Strayed, and Stolen: Prehistoric Social Devolution in the Southeast" and "Rise and Fall of the Mississippian."

6. Marshall Sahlins, *Tribesmen;* for ranked lineages, see Fried, *Evolution,* 120–28; and Steponaitis, "Location Theory," has developed the notion of "Simple Chiefdom."

7. Larson, *Aboriginal Subsistence.*

8. Peebles and Kus, "Ranked Societies."

9. See Friedman, "Tribes, States, and Transformations" for this description of the devolution process. Archaeological correlates are discussed in Peebles, "Paradise Lost," and "Rise and Fall of the Mississippian"; Brain, "Late Prehistoric Settlement Patterning," 54–56; Williams and Brain, *Lake George Site,* 414–16; Sheldon, *Mississippian-Historic Transition,* 88. Brain, *Tunica Archaeology,* 319, has observed that in the lower Yazoo actual contact was directly responsible for devolution.

10. Dobyns has argued this thesis in *Their Number Become Thinned,* and Ramenofsky has explored its implications for the southwest in *Vectors of Death,* 42–71. See also Marvin T. Smith, "Aboriginal Depopulation in the Postcontact Southeast," this volume.

11. Curren, *Protohistoric Period,* 242–48.

12. McNeill, *Plagues and Peoples,* 44–45.

13. See Marvin Smith, *Archaeology of Aboriginal Culture Change in the Interior Southwest,* 54–58, for a summary, and Dobyns, *Their Number Become Thinned,* 254–59, for the fevers, but note that this evidence has been criticized severely by David Henige ("If Pigs Could Fly"). For the smallpox episode, see Dobyns, *Their Number Become Thinned,* 259–60. Dobyns has since suggested, in a 1990 presentation to the Society for American Archaeology, that the effects of this smallpox epidemic may not have been as serious in North America as it was in Mexico; see Dobyns, "New Native World," 543–44.

14. For the range of diseases carried by modern pigs and the details of their communicability to other animals and man, see Leman et al., *Diseases of Swine.*

15. Johnson and Sparks, "Protohistoric Settlement Patterns," 75–76. Jay John-

son, James Atkinson, and David Chase have been formulating this notion of a protohistoric "prairie culture" on the basis of protohistoric site distribution evidence on the Black Prairie in Mississippi and Alabama.

16. Mann, *Ceramics from the Pearl Mounds,* describes the impressive site that was its center.

17. See Peebles, "Paradise Lost," and "Rise and Fall of the Mississippian."

18. Peebles, "Paradise Lost," 30–31. See Ladurie, *Times of Feast, Times of Famine,* for the classic treatment of this phenomenon in Europe.

19. M. T. Smith, *Aboriginal Culture Change,* 65, makes the urn burial/epidemic disease connection. Curren, *Protohistoric Period,* 242–48, argues the case for devolution as a result of Spanish exploration.

20. Charles Hudson et al., "Coosa," outlines the arguments from the Spanish texts for the impressiveness of the chiefdoms of Coosa and Tascaluca.

21. For the implications of secondary processing, see Robert Hertz, *Death and the Right Hand,* 27–86, and Metcalf and Huntington, *Celebrations of Death,* 33–37. Ramenofsky, *Vectors of Death,* 23–24, discusses the archaeological correlates of contagion.

22. Mann, *Pearl Mounds,* reports on the ceramics distribution that justifies the dating of the end of the Pearl Mound site.

23. Brain, "Late Prehistoric Settlement Patterning," 356.

24. I. Brown, *Natchez Indian Archaeology,* 2, 188–96, and Ramenofsky, *Vectors of Death,* 42–71.

25. The two earliest maps are the so-called de Soto map of 1544 and the Chiaves map drawn from it and printed in Ortelius's atlas, both in Cumming, *The Southeast in Early Maps,* 113–17. On the limitations of the "de Soto" map, see Boston, "The 'De Soto' Map," 248.

26. See Atkinson, "Historic Contact Indian Settlement," and Marshall, "Lyon's Bluff Site," for evidence of Alabama-related populations and their continuity into the historic period. There is no archaeological evidence to support the assertion that these "Alabamas" west of the Tombigbee moved anywhere.

27. In Cumming, *Southeast in Early Maps,* 170–73.

28. Le Maire maps survive from 1716; see Cumming, *Southeast in Early Maps,* 184. For "les Aepaetaniche," ibid., 170–73.

29. The names Pedegoe, Pedoge, and Patagahatche are found on the maps of Crisp/Nairne 1711, Popple 1733, and Mitchell 1755, found respectively in Cumming, *Southeast in Early Maps,* 179–80, 198–200, and 223–24. For Ayepategoula, see Swanton, *Social and Ceremonial Life of the Choctaw,* 57, and Rowland, Sanders, and Galloway, *Mississippi Provincial Archives: French Dominion* (hereafter *MPA:FD*), 4: 276, 283.

30. Priestley, *Luna Papers,* contains the documentary evidence supporting this conclusion, which was the one Priestley himself drew; see Priestley, *Tristan de Luna,* 111.

31. Priestley, *Luna Papers,* 1: xxxviii. Paul Hoffman has suggested in planning sessions for a new colonial-period exhibit at the Mississippi State Historical Museum that these conflicting descriptions of Coosa by the de Soto chroniclers and the Luna soldiers may reflect "explorer" rhetoric vs. "settler" hard practicality rather than drastic population decline. See Hoffman, "Nature and Sequence," 52–53.

32. Chester DePratter, Hudson, and Smith, "Route of Juan Pardo's Explorations," 150.

33. Calderón, "A 17th Century Letter," and Hann, *Apalachee*, 189–90.

34. M. Boyd, "Expedition of Marcos Delgado."

35. Leonard, "Spanish Re-exploration."

36. Wright, *The Only Land They Knew*, 126–50, and William Snell, *Indian Slavery*, 63, give good summaries of the known evidence for British-sponsored slave raids. For the French promise of guns for Choctaws, see Galloway, "Henri de Tonti du Village des Chactas," 170.

37. The westward flight of Chickasawhays and Conchas is described in Baudouin to Salmon, Nov. 23, 1732, in Archives Nationales, Paris, Archives des Colonies (hereinafter AC), Series C13A, vol. 14, 182–96. The Scanapa chief's complaint is reported in Regis du Roullet Journal, 1729, in AC, Series C13A, vol. 12, 67–99. Blenville's observations of the Mobile delta are found in McWilliams, *Iberville's Gulf Journals*, 168–70. The constant raids on the Choctaws are mentioned in *MPA:FD*, 3: 34 et passim.

38. DeRosier, *Removal of the Choctaw Indians*, 37.

39. Archives Nationales, Paris, Archives Hydrographiques V. LXVII², No. 14–1, portfolio 135, document 21.

40. Swanton, *Social and Ceremonial Life of the Choctaw*, 79ff.

41. *MPA:FD*, 4: 125, 300. See Galloway, "Choctaw Factionalism and Civil War."

42. Nairne, *Muskogean Journals*, 62.

43. Galloway, "Choctaw Factionalism," 295–96.

44. Evidence with respect to Alibamon Mingo can be found in Noyan to Maurepas, Jan. 4, 1739, AC, Series C13A, vol. 24, 224–35v; for the Yanabe chief's nephew, see Beauchamp Journal, Oct. 19, 1746, AC, Series C13A, vol. 30, 222–40v.

45. Regis du Roullet to Perier, Feb. 21, 1731, AC, Series C13A, vol. 13, 173–80; see also Galloway, "Choctaw Factionalism," for a discussion of the moieties as factions.

46. Swanton, *Social and Ceremonial Life of the Choctaw*, 56.

47. *MPA:FD*, 4: 288.

48. Galloway, "Henri de Tonti du Village des Chactas,", and Regis du Roullet Journal, 1729, AC, Series C13A, vol. 12, 67–99. For Lusser's census, Lusser to Maurepas, Jan. 12–Mar. 23, 1730, Series AC, C13A, vol. 12, 100–134v.

49. Iberville, *Gulf Journals*, 141.

50. A reproduction of this map can be found in Rowland and *MPA:FD*, 1: facing page 154.

51. Blitz, *Mississippi Choctaw Indians*, 40–46, and Baudouin to Salmon, Nov. 23, 1732, AC, Series C13A, vol. 14, 182–96.

52. Moony, "Many Choctaw Standing," 47–48.

53. Parker, "Test Investigations at 1Su7," 70–72. This perception slightly contradicts Blitz, *Mississippi Choctaw Indians*, 51, who separates the rectilinear motifs but subsumes them under the Fatherland Incised type.

54. Swanton, *Social and Ceremonial Life of the Choctaw*, 170–94.

55. Rogers, "Choctaw Mortuary Ceremonialism."

56. See Iberville, *Gulf Journals*, 63, and Du Ru, *Journal*, 20, for the Bayougoulas; Du Ru, *Journal*, 26–27, for the Oumas; and McWilliams, *Fleur de Lys and Calumet*, 111, for the Acolapissas.

57. Swanton, *Chickasaw Indians*, 229–35, and Chambers, "Excavations in Lee County, 1936–7."

58. For example, by James Brown, in his paper "Dimensions of Status."

59. Swanton, *Indian Tribes of the Lower Mississippi Valley*, 138–57.

60. Swanton, *Social Organization and Social Usages*, 388–98.

61. See the papers in J. A. Brown, *Social Dimensions of Mortuary Practices,* especially James Brown, "The Dimensions of Status in the Burials at Spiro"; Lewis H. Larson, Jr., "Archaeological Implications of Social Stratification at the Etowah Site, Georgia"; and Christopher S. Peebles, "Moundsville and Surrounding Sites: Some Structural Considerations of Mortuary Practices, II."

62. Sheldon, *Mississippian-Historic Transition*, 80.

63. Stowe, "Pensacola Variant," 125.

64. The standard sources on the Mobilian jargon are Crawford, *Mobilian Trade Language,* and Drechsel, *Mobilian Jargon: Linguistic, Sociocultural, and Historical Aspects of an American lingua franca.*

65. Nairne to Izard, April 15, 1708, in Nairne, *Muskogean Journals*, 61.

66. Swanton, *Social and Ceremonial Life of the Choctaw*, 124.

67. I. W. Brown discusses the function of cultural brokers in *French-Indian Culture Contact*, 379–82. Bruce Smith discusses the factionalizing tendencies of big-men in "Archaeology of the Southeastern United States," 48–50.

68. See Alibamon Mingo's speech to the 1765 Choctaw Congress held by the British in Rowland, *Mississippi Provincial Archives: English Dominion*, 239–41.

69. See R. White, "Red Shoes."

70. See Galloway, " 'The Chief Who is Your Father'."

WORKS CITED

Adair, James. *Adair's History of the American Indians*. 1775. Reprint edited by Samuel Cole Williams. Johnson City, Tenn.: Watauga Press, 1930.

Akridge, Scott. "De Soto's Route in North Central Arkansas." *Field Notes: Newsletter of the Arkansas Archaeological Society* 211 (1986): 3–7.

Albornoz, Miguel. *Hernando de Soto: Knight of the Americas*. Translated by Bruce Boeflin. New York: Franklin Watts, 1986.

Alegre, Francisco Javier. *Historia de la Compañía de Jesús en Nueva España*. Vol. 1, Books 1–3 (1566–96). Bibliotheca Insituti Historici S.J. Vol. 9 [Original edition 1841–42. Mexico City.] Rome: Institutum Historicum S.J., 1956.

Alonso de Chaves y el libro de su "Espejo de Navegantes." Edited by Pablo Castañeda, M. Cuesta, and P. Hernandez. Madrid, 1977.

Anders, Gary C. "Theories of Underdevelopment and the American Indian." *Journal of Economic Issues* 14 (1980): 681–701.

Anderson, David G. "The Mississippian Occupation and Abandonment of the Savannah River Valley." *Florida Anthropologist* 43 (1990): 13–35.

———. "The Paleoindian Colonization of Eastern North America: A View from the Southeastern United States." In Kenneth B. Tankersley and Barry L. Isaac, editors, *Early Paleoindian Economies of Eastern North America*, 163–216. Research in Economic Anthropology, Supplement 5. Cincinnati: JAI Press, 1990.

———. "The Internal Organization of Chiefdom Level Societies on the Southeastern Atlantic Slope: An Examination of Ethnohistoric Sources." *South Carolina Antiquities* 17 (1985): 35–69.

Anderson, David G., David Hally, and James Rudolph. "The Mississippian Occupation of the Savannah River Valley." *Southeastern Archaeology* 5 (1986): 32–51.

Anderson, David G., and Joseph Schuldenrein. *Prehistoric Human Ecology Along the Upper Savannah River: Excavations at the Rucker's Bottom, Abbeville and Bullard Site Groups*. Atlanta: National Park Service, 1985.

Anghiera, Pietro Martiere d'. *Decadas del Nuevo Mundo*. Edited by Edmundo O'Gorman. 2 vols. Mexico City: Porrua, 1964.

———. *De Orbe Novo, the Eight Decades of Peter Martyr d'Anghera*. Translated by Francis M. MacNutt. 2 vols. New York: G. P. Putnam's Sons, 1912.

———. *De Orbe Nouo Petri Martyris ab Angleria Mediolanensis protonotarij Cesaris senatoria Decades*. Compluti: Michaelem D'Equia, 1530.

Archer, Gabriel. "Relatyon of the Discovery of Our River." In Philip L. Barbour, editor, *The Jamestown Voyages Under the First Charter*. 1607. The Hakluyt Society, ser. 2, vol. 136. Cambridge, 1969.

Arnade, Charles. *Florida on Trial, 1593–1602*. Coral Gables: University of Miami Press, 1959.

———. *The Siege of St. Augustine in 1702*. Gainesville: University of Florida Press, 1959.

Atkinson, James R. "The de Soto Expedition through North Mississippi in 1540–41." *Mississippi Archaeology* 22 (1987): 61–73.

———. "A Historic Contact Indian Settlement in Oktibbeha County, Mississippi." *Journal of Alabama Archaeology* 25 (1979): 61–82.

Avellaneda, Ignacio. *Los Sobrevivientes de la Florida: The Survivors of the de Soto Expedition*. Research Publications of the P. K. Yonge Library of Florida History, no. 2. Gainesville: University of Florida Libraries, 1990.

Ayala y Escobar, Juan de. Letter to the King, St. Augustine, April 18, 1717. Archivo General de Indias, Santo Domingo 843, Stetson Collection of the P. K. Yonge Library of Florida History of the University of Florida.

Badger, Reid R., and Lawrence A. Clayton, editors. *Alabama and the Borderlands, from Prehistory to Statehood*. University, Ala.: University of Alabama Press, 1985.

Balandier, Georges. *Political Anthropology*. London: The Penguin Press, 1967.

Bancroft, Hubert H. *History of Mexico*. 6 vols. San Francisco: 1883–88.

Bandera, Juan de la. "The 'Long' Bandera Relation." Translated by Paul E. Hoffman. In Charles Hudson, *The Juan Pardo Expeditions: Exploration of the Carolinas and Tennessee, 1566–1568*, 205–96. Washington, D.C.: Smithsonian Institution Press, 1990.

Barcía Carballido y Zuñiga, Andrés Gonzalez de. *Chronological History of the Continent of Florida*. 1723. Translated by Anthony Kerrigen. Gainesville: University of Florida Press, 1951.

Barker, Alex W. "Powhatan's Pursestrings: On the Meaning of Surplus in a Seventeenth Century Algonkian Chiefdom." In Alex Barker and Timothy Pauketat, editors, *Lords of the Southeast: Social Inequality and the Native Elites of Southeastern North America*. Archaeological Papers of the American Anthropological Association, no. 3. Washington, D.C.: American Anthropological Association, 1992.

Bartram, William. *Travels through North and South Carolina, Georgia, East and West Florida, the Cherokee Country, the Extensive Territories of the Muscogulges, or Creek Confederacy, and the Country of the Choctaws*. 1791. Reprint. New York: Penguin, 1988.

———. *The Travels of William Bartram*. Edited by Frances Harper. New Haven: Yale University Press, 1958.

Basehart, Harry W. "Ashanti." In David M. Schneider and Kathleen Gough, editors, *Matrilineal Kinship*. Berkeley: University of California Press, 1961.

Bernard-Bossu, Jean. *Travels in the Interior of North America. 1751–1762*. Translated and edited by Seymour Feiler. Norman: University of Oklahoma Press, 1962.

Beverley, Robert. *History and Present State of Virginia*. Edited by Louis B. Wright. Chapel Hill: University of North Carolina Press, 1947.

Biedma. See Hernandez de Biedma

Binford, Lewis R. "Archaeological and Ethnohistorical Investigation of Cultural Diversity and Progressive Development among Aboriginal Cultures of Coastal Virginia and North Carolina." Ph.D. dissertation, University of Michigan, 1964.

Bishop, Morris. *The Odyssey of Cabeza de Vaca.* New York: Century, 1933.

Blake, Alan. *A Proposed Route for the Hernando de Soto Expedition from Tampa Bay to Apalachee Based on Physiography and Geology.* Alabama de Soto Commission Working Papers, no. 2. Tuscaloosa: University of Alabama, State Museum of Natural History, 1987.

Blakely, Robert. "The Life Cycle and Social Organization." In Robert Blakely, editor, *The King Site: Continuity and Contact in Sixteenth-Century Georgia.* Athens: University of Georgia Press, 1988.

Blakely, Robert, and Bettina Detweiler-Blakely. "The Impact of European Diseases in the Sixteenth Century Southeast: A Case Study." *Midcontinental Journal of Archaeology* 14 (1989): 62–89.

Blanton, Dennis B. *Archaeological Data Recovery at Cultural Property GP-HK-08 in Hancock County, Georgia on the Wadley-Wallace Dam Section of the Plant Vogtle–Plant Scherer 500KV Electric Transmission Line Corridor.* Atlanta: Garrow and Associates, 1985.

Blitz, John H. *An Archaeological Study of the Mississippi Choctaw Indians.* Mississippi Department of Archives and History Archaeological Report no. 16. Jackson: Mississippi Department of Archives and History, 1985.

Bogan, Arthur E., and Richard R. Polhemus. "Faunal Analysis: A Comparison of Dallas and Overhill Cherokee Sustenance Strategies." In Richard R. Polhemus, editor, *The Toqua Site: A Late Mississippian Dallas Phase Town.* University of Tennessee Department of Anthropology Report of Investigation, no. 41. Knoxville, 1987.

Bolton, Herbert E., editor. *Arredondo's Historical Proof of Spain's Title to Georgia.* Berkeley: University of California Press, 1952.

Bolton, Herbert E., and Mary Ross. *The Debatable Land: A Sketch of the Anglo-Spanish Contest for the Georgia Country.* Berkeley: University of California Press, 1925.

Booker, Karen, Charles Hudson, and Robert Rankin. "Place Name Identification and Multilinguism in the Sixteenth-Century Southeast." *Ethnohistory* 39 (1992): 399–451.

Bost, David H. "History and Fiction: The Presence of Imaginative Discourse in Some Historical Narratives of Colonial Spanish America." Ph.D. dissertation, Vanderbilt University, 1982.

Boston, Barbara. "The de Soto Map." *Mid-America* 23 (1941): 236–50.

Boulding, Kenneth E. *Three Faces of Power.* Newbury Park, California: Sage Publications, 1989.

Bourne, Edward G., editor. *Narratives of the Career of Hernando de Soto.* 2 vols. New York: Allerton, 1904.

Boyd, Clifford C., and Gerald F. Schroedl. "In Search of Coosa." *American Antiquity* 52 (1987): 840–44.

Boyd, Donna C. M. "A Comparison of Mouse Creek Phase to Dallas and Middle Cumberland Culture Skeletal Remains." In Janet E. Levy, editor, *Skeletal Analysis in Southeastern Archaeology.* Raleigh: North Carolina Archaeological Council, 1986.

Boyd, Mark F. "Fort San Luis: Documents Describing the Tragic End of the Mission Era." In Mark F. Boyd, Hale G. Smith, and John W. Griffin, editors, *Here They Once Stood: The Tragic End of the Apalachee Missions*. Gainesville: University of Florida Press, 1951.

———. "The Expedition of Marcos Delgado from Apalache to the Upper Creek Country in 1686." *Florida Historical Quarterly* 16 (1937): 1–32.

Boyd, Mark F., Hale G. Smith, and John W. Griffin, editors. *Here They Once Stood. The Tragic End of the Apalachee Missions*. Gainesville: University of Florida Press, 1951.

Bradley, James W. *Evolution of the Onondaga Iroquois: Accommodating Change. 1500–1655*. Syracuse: Syracuse University Press, 1987.

Brain, Jeffrey P. "Introduction: Update of de Soto Studies Since the United States de Soto Expedition Commission Reports." In John R. Swanton, editor, *Final Report of the United States de Soto Expedition Commission*. Washington, D.C.: Smithsonian Institution Press, 1985.

———. "Late Prehistoric Settlement Patterning in the Yazoo Bluffs Region of the Lower Mississippi Valley." In Bruce D. Smith, editor, *Mississippian Settlement Patterns*. New York: Academic Press, 1978.

———. *Tunica Archaeology*. Vol. 78. Cambridge, Mass.: Peabody Museum of Archaeology, 1988.

Brasser, T. J. "The Coastal Algonquians: People of the First Frontiers." In Eleanor Burke Leacock and Nancy Oestreich Lurie, editors, *North American Indians in Historical Perspective*. New York: Random House, 1971.

Braun, David P. "Illinois Hopewell Burial Practices and Social Organization: A Reexamination of the Klunk-Gibson Mound Group." In Brose and Greber, editors, *Hopewell Archaeology: The Chillicothe Conference*. Kent, Ohio: Kent State University Press, 1979.

Braun, David P., and Stephen Plog. "Evolution of 'Tribal' Social Networks: Theory and Prehistoric North American Evidence." *American Antiquity* 47 (1982): 504–25.

Braund, Kathryn E. Holland. "Mutual Convenience–Mutual Dependences: The Creeks, Augusta, and the Deerskin Trade, 1733–1783." Ph.D. dissertation, Florida State University, 1986.

Brose, David S., and N'omi Greber, editors. *Hopewell Archaeology: The Chillicothe Conference*. Kent, Ohio: Kent State University Press, 1979.

Brown, Antoinette B. "Diet and Nutritional Stress." In Robert L. Blakely, editor, *The King Site: Continuity and Contact in Sixteenth-Century Georgia*. Athens: University of Georgia Press, 1988.

Brown, Ian W. "The Calumet Ceremony in the Southeast and Its Archaeological Manifestations." *American Antiquity* 54 (1989): 311–31.

———. *Natchez Indian Archaeology: Culture Change and Stability in the Lower Mississippi Valley*. Mississippi Department of Archives and History Archaeological Report no. 15. Jackson: Mississippi Department of Archives and History, 1985.

———. "Early 18th Century French-Indian Culture Contact in the Yazoo Bluffs Region of the Lower Mississippi Valley." Ph.D. dissertation, Brown University, 1979.

Brown, James A. "Long-term Trends to Sedentism and the Emergence of Complexity in the American Midwest." In T. Douglas Price and James A. Brown, editors, *Prehistoric Hunter-Gatherers: The Emergence of Cultural Complexity.* Orlando: Academic Press, 1985.

———. "The Southern Cult Reconsidered," *Midcontinental Journal of Archaeology* 1 (1976): 115–35.

———. "The Dimensions of Status in the Burials at Spiro." In James A. Brown, editor, *Approaches to the Social Dimensions of Mortuary Practices.* Memoirs of the Society for American Archaeology, no. 25. Washington, D.C.: Society for American Archaeology, 1971.

———, editor. *Approaches to the Social Dimensions of Mortuary Practices.* Memoirs of the Society for American Archaeology, no. 25. Washington, D.C.: Society for American Archaeology, 1971.

Brown, M. L. *Firearms in Colonial America.* Washington, D.C.: Smithsonian Institution Press, 1980.

Bullen, Ripley P., and James B. Stoltman, editors. *Fiber-Tempered Pottery in Southeastern United States and Northern Columbia: Its Origins, Context, and Significance.* Florida Anthropological Society Publications, no. 6. Gainesville, 1972.

Bushnell, Amy Turner. "Ruling 'the Republic of Indians' in Seventeenth-Century Florida." In Peter H. Wood, Gregory A. Waselkov, and M. Thomas Hatley, editors, *Powhatan's Mantle, Indians in the Colonial Southeast.* Lincoln: University of Nebraska Press, 1989.

———. *Santa María in the Written Record.* Miscellaneous Project Report Series, no. 21. Gainesville: Florida Museum of Natural History, 1986.

———. *The King's Coffer: Proprietors of the Spanish Florida Treasury, 1565–1702.* Gainesville: University of Florida Press, 1981.

———. "Patricio de Hinachuba: Defender of the Word of God, the Crown of the King, and the Little Children of Ivitachuco." *American Indian Culture and Research Journal* 3, no. 3 (1979): 1–21.

———. "That Demonic Game: The Campaign to Stop Indian Pelota Playing in Spanish Florida, 1675–1684." *The Americas* 35 (1978): 1–19.

———. "The Menéndez-Marquez Cattle Barony at La Chua and the Determinants of Economic Expansion in 17th Century Florida." *Florida Historical Quarterly* 56 (1978): 407–31.

Cabeza de Vaca, See Núñez Cabeza de Vaca.

Caldwell, Joseph R. "Investigations at Rood's Landing, Stewart County, Georgia." *Early Georgia* 2 (1955): 22–49.

Caldwell, Joseph R., and Catherine McCann. *Irene Mound Site, Chatham County, Georgia.* Athens: University of Georgia Press, 1941.

Canner, Thomas. "A Relation of the Voyage Made to Virginia in the Elizabeth of London . . . in the Yeere 1603." In Samuel Purchas, editor, *Hakluytus Posthumus or Purchas His Pilgrimes,* vol. 18, 329–35. Glasgow: James MacLehose and Sons, 1904–6.

Capilla, Joan Baptista de. Letter to the King, St. Augustine, November 4, 1609. Archivo General de Indias, Santo Domingo 224, Woodbury Lowery Collection, reel 3, Florida State University Library copy.

Carneiro, Robert L. "The Chiefdom: Precursor of the State." In Grant Jones and Robert Katz, editors, *The Transition to Statehood in the New World.* Cambridge: Cambridge University Press, 1981.

———. "A Theory of Origin of the State." *Science* 169 (1970): 733–38.

Carroll, Bartholomew Rivers, editor, *Historical Collections of South Carolina.* New York: Harper and Row, 1836.

Cashin, Edward. " 'But Brothers, It is Our Land We are Talking About': Winners and Losers in the Georgia Backcountry." In Ronald Hoffman, Thad W. Tate, and Peter J. Albert, editors, *An Uncivil War: The Southern Backcountry During the American Revolution.* Charlottesville: University Press of Virginia, 1985.

Cassidy, Claire M. "Comparison of Nutrition and Health in Preagricultural and Agricultural Amerindian Skeletal Populations." Ph.D. dissertation, University of Wisconsin, 1972.

Castillo, E. D. "The Native Response to the Colonization of Alta California." In David Hurst Thomas, editor, *Columbian Consequences.* Vol. 1, *Archaeological and Historical Perspectives on the Spanish Borderlands West.* Washington, D.C.: Smithsonian Institution Press, 1989.

Chagnon, Napoleon. "Genealogy, Solidarity, and Relatedness: Limits to Local Group Size and Patterns of Fissioning in an Expanding Population." *Yearbook of Physical Anthropology, 1975* 19 (1976): 95–110.

———. "Social Causes for Population Fissioning: Tribal Social Organization and Genetic Microdifferentiation." In G. A. Harrison and A. J. Boyce, editors, *The Structure of Human Populations.* Oxford: Clarendon Press, 1972.

Chambers, Moreau B. C. "Field Notes, Excavations in Lee County, 1936–37." Mississippi Department of Archives and History, Jackson, Record Group 31, vol. 218.

Chapman, Jefferson, Hazel R. Delcourt, and Paul A. Delcourt. "Strawberry Fields, Almost Forever: Generations of Prehistoric Native Americans Transformed the Landscape of Eastern Tennessee." *Natural History* 9 (1989): 50–59.

Chardon, Roland. "Response to Eubanks." *Florida Anthropologist* 43 (1990): 43–44.

———. "The Elusive Spanish League: A Problem of Measurement in Sixteenth-Century New Spain." *Hispanic American Historical Review* 60 (1980): 294–302.

———. "The Linear League in North America." *Annals of the Association of American Geographers.* 70 (1980): 129–53.

Cherry, J. F. "Power in Space: Archaeological and Geographical Studies." In J. M. Wagstaff, editor, *Landscape and Culture: Geographical and Archaeological Perspectives.* Oxford: Basil Blackwell, 1987.

Cheves, Langdon, editor. "The Shaftesbury Papers and Other Records Relating to Carolina and the First Settlement on Ashley River Prior to the Year 1676." *Collections of the South Carolina Historical Society* 5 (1897): 1–523. Charleston.

Chiefs of Apalachee. Letter to the King, San Luis de Abalachi, 21st Day of the Moon that is called January, 1688. Translation from Apalachee to Spanish by Fray Marcelo de San Joseph. Archivo General de Indias, Santo Domingo 839, Stetson Collection of the P. K. Yonge Library of Florida History of the University of Florida.

Chipman, Donald. "In Search of Cabeza de Vaca's Route Across Texas: An Historiographical Survey." *Southwestern Historical Quarterly* 91 (1987): 127–48.

Chmurny, William W. "The Ecology of the Middle Mississippian Occupation of the American Bottom." Ph.D. dissertation, University of Illinois, 1973.

Clausen, Carl J., A. D. Cohen, Cesare Emiliani, J. A. Holman, and J. J. Stipp. "Little Salt Spring, Florida: A Unique Underwater Site." *Science* 203 (1979): 609–14.

Cockrell, Wilburn A., and Larry Murphy. "Pleistocene Man in Florida." *Archaeology of Eastern North America* 6 (1978): 1–12.

Coker, William S., and Thomas Watson. *Indian Traders of the Southeastern Spanish Borderlands, Panton, Leslie and Company, 1783–1847.* Pensacola: University of West Florida Press, 1986.

Colección de documentos inéditos relativos al descubrimiento, conquista, y organización de las antiguas posesiones españolas de América y Oceanía, sacados de los archivos del reino y muy especialmente del de Indias. Edited by Joaquín Pacheco, Francisco de Cardenas, and Luis Torres de Mendoza. 42 vols. Madrid, 1864–84.

Cook, Sherburne F. *Prehistoric Demography.* Addison-Wesley Modular Publications, module 16. Reading, Mass., 1972.

Cook, Sherburne F., and Woodrow Borah. *The Indian Population of Central Mexico, 1531–1610.* Berkeley: University of California Press, 1960.

Corkran, David H. *The Creek Frontier. 1540–1783.* Norman: University of Oklahoma Press, 1967.

Covey, Cyclone. *Cabeza de Vaca's Adventures in the Unknown Interior of America.* New York: Collier, 1961.

Covington, James W. "Apalachee Indians, 1704–1763." *Florida Historical Quarterly* 50 (1972): 366–84.

———. "The Apalachee Indians Move West." *Florida Anthropologist* 17 (1964): 221–25.

———, editor. *Pirates, Indians, and Spaniards: Father Escobedo's La Florida.* St. Petersburg, Fla.: Great Outdoors Publishing Company, 1963.

Cowdrey, Albert E. *This Land, This South: An Environmental History.* Lexington: University Press of Kentucky, 1983.

Crane, Verner W. *Southern Frontier.* Durham: Duke University Press, 1928.

Crawford, James. *The Mobilian Trade Language.* Knoxville: University of Tennessee Press, 1978.

———. "Southeastern Indian Languages." In James M. Crawford, editor, *Studies in Southeastern Indian Languages.* Athens: University of Georgia Press, 1975.

Crook, Morgan R., Jr. *Mississippi Period Archaeology of the Georgia Coastal Zone.* Georgia Archaeological Research Design Papers, no. 1. Laboratory of Archaeology Series Report no. 23. Athens: University of Georgia Department of Anthropology, 1986.

Crosby, Alfred W. *The Columbian Exchange.* Westport, Conn.: Greenwood Press, 1972.

Crumley, Carol L. *Celtic Social Structure: The Generation of Archaeologically Testable Hypotheses from Literary Evidence.* University of Michigan Museum of Anthropology Papers, no. 54. Ann Arbor: University of Michigan, 1974.

Cumming, William P. *The Southeast in Early Maps with an Annotated Check List of Printed and Manuscript Regional and Local Maps of Southeastern North America.* Princeton: Princeton University Press, 1958.

Cumming, W. P. "French, Spanish, and English Attempts to Colonize the East Coast before 1600." In W. P. Cumming, R. A. Skelton, and D. B. Quinn, editors, *The Discovery of North America.* New York: American Heritage Press, 1971.

Curren, Caleb. *The Protohistoric Period in Central Alabama.* Camden, Ala.: Alabama-Tombigbee Regional Commission, 1984.

Curren, Caleb, Keith J. Little, and Harry O. Holstein. "Aboriginal Societies Encountered by the Tristán de Luna Expedition." *Florida Anthropologist* 42 (1989): 381–95.

Davenport, Harbert, editor. "The Expedition of Panfilo de Narvaez by Gonzalo Fernandez de Oviedo y Valdés." *Southwestern Historical Quarterly.* 27 (1923): 120–39, 217–41, 276–304; 28 (1924): 56–74, 122–63.

Davis, Dave D. *Perspective on Gulf Coast Prehistory.* Ripley P. Bullen Monographs in Anthropology and History, no. 5. Gainesville: University Presses of Florida, 1984.

Davis, William W. H. *Spanish Conquest of New Mexico.* Doylestown, Penn., 1869.

Deagan, Kathleen A. "Cultures in Transition: Fusion and Assimilation Among the Eastern Timucua." In Jerald T. Milanich and Samuel Proctor, editors, *Tacachale: Essays on the Indians of Florida and Southeastern Georgia During the Historic Period.* Ripley P. Bullen Monographs in Anthropology and History, no. 1. Gainesville: University Presses of Florida, 1978.

———. "Fig Springs: The Mid-Seventeenth Century in North-Central Florida." *Historical Archaeology* 6 (1972): 23–46.

Debo, Angie. *The Road to Disappearance.* Norman: University of Oklahoma Press, 1941.

Decker, Deena S. "Origin(s), Evolution, and Systematics of *Cucurbita pepo* (Cucurbitaceae)." *Economic Botany* 42 (1988): 3–15.

DeJarnette, David, and Asael T. Hansen. *The Archaeology of the Childersburg Site, Alabama.* Tallahassee: Florida State University Notes in Anthropology, 1960.

DePratter, Chester B. *Late Prehistoric and Early Historic Chiefdoms in the Southeastern United States.* New York: Garland Publishing, 1991.

———. "Cofitachequi: Ethnohistorical Sources and Archaeological Evidence." In Albert C. Goodyear, II, and Glenn T. Hanson, editors, *Studies in South Carolina Archaeology: Essays in Honor of Robert L. Stephenson.* Columbia, S.C.: Institute of Archaeology and Anthropology, 1989.

———, editor. "Explorations in the Interior South Carolina by Hernando de Soto (1540) and Juan Pardo (1566–1568)." *South Carolina Institute of Archaeology and Anthropology Notebook* 19 (1987): 1–61.

———. "Adamson Site (38KE11)." *South Carolina Institute of Archaeology and Anthropology Notebook* 17 (1985): 37.

———. "1985 Archaeological Field School: Mulberry Site (38KE12), South Carolina." *South Carolina Institute of Archaeology and Anthropology Notebook* 17 (1985): 31–36.

———. "Late Prehistoric and Early Historic Chiefdoms in the Southeastern United States." Ph.D. dissertation, University of Georgia, 1983.

DePratter, Chester, Charles Hudson, and Marvin T. Smith. "The Juan Pardo Expeditions: North from Santa Elena." *Southeastern Archaeology* 9 (1990): 140–46.

———. "The Hernando de Soto Expedition: From Chiaha to Mabila." In Reid R. Badger and Lawrence A. Clayton, editors, *Alabama and the Borderlands, from Prehistory to Statehood.* Tuscaloosa: University of Alabama Press, 1985.

———. "The Route of Juan Pardo's Explorations in the Interior Southeast, 1566–1568." *Florida Historical Quarterly* 62 (1983): 125–58.

DePratter, Chester, and Marvin T. Smith. "Sixteenth Century European Trade in the Southeastern United States: Evidence from the Juan Pardo Expeditions (1566–1568)." In Henry F. Dobyns, editor, *Spanish Colonial Frontier Research.* Albuquerque: Center for Anthropological Research, 1980.

DeRosier, Arthur H. *The Removal of the Choctaw Indians.* Knoxville: University of Tennessee Press, 1970.

Detweiler-Blakely, Bettina. "Stress and the Battle Casualties." In Robert L. Blakely, editor, *The King Site: Continuity and Contact in Sixteenth-Century Georgia.* Athens: University of Georgia Press, 1988.

De Vorsey, Louis. "The Colonial Georgia Backcountry." In Edward J. Cashing, editor, *Colonial Augusta: "Key of the Indian Country."* Macon, Ga.: Mercer University Press, 1986.

Dickens, Roy S. *Cherokee Prehistory.* Knoxville: University of Tennessee Press, 1976.

Dickinson, Jonathan. *Jonathan Dickinson's Journal: or, God's Protecting Providence.* Edited by Evangeline Andrews and Charles Andrews. New Haven: Yale University Press, 1945. Reprint. Stuart, Fla.: Southeastern Printing, 1981.

Dobyns, Henry F. "New Native World: Links between Demographic and Cultural Changes." In David Hurst Thomas, editor, *Columbian Consequences.* Vol. 3, *The Spanish Borderlands in Pan-American Perspective.* Washington, D.C.: Smithsonian Institution Press, 1991.

———. *Their Number Become Thinned: Native American Population Dynamics in Eastern North America.* Knoxville: University of Tennessee Press, 1983.

———. "Estimating Aboriginal American Population: An Appraisal of Techniques with a New Hemispheric Estimate." *Current Anthropology* 7 (1966): 395–416.

———. "An Outline of Andean Epidemic History to 1720." *Bulletin of the History of Medicine* 37 (1963): 493–515.

Documents Ancillary to the Vaca Journey. Translated by Basil C. Hedrick and Carroll L. Riley. Carbondale: University Museum, Southern Illinois University, 1976.

Doster, James F. *The Creek Indians and Their Florida Lands, 1740–1823.* 2 vols. New York: Garland, 1974.

Douglas, Mary. "Is Matrilineality Doomed in Africa?" In Mary Douglas and Phyllis M. Kaberry, editors, *Man in Africa.* Garden City: Doubleday, 1971.

Drechsel, Emanuel. *Mobilian Jargon: Linguistic, Sociocultural, and Historical Aspects of an American lingua franca.* Ph.D. dissertation, University of Wisconsin, 1979.

Du Ru, Paul. *Journal of Paul Du Ru.* Edited and translated by Ruth Lapham Butler. Chicago: Caxton Club, 1934.

Dye, David H., and Cheryl Anne Cox, editors, *Towns and Temples along the Mississippi.* Tuscaloosa: University of Alabama Press, 1990.

Dyson, S. *The Creation of the Roman Frontier.* Princeton: Princeton University Press, 1985.

Earle, Timothy K. "The Evolution of Chiefdoms." *Current Anthropology* 30 (1989): 84–88.

———. "Chiefdoms in Archaeological and Ethnohistoric Perspective." *Annual Review of Anthropology* 16 (1987): 279–308.

———. "A Model of Subsistence Change." In Timothy K. Earle and Andrew Christenson, editors, *Modeling Change in Prehistoric Subsistence Economies.* New York: Academic Press, 1980.

———. "A Reappraisal of Redistribution." In Timothy K. Earle and Jonathan Ericson, editors, *Exchange Systems in Prehistory.* New York: Academic Press, 1977.

Early, Ann M. "Caddoan Settlement Systems in the Ouachita River Basin." In Neal L. Trubowitz and Marvin D. Jeter, editors, *Arkansas Archaeology in Re-*

view. Arkansas Archeological Survey Research Series, no. 15. Fayetteville, 1982.

Elliot, Daniel T. "Finch's Survey." *Early Georgia* 9 (1981): 14–24.

Elvas, Gentleman of. "True Relation of the Vicissitudes that Attended the Governor Don Hernando de Soto and Some Nobles of Portugal in the Discovery of the Province of Florida." Translated by Buckingham Smith. In E. G. Bourne, editor, *Narratives of the Career of Hernando de Soto*, vol. 1. New York: Allerton, 1904.

Eubanks, W. S., Jr. "Studying de Soto's Route: A Georgia House of Cards." *Florida Anthropologist* 42 (1989): 369–80.

Ewan, Joseph, and Nesta Ewan. *John Banister and His Natural History of Virginia. 1678–1692.* Urbana: University of Illinois Press, 1970.

Ewen, Charles R. "Soldier of Fortune: Hernando de Soto in the Territory of the Apalachee, 1539–1540." In David Hurst Thomas, editor, *Columbian Consequences.* Vol. 2, *Archaeological and Historical Perspectives on the Spanish Borderlands East.* Washington, D.C.: Smithsonian Institution Press, 1990.

——— . *The Discovery of de Soto's First Winter Encampment in Florida.* Alabama de Soto Commission Working Papers, no. 7. Tuscaloosa: University of Alabama, State Museum of Natural History, 1988.

Fairbanks, Charles H. "Some Problems of the Origin of Creek Pottery." *Florida Anthropologist* 11 (1958): 53–64.

——— . "Creek and Pre-Creek." In James B. Griffin, editor, *Archaeology of Eastern United States.* Chicago: University of Chicago Press, 1952.

Farnsworth, Kenneth B., and Thomas E. Emerson, editors. *Early Woodland Archeology.* Kampsville, Ill.: Center for American Archaeology Press, 1986.

Fausz, J. Frederick. "Patterns of Anglo-Indian Aggression and Accommodation Along the Mid-Atlantic Coast, 1584–1634." In William Fitzhugh, editor, *Cultures in Contact: The Impact of European Contacts on Native American Cultural Institutions, A.D. 100–1800.* Washington, D.C.: Smithsonian Institution Press, 1985.

——— . "Fighting 'Fire' with Firearms: The Anglo-Powhatan Arms Race in Early Virginia." *American Indian Culture and Research Journal* 3 (1979): 33–50.

Feest, Christian F. "Seventeenth Century Virginia Algonquian Population Estimates." *Quarterly Bulletin of the Archeological Society of Virginia* 28 (1973): 66–79.

Ferguson, Leland, editor. "Archaeological Investigations at the Mulberry Site." *South Carolina Institute of Archaeology and Anthropology Notebook* 6 (1974).

——— . "Exploratory Archaeology at the Scott's Lake Site (38CR1), Santee Indian Mound—Ft. Watson, Summer 1972." *South Carolina Institute of Archaeology and Anthropology Research Manuscript Series*, no. 36 (1973).

——— . "Mulberry Plantation Exploratory Archeology." *South Carolina Institute of Archaeology and Anthropology Research Manuscript Series*, no. 54 (1973).

Fernández de Florencia, Juan. Letter to Pablo de Hita Salazar, San Luis, August 30, 1678. Archivo General de Indias, Santo Domingo 226, Woodbury Lowery Collection, reel 4.

Fernández de Olivera, Juan. Letter to the King, St. Augustine, October 13, 1612. Archivo General de Indias, Santo Domingo 229, Woodbury Lowery Collection, reel 3.

Fish, Suzanne K., and Richard W. Jefferies. "The Site Plan at Cold Springs, 9Ge10." *Early Georgia* 11 (1983): 61–73.

Floyd, Troy. *The Columbus Dynasty in the Caribbean, 1492–1526.* Albuquerque: University of New Mexico, 1973.

Fogelson, Raymond D. "Who Were the Aní Kuatani? An Excursion into Cherokee Historical Thought." *Ethnohistory* 31 (1984): 255–63.

Fontaneda, Hernando d'Escalante. *Memoir of Do. d'Escalante Fontaneda Respecting Florida.* Translated by Buckingham Smith, annotated by David True. Miami, Fla.: Greater Miami Bicentennial Project, 1976.

Ford, Richard I. "Gathering and Gardening: Trends and Consequences of Hopewell Subsistence Strategies." In David S. Brose and N'omi Greber, editors, *Hopewell Archaeology: The Chillicothe Conference.* Kent, Ohio: Kent State University Press, 1979.

———. "Evolutionary Ecology and the Evolution of Human Ecosystems: A Case Study from the Midwestern U.S.A." In James N. Hill, editor, *Explanation of Prehistoric Change.* Albuquerque: University of New Mexico Press, 1977.

Fortes, Meyer. "Kinship and Marriage Among the Ashanti." In A. R. Radcliff-Brown and Daryll Forde, editors, *African Systems of Kinship and Marriage.* London: Oxford University Press, 1950.

Fowler, Melvin L. "Cahokia and the American Bottom: Settlement Archaeology." In Bruce D. Smith, editor, *Mississippian Settlement Patterns.* New York: Academic Press, 1978.

Fox, Robin. *Kinship and Marriage.* Baltimore: Penguin, 1967.

Frank, Andre Gunder. *Capitalism and Underdevelopment in Latin America.* New York: Monthly Review, 1969.

[Friar]. Letter to the King, St. Augustine, February 2, 1635. Archivo General de Indias, Santo Domingo 225, Woodbury Lowery Collection, reel 4.

Fried, Morton H. *The Evolution of Political Society.* New York: Random House, 1967.

Friedman, Jonathan. "Tribes, States, and Transformations." In Maurice Bloch, editor, *Marxist Analyses and Social Anthropology.* New York: John Wiley and Sons, 1975.

Fritz, Gayle J. "Crops before Corn in the East: Early and Middle Woodland Period Paleoethnobotany," 55–77. In C. Margaret Scarry, editor, *Foraging and Farming in the Eastern Woodlands.* Ripley P. Bullen Monographs in Anthropology and History. Gainesville: University Presses of Florida, 1993.

———. "Multiple Pathways to Farming in Precontact Eastern North America." *Journal of World Prehistory* 4 (1990): 387–435.

Fritz, Gayle J., and Bruce D. Smith. "Old Collections and New Technology: Documenting the Domestication of Chenopodium in Eastern North America." *Midcontinental Journal of Archaeology* 13 (1988): 3–27.

Galloway, Patricia. " 'The Chief Who Is Your Father': Choctaw and French Views of the Diplomatic Relation." In Peter H. Wood, Gregory A. Waselkov, and M. Thomas Hatley, editors, *Powhatan's Mantle: Indians in the Colonial Southeast.* Lincoln: University of Nebraska Press, 1989.

———, editor. *The Southeastern Ceremonial Complex: Artifacts and Analysis.* Lincoln: University of Nebraska Press, 1989.

———. "Technical Origins for Chickachae Combed Ceramics: An Ethnohistorical Hypothesis." *Mississippi Archaeology* 19 (1984): 58–66.

———. "Choctaw Factionalism and Civil War, 1746–1750." *Journal of Mississippi History* 44 (1982): 289–328.

————. "Henri de Tonti du Village des Chactas: The Beginning of the French Alliance." In Patricia Galloway, editor, *La Salle and His Legacy*. Jackson: University Press of Mississippi, 1982.

Gannon, Michael. *The Cross in the Sand*. Gainesville: University Presses of Florida, 1983.

————. "Sebastian Montero, Pioneer American Missionary, 1566–1572." *Catholic Historical Review* 51 (1965): 335–53.

Garcilaso de la Vega, El Inca. *La florida del Inca*. Edited by Sylvia Hilton. Madrid: Historia, 1986.

————. *La florida del Inca*. Facsimile edition with introduction and notes by Sylvia Hilton. Madrid: Fundación Universitaria Española, 1982.

————. *The Florida of the Inca*. Translated and edited by John G. Varner and Jeannette J. Varner. Austin: University of Texas Press, 1951.

Garrow, Patrick H. "The Mouse Creek 'Focus': A Reevaluation." *Southeastern Archaeological Conference Bulletin* 18 (1975): 76–85.

Garst, Daniel. "Wallerstein and His Critics." *Theory and Society* 14 (1985): 469–95.

Gatschet, Albert S. *A Migration Legend of the Creek Indians, with a Linguistic, History, and Ethnographic Introduction*. Philadelphia: Brinton's Library of Aboriginal American Literature, vol. 1, part 4, 1884.

Geiger, Maynard J. *Biographical Dictionary of the Franciscans in Spanish Florida and Cuba (1528–1842)*. Paterson, N.J.: St. Anthony Guild Press, 1940.

————. *The Franciscan Conquest of Florida, 1573–1618*. Washington, D.C.: Catholic University Press, 1937.

Gilmary, John. *Discovery and Exploration of the Mississippi Valley*. New York, 1852.

Goad, Sharon I. "Middle Woodland Exchange in the Prehistoric Southeastern United States." In David S. Brose and N'omi Greber, editors, *Hopewell Archaeology: The Chillicothe Conference*. Kent, Ohio: Kent State University Press, 1979.

Goggin, John M. *Space and Time Perspective in Northern St. Johns Archeology*. Yale University Publications in Anthropology, no. 47. New Haven: Yale University Press, 1952.

Goggin, John M., and William C. Sturtevant. "The Calusa: A Stratified, Nonagricultural Society (with Notes on Sibling Marriage)." In Ward H. Goodenough, editor, *Explorations in Cultural Anthropology: Essays in Honor of George Peter Murdock*. New York: McGraw-Hill, 1964.

Goldman, Irving. *Ancient Polynesian Society*. Chicago: University of Chicago Press, 1970.

Gómez de Engraba, Juan. Letter to Francisco Martínez, St. Augustine, April 4, 1657. In John Hann, *Translation of Governor Rebolledo's 1657 Visitation of Three Florida Provinces and Related Documents*. Florida Archaeology, no. 2. Tallahassee: Florida Bureau of Archaeological Research, 1986.

Goodwin, Gary. *Cherokees in Transition: A Study of Changing Culture and Environment Prior to 1775*. Chicago: University of Chicago Press, 1977.

Goody, Jack. *Production and Reproduction*. Cambridge: Cambridge University Press, 1976.

Gradie, Charlotte. "Spanish Jesuits in Virginia: The Mission That Failed." *Virginia Magazine of History and Biography* 96 (1988): 131–56.

Green, Michael D. *The Politics of Indian Removal: Creek Government and Society in Crisis.* Lincoln: University of Nebraska Press, 1982.

Griffin, James B. "Changing Concepts of the Prehistoric Mississippian Cultures of the Eastern United States." In Reid Badger and Lawrence Clayton, editors, *Alabama and the Borderlands: From Prehistory to Statehood.* Tuscaloosa: University of Alabama Press, 1985.

Griffin, John W. *The Archeology of Everglades National Park: A Synthesis.* Tallahassee: National Park Service Southeast Archeological Center, 1988.

Griffin, John W., Sue B. Richardson, Mary Pohl, Carl D. McMurray, C. Margaret Scarry, Suzanne K. Fish, Elizabeth S. Wing, L. Jill Loucks, and Marcia K. Welsh. *Excavations at the Granada Site.* Archaeology and History of the Granada Site, vol. 1. Tallahassee: Florida Division of Archives, History and Records Management, 1984.

Gutiérrez, Ramón A. *When Jesus Came, the Corn Mothers Went Away: Marriage, Sexuality, and Power in New Mexico, 1500–1846.* Stanford: Stanford University Press, 1991.

Haas, Jonathan. *The Evolution of the Prehistoric State.* New York: Columbia University Press, 1982.

Hallenbeck, Clive. *Alvar Núñez Cabeza de Vaca: The Journey and Route of the First European to Cross the Continent of North America, 1534–1536.* 1940. Reprint. Port Washington, N.Y.: Kennikat Press, 1971.

Hally, David J. "Archaeology and Settlement Plan of the King Site." In Robert Blakely, editor, *The King Site: Continuity and Contact in Sixteenth-Century Georgia.* Athens: University of Georgia Press, 1988.

———. "Domestic Architecture and Domestic Activities in the Native South." *Early Georgia* 10 (1982): 40–52.

———. "Plant Preservation and the Content of Paleobotanical Samples: A Case Study." *American Antiquity* 46 (1981): 723–42.

Hally, David J., and James B. Langford, Jr. *Mississippi Period Archaeology of the Georgia Valley and Ridge Province.* University of Georgia Laboratory of Archaeology Series, no. 25. Athens: University of Georgia Laboratory of Archaeology, 1988.

Hally, David J., and James Rudolph. *Mississippian Period Archaeology of the Georgia Piedmont.* University of Georgia Laboratory of Archaeology Series, no. 24. Athens: University of Georgia Laboratory of Archaeology, 1986.

Hally, David J., Marvin T. Smith, and James B. Langford, Jr. "The Archaeological Reality of de Soto's Coosa." In David Hurst Thomas, editor, *Columbian Consequences.* Vol. 1, *Archaeological and Historical Perspectives on the Spanish Borderlands.* Washington, D.C.: Smithsonian Institution Press, 1990.

Hamor, Ralph. *A Tru Discourse of the Present State of Virginia.* 1615. Reprint. Richmond: Virginia State Library, 1957.

Hanke, Lewis U. *The Spanish Struggle for Justice in the Conquest of America* (1949). Reprint. Boston: Little, Brown, 1965.

Hann, John H. *Visitations and Revolts in Florida, 1656–1695.* Florida Archaeology, no. 7. Tallahassee: Florida Bureau of Archaeological Research. In press.

———. *Missions to the Calusa.* Gainesville: University of Florida Press, 1991.

———. "De Soto, Dobyns, and Demography in Western Timucua." *Florida Anthropologist* 43 (1990): 3–12.

———. "Summary Guide to Spanish Florida Missions and Visitas with Churches in the Sixteenth and Seventeenth Centuries." *The Americas* 46 (1990): 417–513.

———. "St. Augustine's Fallout from the Yamasee War." *Florida Historical Quarterly* 68 (1989): 180–200.

———. *Apalachee: The Land Between the Rivers.* Ripley P. Bullen Monographs in Anthropology and History, no. 7. Gainesville: University Presses of Florida, 1988.

———. "Apalachee Counterfeiters in St. Augustine." *Florida Historical Quarterly* 67 (1988): 52–68.

———. "Florida's Terra Incognita: West Florida's Natives in the Sixteenth and Seventeenth Century." *Florida Anthropologist* 41 (1988): 61–107.

———. "Twilight of the Mocamo and Guale Aborigines as Portrayed in the 1695 Visitation." *Florida Historical Quarterly* 66 (1987): 1–24.

———. *Church Furnishings, Sacred Vessels and Vestments Held by the Missions of Florida: Translation of Two Inventories.* Florida Archaeology, no. 2. Tallahassee: Florida Bureau of Archaeological Research, 1986.

———. "Demographic Patterns and Changes in Mid-Seventeenth Century Timucua and Apalachee." *Florida Historical Quarterly* 64 (1986): 371–92.

———. *Translation of Alonso de Leturiondo's Memorial to the King of Spain.* Florida Archaeology, no. 2. Tallahassee: Florida Bureau of Archaeological Research, 1986.

———. *Translation of Governor Rebolledo's 1657 Visitation of Three Florida Provinces and Related Documents.* Florida Archaeology, no. 2. Tallahassee: Florida Bureau of Archaeological Research, 1986.

———. *Translation of the Ecija Voyages of 1605 and 1609 and the Gonzalez Derrotero of 1609.* Florida Archaeology, no. 2. Tallahassee: Florida Bureau of Archaeological Research, 1986.

Hantman, Jeffrey L. "Between Powhatan and Quirank: Reconstructing Monacan Culture and History in the Context of Jamestown." *American Anthropologist* 92 (1990): 676–90.

Hariot, Thomas. *A Briefe and True Report of the New Found Land of Virginia.* 1590. Reprint. New York: Dover, 1972.

Harris, Walter. *Here the Creeks Sat Down.* Macon, Ga.: J. W. Burke, 1958.

Haselgrove, C. "Culture Process on the Periphery: Belgic Gaul and Rome During the Late Republic and Early Empire." In Michael Rowlands, Mogens Larsen, and Kristian Kristiansen, editors, *Center and Periphery in the Ancient World.* Cambridge: Cambridge University Press, 1987

———. "Wealth, Prestige, and Power: The Dynamics of Political Centralization in Southeast England." In C. Renfrew and S. Shennan, editors, *Ranking, Resources, and Exchange.* Cambridge: Cambridge University Press, 1982.

Hassan, Fekri A. *Demographic Archaeology.* New York: Academic Press, 1981.

Hatch, James W. "The Citico Site (40HA65): A Synthesis." *Tennessee Anthropologist* 1 (1976): 76–104.

———. "Status in Death: Principles of Ranking in Dallas Culture Mortuary Remains." Ph. D. dissertation, Pennsylvania State University, 1976.

Hatch, James W., and Richard A. Geidel. "Tracing Status and Diet in Prehistoric Tennessee." *Archaeology* 36:1 (1983): 56–59.

Hatch, James W., and Patrick S. Willey. "Stature and Status in Dallas Society." *Tennessee Archaeologist* 30 (1974): 107–31.

Hatch, James W., Patrick S. Willey, and Edward E. Hunt, Jr. "Indicators of Status-Related Stress in Dallas Society: Transverse Lines and Cortical Thickness in Long Bones." *Midcontinental Journal of Archaeology* 8 (1983): 49–71.

Hatley, Thomas. "The Dividing Paths: The Encounters of the Cherokees and the South Carolinians in the Southern Mountains, 1670–1785." Ph.D. dissertation, Duke University, 1988.

Hawkins, Benjamin. *A Sketch of the Creek Country in the Years 1798 and 1799.* 1848. Spartanburg, S.C.: The Reprint Co., 1982.

Hedeager, Lotte. "Empire, Frontier, and Barbarian Hinterland: Rome and Northern Europe from A.D. 1–400." In Michael Rowlands, Mogens Larsen, and Kristian Kristiansen, editors, *Center and Periphery in the Ancient World.* Cambridge: Cambridge University Press, 1987.

Helms, Mary W. *Ulysses' Sail: An Ethnographic Odyssey of Power, Knowledge, and Geographical Distance.* Princeton: Princeton University Press, 1988.

―――. *Ancient Panama: Chiefs in Search of Power.* Austin: University of Texas Press, 1979.

Hemming, John. *Red Gold: The Conquest of the Brazilian Indians.* Cambridge: Harvard University Press, 1978.

Hemmings, E. Thomas, and John H. House, editors. *The Alexander Site, Conway County, Arkansas.* Arkansas Archeological Survey Research Series, no. 24. Fayetteville, 1985.

Henige, David "The Context, Content, and Credibility of La Florida del Ynca." *The Americas* 43 (1986): 1–23.

―――. "If Pigs Could Fly: Timucuan Population and Native American Historical Demography." *Journal of Interdisciplinary History* 16 (1986): 701–20.

―――. "Primary Source by Primary Source? On the Role of Epidemics in New World Depopulation." *Ethnohistory* 33 (1986): 293–312.

Hering, William Waller, compiler. *The Statutes at Large . . .* 13 vols. New York: R. W. & G. Bartow, 1809–23.

Hernandez de Biedma, Luis. "Account of the Island of Florida." Translated by Buckingham Smith in Edward Gaylord Bourne, editor, *Narratives of the Career of Hernando de Soto,* vol. 2. New York: Allerton, 1922.

―――. "Relation of the Conquest of Florida." In E. G. Bourne, editor, *Narratives of the Career of Hernando de Soto* 2:1–40. New York: Allerton, 1904.

―――. "Relación de la isla de la Florida." In *Colección de Documentos Inéditos,* vol. 3. Madrid, 1865.

―――. "Relación de la isla de la Florida." In Buckingham Smith, editor, *Colección de varios documentos para la historia de la Florida y tierras adyacentes.* London, 1857.

Hertz, Robert. *Death and the Right Hand.* Translated by Rodney and Claudia Needham. Glencoe, Ill.: Free Press, 1960.

Heye, George, Frederick Hodge, George Pepper. "The Nacoochee Mound in Georgia." *Museum of the American Indian.* Heye Foundation Contribution no. 2. New York: Heye Foundation, 1918.

Higginbotham, Jay. *Old Mobile, Fort Louis de la Louisiane, 1702–1711.* Mobile: Museum of the City of Mobile, 1977.

Hita Salazar, Pablo de. Letter to the Queen, St. Augustine, August 24, 1675, Archivo General de Indias, Santo Domingo 839, Stetson Collection of the P. K. Yonge Library of Florida History of the University of Florida.

Hoebel, E. Admonson. *Anthropology: The Study of Man.* 3d ed. New York: McGraw-Hill, 1966.

Hoffman, Bernard G. *Observations on Certain Ancient Tribes of the Northern Appalachian Province.* Bulletin of Bureau of American Ethnology, no. 191. Washington, D.C.: Government Printing Office, 1964.

Hoffman, Paul E. "Nature and Sequence of the Borderlands." In Patricia Galloway, editor, *Native, European, and African Cultures in Mississippi, 1500–1800.* Jackson: Mississippi Department of Archives and History, 1991.

————. *A New Andalucia and a Way to the Orient: The American Southeast During the Sixteenth Century.* Baton Rouge: Louisiana State University Press, 1990.

————. "The Chicora Legend and Franco-Spanish Rivalry in *La Florida.*" *Florida Historical Quarterly* 58 (1980): 415–26.

————. "A New Voyage of North American Discovery: The Voyage of Pedro de Salazar to the Island of Giants." *Florida Historical Quarterly* 58 (1980): 415–26.

Hornbeck, David. "Economic Growth and Change at the Missions of Alta California, 1769–1846." In David Hurst Thomas, editor, *Columbian Consequences.* Vol. 1, *Archaeological and Historical Perspectives on the Spanish Borderlands West.* Washington, D.C.: Smithsonian Institution Press, 1989.

Horruytiner, Luis de. Letter to the King, St. Augustine, November 15, 1633. Archivo General de Indias, Santo Domingo, 233, Stetson Collection of the P. K. Yonge Library of Florida History of the University of Florida.

House, John H. "Kent Phase Investigations in Eastern Arkansas, 1978–1984." *Mississippi Archaeology* 22 (1987): 46–60.

Hudson, Charles. "The Social Context of the Chiefdom of Ichisi." In David Hally, editor, *Ocmulgee Archaeology, 1936–1986.* Athens: University of Georgia Press. In press.

————. "Evidence for a New De Soto Route West of the Mississippi River." In Gloria A. Young and Michael P. Hoffman, editors, *The De Soto Expedition in the West.* Fayetteville: University of Arkansas Press, 1993.

————. *The Juan Pardo Expeditions: Exploration of the Carolinas and Tennessee, 1566–68.* Washington, D.C.: Smithsonian Institution Press, 1990.

————. "A Synopsis of the Hernando de Soto Expedition, 1539–1543." In *De Soto Trail: De Soto National Historic Trail Study.* Final Report Prepared by the National Park Service. National Park Service, March 1990.

————. "A Spanish-Coosa Alliance in Sixteenth-Century North Georgia." *Georgia Historical Quarterly* 72 (1988): 599–626.

————. "Juan Pardo's Excursion Beyond Chiaha." *Tennessee Anthropologist* 12 (1987): 74–87.

————. "An Unknown South: Spanish Explorers and Southeastern Chiefdoms." In George Sabo, III, and William M. Schneider, editors, *Visions and Revisions: Ethnohistoric Perspectives on Southern Cultures. Southern Anthropological Society Proceedings* 20 (1987): 6–24.

————. *The Uses of Evidence in Reconstructing the Route of the Hernando de Soto Expedition.* Alabama de Soto Commission Working Papers, no. 1. Tuscaloosa: University of Alabama, State Museum of Natural History, 1987.

————. "Some Thoughts on the Early Social History of the Cherokees." In David G. Moore, editor, *The Conference on Cherokee Prehistory.* Swannanoa, N.C.: Warren Wilson College, 1986.

———. "De Soto in Arkansas: A Brief Synopsis." *Field Notes: Newsletter of the Arkansas Archaeological Society* 205 (1985): 3–12.

———. "The Genesis of Georgia's Indians." In H. H. Jackson and Phinizy Spalding, editors, *Forty Years of Diversity: Essays on Colonial Georgia.* Athens: University of Georgia Press, 1984.

———. *The Southeastern Indians.* Knoxville: University of Tennessee Press, 1976.

Hudson, Charles, Chester DePratter, and Marvin Smith. "Hernando de Soto's Expedition through the Southern United States." In Jerald T. Milanich and Susan Milbrath, editors, *First Encounters: Spanish Explorations in the Caribbean and the United States, 1492–1570.* Gainesville: University of Florida Press, 1989.

———. "The Victims of the King Site Massacre: A Historical Detectives' Report." In Robert L. Blakely, editor, *The King Site: Continuity and Contact in Sixteenth-Century Georgia.* Athens: University of Georgia Press, 1988.

Hudson, Charles, and Marvin Smith. "Reply to Eubanks." *Florida Anthropologist* 43 (1990): 36–42.

Hudson, Charles, Marvin Smith, and Chester DePratter. "The Hernando de Soto Expedition: From Mabila to the Mississippi." In David Dye and Cheryl Anne Cox, editors, *Towns and Temples along the Mississippi.* Tuscaloosa: University of Alabama Press, 1990.

———. "The Hernando de Soto Expedition: From Apalachee to Chiaha." *Southeastern Archaeology* 3 (1984): 65–77.

Hudson, Charles, Marvin Smith, Chester B. DePratter, and Emilia Kelley. "The Tristán de Luna Expedition, 1559–1561." *Southeastern Archaeology* 8 (1989): 31–45.

Hudson, Charles, Marvin Smith, David Hally, Richard Polhemus, and Chester DePratter. "Reply to Boyd and Schroedl." *American Antiquity* 52 (1987): 845–56.

———. "Coosa: A Chiefdom in the Sixteenth-Century Southeastern United States," *American Antiquity,* 50 (1985): 723–37.

Hudson, Charles, John Worth, and Chester B. DePratter. "Refinement in de Soto's Route through Georgia and South Carolina." In David Hurst Thomas, editor, *Columbian Consequences.* Vol. 2, *Archaeological and Historical Perspectives on the Spanish Borderlands East.* Washington, D.C.: Smithsonian Institution Press, 1990.

Hulton, Paul. *America 1585: The Complete Drawings of John White.* Chapel Hill: University of North Carolina Press, 1984.

Hunter, Donald G. "The Apalachee on Red River, 1763–1834: An Ethnohistory and Summary of Archaeological Testing at the Zimmerman Hill Site, Rapides Parish, Louisiana." *Louisiana Archaeology,* no. 12 (1985): 7–127.

Ibarra, Pedro de. Letter to the King, St. Augustine, September 1, 1609. Archivo General de Indias, Santo Domingo 128, Stetson Collection of the P. K. Yonge Library of Florida History of the University of Florida.

Jacobs, William R. *Indians of the Southern Colonial Frontier: The Edmond Atkin Report and Plan of 1755.* Columbia: University of South Carolina Press, 1954.

Jennings, Francis. *The Ambiguous Iroquois Empire: The Covenant Chain Confederation of Indian Tribes with English Colonies from its Beginnings to the Lancaster Treaty of 1744.* New York: Norton, 1984.

Jester, Annie Lash, and Martha Woodroof Hiden. *Adventurers of Purse and Person: Virginia 1607–1625.* Princeton: Princeton University Press, 1956.

Jesus, Alonso de. Letter to Luis de Rojas y Borja, [ca. 1630]. Archivo General de Indias, Santo Domingo 235, microfilm 28K, reel 36 (Letters and dispatches of ecclesiastical persons of Florida) of the P. K. Yonge Library of Florida History of the University of Florida.

Johannessen, Sissel. "Farmers of the Late Woodland," 55–77. In C. Margaret Scarry, editor, *Foraging and Farming in the Eastern Woodlands*. Ripley P. Bullen Monographs in Anthropology and History. Gainesville: University Presses of Florida, 1993.

John, Elizabeth A. H. *Storms Brewed in Other Men's Worlds. The Confrontation of Indians, Spanish, and French in the Southwest, 1540–1795*. College Station: Texas A & M University Press, 1975.

Johnson, Allen W., and Timothy Earle. *The Evolution of Human Societies*. Stanford: Stanford University Press, 1987.

Johnson, Cecil. *British West Florida. 1763–1783*. New Haven: Yale University Press, 1943.

Johnson, Gregory A. "The Changing Organization of Uruk Administration on the Susiana Plain." In Frank Hole, editor, *The Archaeology of Western Iran*. Washington, D.C.: Smithsonian Institution Press, 1987.

———. "Organizational Structure and Scalar Stress." In Colin Renfrew, Michael Rowlands, and Barbara Segraves, editors, *Theory and Explanation in Archaeology: The Southampton Conference*. New York: Academic Press, 1982.

———. "Information Sources and the Development of Decision-making Organizations." In Charles Redman, Mary Berman, Edward Curtin, William Langhorne, Nina Versaggi, and Jeffrey Wanser, editors, *Social Archeology: Beyond Subsistence and Dating*. New York: Academic Press, 1978.

Johnson, Jay, and John Sparks. "Protohistoric Settlement Patterns in Northeastern Mississippi." In David H. Dye and Ronald C. Brister, editors, *The Protohistoric Period in the Mid-South: 1500–1700*. Mississippi Department of Archives and History Report no. 18. Jackson: Mississippi Department of Archives and History, 1986.

Johnson, Kenneth W. "The Utina and the Potano Peoples of Northern Florida: Changing Settlement Systems in the Spanish Colonial Period." Ph.D. dissertation, University of Florida, 1991.

Johnson, Nathaniel. "Report of the Governor and Council, 1708." In H. Roy Merrens, editor, *The Colonial South Carolina Scene: Contemporary Views, 1697–1774*. Columbia: University of South Carolina Press, 1977.

Jones, B. Calvin. "Southern Cult Manifestations at the Lake Jackson Site, Leon County, Florida: Salvage Archaeology of Mound 3." *Midcontinent Journal of Archaeology* 7 (1982): 3–44.

———. *Colonel James Moore and the Destruction of the Apalachee Missions in 1704*. Miscellaneous Project Report Series, no. 2. Tallahassee: Florida Bureau of Historic Sites and Properties, 1972.

Jones, B. Calvin, and Gary Shapiro. "Nine Mission Sites in Apalachee." In David Hurst Thomas, editor, *Columbian Consequences*. Vol. 2, *Archaeological and Historical Perspectives on the Spanish Borderlands East*. Washington, D.C.: Smithsonian Institution Press, 1990.

Keegan, William F., editor. *Emergent Horticultural Economies of the Eastern*

Woodlands. Occasional Paper no. 7. Carbondale: Southern Illinois University Center for Archaeological Investigations, 1987.

Keegan, William F., and Morgan D. Maclachlan. "Taíno Kinship and Politics." *American Anthropologist* 91 (1989): 613–30.

Keel, Bennie C. *Cherokee Archaeology: A Study of the Appalachian Summit.* Knoxville: University of Tennessee Press, 1976.

Kelly, Arthur R. *A Preliminary Report on Archaeological Excavations at Macon, Georgia.* Bureau of American Ethnology Bulletin no. 119. Washington, D.C.: Smithsonian Institution, 1938.

Kelly, John E. "The Emergence of Mississippian Culture in the American Bottom." In Bruce Smith, editor, *The Mississippian Emergence: The Evolution of Ranked Agricultural Societies in Eastern North America.* Washington, D.C.: Smithsonian Institution Press, 1990.

———. "Range Site Community Patterns and the Mississippian Emergence." In Bruce D. Smith, editor, *The Mississippian Emergence: The Evolution of Ranked Agricultural Societies in Eastern North America.* Washington, D.C.: Smithsonian Institution Press, 1990.

Kessell, John L. "Spaniards and Pueblos: From Crusading Intolerance to Pragmatic Accommodation." In David Hurst Thomas, editor, *Columbian Consequences.* Vol. 1, *Archaeological and Historical Perspectives on the Spanish Borderlands West.* Washington, D.C.: Smithsonian Institution Press, 1989.

———. *Kiva, Cross, and Crown: The Pecos Indians and New Mexico, 1540–1840.* Albuquerque: University of New Mexico Press, 1987.

Kestle, Sharon. "Subsistence and Sex Roles." In Robert L. Blakely, editor, *The King Site: Continuity and Contact in Sixteenth-Century Georgia.* Athens: University of Georgia Press, 1988.

Ketcham, Herbert E. "Three Sixteenth Century Spanish Chronicles Relating to Georgia." *Georgia Historical Quarterly.* 38 (1954): 66–82.

Kimball, Larry R., editor. *The 1977 Archaeological Survey: An Overall Assessment of the Archaeological Resources of Tellico Reservoir.* Knoxville: University of Tennessee Department of Anthropology, 1985.

Kipp, Rita S., and Edward M. Schortman. "The Political Impact to Trade in Chiefdoms." *American Anthropologist* 91 (1989): 370–85.

Kirchhoff, Paul. "Principles of Clanship in Human Society." *Davidson Anthropological Society Journal* 1 (1955): 1–11.

Knight, Vernon J., Jr. "Social Organization and the Evolution of Hierarchy in Southeastern Chiefdoms." *Journal of Anthropological Research* 46 (1990): 1–23.

———. *A Summary of Alabama's de Soto Mapping Project and Project Bibliography.* Alabama de Soto Working Papers, no. 9. Tuscaloosa: University of Alabama, State Museum of Natural History, 1988.

———. "The Institutional Organization of Mississippian Religion." *American Antiquity* 51 (1986): 675–87.

———. *East Alabama Archaeological Survey: 1984 Season.* Report of Investigations, no. 44. Moundville: University of Alabama Office of Archaeological Research, 1985.

———. *Tukabatchee: Archaeological Investigations at an Historic Creek Town, 1984.* Report of Investigations, no. 45. Moundville: University of Alabama Office of Archaeological Research, 1985.

————. "Mississippian Ritual." Ph.D. dissertation, University of Florida, 1981.

Knight, Vernon J., Jr., and Tim S. Mistovich. *Walter F. George Lake: Archaeological Survey of Free Owned Lands.* Report of Investigations, no. 49. Moundville: University of Alabama Office of Archaeological Research, 1984.

Knight, Vernon J., Jr., Gloria G. Cole, and Richard Walling. *An Archaeological Reconnaissance of the Coosa and Tallapoosa River Valleys, East Alabama: 1983.* Report of Investigations, no. 43. Moundville: University of Alabama Office of Archaeological Research, 1984.

Knowles, Nathaniel. "The Torture of Captives by the Indians of Eastern North America." *Proceedings of the American Philosophical Society* 82 (1940): 151–225.

Kohl, Johann Georg. *A History of the Discovery of the East Coast of North America.* Vol. 1 of *Documentary History of the State of Maine.* 24 vols. Portland: Maine Historical Society, 1869–1916.

Kowalewski, Stephen A., and James W. Hatch. "The Sixteenth-Century Expansion of Settlement in the Upper Oconee Watershed, Georgia." *Southeastern Archaeology* 10 (1991): 1–17.

Krieger, Alex D. "The Travels of Alvar Núñez Cabeza de Vaca in Texas and Mexico, 1534–1536." *Homenaje a Pablo Martínez del Río en el vigésimoquinto aniversario de la primera edición de "Los orígenes americanos."* Mexico City: Instituto Nacional de Antropologia e Historia, 1961.

————. "Un nuevo estudio de la ruta seguida por Cabeza de Vaca através de Norte América." Ph.D. dissertation, Universidad Nacional Autónoma de México, 1955.

Kroeber, Alfred L. *Cultural and Natural Areas of Native North America.* Berkeley: University of California Press, 1939.

Ladurie, Emmanuel Le Roy. *Times of Feast, Times of Famine: A History of the Climate Since the Year 1000.* Translated by Barbara Bray. Garden City, N.Y.: Doubleday, 1971.

Lallo, J. W. "The Skeletal Biology of Three Prehistoric American Indian Societies from Dickson Mounds." Ph.D. dissertation, University of Massachusetts, 1973.

Lankford, George E., III. "Saying Hello to the Timucua." *Mid America Folklore* 12 (1984): 7–23.

Larsen, Clark Spencer. *The Anthropology of St. Catherines Island.* Vol. 3. *Prehistoric Human Biological Adaptation.* Anthropological Papers of the American Museum of Natural History, vol. 57, no. 2. New York: American Museum of Natural History, 1982.

Larson, Lewis H. "The Pardo Expedition: What was the Direction at Departure?" *Southeastern Archaeology* 9 (1990): 124–39.

————. *Aboriginal Subsistence Technology on the Southeastern Coastal Plain During the Late Prehistoric Period.* Gainesville: University Presses of Florida, 1980.

————. "Historic Guale Indians of the Georgia Coast and the Impact of the Spanish Mission Effort." In Jerald T. Milanich and Samuel Proctor, editors, *Tacachale Essays on the Indians of Florida and Southeastern Georgia During the Historic Period.* Gainesville: University of Florida Press, 1978.

————. "Functional Considerations of Warfare in the Southeast During the Mississippi Period." *American Antiquity* 37 (1972): 383–92.

Las Casas, Fray Bartolemé de. *Historia de las Indias.* Mexico City: Fondo de Cultura Económica, 1959.

Laudonnière, René Goulaime de. *Three Voyages*. Translated with an introduction and notes by Charles E. Bennett. Gainesville: University Presses of Florida, 1975.

Lawson, Samuel J., III, "La Tama de la Tierra Adentro." *Early Georgia* 15 (1987): 1–18.

Lederman, Rena. "Changing Times in Mendi: Notes Towards Writing Highland New Guinea History." *Ethnohistory* 33 (1986): 1–30.

Lefler, Hugh, editor. *A New Voyage to Carolina*. Chapel Hill: University of North Carolina Press, 1967.

Leman, A. D., Barbara Straw, Robert D. Glock, William L. Mengeling, R. H. C. Penny, and Erwin Scholl, editors. *Diseases of Swine*. 6th ed. Ames: Iowa State University Press, 1986.

Le Moyne De Morgues, Jacques. *Brevis Narratio Eorum qua in Floarida America Provincia Gallis Acciderunt*. In Theodore de Soto Bry, editor, *America (Historia America Sive Novi Orbis)*, Part II. Frankfurt, 1591.

León, Antonio G., translator. n.d. Synod of the Diocese of Santiago de Cuba, Jamaica, Habana, and Florida, Bishop Juan García de Palacios, 1682.

Leonard, Irving A. "The Spanish Re-exploration of the Gulf Coast in 1686." *Mississippi Valley Historical Review* 22 (1936): 547–57.

Le Page Du Pratz, Antoine. *Historie de la Louisiane*. Paris, 1758.

Leturiondo, Domingo de. *Translation of Alonso de Leturiondo's Memorial to the King of Spain*. Translated by John H. Hann. Florida Archaeology, no. 2. Tallahassee: Florida Bureau of Archaeological Research, 1986.

———. Letter to the King (extracts), St. Augustine, December 30, 1672. Archivo General de Indias, Santo Domingo 848, Woodbury Lowery Collection, reel 4.

Lewis, Clifford M., and Albert J. Loomie. *The Spanish Jesuit Missions in Virginia: 1570–1572*. Chapel Hill: University of North Carolina Press, 1953.

Lewis, Thomas M. N., and Madeline Kneberg. *Hiwassee Island: An Archaeological Account of Four Tennessee Indian Peoples*. Knoxville: University of Tennessee Press, 1941.

Littlefield, Daniel F., Jr. *Africans and Creeks: From the Colonial Period to the Civil War*. Westport, Conn.: Greenwood Press, 1979.

Lockhart, James. *The Men of Cajamarca: A Social and Biographical Study of the First Conquerers of Peru*. Austin: University of Texas Press, 1972.

Long, S. H. *Report of Examinations and Surveys with a View of Improving the Navigation of the Holston and Tennessee Rivers*. Executive Document no. 176. 43d Cong., 2d. sess. Washington, D.C.: Government Printing Office, 1875.

López, Atanasio. *Relación Histórica de la Florida, escrita en el Siglo XVII*. Madrid: Ramona Velasco, 1936.

López, Baltasar. Letter to the King, St. Augustine, September 15, 1602. Archivo General de Indias, Santo Domingo 235, Stetson Collection of the P. K. Yonge Library of Florida History of the University of Florida.

López de Gómera, Francisco. *Historia general de las Indias*. 2 vols. 1552. Reprint. Barcelona: Editorial Iberia, 1954.

Lorant, Stefan. *The New World: The First Pictures of America*. New York: Duell, Sloan and Pearce, 1946.

Loucks, L. Jill. "Political and Economic Interactions between the Spaniards and the Indians: Archaeological and Ethnohistorical Perspectives on the Mission System in Florida." Ph.D. dissertation, University of Florida, 1978.

Lowery, Woodbury. *Spanish Settlements within the Present Limits of the United States*. 2 vols. 1901–11. Reprint. New York: Russell and Russell, 1959.

Lowie, Robert H. *The Origin of the State*. New York: Harcourt, Brace and Co., 1927.

Luna, Tristán de. *The Luna Papers*. Edited and translated by Herbert I. Priestley. 2 vols. Deland: Florida State Historical Society, 1928.

Lyon, Eugene. *The Enterprise of Florida, Pedro Menéndez de Avilés and the Spanish Conquest of 1565–1568*. Gainesville: University of Florida Press, 1976.

McCartney, Martha W. "Cockacoeske, Queen of Pamunkey: Diplomat and Suzerain." In Peter H. Wood, Gregory A. Waselkov, and M. Thomas Hatley, editors, *Powhatan's Mantle: Indians in the Colonial Southeast*. Lincoln: University of Nebraska Press, 1989.

McCracken, Grant. *Culture and Consumption*. Bloomington: Indiana University Press, 1988.

McDowell, W. L., editor. *Documents Relating to Indian Affairs, May 21, 1750– August 7, 1754*. Columbia: South Carolina Archives Department, 1958.

McDowell, William L., Jr., editor. *Journals of the Commissioners of the Indian Trade. September 20, 1710-August 29, 1718*. Columbia: South Carolina Archives Department, 1955.

McEwan, Bonnie G., editor. *The Missions of Spanish Florida*. The Florida Anthropologist [Special Issue] 44 (1991): 104–330.

Machado, Francisco. Accounting of gifts to Indians, St. Augustine, June–July 1597. Archivo General de Indias, Santo Domingo 231, Woodbury Lowery Collection, reel 2.

McNeill, William H. *Plagues and Peoples*. New York: Anchor-Doubleday, 1989.

———. "San Luis de Talimali: The Archaeology of Spanish-Indian Relations at a Florida Mission." *Historical Archaeology* 25 (1991): 36–60.

McWilliams, Richebourg Gaillard, editor and translator. *Iberville's Gulf Journals*. University: University of Alabama Press, 1981.

———, editor and translator. *Fleur de Lys and Calumet, Being the Penicault Narrative of French Adventure in Louisiana*. Baton Rouge: Louisiana State University Press, 1953. Reprint. Tuscaloosa: University of Alabama Press, 1988.

Mair, Lucy. *Primitive Government*. London: Penguin Books, 1962.

Mann, Cyril Baxter. "An Archaeological Classification of Ceramics from the Pearl Mounds (22LW510) Lawrence County, Mississippi." M.A. thesis, University of Southern Mississippi, 1988.

Manning, Mary K. *Archaeological Investigations at 9Pm260*. Wallace Reservoir Project Contribution, no. 16. Athens: University of Georgia Department of Anthropology, 1982.

Marotti, Frank, Jr. "Juan Baptista de Segura and the Failure of the Florida Jesuit Mission, 1566–1572." *Florida Historical Quarterly* 63 (1985): 267–79.

Marquardt, William H. "The Calusa Social Formation in Protohistoric South Florida." In Thomas Patterson and Christine Gailey, editors, *Power Relations and State Formation*. Washington, D.C.: American Anthropological Association, 1987.

———. "Complexity and Scale in the Study of Fisher-Gatherer-Hunters: An Example from the Eastern United States." In T. Douglas Price and James A. Brown, editors, *Prehistoric Hunter-Gatherers: The Emergence of Cultural Complexity.* Orlando: Academic Press, 1985.

Marrinan, Rochelle A. "The Archaeology of the Spanish Missions of Florida: 1566–1704." In K. W. Johnson, J. M. Leader, and R. C. Wilson, editors, *Indians, Colonists, and Slaves, Essays in Memory of Charles H. Fairbanks. Florida Journal of Anthropology,* Special Publication. Gainesville, 1985.

Marrinan, Rochelle A., John F. Scarry, and Rhonda Majors. "Prelude to De Soto: The Ill-fated Expedition of Pánfilo de Narváez." In David Hurst Thomas, editor, *Columbian Consequences.* Vol. 2, *Archaeological and Historical Perspectives on the Spanish Borderlands East.* Washington, D.C.: Smithsonian Institution Press, 1990.

Marshall, Richard A. *The Emergent Mississippian.* Occasional Papers, no. 87–01. Starkville, Miss.: Cobb Institute of Archaeology, Mississippi State University, 1987.

———, editor. "Lyon's Bluff Site (22OK1) Radiocarbon Dated." *Journal of Alabama Archaeology* 23 (1977): 53–57.

Martin, Joel W. *Sacred Revolt: The Muskogees' Struggle for a New World.* Boston: Beacon Press, 1991.

Martínez, Lorenzo. Letter to the King, St. Augustine, September 14, 1612. Archivo General de Indias, Santo Domingo 232, Stetson Collection of the P. K. Yonge Library of Florida History of the University of Florida.

Martyr, Peter. See Anghiera, Pietro Martiere D'

Matheos, Antonio. Testimony from the record of the *residencia,* 1687–1688. Archivo General de Indias, Escribanía de Cámara, leg. 156C, pieza 25 (E. 20), folios 50–116.

Mathews, David S. "The Massacre: The Discovery of De Soto in Georgia." In Robert Blakely, editor, *The King Site: Continuity and Contact in Sixteenth-Century Georgia.* Athens: University of Georgia Press, 1988.

Matter, Robert Allen. "Economic Basis of the Seventeenth-Century Florida Missions." *Florida Historical Quarterly* 52 (1973): 18–38.

Meltzer, David J. "Late Pleistocene Human Adaptations in Eastern North America." *Journal of World Prehistory* 2 (1988): 1–53.

Meltzer, David J., and Bruce D. Smith. "Paleo-Indian and Early Archaic Subsistence Strategies in Eastern North America." In Sarah Neusius, editor, *Foraging, Collecting, and Harvesting: Archaic Period Subsistence and Settlement in the Eastern Woodlands.* Carbondale: Southern Illinois University Center for Archaeological Investigations, 1986.

Méndez de Canzo, Gonzalo. Letter to the King, St. Augustine, September 22, 1602, Archivo General de Indias, Santo Domingo 224, Jeannette Thurber Connor Collection, reel 2.

———. Letter to the King, St. Augustine, April 24, 1601. Archivo General de Indias, Santo Domingo 235, Stetson Collection of the P. K. Yonge Library of Florida History of the University of Florida.

Menéndez Marquez, Francisco. Letter to the King, St. Augustine, February 8, 1648. Archivo General de Indias, Santo Domingo 229, Jeannette Thurber Connor Collection, reel 3.

Menéndez Marquez, Francisco, and Pedro Benedit Horruytiner. Letter to the King,

St. Augustine, July 27, 1647. Archivo General de Indias, Santo Domingo 235, Jeannette Thurber Connor Collection, reel 4.

Merrell, James. *The Indians' New World: Catawbas and Their Neighbors from European Contact through the Era of Removal.* Chapel Hill: University of North Carolina Press, 1989.

———. "'Our Bond of Peace': Patterns of Intercultural Exchange in the Carolina Peidmont, 1650–1750." In Peter H. Wood, Gregory A. Waselkov, and M. Thomas Hatley, editors, *Powhatan's Mantle: Indians in the Colonial Southeast.* Lincoln: University of Nebraska Press, 1989.

———. "The Indians' New World: The Catawba Experience." *William and Mary Quarterly* 41 (1984): 537–65.

Merry, Carl, and Sharon Pekrul. "A Summary of the 1981 Ditch Excavations at the Mulberry Site." *South Carolina Antiquities* 15 (1983): 61–62.

Metcalf, Peter, and Richard Huntington. *Celebrations of Death: The Anthropology of Mortuary Ritual.* 2d ed. Cambridge: Cambridge University Press, 1991.

Meyer, William E. *Ancient Trails in the Southern United States.* Washington, D.C.: Government Printing Office, 1928.

———. "Indian Trails of the Southeast." In *42nd Annual Report, 1924–25.* Washington, D.C.: Bureau of American Ethnology, Smithsonian Institution, 1928.

Milanich, Jerald T. "Hernando de Soto and the Expedition in Florida: An Overview." *Florida Anthropologist* 42 (1989): 307–13.

———. "Corn and Calusa: DeSoto and Demography." In S. Gaines, editor, *Coasts, Plains and Deserts: Essays in Honor of Reynold J. Ruppé.* Anthropological Research Papers, no. 38. Tempe: Arizona State University Press, 1987.

———. Review of *Their Number Become Thinned* by Henry Dobyns. *Agriculture and Human Values* 2 (1985): 83–85.

———. "The Western Timucua: Patterns of Acculturation and Change." In Jerald T. Milanich and Samuel Proctor, editors, *Tacachale: Essays on the Indians of Florida and Southeastern Georgia During the Historic Period.* Ripley P. Bullen Monographs in Anthropology and History, no. 1. Gainesville: University Presses of Florida, 1978.

———. *Excavations at the Richardson Site, Alachua County, Florida: An Early Seventeenth Century Potano Indian Village (with Notes on Potano Culture Change).* Miscellaneous Project Report Series, no. 2. Tallahassee: Florida Bureau of Historic Sites and Properties, 1972.

———. *The Alachua Tradition of North-Central Florida.* Contributions of the Florida State Museum, Anthropology and History, no. 17. Gainesville: Florida State Museum, 1971.

Milanich, Jerald T., Ann Cordell, Vernon J. Knight, Jr., Timothy Kohler, and Brenda Sigler-Lavelle. *McKeithen Weeden Island: The Culture of Northern Florida, A.D. 200–900.* Orlando: Academic Press, 1984.

Milanich, Jerald T., and Charles H. Fairbanks. *Florida Archaeology.* New York: Academic Press, 1987.

Milanich, Jerald, and Charles Hudson. *Hernando de Soto and the Indians of Florida.* Gainesville: University of Florida Press, 1993.

Milanich, Jerald T., and Kenneth W. Johnson. *Santa Fé: A Name Out of Time.* Miscellaneous Project Report Series, no. 41. Gainesville: Florida Museum of Natural History, 1989.

Milanich, Jerald T., and Rebecca Saunders. *The Spanish Castillo and the Franciscan Doctrina of Santa Catalina, at Santa Maria, Amelia Island, Florida (8Na41)*. Miscellaneous Project Report Series, no. 20. Gainesville: Florida Museum of Natural History, 1986.

Milanich, Jerald T., and William C. Sturtevant. *Francisco Pareja's 1613 Confessionario: A Documentary Source for Timucuan Ethnography*. Tallahassee: Florida Department of State, 1972.

Miller, Christopher L., and George R. Hamell. "A New Perspective on Indian-White Contact: Cultural Symbols and Colonial Trade." *Journal of American History* 73 (1986): 311–28.

Milling, Chapman. *Red Carolinians*. Columbia: University of South Carolina Press, 1969.

Milner, George R. "The Late Prehistoric Cahokia Cultural System of the Mississippi River Valley: Foundations, Florescence, and Fragmentation." *Journal of World Prehistory* 4 (1990): 1–43.

———. "Measuring Prehistoric Levels of Health: A Study of Mississippian Period Skeletal Remains from the American Bottom, Illinois." Ph.D. dissertation, Northwestern University, 1982.

———. "Epidemic Disease in the Postcontact Southeast: A Reappraisal." *Midcontinental Journal of Archaeology* 5 (1980): 39–56.

Mistovich, Tim S., and Vernon J. Knight, Jr. *Excavations at Four Sites on Walter F. George Lake, Alabama and Georgia*. Report of Investigations, no. 49. Moundville: University of Alabama Office of Archaeological Research, 1986.

Mitchem, Jeffrey. "Ethnohistoric and Archaeological Evidence for a Protohistoric Provincial Boundary in West Peninsular Florida." Paper presented at the forty-sixth annual Southeastern Archaeological Conference, Tampa, Florida, November 10, 1989.

———. "Redefining Safety Harbor: Late Prehistoric/Protohistoric Archaeology in West Peninsula Florida." Ph.D. dissertation, University of Florida, 1989.

Mitchem, Jeffrey, and Dale Hutchinson. "Interim Report on Archaeological Research at the Tatham Mound, Citrus County, Florida: Season III." *Miscellaneous Project Report Series*, no. 30. Gainesville: Florida State Museum, 1987.

Mooney, James. *The Aboriginal Population of America North of Mexico*. Smithsonian Miscellaneous Collections, no. 80. Washington, D.C.: Government Printing Office, 1928.

———. *The Siouan Tribes of the East*. Bureau of American Ethnology Bulletin no. 22. Washington, D.C.: Smithsonian Institution, 1894.

Mooney, Timothy. "Many Choctaw Standing: An Inquiry into Culture Compromise and Culture Survival Reflected in Seven Choctaw Sites in East-Central Mississippi." 1991. Typescript in author's possession.

Moore, Clarence B. "Certain Sand Mounds on the St. Johns River, Florida, Part I." *Journal of the Academy of Natural Sciences of Philadelphia* 10 (1894): 5–103.

Moreno Ponce de León, Pedro. Letter to the King, St. Augustine, July 9, 1648, and July 21, 1648. Archivo General de Indias, Santo Domingo 235, Woodbury Lowery Collection, reel 3.

Morgan, Edmund S. "The First American Boom: Virginia 1618 to 1630." *William and Mary Quarterly* 28 (1971): 167–98.

Morrell, L. Ross, and B. Calvin Jones. "San Juan de Aspalaga: A Preliminary

Architectural Study." *Florida Bureau of Historic Sites and Properties* 1 (1979): 25–43.

Morse, Dan F. "ASU Spring Break Archaeology Project." Report to Hester A. Davis, March 21, 1989. Typescript in author's possession.

———. "Protohistoric Hunting Sites in Northeastern Arkansas." In David H. Dye and Ronald C. Brister, editors, *The Protohistoric Period in the Mid-South: 1500–1700*. Mississippi Department of Archives and History Archaeological Report no. 18. Jackson: Mississippi Department of Archives and History, 1986.

Morse, Dan F., and Phyllis A. Morse. *Archaeology of the Central Mississippi Valley*. New York: Academic Press, 1983.

Morse, Phyllis, and Dan F. Morse. "The Zebree Site: An Emerged Early Mississippian Expression in Northeast Arkansas." In Bruce D. Smith, editor, *The Mississippian Emergence: The Evolution of Ranked Agricultural Societies in Eastern North America*. Washington, D.C.: Smithsonian Institution Press, 1990.

Muller, Jon D. "Mississippian Specialization and Salt." *American Antiquity* 49 (1984): 489–507.

Nairne, Thomas. *Nairne's Muskhogean Journals: The 1708 Expedition to the Mississippi River*. Edited by Alexander Moore. Jackson: University Press of Mississippi, 1988.

Naroll, Raoul. "Floor Area and Settlement Population." *American Antiquity* 27 (1962): 587–89.

Nash, June. "Ethnographic Aspects of the World Capitalistic System." *Annual Review in Anthropology* 10 (1981): 393–423.

Navarrete, Martín Fernandez, editor. *Colección de los viages y descubrimientos que hicieron por mar los Españoles desde fines del siglo XV*. 5 vols. Madrid: Imprenta Real, 1825.

Netting, Robert M. "Sacred Power and Centralization: Aspects of Political Adaptation in Africa." In Brian Spooner, editor, *Population Growth: Anthropological Implications*. Cambridge: M.I.T. Press, 1972.

Neusius, Sarah W., editor. *Foraging, Collecting, and Harvesting: Archaic Period Subsistence and Settlement in the Eastern Woodlands*. Occasional Paper no. 6. Carbondale: Southern Illinois University Center for Archaeological Investigations, 1986.

Nunez, Theron A., Jr. "Creek Nativism and the Creek War of 1813–1814." *Ethnohistory* 5 (1958): 1–47, 131–75, 292–301.

Núñez Cabeza de Vaca, Alvar. *La Relación o Naufragios de Alvar Núñez Cabeza de Vaca*. Edited by Martin A. Favata and José B. Fernandez. Potomac, Md.: Scripta Humanistica, 1986.

———. *The Journey of Alvar Núñez Cabeza de Vaca*. Translated by Fanny Bandelier. 1905. Reprint. Chicago: Rio Grande Press, 1964.

———. *Relation of Alvar Núñez Cabeça de Vaca*. Translated by Buckingham Smith, 1871. Ann Arbor: University Microfilms, 1966.

———. "The Narrative of Alvar Núñez Cabeza de Vaca." In Frederick W. Hodge, and Theodore H. Lewis, editors, *Spanish Explorers in the Southern United States 1528–1543*. New York: Charles Scribner's Sons, 1907.

Oberg, Kalervo. "Types of Social Structure Among the Lowland Tribes of Central and South America." *American Anthropologist* 57 (1955): 472–88.

O'Donnell, James H. *Southern Indians in the American Revolution.* Knoxville: University of Tennessee Press, 1973.

Oré, Luis Gerónimo. *The Martyrs of Florida,* (1513–1616). Translated by Maynard Geiger. New York: Joseph F. Wagner, 1936.

Oviedo y Valdés, Gonzalo Fernandez de. *The Journey of the Vaca Party: The Account of the Narváez Expedition 1528–1536. As Related by Gonzalo Fernandez de Oviedo y Valdés.* Translated by Basil C. Hedrick and Carroll L. Riley. Carbondale: University Museum, Southern Illinois University, 1974.

―――. *Historia general y natural de las Indias.* 5 vols. Biblioteca de Autores Españoles, vols. 117–21. Madrid: Graficas Orbe, 1959.

―――. *Historia general y natural de las Indias.* 4 vols. Madrid: Real Academia de la Historia, 1851–55.

Pareja, Francisco de. Letter to the King, St. Augustine, September 14, 1602. Archivo General de Indias, Santo Domingo 235, Stetson Collection of the P. K. Yonge Library of Florida History of the University of Florida.

Pareja, Francisco de., et al. Letter to the King, St. Augustine, January 17, 1617. Archivo General de Indias, Santo Domingo 235, Woodbury Lowery Collection, reel 3.

Pareja, Francisco de., and Alonso de Peñaranda. Letter to the King, St. Augustine, November 6, 1607. Archivo General de Indias, Santo Domingo 224, Stetson Collection of the P. K. Yonge Library of Florida History of the University of Florida.

Parham, Kenneth. "Toqua Skeletal Biology: A Biological Approach." In Richard D. Polhemus, editor, *The Toqua Site: A Late Mississippian Dallas Phase Town.* University of Tennessee Department of Anthropology Report of Investigation, no. 41. Knoxville, 1987.

Parham, Kenneth, and Gary T. Scott. "Porotic Hyperostosis: A Study of Disease and Culture at Toqua (40MR6), A Late Mississippian Site in Eastern Tennessee. In Patrick Willey and Fred H. Smith, editors, *The Skeletal Biology of Aboriginal Populations in the Southeastern United States.* Miscellaneous Papers, no. 5. Knoxville: Tennessee Anthropological Association, 1980.

Parker, James W. "Archaeological Test Investigations at 1Su7: The Fort Tombecbe Site." *Journal of Alabama Archaeology* 28 (1982): 1–104.

Pastor, Beatriz. *Discursos narrativos de la conquista: mitificación y emergencia.* Hanover, N.H.: Ediciones del Norte, 1988.

Pauketat, Timothy R. "Mississippian Domestic Economy and Formation Processes: A Response to Prentice." *Midcontinental Journal of Archaeology* 12 (1987): 77–88.

Paynter, Robert. "Surplus Flow between Frontiers and Homelands." In Stanton W. Green and Stephen M. Perlman, editors, *The Archaeology of Frontiers and Boundaries.* Orlando: Academic Press, 1985.

Pearson, Fred Lamar, Jr. "Spanish-Indian Relations in Florida, 1602–1675: Some Aspects of Selected Visitas." *Florida Historical Quarterly* 52 (1974): 261–73.

Peebles, Christopher S. "The Rise and Fall of the Mississippian in West Central Alabama: The Moundville and Summerville Phases, A.D. 1000 to 1600." *Mississippi Archaeology* 22 (1987): 1–31.

―――. "Paradise Lost, Strayed, and Stolen: Prehistoric Social Devolution in the

Southeast." In Miles Richardson and Malcom C. Webb, editors, *The Burden of Being Civilized: An Anthropological Perspective on the Discontents of Civilization*. Athens: University of Georgia Press, 1986.

———. "Moundville and Surrounding Sites: Some Structural Considerations of Mortuary Practices II." In James A. Brown, editor, *Approaches to the Social Dimensions of Mortuary Practices*. Memoirs of the Society for American Archaeology, no. 25. Washington, D.C.: Society for American Archaeology, 1971.

Peebles, Christopher S., and Susan M. Kus. "Some Archaeological Correlates of Ranked Societies." *American Antiquity* 42 (1977): 421–48.

Penman, John T. "The Lamar Phase in Central Georgia." *Southeastern Archaeological Conference Bulletin* 19 (1976): 18–21.

Pepper, Dannll. "Dannll Pepper to Governor Lyttelton." In W. L. McDowell, editor, *Documents Relating to Indian Affairs. 1754–1765*. Columbia: South Carolina Archives Department, 1958.

Percy, George. "Observations Gathered out of a Discourse of the Plantation of the Southern Colonie in Virginia by the English 1606." In Philip L. Barbour, editor, *The Jamestown Voyages Under the First Charter*. The Hakluyt Society, ser. 2, vol. 136. Cambridge, 1969.

Perdue, Theda. *Slavery and the Evolution of Cherokee Society, 1540–1866*. Knoxville: University of Tennessee Press, 1979.

Pérez, Francisco. Letter to the King, St. Augustine, 1646. Archivo General de Indias, Santo Domingo 235, Woodbury Lowery Collection, reel 3.

Phillips, James L., and James A. Brown, editors. *Archaic Hunters and Gatherers in the American Midwest*. San Diego: Academic Press, 1983.

Phillips, Philip. *Archaeological Survey in the Lower Yazoo Basin, Mississippi, 1949–1955*. Vol. 60. Cambridge, Mass.: Peabody Museum of Archaeology, 1970.

Phillips, Philip, and James A. Brown. *Pre-Columbian Shell Engravings from the Craig Mound at Spiro, Oklahoma*, Cambridge, Mass.: Peabody Museum Press, 1978.

Phillips, Philip, James A. Ford, and James B. Griffin. *Archaeological Survey in the Lower Mississippi Alluvial Valley, 1940–1947*. Vol. 25. Cambridge, Mass.: Peabody Museum of Archaeology, 1951.

Phinney, A. D. "Narvaez and de Soto: Their Landing Places and the Town of Espiritu Santo." *Florida Historical Quarterly* 3 (1925): 15–16.

Pickett, Albert J. *History of Alabama, and Incidentally of Georgia and Mississippi from the Earliest Period*. Charleston, S.C.: Walker and James, 1851.

Polhemus, Richard. *Toqua: A Late Mississippian Dallas Town*. Tennessee Valley Authority Publications in Anthropology, no. 44. 1987.

———. "The Early Historic Period in the East Tennessee Valley." University of Georgia Department of Anthropology. Athens, 1982. Photocopy.

Porter, Kenneth Wiggins. *The Negro on the American Frontier*. New York: Arno Press and the *New York Times*, 1971.

Potter, Stephen R. "Early English Effects on Virginia Algonquian Exchange and Tribute in the Tidewater Potomac." In Peter H. Wood, Gregory A. Waselkov, and M. Thomas Hatley, editors, *Powhatan's Mantle: Indians in the Colonial Southeast*, Lincoln: University of Nebraska Press, 1989.

———. "An Analysis of Chicacoan Settlement Patterns." Ph.D. dissertation, University of North Carolina, 1982.

Powell, Mary Lucas. *Status and Health in Prehistory: A Case Study of the Moundville Chiefdom*. Washington, D.C.: Smithsonian Institution Press, 1988.

Prentice, Guy. "Economic Differentiation Among Mississippian Farmsteads." *Midcontinental Journal of Archaeology* 10 (1985): 77–122.

Priestley, Herbert I. *Tristán de Luna: Conquistador of the Old South*. Glendale, Calif.: Arthur H. Clark, 1936.

Prince, Le Baron Bradford. *A Concise History of New Mexico*. 2d ed. Cedar Rapids: Torch Press, 1914.

Purchas, Samuel. *Purchas His Pilgrimes*. 3d ed. London, 1617.

Quattlebaum, Paul. *The Land Called Chicora: The Carolinas Under Spanish Rule with French Intrusions, 1520–1670*. Gainesville: University of Florida Press, 1956.

Quinn, David B. *Set Fair for Roanoke: Voyages and Colonies, 1584–1606*. Chapel Hill: University of North Carolina Press, 1985.

———. *North America from the Earliest Discovery to First Settlements: The Norse Voyages to 1612*. New York: Harper and Row, 1977.

———. *England and the Discovery of America, 1481–1620*. New York: Alfred A. Knopf, 1974.

———, editor. *The Roanoke Voyages, 1585–1590*. The Hakluyt Society, ser. 2, vol. 104. Cambridge, 1955.

Ramenofsky, Ann F. *Vectors of Death: The Archaeology of European Contact*. Albuquerque: University of New Mexico Press, 1987.

Ranjel, Rodrigo. "A Narrative of de Soto's Expedition." In E. G. Bourne, editor, *Narratives of the Career of Hernando de Soto*, vol. 2. New York: Allerton, 1904.

Ray, Arthur J. "Indians as Consumers in the Eighteenth Century." In Carol M. Judd and Arthur J. Ray, editors, *Old Trails and New Directions: Papers of the Third North American Fur Trade Conference*. Toronto: University of Toronto Press, 1980.

Rebolledo, Diego de. Letter to the Franciscans, St. Augustine, August 5, 1657. In John Hann, *Translation of Governor Rebolledo's 1657 Visitation of Three Florida Provinces and Related Documents*. Florida Archaeology, no. 2. Tallahassee: Florida Bureau of Archaeological Research, 1986.

Reding, Katherine, translator. "Letter of Gonzalo Mendez de Canço, Governor of Florida, to Philip II of Spain, June 28, 1600." *Georgia Historical Quarterly* 8 (1924): 215–28.

Reitz, Elizabeth J. "Zooarchaeological Evidence for Subsistence at La Florida Missions." In David Hurst Thomas, editor, *Columbian Consequences*. Vol. 2, *Archaeological and Historical Perspectives on the Spanish Borderlands East*. Washington, D.C.: Smithsonian Institution Press, 1990.

Reitz, Elizabeth J., and C. Margaret Scarry. *Reconstructing Historic Subsistence with an Example from Sixteenth-century Spanish Florida*. Special Publication Series, no. 3. Glassboro, N.J.: Society for Historical Archaeology, 1985.

Renfrew, Colin. *Approaches to Social Archaeology*. Cambridge: Harvard University Press, 1984.

———. "Trade as Action at a Distance: Questions of Integration and Communication." In Jeremy A. Sabloff and C. C. Lamberg-Karlovsky, editors, *Ancient Civilization and Trade*. Albuquerque: University of New Mexico Press, 1975.

————. *Before Civilization: The Radiocarbon Revolution and Prehistoric Europe.* London: Penguin Books, 1973.

Renfrew, C., and J. Cherry, editors. *Peer Polity Interaction and Socio-Political Change.* Cambridge: Cambridge University Press, 1986.

Richards, Audrey I. "Some Types of Family Structure Among the Central Bantu." In A. R. Radcliff-Brown and Daryll Forde, editors, *African Systems of Kinship and Marriage.* London: Oxford University Press, 1950.

Rivers, William James. *A Sketch of the History of South Carolina to the Close of the Proprietary Government.* Charleston: McCarter and Co., 1856.

Robertson, James A., translator and editor. *True Relation of the Hardships Suffered by Governor Fernando de Soto & Certain Portuguese Gentlemen During the Discovery of the Province of Florida. Now Newly Set Forth by a Gentleman of Elvas.* 2 vols. Deland: Florida State Historical Society, 1933.

Rochefort, Charles. *The History of the Caribby-Islands.* Translated by John Davies. London, 1666.

Rogel, Juan. Letter to Jerónimo Ruiz del Portillo, Havana, April 25, 1568. In John Hann, editor, *Missions to the Calusa.* Gainesville: University of Florida Press, 1991, and Felix Zubillaga, editor, *Monumenta Antiquae Floridae (1566–1572).* Monumenta Historica Societies Iesu, vol. 69. Rome: Monumenta Historica Societis Iesu, 1946.

Rogers, Victor A. "Choctaw Mortuary Ceremonialism: Implications for Social Structure." Paper prepared for seminar on Indian Studies, Mississippi State University, 1982.

Rolingson, Martha Ann. "The Toltec Mounds Site, A Ceremonial Center in the Arkansas River Lowland." In Bruce D. Smith, editor, *The Mississippian Emergence: The Evolution of Ranked Agricultural Societies in Eastern North America.* Washington, D.C.: Smithsonian Institution Press, 1990.

————, editor. *Emerging Patterns of Plum Bayou Culture: Preliminary Investigations of the Toltec Mounds Research Project; Toltec Papers II.* Arkansas Archeological Research Series, no. 18. Fayetteville, 1982.

Rose, Jerome C., and Murray K. Marks. "Bioarchaeology of the Alexander Site." In E. Thomas Hemmings and John H. House, editors, *The Alexander Site, Conway County, Arkansas.* Arkansas Archaeological Survey Research Series, no. 24. Fayetteville, 1985.

Ross, Mary. "With Pardo and Moyano on the Fringes of the Georgia Land." *Georgia Historical Quarterly* 14 (1930): 267–85.

Roth, Janet A. "Analysis of Faunal Remains." In David J. Hally, editor, *Archaeological Investigations of the Little Egypt Site (9MU102), Murray County, Georgia, 1970–72 Seasons.* Atlanta: Archaeological Services Division, National Park Service, 1980.

Rothschild, Nan A. "Mortuary Behavior and Social Organization at Indian Knoll and Dickson Mounds." *American Antiquity* 44 (1979): 658–75.

Rountree, Helen C. "The Powhatans and the English: A Case of Multiple Conflicting Agendas." In Helen C. Rountree, editor, *Powhatan Foreign Relations, 1500–1722.* Charlottesville: University Press of Virginia, 1993.

————. *Pocahontas's People: The Powhatan Indians of Virginia Through Four Centuries.* Norman: University of Oklahoma Press, 1990.

———. *The Powhatan Indians of Virginia: Their Traditional Culture.* Norman: University of Oklahoma Press, 1989.

Rowland, Dunbar, editor. *Mississippi Provincial Archives: English Dominion,* vol. 2. Jackson: Mississippi Department of Archives and History, 1911.

Rowland, Dunbar and Albert Godfrey Sanders, editors and translators. *Mississippi Provincial Archives: French Dominion,* vol. 3. Jackson: Mississippi Department of Archives and History, 1932.

———. *Mississippi Provincial Archives, 1701–1729, French Dominion.* Jackson: Mississippi Department of Archives and History, 1929.

———. *Mississippi Provincial Archives: French Dominion,* vol. 1. Jackson: Mississippi Department of Archives and History, 1927.

Rowland, Dunbar, Albert Godfrey Sanders, and Patricia Galloway, editors and translators, *Mississippi Provincial Archives: French Dominion,* vols. 4 and 5. Baton Rouge: Louisiana State University Press, 1984.

Royal Officials. Letter to the King, St. Augustine, March 18, 1647. Archivo General de Indias, Santo Domingo 229, Stetson Collection of the P. K. Yonge Library of Florida History of the University of Florida.

———. Letter to the King, St. Augustine, May 22, 1647. Archivo General de Indias, Santo Domingo 235, Jeannette Thurber Connor Collection, reel 3.

Rudolph, James. "Earthlodges and Platform Mounds: Changing Public Architecture in the Southeastern United States." *Southeastern Archaeology* 3 (1984): 33–45.

Rudolph, James L., and Dennis B. Blanton. "A Discussion of Mississippian Settlement in the Georgia Piedmont." *Early Georgia* 8 (1980): 14–37.

Rudolph, James L., and David J. Hally. *Archaeological Investigations at the Beaverdam Creek Site (9EB85), Elbert County, Georgia.* Atlanta: Archaeological Services Division, National Park Service, 1985.

———. *Archaeological Investigations at Site 9Pm220.* Wallace Reservoir Project Contribution, no. 19. Athens: University of Georgia Department of Anthropology, 1982.

Ruhl, Donna L. "Spanish Mission Paleoethnobotany and Culture Change: A Survey of the Archaeobotanical Data and Some Speculations on the Aboriginal and Spanish Agrarian Interactions in La Florida." In David Hurst Thomas, editor, *Columbian Consequences.* Vol. 2, *Archaeological and Historical Perspectives on the Spanish Borderlands East.* Washington, D.C.: Smithsonian Institution Press, 1990.

Ruiz de Salazar y Vallecilla, Benito. Letter to the King, St. Augustine, May 22, 1647, Archivo General de Indias, Santo Domingo 229, Jeannette Thurber Connor Collection, reel 3.

Russell, Margaret Clayton. "Lamar and the Creeks, An Old Controversy Revisited." *Early Georgia* 3 (1975): 53–67.

Ryan, Thomas. "Test Excavations at McCollum Site." *South Carolina Institute of Archaeology and Anthropology Notebook* 5 (1971): 104–10.

Sahlins, Marshall D. *Islands of History.* Chicago: University of Chicago Press, 1985.

———. *Stone Age Economics.* Chicago: Aldine, 1972.

———. *Tribesmen.* Englewood Cliffs, N.J.: Prentice-Hall, 1968.

———. *Social Stratification in Polynesia.* Seattle: University of Washington Press, 1958.

Salisbury, Neal. *Manitou and Providence: Indians, Europeans, and the Making of New England, 1500–1643*. New York: Oxford University Press, 1982.

Salley, Alexander S., editor. *Records in the British Public Records Office Relating to South Carolina*. 5 vols. Columbia: Historical Society of South Carolina, 1928–47.

——, editor. *Journals of the Commons House of Assembly of South Carolina*. Columbia: Historical Society of South Carolina, 1907–49.

San Antonio, Francisco de., et al. Letter to the King, St. Augustine, September 10, 1657. In John Hann, *Visitations and Revolts in Florida, 1656–1695*. Florida Archaeology, no. 7. Tallahassee: Florida Bureau of Archaeological Research. In press.

Santa Cruz, Alonso de. *Islario General de todas las islas del mundo*. 2 vols. Madrid, 1918.

Sauer, Carl O. *Sixteenth Century North America: The Land and the People as Seen by Europeans*. Berkeley: University of California Press, 1971.

Saunders, Rebecca. *Excavations at 8Na41, Two Mission Period Sites on Amelia Island, Florida*. Miscellaneous Project Report Series, no. 35. Gainesville: Florida Museum of Natural History, 1989.

Scarry, C. Margaret. "Agricultural Risk and the Development of Mississippian Chiefdoms: Prehistoric Moundville as a Case Study," 57–181. In C. Margaret Scarry, editor, *Foraging and Farming in the Eastern Woodlands*. Ripley P. Bullen Monographs in Anthropology and History. Gainesville: University Presses of Florida, 1993.

——. "Variability in Mississippian Crop Production Strategies," 78–90. In C. Margaret Scarry, editor, *Foraging and Farming in the Eastern Woodlands*. Ripley P. Bullen Monographs in Anthropology and History. Gainesville: University Presses of Florida, 1993.

——. "Plant Production and Procurement in Apalachee Province." *Florida Anthropologist* 44 (1991): 285–294.

——. "Plant Remains from the San Luis Mission Church." In Richard Vernon and Bonnie McEwan, editors, *Investigations in the Church Complex and Spanish Village at San Luis*. Florida Archaeological Reports, no. 18. Tallahassee: Florida Bureau of Archaeological Research, 1990.

——. "Plant Remains from the Walling Truncated Mound: Evidence for Middle Woodland Horticultural Activities." In Vernon J. Knight, Jr., editor, *Excavation of the Truncated Mound at the Walling Site*. Report of Investigations, no. 56. Moundville: University of Alabama Office of Archaeological Research, 1990.

——. "Preliminary Examination of Plant Remains." In G. Shapiro, editor, *Archaeology at San Luis: 1984–1985 Broad-Scale Testing*. Florida Archaeology, no. 3. Tallahassee: Florida Bureau of Archaeological Research, 1987.

——. "Change in Plant Procurement and Production during the Emergence of the Moundville Chiefdom." Ph.D. dissertation, University of Michigan, 1986.

——. "Paleoethnobotany of the Granada Site." In John W. Griffin, Sue B. Richardson, Mary Pohl, Carl D. McMurray, C. Margaret Scarry, Suzanne K. Fish, Elizabeth S. Wing, L. Jill Loucks, and Marcia K. Welsh, *Excavations at the Granada Site: Archaeology and History of the Granada Site*, vol. 1. Tallahassee: Florida Division of Archives, History and Records Management, 1984.

Scarry, C. Margaret, and Elizabeth J. Reitz. "Herbs, Fish, Scum, and Vermin: Subsistence Strategies in Sixteenth-Century Spanish Florida." In David Hurst

Thomas, editor, *Columbian Consequences*. Vol. 2, *Archaeological and Historical Reflections on the Spanish Borderlands East*. Washington, D.C.: Smithsonian Institution Press, 1990.

Scarry, John F. "Political Offices and Political Structure: Ethnohistoric and Archaeological Perspectives on the Native Lords of Apalachee." In Alex Barker and Timothy K. Pauketat editors, *Lords of the Southeast: Social Inequality and the Native Elites of Southeastern North America*. Archaeological Papers of the American Anthropological Association, no. 3. Washington, D.C.: American Anthropological Association, 1992.

——. "Mississippian Emergence in the Fort Walton Area: The Evolution of the Cayson and Lake Jackson Phases." In Bruce D. Smith, editor, *The Mississippian Emergence*. Washington, D.C.: Smithsonian Institution Press, 1990.

——. "The Rise, Transformation, and Fall of Apalachee: A Case Study of Political Change in a Chiefly Society." In Mark Williams and Gary Shapiro, editors, *Lamar Archaeology: Mississippian Chiefdoms in the Deep South*. Tuscaloosa: University of Alabama Press, 1990.

——. "A Proposed Revision of the Fort Walton Ceramic Typology: A Type-Variety System." *Florida Anthropologist* 38 (1985): 199–233.

——. "Fort Walton Development: Mississippian Chiefdoms in the Lower Southeast." Ph.D. dissertation, Case Western Reserve University, 1984.

Scarry, John F., and Claudine Payne. "Mississippian Polities in the Fort Walton Area: A Model Generated from the Renfrew-Level XTENT Algorithm." *Southeastern Archaeology* 5 (1986): 79–90.

Schambach, Frank F. "The End of the Trail: The Route of Hernando de Soto's Army through Southwest Arkansas and East Texas." *The Arkansas Archaeologist* 27/28 (1986/1987): 9–33.

——. "The Archaeological Background." In Frank F. Schambach and Frank Rackerby, editors, *Contributions to the Archaeology of the Great Bend Region of the Red River Valley, Southwest Arkansas*. Arkansas Archeological Survey Research Series, no. 22. Fayetteville, 1982.

Schneider, Jane. "Was There a Pre-Capitalist World-System?" *Peasant Studies* 6 (1977): 20–29.

Schnell, Frank T. "The Beginning of the 'Creeks': Where Did They First 'Sit Down,'" *Early Georgia* 17 (1989): 24–29.

Schroedl, Gerald F., editor. *Overhill Cherokee Archaeology at Chota-Tanasee*. Knoxville: University of Tennessee Department of Anthropology, 1986.

Scott, Cary, and Richard Polhemus. "Mortuary Patterning." In Richard Polhemus, editor, *The Toqua Site: A Late Mississippian Dallas Phase Town*. University of Tennessee Department of Anthropology Report of Investigation, no. 41. Knoxville, 1987.

Scott, Elizabeth. "The Route of the Narvaez Expedition through Florida." *Florida Journal of Anthropology* 6 (1981): 52–63.

Scurry, J. D., J. W. Joseph, and F. Hamer. *Initial Archaeological Investigations at Silver Bluff Plantation, Aiken County, South Carolina*. South Carolina Institute of Archaeology and Anthropology Research Manuscript Series, no. 168 (1980).

Sears, Elsie, and William H. Sears. "Preliminary Report on Prehistoric Corn Pollen from Fort Center, Florida." *Southeastern Archaeological Conference Bulletin* 19 (1976): 53–56.

Sears, William H. "The State and Settlement Patterns in the New World." In K. C. Chang, editor, *Settlement Pattern Archaeology*. Palo Alto: National Press, 1968.

———. "The State in Certain Areas and Periods of the Prehistoric Southeastern United States." *Ethnohistory* 9 (1962): 109–25.

———. "Creek and Cherokee Culture in the 18th Century." *American Antiquity* 21 (1955): 143–49.

———. *Excavations at Kolomoki, Season III and IV, Mound D*. University of Georgia Series in Anthropology, no. 4. Athens: University of Georgia Press, 1953.

———. *Excavations at Kolomoki, Season II, Mound E*. University of Georgia Series in Anthropology, no. 3. Athens: University of Georgia Press, 1951.

Serrano y Sanz, Manuel, editor. *Documentos históricos de la Florida y la Luisiana. Siglos XVI al XVIII*. Madrid: Libreria General de Victoriano Suarez, 1912.

Service, Elman R. *Origins of the State and Civilization*. New York: Norton, 1975.

———. *Primitive Social Organization: An Evolutionary Perspective*. 2d ed. New York: Random House, 1971.

———. *Profiles in Ethnology*. New York: Harper and Row, 1963.

———. *Primitive Social Organization*. New York: Harper and Row, 1962.

Shapiro, Gary. "Bottomlands and Rapids: A Mississippian Adaptive Niche in the Georgia Piedmont." In Mark Williams and Gary Shapiro, editors, *Lamar Archaeology: Mississippian Chiefdoms in the Deep South*. Tuscaloosa: University of Alabama Press, 1990.

———. *Archaeology at San Luis: Broad-Scale Testing, 1984–85*. Florida Archaeology, no. 3. Tallahassee: Florida Bureau of Archaeological Research, 1987.

———. "Inside the Apalachee Council House at San Luis." Paper presented at the forty-eighth annual Southeastern Archaeological Conference. Charleston, S.C., November 12, 1987.

———. "Site Variability in the Oconee Province: A Late Mississippian Society of the Georgia Piedmont." Ph.D. dissertation, University of Florida, 1983.

———. *Archaeological Investigations at Site 9Ge175*. Wallace Reservoir Project Contribution, no. 13. Athens: University of Georgia Department of Anthropology, 1981.

Shapiro, Gary N., and John H. Hann. "The Documentary Image of the Council Houses of Spanish Florida Tested by Excavations at the Mission of San Luis de Talimali." In David Hurst Thomas, editor, *Columbian Consequences*. Vol. 2, *Archaeological and Historical Perspectives on the Spanish Borderlands East*. Washington, D.C.: Smithsonian Institution Press, 1990.

Shea, Andrea, Richard Polhemus, and Jefferson Chapman. "The Paleoethnobotany of the Toqua Site." In Richard R. Polhemus, editor, *The Toqua Site: A Late Mississippian Dallas Phase Town*. University of Tennessee Department of Anthropology Report of Investigation, no. 41. Knoxville, 1987.

Shea, John Gilmary. "Ancient Florida." In Justin Windsor, editor, *Spanish Exploration in America from the Fifteenth to the Seventeenth Century*. Vol. 2 of *Narrative and Critical History of the United States*. 8 vols. Boston and New York: Houghton Mifflin, 1884–89.

Sheldon, Craig Turner, Jr. "The Mississippian-Historic Transition in Central Alabama." Ph.D. dissertation, University of Oregon, 1974.

Smith, Bruce D., editor. *The Mississippian Emergence: The Evolution of Ranked*

Agricultural Societies in Eastern North America. Washington, D.C.: Smithsonian Institution Press, 1990.

———. "The Archaeology of the Southeastern United States: From Dalton to de Soto, 10,500–500 B.P." In Fred Wendorf and Angela Close, editors, *Advances in World Archaeology*, vol. 5. New York: Academic Press, 1986.

———. "Mississippian Patterns of Subsistence and Settlement." In R. Reid Badger and Lawrence A. Clayton, editors, *Alabama and the Borderlands: From Prehistory to Statehood.* Tuscaloosa: University of Alabama Press, 1985.

———. "Mississippian Expansion: Tracing the Historical Development of an Explanatory Model." *Southeastern Archaeology* 3 (1984): 13–32.

———, editor. *Mississippian Settlement Patterns.* New York: Academic Press, 1978.

———. "Variation in Mississippian Settlement Patterns." In Bruce D. Smith, editor, *Mississippian Settlement Patterns.* New York: Academic Press, 1978.

Smith, Buckingham, editor. *Narratives of de Soto in the Conquest of Florida as Told by a Gentleman of Elvas and in a Relation by Luys Hernandez de Biedma.* 1st ed., 1866.

Smith, Hale G. *Analysis of the Lamar Site (9Bi7) Materials at the Southeastern Archaeological Center.* Tallahassee: Florida State University Department of Anthropology, 1973.

Smith, John. "The General Historie of Virginia, New England, and the Summer Isles, 1624." In Philip L. Barbour, editor, *The Complete Works of Captain John Smith (1580–1631)*, vol. 2 Chapel Hill: University of North Carolina Press, 1986.

———. "A Map of Virginia." In Philip L. Barbour, editor, *The Complete Works of Captain John Smith (1580–1631)*, vol. 1. Chapel Hill: University of North Carolina Press, 1986.

———. "A True Relation." In Philip L. Barbour, editor, *The Complete Works of Captain John Smith (1580–1631)*, vol. 1. Chapel Hill: University of North Carolina Press, 1986.

Smith, Louis R., Jr. "British-Indian Trade in Alabama, 1670–1756." *Alabama Review* (1974): 65–75.

Smith, Marion F., Jr., and John F. Scarry. "Apalachee Settlement Distribution: The View from the Florida Master Site File." *Florida Anthropologist* 41 (1988): 351–64.

Smith, Marvin T. "Aboriginal Population Movements in the Early Historic Period Interior Southeast." In Peter H. Wood, Gregory A. Waselkov, and M. Thomas Hatley, editors, *Powhatan's Mantle: Indians of the Colonial Southeast.* Lincoln: University of Nebraska Press, 1989.

———. "Early Historic Vestiges of the Southern Cult." In Patricia Galloway, editor, *The Southeastern Ceremonial Complex: Artifacts and Analysis.* Lincoln: University of Nebraska Press, 1989.

———. "In the Wake of de Soto: Alabama's Seventeenth Century Indians on the Coosa River." Report to the Alabama de Soto Commission. Tuscaloosa: University of Alabama, State Museum of Natural History, 1989.

———. *Archaeology of Aboriginal Culture Change in the Interior Southeast: Depopulation During the Early Historic Period.* Gainesville: University of Florida Press, 1987.

———. *Archaeological Investigations at the Dyar Site, 9Ge5*. Wallace Reservoir Project Contribution, no. 11. Athens: University of Georgia Department of Anthropology, 1981.

———. "The Route of de Soto through Tennessee, Georgia and Alabama: The Evidence from Material Culture." *Early Georgia* 4 (1976): 27–47.

Smith, Marvin T., David J. Hally, and Gary Shapiro. "Archaeological Investigations at the Ogeltree Site, 9GE153." *Wallace Reservoir Project Contribution*, no. 10. Athens: University of Georgia Department of Anthropology, 1981.

Smith, Marvin T., and Stephen A. Kowalewski. "Tentative Identification of a Prehistoric 'Province' in Piedmont Georgia." *Early Georgia* 8 (1980): 1–13.

Smith, Marvin T., and James B. Langford. "Recent Investigations in the Cone of the Coosa Province." In Mark Williams and Gary Shapiro, editors, *Lamar Archaeology: Mississippian Chiefdoms in the Deep South*. Tuscaloosa: University of Alabama Press, 1990.

Smith, Robin L. "Coastal Mississippian Period Sites at Kings Bay: A Model-Based Archaeological Analysis." Ph.D. dissertation, University of Florida, 1982.

Snell, William R. "Indian Slavery in Colonial South Carolina, 1671–1795. Ph.D. dissertation, University of Alabama, 1972.

Snow, Frankie. "Pine Barrens Lamar." In Mark Williams and Gary Shapiro, editors, *Lamar Archaeology: Missippian Chiefdoms in the Deep South*. Tuscaloosa: University of Alabama Press, 1990.

Solana, Manuel. "Memorandum and Accounting for 500 Yards of Jerqueta." San Luis, [ca. 1703]. In Mark F. Boyd, Hale G. Smith, and John W. Griffin, editors, *Here They Once Stood: The Tragic End of the Apalachee Missions*. Gainesville: University of Florida Press, 1951.

South, Stanley. *The Discovery of Santa Elena*. South Carolina Institute of Archaeology and Anthropology Research Manuscript Series, no. 65. Columbia, S.C.: South Carolina Institute of Archaeology, 1980.

Spelman, Henry. "Relation of Virginea." In Edward Arber and A. G. Bradley, editors, *The Travels and Works of Captain John Smith*. New York: Burt Franklin, 1910.

Squier, Ephraim, and E. G. Davis. *Ancient Monuments of the Mississippi Valley*. Smithsonian Institution Contributions to Knowledge, no. 1. Washington, D.C.: Smithsonian Institution, 1848.

Steinen, Karl T. "Ochlockonee River Weeden Island Project." West Georgia College Department of Sociology and Anthropology, 1988. Typescript.

Steponaitis, Vincas P. "Prehistoric Archaeology in the Southeastern United States, 1970–1985." *Annual Review of Anthropology* 15 (1986): 363–404.

———. *Ceramics, Chronology, and Community Patterns: An Archaeological Study at Moundville*. New York: Academic Press, 1983.

———. "Locational Theory and Complex Chiefdoms: A Mississippian Example." In Bruce D. Smith, editor, *Mississippian Settlement Patterns*. New York: Academic Press, 1978.

Steward, Julian H. "The Direct Historical Approach to Archaeology." *American Antiquity* 7 (1942): 337–43.

———. "Ecological Aspects of Southwestern Society." *Anthropos* 32 (1937): 87–104.

Steward, Julian H., and Louis Faron. *Native Peoples of South America*. New York: McGraw-Hill, 1959.

Storey, Rebecca. Review of *Their Number Become Thinned* by Henry Dobyns. *American Anthropologist* 87 (1985): 455–56.

Stowe, Noel Read. "The Pensacola Variant and the Southern Ceremonial Complex." In Patricia Galloway, editor, *Southeastern Ceremonial Complex: Artifacts and Analysis*. Lincoln: University of Nebraska Press, 1989.

Strachey, William. *The Historie of Travell into Virginina Britania*. 1612. Reprint edited by Louis B. Wright and Virginia Freund. London: The Hakluyt Society, 1953.

Stuart, George. "The Post-Archaic Occupation of Central South Carolina." Ph.D. dissertation, University of North Carolina, 1975.

Sturtevant, William. Foreword to John R. Swanton, editor, *Final Report of the United States de Soto Expedition Commission*. 1939. Reprint. Washington, D.C.: Smithsonian Institution Press, 1985.

Sullivan, Lynne P. "The Mouse Creek Phase Household." *Southeastern Archaeology* 6 (1987): 16–29.

Swanton, John R. *Final Report of the United States de Soto Expedition Commission*. First published in 1939 as United States House of Representatives Document no. 71, 76th Cong., 1st sess. Reprint. Washington, D.C.: Smithsonian Institution Press, 1985.

———. *The Indians of the Southeastern United States*. Classics of Smithsonian Anthropology. 1946. Reprint. Washington, D.C.: Smithsonian Institution Press, 1979.

———. *Indian Tribes of the Southeastern United States*. Bureau of American Ethnology Bulletin no. 137. Washington, D.C.: Government Printing Office, 1946.

———. "The Early History of the Eastern Siouan Tribes." In *Essays Presented to A. L. Kroeber*. Berkeley: University of California Press, 1936.

———. "Ethnological Value of the de Soto Narratives." *American Anthropologist*, n.s. 34 (1932): 570–90.

———. *Source Material for the Social and Ceremonial Life of the Choctaw Indians*. Bureau of American Ethnology Bulletin no. 103. Washington, D.C.: Government Printing Office, 1931.

———, editor. "Social and Religious Beliefs and Usages of the Chickasaw Indians." *44th Annual Report of the Bureau of American Ethnology*. Washington, D.C.: Government Printing Office, 1928.

———. "Social Organization and Social Usages of the Creek Confederacy." *42nd Annual Report of the Bureau of American Ethnology*. Washington, D.C.: 1928.

———. *The Early History of the Creek Indians and Their Neighbors*. Bureau of American Ethnology Bulletin 73. Washington, D.C.: 1922.

———. "De Soto's Line of March from the Viewpoint of an Ethnologist." *Mississippi Valley Historical Association Proceedings* 5 (1912): 147–57.

———. *Indian Tribes of the Lower Mississippi Valley and Adjacent Coast of the Gulf of Mexico*. Bureau of American Ethnology Bulletin no. 43. Washington, D.C.: Government Printing Office, 1911.

Symes, M. I. and M. E. Stephens. "A-272: The Fox Pond Site." *Florida Anthropologist* 18 (1965): 65–76.

Taitt, David. "Journal of David Taitt's Travels from Pensacola, West Florida, to and through the Country of the Upper and Lower Creeks, 1772." In Newton D. Mereness, editor, *Travels in the American Colonies*. New York: Macmillan, 1916.

Tally, Lucy. "Preliminary Demographic Analysis of the King Site Burial Population." *Southeastern Archaeological Conference Bulletin* 18 (1975): 74–85.

Tanner, Helen Hornbeck. "The Land and Water Communication Systems of the Southeastern Indians." In Peter H. Wood, Gregory A. Waselkov, and M. Thomas Hatley, editors, *Powhatan's Mantle: Indians in the Colonial Southeast*. Lincoln: University of Nebraska Press, 1989.

Taylor, Donna. "Some Locational Aspects of Middle-Range Hierarchical Societies." Ph.D. dissertation, City University of New York, 1975.

TePaske, John J. "French, Spanish, and English Indian Policy on the Gulf Coast, 1513–1763: A Comparison." In Ernest F. Dibble and Earle W. Newton, editors, *Spain and Her Rivals on the Gulf Coast*. Pensacola: University of West Florida Press, 1971.

Tesar, Louis D. *The Leon County Bicentennial Survey Report: An Archaeological Survey of Selected Portions of Leon County, Florida*. Miscellaneous Project Report Series, no. 49. Tallahassee: Florida Bureau of Historic Sites and Properties, 1980.

Theisen, Gerald, translator. "Oviedo's Version of the Lost Joint Report Presented to the Audienceia of Santo Domingo." In *The Narrative of Alvar Núñez Cabeza de Vaca*. Translated by Fanny Bandelier. Barre, Mass.: The Imprint Society, 1972.

Thomas, Cyrus. "Report on the Mound Explorations of the Bureau of Ethnology." *Bureau of American Ethnology 12th Annual Report*. Washington, D.C.: Government Printing Office, 1894.

Thomas, David Hurst. *The Archaeology of Mission Santa Catalina de Guale*. Vol. 1, *Search and Discovery*. Anthropological Papers of the American Museum of Natural History. New York: American Museum of Natural History, 1987.

Thomas, David Hurst, Grant Jones, Roger Durham, and Clark S. Larsen. *The Anthropology of St. Catherines Island*. Vol. 1, *Natural and Cultural History*. Anthropological Papers of the American Museum of Natural History, vol. 55, no. 2. New York: American Museum of Natural History, 1978.

Todorov, Tzvetan. *The Conquest of America*. New York: Harper and Row, 1984.

Turnbaugh, William. "Wide-Area Connections in Native North America." *American Indian Culture and Research Journal* 4 (1976): 22–28.

Turner, E. Randolph, III. "Difficulties in the Archaeological Identification of Chiefdoms as Seen in the Virginia Coastal Plain During the Late Woodland and Early Historic Periods." In Jay F. Custer, editor, *Late Woodland Cultures of the Middle Atlantic Region*. Newark: University of Delaware Press, 1989.

———. "Socio-Political Organization within the Powhatan Chiefdom and the Effects of European Contact, A.D. 1607–1646." In William Fitzhugh, editor, *Cultures in Contact: The Impact of European Contacts on Native American Cultural Institutions in Eastern North America, A.D. 1000–1800*. Washington, D.C.: Smithsonian Institution Press, 1985.

———. "The Archaeological Identification of Chiefdom Societies in Southwestern Virginia." In C. Geier and M. Barber, editors, *Upland Archaeology in the East*. Cultural Resources Report no. 2. United States Forest Service, 1983.

———. "A Reexamination of Powhatan Territorial Boundaries and Population, ca. A.D. 1607." *Quarterly Bulletin of the Archaeological Society of Virginia* 37 (1982): 45–64.

———. "An Archaeological and Ethnohistorical Study on the Evolution of Rank Societies in the Virginia Coastal Plain." Ph.D. dissertation, Pennsylvania State University, 1976.

Vega, Damian de Castro y Pardo. Letter to the King, St. Augustine, July 9, 1643. Archivo General de Indias, Santo Domingo 224, Woodbury Lowery Collection, reel 3.

———. Letter to the King, St. Augustine, August 12, 1639. Archivo General de Indias, Santo Domingo 225, Stetson Collection of the P. K. Yonge Library of Florida History of the University of Florida.

Vega, Garcilaso de la. See Garcilaso de la Vega, El Inca.

Vernon, Richard. *17th Century Apalachee Colono-Ware as a Reflection of Demography, Economics, and Acculturation.* Historical Archaeology, no. 22. Columbia: South Carolina Institute of Archaeology, 1988.

Voegelin, Charles F. *Map of North American Indian Languages.* New York: J. J. Augustin, 1944.

Waddell, Gene. *Indians of the South Carolina Lowcountry, 1562–1751.* Spartanburg, S.C.: Reprint Company, 1980.

Wallerstein, Immanuel. *The Modern World System: Capitalist Agriculture and the Origin of the European World Economy in the Sixteenth Century.* New York: Academic Press, 1974.

Waring, Antonio J., Jr., and Preston Holder. "A Prehistoric Ceremonial Complex in the Southeastern United States." In Stephen Williams, editor, *The Waring Papers: The Collected Works of Antonio J. Waring, Jr.* Revised ed. Papers of the Peabody Museum of Archaeology, no. 58. Cambridge: Peabody Museum Press, 1977.

Waselkov, Gregory A. "Seventeenth Century Trade in the Colonial Southeast." *Southeastern Archaeology* 8 (1989): 117–33.

———. "Lower Tallapoosa Cultural Resources Survey." Phase I Report. Auburn University Department of Sociology and Anthropology. Auburn, 1981.

Waselkov, Gregory A., and John C. Cottier. "European Perceptions of Eastern Muskogean Ethnicity." In G. A. Waselkov, editor, *Culture Change on the Creek Indian Frontier.* Unpublished report submitted to the National Science Foundation, 1985.

Wauchope, Robert. *Archaeological Survey of Northern Georgia with a Test of Some Cultural Hypotheses.* American Antiquity Memoir no. 21. Salt Lake City: Society for American Archaeology, 1966.

Webb, William S. *Indian Knoll.* 2d ed. Knoxville: University of Tennessee Press, 1974.

Weddle, Robert. *Spanish Sea: The Gulf of Mexico in North American Discovery, 1500–1685.* College Station: Texas A & M University Press, 1985.

Weddle, Robert, Mary Christine Morkovsky, and Patricia Galloway, editors. *La Salle, the Mississippi, and the Gulf: Three Primary Documents.* College Station: Texas A & M University Press, 1987.

Weiner, Annette B. *The Trobrianders of Papua New Guinea.* New York: Holt, Rinehart and Winston, 1988.

Weisman, Brent. *Excavations on the Franciscan Frontier: Archaeology at the Fig Springs Mission.* Gainesville: University of Florida Press, 1992.

———. *1988 Excavations at Fig Springs (8Co1), Season 2, July–December, 1988.* Florida Archaeological Reports, no. 4. Tallahassee: Florida Bureau of Archaeological Research, 1988.

Welch, Paul D. *Moundville's Economy.* Tuscaloosa: University of Alabama Press, 1990.

Wells, Peter S. *Farms, Villages, and Cities: Commerce and Urban Origins in Late Prehistoric Europe.* Ithaca: Cornell University Press, 1984.

———. *Culture Contact and Culture Change: Early Iron Age Central Europe and the Mediterranean World.* Cambridge: Cambridge University Press, 1980.

Wenhold, Lucy L. "A 17th Century Letter of Gabriel Diaz Vara Calderón, Bishop of Cuba, Describing the Indians and Indian Missions of Florida." *Smithsonian Miscellaneous Collections,* no. 95. Washington, D.C.: Smithsonian Institution, 1936.

White, Douglas R., George P. Murdock, and Richard Scaglion. "Natchez Class and Rank Reconsidered." *Ethnology* 10 (1971): 369–88.

White, Nancy M., with Stephanie J. Belovich and David S. Brose. *Archaeological Survey at Lake Seminole: Jackson and Gadsden Counties, Florida, Seminole and Decatur Counties, Georgia.* Archaeological Research Reports, no. 29. Cleveland: Cleveland Museum of Natural History, 1981.

White, Richard. *The Roots of Dependency: Subsistence, Environment, and Social Change Among the Choctaws, Pawnees, and Navajos.* Lincoln: University of Nebraska Press, 1983.

———. "Red Shoes: Warrior and Diplomat." In David G. Sweet and Gary B. Nash, editors, *Struggle and Survival in Colonial America.* Berkeley: University of California Press, 1981.

Widmer, Randolph J. *The Evolution of the Calusa: A Nonagricultural Chiefdom on the Southwest Florida Coast.* Tuscaloosa: University of Alabama Press, 1988.

———. "Social Organization of the Natchez Indians." *Southern Anthropologist* 5 (1975): 1–7.

Williams, Mark. *Archaeological Excavations at Shoulderbone Mounds and Village, 9HK1.* Watkinsville, Ga.: LAMAR Institute, 1990.

———. *Archaeological Excavations at the Shinholser Site (9B11): 1985 and 1987.* Watkinsville, Ga.: LAMAR Institute, 1990.

———. "The Hernando De Soto Expedition in Northeast Georgia." Watkinsville, Ga.: LAMAR Institute, 1989. Typescript in author's possession.

———. *Early History of the Indians along the Savannah and Oconee Rivers.* Watkinsville, Ga.: LAMAR Institute, 1988.

———. *Scull Shoals Revisited.* Cultural Resource Report, no. 1. Gainesville, Ga.: U.S. Forest Service, 1988.

———. *Archaeological Testing at the Lingerlonger Mound, 9Ge35.* Watkinsville, Ga.: LAMAR Institute, 1987.

———. *Preliminary Report of Excavation at 9Pm211.* Athens: University of Georgia Department of Anthropology, 1987.

———. *Archaeological Excavations at Scull Shoals Mounds (9Ge4).* Cultural Resources Report, no. 6. Gainesville, Ga.: U.S. Forest Service, 1984.

———. "The Joe Bell Site: Seventeenth Century Lifeways on the Oconee River." Ph.D. dissertation, University of Georgia, 1983.

———. "Indians Along the Oconee after de Soto: The Beginning of the End." *Early Georgia* 10 (1982): 27–39.

Williams, Mark, and Gary Shapiro, editors. *Archaeological Excavations at Little River (9Mg46): 1984–1987*. Watkinsville, Ga.: LAMAR Institute, 1990.

———. *Lamar Archaeology: Mississippian Chiefdoms in the Deep South*. Tuscaloosa: University of Alabama Press, 1990.

———. "Paired Towns." In Mark Williams and Gary Shapiro, editors, *Lamar Archaeology: Mississippian Chiefdoms in the Deep South*. Tuscaloosa: University of Alabama Press, 1990.

Williams, Marshall, and Carolyn Branch. "The Tugalo Site, 9St1." *Early Georgia* 6 (1978): 32–37.

Williams, Stephen, and Jeffrey P. Brain. *Excavations at the Lake George Site, Yazoo County, Mississippi, 1958–1960*. Papers of the Peabody Museum of Archaeology and Ethnology. Vol. 74. Cambridge, Mass.: Peabody Museum of Archaeology, 1983.

Willis, William S., Jr. "Anthropology and Negroes on the Southern Colonial Frontier." In James C. Curtis and Lewis L. Gould, editors, *The Black Experience in America: Selected Essays*. Austin: University of Texas Press, 1970.

Wingfield, Edward Maria. "Discourse." In Philip L. Barbour, editor, *The Jamestown Voyages Under the First Charter*. Cambridge: The Hakluyt Society, 1969.

Witthoff, John. *Green Corn Ceremonialism in the Eastern Woodlands*. Occasional Contributions, no. 13. Ann Arbor: University of Michigan Museum of Anthropology, 1949.

Wood, Peter H. "Indian Servitude in the Southeast." In Raymond D. Fogelson, editor, *Handbook of North American Indians: Southeast*. Washington, D.C.: Smithsonian Institution Press. In press.

———. "The Changing Population of the Colonial South: an Overview by Race and Region, 1685–1790." In Peter H. Wood, Gregory A. Waselkov, and M. Thomas Hatley, editors, *Powhatan's Mantle: Indians in the Colonial Southeast*. Lincoln: University of Nebraska Press, 1989.

———. *Black Majority: Negroes in Colonial South Carolina from 1670 through the Stono Rebellion*. New York: Alfred A. Knopf, 1974.

Worth, John R. "The Timucuan Missions of Spanish Florida and the Rebellion of 1656." Ph.D. dissertation, University of Florida, 1992.

———. "Mississippian Occupation of the Middle Flint River." M.A. thesis, University of Georgia, 1988.

Wright, Henry T. "Prestate Political Formations." In Timothy K. Earle, editor, *On the Evolution of Complex Societies: Essays in Honor of Harry Hoijer, 1982*. Malibu: Undena Publications, 1984.

Wright, J. Leitch, Jr. *Creeks and Seminoles: The Destruction and Regeneration of the Muscogulge People*. Lincoln: University of Nebraska Press, 1986.

———. *The Only Land They Knew: The Tragic Story of the American Indians in the Old South*. New York: Free Press, 1981.

Wyckoff, Donald G. *The Caddoan Cultural Area: An Archaeological Perspective*. New York: Garland, 1974.

Yarnell, Richard A. "Domestication of Sunflower and Sumpweed in Eastern North America." In Richard I. Ford, editor, *The Nature and Status of Ethnobotany*.

University of Michigan Anthropology Papers, no. 67. Ann Arbor: University of Michigan Museum of Anthropology, 1978.

Yerkes, Richard W. "Microwear, Microdrills, and Mississippian Craft Specialization." *American Antiquity* 48 (1983): 499–518.

Zubillaga, Felix, editor. *Monumenta Antiquae Floridae (1566–1572)*. Monumenta Historica Societis Iesu, vol. 69. Rome: Monumenta Historica Societis Jesu, 1946.

Zúñiga y Zerda, Joseph de. Letter to Manuel Solana, St. Augustine, March 14, 1701, in Mark F. Boyd, Hale G. Smith, and John W. Griffin, editors, *Here They Once Stood. The Tragic End of the Apalachee Missions*. Gainesville: University of Florida Press, 1951.

CONTRIBUTORS

Chester B. DePratter is a research associate professor at the South Carolina Institute of Archaeology and Anthropology, University of South Carolina. He has conducted extensive research, both archaeological and ethnohistorical, on the contact period in the southeastern United States, and he has coauthored papers on the sixteenth-century expeditions of Hernando de Soto, Juan Pardo, and Tristán de Luna.

Patricia Galloway is a special projects officer at the Mississippi Department of Archives and History. Her research interests include the ethnohistory of the western Muskogean tribes, colonial French Louisiana history, and ethnohistorical epistemology. The current editor of *Mississippi Archaeology* and the *MDAH Archaeological Reports* series, she has completed a book on the ethnogenesis of the Choctaw Indians and has also edited *La Salle and His Legacy*, volumes 4 and 5 of the *Mississippi Provincial Archives: French Dominion*, and *Southeastern Ceremonial Complex: Artifacts and Analysis.*

David J. Hally received his doctorate from Harvard University in 1972. He is an associate professor of anthropology at the University of Georgia where he specializes in the investigation of the late prehistoric and early historic inhabitants of the southeastern United States.

John H. Hann is a historian and translator for the San Luis Archaeological and Historic Site administered by the Florida Bureau of Archaeological Research under the secretary of state. He has taught Latin American history at Florida State University and New Mexico State University. He has published articles and translations on the Indians and Spanish missions of the Southeast and volumes on the Apalachee and the Calusa.

Paul E. Hoffman is professor of history at the Louisiana State University. He is author of *The Spanish Crown and the Defense of the Caribbean, 1535–1585* and *A New Andalucia and a Way to the Orient: The American Southeast During the Sixteenth Century.*

Charles Hudson is a professor of anthropology at the University of Georgia. He is author of *The Southeastern Indians* and *The Juan Pardo Expeditions: Exploration of the Carolinas and Tennessee, 1566–1568.*

Vernon James Knight, Jr. is an associate professor of anthropology at the University of Alabama. His research on Creek Indian culture and history is primarily archaeological, involving fieldwork in the Coosa, Tallapoosa, and Chattahoochee River valleys of Alabama and Georgia. His publications on this topic include investigations of the archaeological sites of Tukabatchee and Big Tallassee.

Joel W. Martin is an assistant professor of religious studies at Franklin and Marshall College and a visiting fellow at the Center for the Study of American Religion, Princeton University. He is the author of *Sacred Revolt: The Muskogees' Struggle for a New World*.

Jerald T. Milanich is the curator of archaeology at the Florida Museum of Natural History, where he was a member of the team responsible for the traveling exhibit, "First Encounters: Spanish Explorations in the Caribbean and United States, 1492–1570." He has carried out archaeological and ethnohistorical research on the native peoples of the southeastern United States, especially Florida and Georgia. His recent research has focused on the history and peoples of sixteenth- and seventeenth-century La Florida.

Helen C. Rountree received her doctorate in 1973 from the University of Wisconsin-Milwaukee and is a professor of anthropology at Old Dominion University in Norfolk, Virginia. A cultural anthropologist and ethnohistorian, she has done historical research and ethnographic fieldwork with the modern Powhatans since 1969. She has published several articles on the historic and modern Indians of Virginia and is the author of two books: *The Powhatan Indians of Virginia: Their Traditional Culture* and *Pocahontas's People: The Powhatan Indians of Virginia Through Four Centuries*.

John F. Scarry is the director of the Program for Cultural Resource Assessment and adjunct assistant professor of anthropology at the University of Kentucky. He received his doctoral degree from Case Western Reserve University in 1984. His research has focused on the evolution and structure of the Mississippian chiefdoms and their interaction with European explorers and missionaries. He has published papers on the emergence of the Apalachee chiefdom and political change during the life of the Apalachee chiefdom. He is also coauthor (with B. Calvin Jones and John H. Hann) of a monograph on the seventeenth-century Apalachee mission San Pedro y San Pablo de Patale.

Marvin T. Smith, an adjunct assistant professor of anthropology at the University of South Alabama, holds a doctoral degree in anthropology from the University of Florida. His research has focused on Spanish exploration of the southeastern United States and its effects upon native societies. He is an authority on early Spanish material culture traded to Indians. Dr. Smith is the author of several articles and a book, *The Archaeology of Aboriginal Culture Change: Depopulation during the Early Historic Period*.

Carmen Chaves Tesser is a professor of Romance languages at the University of Georgia. Her current research deals with third world texts and their reception in the United States.

E. Randolph Turner III received his doctorate in 1976 from the Pennsylvania State University and is the senior prehistoric archaeologist with the Commonwealth of Virginia's Department of Historic Resources. An archaeologist and ethnohistorian, his current work covers all periods and ethnic groups throughout the state, but his specialty has long been the development of the Powhatan paramount chiefdom. He is the author of several articles, notably chapters in *Cultures in Contact* and *Late Woodland Cultures of the Middle Atlantic Region,* and many research reports.

Randolph J. Widmer is an associate professor of anthropology at the University of Houston. He is the author of *The Evolution of the Calusa: A Nonagricultural Chiefdom on the Southwest Florida Coast.*

Mark Williams is the president of the LAMAR Institute and an archaeologist associated with the University of Georgia. He holds a doctorate from that school.

John E. Worth holds a doctoral degree from the University of Florida and is an educational coordinator and anthropologist at the Fernbank Museum of Natural History in Atlanta, Georgia. He has done archaeological fieldwork at late prehistoric and early historic period aboriginal sites in Georgia, Florida, and South Carolina and spent four months in 1991 conducting documentary research in the Archivo General de Indias in Sevilla, Spain. His archaeological and ethnohistorical investigations relative to the Spanish colonial system have included the expedition of Hernando de Soto and the seventeenth-century mission provinces of Timucua, Guale, and Mocama.

INDEX